IMPORTANT

HERE IS YOUR REGISTRATION CODE TO ACCESS MCGRAW-[HILL]
PREMIUM CONTENT AND MCGRAW-HILL ONLINE RESOURCES

For key premium online resources you need THIS CODE to gain access. Once the code is entered, you will be able to use the web resources for the length of your course.

Access is provided only if you have purchased a new book.

If the registration code is missing from this book, the registration screen on our website, and within your WebCT or Blackboard course will tell you how to obtain your new code. Your registration code can be used only once to establish access. It is not transferable.

To gain access to these online resources

1. USE your web browser to go to: **http://www.mhhe.com/federpip4**
2. CLICK on "First Time User"
3. ENTER the Registration Code printed on the tear-off bookmark on the right
4. After you have entered your registration code, click on "Register"
5. FOLLOW the instructions to setup your personal UserID and Password
6. WRITE your UserID and Password down for future reference. Keep it in a safe place.

If your course is using WebCT or Blackboard, you'll be able to use this code to access the McGraw-Hill content within your instructor's online course.

To gain access to the McGraw-Hill content in your instructor's WebCT or Blackboard course simply log into the course with the user ID and Password provided by your instructor. Enter the registration code exactly as it appears to the right when prompted by the system. You will only need to use this code the first time you click on McGraw-Hill content.

These instructions are specifically for student access. Instructors are not required to register via the above instructions.

The McGraw·Hill Companies

Mc Graw Hill **Higher Education**

Thank you, and welcome to your McGraw-Hill Online Resources.

10 Digit: 0-07-325496-7
t/a Feder
Past in Perspective, 4/e

UY7P-7EJB-BRAG-Qk

REGISTRATION CODE
REGISTRATION CODE

The Past in Perspective

AN INTRODUCTION TO HUMAN PREHISTORY

FOURTH EDITION

Kenneth L. Feder

Central Connecticut State University

Boston   Burr Ridge, IL   Dubuque, IA   Madison, WI   New York   San Francisco   St. Louis
Bangkok   Bogotá   Caracas   Kuala Lumpur   Lisbon   London   Madrid   Mexico City
Milan   Montreal   New Delhi   Santiago   Seoul   Singapore   Sydney   Taipei   Toronto

For Josh and Jacob

Mc Graw Hill **Higher Education**

Published by McGraw-Hill, an imprint of The McGraw-Hill Companies, Inc., 1221 Avenue of the Americas, New York, NY 10020. Copyright © 2007. All rights reserved. No part of this publication may be reproduced or distributed in any form or by any means, or stored in a database or retrieval system, without the prior written consent of The McGraw-Hill Companies, Inc., including, but not limited to, in any network or other electronic storage or transmission, or broadcast for distance learning.

This book is printed on acid-free paper.

1 2 3 4 5 6 7 8 9 0 VNH/VNH 0 9 8 7 6

ISBN-13: 978-0-07-310770-7
ISBN-10: 0-07-310770-0

Editor in Chief: Emily Barrosse
Publisher: Phil Butcher
Sponsoring Editor: Kevin Witt
Marketing Manager: Dan Loch
Project Manager: Anne Fuzellier
Manuscript Editor: Joan Pendleton
Art Director: Jeanne M. Schreiber
Text Designers: Glenda King/Cassandra Chu

Cover Designer: William Stanton
Art Manager: Robin Mouat
Illustrators: John and Judy Waller, Patti Isaacs
Photo Research: Brian J. Pecko
Production Supervisor: Randy Hurst
Media: Shannon Gattens/Michele Borrelli

Composition: 10/12 Palatino by Thompson Type
Printing: Von Hoffman Corporation

Cover: Anthropomorphic Mask (stone, turquoise, obsidian, and shell) (157743), Teotihuacán/Museo Nacional de Antropologia, Mexico City, Mexico, Jean-Pierre Courau/© The Bridgeman Art Library

Library of Congress Cataloging-in-Publication Data
Feder, Kenneth L.
    The past in perspective : an introduction to human prehistory / Kenneth L. Feder.—4th ed.
        p. cm.
    Includes bibliographical references and index.
    ISBN 0-07-310770-0
    1. Prehistoric peoples. 2. Human evolution. 3. Fossil hominids.
4. Human remains (Archaeology) I. Title.
    GN766.F43 2006
    569.9—dc22   2005056224

The Internet addresses listed in the text were accurate at the time of publication. The inclusion of a website does not indicate an endorsement by the authors or McGraw-Hill, and McGraw-Hill does not guarantee the accuracy of the information presented at these sites.

www.mhhe.com

Preface

"The past is a bucket of ashes," said the poet Carl Sandburg. Surely he was wrong. The past is not cold, dead, and spent. It is alive in everything we are and will be. We live in a universe filled with its traces. The stars in the night sky shine with a light that began its journey millions of years ago. The fossilized remnants of remarkable creatures that once walked the earth lie entombed in the soil beneath our feet. Cooking hearths and food scraps, pyramids and pottery, stone tools and bone awls, cave paintings and ivory sculptures—all date to the ancient human past, yet exist in the present. The past is not a bucket of ashes, but rather, as writer L. P. Hartley put it, "the past is a foreign country." In this book, we will visit that country.

The Past in Perspective: An Introduction to Human Prehistory focuses on the dim echoes of the human past, presenting an accessible chronicle of human physical and cultural evolution. The readers of this text are undergraduates with no previous coursework in archaeology; for many it will be their only academic exposure to our prehistoric past. Rather than overwhelm beginning students with an all-inclusive, detailed survey of human antiquity, this text looks at the major themes of the human evolutionary story. It begins with the evolution of our earliest hominid ancestors, traces the evolution of the modern human species, and follows the various pathways our ancestors took in the development of food-producing societies and complex civilizations. My goal throughout is to instill in readers an appreciation for the long chronicle of humanity and the ongoing processes we use to construct and assess that story.

HOW THE TEXT IS ORGANIZED

Chapters 1 and 2 provide context and background for the discussion of human prehistory. Chapter 1 places the study of the human past in the context of science, specifically the science of anthropology. Chapter 1 also explains how a scientific approach to the study of prehistory developed. Chapter 2 is a brief overview of key methodologies employed by archaeologists and paleoanthropologists in their study of the human past. It represents a brief introduction to archaeology.

Following these introductory chapters, Chapters 3–15 go on to present a chronological survey of the human past. Each chapter follows a consistent format with these headings: Chapter Overview, Prelude, Chronicle, Issues and Debates, Case Study Close-Up, Visiting the Past, Summary, and To Learn

More. A consistent format provides a pedagogical advantage, and the trajectory of human physical and cultural evolution becomes far more apparent and connected. What we know, what we don't know, and what are still topics of vigorous debate will be clear to the reader.

The **CHAPTER OVERVIEW** introduces the primary topic of the chapter in several brief paragraphs.

The **PRELUDE** represents a conscious attempt on my part to provide a pedagogical "hook" for each chapter. Personal anecdotes or fascinating historical incidents, for example, immediately engage students in the key issue or issues of the chapter, whether it is upright locomotion, the origins of artistic expression, or the power of ancient civilizations.

The **CHRONICLE** presents in narrative form a consensus view of that part of the human past that is the chapter's focus. It represents the heart of each chapter, providing our current understanding of the time period covered, the hominids discussed, and the cultural evolutionary developments reflected in the time period.

ISSUES AND DEBATES discusses the answers we have been able to provide for key questions about human physical and cultural evolution as well as the unresolved issues that remain and the ongoing debates. These sections provide differing—and sometimes competing—perspectives. Students are thus exposed to the sometimes messy, always exciting, and inevitably human process of science fraught with disagreements, reassessments, shifting paradigms, and only hard-won consensus.

The **CASE STUDY CLOSE-UP** is a detailed examination of one or more sites considered diagnostic or emblematic of the time period or primary issue of the chapter.

VISITING THE PAST directs readers to key sites mentioned in the chapter that are open to the public, suggests museums where the materials from important sites discussed in the chapter are displayed, and directs the reader to Internet sites that provide the opportunity for "virtual visits" with detailed discussions, photographs, videos, and animations related to the chapter topic.

Each chapter **SUMMARY** provides a brief recapitulation of the key issues in the chapter.

TO LEARN MORE is divided into four sections: (1) "Technical Summaries," where students can find primary sources, including articles in professional journals and books; (2) "Popular Summaries," including secondary sources like magazine articles and trade books; (3) "On the Web," providing Internet sources related to the chapter topic; and (4) "Online Learning Center," describing the resources available at the Web site that accompanies this book.

ADDITIONAL FEATURES

In addition to a consistent chapter format, I've included a number of other features that make this text a more useful learning tool.

- A **timeline** opens every chapter and helps place the key events and sites mentioned in the body of the chapter within a global historical context.
- To help students better orient themselves on the world stage, I've included abundant **maps** throughout the book. Each chapter (3–15) presents a map or, in some cases, multiple maps in which each of the sites mentioned in the chapter are located. Chapters 3–15 also include a **list of sites**—broken out by continent, region, or country—that are mentioned in the chapter, along with the page number where they can be found.
- A list of **Key Terms** at the end of each chapter provides an alphabetical listing of important terms that appear in boldfaced type within the chapters and includes page numbers for where they can be found. Definitions can be found in the end-of-book glossary.
- The text's **visual appeal** enhances its readability. Full-color photographs are cross-referenced to pertinent text discussions. Detailed, colorful charts and drawings, as well as abundant color photographs, underscore significant points in the text. Captions add information rather than simply label the art.
- The **Glossary, References,** and a comprehensive **Index** make information readily accessible.
- An **Online Learning Center (OLC),** found at http://www.mhhe.com/feder4, now accompanies *The Past in Perspective.* The OLC includes learning objectives for each chapter, interactive timeline study guides to reinforce the information in the text, links to Web sites with more information about the archaeological sites in the text, and self-quizzes to test understanding of the material in each chapter.

ONLINE LEARNING CENTER

WHAT'S DIFFERENT ABOUT THE FOURTH EDITION?

Anyone familiar with previous editions of *The Past in Perspective* will find the features that have made this book unique—the engaging writing style, the consistent organization of chapters, the personalization of the past—are all still there. These key aspects have not been altered. At the same time, the focus of the content of the book has been, not so much shifted, but expanded. In this, the fourth edition, there have been substantial additions of material pertinent to the more recent past, especially the development of early state societies. Specifically, there have been significant changes, improvements in, and additions to the following chapters:

- Following its substantial reconfiguration in the previous edition, **Chapter 1** has been reworked only slightly.

- **Chapter 2** provides additional discussion of the ways in which archaeological sites come into existence and how they are preserved. Also, the section on how archaeologists trace raw materials has been improved.
- When I began writing the first edition of this book more than ten years ago, all I could say about the period between 7 and 4 million years ago was how important it was in the evolution of the hominids while I bemoaned the fact that we knew so little about it. In **Chapter 3** of this edition of the book, there is a substantial discussion of a number of different hominids who may have taken the first literal and figurative steps in human evolution sometime around 6 million years ago.
- New material in **Chapter 4** reflects the exciting, if vexing fact that nothing about hominid evolution is entirely settled. The specimen called the "Hobbit" found on the island of Flores is examined here, along with other new fossil discoveries that have expanded our understanding of the geographical expansion of the hominid family beyond Africa.
- Previous editions of the book presented the evolution of premodern and modern human beings in separate chapters. This was never completely satisfying and led to redundancy with, especially, material on the Neandertals presented in each of those separate chapters. **Chapter 5** here combines the material presented in those two chapters (5 and 6 in the previous edition of the book). All of the important information remains, but redundancy has been eliminated.
- New material is presented in **Chapter 6** showing that the production of art and the use of symbols precedes the Upper Paleolithic.
- As soon as the book is printed, new sites are found that cause us at least to reconsider the nature and timing of the earliest human settlement of Australia and the New World. **Chapter 7** presents the data produced since the last edition went to press.
- **Chapter 8** provides a greatly expanded discussion of post-Pleistocene adaptations, especially in Europe, North America, and Australia.
- The discussion of phytoliths, genetics, and isotope analysis as these relate to the origins of domestication, has been enhanced in **Chapter 9.** The demographic implications of the Food Producing Revolution are presented in far greater detail.
- There is a new and greatly expanded discussion of the roots of complexity in Mesoamerica and South America in **Chapter 10.**
- The most substantial changes to *The Past in Perspective* occur in its final chapters, effectively, the last one-third of the book. Where previous editions provided only two, albeit lengthy and dense chapters on the development of civilization—one on the Old World and the other on the New World—this edition presents a greatly expanded presentation of the evolution of the state in four chapters. **Chapter 11**'s focus is on Mesopotamia, Egypt, and Pakistan. **Chapter 12** moves on to China, southeast Asia, and Crete. **Chapter 13** now presents the development of civilization in Mesoamerica with far more detailed examinations of the

Maya and Teotihuacán. **Chapter 14** focuses on the evolution of the state in South America. These chapters have been, essentially, rewritten from the ground up with substantially more content, but presented in the same, accessible and engaging format and style that has always characterized the book.

- **Chapter 15** provides an expanded look at Adena and Hopewell.

In an old television ad, viewers were told that "the world is a carousel of color." You will immediately notice that now, so is *The Past in Perspective*. There no longer are a limited number of color images in a handful of inserts in the book; the fourth edition of *The Past in Perspective* has color imagery throughout. The use of color is far more than simply a cosmetic change; students will gain a far greater appreciation, especially for the artistic achievements of ancient humanity, when they can view images of these achievements in color.

SUPPLEMENTARY MATERIAL FOR INSTRUCTORS

- Instructor's Manual and Testbank include multiple-choice and short-answer/essay questions, as well as chapter overviews, lists of key words, and suggested sources for videos, CD-ROMs, and Internet sites.
- Instructor's Online Learning Center is password-protected access to additional professional and teaching resources.
- PageOut allows instructors to create a course Web site using a template provided by McGraw-Hill.

ACKNOWLEDGMENTS

Textbooks, perhaps especially those about human biological and cultural evolution, are themselves evolutionary journeys. My invaluable guides on this voyage included colleagues who have made many useful suggestions concerning my route, both formally as reviewers and informally through letters, phone calls, and e-mails. Also assisting in this endeavor have been students, many of whom were generous with criticism, complaints, encouragement, and assistance. In particular, I wish to thank the reviewers of the fourth edition:

Michael Love
CSU Northridge

Doug Bamforth
University of Colorado at Boulder

Mark A. Rees
University of Louisiana at Lafayette

Arthur Rostoker
Queen's College CUNY

Celeste Ray
University of the South

Sean Rafferty
University of Albany SUNY

Textbooks require the enthusiastic support and tireless assistance of a wide group of people; *The Past in Perspective* has been lucky enough to have always had the highest levels of such support and assistance. For this edition I have been the grateful recipient of the wonderful work of the best copyeditor on the planet, maybe even the whole galaxy, Joan Pendleton. Cassandra Chu's design of the book takes my breath away, and Art Editor Robin Mouat constantly performs the miracle of making the book look as good as I hope it reads. I have worked on several books with Photo Researcher Brian Pecko and I have come to the conclusion that there's simply no image Brian can't track down. Brian's work contributed greatly to the appearance of this book. Margeting Manager Dan Loch is relentless and, my best suggestion to you is to simply adopt the book just to get Dan off your case.

Editorial Coordinator Teresa Treacy was the first person I would e-mail on any issue—and usually the last I would have to—she simply took care of whatever it was. It was a joy to have Anne Fuzellier as the Project Manager for *The Past in Perspective*. With Anne managing I could actually focus on the little things; you know, research and writing. Thanks Anne and, as always, "des saucisses, sans doute!"

Especially at a large publishing house, every project needs a champion, someone who makes sure the book isn't constrained by the practical concerns of the publisher. Senior Editor Kevin Witt has been *The Past in Perspective*'s champion. Kevin never doubted that the new, "colorful" edition was worth the effort, energy, and resources and I am enormously in his debt.

In the way of personal thanks, I am grateful for having a colleague like Michael Alan Park. My sense of excitement about the world around me was kindled by my parents, and I thank them both. A special thanks goes to my globetrotting father for his wonderful photographs. Of course, no acknowledgment is complete without crediting one's immediate family. Thanks to my kids, Josh and Jacob, whose mere existence reminds me of my own very small place in evolution's drama. And expansive thanks to my wife, Melissa, the sweetest person on the planet. I can't lift heavy objects or fix cars, but I can write books. I think she's impressed. Finally, I must acknowledge my multiple partners in crime, kitties Randolph and Harpo, who are gone now, but who, in sharing their lives with me, disabused me of any foolish notion I may have had about the superiority of the human species. And thanks to our current generation of beasts, Busterella, Groucho, and our latest, Aslan, who are quick to remind me that a scratch behind the ear and a clean litter box are more pressing than whatever it is I am staring at on the computer screen.

Contents

4 The Human Lineage   116

5 The First Humans   160
THE EVOLUTION OF *HOMO SAPIENS*

6 Expanding Intellectual Horizons 218
ART AND IDEAS IN THE UPPER PALEOLITHIC AND LATE STONE AGE

7 Expanding Geographic Horizons 256
NEW WORLDS

8   After the Ice   308
CULTURAL CHANGE IN THE POST-PLEISTOCENE

9 The Food-Producing Revolution 344

10 The Roots of Complexity   408
THE ORIGINS OF CIVILIZATION

11 An Explosion of Complexity 450
THE FLOWERING OF CIVILIZATION IN THE OLD WORLD: MESOPOTAMIA, EGYPT, AND THE INDUS VALLEY

12 An Explosion of Complexity 502
THE FLOWERING OF CIVILIZATION IN THE OLD WORLD: SHANG, MINOAN, AND KHMER

13 An Explosion of Complexity 528
THE FLOWERING OF CIVILIZATION IN THE NEW WORLD: MESOAMERICA

14 An Explosion of Complexity 560
THE FLOWERING OF CIVILIZATION IN THE NEW WORLD: SOUTH AMERICA

Evolutionary Epilogue   631

The Past in Perspective

1

Encountering the Past

CHAPTER OVERVIEW

This book focuses on the work of archaeologists. Archaeology is a subdiscipline within the broader field of anthropology—the study of humanity. Whereas other anthropologists study living people, archaeologists concentrate on the cultural evolution of past human beings. Archaeologists accomplish this through the study of our ancestors' biological remains and the analysis of the physical objects that they made, used, and left behind.

Recognizing that the world and humanity were ancient and understanding that elements of this ancient past were preserved and could be studied in the present was difficult for past thinkers whose concepts of time were constrained by their traditional beliefs. Some past thinkers viewed the world as the static product of a relatively recent, divine creation. Others came to understand that the earth is the result of slow-acting, natural causes that continue to operate in the present. In this now accepted view, the world and all of its inhabitants, including human beings, have a lengthy history and are ever-changing. Only by recognizing that the world is vastly ancient and is characterized by change can the lengthy archaeological record of an ancient humanity be accommodated.

	1640	1650	1660	1670	1680	1690	1700	1710
GEOLOGY		Bishop Ussher determines that creation took place in 4004 B.C., 1650				*The Wisdom of God* by John Ray is published, 1691 William Whiston proposes that a collision between earth and a comet caused Noah's flood, 1696		
BIOLOGY								
ARCHAEOLOGY								

1720	1730	1740	1750	1760	1770	1780	1790	1800	1810	1820	1830	1840	1850	1860	1870	1880

Theory of the Earth by James Hutton published, 1788

Principles of Geology by Charles Lyell published, 1830

William Smith's stratigraphic tables first circulated, 1799

William Smith's stratigraphic tables published, 1815

Linnaeus publishes his taxonomy for all living things, 1758

Philosophie Zoologique by Jean-Baptiste Lamarck published, 1809

Darwin begins his voyage on the *Beagle*, 1831

Darwin writes a synopsis of his theory of evolution, 1844

The Origin of Species by Charles Darwin published, 1859

The Descent of Man by Charles Darwin published, 1872

John Frere finds flint tools in soil layer deep in quarry in Hoxne, England, 1797

Flint tools and bones of extinct animals found in Kent's Cavern, England, 1824

C. J. Thomsen publishes museum guide and introduces three-age system, 1836

Primitive skull found in Neander Valley, Germany, 1856

Ancient Society by Lewis Henry Morgan published, 1877

Human bones found with bones of extinct animals in French cave, 1828

Geological Evidences of the Antiquity of Man by Charles Lyell published, 1863

Boucher de Perthes finds ancient flint axes, 1837

Researches in the Early History of Mankind by Edward Tyler published, 1865

ONLINE LEARNING CENTER

Go to **www.mhhe.com/feder4** for an interactive study guide version of this timeline.

PRELUDE

The past is dead and gone. At least that's what we usually think and say. Surely there is nothing much left of it beyond our dim memories. Perhaps the past is like the faces of people in an old photograph, people we once knew—people we once were. The focus is crisp soon after the photo is taken, but gradually the image fades as time hurries on, blurring into vague splotches of color on photo paper. Ultimately, the past, like these images, grows faint, becoming little more than an indistinct haze. Indeed dead. Indeed gone. But is this common impression entirely accurate? In fact, it isn't. In a very real way, the past sometimes and unexpectedly endures into the present. When we are lucky, its image can be brought into sharp focus again.

For example, take a walk out toward the margins of just about any modern town. Follow a trail into the desert or deep into the piney woods and recognize that, in a sense, the trail conveys the hiker back through time. Consider my own town of Simsbury, Connecticut. In the rural, northwest corner of town, out beyond the beautiful homes with their splendid views of the valley below, is a trail that meanders into the McLean Game Refuge, a 4,000-acre sanctuary for animals, fish, birds, and trees. The trail into the refuge surges downhill, propelling the hiker past stands of hemlock, white and red pine, maple, and oak. As you gaze around the curiously broad trail and scan the higher ground on either side, you notice that this uninhabited woodland bears witness to something far different in its past. Low-lying stone walls demarcate the edges of the wide path, and that in itself is a puzzle (Figure 1.1). No one in living memory built these walls, yet there they stand, mysteriously lining the edges of a hiking trail far wider than it needs to be, in the middle of a game refuge. And there is more. Look beyond the walls along the trail and you will notice a web of more stone walls, often rather elaborate and well made, as much as 4 feet high, and in some cases stretching for more than 100 feet before intersecting with yet other fieldstone walls. These walls serve to enclose segments of land, each several acres in size, as if demarcating the property holdings of invisible homesteads. But whose property? Whose homesteads? Again, mysterious. Why would anyone feel compelled to do all the work necessary to segregate sections of land by piling up thousands of heavy, dense fieldstones in the middle of a thick, damp woodland whose sole purpose today is to provide a home to deer, raccoons, and opossums and to afford a place for quiet contemplation of nature by its human visitors?

As you continue farther along the trail into the woods and farther from the magnificent homes with their precisely groomed lawns and beautifully landscaped surroundings, the stone walls seem to loom larger around you. They are taller, more elaborately made, and increasingly out of place in the apparent long-standing wilderness that surrounds you. Then, in the distance, along the trail, an opening in the trees becomes apparent. Upon arrival at the clearing, you spy a complex, well-made, fieldstone foundation of a large structure with a substantial square block of stones presenting large fireplaces on

FIGURE 1.1
Now deep in a thickly wooded game refuge, stone walls like this one once lined the roadways and gridded the fields used by the inhabitants of Pilfershire and hundreds of other communities scattered throughout New England.
(K. L. Feder)

each of its four faces (Figure 1.2). It is obviously the remnant base of the center chimney of a substantial house whose superstructure, likely wood-framed and sheathed in clapboard siding, is gone now, but whose stone-piled foundation clearly indicates its size and configuration. Walking around the foundation, it is easy to locate the well. Sprinkled about you on the ground, mixed in with oak and maple leaves, pine cones and needles are bits and pieces of ceramic vessels; large chunks of thick-walled, utilitarian stoneware crocks; more delicate shards of plain, white-glazed dishes; spalls of oddly thick, green glass; and deeply rusted iron nails, not round like our modern ones but squared off, looking more like little pegs of metal than nails.

Curious enough that this foundation sits in the middle of the woods, a healthy walk from the nearest inhabited home, but even more curious when you continue past the large foundation and realize it is but one of several, perhaps as many as 50 altogether, stone foundations and simple cellar holes, embedded deeply in the woods, some distance from the modern neighborhood of elegant homes.

What was this place? When was it inhabited? Who lived here? What happened to their seemingly once thriving small community? Why was it abandoned? Where did the inhabitants go?

FIGURE 1.2

This stone foundation is all that remains of one of the structures that made up the long-since-deserted Pilfershire community located in north-central Connecticut. Stone walls, foundations, wells—along with the objects used and then lost, abandoned, or discarded by the inhabitants of the community—represent the part of the past that endures into the present. This book presents what we know about the grand sweep of human history through the analysis of the enduring physical remains of the past. (K. L. Feder)

These are vexing questions, but one thing is certain: A specter of the past surely endures into the present at this place. Though now little more than a collection of stone walls and cellar holes in the middle of the woods, 200 years ago this was the nucleus of a thriving community called Pilfershire, with homes, cleared fields, farms, barns, a cider mill, a school, various small industries, and shops. The children of Pilfershire once ran along paths in a village that are now hiking trails in a wildlife sanctuary. The path taken to get to this place, curiously broad for a simple hiking trail and mysteriously bounded by stone walls, is what remains of the old coach road that conveyed people and goods to and from the village. People worked, prayed, laughed, loved, lived out their lives, and ultimately died at this place. Now they are ghosts, and their community is little more than a point of interest in a nature trail guide. Oh, and one more thing: What was once their community is now an **archaeological site,** an enchanted place where the past resides in the present.

A FOREIGN COUNTRY

In the wonderful title of David Lowenthal's (1988) book whose wording he took from the English novelist L. P. Hartley, it is phrased in this way: *The Past Is a Foreign Country*. With that literary image in mind, we might say that the site where the remnants of the Pilfershire community can be found today represents a place where we in the present can visit that exotic land that is the past. This past seems foreign and exotic because it is so unexpected. It is a

FIGURE 1.3

Carnac, in northwest France (top), a spectacular, 5,000-year-old display of several thousand upright stones arrayed in more than a dozen neatly parallel rows, and the well-known Colosseum in Rome, a stadium that could hold nearly 50,000 spectators upon its completion in A.D. *80 (bottom), are examples of very impressive ancient archaeological sites.* (K. L. Feder)

past that reflects common people living ordinary lives, lives too often ignored or only briefly glided over by history.

In a sense, Pilfershire represents an abandoned, forgotten part of human history, but it is not unique. All over Connecticut, throughout New England, scattered around the United States, and, in fact, densely dispersed across the globe (Figure 1.3), there are innumerable "lost villages," places where the detritus of past people lays abandoned in the woods, nestled under meters of sand, ensconced in ancient layers of soil, hidden deep in the recesses of dark caverns, and even embedded in rock (Figure 1.4). The pasts reflected in these lost villages—and lost quarries, encampments (Figure 1.5), killing fields, fishing stations, sacred places (see Figure 1.5), trading posts, mines, hunting camps, and burial grounds (Figure 1.6)—reside in our present in the form of material remains left behind by human beings who lived their lives centuries, millennia, and even millions of years ago. The remnants of their homes and

FIGURE 1.4

Hidden in a niche in a cliff in northern Arizona, Montezuma's Castle was the site of a small community of Native Americans who inhabited the area more than 600 years ago. These Easter Island Moai were never completed and still rest in the quarry where they were being sculpted nearly a thousand years ago. Ancient communities and places of work, like quarries, mines, hunting grounds, can all become part of the archaeological record. (K. L. Feder)

FIGURE 1.5

Called Newspaper Rock, this panel of petroglyphs or "rock-writing" (left) represents another way in which people alive decades, centuries, and millennia ago have left messages that archaeologists in the present attempt to understand. Even something as mundane as a stone tool, like this broken arrowpoint (right) found in a small village site in West Simsbury, Connecticut, can speak volumes to the archaeologist hoping to examine the lives of people who lived long ago. (K. L. Feder).

FIGURE 1.6

The dead can speak to archaeologists directly, as seen here (right) in the gravestone of Hephzibah Cornish who died in 1755, leaving behind a grieving husband who truly loved her. People in the distant past also left memorials to those they loved and respected and for whom they grieved; here (left), a burial mound in Collinsville, Illinois, specifically, Mound 72 at Cahokia (see chapter 15), marks the location of the grave of an important ruler of the community, interred alongside a retinue of human sacrifices including 53 young women and four men. (K. L. Feder)

possessions—even the remains of their own bodies—continue their slow descent into oblivion, but at least for some of them, we have arrived before they have turned to dust, before they are, in fact, dead and gone. In these providential instances, we have arrived in time to tell their stories.

This book strives to accomplish that task of storytelling through the application of the sciences of **paleoanthropology** and **archaeology.** This book is not about the story of a single time or place but of all the times and all the places of humanity. It is a travelogue, of sorts, in which together we will visit the "foreign country" that is our species' enduring past.

AN ANTHROPOLOGICAL PERSPECTIVE

Paleoanthropology and archaeology are subfields within the broader discipline of **anthropology** (Figure 1.7). Contemporary anthropology is the study of people. Of course, the other social sciences—economics, political science, psychology, sociology—also study people but from very particular perspectives, focusing on specific aspects of human behavior. Anthropology, on the other hand, attempts to be holistic and integrative in its approach. If other social scientists specialize in the workings of specific systems within human society, anthropologists tend to be generalists who want to know how human society, with all its interrelated parts, works as a whole and how it came into existence.

Some anthropologists—called **ethnographers**—study humans by residing in particular societies and observing the behaviors of the people living in them. Margaret Mead, who spent many years among the Samoans (people inhabiting an island chain in the Pacific Ocean), is probably the most famous

FIGURE 1.7

The major subdivisions of the field of anthropology. Though these subdivisions represent distinct approaches, there are numerous connections among them. Moreover, each can be further subdivided into subspecialities.

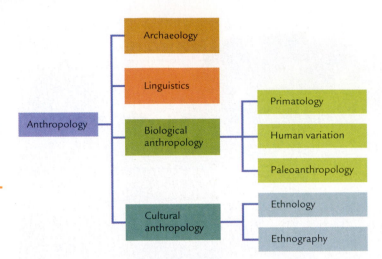

ethnographer (Figure 1.8). In the past, many ethnographers, most of whom were members of Western societies, chose to focus on exotic, non-Western people. Today, ethnographers study inner-city youth gangs, rural farming communities, factory workers, and even the community of academic anthropologists. Each group, in its own way, represents a society—or a part of a larger society—the study of which can tell us something about the human condition.

Researchers who go beyond examining a particular group of people to compare the behaviors of different cultures are conducting **ethnology.** An ethnologist might take the work of several ethnographers who have conducted detailed studies of specific human groups and investigate, for example, how those various peoples deal with death, discipline their children, choose a mate, or build their houses. A highly specialized subfield of anthropology is **anthropological linguistics.** Here, the focus is language—how it evolved and the historical relationships among the known languages.

Primatologists also live with the groups they study (Figure 1.9). Instead of living among and studying people, these anthropologists focus their attention on the group of animals called the nonhuman **primates.** Prosimians, monkeys, apes, and humans are all primates (see Chapter 3). Primatologists aim to better understand our nearest living relatives. Believing that all primates share a common evolutionary heritage, primatologists hope to gain insights into our ancestral line. Jane Goodall, who has devoted much of her life to living among and learning about chimpanzees in the wild, is perhaps the best-known primatologist. Dian Fossey lived and worked with gorillas in the African nation of Rwanda. Her life and work as a primatologist was the subject of a biography by Farley Mowat, *Woman in the Mists* (1987), and the Hollywood movie *Gorillas in the Mist.*

Paleoanthropologists and archaeologists investigate the evolutionary history of humanity, both the biological evolution of our species and its cultural

FIGURE 1.8
Margaret Mead, in native dress (on the left), poses with a native Polynesian woman. (Courtesy of the Institute for Intercultural Studies, Inc., New York. Photo from the Library of Congress)

FIGURE 1.9
Jane Goodall's work among the chimpanzees has provided enormous insight into the lives of chimps and, indirectly, into the lives of our ancient ancestors (see Chapter 3). (Courtesy of the Jane Goodall Institute. Photo by Ken Regan)

evolution. Paleoanthropologists have as their database the early biological history of our species; they focus on the skeletal remains of our ancient human ancestors (Figure 1.10). Paleoanthropologists search for and analyze the fossils of our ancestors, and they rely increasingly on the analysis of modern human DNA in an attempt to solve the puzzle of our genetic roots. In a few lucky instances, they have even been able to extract DNA from ancient bones, reading the genetic instructions for some of our ancestors (see Chapter 5).

Archaeologists, on the other hand, rely on the material remains left behind by past peoples, including those same varieties of human beings whose bones the paleoanthropologists unearth (Figure 1.11). Material remains may include the things people made and used, from simple stonecutting tools to complex monuments. Although archaeology is often perceived as being a

romantic enterprise, it is perhaps better described as the study of "other people's garbage," as a PBS TV documentary called it (PBS 1980).

We humans are not only biological organisms whose adaptation is rooted in our genes but also cultural organisms whose uniquely great intelligence allows us to invent much of our strategy for survival. As researchers first recognized in the eighteenth century, these invented adaptations—our **cultures**—have evolved just as surely as have our bodies and brains. Not only did our human ancestors leave behind their physical remains, which reflected their biological adaptation, but they also left behind the material objects they made and used as part of their cultural adaptation. The study of these two sources of information—their bones and artifacts—allows us to paint a picture of the lives of our ancient human ancestors.

FIGURE 1.10

Donald Johanson, whose work in East Africa has revealed the remains of some of our most ancient hominid ancestors, is shown here at Hadar, a fossil locality that has provided the remains of Lucy and other members of the species Australopithecus afarensis *(see Chapter 3).* (© Institute of Human Origins)

AN ANCIENT WORLD

An understanding of the context of time is crucial in our journey to the "foreign country" of the past. Any discussion of ancient societies requires the recognition that time itself is ancient, and this recognition is relatively recent in Western thought.

The Age of the Earth

It was commonly believed by Europeans in the sixteenth and seventeenth centuries that the world was only a few thousand years old. For example, in Shakespeare's play *As You Like It*, written in about 1600, one of the characters states, "The poor world is almost six thousand years old." In 1642 John Lightfoot calculated creation's date at 3928 B.C., making the world 5,570 years old at that time (Brice 1982:19). There were other, similar estimates.

FIGURE 1.11

Archaeologist Melinda Zeder of the Smithsonian Institution has worked extensively in the Middle East, exploring some of the world's most ancient Neolithic sites (see Chapter 9, especially the "Case Study Close-Up").
(Courtesy of Melinda Zeder)

Ultimately, most people in the Western world came to accept the determination of Irish archbishop James Ussher that the earth had been created in 4004 B.C. and that God had begun the work "upon the entrance of the night preceding the twenty-third day of October" (from Archbishop Ussher's *Annales,* in Brice 1982:18). This date later became widely accepted; beginning in 1701, it was printed as a marginal note in all English Bibles. Though Ussher's precise figure is often maligned by modern scientists and writers, he arrived at it in 1650 through detailed historical research, analysis of astronomical cycles, and reference to biblical genealogies (Gould 1991).

Along with a young earth, many Western thinkers believed the world to have been created by God, just as we now see it, during the creation week discussed in the Old Testament of the Bible. Most believed that the world was "fixed" or set at creation and that everything that was a part of that world—plant and animal species, as well as human beings—had changed little, if at all, since creation less than 6,000 years previously. John Ray, a reverend, naturalist, and scientist, was perhaps the most eloquent spokesman for this **creationist** perspective. In his view (1691, Preface), the world around him reflected "the works created by God at first and by him conserved to this day in the same state and condition in which they were first made."

A WRECK OF A WORLD

Other Western thinkers disagreed with Ray's perspective, believing, instead, that the earth had changed radically from the original creation and that this change had been decidedly for the worse. They agreed that the world God created had been perfect and that some of that perfection could still be seen and used as an argument for God's existence, but they also viewed the modern world as a pale reflection of the perfect place God had created. Benjamin Franklin summed up this perspective best when he characterized the earth of his time as "this wreck of a world we live on" (Greene 1959:39).

Most naturalists in the late seventeenth through eighteenth centuries were **catastrophists.** They believed the world had changed dramatically since creation through a series of catastrophic, natural processes set in motion by God upon his original creation of the world. Catastrophists generally believed that these natural processes could be understood through careful study.

Noah's Flood

One example catastrophists pointed to as evidence of the process of catastrophic deterioration of the earth was Noah's flood. The Bible states that God decided to destroy the world and all its living things through a great universal deluge, saving only the family of Noah and representatives of each kind of animal. Astronomer Edmund Halley (after whom the famous comet is named) proposed in 1694 that a comet crashing into the earth (sent, of

FIGURE 1.12

Following Edmund Halley, William Whiston suggested that a comet striking the earth had been the cause of Noah's flood. In this illustration, a comet passes by the earth, deforming the planet into an oblong shape. According to Whiston, the flood resulted from water in the comet's tail (shown here on the right) as well as water gushing up from the earth's interior when the surface cracked because of its deformation. (William Whiston, *New Theory of the Earth*, 1696)

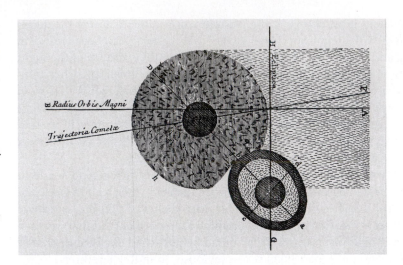

course, by God) might have initiated the great flood. Halley feared the reaction if he published such a seemingly mechanical or naturalistic explanation for divine retribution for human depravity, so he circulated his idea only among friends. In 1696, however, another writer, William Whiston, published precisely this hypothesis in *A New Theory of the Earth* (Figure 1.12). To accommodate this physical explanation to theology, Whiston suggested that God had known during the creation week that the human species would descend into a depraved state and immediately set in motion the comet, preordained to encounter the earth at just the right time!

Some catastrophists believed that great floods, like Noah's but at a smaller magnitude, had been the primary natural agency by which God caused his creation to wind down. Imagine devastating tsunamis, like the one that ravaged Indonesia, Sri Lanka, and India in late 2004, afflicting the planet on a regular basis. Others suggested that earthquakes and volcanoes were more important processes in the deterioration of the earth since creation. The south Asian tsunami was caused by a submarine earthquake, so this modern catastrophe would fit here as well. In either case, catastrophists faced a problem of scale. For example, flooding was a common natural phenomenon that often wrought great destruction, and volcanoes were understood as capable of incredible devastation; but the power of these processes seemed far too limited to produce, in the accepted time frame provided by Bishop Ussher, the kinds of planetary decay catastrophists believed characterized the earth. Though enormous on a human scale, great floods and powerful volcanic eruptions seemed trifling on a planetary scale. The tsunami of 2004 wiped out hundreds of communities, killed as many as 150,000 people, and was an enormous human tragedy, but it was not a catastrophe on a planetary scale. Most of the earth and most of its people did not suffer its direct effects. Catastrophists had to posit that calamities—the likes of which human history had never witnessed or recorded—had occurred in the past in order to produce the degree of degeneration they perceived in the physical world.

EQUABLE AND STEADY CHANGE

Scottish scientist James Hutton became one of the first proponents of a hypothesis that stood in opposition to catastrophism (Figure 1.13). In his view, first espoused in his seminal and revolutionary work *Theory of the Earth,* "The operations of nature are equable and steady," not unpredictable and catastrophic (1795:19). This viewpoint, held by others as well, gave rise to the new perspective of **uniformitarianism.**

Hutton viewed the world as a marvelously constructed, perfectly synchronized machine—not merely switched on at creation and destined to run down, but brilliantly conceived to readjust and re-create itself continually. Certainly Hutton believed in God, but not one who would create a perfect world programmed to begin to disintegrate immediately after its creation. Hutton proposed a world designed by a creator so clever that slow and steady processes of decay were eternally offset by slow and steady processes of rejuvenation.

For example, catastrophists interpreted the discovery of the fossil remains of marine organisms at locations hundreds or even thousands of miles from the coast and at elevations of several thousand feet above sea level as evidence for a universal flood as described in the Bible. Hutton viewed these data quite differently. He believed that the presence of fossilized marine organisms on dry land indicated that these places had at one time been under the ocean. He suggested that during earth's history the hardest mountains erode, producing fresh soil in which plants can grow and on which humans can subsist. These soils are continually washed out across the land into rivers and ultimately flow into the oceans, where they become part of the seabed. Marine organisms live and die on these surfaces, depositing their shells. All of the loose materials at the bottom of the sea—including those fossil remains—eventually are consolidated through heat and pressure back into rock again, and through volcanic action the rock is slowly raised up to become mountains once more. Eventually, these mountains also will erode back into soil, the soil will be washed back into the sea, and so on, ad infinitum. Because of this endless cycle, any investigation of the history of the earth reveals "no vestige of a beginning—no prospect of an end" (Hutton 1795:200).

In a conceivably indirect criticism of Bishop Ussher's calculation, Hutton maintained that "time, which means everything in our ideas and is often deficient in our schemes, is to nature, endless" (1795:15). Processes like **erosion** and **weathering**—seen every day in rivers cutting their channels, in tides resculpting the shore, or in wind carving canyons—could have produced the present appearance of the earth if afforded sufficient time. Hutton argued

FIGURE 1.13
Eighteenth-century Scottish geologist James Hutton, one of the first and most persuasive proponents of uniformitarianism. (James Hutton, *Theory of the Earth,* 1795)

that once it was accepted that these ordinary processes were responsible for earth's alteration since creation, earth's actual age could be deduced. Through the careful scientific study of the rates and patterns of ordinary processes of erosion and weathering, "we find . . . means for concluding a certain portion of time to have necessarily elapsed, in the production of those events of which we see the effects" (1795:19).

For the earth to have attained its appearance, modern observable phenomena must have been operating long enough to have produced mountain chains, meandering rivers, great canyons, and eroded valleys. Because the rates of erosion and weathering could be measured, one needed only to ask how long such processes must have been operating in order for modern features to have formed.

ANCIENT HUMANS?

In 1797, only two years after the publication of Hutton's expanded version of *Theory of the Earth*, John Frere, a young Englishman, found some curious stone tools in a brick-earth quarry in the small English village of Hoxne (Figure 1.14). His letter describing the artifacts to the London Society of Antiquaries was read before the group in the same year and printed in its journal in 1800 (Frere 1800).

Some of the objects Frere reported on were finely made, as were other stone tools of sharp flint previously found throughout England and elsewhere in Europe. With Hutton's concept of an ancient earth still quite controversial, however, all of human history—including a period when cultures made stone

FIGURE 1.14

Two views of one of the flint implements discovered and reported on in 1797 by John Frere. Frere believed that the great depth at which the implements were found, as well as their position in a soil layer beneath one in which the bones of extinct animals had been located, indicated great antiquity for the makers of such tools.
(© Society of Antiquaries, London)

tools instead of metal ones—had to be shoehorned into Bishop Ussher's calculation of a less than 5,700-year-old earth.

This time frame resulted in some remarkable suggestions about the primitive-looking stone objects that Frere and others had found. Some seventeenth-century observers proposed that they had been fashioned, not by ancient people but by modern elves and fairies! In the mid-1600s, in a more naturalistic but equally improbable explanation, Ulisse Aldrovandi suggested that such objects were produced by nature through "the admixture of a certain exhalation of thunder and lightning with metallic matter . . . which is coagulated by the circumfused moisture and conglutinated into a mass" (Daniel and Renfrew 1988:29–30).

Other scientists in the seventeenth century were not quite so enamored of explanations that relied on fairies and elves or thunder and lightning. They suggested that these flint objects had been made by people in the past. But this explanation still was hampered by the restriction that a previous race of stone-tool-using humans could be no more than about 6,000 years old because that was the age of the earth and the universe that God had created. Some scientists suggested that the tools were made by pre-Adamites (literally, people "before Adam," created by God in a previous construction of the world not mentioned in the Bible). Another approach that conformed better to the 6,000-year restriction and a more standard biblical view was to credit the manufacture of the implements to a race of barbaric people who had lived after Adam and before Noah's flood.

The Implications of Frere's Discovery

What made Frere's discovery so significant was that for perhaps the first time, primitive stone tools could be shown to have originated at great depth (in this case, 12 ft below the surface) and that the bones of extinct animals were found *above* the tools, in more recent soil layers. Frere recognized that from a uniformitarian perspective, this placement implied a great age for the tools and, in turn, a significant age for the humans who had made them.

Frere's argument for the antiquity of the artifacts he found was based on their **stratigraphic** position in the quarry. Frere and members of the London Society of Antiquaries may have been aware of the work of surveyor William Smith, who a few years earlier had recognized that the soil beneath the earth's surface occurred in layers and that the layers produced ordered and regular groups of fossils. Smith showed that the layers could be identified and distinguished by their population of fossil species, with sequentially lower layers representing increasingly ancient time periods. In 1799 Smith circulated a handwritten table showing the order of strata he had encountered, but he did not publish a detailed report until 1815, laying the groundwork for the analysis of **stratigraphy** (see Chapter 2; Grayson 1983).

Frere's excursion to Hoxne may have put him at the right place to add to the mounting evidence for the uniformitarian perspective of an ancient earth—and to show that the human species was a part of that story—but he surely had made his discovery at the wrong time. Frere had figured out that the clay pit at Hoxne was a place where the past endured into the present, but he couldn't prove that this past was ancient. Smith's stratigraphic work was quite new, and Hutton and his supporters were in the midst of the first skirmishes of a battle to defend uniformitarianism against the attacks of a hostile scientific and religious community. Hutton and his followers were more interested in evidence related directly to the age of the earth than in other, somewhat incidental, and even more controversial evidence confirming a human presence on an ancient earth. As scholar A. Bowdoin Van Riper (1993) points out, even many ardent uniformitarianists continued to maintain that humans were a recent addition to an ancient earth that had passed through a series of stages leading up to the modern world. Sadly, Frere's letter to the society about the stone tools and their apparent great age was promptly forgotten.

More Stone Tools . . . and Bones

Additional evidence discovered in the early 1800s provided tantalizing evidence for the great antiquity of humanity, but it also failed to convince most scientists. For example, in 1828, in the town of Narbonne, France, a museum curator reported the discovery of human bones together in the same cave deposit with the bones of extinct animals. The gentleman who made the discovery, however, elected not to make any connection between the human and animal remains, suggesting that their co-occurrence was a result of chance (Daniel and Renfrew 1988:33).

At about the same time, Father John MacEnery announced the discovery of flint tools and the bones of extinct animals in Kent's Cavern in Torquay in southern England. MacEnery's evidence, gathered between 1824 and 1829, strongly suggested that the tools and animal remains were of equal age; they were found together, sealed beneath a stalagmite in the cavern. MacEnery's writings show him initially to have been quite excited about the implications of his discovery as it related to the antiquity of humanity. Nevertheless, MacEnery ultimately backed off from any claim of association between the tools and the bones of extinct animals (Grayson 1983). Most scientists believed, despite the lack of evidence, that the stone tools had gotten under the stalagmites only recently, when humans dug out ovens in the cave floor (Daniel and Renfrew 1988:33–34).

Jacques Boucher de Perthes was a French customs official with a passion for artifact collecting, finding hundreds of flint implements in his excavations in the high gravel terraces overlooking the River Somme in northern France. In the title of the book he wrote presenting his work, published in 1847, he labeled these chipped stone tools *antediluvian,* meaning, literally, "from before the flood." Certainly the tools appeared to be primitive and ancient, but, just as important, Boucher de Perthes found the artifacts in deep excavations, in the same layers where he also recovered the bones of extinct animals, including those of bison, woolly mammoth, woolly rhinoceros, and cave bears (Stiebing 1993). As had been the case with the stone tools unearthed by John Frere in England, it was the stratigraphic context and association of the tools with fossil bones that provided strong evidence for their great antiquity, dating, in fact, from a time when people relied on stone, not metal, for their weapons and tools and when animals long since extinct roamed the European countryside.

These and other discoveries made in the early years of the nineteenth century implied a greater antiquity of the human species than was allowed for in Bishop Ussher's biblically based chronology. The unearthing of tools and bones seemed to place our species deep in time in Hutton's uniformly changing, ancient earth. Yet none of these discoveries separately or together were viewed as compelling by most scientists.

The denial of great human antiquity might be ascribed to pressure applied by the church or simply to a stubborn refusal to accept the evidence. But, as archaeologist Donald Grayson (1983) shows, this is an unfair assumption. Certainly there was a desire to reject the claim of great age for our species, but until about 1859 the evidence supporting this claim just wasn't that strong. Stratigraphy was a new approach, and archaeological excavation methods were not well developed. In the court of scientific opinion, the physical association between artifacts and the bones of extinct animals could not be proved beyond a reasonable doubt.

THE SLOW AGENCY OF EXISTING CAUSES

Hutton had fired the first salvos in a revolution in thinking about the processes responsible for the physical features of the earth and the age of the planet. But in the intellectual battle that ensued, Hutton barely was able to hold his position. The human place in time could not be established when time itself was still a point of such great contention. It became the task of the brilliant British geologist Charles Lyell (Figure 1.15) to continue this revolution in thinking about the past and to provide time enough for an ancient humanity. The subtitle of Lyell's seminal work, *Principles of Geology,* first published in 1830, conveys the essence of his approach: "An attempt to explain the former changes of the earth's surface by reference to causes now in operation" (Lyell 1830).

To come to a rational understanding of the earth, Lyell felt it necessary to dispense entirely with "imaginary pictures of catastrophes and confusion such as haunted the imagination of the early cosmogonists" (1830:72). His fundamental assertion was that "all past changes on the globe had been brought about by the slow agency of existing causes" (1830:63).

Perhaps the most revolutionary and problematic deduction from such a hypothesis concerned the time necessary to produce the kinds of geological features seen on the earth if only the "slow agency of existing causes" was considered. Lyell himself admitted, "The imagination was first fatigued and

FIGURE 1.15
Nineteenth-century English geologist Charles Lyell. Lyell was the most eloquent and thorough of the uniformitarianists. (Charles Lyell, *Principles of Geology,* 1830)

overpowered by endeavoring to conceive the immensity of time required for the annihilation of whole continents by so insensible a process" (1830:63). But he went on to apply his fundamental axiom of uniformitarianism to estimate the ages of significant geological features. In a work published in 1863, for example, Lyell calibrated the modern rate at which the Mississippi Delta was growing and concluded that at its current rate of growth it must have taken 100,000 years to have attained its size.

Needless to say, such an estimated age for the Mississippi Delta was shocking to those who accepted Bishop Ussher's determination for the age of the entire earth. Lyell was viciously attacked in print and charged with heresy, but such allegations rang hollow. Though the Bible measures the period of creation as six days, it does not place that creation week in time; nowhere does the Bible actually record the age of the universe, earth, or life. Hutton and Lyell's view and that of uniformitarianism may have contradicted the interpretation of an archbishop, but they did not disclaim the word of God.

Lyell was a great scientist and a persuasive proponent of the uniformitarian perspective. His work resonated in the minds of many geologists, biologists, and archaeologists and freed them from the perspective of a recent earth into whose chronology all of their observations and deductions had to be crammed. Charles Darwin later was to state, without too much exaggeration, "The science of geology is enormously indebted to Lyell—more so, as I believe, than to any other man who ever lived" (F. Darwin 1961:51).

ANCIENT HUMANS REVISITED

With Lyell, uniformitarianism was to become the orthodox perspective in geology. The earth was old, and its story could be read in its ancient layers. Discoverers of primitive-looking stone artifacts found at a great depth began to suggest great antiquity for humanity as well—how old was still a matter of conjecture but certainly far greater than Bishop Ussher's calculation of about 5,700 years. With the discovery of clusters of such stone tools and with no evidence of the use of metals found alongside, it became increasingly obvious that human cultures had changed dramatically since the makers of those stone tools had lived.

Cultures Ancient and Changing

Just six years after the initial publication of Lyell's *Principles of Geology*, a guidebook was published describing the artifacts that could be seen in the Danish National Museum in Copenhagen. Written by Danish museum curator Christian Jurgensen Thomsen, the guidebook organized the museum's collection chronologically into three prehistoric ages—stone, bronze, and iron—based on the most-favored raw materials used to make tools during each of the three epochs.

Inherent in Thomsen's **three-age system** was the notion that culture had changed through time, in a predictable sequence. The three ages were developmental as well as chronological. There was an implied succession of increasing technological sophistication, an evolution toward tools that were better (more effective, more durable) but also more difficult to manufacture.

That culture had been undergoing great change during human tenure on the planet was no more evident in the nineteenth century than was the notion of an ancient earth. In fact, it was surprising to some Western thinkers that the very oldest traces of human culture did not include metal tools. They assumed that metallurgy had been around at least since the time of Noah. Thomsen deserves credit for recognizing and making explicit in his guidebook that the archaeological record clearly shows great changes in human technological abilities.

FIGURE 1.16
Charles Darwin, the father of modern biological evolutionary theory. (Neg. # 108781, courtesy of Department of Library Services, American Museum of Natural History)

CHARLES DARWIN AND THE ANTIQUITY OF LIFE

In 1828 a bright, young Englishman entered Cambridge University in pursuit of a degree in theology. His name was Charles Darwin (Figure 1.16).

Darwin took a natural science course at Cambridge under a brilliant scientist and charismatic professor, John Stephens Henslow, a remarkable teacher who became a mentor to many of his students. Henslow genuinely liked Darwin and felt that he had a real knack for observing nature. He recommended his young student to a position aboard a British government survey ship, the *Beagle,* which was to produce detailed sailing charts of the coast of South America and then circumnavigate the world. The voyage would begin in 1831 when Darwin was just 22 years old. Despite some initial misgivings on the part of his father, who was still supporting him financially, Darwin agreed to the position and began a mission that was supposed to last 2 years but actually lasted closer to 5. Though officially hired to be a companion to the ship's young captain, Darwin's training was as a naturalist, and he spent much of his time on the voyage around the world observing nature and collecting plant and animal specimens in places far removed from England. Thus, events had conspired to push the young theology student to collect the data that would, 28 years later, lead to one of the most important books ever published in the name of science.

AN EVOLUTIONARY PHILOSOPHY

Evolution is the focus of Darwin's work and the organizing theme of this book. The term itself evokes so much emotion and misunderstanding that it is important first to put it in context.

Biological evolution simply implies a process of systematic change through time. The natural world is vast and diverse, and many living things are born into it. Some of those living things possess, by chance, characteristics that increase the likelihood of their survival and of their having descendants who share those advantageous characteristics. An individual may be faster, stronger, more dexterous, or able to move more efficiently through its habitat. It may be better camouflaged, have better visual acuity, be better at attracting a mate, or possess greater intelligence. These advantages may make it more likely to survive and more likely, therefore, to pass those characteristics on to subsequent generations.

Over vast spans of time, an entire species can be moved toward these advantageous characteristics, because those who lack them tend to die more quickly—often before becoming old enough to mate and produce descendants who also lack them. Through the slow and steady accumulation of advantageous characteristics or as the result of the rapid appearance of a dramatically different and advantageous feature, a species can become so different that it no longer is even the same kind of animal. It has become a new and different species: It has evolved.

The varied and changing natural world provides the context in which an organism must live and to which it must adjust. Biological evolution is not directed; species do not actively develop strategies for survival—called **adaptations.** And biological evolution has no direction; species do not necessarily become bigger, stronger, or faster. In fact, the fossil record shows that most species become extinct. Those that survive do so because at least some individual members are lucky enough to possess physical or behavioral adaptations that allow them to.

For some species, the means of adjustment go beyond the solely biological. Such species are able, as a result of their great intelligence, to develop new adaptations virtually instantly. They can invent new ways of surviving and teach these new ways to other members of their species and to their offspring. These survival methods are not genetically determined in the manner of a thick coat of fur, powerful jaws, or grasping hands and feet; they are cultural. Though made possible by the biological feature of a large and complex brain, culture represents a strategy for survival beyond that which is provided by an animal's genes. Modern human beings rely, as did our ancient human ancestors, on cultural adaptations for survival. A discussion of these adaptations and how they, too, have systematically changed through time makes up a large portion of this book.

The Mutability of Species

Although he didn't think it was important at the time, Darwin recognized that animals he encountered on islands off the coast of South America resembled, but were not identical to, animals found on the mainland, where they must have originated. The island descendants of mainland species seemed to have altered from their original state after migrating. The descendants must have become better adjusted, or **adapted,** to the different environmental conditions in their new habitats. Even on different islands within island chains, individual kinds of animals resembled each other, though differing in significant attributes from island to island.

For example, on the Falkland Islands, off the southeastern coast of South America, foxes were recognizably different from one island to the next. All these island foxes must have come from the mainland, so why were they different from mainland foxes, why did they vary from island to island, and how could this variety have occurred? On the Galápagos Islands, 500 miles west of the northwestern coast of South America, Darwin found that tortoises living on each of the dozen large islands could be differentiated, and so could finches—small birds whose source was certainly the mainland. The finches did not look precisely like any other South American finch, and they differed in form and behavior among islands. How had each type of finch become uniquely adjusted to the particular features of its island if the finch species was immutable and fixed at creation? This mystery simply could not be explained within the accepted paradigm of the fixity of species.

In 1836, after a long and successful voyage, Darwin and the *Beagle* returned triumphantly to England. Many of Darwin's reports and specimens had preceded him, and he returned to find his work roundly praised by the scientific community. Darwin met and was befriended by geologist Charles Lyell, who was extremely grateful that Darwin's geological observations matched precisely his uniformitarian view of the evolution of the earth.

THE ORIGIN OF SPECIES

Darwin's masterpiece, *The Origin of Species by Means of Natural Selection,* was published in 1859. In the introduction to the book, Darwin succinctly articulates the essence of his theory:

> As many more individuals of each species are born than can survive; and as, consequently, there is a frequently recurring struggle for existence, it follows that any being, if it vary, however slightly in any manner profitable to itself, under the complex and sometimes varying conditions of life, will have a better chance of surviving, and thus be *naturally selected.* From the strong principle of inheritance, any selected variety will tend to propagate its new and modified form. (Darwin 1859:7)

As Darwin saw it, variation within a species—of foxes, tortoises, finches, and so on—provided some individuals with characteristics that allowed them a better chance for survival under the conditions established by nature. He called this process "**natural selection**" because, in essence, those individuals were "selected" by nature to survive and pass along their advantageous characteristics to their offspring. In this way, for example, finches of a single species might lose their way in a storm and get blown to an island where conditions were quite different from those at their mainland home. Many of the finches would die, unable to survive in their new circumstances; but a few might, by chance, possess characteristics that would enable them to endure. They would pass those features on to their offspring; and over many generations, birds with those qualities would continue to be selected for—that is, to survive. After a time, the island finches would no longer resemble the mainland finches. Given sufficient time, they might become so different that they would be a different species entirely.

Human Evolution

As astounding as Darwin's suggestions were, perhaps what bothered people most was the deduction that this process could be applied to the evolution of human beings. An ape with a slightly larger brain and greater intelligence might be more apt to survive than his or her slower cousins. Over time, through natural selection, large brains would be increasingly selected for and eventually the ape would become human. The implication so shocked Charles Lyell that, though by and large a supporter of Darwin and a close personal friend, he never quite accepted that human intellect could be produced via such a mechanism.

Darwin knew how delicate the subject of human evolution might be. In 1857 he wrote to his colleague Alfred Russell Wallace: "You ask whether I shall discuss 'man.' I think I shall avoid the whole subject, as so surrounded with prejudices; though I fully admit that it is the highest and most interesting problem for the naturalist" (Bowlby 1990:325). He hinted at the applicability of natural selection to humanity in *Origin* when he concluded that, by the application of the theory, "Much light will be thrown on the origins of man and his history" (Darwin 1859:243). As we will see throughout this book, Darwin was right.

The Human Factor

In 1856, the year before Darwin indicated to Wallace his desire to steer clear of any mention of humanity in his discussion of evolution, a partial fossil skull was found in the Neander Valley in Germany (see Figure 5.11). At least two similar skulls had been found previously in Europe (in Belgium and on Gibraltar), but these largely were ignored. The Neander Valley skull, like those found previously, was as large as a modern human skull, though it looked quite different. As we will see in Chapter 5, whereas some scientists declared the large, flat skull with great ridges of bone above where the eyes had been to be a pathological oddity, others saw it as representative of an ancient race of humans.

Discoveries related to the question of human antiquity accelerated in the late 1850s. A few months before the November 1859 publication of Darwin's *The Origin of Species,* the respected geologist John Prestwich delivered an address to the Royal Society of London announcing his belief that flint tools he had seen in France, which had been excavated by Boucher de Perthes, provided convincing evidence of the great antiquity of humanity. The archaeologist John Evans had accompanied Prestwich to France and had come to the same conclusion. The week after Prestwich's speech, Evans delivered a speech to the London Society of Antiquaries—the same society John Frere had written to 62 years earlier—in which he asserted that Frere had been right after all. The sites he saw in France convinced him of the great age of the flint artifacts he saw there—they looked just like the artifacts Frere had discovered, and they were in a similar stratigraphic position. Evans concluded: "This much appears to be established beyond doubt, that in a period of antiquity remote beyond any of which we have hitherto found traces, this portion of the globe was peopled by man" (Daniel and Renfrew 1988:37).

With the notion of a uniformly changing, very ancient earth in place, the new artifactual and skeletal evidence began to convince many people of the great antiquity of the human species. There still was substantial debate over what "great antiquity" meant on any kind of a fixed time scale. No date could be assigned to the early humans who had made the stone tools, nor could any age be assigned to the German skull. But scientists were clearly shifting their opinion and beginning to view the earth and the human species as ancient— far older than 6,000 years.

Also in 1859, the venerable Charles Lyell announced that he was now convinced of the chronological length of the human presence on the earth, which he knew to be ancient (Daniel and Renfrew 1988:37). His publication of *The Geological Evidences of the Antiquity of Man* would come four years later (1863), providing a massive compendium of the evidence for ancient human traces. Lyell's initial statement of support for great age for humanity and especially the publication of *Geological Evidences* meant the previous heresy of a greatly ancient human species now bore "the stamp of scientific orthodoxy" (Van Riper 1993:9).

CULTURES EVOLVING

Led first by Hutton and then Lyell, the uniformitarianists had shown that the earth was old; the pages of its ancient history were the strata that lay beneath our feet. Archaeologists had discovered human-made objects on those ancient pages, proving the great antiquity of humanity within the stratigraphic history of the planet.

Darwin had gone on to show that within the lengthy history of the earth, plants and animals had changed dramatically; they had, in fact, evolved. And now, the ancient human-made objects found by the early archaeologists—the stone tools—provided clear evidence that human culture had evolved over an enormous period of time as well. As Charles Lyell himself pointed out (1863:379), if culture had remained constant throughout human history, then archaeologists should have been finding "buried railways or electrical telegraphs" along with other scientifically advanced artifacts in ancient stratigraphic layers. Instead, archaeologists were finding stone tools, admittedly finely made but essentially and fundamentally primitive, associated with the bones of extinct animals in ancient stratigraphic levels. Clearly this was evidence of great change from the culture of the earliest humans to that of the modern (nineteenth-century) world. As surely as geologists had shown that the earth had sustained enormous change over a vast expanse of time and as surely as biologists now were showing that life itself had experienced great change, so archaeologists were showing that human behavior had also changed greatly during our species' history on earth.

The recognition of great cultural changes from earliest times to the present lent support for the three-age system and its identification of all that had happened in between. What Christian Jurgensen Thomsen understood and made concrete others now began to build on in constructing broad theories of cultural evolution. For example, Edward Tylor's *Researches into the Early History of Mankind and the Development of Civilization* (1865) expanded on Thomsen's chronology, subdividing his stone age into an "unground stone" phase (in which tools were produced by the presumably more primitive method of flaking or striking) and a "ground stone" phase (in which tools were produced by the presumably more advanced method of grinding and polishing).

For most Western thinkers in the nineteenth century, the cultural evolution they perceived in the archaeological record was synonymous with cultural progress. Tylor (1871:198) characterized culture change as "in the main, an upward development." Tylor and others assumed that if the world and even human beings were not the stable, safe, reassuring entities they had once been presumed to be, at least the human past told a story of continual, if slow, improvement. And not surprisingly, nineteenth-century European scientists assumed that the pinnacle of cultural development was nineteenth-century Europe. To them, the archaeological record presented a long and remarkable tale of a species hoisting itself up from its original primitive state to an ever-increasing level of civilization.

Some scholars suggested specific sequences of culture change that most of humanity had passed through in the long ascent toward modern civilization. For example, anthropologist Lewis Henry Morgan (1877:8) theorized that "the experience of mankind has run in nearly uniform channels." In Morgan's view, cultures evolve through stages he labeled savagery, barbarism, and civilization (with each stage involving substages) and are marked by increasingly complex material culture and greater sophistication in how people feed themselves. Where Thomsen's sequence dealt only with the advancement in the raw materials used to make tools, Morgan's included the invention of fire and pottery, the development of farming and animal husbandry, the use of iron tools, and, finally, the invention of a written, alphabetic language. In Morgan's view, virtually all cultures in human history had passed through his various stages, and those that were still in one of the more primitive levels by the nineteenth century had simply become "stuck" at some stage in this universal sequence as the result of something lacking in their society—for example, an important invention like metal or an alphabet.

We now view culture as adaptation, as the fundamental way in which people adjust to their surroundings. Cultures change as conditions change, and there is no necessary "upward" movement or progress. Cultures survive not because they become better but because they become better adapted to their world. Nevertheless, thinkers like Thomsen, Tylor, and Morgan made the important observation, not self-evident in the nineteenth century, that human behavior has vastly changed through time. This behavior became translated into the material record, which provided the data the early archaeologists used to frame their cultural evolutionary constructs. That same material record—now much expanded—continues to provide much of the data on which this book is based. The methods by which archaeological data are gathered and analyzed are the focus of the next chapter.

OUR MODERN VIEW

We began our historical discussion with a belief in an unchanging universe that was created less than 6,000 years ago by an omnipotent God and that was populated by plants, animals, and people whose forms and qualities were forever fixed at creation. That universe was simple, predictable, and reassuring.

We now hold the modern scientific view of the universe and life, initially espoused by Lyell and Darwin, as ancient and dynamic, unpredictable and serendipitous, awesome and awful.

What we have lost in terms of a pleasant and comforting view of the world and the human species' place in it is more than made up for in the infinitely fascinating story we can now tell of the evolution of our species. And as seventeenth-century scientist and clergyman John Ray stated, "Those who scorn and decry knowledge should remember that it is knowledge that makes us men, superior to the animals and lower than the angels, that makes us capable of virtue and happiness such as animals and the irrational cannot attain" (Raven 1950:251).

SUMMARY

Though many people assume that the past is merely dead and gone, in fact it can endure into the present in the form of the material remains of the things ancient people made and used. The sciences of archaeology and paleoanthropology endeavor to find and analyze those remains in an attempt to tell the story of human antiquity. That story is the focus of this book.

Time is the backdrop against which the story of humanity is played out, and until fairly recently the depth of time was unknown. Most Western thinkers in the seventeenth century believed that the world and all life within it had been established during a creation week that had occurred not even 6,000 years previously. They further believed that their world was just as God had made it and reflected the perfection of creation.

Some natural scientists, on the other hand, saw the world as a "wreck," which had decayed since the time of creation. Viewing the world as quite young, perhaps no more than 6,000 years old, these thinkers suggested that the history of the earth had been marked by a string of catastrophes.

James Hutton and Charles Lyell were spokesmen for a different perspective. Rejecting claims of hypothetical catastrophes, they explained the appearance of the earth on the basis of observable, slow, steady, and uniform natural processes. They asserted that such observable natural phenomena could produce the current state of the earth if afforded sufficient time. They measured the age of the earth not in thousands of years but in hundreds of thousands and even millions of years. Especially during the nineteenth century, researchers began uncovering tantalizing bits of evidence—in the form of flint implements together with the bones of extinct animals and even those of human beings—that suggested this ancient earth had been populated by early forms of humanity.

Charles Darwin viewed the biological world as the result of natural processes of change. His theory of natural selection provided an overarching explanation for the diversity of life on the planet. With the amount of time provided by Hutton and Lyell's perspective of earth history, the process of natural selection could have produced the great diversity of life seen on the planet, the differences and similarities among different kinds of organisms, even the evolution of humanity.

TO LEARN MORE

Technical Summaries

For a firsthand glimpse of how the scientists discussed in this chapter worked out the problems presented by the study of the origins of life and the planet and of how they reached the conclusion that the earth was ancient and changing, there is no better place to go than the original works. These sources are cited in the text.

Popular Summaries

Two excellent sources on the history of archaeological and paleoanthropological thoughts are Glyn Daniel and Colin Renfrew's *The Idea of Prehistory* (1988) and William Stiebing Jr.'s *Uncovering the Past: A History of Archaeology* (1993). For more detailed coverage of the early history of the discipline, see Donald Grayson's *The Establishment of Human Antiquity* (1983) and A. Bowdoin Van Riper's *Men Among the Mammoths: Victorian Science and the Discovery of Human Prehistory* (1993). If you are interested in a detailed discussion of the life of Charles Darwin, John Bowlby's 1990 monograph, *Charles Darwin: A New Life,* is simply terrific. Charles Raven's 1950 biography, *John Ray, Naturalist: His Life and Works,* shows how a great seventeenth-century thinker accommodated both his religious faith and his scientific perspective.

On the Web

For a comprehensive listing of Internet sites related to the field of anthropology in general, with many sites focusing on archaeology and paleoanthropology, one of the best places to visit is Anthro.Net at http://www.anthro.net/. Here you will find a huge number of links to Web sites focusing on various subdisciplines in anthropology, including topics that are addressed in this book (human origins and evolution, the Paleolithic, ancient civilizations). Anthro.Net also provides links to the Web sites of anthropology journals and academic departments that offer anthropology programs.

Online Learning Center: www.mhhe.com/feder4

The Online Learning Center (OLC) Web companion to *The Past in Perspective* features a variety of supplemental study aids. For each chapter, this free Web site includes:

ONLINE LEARNING CENTER

- Self-Quizzes to take as pretests prior to exams
- Interactive Timeline Study Guides for additional review and reinforcement of key information
- Learning Objectives
- Chapter Site links with Web addresses for many of the fossil and archaeological sites mentioned in the text

KEY TERMS

adaptation, 22	creationist, 13	primate, 10
adapted, 22	culture, 12	primatologist, 10
anthropological linguistics, 10	erosion, 15	stratigraphic, 17
	ethnographer, 9	stratigraphy, 17
anthropology, 9	ethnology, 10	three-age system, 21
archaeological site, 6	evolution, 21	uniformitarianism, 15
archaeology, 9	natural selection, 23	weathering, 15
catastrophist, 13	paleoanthropology, 9	

2

Probing the Past

CHAPTER OVERVIEW

Paleoanthropologists and archaeologists study the actual physical remains of human beings and those of our evolutionary ancestors. They also examine the material remains of the behavior of these ancient ancestors: the things that past humans made and used and then lost or discarded. Through the investigation of the bones of humans and human ancestors, as well as the analysis of the objects they left behind—tools, weapons, items of adornment, works of art, structures, and so on—paleoanthropologists and archaeologists hope to better understand the ways in which our ancestors evolved and adapted. This chapter summarizes many of the most important and widely used techniques relied on by these scientists to paint a picture of the human past.

Applicable range of major dating techniques

	2 million	1 million	900,000
Radiocarbon Radioactive decay			
Archaeomagnetism Alignment of particles in cultural deposits with the earth's magnetic field			
Dendrochronology Counting of annual growth rings of trees			
Uranium series* Radioactive decay		▪▪▪▪▪▪▪▪▪▪▪	
Obsidian hydration Chemical process: accumulation of weathering rind on artifact			
Fission track Radioactive decay leaves microscopic tracks in crystals at known rate	▬▬▬▬▬▬		
Luminescence Radiation damage: accumulation of energy in crystals			
Electron spin resonance Radiation damage: accumulation of unpaired electrons in crystals	◀▬▬▬▬		
Potassium argon (K/Ar) Radioactive decay		◀▬▬▬	
Paleomagnetism Alignment of particles in natural deposits with the earth's magnetic field	◀▬▬▬▬		

*Uranium series results older than 300,000 years are statistically questionable.

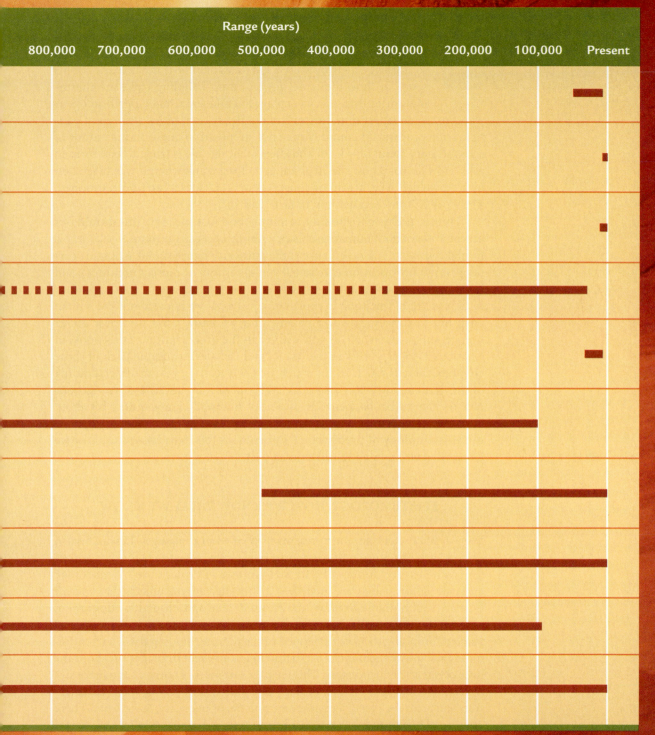

ONLINE
LEARNING
CENTER

Go to **www.mhhe.com/feder4** for an
interactive study guide version of this timeline.

31

PRELUDE

Do you remember hearing or reading any of Rudyard Kipling's "just so stories" when you were a kid, tales like "how the leopard got his spots" or "how the camel got his hump"? Kipling's tales are charming stories that seek to explain to children, usually in a humorous way, how some aspect of nature or human behavior attained its present configuration or form. Of course, you're not supposed to question the author of a just so story about how he or she knows that the tale is true; it's bad form to ask, "How do you know the elephant got a long trunk when it was tugged on by a crocodile?" The "truth" of a just so story, of course, can't be questioned. The story is "true" because it is, in fact, "just so."

Human prehistory should not simply be a just so story. You should not accept a story about human prehistory simply because on some level it seems to make sense to you or because some authority figure said it was so. It certainly is not my intention here to tell you the stories of human prehistory and have you believe or accept them just because I say they are so. It is important in the context of this book to explain not just what we know about the human past, but to convey, however briefly, how we know what we know about human antiquity. In fact, as you will see in the organization of this book, in Chapters 3–15, especially in the "Issues and Debates" section of each of those chapters, there is much about which we are uncertain in our understanding of the human past. Many issues are still contentious, and there are vigorous debates about what happened in antiquity. But we do know quite a bit about the human past, even our most ancient antiquity. The focus of this chapter is the **epistemology** of prehistory. Its purpose is to briefly introduce how we know what we know about the human past.

EPISTEMOLOGY: HOW WE KNOW WHAT WE KNOW

Every field of scientific study presents its own set of challenges. Researchers in each branch of science must develop a specific set of methods for data collection as well as techniques of data analysis and interpretation. Archaeology and paleoanthropology are no different. Our data are the objects that ancient humans and human ancestors made, used, lost, abandoned, or discarded, along with the physical remains of the species themselves. Archaeologists and paleoanthropologists have developed procedures for finding these ancient remains along with techniques for extracting from them information about the lives of our ancient ancestors. This chapter summarizes some of the more significant methods used in archaeology and paleoanthropology for data collection and analysis. The discussion here will be, of necessity, quite brief. There are several fine textbooks whose primary focus is the methodology of archaeology and paleoanthropology, examining in detail how we know what we know about the human past. A listing of these sources is provided in the "To Learn More" section of this chapter.

The "Science" in the Study of the Past

Science often begins with objective observation of the world or universe. For example, biologists examine living things; astronomers focus on other planets, stars, and galaxies; and geologists observe the earth itself. Anthropologists, on the other hand, concentrate on humanity, with paleoanthropologists and archaeologists focusing more specifically on the human past.

All scientists observe the world and look for patterns or correlations, cause-and-effect relationships, trends, and trajectories in an attempt to puzzle out the rules that govern how the world works—how the earth was formed, how rivers flow, how life originated, how humanity evolved, or how people adapt through their cultures. To be sure, scientists are not blank slates or passive receptors of the data they encounter in research. Dominant perspectives called **paradigms**—think of a paradigm as scientific worldview or conceptual framework—play a significant role in how we structure our research, in the kinds of research that receive funding, in what kinds of evidence we look for, and in how we interpret and interpolate what we do find. The hallmark of science, however, rests in its constant assessment, testing, probing, and revision. New approaches and new interpretations, in archaeology, paleoanthropology, and all other sciences, are constantly being proposed and then tested. One of the great strengths of science rests in its ability to accept data that are surprising and unexpected.

From the things they observe and the patterns they perceive, scientists come up with general explanations, or **hypotheses,** for what they have observed. Scientists are not content, however, just to generalize about the world. They also need to test these hypotheses by predicting what other data will be found if a hypothesis is valid, if it accurately explains how things work. Paleoanthropologists and archaeologists accomplish these tasks by applying the procedures outlined in this chapter and by a rigorous adherence to the scientific method.

Our goal may be to understand the mysteries of life, but science is a process as much as a result and rarely provides absolute answers to our questions in any field. With our imperfect knowledge and incomplete understanding, usually we can expect no more than increasingly better approximations about how things are—or were. Certainty is a rare commodity in any of the sciences.

In archaeology and paleoanthropology we are examining our own human past and time periods enormously distant from our own. It is one thing for a chemist to examine a chemical reaction and suggest a rule that governs how those reactions progress; it is one thing for a microbiologist to focus on a colony of bacteria and suggest a hypothesis for how those bacteria react to heat or an overabundance of food. These chemical reactions and bacteria are of the here and now, and they are apart from us. It is quite another thing for paleoanthropologists and archaeologists, who gaze back across the centuries, millennia, and eons of human history where the data are ancient, elusive, and rare and where our interpretations impinge on how we view ourselves. Did we humans begin our journey as a "killer ape," and what does it mean to us if we did? Were the world's first civilizations dependent on slavery and warfare, and if so, what does this knowledge tell us about our twenty-first-century civilization?

As scientists, we must always be aware of and try to transcend our own preconceptions of what we think the past *should* tell us—or what we would like it to tell us—about ourselves. Our constructs of the past should be objective and free of our own temporal and cultural biases. This ideal is not easy to achieve, and we archaeologists and paleoanthropologists have sometimes fallen short of these goals. Further, we must recognize that our interpretations of the human past are approximations subject to continual refinement, major overhaul, or even complete abandonment as new data and new ways of looking at the same data come to the fore.

PALEOANTHROPOLOGICAL AND ARCHAEOLOGICAL SITES

Paleoanthropological and archaeological **sites** are places where physical evidence of a past human presence can be recovered. Such evidence consists of (1) the skeletal remains of human beings or human ancestors, (2) **artifacts**—objects made and used by past peoples (Figure 2.1), and (3) **ecofacts**—environmental elements that exhibit traces of human use or activity, such as the bones of butchered animals (see Figure 7.22, for example).

Wherever people lived or worked, they used material from the surrounding environment: stone, clay, metal, wood, bone, plant fiber, seeds, antler, animal hides, and so on. These materials ultimately are lost, used up and discarded, abandoned, or hidden away for future use. Where conditions in the soil allow for their preservation, these items can be found and recovered for analysis by scientists who study the human past. Together, these physical remnants make up the archaeological site. A site was once a home, a community, a place of work. It now is a place where data can be collected that will enable us to tell the story of that home, that community, and that workplace.

Sites are defined not only by the recovered objects themselves but also by the physical arrangement of the remains. The preserved spatial context of archaeological remains—where things were used and left by an ancient people—allows us to reconstruct the activities that took place at a site. Most reconstructions of past times are based on analysis of human remains, artifacts, and ecofacts, as well as their spatial arrangement at sites where people lived or performed special tasks. Sites can be small and short-term, like hunting camps, or large and permanent, like the sites of the world's first cities in Mesopotamia (see Chapter 11).

How Sites Are Formed

Sites come into existence through a series of site formation processes (Schiffer 1976): Tools can be discarded or lost; food remains can be thrown in a trash

FIGURE 2.1
Artifacts, features, and sites are primary elements of archaeological analysis. For example, all of these 1,500-year-old stone blades from Connecticut are artifacts: objects that ancient people made and used (top). This 4,000-year-old stone platform represents a cooking feature: it is the physical manifestation of an activity conducted along the banks of the Farmington River (middle). Hovenweep, located in southwestern Colorado, is a nearly 1,000-year-old site, a place where people lived and worked (bottom). (K. L. Feder)

pit or pile; dead bodies may be casually abandoned or intentionally and cere-monially buried; valuable objects may be "cached," or hidden away, for a future retrieval that never takes place; human ancestors may be killed by animals and their remains dragged into a lair; and so forth. The study of how paleontologi-cal remains ended up in a particular place is called **taphonomy;** we can also apply this term to the study of how paleoanthropological or archaeological remains came to rest in their place of discovery. Recognition of how items be-came part of the paleoanthropological or archaeological record provides in-sights into the behavior of the human beings who left those artifacts behind.

Archaeological artifacts and ecofacts used or produced together to accom-plish a task—to make stone tools, to prepare food, to carry out a ceremony—often are deposited together on the ground in a pattern that reflects the spatial arrangement of the activity. These clusters of archaeological material are called **features** and can be analyzed in our attempt to reconstruct a particular activity or set of behaviors. When **activity areas** are intact—in other words, where the items used together and deposited together are left exactly where they fell by ancient people—we use the term **primary refuse.** The next time you see inconsiderate folks leave the remnants of their picnic lunch behind on the ground, don't think of it as a gross mess, think of it as primary refuse. The remnants of that lunch, the waste flakes resulting from the production of stone tools left where they fell and the skeletal elements of an animal left where it was butchered are examples of primary refuse.

The Simsbury trash dump, now called the landfill, was used as the collec-tive garbage disposal point for residents of my town for nearly 70 years. The landfill began as a deep, broad depression where, beginning in 1920, residents would haul their trash for disposal. Slowly, the depression became filled with trash, but town residents kept coming; and by 1988, what was once a trash pit had become a substantial trash mountain more than 60 feet high. The Sims-bury landfill and countless others throughout the world represent **secondary refuse** accumulations, places where members of a community disposed of their trash. Just like us in the modern world, ancient people also often cleaned up the places where they carried out tasks, removing the objects used and produced from their primary contexts to a designated refuse area or areas. Just as we use refuse dumps and recycling facilities in our towns and cities, people in the past often took their trash to a pile or pit, removing from the immediate vicinity of their living quarters material that might be dangerous, that might attract wild animals or noxious insects, or that might simply oth-erwise be a nuisance (perhaps because of its smell).

How Sites Are Preserved

Once material objects are laid on or in the earth, natural processes may cover, protect, and preserve them. Volcanic ash or lava, silt from a flooding river, sand blown by the wind, a collapsed cave roof, an avalanche—all may cover the objects left behind by people, preserving them until nature or anthropologists uncover them many years later. Some of the materials used by people, especially stone tools and pottery, preserve very well under most circumstances. Other materials, like bone and plant remains, require particular conditions for preservation. When archaeologists and paleoanthropologists are lucky, an archaeological site is itself like a fossil, a preserved physical representation of a past people and way of life.

In certain cases, the catastrophic agency of a community's destruction ironically acts, at least in part, to preserve the archaeological site left behind. There is no better known example of this than what occurred at the beautiful Roman harbor town of Pompeii (Cooley 2003).

Nestled between the Bay of Naples and the foot of a towering volcanic mountain named Vesuvius, the residents of Pompeii had long been subject to the rumblings of their looming neighbor. We know that an enormous earthquake rocked Pompeii in A.D. 62, causing significant damage. In the years following this, numerous smaller tremors were felt by the city's residents, who likely became inured to the bad behavior of the volcano. Those tremors increased in frequency and amplitude in the early summer of A.D. 79 and then, on August 24, Vesuvius erupted catastrophically, hurling what is estimated to have been about 4 cubic km (a cubic mile) of ash into the atmosphere, some of it reaching an altitude of as much as 30 km (more than 18 mi; that's three times higher than the cruising altitude of a standard commercial jet). The prevailing wind, along with gravity, brought the plume of **ejecta** over the city, resulting in a shower of **pumice** that accumulated like an eerie, ashy snow on the streets and rooftops. Falling at an estimated rate of 15 cm (about 6 in.) per hour (faster, by far, than any snowfall you have experienced), the weight of the accumulating pumice eventually collapsed roofs and filled the streets and houses of Pompeii, attaining a height of about 2.8 m (9 ft) (Cooley 2003:40).

It is believed that the accumulating pumice killed only a few hundred residents of Pompeii, but it was a series of **pyroclastic** surges—what amounts to a sequence of extraordinarily hot avalanches—on August 25 racing down the slopes of Vesuvius at speeds approaching 200 km (almost 125 mi) per hour that killed thousands more and, essentially, killed the city as well (Cooley 2003:42). Pompeii had succumbed to one of the most awesome forces in nature and lay as a great sepulcher, undisturbed, for more than 1,500 years

After its destruction, Pompeii and the area surrounding the city were abandoned by any who had survived the eruption of Vesuvius, and no attempt was made to rebuild. Once abandoned, Pompeii slowly faded from memory until it was all but forgotten.

The initial fall of pumice had killed hundreds and destroyed most of the homes of Pompeii's residents, but it also protected the walls of those homes from the destructive force of the pyroclastic flow on the following day. Sealed in pumice, these walls—as well as the boulevards, avenues, and back alleys of Pompeii—were neither burned nor crushed, but preserved, insulated from the elements and looters. Then, in A.D. 1595, just a little more than 400 years ago and more than 1,500 years after its tragic destruction, the city was rediscovered

FIGURE 2.2
Volcanic ash was long ago removed by archaeologists from around the columns, arches, walls, and stairways of Pompeii, here dramatically framed by the jagged caldera of Vesuvius, the volcano that destroyed the city and killed many of its residents. (K. L. Feder)

by excavators. Researchers soon began the arduous task of removing the hardened ash and pumice layer, revealing the homes, theaters, and civic buildings of Pompeii, with their sometimes well-preserved wall paintings and tiled mosaics. Though the roofs are gone, today the city is a strange place, a ghost town that appears to have been abandoned months or only a few years ago (Figure 2.2).

Even some of the inhabitants of Pompeii were preserved, in a way, when their bodies were entombed by the ash deposited by the pyroclastic surges on August 25. Entombed in a hard crust of ash, the bodies decayed away, leaving a hollow in the shape of the deceased. When discovered, these hollows were filled with plaster and the ash chipped away, revealing a series of extraordinary phantasms—crudely cast, three-dimensional images of human tragedies (Figure 2.3).

How Sites Are Found

Archaeological sites are found in a number of ways. While some natural processes may preserve sites, other such processes may expose them. Rivers cutting into their banks, wind blowing sand away from an area, or waves eroding a beach may bring to light ancient, buried remains (Figure 2.4). Many of the sites related to the earliest history of humanity have been exposed by these processes of erosion. Places such as Olduvai Gorge in Tanzania and the Hadar region of Ethiopia (see Chapters 3 and 4) present naturally exposed layers of ancient geological deposits (Figure 2.5). By walking over these places systematically in a procedure called **pedestrian survey,** paleoanthropologists and archaeologists found many of the important ancestral human fossils discussed in this book.

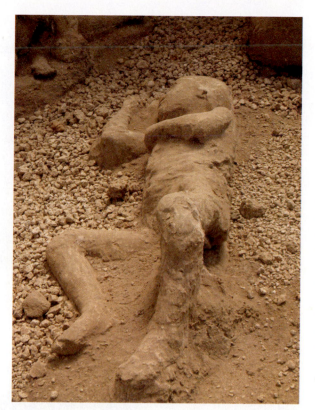

FIGURE 2.3
Eerie images of people, like this one of what appears to be a sleeping child, were made when archaeologists found gaps in the volcanic ash that covered Pompeii, which they then filled with plaster. The child depicted here was not sleeping, but dead, a victim of the eruption. The falling ash first killed the child and then hardened before the body decomposed, leaving a hollow, a perfect child-shaped mold of one of those unfortunate enough to have been caught in the catastrophic eruption of Vesuvius in A.D. 79.
(K. L. Feder)

FIGURE 2.4
At Skara Brae, in the Orkney Islands north of Scotland, an ancient site a few thousand years old was exposed by the winds and waves of a North Atlantic storm. (K. L. Feder)

FIGURE 2.5
The ancient soil levels and many sites of Hadar have been revealed through the slow-acting process of erosion. Much of Don Johanson's work on the fossil species Australopithecus afarensis *(see Chapter 3) has been conducted at Hadar (see also Figure 1.10).* (© Institute of Human Origins)

FIGURE 2.6
In areas of the world where natural processes have not exposed ancient sites, archaeologists must dig to reveal buried cultural deposits. Test pits are often excavated to explore an area for buried archaeological material. (K. L. Feder)

In other cases, archaeologists do not have the luxury of naturally exposed ancient layers in which to search for artifacts, ecofacts, or human skeletons. In these areas, scientists search for sites through a process of subsurface sampling, placing **test pits** at regular intervals in an attempt to locate ancient material buried by natural processes (Figure 2.6). In some cases, sophisticated **remote-sensing** devices—ground-penetrating radar, proton magnetometers, electrical resistivity meters—can help in the search for sites by probing for anomalous readings under the surface that may indicate the presence of buried cultural material or soil disturbance by ancient people (Conyers 2004). Aerial photography can help identify large-scale land modifications or buried remains that affect the growth of vegetation.

The strategies we employ in archaeological survey are determined by the interaction of a number of variables. Most important among these are **visibility** and **obtrusiveness** (Schiffer et al. 1978). Visibility is a factor of the local environment and refers to the ease with which an observer can detect the presence of archaeological remains at a given place. Regions where (1) there is little vegetation growth to obscure above-ground remains; (2) soil deposition is minimal and, therefore, material exposed on the surface is not buried; (3) natural processes, like wind or flowing water, do not remove archaeological material on the surface; or (4) loose material burying archaeological remains is regularly removed by erosion present the archaeologist with high visibility. Pedestrian surveys can be highly effective in areas where any combination of these factors applies. Places where vegetation grows quickly and thickly or where local geological processes quickly deposit materials on anything left on the surface, and where erosion does not act to remove those deposits, are said to be of low archaeological visibility. In areas marked by low visibility, archaeological material is buried, and there may be no obvious evidence on the surface that there are remains underfoot. Here, test pits and the use of remote-sensing devices may be necessary to find sites.

Obtrusiveness is a factor of culture and refers to the size, durability, and density of the remains left behind by an ancient people. Monumental, durable architectural remains—pyramids made of stone, adobe pueblos, brick citadels—are highly obtrusive in that they preserve for long periods of time and, as a result of their size, are often easy to discern on the surface, even many years after they were abandoned.

Sedentary groups that did not build large structures may still have left behind obtrusive remains; living in one place for a substantial period of time can produce sites where small, individually unobtrusive items build up into dense deposits that are highly obtrusive. The sites produced by a nomadic people, living for only short periods of time at any given place, who made small tools of fragile material, leave behind clues of their presence that are far more subtle and difficult to discern.

Finally, the complex interaction of natural visibility and cultural obtrusiveness determines the ease with which sites will be found and prescribes the procedures that will most effectively find them (Figure 2.7). A sedentary people who lived in dense populations and who constructed great monuments of stone in an environment with little vegetation growth and a slow-acting process of geological deposition—think ancient Egypt—produce sites that are relatively easy to find through pedestrian survey. Of course, these people may also intentionally bury materials—most obviously, the remains of the dead and their accompanying grave goods—rendering those remains less obtrusive than materials left on the surface. A nomadic group that built small, portable structures of fragile material and who left behind only dispersed

FIGURE 2.7

A large-scale monument, like the Great Sphinx of ancient Egypt, made of durable material in a region without quickly growing vegetation may be both highly obtrusive and highly visible (top). A small nineteenth-century Connecticut village where foundations were made of stone may be obtrusive, but visibility may not be high where vegetation grows quickly (middle). Finally, a small, thousand-year-old village whose inhabitants made no large or permanent structures may disappear completely from the surface as organic material decays, and durable material is covered by floodborne deposits. The site in the bottom photograph was discovered through excavation.

(K. L. Feder)

FIGURE 2.8
To maintain the spatial relationships among the materials found at a site, archaeologists often excavate in square units, slowly peeling away soil layers. (K. L. Feder)

scatters of small stone tools in an environment where vegetation grows quickly and where streams and rivers flood regularly, depositing sometimes thick layers of **alluvium**—think the United States, east of the Mississippi River—produces sites that require a different set of procedures to locate, including test pitting and remote sensing.

How Information Is Recovered

Once a site has been found, the arduous task of extracting the physical evidence from the ground begins. Paleoanthropological and archaeological evidence is rare, precious, and often fragile, so the methods used to unearth it have been designed accordingly.

We must recover our data with great care. Though we may use power equipment and picks and shovels to remove the culturally sterile overburden, once within the zone of a site, we ordinarily rely on handheld trowels, dental picks, and brushes to remove the soil enclosing site materials (Figure 2.8). Material may be left exactly where found in order to expose the possible **associations** among the remains. For example, a single stone, found and then tossed in a bag, is not nearly as informative as a series of stones, each one left in place, that together denote an earth oven (Figure 2.9).

Context is the key here. A single artifact, devoid of any context—where it was found, what items it was found in proximity to—provides the archaeologist or paleoanthropologist with only a fraction of the information provided by an object for which context has been preserved and recorded. Consider the various possible contexts of a spearpoint in Figure 2.10. In 2.10b the spearpoint is found embedded in an animal bone. In 2.10c the same artifact is depicted as part of a **cache,** or collection, of other spearpoints. In 2.10d, again the same artifact is shown, this time stuck in the eye orbit of a human being. Finally, in 2.10e the spearpoint is shown as one of two next to the skeletal

FIGURE 2.9
The stones lining the bottom of a 4,000-year-old earth oven demarcate this archaeological feature. The stones were heated in a fire and then placed in the bottom of a pit, where the heat radiated by the stones was used for cooking.
(K. L. Feder)

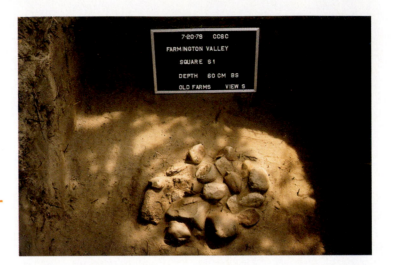

remains of a person. In each case the spearpoint is exactly the same, but its setting and spatial associations differ, suggesting different uses or meanings of the object, respectively: a hunting weapon, part of a tool kit, a weapon of war, an offering to a deceased member of the group.

Though it might be an exaggeration to say that in archaeology context is everything, context certainly is crucial. This should explain in part why archaeologists and paleoanthropologists are meticulous and exacting in excavating sites. A site is much more than just the sum of its individual parts (artifacts and ecofacts). Objects need to be carefully exposed, leaving them, at least initially, in place in order to preserve their spatial contexts and associations. This also explains why detailed and time-consuming record keeping is important before specimens are removed from the ground and returned to the lab for analysis.

As careful as we are in excavating a site, we can miss small fragmentary remains. All excavated soil ordinarily is sifted through wire screening of ¼-inch, ⅛-inch, or even smaller mesh, to ensure 100% recovery. In some cases the soil matrix may be taken to an on- or off-site lab, where standing water may be used to help in separating artifacts, ecofacts, or human bone from the surrounding soil.

ANALYZING ARCHAEOLOGICAL DATA

Like detectives at the scene of a crime, archaeologists collect physical evidence at the scene of a life. We can break this archaeological evidence down into the following categories: artifacts, ecofacts, and human skeletons. Each category requires its own forms of analysis.

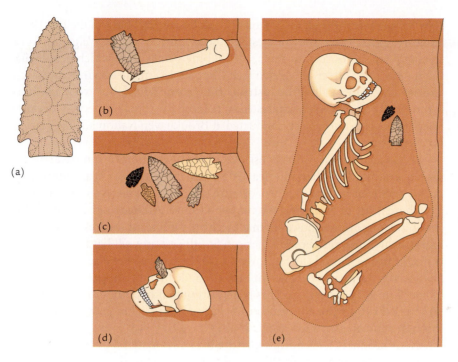

(a)

(b)

(c)

(d)

(e)

FIGURE 2.10
*An isolated artifact may
reveal much about an
ancient technology, but to
determine the use and
meaning an object had to a
past people, context is
crucial. Consider the same
hypothetical artifact (a)
recovered archaeologically
from very different con-
texts; (b) embedded in
an animal bone; (c) as one
in a cluster of spearpoints
found in an ancient hiding
place; (d) stuck in the skull
of a human being; (e) as a
grave offering to a deceased
hunter. In each case the
artifact looks exactly the
same, but its context—and,
therefore, its deduced use
and meaning—is different.*
(From Kenneth Feder and
Michael Park, *Human Antiquity:
An Introduction to Physical
Anthropology and Archaeology,*
Fourth Edition, Mayfield Publishing Company, 2001. Reprinted with permission from
The McGraw-Hill Companies.)

How Artifacts Are Analyzed

In analyzing artifacts, at a minimum we want to know where the raw materials for the objects came from, how the items were manufactured, how they
were used, and the social context in which they were made and used.

The Sources of Raw Materials   We can figure out where ancient people obtained their raw materials through a process called **trace element analysis,** in
which impurities present in tiny or "trace" amounts are scanned for. Essentially,
this involves a precise determination of the chemical makeup of artifacts and of
potential geographic sources for the raw materials from which artifacts were
made by any one of a number of procedures such as **neutron activation analysis** and **X-ray fluorescence.** The percentages of particular impurities often are
unique and diagnostic of specific sources and can serve as a fingerprint for place
of origin. Artifacts are examined for their particular percentages of these trace
elements. Possible sources for the raw material from which the artifact was
made are also examined for their trace element percentages. If a raw material
source and the artifact have matching trace element profiles, a scientist can usually suggest that the raw material for the artifact derived from that source.

When I retrieved my copy of the January/February 2005 issue of *Archaeology* magazine from the mailbox, I briefly glanced at the table of contents and
immediately saw the name Phil Weigand. Phil had been one of my professors
when I was an undergraduate archaeology student at the State University of

New York at Stony Brook (now Stony Brook University) back in the late 1960s and early 1970s. Even more interesting, the article focused on Weigand's work tracing possible sources for the beautiful blue stones from which people like the Aztecs and Toltecs of Mexico (see Chapter 13) made carvings, mosaics, and jewelry. They called the lustrous blue stone *xiuitl*, but we know it as turquoise. I was extremely interested in reading the article, especially because I had worked on the project, conducted at Brookhaven National Laboratories, for a semester.

It has been conservatively estimated that a million turquoise artifacts have been found in Mesoamerica (Powell 2005), but there is an interesting problem; there aren't any known, extensive turquoise sources in central Mexico where most of the artifacts have been found. Archaeologists and geologists have long known, however, that there are significant sources of extremely high-quality turquoise in the American Southwest, not all that far away from central Mexico. Could the Southwest turquoise have been the raw material from which the artisans of ancient Mexico made their often spectacular works of art (Figure 2.11)? Weigand has been testing that hypothesis for more than 30 years through the application of trace element chemistry, specifically through neutron activation analysis (NAA).

NAA produces a chemical signature for a raw material by bombarding it with neutrons. Every chemical component of the bombarded material, in turn, emanates a unique signature of energy, providing a precise picture of the composition of a raw material, down to the tiniest proportions of impurities. This aspect of NAA is useful to archaeologists tracing raw materials because, for many raw materials, different sources have distinguishable and diagnostically different chemical signatures. In other words, two pieces of turquoise (or obsidian or copper, etc.) may look entirely alike, but have distinctive chemical compositions traceable to different sources.

Weigand has collected samples of raw turquoise from 44 sources in the American Southwest and California. I was one of several students who prepared turquoise samples from these sources for NAA, which established the chemical signatures of each of these sources. With Brookhaven Lab physicist Garman Harbottle, Weigand was able, again through the application of NAA, to determine the chemical composition of finished artifacts excavated from sites in Mexico and compare those signatures with sources in the Southwest. And, in fact, many of the artifacts found in Mexico revealed chemical signatures comparable to those of sources located in the American Southwest.

Tool Manufacture and Use   Through **experimental replication,** the process of attempting to authentically re-create ancient artifacts, researchers can assess how an item was made. They also examine historically described groups that possessed a technology analogous to that of the ancient people being studied. Scientists can deduce the use an artifact served from its **morphology**—its form, what it looked like—and by the evidence of **wear patterns.** Different actions (piercing, cutting, scraping, engraving, chopping) performed by dif-

FIGURE 2.11
The raw materials from which artifacts were made can sometimes be traced to their geographic sources through the analysis of their trace element chemistry. In this way, for example, archaeologist Phil Weigand has been able to show that much of the turquoise used to produce jewelry and other items of adornment in ancient Mexico was obtained by the artisans from sources in Arizona and New Mexico.
(© Werner Foreman/Art Resource, NY)

ferent tools on different raw materials (stone, wood, leather, bone, antler) leave distinctive and diagnostic wear traces, or "edge damage" (striations, polish, scars) that can be assessed through replication (Shea 1992). In an experiment conducted by archaeologist Lawrence Keeley (1980), researchers used stone-tool replicas to perform different tasks on particular raw materials. For example, some tools were used to cut animal hide, some were used to saw wood, some were used to scrape meat off of bone, while others were used to drill in antler. Each tool used was then examined carefully under a microscope, and the particular kinds of resulting polish, damage, or wear on each were catalogued. This experiment essentially defined the damage or wear that accompanies each kind of use so that these tools and those from subsequent experiments and experimenters can serve as models for stone-tool wear patterns in the analysis of ancient specimens. If the ancient wear patterns match those seen on a particular experimental tool, researchers can conclude that the archaeological implement was used in much the same way.

Social Patterns   Along with providing insights into technology and use, artifacts can sometimes help illuminate less concrete aspects of ancient lifeways. The particular style of an artifact made by an individual may tell us something about who taught the maker. How people learn to make objects within a culture is a social decision. For example, they may learn from a parent who is passing down a family tradition of spearpoint or ceramic styles. The style seen in the archaeological remains, therefore, embodies this aspect of an ancient social system.

Some archaeological features even more directly reveal the nonmaterial practices of a people. Most obvious here are burials, which often directly

FIGURE 2.12

Burials are archaeological features. They represent a moment in time when a community laid to rest a companion, friend, loved one—or ruler. Burials often reflect the social and economic status of the deceased and, of course, the religious beliefs of the community, especially as these relate to the meaning of death. This museum representation of the main burial of Mound 72, at Cahokia (see Chapter 14) reflects the care with which the residents of this complex community disposed of the remains of an important ruler. (Courtesy of Cahokia Mounds Historic Site)

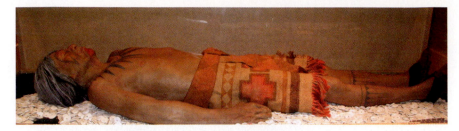

reflect a group's religious ideology as it relates to recognition of the significance of death as well as possible belief in an afterlife (Figure 2.12). Neandertals (see Chapter 5) interred their dead with tools and food 60,000 years ago, and what we uncover may tell us much about their perspective on life and death. Egyptian pharaohs were laid to rest in sumptuous splendor (see Chapter 11), and what we unearth in their pyramids informs us of their beliefs about the meaning of death.

How Ecofacts Are Analyzed

Animal bones, charred seeds, nut fragments, the shells of marine organisms, and fruit pits recovered at sites may represent the food remains of past people. Because diet is an important part of a culture, scientists would like to reconstruct the subsistence practices of prehistoric people.

Because the skeletons of different animal species are usually distinctive, the kinds of animals present in an archaeological deposit can often be identified if remains are not too fragmented. Cut marks on bone are evidence of butchering, and charring from a fire signifies cooking. Both are good indicators that the animal was used for food. Many archaeology labs possess **osteological comparative collections,** or bone libraries, where ancient specimens can be compared to known, labeled specimens to help identify the species recovered in excavation.

The minimum number of animals represented in the **faunal assemblage** at a site can also be reconstructed. Because most animals exhibit two distinct forms on the basis of sex—that is, **sexual dimorphism**—scientists often can distinguish male from female animals. In addition, because animals go through a number of **osteological** developmental stages—changes in their bones as they grow and mature—it is also often possible to determine the age at death of an animal hunted, killed, cooked, and eaten by a prehistoric people. Furthermore, scientists can differentiate the bones of wild animals from those of domesticated animals: Domesticated animals frequently are smaller than their wild ancestors; the teeth of domesticated dogs are more crowded than those of their wolf progenitors; and the bones of wild animals are often denser than those of their domesticated descendants. We can learn much about the subsistence strategies of an ancient people if we can determine the species of an animal and its sex and age, whether the people hunted only older animals, and whether they avoided killing females or killed most of the young males but allowed females to survive to adulthood (a common pattern among domesticated animals).

Plant remains, including seeds, nuts, and wood, can be recovered and analyzed, and the contribution of plant foods to the diet can be assessed. Because plants are available seasonally, the yearly schedule of a people can be reconstructed based on which plant foods are present at a site and which are absent. We usually can differentiate the seeds, grains, or fruits of wild species from those that have been altered by humans through **artificial selection** (see Chapter 9) in the process of domestication.

Ecofacts contribute to our understanding of past human adaptations beyond just enabling a direct reconstruction of diet. These remains also allow us to paint a detailed picture of the past environments in which ancient people lived. From the recovered remains of flora and fauna, we can reconstruct the plant and animal communities that were contemporaneous with ancient societies. Plant and animal communities often rely on a particular, sometimes rather narrow, range of climatic variables including amount of rainfall, length of the growing season, and high and low temperatures. By identifying the existence of particular plant and animal communities in the past, we can deduce the presence of climatic conditions such communities required for their survival.

Macroscopic remains found at archaeological or paleoanthropological sites—as well as materials found off-site dating to the time period the site was occupied, including animal bones, seeds, nut fragments and nutshells, fruit pits, and rinds—can be recovered and identified. The climatic regime that most likely prevailed during the period of human occupation can be deduced based on the requirements of the mix of plant and animal species found. For example, caribou are not native to southern New York State, yet their remains have been found there—apparently they were on the menu—at the Dutchess Quarry Cave site, a more than 10,000-year-old occupation of the Hudson River valley near the modern town of Athens in Orange County. Today, caribou live far to the north in Canada and require a much colder climate than the one that currently characterizes southern New York. Their presence there 10,000 years ago implies a much colder climate then. This, in turn, provides archaeologists with important information about the environment to which human beings living in this same place adapted.

Palynology   One of the most important sources of information about past plant communities is **pollen,** the male gamete in plant sexual reproduction. Pollen grains tend to be rather durable and can preserve for thousands and even tens of thousands of years. Beyond this, pollen morphology is species specific: The pollen produced by each species is unique and distinguishable from the pollen produced by other kinds of plants. In other words, each species produces pollen that can serve in the manner of a fingerprint by which the presence of a species at a particular place in the past can be verified (Figure 2.13).

FIGURE 2.13
*Examples of the pollen
grains of eight different
plant species, magnified
5,000 times. Pollen grain
form is species-specific. By
recovering pollen from
archaeological levels,
palynologists can identify
the plants growing in an
area when it was occupied
in the past, reconstruct the
makeup of a previous plant
community, and deduce the
nature of the environment
that must have been in
place for the reconstructed
plant community to have
survived.* (From Kenneth
Feder and Michael Park, *Human
Antiquity: An Introduction to
Physical Anthropology and
Archaeology,* Fourth Edition,
Mayfield Publishing Company,
2001. Reprinted with permission from The McGraw-Hill
Companies.)

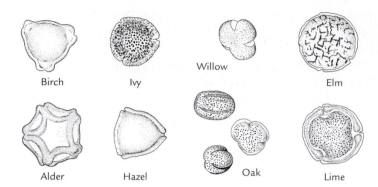

Birch   Ivy   Willow   Elm

Alder   Hazel   Oak   Lime

Upon recovery of pollen from an ancient soil layer at or nearby an archaeological site, researchers can calculate the percentages of the various kinds of pollen falling on a site when it was occupied. Next, they attempt to locate modern locations where the **pollen rain**—the percentages of the pollen of different plant species that rains down in the spring today—is a close match for the percentages derived for an ancient time and place. When a good match can be found, it is reasonable to conclude that the ancient climate in which the site's inhabitants found themselves was similar to the climate of the modern location with a similar pollen rain.

My own state of Connecticut, for example, has four distinct seasons including long, hot, humid summers and cold, snowy winters. Today's profile contains an abundance of pollen from cold-loving trees like pine and birch, but there also is plenty from temperate-climate species like oak, maple, and hickory. Fourteen thousand years ago, however, the pollen falling on the state included only one of these species, pine; 60% of the pollen in that period came from bushes that don't even grow in Connecticut today but can be found thriving only in the Canadian Arctic (Davis 1969). The pollen species percentages as a whole falling on Connecticut 14,000 years ago look nothing like the modern breakdown but are a reasonably good match for what falls in northeastern Canada today. From this we can deduce that the climate of Connecticut 14,000 years ago was probably quite similar to what we find in the modern Canadian Arctic. **Palynology** provides a vital, direct link to the plant communities that characterized given places and times. This, in turn, allows us to suggest what the overall climate was like at those times and places.

Carbon Isotopes   All plants conduct photosynthesis, but not all photosynthesis is the same. In fact, there are a number of different **photosynthesis pathways.** For example, the **C3 pathway** characterizes most trees, and the **C4 pathway** typifies most grasses. These two pathways do essentially the same thing: They are the processes by which plants extract carbon from the carbon dioxide they respire and then use that carbon to produce leaves, stems, roots, bark, wood, and so on. These two pathways differ, however, in how they treat the different varieties (**isotopes**) of carbon in the atmosphere. We will see later in this chapter that one carbon variety, ^{14}C, is valuable in dating archaeological material. Here, an analysis of the concentration of another version of carbon, ^{13}C, provides data that can be useful in environmental reconstruction. C3 pathway plants, the trees, select against ^{13}C during photosynthesis. After trees extract carbon atoms from carbon dioxide, those atoms that happen to be ^{13}C tend to be filtered out and then eliminated. C4 pathway plants, most grasses and sedges, have no such bias. They use whatever ^{13}C they take in and incorporate this carbon into their various parts. As a result, C4 pathway plants have a higher concentration of ^{13}C than do C3 pathway plants.

The soil in which plants grow and even the bones of the animals that ate the plants all reflect the concentration of ^{13}C in the preponderance of plants growing in an area at a particular time period. When and where **carbon isotope analysis** shows that concentration was relatively high, it means that grasses dominated the plant community. When the ^{13}C concentration was relatively low, it means that trees dominated.

As we will see in Chapter 3, an analysis of dramatic changes in ^{13}C concentrations over time suggests fundamental changes in the kinds of plant communities that characterized regions, continents, and even the entire planet. For example, evidence found at multiple locations indicates a worldwide contraction of forests and their replacement by grasslands beginning about 7 million years ago. The time of these shrinking forests is also characterized by a wave of extinction of forest-dwelling ape species and may have helped set the stage for the success of an apelike creature that could thrive in grasslands. That creature may very well have been our ancestor.

Phytoliths   Plants also produce a nonorganic residue consisting of microscopic mineral particles called **phytoliths** (Figure 2.14). Phytoliths are quite durable and can last in soil deposits or, when we are lucky, on the edges of tools used to process the plants that produced them. Phytolith form is unique to each plant species, so, when phytoliths are recovered at an archaeological site, specialists can determine the species of plants growing in the area when the site was occupied and might even be able to tell the species of plants cut, pounded, or ground with the tool.

Oxygen Isotopes   Planetwide changes in climate can also be read in the oxygen isotope record preserved in the fossil shells of ancient marine microorganisms called **foraminifera** ("forams" to those in the know). Foram shells reflect the ratio of two isotopes of oxygen, ^{16}O and ^{18}O, in seawater when these organisms were alive. Because ^{16}O is lighter than ^{18}O, water molecules (H_2O) with the lighter oxygen isotope evaporate more readily than do those with the heavier variety. Ordinarily, this makes little difference because the water that evaporates from the ocean returns as rain or as meltwater from frozen precipitation. However, during cold periods, water evaporates from the ocean and some of it falls as snow on land in higher elevations and upper

FIGURE 2.14
Phytoliths are inorganic, silica bodies produced by plants. Phytoliths are useful to archaeologists because they are durable and each species produces distinct forms; specialists can identify the plant from the phytolith. Pictured here are maize phytoliths. (Courtesy Deborah Pearsall/University of Missouri Paleoethnobotany Lab)

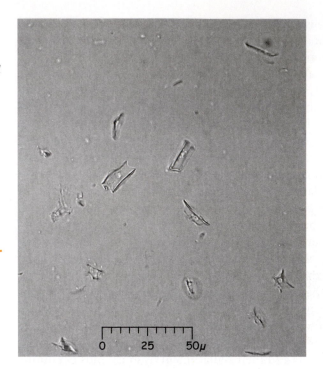

latitudes. During periods of worldwide temperature decline, an increasing amount of that frozen precipitation remains locked as ice, not returning to the ocean. As a result, a disproportionate amount of lighter oxygen water is removed from the evaporation-precipitation cycle during these cold periods. The oceans, therefore, become depleted of ^{16}O relative to ^{18}O. Foram shells reflect this depletion as they incorporate oxygen in the surrounding seawater into their shells. Therefore, when the proportion of ^{16}O in foram shells exhibits a drop, it's a good bet that worldwide temperature was experiencing a decline as well. When later foram shells show a return of higher ^{16}O levels, this indicates a change toward warmer temperatures. The oxygen isotope proportion curve (see Figure 4.12) has been worked out for the past 780,000 years or so based on ancient dated submarine strata in which foram shells have been recovered and analyzed (Shackleton and Opdyke 1973, 1976). Scientists have used this curve to figure out changes in worldwide temperature and glacial ice coverage during the Pleistocene epoch or the Ice Age.

Although the environment cannot cause a particular adaptation to develop, and a change in the environment does not guarantee any specific evolutionary change or behavioral adjustment, it does serve as the stage on which adaptations, evolutionary developments, and behavioral adjustments are played out. Clearly, to understand human adaptation, archaeologists and paleoanthropologists need to understand the nature of the ancient environments to which humans adapted. Reconstructing animal communities through the identification of their bones and reconstructing plant communities on the basis of their macroscopic remains, through palynology, and by carbon isotope analysis contribute to our understanding of the environments that played a crucial role in shaping the human story.

How Human and Prehuman Skeletal Remains Are Analyzed

The bones of human ancestors are an invaluable resource to paleoanthropologists and archaeologists. To begin with, the fact that archaic forms of human beings existed is shown most clearly by the presence of their bones, which are different from those of either apes or modern humans. (See the many photographs in Chapters 3–5 of creatures who were ancestral to us but, at the same time, were not quite us.) These bones can inform us about how human ancestors walked, the kinds of climates to which they were adapted, the foods they ate, their general level of nutrition, and the diseases and traumas from which they suffered. Comparing the bones of ancient human ancestors to those of modern people can help us place these specimens accurately in the human evolutionary line.

The Species Represented by a Bone   Ordinarily, the first question scientists ask about a bone concerns its species. When bones are complete, species identification is relatively straightforward because the precise form of each bone in an animal's body is unique to its species. For example, each of the 212 bones of the human body is uniquely human and cannot be mistaken for the bones of any other animal species. As a result, for the most part, the species of an intact bone found at an ancient archaeological site can be identified with great accuracy.

The identification of species can be tricky when we deal with the remains of possible human ancestors. A first step is to compare the excavated bones with those of modern people. When the recovered bones exhibit features or landmarks that are uniquely human—for example, the position of the point of connection between the top of the spinal column and the base of the cranium reflecting the diagnostically human pattern of walking on two feet rather than four—we can confidently conclude at least that the bones being examined belonged to an individual in the human family. Also, very detailed and careful measurements can be taken of the bones and teeth of excavated specimens. Ordinarily, if those measurements—for example, the thickness of tooth enamel or the proportions of the bones in the hands—fall outside the range of those same measurements taken on human beings, we may conclude that the bones do not belong to a modern human being.

What happens when the bones being examined fall outside the range of variation of any living species, as do many of the bones discussed in Chapters 3–5? Sometimes, a new designation is created—for example, *Ardipithecus, Sahelanthropus,* or *Australopithecus*—to reflect the fact that the bones do not belong to any known, living creature but rather to an extinct variety that had not been recognized previously (Chapter 3). The next problem that may arise, however, concerns the interpretation of subsequent discoveries. Does a new fossil with features that indicate it did not belong to any living species belong to an already defined fossil species, or should we invent a new species designation for the newly discovered bones?

Remember, when judging whether or not a bone belonged to an animal of a known, living species, we need to determine whether its various measurements fall within the ranges of variation calculated for the living group. These ranges are very well known for modern human beings. A bone's identity as human or not can be determined. But how do we determine if a newly discovered bone whose measurements fall outside the human range belonged to an extinct species that has already been defined? Here we don't have nearly as good an idea of what the range of variation is for the bones of an extinct species. You cannot figure out a range of variation when there is only one specimen. The accuracy of a range cannot be meaningful when there are only a few examples. So it can be extremely difficult to figure out if the new bone's statistics fall within or outside that poorly known range. Beyond this, perhaps instead of placing a new specimen in a new species, we should expand the metrical definition of our own species to include it as well.

As a result, there is an element of subjectivity in inserting a fossil into a given extinct species or using the fossil to name a new species. Some paleoanthropologists are "lumpers," accepting a wide range of variation in ancient species and lumping most new finds into one of the already existing categories. Others are "splitters," assuming a narrow range of acceptable variation and naming new species with nearly every new discovery on the basis of rather small differences between the new find and already defined groups.

There is no right and wrong here. Naming new species and categorizing new finds cannot be absolutely objective, and there is much disagreement about the number of ancient, extinct species in the human evolutionary line. Keep this in mind when reading Chapters 3–5.

The Sex of a Skeleton   This book will refer to specific fossils as being male or female. This identification is possible because of the recognition of sexual dimorphism. Human and ape males, for example, have skeletons that often are readily distinguishable from those of females of the same species. Among humans and apes, males tend to be larger, with heavier, denser, and rougher bones than females.

In addition, males tend to have larger, heavier skulls, with larger and rougher areas for muscle attachment. In some ape species, males have a bony crest on the top of their skulls, whereas females lack this feature. Also, in some species, males have a large ridge of bone above the eye orbits (sockets). Females either lack this feature or have a smaller bony ridge.

Among human beings, all of the various angles of the pelvis that control the overall size of the birth canal are, of necessity, larger in the vast majority of females than in males. With enough skeletal elements recovered, anthro-

Ages of epiphyseal union

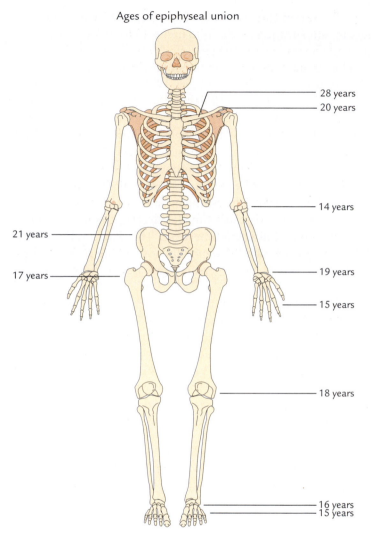

28 years
20 years

14 years

21 years —

17 years —

19 years

15 years

18 years

16 years
15 years

Age at which the epiphyses in the indicated area fuse to the shafts.

Ages of tooth eruption

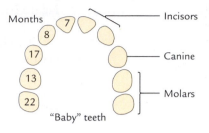

Months

7 — Incisors
8
17 — Canine
13
22 — Molars

"Baby" teeth

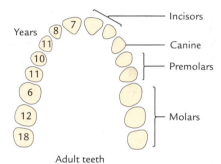

Years

7 — Incisors
8
11 — Canine
10 — Premolars
11
6
12 — Molars
18

Adult teeth

FIGURE 2.15
*These diagrams show
epiphyseal fusion for
human beings and the age
order of tooth eruption.
Careful analysis of skeletal
remains can reveal species,
sex, age at death, nutri-
tional status, cause of
death, and geographic
origin of the individual.*

pologists can correctly distinguish males and females more than 95% of the
time (Krogman 1973).

The Age at Death   Our discussion of human skeletons will occasionally mention an individual's approximate age at death. As with animals, the bones of
human children go through a series of developmental changes during the
course of their lives. For example, tooth eruption and replacement provide
developmental time-posts in human maturation. The **deciduous dentition**—
the baby teeth—erupt above the gum line in a regular order and at fairly well
established times (Figure 2.15). The permanent teeth then replace the baby
teeth, also in a regular pattern, at reasonably well fixed ages until, finally, the

wisdom teeth—the 18-year molars—come in. Using a chart like that shown in Figure 2.15, one can estimate the age of a child under 18 based on which teeth have already erupted above the gum line and which teeth have yet to appear.

Another developmental time-post can be found on the long bones—the various bones of the arms, legs, hands, and feet. When we are born, each of the long bones in our extremities is in three sections: a shaft, or **diaphysis,** and two endcaps, or **epiphyses** (*sing.,* epiphysis). In a process called **epiphyseal fusion,** the shafts and endcaps fuse to one another during growth at more or less set times during our teen years; this fusion reflects maturity and full growth (see Figure 2.15). Once again, by reference to the time range when each of the individual epiphyses fuses to its respective diaphysis, the age at death of an immature individual can be estimated fairly accurately.

Later in life, changes are less regularly timed, reflecting gradual deterioration of our bones rather than consistent time-posts. This deterioration, while inevitable, is subject to great variability depending on the life and work history of the individual, so determining a person's age based on his or her state of deterioration can be problematic.

There are, however, some changes in the adult skeleton that are more consistently timed. For example, **cranial sutures**—the places where the different cranial plates come together—fuse through time. Young adults usually exhibit well-defined sutures, whereas aged people may have had their sutures disappear entirely. The region where the pubic bones come together—the **pubic symphysis**—can also be used to estimate the age at death of an individual. At their point of articulation, the faces of the left and right pubic bones go through a fairly regular, age-dependent sequence of changes.

Geographic Origin   We all recognize that people's physical features differ based on the geography of their origins; humans from different parts of the world possess a constellation of physical traits—skin color, nose shape, hair texture, body proportions—that distinguish them from people from other parts of the world. Skeletal traits also vary geographically; so in some instances, the skeletal remains of individuals can be traced to the part of the world from which they came. For example, one reason we know that Native Americans originated in Asia is that the oldest skeletal remains in North America share a group of skeletal characteristics with Asian people (see Chapter 7).

Pathology and Disease   The bones in a human body are like a book on which some of that human's life experiences are written. Healed bone breaks, episodes of malnutrition during growth, specific dietary deficiencies, the ingestion of certain poisons, arthritis, tuberculosis, syphilis, cancers, and many other conditions leave recognizable traces on bones. These marks can be read by the specialist in **paleopathology.** The paleopathological evidence on the bones of European Neandertals will be discussed in Chapter 5; the high level of malnutrition evident on their bones may explain why the Neandertals became extinct.

As mentioned previously in this chapter, two photosynthesis pathways, C3 and C4, differ in the degree to which they utilize one of the stable varieties of the element carbon (specifically, ^{13}C); C3 plants (mostly trees) tend to filter out ^{13}C, while C4 plants (mostly grasses and sedges) do not. As a result, as mentioned earlier, C3 plants tend to have a measurably lower ^{13}C "signal" or concentration than do C4 plants. The bones of animals, including those of people, who eat plant products reflect the ^{13}C levels of their foods. So, the bones of a people who subsisted on tree foods (fruits and nuts) will exhibit a lower ^{13}C signal than those bones of a people who relied to a greater extent on the seeds, leaves, or roots of grasses (and remember, wheat, barley, oats, and maize are all C4 pathway grasses). When the bones of these two different people are studied, their ^{13}C signals can be determined, and the source of the bulk of their foods—C3 or C4 plants—can be deduced.

Preserved Bodies   Human skeletal remains are poignant reminders of our own mortality as well as valuable sources of information about the lives of ancient people. It is not hard to imagine flesh on the bone and to consider that the dry, hard "specimen" analyzed by the archaeologist was once part of a living human being. But on rare occasions, the human being behind the osteological remains does not have to be imagined. Some complete—or nearly complete—bodies of ancient humans have been remarkably preserved. These rare discoveries offer the archaeologist a uniquely clear window on the past.

Nearly intact bodies 2,000, 3,000, even 4,000 years old have been recovered from Danish peat bogs (Glob 1969). The anaerobic character—the complete lack of oxygen—of the bogs prevents the survival of bacteria that eat flesh. Several partially complete bodies have been removed from the bogs, with internal organs intact, the skin—including fingerprints and body markings such as tattoos—fully preserved, facial expressions clearly discernible, and even the hair on their heads and eyebrows and eyelashes preserved virtually completely. The equivalent of autopsies conducted on the modern deceased can be performed on these ancient corpses. Diseases, traumas, parasites, and even the immediate cause of death can be diagnosed. Some of the bog bodies were the remains of people who had been executed by strangulation; in at least one case, the rope used was preserved along with its victim and was discovered intact and in place around the deceased's neck.

The so-called Ice Man, also known as Ötzi, was essentially freeze-dried beneath a glacier in the Italian Alps (Roberts 1993; Sjøvold 1992; Spindler 1994). When discovered accidentally by two German hikers, his body was just peeking out from the ice; they first thought it was a doll (Figure 2.16). Officials who arrived on the scene presumed the body was the remains of one of the many hikers who had died in recent, unexpected blizzards. Only when the body was removed from the ice and the surrounding area searched for evidence were ancient tools and clothing found: grass-lined shoes, a hafted copper axe, an ash-handled flint knife and woven grass sheath, an antler-tipped stick for sharpening the flint tool, twelve unfinished arrows, an unfinished

FIGURE 2.16

Affectionately known as Ötzi, or the Ice Man, this more than 5,000-year-old body was found in the Italian Alps in 1991. Modern medical procedures have been applied to this remarkably well preserved body, enabling the reconstruction of this individual's final meal and even the cause of his death—an arrow that pierced his left shoulder. (© Corbis Sygma)

bow, and a deerskin quiver. Radiocarbon dating (see the next section) indicates that the Ice Man lived about 5,300 years ago, yet his organs are intact and his flesh preserved; enigmatic tattoos—consisting of a series of parallel lines on his body—are still visible.

Ötzi was in his 40s or 50s when he died. X-rays show clearly that he suffered from arthritis in the neck as well as the lower back and right hip. His body also displays evidence of a number of traumas sustained during his life: Eight ribs show evidence of healed or healing fractures; the bones of at least one toe exhibit evidence typical of frostbite; the single preserved fingernail shows furrows that probably represent periods of reduced nail growth attributable to malnutrition or other bodily stress.

But arthritis, broken ribs, malnutrition, or even the freezing cold didn't kill the Ice Man. Other people did. An arrowhead was found deeply embedded in his left shoulder. The weapon apparently did not sever any major arteries nor did it pierce any of Ötzi's internal organs. However, the pathologist who examined the body concluded that the wound from the arrow bled heavily and the Ice Man likely suffered a prolonged and painful death (Shouse 2001).

Biological anthropologists are fascinated by the bones of our ancient as well as our not-so-ancient ancestors precisely because those remains are laden with information. As Dorothy Lippert (1997:126), an anthropologist at the Smithsonian National Museum of Natural History, phrases it, bones allow the deceased to "tell us their stories."

It is always important to remember, however, that those bones represent real people, once flesh and blood, now gone, people with descendants who may not be particularly interested in having the remains of their relatives dug up, poked and prodded, and then stored in laboratories and even put on display in museums. This issue is most sensitive where a native people with a history of being exploited and, perhaps, even having been the victim of genocidal practices, see the remains of their ancestors removed from the earth and treated like mere specimens by members of the same cultural group who victimized their people in the first place. In his discussion of the Kennewick remains to be discussed in Chapter 7, David Hurst Thomas (2000) chronicles the often shocking behavior of some scientists in the nineteenth century in their desire to collect the skeletal remains of Native Americans. Aware of this history, Native Americans, Native Australians, and other aboriginal people may be skeptical of the argument that the analysis of the bones of their ancestors is of value to them and not just another form of exploitation.

Archaeologists and biological anthropologists have to do a much better job communicating the importance of their work and respecting the perspectives of native peoples. Dorothy Lippert, mentioned earlier, has contributed an important approach to this problem. In fact, she is an anthropologist *and* a Native American who views archaeology as a tool that native people can use to enable their ancestors to tell their own stories.

DETERMINING THE AGE OF A SITE OR SPECIMEN

It may be the first question people ask about an archaeological site or artifact: "How old is it?" In fact, it is one of the key questions that archaeologists and paleoanthropologists hope to answer about the sites they excavate and the artifacts they uncover. In attempting to illuminate the chronology of human evolution, paleoanthropologists need to know the ages of the various fossils discussed in this book. In their efforts to produce a narrative of the lengthy history of the human race before there was writing and to expose the cultural processes at work that produced that narrative, archaeologists need to know when major developments—the earliest production and use of tools, the origins of hunting, the development of agriculture, the growth of class societies— took place.

Chronology has always been important in paleoanthropology and archaeology, but until fairly recently in the history of these disciplines, dating fossils and sites depended on sequences based on **stratigraphic** layering of the earth's surface—and a lot of guesswork. The fundamental technique had changed little since William Smith recognized its applicability in the late eighteenth and early nineteenth centuries (see Chapter 1). Dating was not absolute, but relative; scientists could determine whether a fossil or site was older or younger than another fossil or site depending on whether it was in a higher or lower stratigraphic layer. Fossil specimens and archaeological sites were assigned to particular stratigraphic layers. Though no certainty could be achieved, scientists derived dates based on assumed rates of formation of the layers above and below, on the guessed ages of fossils of extinct species found in association with human remains, and on a bit of intuition.

Dating Techniques Based on Radioactive Decay

Stratigraphic sequences, fossil associations, and even intuition are still used by paleoanthropologists and archaeologists in dating specimens, but these are no longer the only or primary methods of dating. Researchers can now rely on **radiometric** dating techniques based on the known rates of decay of several radioactive (unstable) isotopes (varieties) of common elements such as carbon (^{14}C dating), uranium (uranium series dating), and potassium (potassium/argon, or K/Ar, dating). These techniques provide **absolute dates** rather than **relative dates.** This does not necessarily mean they are accurate or precise, though we strive for both. The term *absolute* means only that we can associate a year or range of years with an object or site rather than place the sites or objects only in chronological order, as is the case in relative dating. Absolute dating is also referred to as *chronometric,* meaning, literally, that in its application we are attempting to measure time.

K/Ar Dating   One technique that has been particularly useful when applied to early human ancestors is **K/Ar dating** (Dalrymple and Lanphere 1969). A newer version of the technique, $^{40}Ar/^{39}Ar$, is more accurate and is used more often than the older procedure, but it is still based on measuring the amount of argon 40 buildup in volcanic rock (Deino, Renne, and Swisher 1998).

Potassium is a common element found in volcanic deposits. A radioactive variety of potassium decays into argon gas. When a volcanic layer is deposited, all of the argon already present from previous potassium decay bubbles off into the atmosphere. In a sense, the atomic clock in the ash or lava is set to zero and there is no argon left in the deposit. When the volcanic rock solidifies, the unstable potassium continues its slow decay to argon, which is trapped in the rock. Because we know the rate at which the radioactive variety of potassium decays to argon—its **half-life** is 1.250 billion years—by measuring how much argon has accumulated in the rock, we can determine how long the argon has been building up since the rock was last liquefied (that is, since the volcanic eruption deposited the lava) and, therefore, when that rock was deposited.

Potassium/argon and argon/argon dating provide an age for the rock itself. You can't use the technique directly to date an artifact made from the rock. For example, there is a volcanic deposit in my home town that has been dated to about 180 million years ago. People living in the valley bordering the mountain where exposures of that volcanic rock can be found quarried some of it and made tools about 5,000 years ago. The tools are 5,000 years old, even though potassium/argon or argon/argon dating would still provide a date of 180 million years; that date indicates when the molten lava solidified and not when people made artifacts from that rock.

In most applications of potassium/argon and argon/argon dating, human fossils are found above or below a datable layer. When a fossil is found above a dated layer, the fossil must be younger than that layer; that is, the creature was alive at some point after the volcanic layer was deposited. The date on the layer below a fossil represents a maximum age for the fossils; they cannot be any older than the age of the volcanic flow that underlies them. When a fossil is found beneath a dated layer, we can be sure it is older than that deposit; that is, the creature was living in the area before the dated layer was deposited. The date on a layer above a fossil represents a minimum age; the fossils may date to any time before the volcanic layer that overlies them, but they cannot be any younger. Under the best of circumstances, the fossils can be associated with layers both above and below them, enabling us to bracket their age.

There is one notable exception to the indirect application of these dating procedures. The humanlike footprints found in hardened volcanic ash at Laetoli in Tanzania, to be discussed in more detail in Chapter 3, must be the same age as the rock itself; the ash fell, was moistened by a soft rain, and then two individuals walked across it, leaving their trails. The wet ash quickly hardened, was covered by additional ash, and, in this way, was preserved. Dating the rock therefore allows for a precise, direct determination of the age of the footprints.

^{14}C Dating   Carbon is an extremely abundant element and one of the building blocks of life on earth; every living thing contains carbon. The most common and stable variety of carbon is ^{12}C. The numeral 12 refers to the number of particles in the carbon atom's nucleus: 6 positively charged particles, or protons, and 6 neutral particles, or neutrons. A radioactive isotope of carbon is produced when free neutrons originating in the sun stream toward earth and collide with nitrogen atoms in the earth's atmosphere. When the neutron displaces a proton in the nitrogen nucleus in such collisions, the resulting atom has only 6 protons left $(7 - 1)$ and no longer 7 but 8 neutrons $(7 + 1)$. Having 6 protons changes the atom from nitrogen to carbon. The resulting variety of the element is carbon 14 (^{14}C) for the 14 particles in its nucleus (6 protons and 8 neutrons).

Because ^{14}C and ^{12}C are nearly identical chemically, they combine equally with oxygen to produce carbon dioxide, which plants take in through respiration. Plants exhale oxygen and keep the carbon atoms—both ^{14}C and ^{12}C— which they then use in the production of leaves, branches, roots, nuts, seeds, or fruits. Again, because ^{12}C and ^{14}C are so similar chemically, the proportion of ^{12}C to ^{14}C in grasses, trees, and bushes is the same as it is in the atmosphere (one trillion ^{12}C atoms for every one ^{14}C atom). When animals eat the products of these plants and again when other animals eat these animals, the ratio of ^{12}C to ^{14}C across the food web remains the same. In fact, all living things on earth are part of the carbon cycle and maintain the same proportion of stable ^{12}C to unstable ^{14}C during their lifetimes—a proportion that is, in turn, the same proportion as is seen in the atmosphere.

As an unstable isotope, ^{14}C ultimately decays, reverting back to the nitrogen atom from which it was produced. Like radioactive potassium, ^{14}C decays at a regular, naturally fixed half-life—in its case, 5,730 years. Once an organism dies, no new carbon is respired or ingested, and so the constantly decaying ^{14}C is no longer replenished. When an organism has been out of this carbon cycle for a substantial amount of time—measured in the hundreds, thousands, or tens of thousands of years—it contains significantly less ^{14}C than it did when it was alive. How much less can be measured and the amount of time it must have taken based on its known, fixed rate of decay for that much loss to have occurred can be determined based on the known rate of decay.

So the decay of ^{14}C provides a natural clock, a kind of hourglass where the rate at which the sand pours into the bottom of the glass is known. One need only determine how much sand (^{14}C) was present initially in the hourglass (organism) and how much now remains to establish approximately when the glass was overturned (when the organism died). For the **radiocarbon dating** (**carbon dating,** ^{14}C dating) to produce accurate results, the item being dated needs to be at least a few hundred and ordinarily less than about 40,000 years old. **Accelerator mass spectrometry (AMS)**, another method of ^{14}C dating, may ultimately extend the viable dating range back 10,000 to 30,000 years beyond this. For now, AMS dating allows for much smaller samples to be radiocarbon-dated.

Fluctuations in solar radiation cause changes in the production of ^{14}C in the atmosphere over broad stretches of time, and this variation has an effect on the dates derived through radiocarbon dating. During periods when ^{14}C was being produced at a slightly higher rate, dated items will produce dates that are a little younger than their actual, or "calendar," age. On the other hand, during periods when ^{14}C was being produced at a lower rate, dated items produce dates that are a little older than their actual age. A partial solution to this complication is provided by dendrochronology.

Dating Techniques Based on Biology

Dendrochronology, or tree-ring dating, is an extremely accurate biological dating technique. Its usefulness in dating archaeological sites results from four factors that apply in some areas of the world.

1. Trees add one growth ring every year.
2. The width of each year's tree ring is controlled by an environmental condition or set of conditions such as spring rainfall amount or temperature.
3. Any sequence of varying tree-ring widths over a long period of time is unique.
4. All trees in a given area reflect the same pattern of changes through time in tree-ring width.

By overlapping ring sequences of living trees with those of old dead trees, a **master sequence** of tree-ring width-variation over many years has been developed. By analysis of bristlecone pine trees, a master sequence greater than 9,000 years has been produced for the American West. The master sequence

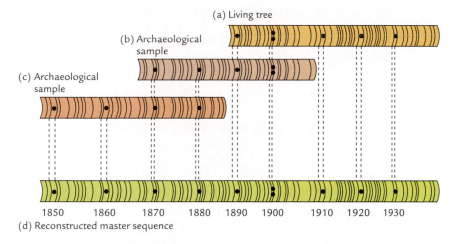

(a) Living tree

(b) Archaeological sample

(c) Archaeological sample

1850   1860   1870   1880   1890   1900   1910   1920   1930

(d) Reconstructed master sequence

FIGURE 2.17

Cross section of tree rings from a living tree (a) overlaps the ring sequence from an archaeological sample (b), which, in turn, overlaps part of the sequence of another archaeological sample (c). The overlapping of many samples allows for the construction of a "master sequence" of tree-ring width patterns (d). (From Robert J. Sharer and Wendy Ashmore, *Archaeology: Discovering Our Past,* Mayfield Publishing Company, 1993. Reprinted with permission from The McGraw-Hill Companies.

constructed in England extends to 7,000 years ago; the master sequence developed in western Germany extends back even further to about 10,000 years ago. When an archaeological site is located that contains wood or even entire cross sections of logs, the succession of thick and thin rings in the ancient specimens can be compared to the master sequence. By determining where the individual sequence overlaps with the master sequence, the life span of the tree can be fixed in time (Figure 2.17). By seeing in what year these archaeological specimens were cut down—the actual year in which the tree's final ring was added—an exact date can be associated with the site.

Individual tree rings have been carbon-dated. Old rings are no longer growing and are, therefore, removed from the carbon cycle; ^{14}C is not being replenished in them. A ring laid down 1,000 years ago in a *living* redwood tree, for example, will produce a carbon date of about 1,000 years. A very large sample of carbon dates derived from old tree rings has been carefully compared to the actual calendar age of each ring as determined by dendrochronology. The resulting **calibration curve,** now extending back to 12,400 years ago, allows a radiocarbon date within this period to be converted to a calendar year date (Reimer et al. 2004) (Figure 2.18).

There are not enough preserved samples of ring sequences from old enough trees to extend the calibration curve to the period before 12,400 years ago. **Varves,** layers of sediment that are deposited annually along lake and ocean shorelines and whose ages, therefore, can be calculated directly by counting back from the present, have been used to calibrate older radiocarbon dates in an approach conceptually similar to tree-ring dating. Radiocarbon dates derived from organic samples recovered from precisely dated varves have been compared to their respective varve "calendar" dates. The degree of error and the amount of correction needed to convert carbon dates to calendar dates for the period 12,400 to 26,000 years ago have been calculated in this way (Kitagawa and van der Plicht 1998; Reimer et al. 2004). In general,

FIGURE 2.18

Calibration curve for radiocarbon dates. The vertical axis represents the radiocarbon dates derived for a large number of tree-ring samples, and the horizontal axis represents the actual dendrochrono-logically derived dates for those same tree rings. As you can see, for tree rings that are more than about 3,000 years old, radiocarbon dates (the jagged line) generally understate the true age of a sample.

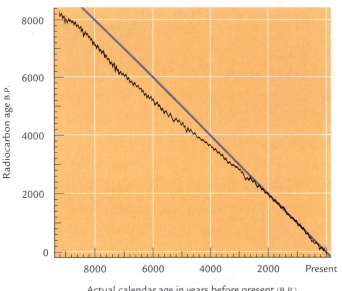

the further back in time, the more a radiocarbon date will underestimate the actual age of whatever is being dated; this underestimation can amount to several thousand years.

Dating Techniques Based on Radiation Damage

Electron spin resonance dating (**ESR**) is one of a number of techniques that date materials through the measurement of radiation damage—in this case, the buildup of electrons trapped in crystalline materials at a site (Grün 1989, 1993; Grün and Stringer 1991). When, for example, a tooth is formed, the electrons in the atoms of that tooth are technically in an unexcited state, or "ground state." As a result of natural radioactivity in the tooth itself, as well as in the soil in which the tooth is deposited, some of those electrons get trans-ferred to higher energy levels and get "trapped" there. The number of trapped electrons is a function of characteristics of the material (in this case, tooth enamel), the amount of background radiation, and time—how long since the tooth formed. Because the trapping characteristics of different materials as well as background radiation levels can be measured and accounted for, the number of electrons trapped in a sample can be used to determine the age of the sample. ESR can date teeth that are more than a few thousand years old, but its key contribution is in dating sites that are too old for radiocarbon dating—in other words, sites more than 50,000 years old. The upper limit for ESR is unknown; it has been estimated at somewhere between 10 million and 100 million years (Grün and Stringer 1991:165). Even the lower limit renders the technique applicable to sites directly related to human evolution. Greatest success has been achieved on mollusk shells, speleothems (cave deposits), corals, volcanic rock, and tooth enamel. ESR does not, however, work well on bone (Grün and Stringer 1991:155).

Luminescence dating, like ESR, measures the amount of energy that is trapped in material recovered at archaeological sites as a result of natural radioactive decay in the surrounding soil. Again, such energy is released at a set rate in a given soil, so the amount captured in site materials reflects their age. The amount of energy captured by the archaeological material over time and, hence, its age can be measured after releasing the energy by heat (in the application called **thermoluminescence,** or **TL**) or by laser light (in the application called **optically stimulated luminescence,** or **OSL**).

Luminescence dating has been applied successfully to fired clay objects, especially pottery, as well as to stone that has been heated to a high temperature—for example, the rocks lining a fireplace. In both cases the application of heat—the firing of the pot or the heating of the stone in a fire—releases all of the energy previously trapped in the material. This effectively sets the trapped-charge clock to zero. Then once the pot or stone is returned to the earth, it again begins to accumulate energy at the set rate produced by the natural radioactivity of the surrounding soil. Knowing that rate allows calculation of how much time has elapsed since the object was heated and, therefore, when people were present at the site making pots or banking their hearths with stones.

Fission-track dating, another radiation-damage measurement, bases age estimates on the number of visible "tracks" left by radioactive decay in site materials; these microscopic tracks build up at a regular rate.

Dating by Measuring Chemical Processes

Obsidian hydration measures the regular buildup of a "hydration layer" on freshly exposed volcanic glass; a fresh surface is exposed when a human hammers off a stone flake while making obsidian tools. The exposed surface immediately begins to combine chemically with water in the air around it or in the soil in which it is deposited. The thickness of the layer on an exposed obsidian surface is a function of time, the moisture level and temperature of its environment of deposition, and characteristics of the particular obsidian. Where that moisture level can be measured and controlled for, the age of the flake can be determined. Where the rate of hydration-layer development can be determined, an absolute date can be derived for the artifact. In other cases, only relative dates can be determined; we can figure out which objects are older than others on the basis of their thicker hydration layer.

Dating by Measuring Paleomagnetism

Paleomagnetic dating is based on the fact that the position of magnetic north has fluctuated over time. The orientation of naturally magnetic particles in a lava flow is measured to determine the direction of magnetic north when the

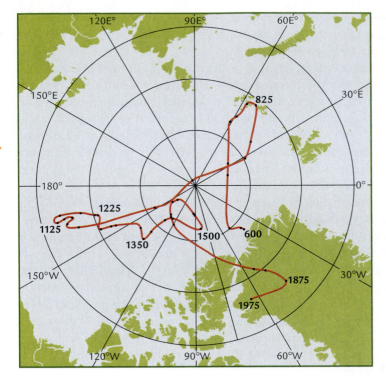

flow was hot. Because the location of magnetic north has been determined for long periods of time, scientists can date volcanic layers that preserve evidence of the location of north when the deposits were laid down (Kappelman 1993).

In certain circumstances, remnant magnetism in recent geological and cultural features can also be useful in dating sites. Just as the orientation of magnetic particles in an ancient lava flow may become fixed, in **archaeomagnetism** magnetic orientation can become "fossilized" in cultural features. For example, the magnetic particles in sediments that have infilled a canal may become lined up with the earth's magnetic field at the time of their deposition (Eighmy and Howard 1991). Similarly, the magnetic particles in clay making up the bricks of a kiln, like so many natural compass needles, may point to the location of magnetic north at the time they were heated. Careful study of dated sites with features exhibiting evidence of past magnetic orientation has provided data necessary for the production of a "master curve" showing the location of magnetic north as it changed through time (Eighmy and Sternberg 1990). Figure 2.19 shows the deduced location of magnetic north based on archaeomagnetism between A.D. 600 and 1975. When the orientation of the earth's magnetic field has been preserved in features found at an archaeological site dating to sometime in that period, a more precise estimate of the site's age can be deduced based on the dated location of magnetic north along this curve during the site's occupation.

SUMMARY

Archaeologists and paleoanthropologists apply a broad array of techniques in their investigation of the human past. This chapter has briefly surveyed some of the more important procedures for recovering and analyzing the data on which the rest of the book is based.

How sites are formed, how they are preserved, and how they are discovered are key questions for archaeologists and paleoanthropologists. Once found, data can be analyzed to determine the age of the materials, how tools were made and used, the subsistence base of the people, and aspects of their social and even religious lives. Past peoples can also be investigated directly through analysis of their physical remains, which determines the age, sex, health status, and geographic origin of ancient individuals. The evolutionary relationship between a prehistoric person and modern human beings can therefore be determined.

Using the general procedures outlined in this chapter and many other very specific analytical techniques mentioned throughout this book, archaeologists and paleoanthropologists can reveal the chronicle of the human past. We begin that chronicle in Chapter 3.

TO LEARN MORE

Technical Summaries

The point of this chapter was merely to introduce you to some of the more important methods employed by archaeologists. For a far more thorough introduction, there are many fine textbooks that describe the way archaeologists and paleoanthropologists collect and interpret data about the human past. Any one of the following textbooks would be a good choice to continue your study of archaeological method: *Discovering Our Past: A Brief Introduction to Archaeology* by Wendy Ashmore and Robert J. Sharer (2000); *Back to the Earth* by John Staeck (2002); *Archaeology: A Brief Introduction* (2003) and *In the Beginning: An Introduction to Archaeology* (2000b), both by Brian Fagan; *Archaeology: Down to Earth* (1999) and *Archaeology* (1998), both by David Hurst Thomas, and *Linking to the Past: A Brief Introduction to Archaeology,* by Kenneth L. Feder (2004). For the analysis of human skeletal material, see Wilton Marion Krogman's *The Human Skeleton in Forensic Medicine* (1973) for a classical treatment. There is probably no better recent source than Tim White and Pieter Folken's *Human Osteology* (1991).

Popular Summaries

Brian Fagan has written two wonderful treatments of archaeology and its history: *Quest for the Past* (1994), which focuses on several famous discoveries in archaeology (such as King Tut's tomb), and *Eyewitness to Discovery* (1998), which consists of more than 50 original, first-person accounts of archaeological discovery. Two anthologies of popular articles discussing archaeological method and meaning are available: *Annual Editions: Archaeology* (2005; edited by Linda Hasten) and *Lessons from the Past: A Reader in Introductory Archaeology* (1999; edited by Kenneth L. Feder).

On the Web

There is no shortage of Internet sites devoted to archaeology. Detailed Web pages focus on virtually every topic discussed in this chapter. Many of these sites are associated with museums with displays about archaeology, university courses in which these topics are taught, and laboratories that conduct the analytical procedures discussed here. A helpful clearinghouse of archaeological information available on the Net can be found online at the ArchNet site (http://archnet.asu.edu/). On the ArchNet home page, click on the Subject Area link for a list of topics, each with a lengthy set of links to Web sites devoted to, for example, palynology, faunal analysis, stone tools, and mapping.

Online Learning Center: www.mhhe.com/feder4

ONLINE
LEARNING
CENTER

The Online Learning Center (OLC) Web companion to *The Past in Perspective* features a variety of supplemental study aids. For each chapter, this free Web site includes:

- Self-Quizzes to take as pretests prior to exams
- Interactive Timeline Study Guides for additional review and reinforcement of key information
- Learning Objectives
- Chapter Site links with Web addresses for many of the fossil and archaeological sites mentioned in the text

KEY TERMS

absolute date, 60
accelerator mass
   spectrometry (AMS),
   62
activity area, 36
alluvium, 43
archaeomagnetism, 66
artifact, 34
artificial selection, 49
association, 43
C3 pathway, 50
C4 pathway, 50
cache, 43
calibration curve, 63
carbon dating, 62
carbon isotope analysis, 51
cranial suture, 56

deciduous dentition, 55
dendrochronology, 62
diaphysis, 56
ecofact, 34
ejecta, 37
electron spin resonance
   dating (ESR), 64
epiphyseal fusion, 56
epiphysis, 56
epistemology, 32
experimental replication,
   46
faunal assemblage, 48
feature, 36
fission-track dating, 65
foraminifera, 51
half-life, 60

hypothesis, 33
isotope, 51
K/Ar dating, 60
luminescence dating, 65
master sequence, 62
morphology, 46
neutron activation
   analysis, 45
obsidian hydration, 65
obtrusiveness, 41
optically stimulated
   luminescence (OSL), 65
osteological, 48
osteological comparative
   collection, 48
paleomagnetic dating, 65
paleopathology, 56

3

African
Roots

CHAPTER OVERVIEW

Though human beings are distinguished by large brains, great intelligence, and a reliance on culture, fossil evidence shows that large brains were not characteristic of our earliest ancestors. The first steps of the hominid family were literal first steps: Walking on two rather than four feet was what differentiated them from the apes.

The oldest members of the human family date to more than 5 million years ago, about the time our ancestors diverged from those of the modern apes. The different names we have assigned to these specimens—*Sahelanthropus, Ardipithecus, Orrorin,* and, after 4 million years ago, several varieties of *Australopithecus*—reflect actual physical differences as well as modern arguments about what those differences mean. These creatures share in common the fact that their brains were no larger than those of modern chimpanzees. What they all also seem to share is a skeletal anatomy suited to walking on two feet.

A fork in the hominid road appears about 2.5 million years ago, when a new hominid form is seen in the fossil record. Along with an anatomy suited to upright walking, *Homo habilis* had a brain size beyond the range of the apes and exhibited a greater reliance on culture as seen in the production of stone tools. *Homo habilis* and some of the Australopithecines were contemporaries. Whereas the latter were highly specialized and became extinct, the former are directly ancestral to modern humanity.

		Millions of years ago							
		7	6	5	4	3	2	1	0
Sahelanthropus tchadensis		▬							
Orrorin tugenensis			▬						
Ardipithecus ramidus			▬▬						
Australopithecus anamensis					▪				
Australopithecus afarensis					▬▬				
Kenyanthropus platyops					▬				
Australopithecus africanus						▬▬			
Australopithecus aethiopicus						▪			
Homo habilis						▬			
Australopithecus robustus							▬		
Australopithecus boisei							▬▬		

ONLINE LEARNING CENTER

Go to **www.mhhe.com/feder4** for an interactive study guide version of this timeline.

Wearing shoes most of the time, few of us think about the actual mechanics of walking. Our feet are ordinarily enclosed in footwear with stiff, hard soles, and we walk on even harder pavement. In a sense, walking in shoes on a paved surface insulates us from part of the process of locomotion as practiced by our ancient human ancestors. Walking barefoot on the soft sand of a beach, however, reminds us with each step of the natural process. No longer is walking a matter of two flat slabs of leather or rubber alternately clomping down on the pavement. Instead, we can sense our feet actually interacting with the earth, gripping into the soil beneath them, pushing us forward in our desire to get from here to there. In the instant of each step, our heel strikes first, leaving deep impressions as the sand compresses beneath our weight, all of it focused on that small point at the heel. Then the foot rolls forward, the arch lightly curving over the sand and leaving a thin, sharp indentation with the side of the sole. Next, all in a fraction of a second, we rock up onto the balls of our feet, thrusting our center of gravity forward, as we push our alternate leg in front of us. Finally, our toes push down, gripping into the earth, with sand squishing up between and around them, as we propel our bodies forward, ready to catch ourselves in the next step with the other foot.

Most of us have, at one time or another, walked barefoot on wet sand in this way, leaving a uniquely human trail of footprints behind us. I remember in particular one time when I walked on a beach with my then 6-year-old son Josh and glanced back at our two sets of footprints, one big, one small, as the waves began the inevitable process of erasing them from the sand. Our disappearing trail of footprints reminded me of another such trail, made in a far distant time by two people who passed together across a landscape far different from the Cape Cod beach where my son and I walked. Those footprints, however, were not erased by the tide or blown away by the wind. Those prints, left in a fine volcanic ash on an East African plain in a place called Laetoli, in the modern nation of Tanzania, were preserved, allowing us in the present to examine the way our most ancient ancestors walked (Hay and Leakey 1982; Leakey and Hay 1979; White and Suwa 1987).

The conditions and sequence of events had to be perfect for those footprints to be preserved. First, a thin ash layer had to be deposited. Soon after, a mild rain had to fall, turning the ash into the consistency of wet cement. Immediately following this, and before the ash had hardened, the two people (and, perhaps, another) had to walk across its surface, leaving their footprints in the still-damp ash. Then the sun needed to come out to dry the ash bed to the hardness of rock before another rainfall might wash it all away. Finally, another ash layer had to be deposited, covering the footprint trail and protecting it from the natural erosion that might otherwise have destroyed it. Even ordinarily impassive scientists have characterized the preservation of the Laetoli footprint trails as "miraculous" (Johanson and Edey 1981).

FIGURE 3.1

On the left is the Laetoli pathway, the fossilized footprints of at least two human ancestors who walked in a remarkably modern fashion. On the right is the recent pathway of a father and his 6-year-old son. Though separated in time by more than 3.5 million years, the two sets of footprints clearly show the continuity of bipedal locomotion in the hominid family. (Left: John Readers/ SPL/Photo Researchers, Inc.; *right:* K. L. Feder)

Those footprints were found more than 3.5 million years after the two people, possibly a child and an adult, and perhaps a third person, strode across the surface (Leakey and Lewin 1992; Figure 3.1). We will never know their names or why they were walking, apparently in cadence and, perhaps, giving our imagination free rein, arm and arm across the ash bed (Figure 3.2). Yet, in taking those steps, they achieved a kind of immortality. Perhaps most remarkably, their footprints show that those anonymous folk, whose life journey occurred so many years ago, walked in a fashion that is nearly indistinguishable from the way modern humans walk (Charteris, Wall, and Nottrodt 1981; Day and Wickens 1980; T. White 1980; White and Suwa 1987). Those people were among the earliest **hominids,** with whom all living people share a temporally distant but biologically intimate connection. This chapter is about the first people and the world in which they lived.

FIGURE 3.2

Based on a careful analysis of their preserved footprints as well as skeletal remains of hominids that lived at the same time, artists have produced models of the human ancestors who left their trail at Laetoli, Tanzania. (Neg. #4744[5]. Photo by D. Finnin/C. Chesek. Courtesy Department of Library Services, American Museum of Natural History)

CHRONICLE

Imagine a 2-hour movie representing the history of the universe; the very first moment of the film represents the first instant of the beginning of everything, the event cosmologists call "the Big Bang."

In our imaginary movie, everything happens proportionally to when it actually happened in the history of the universe. In such a movie, the earth does not form until more than 80 minutes after the first flash on the screen, the first living things make their appearance at about 90 minutes into the film, dinosaurs briefly flash across the screen at the 118-minute mark, the first of the apes do not appear until 119 minutes 50 seconds after the movie began, and, finally, the earliest members of the human family do not appear until 1 hour 59 minutes 57 seconds into our metaphorical 2-hour movie. The entire human story, in other words, is contained in the final *3 seconds* of the film! Though this period may not seem very important from a universal perspective, in human terms we are talking about more than 6 million years, or

Era	Period	Epoch	Million years ago
Cenozoic	Quaternary	Holocene	0.01
		Pleistocene	1.7
	Tertiary	Pliocene	5
		Miocene	23
		Oligocene	38
		Eocene	55
		Paleocene	65
Mesozoic	Cretaceous		135
	Jurassic		190
	Triassic		225
Paleozoic	Permian		270
	Carboniferous		345
	Devonian		400
	Silurian		425
	Ordovician		500
	Cambrian		600
Precambrian	Proterozoic		1,000
	Archeozoic		3,000
	Azoic		4,600

FIGURE 3.3
Humans appear extremely late on this standard time scale for earth history. The earliest hominids date to the end of the Miocene.

300,000 generations of human ancestors. These metaphorical final 3 seconds are the focus of paleoanthropologists and archaeologists.

MIOCENE PREFACE

Let's go back to look at the world at the 119-minute 50-second mark in the movie, when our nearest living nonhuman relatives first make their appearance. The world of this period, called the **Miocene** (from about 23 million to 5 million years ago; Figure 3.3), is one we can scarcely imagine. During this epoch, our planet was a matchless place for forest-dwelling creatures, and many ape species evolved to fill the varied **niches** offered by this rich world. Places that today are covered with grassland, prairie, and agricultural crops were then fertile forests, populated by an astounding bestiary of tree-loving species.

Fossil Apes of the Miocene

Primatologists now estimate that there were more than 40 general varieties—technically, **genera**—of apes living during the Miocene. Each genus encompassed multiple species; by a recent count there were nearly 100 ape species during this time (Begun 2003). Compare this situation to the present, with our paltry assemblage of only three genera of large or "great" apes divided

FIGURE 3.4
Phylogeny for apes and humans, based on the fossil record.

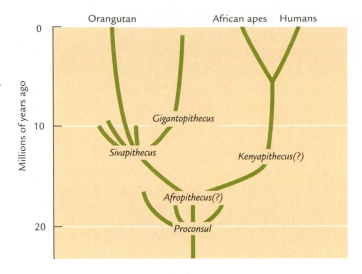

into four species (chimp, bonobo, gorilla, and orangutan) and a single genus of the small or "lesser" apes divided into nine species of gibbons and siamangs. Even more significant than actual number of ancient ape genera and species is the great geographic range and the broad diversity reflected among these apes.

The Miocene apes flourished in a broad and diverse array of habitats, including the tropical forests of Africa and Asia, where the modern apes currently live, but also in cooler, drier temperate forests in Europe, where Miocene ape fossils have been found in Spain, France, Italy, Greece, and Hungary. Morphological diversity was great as well; both the smallest apes (weighing just a bit more than 3.5 kg [7.7 lbs]) and the largest (300 kg [660 lbs], or about 50% larger than a modern, adult male gorilla) lived during the Miocene (Figure 3.4). Some Miocene apes had long, thin arms, ideal for **brachiating,** and others seem better adapted to climbing and leaping from branch to branch. One species, *Oreopithecus bamboli,* may even have been adept at walking on two feet, a hallmark of the human lineage. Based on an analysis of teeth, it appears that the diets of different Miocene ape species were diverse as well, with some adapted to chewing soft fruits, while others chewed leaves, and others still focused on seeds and nuts.

Why the Study of Apes Is Relevant to the Study of Humanity

We are not descended from chimps, bonobos, gorillas, or orangutans. We did not evolve from them. In fact, they have been evolving separately from us for as long as we have been evolving separately from them. But we share with them a common ancestor. Our evolutionary connection is apparent in our appearance and even in our genes. Human and chimp DNA, in particular, are amazingly similar. In fact, a comparison of modern human, chimp, and gorilla DNA found that human beings and chimps are more similar to each other then either humans or chimps are to gorillas (Wildman, Grossman, and Goodman 2001). Figure 3.4, based in part on DNA evidence, presents a general **phylogeny** for the fossil and modern apes, showing how we currently conceive of their evolutionary relationships. The figure also shows how we view the human position on this phylogeny, and we will focus our energies on that branch in the rest of this book.

By studying modern apes in a natural setting, primatologists hope to catch glimpses of behaviors the apes share with us: A chimp infant runs to its mother when it is frightened, and two adults embrace and pat each other's backs; chimps live in tightly knit social groups, make and use tools, and occasionally walk on two feet while carrying objects in their hands. In these shared elements we likely are recognizing behaviors we have inherited from a common ancestor who lived more than 6 million years ago and from whom both chimpanzees and humans descended.

By studying both modern and fossil apes, therefore, primatologists are able to get a glimpse, however fleeting and indirect, of our own distant past. To comprehend the environmental and evolutionary context in which our human ancestors first appeared, we have to understand what preceded them and, in essence, where they came from.

What Happened to the Apes at the End of the Miocene?

Today, the surviving ape species are threatened with extinction as a result of habitat destruction at the hands of humanity. As the tropical forests of Africa and Asia that are home to the apes are cleared for agriculture to support the burgeoning human population, the apes are pushed into smaller and smaller enclaves. Without a concerted effort by our species, the same species that is responsible for their current precarious position, our nearest living evolutionary relatives may become extinct except in zoos and animal parks.

At the end of the Miocene, the many species of apes that are represented in the fossil record also faced extinction, but not by any human agency; our direct ancestors had not yet evolved. Instead, a natural environmental change began to shrink the rich forest world. Though paleoclimatologists and paleobotanists disagree about how and why this change took place, almost all agree that large areas of the extensive forestlands began to contract sometime during the middle or late Miocene, to be replaced largely by grasslands, or **savannas,** by the beginning of the next epoch, the **Pliocene,** about 5 million years ago. And with the contraction of the forests, most of the ape species that had thrived there became extinct.

For example, geologists Thure Cerling, Yang Wang, and Jay Quade (1993) have shown that soils and fossil teeth in south-central Asia (Pakistan) and North America (the western United States) exhibit a simultaneous, dramatic increase between 7 million and 5 million years ago in their concentration of the ^{13}C **isotope** (variety) of the element carbon (Figure 3.5). We discussed in

FIGURE 3.5
This graph shows the dra-matic proportional increase of ^{13}C in fossil teeth and soils at the end of the Mio-cene. (From Cerling, Yang, and Quade 1993)

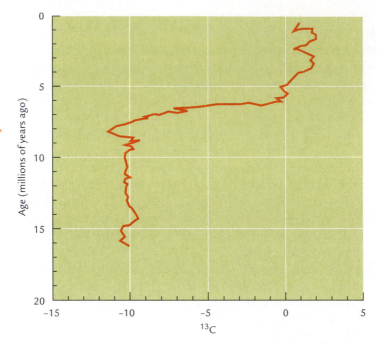

Chapter 2 how most tree species are C3 photosynthesis pathway plants, which tend to select against the ^{13}C variety of carbon. As a result, when a region, continent, or even the world is dominated by the C3 photosynthesis pathway, ^{13}C levels in the soil, in the bones of animals that eat plant by-products, and in the bones of the animals that eat the animals that eat the plants all tend to have lower levels of ^{13}C than they do in times when C4 photosynthesis pathway plants—grasses and sedges—dominate. And, in fact, toward the end of the Miocene, there is a marked increase in the worldwide ^{13}C concentration.

Cerling and co-workers interpret the overall and dramatic increase in ^{13}C concentration at the end of the Miocene as an indication of "a rapid expansion of C4 biomass [that is, grasses and sedges] in both the Old and the New World starting 7 to 5 million years ago" (1993:334). They further point out that the "synchronous expansion of C4 ecosystems in both the New and Old World suggests a change in global conditions rather than local development" (345). More recent research (Morgan, Kingston, and Marino 1994) in Pakistan and Kenya questions the rate the previous study suggested for the expansion of sa-vannas and contraction of the forests worldwide but still supports the general contention that this was a significant, worldwide phenomenon.

The Irony of Extinction

Evolution and extinction are serendipitous and unpredictable. Extinction is, in fact, the norm; it is estimated that 99% of the plant and animal species that have existed during the 3.5-billion-year history of life on earth are extinct.

The role of extinction in evolution also is sadly ironic. Sometimes it is the extinction of one species, genus, or family of animals that opens up the evolutionary field to another. In fact, it was the extinction of the dinosaurs that allowed a previously insignificant class of animals, the mammals—of which we are one—to explode into prominence. Just as surely, the massive wave of ape extinctions resulting from the great climatic and habitat changes that accompanied the end of the Miocene provided the catalyst for the flourishing of the small number of ape species that were able to adapt, adjust, and survive (Gingerich 1986; Pickford 1983).

Almost certainly, those ape species that survived the terminal Miocene possessed some characteristics that, by chance, gave them an advantage in the very different world that was establishing itself. Perhaps it was their remarkable ability for brachiation that ensured the survival of the ancestors of today's gibbons and siamangs when forests were shrinking and competition for remaining space was fierce. Maybe it was the strength, size, intelligence, and social systems of the ancestors of modern gorillas that allowed for their survival. The intelligence and behavioral flexibility of the ancestors of chimps and bonobos probably provided them with an advantage as the myriad Miocene ape species vied for space in the diminishing forests of 7 million years ago.

The modern apes, therefore, can be viewed as the descendants of the winners of this evolutionary struggle. The losers were those who, at the end of the Miocene, found themselves in an alien habitat in which their physical and behavioral characteristics, honed by millions of years of evolution to life in a thick, humid forest, were useless—those that could not survive on the savannas.

All living apes can walk on two feet with varying degrees of success. But **bipedal locomotion** is inefficient and tiring for them; the bones and muscles of their hips and legs simply are not compatible with that form of locomotion. The same was probably true for the apes of the Miocene. But at least one and possibly several Miocene ape species could stand up and walk on two legs better than the others. While providing some advantage in the forests, this ability was particularly valuable in the expanding grasslands that replaced the Miocene woodlands. Natural selection, as discussed in Chapter 1, feeds on variability. The nascent ability for upright locomotion within one or more Miocene ape species provided natural selection with the raw material needed to produce a creature fully capable of bipedal locomotion, one that habitually and efficiently walked on two feet. The species that had this ability was the first human ancestor.

THE FIRST HOMINIDS

The first bipeds did not suddenly develop at the end of the Miocene, the product of evolutionary forcing as grasslands replaced forest habitat rendering bipedal locomotion beneficial. They didn't evolve bipedality because they needed to in the grasslands; evolution does not work that way. Novel features are not made to order. Instead, the paleoenvironmental record of carbon isotopes, as well as plant and animal remains dating to the times and places in which our first upright ancestors lived, shows that they were already thriving as bipeds in forested environments at the end of the Miocene (Gibbons 2002). The first hominids, in fact, were apelike creatures who lived in areas that provided a mosaic of differing habitats including humid forests and dry savannas, low-lying lakesides, and uplands. These apes also just happened to already have the ability to efficiently and, perhaps, habitually walk on two legs. Perhaps because of their adaptation to an environment that already included—but was not restricted to—grasslands and perhaps because of their ability to walk upright, these apes were able to flourish at the end of the Miocene as the grasslands expanded at the expense of the forests while most other ape species could not. It is the fossil record of this turning point in human evolution that commands our attention here.

Late Miocene Hominids

When I began writing anthropology textbooks in the late 1980s, I had to admit that the fossil evidence simply didn't yet exist to assess the conclusion drawn from the analysis of modern human and ape genetics that our evolutionary divergence—our branching off from a common ancestor with the apes—probably occurred between 5 and 7 million years ago. When I began writing, there were ape fossils dating back to 7 or 8 million years ago, but the oldest hominid fossils dated back to less than 4 million years ago. Paleoanthropologists universally bemoaned this fossil gap, particularly because it represented a momentous period of time in our evolution, a time when a behavioral characteristic was established that fundamentally distinguished us from the line that led to the modern apes: habitual upright walking.

In numerous lectures delivered in my classes back in the 1980s, I admitted that the fossils simply hadn't been found to allow us to assess the nature of the divergence of our ancestors from those of modern apes. I always held out hope in those lectures, however, that at some point in the future the fossil gap would be filled. Fortunately, that time has come; and while, as yet, the picture is still rather murky, the fossil gap is beginning to be filled.

It now appears that there is at least one and perhaps as many as four different upright species in Africa dating to more than 5 million years ago (Figure 3.6). Some of the most recently discovered specimens, found in the Asa Koma locality in the Middle Awash region of Ethiopia, have led researchers to name a new species, *Ardipithecus kadabba* (Haile-Selassie, Suwa, and White 2004). So far, the species is represented only by fossil teeth dating to sometime between 5.6 and 5.8 million years ago. The researchers felt justified in naming a new species because, in their overall shape and in how they have worn against one another during chewing, the teeth do not look like those of any of the fossil apes, nor are they a match for hominid teeth yet found. Because, in certain aspects the teeth look to be intermediate between apes and

FIGURE 3.6
Fossil localities of early hominids.

hominids, the researchers hypothesized that the teeth are, in fact, from a hominid very early in the line toward humanity.

Another cluster of fragmentary bones, representing at least five individuals, has been unearthed in the Middle Awash since 1997; the bones have been identified as belonging to another variety of the species *Ardipithecus,* this one called *ramidus* (Haile-Selassie 2001). The *ramidus* specimens have been dated to between 5.2 and 5.8 million years ago (Figure 3.7).

Ardipithecus ramidus is considered to be a hominid also in part because of its dental anatomy. As was the case with *Ardipithecus kadabba,* some very detailed measurements of its teeth exhibit significant differences when compared to those of any ape, living or extinct, and they show substantial similarities to the teeth of all the hominids that followed it. Of far greater importance, however, is the fact that one of the preserved *ramidus* bones, specifically one of the bones of the feet—a toe bone—is very different from that of the apes and quite similar to that of a modern human. The configuration of the *ramidus* toe bone suggests that it had a humanlike foot; and, therefore, it appears that this animal was a biped, rather obviously like us, and not like the other apes.

Ardipithecus ramidus appears to have been a successful hominid, with later specimens dating to 4.4 million years ago (White, Suwa, and Asfaw 1994;

Semaw et al. 2005). Though fragmentary, details of the arm bones and teeth show some similarities to those of human beings. Most important, the cranial fragment recovered in 1992 provided researchers with part of the **foramen magnum,** the large hole at the bottom of the skull through which nerves and blood vessels pass, connecting the brain to the rest of the body. The bony ridge circling the foramen magnum represents the place where the skull rests on top of the vertebral column. The location of the foramen magnum dictates whether a creature is a quadruped or a biped. A cat, for example, has a foramen magnum toward the back of the skull, and the vertebral column lies horizontally toward the rear. In a bipedal human, the foramen magnum is located at the very bottom of the cranium and the vertebral column sits in a vertical position below. There was enough of the foramen magnum preserved on the *Ardipithecus ramidus* specimen to indicate that it was positioned more toward the bottom of the skull than the back. This implies that *Ardipithecus ramidus* was upright and, in fact, one of the oldest hominids yet discovered.

   Ardipithecus ramidus was not the only hominid literally walking around in Africa at around 6 million years ago. Another set of possible hominid bones, these from the Tugen Hills of northwestern Kenya, have been dated to before 5.7 million years ago and may be as much as 6.1 million years old (Aiello and Collard 2001). Called *Orrorin tugenensis* by its discoverers, its status as an early hominid is suggested by its teeth, but the primary evidence used to support this claim is the fragments of three femurs recovered in the excavation. The upper sections of these femurs, representing the place where they connect to the pelvis, suggest a humanlike configuration and, therefore, a pattern of upright walking at about 6 million years ago. A computerized

tomography (CT) scan shows a modern configuration of the internal structure of the bone as well (Galik et al. 2004).

Far to the north and west of the Middle Awash valley home of *Ardipithecus* and the Tugen Hills of *Orrorin,* archaeologists have discovered the remains
of another possible hominid dating to about 6 million years ago. They recovered a spectacularly preserved **cranium** and later some mandibular and dental
fragments from another, very similar individual in the Djourab Desert in the
African nation of Chad along the shoreline of an ancient lake (Brunet et al
2005; Gibbons 2002). This hominid was called *Sahelanthropus tchadensis* and
nicknamed "Toumai" by its discoverers. Its nearly complete cranium is about
the size of a chimpanzee's, indicating that it possessed a chimp-sized brain
(Figure 3.8). However, in the shape of the face, *Sahelanthropus* was decidedly
un-chimplike. A chimpanzee face, like that of all the great apes, thrusts forward, presenting a profile with, essentially, a snout. *Sahelanthropus* is quite
different in this regard, with a very flat face, especially below its lower jaw.
The significant thing about this is that in this feature *Sahelanthropus* resembles the modern human configuration. A virtual reconstruction of Toumai's
skull based on computed tomography (CT) scans, similar to what you might
have done at a medical lab or hospital, allowed for the detailed examination
of 39 cranial landmarks and then the accurate measurement of their spatial

FIGURE 3.9

Looking not quite like an ape, but certainly not human either, this reconstruction of the probable appearance of the face and head of "Toumai,"otherwise known as Sahelanthropus tchadensis, *was produced through computed tomography of the very complete cranium found in the African nation of Chad. You are looking at our best guess of what a very early hominid may have looked like.* (© M.P.F.T.)

relationships, one to another (Zollikofer et al. 2005). The measurements determined from Toumai's CT scans were then compared to the same measurements performed on modern chimpanzees and gorillas, as well those calculated for a sample of ancient hominid skulls. Toumai's measurements fell firmly within the range of the hominids and outside of those computed for the apes. Further, at least one of the measurements, the angle between an imaginary line connecting the top and bottom of each of Toumai's eye orbits and another imaginary line drawn at the base of his cranium is perpendicular, just as it is in hominids as a result of their upright orientation. This further implies that Toumai was upright and, therefore, a hominid.

Toumai's scans have been translated into a clay sculpture providing us our best guess at what he may have looked like in life (Figure 3.9). Toumai's overall look is alien but eerily familiar at the same time. His face and head are apelike, to be sure, but at the same time something quite different from an ape, something far more human. In looking at the reconstruction of Toumai's face and head, we very well may be looking back at one of the oldest members of our hominid family.

Though bones most directly reflective of locomotor patterns—those of the hips and legs—were not recovered, there is a strong indicator of upright posture in the well-preserved cranium. The same characteristic that indicated the 4.4-million-year-old variety of *Ardipithecus* was upright, the position of its foramen magnum, indicates that *Sahelanthropus* was upright as well. It is positioned not at the back but at the bottom of the cranium. This is a clear indication of upright posture and bipedal locomotion.

FIGURE 3.10

Two fragments of a tibia (the larger, lower leg bone) belonging to a member of the species Australopithecus anamensis. *The top part of the tibia, shown on the right, exhibits two concave surfaces on the left and right condyles that meet the upper leg (femur) at the knee, typical of upright walkers and unlike the convex surfaces of an ape tibia.* (Copyright © Kenneth Garrett/NGS Image Collection)

It is too early to determine the precise evolutionary relationships among the 6-million-year-old probable hominids discussed here. Some researchers suggest that they actually represent four separate, distinct hominid species (Begun 2004) while others suggest that, along with their age, they share so much in common in terms of their appearance—based, admittedly, on very few, often fragmentary bones and teeth—they might all represent a single species of early hominid (Haile-Selassie, Suwa, and White 2004). There simply isn't enough information to come to a clear consensus on this issue. What is clear is that they all lived at a time soon after the human lineage diverged from that of the apes. Genetic analysis of human beings and chimps shows that we have been evolving separately for no more than about 7 million years. *Ardipithecus, Orrorin,* and *Sahelanthropus,* therefore, appear to be examples of what our ancestors looked like at the genesis of the human family.

The Genus Australopithecus

Dating to sometime between 4.17 and 4.07 million years ago are the exciting discoveries made in Kanapoi and Allia Bay, Kenya, between 1995 and 1997 (Leakey et al. 1998). The 12 specimens from Allia Bay and the 9 from Kanapoi, including teeth, cranial fragments, and some bones below the skull, have been assigned the species name *Australopithecus anamensis* (Figure 3.10).

The *anamensis* jaw fragments and fossil teeth are apelike. The configuration of the jaw is boxlike in both apes and *anamensis*. Human jaws, on the other hand, expand or open up toward the back of the mouth. An upper arm bone found more than 30 years ago—now assigned to this species based on its stratigraphic position—exhibits many humanlike features. In addition, and more significant, both ends of a tibia (shin bone) that were recovered are very humanlike; its discoverers identify this bone as clearly indicating bipedal

FIGURE 3.11
*This 45% complete skeleton
of the fossil known as Lucy
plus a series of 13 other*
Australopithecus afarensis
*specimens have been dated
to 3.18 million years ago.*
(© 1995 John Reader/SLP/
Photo Researchers, Inc.)

locomotion nearly half a million years before the Laetoli footprints. The environment in which *Australopithecus anamensis* lived was characterized by open woodland or bushland conditions.

The discoverers of *anamensis* suggest that it provides the clearest picture of a human ancestor from about 4 million years ago. As such, this fossil may represent the species ancestral to the well-known hominid we will discuss next and, perhaps, to all of the later hominids to be discussed in this book (Leakey and Walker 1997).

Australopithecus afarensis

Far better known and with a far larger sample of remains is a later, somewhat less apelike form of the same genus, *Australopithecus afarensis*—most likely the creature that left the footprint trail described in this chapter's "Prelude." A significant number of *afarensis* fossils have been discovered. The great majority of these fossils date to the period from 4 million to 3 million years ago. The most significant *afarensis* fossils were found in the Afar geographical region of Ethiopia, where the first and most complete specimens were discovered at the site of Hadar (Figure 3.11), highlighted in this chapter's "Case Study Close-Up."

Some individuals are critical of the evolutionary conclusions of paleoanthropology because they believe the data always to be scanty and equivocal. In fact, thousands of hominid fossil bones have been found. *Afarensis* alone has produced more than 300 individual specimens. Among the key elements of the *afarensis* skeleton that have been found and used to define the species are the pelvis, vertebrae, leg bones, fingers, feet, jaws, skull fragments, a nearly complete cranium, and teeth. Together, these skeletal elements allow us to paint a reliable picture of a creature that, beginning about 4 million years ago, was not becoming bipedal but already was fully upright (see this chapter's "Issues and Debates").

The **postcranial** skeleton (everything below the skull) of *afarensis* is diagnostic of a creature far more like a human than like an ape. The feet of *afarensis* were quite modern, lacking the divergent big toe of the apes. The ape's big toe is positioned on its foot just as our thumbs are positioned on our hands, allowing the ape to grasp objects with its feet (for example, to grasp tree branches when climbing) far better than we can. *Afarensis* possessed the feet of a walker, not those of a climber. Also, the pelvis was quite similar to ours and is easily distinguished from an ape's (see Figure 3.22); the configuration of the pelvis is an accurate indicator of a creature's mode of locomotion (see this chapter's "Issues and Debates").

A computer simulation of *afarensis* locomotion tested various models, including a chimplike gait and a more fully upright, humanlike mode of walking (Crompton et al. 1998). Using the shapes of the preserved bones of the fossil called Lucy in the computer simulation of *afarensis* locomotion, these researchers concluded that a humanlike gait was far more likely. Though Lucy certainly possessed some apelike characteristics, she walked on two feet, not clumsily like a chimp but efficiently like a modern human being. (See this chapter's "Case Study Close-Up" for more on Lucy.)

Compared to human beings, the apes have proportionally very long arms in relation to their trunk and legs. Long, powerful arms allow the apes to climb or swing through trees as well as to walk quadrupedally on the ground. Human arms are, by comparison, short in relation to human legs; try walking on your hands and feet, and you will soon discover that either your legs are far too long or your arms are simply too short. Analysis of the proportions of upper and lower limbs in *afarensis* shows quite clearly that in this respect as well the species was proportioned far more like modern humans than like apes (Shreeve 1996).

On the other hand, *afarensis* had not left its ape heritage behind entirely. In some specimens the finger bones were long and curved, like an ape's (Susman, Stern, and Jungers 1984). This evidence may indicate that *afarensis* retained some of the **arboreal** ability of its ape ancestors at the same time that it walked bipedally on the ground.

Though *afarensis* may have been a proficient climber, evidence shows clearly that this first hominid species had moved away from the heavily arboreal adaptation of apes. Paleoanthropologist Tim White (see Bower 1993d) excavated fragments of an upper and lower arm from a deposit dated to 3.4 million years ago at the site of Maka in Ethiopia. The upper arm bone (the **humerus**) is proportionally short, like a modern human's and unlike the relatively long arm of the ape, with its adaptation for life in the trees. The discovery of one of the lower arm bones (**ulna**) of an *afarensis* specimen lends further support to the notion that the arms were more like a human's than like an ape's. The specimen exhibits some apelike characteristics, but in general the pattern is more like that of a modern human (Aiello 1994; Kimbel, Johanson, and Rak 1994).

All of the essentially human qualities of the postcranial skeleton of *Australopithecus afarensis* must be contrasted with the almost entirely apelike features of its skull, as exhibited in the nearly complete cranium discovered at Hadar (Kimbel, Johanson, and Rak 1994). This cranium, labeled A.L. 444-2 by its excavators, is the most complete *afarensis* skull yet found. It dates to about 3 million years ago, making this specimen one of the youngest yet identified in the *afarensis* fossil species. A detailed description has not yet been published. Nevertheless, it is apparent that in its overall form, A.L. 444-2 is certainly more apelike than any subsequent human ancestor, including other, later versions of *Australopithecus* we will discuss. Cranial capacity is apelike, in the range of 400–500 cc—like that of a modern chimpanzee and about one-third the human mean for brain size (see Figure 3.21). The upper portion of the face is small when compared to the lower part (as in apes), which is the opposite of the pattern in modern human beings. The jaws jut out and are snoutlike—they are said to be **prognathous**—just like those in an adult ape and again quite different from the relatively flat face of a modern human.

FIGURE 3.12

From this comparison of the maxillae (upper jaws) of chimps, Australopithecus, *and modern human beings, it is clear that the teeth in a chimp's mandible are arranged in a boxlike pattern, like those of* Australopithecus. *Modern human teeth form a curve, or arch.* (From *Lucy: The Beginnings of Humankind.* © 1981 Donald C. Johanson & Maitland A. Edey. Drawings © Luba Dmytryk Gudz.)

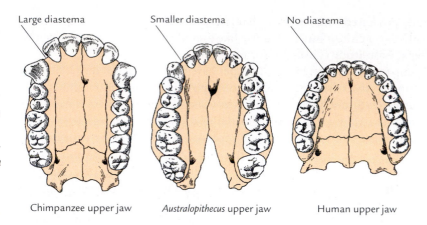

Large diastema   Smaller diastema   No diastema

Chimpanzee upper jaw   *Australopithecus* upper jaw   Human upper jaw

The *afarensis* jaw presents a combination of apelike and humanlike features (Figure 3.12). Humans and apes have the same numbers and kinds of teeth: two incisors, one canine, two premolars, and three molars in each quadrant of the adult mouth. Human teeth, however, in both the upper jaw—the **maxilla**—and the lower jaw—the **mandible**—are positioned in a curving arch that expands to the rear of the mouth; ape teeth present a more boxlike appearance, with the premolars and molars set in nearly parallel rows perpendicular to the incisors. Also, apes have proportionally much larger canine teeth and a gap in the teeth of the opposing jaw to allow room for the large canines when the mouth is closed. This gap, or **diastema,** is not present in the human jaw; our canines are much smaller, and so no gap in the opposing jaw is needed. The *afarensis* jaw is not quite like an ape jaw but not quite like a human jaw either. The configuration of the teeth is more like a box than an arch; there is a small diastema, and tooth size, including that of the canines, that is more apelike than human.

The evidence, then, is quite clear: *Australopithecus afarensis* seems to have been a bipedal ape living between 4 million and 3 million years ago. It looked like a chimpanzee standing on two short but otherwise humanlike legs, with no diverging big toe (Figure 3.13). What we share with *afarensis* is a mode of locomotion, but not a level of intelligence or a reliance on culture.

Just as we saw for the period around 6 million years ago, there appear to have been multiple versions of hominids between 4 and 3 million years ago. For example, a species called *Kenyanthropus platyops* has been defined on the basis of a series of teeth and bones recovered in northern Kenya on the west side of Lake Turkana and dated to 3.5 million years ago (Leakey et al. 2001).

The most significant remains recovered of *Kenyanthropus* are those of a nearly complete, but severely distorted, cranium. In fact, paleoanthropologist Tim White (2003) rejects this species, ascribing its unique appearance to this distortion. Nevertheless, like the *Sahelanthropus* cranium from Chad, the *Kenyanthropus* cranium is evidence of a chimp-sized head but a flat face similar to that of later hominids and modern humans. In fact, its flat profile is

FIGURE 3.13
This artist's conception of Australopithecus afarensis *shows the ability of this ancestral hominid to walk on two feet and also to climb trees.* (Courtesy of John Fleagle/Academic Press; © Stephen Nash)

what led to its species name; *platus* means flat in Greek. In this feature, *Kenyanthropus* differs from apes, but also from some contemporary—for example, *Australopithecus afarensis*—and even later hominids who, though clearly bipedal, had forward-thrusting, apelike faces. And like the other hominids discussed earlier, a reconstruction of the environment of *Kenyanthropus* shows that these later hominids lived in a rich and diverse habitat that included both woodlands and grasslands.

A FORK IN THE HOMINID ROAD

At about 3 million years ago, there is evidence of the evolution of a somewhat different form of hominid. We call these new fossils by the name *Australopithecus africanus*. Like its evolutionary progenitors, *africanus* was bipedal and still walked in an essentially modern human fashion. It also retained a basically apelike skull and brain. There are a number of fairly well preserved *africanus* crania, all apelike, with a sloping forehead and large ridges of bone above the eyes (Figure 3.14). On the other hand, the jaw and its teeth are a bit more humanlike and the face not so prognathous as that of *afarensis,* so in some ways it seems more human in appearance. Nevertheless, its brain size still falls into the range of that of the great apes (see Figure 3.21).

Australopithecus africanus dates to no more than 3 million years ago and seems to fade out of the picture by about 2.2 million years ago. At that point, a larger bipedal form seems to have taken its place (Figure 3.15). Called *Australopithecus robustus,* it was a biped, and its brain size was a bit greater than

FIGURE 3.14
The cranium of Australopithecus africanus, *a lightly
built, or "gracile," australopithecine form that followed*
afarensis *in southern Africa.*
Africanus *flourished after
3 million years ago and
appears to have become
extinct by 2.2 million years
ago.* (Transvaal Museum,
D. C. Panagos)

FIGURE 3.15
The cranium of Australopithecus robustus. Robus-
tus *appears to have been a
highly specialized hominid,
with extremely powerful
jaws adapted to processing
a diet of hard, gritty foods.*
Robustus, *which may have
replaced* africanus, *became
extinct around 1 million
years ago.* (Transvaal Museum, D. C. Panagos)

in *africanus.* More significant is the difference in the cranial architecture of
robustus: Where the top of the *africanus* skull is round and smooth, the top of
the *robustus* skull sports a thin ridge of bone called a **sagittal crest.** Such a
crest allows for a much larger, stronger temporalis muscle, which powers the
movement of the mandible while chewing.

   This feature of the *robustus* skull, along with its much larger surfaced molars and microscopic evidence of wear on the molar surfaces (Figure 3.16), is
a good indication of a shift in dietary emphasis in *robustus,* when compared

to *africanus,* toward a diet of hard foods such as seeds and nuts rather than roots, fruits, or leaves (Grine 1987). Analysis of the mineral content of their bones indicates that the *robustus* diet may have included meat as well (Bower 1992a). *Robustus* fossils disappear from the paleontological record by about 1 million years ago.

The *robustus* pattern of powerful cranial architecture is even more pronounced in another fossil hominid, *Australopithecus boisei,* whose specimens date from 2.2 million years ago to 1.4 million years ago, making it partially contemporaneous with *robustus* (Suwa et al. 1997). *Boisei* is different enough from *robustus* to warrant separate species status. In other words, there was more than one distinct hominid species living in Africa during the same period, a situation similar to the modern situation for **pongids,** in which there are two extant species of chimp (the common chimp and the bonobo).

To complicate matters further, there is a well-preserved, virtually intact cranium (specimen designation KNM WT-17000), called "the Black Skull" for its darkly stained appearance, that is even more robust than *boisei* but older than either *robustus* or *boisei.* Dating to about 2.5 million years ago, the Black Skull has a smaller cranial capacity than even *afarensis* (Johanson 1993; Walker et al. 1986). Because of its extreme robustness, its small cranial capacity, and its early date, no one is quite sure how to interpret the Black Skull, though it might represent a form ancestral to *boisei* or, perhaps, to both *boisei* and *robustus.* Some paleoanthropologists label the Black Skull *Australopithecus aethiopicus.*

A FOREST OF HOMINIDS

To be sure, at this point it is impossible to come to a definitive determination of how all the various fossil species discussed in this chapter—and others left undiscussed—were related to the lineage of modern human beings. Though a chronological chart can help you sort out when the various species lived (Figure 3.17), there is no nice, neat chronological sequence we can come up that shows ancient hominids becoming continuously more modern looking in each of their characteristics through time, leading to individuals that look like modern people. In fact, it appears that there were a number of false starts and dead ends, creatures that were hominids but that became extinct, representing side branches on a densely thick evolutionary bush with modern human beings representing the only surviving branch. We simply don't have large enough samples of the different kinds of hominids that were alive in the period between 6 and 2.5 million years ago to accurately determine which species faded into extinction and which species are directly ancestral to modern human beings. In all likelihood, there are additional extinct hominid species whose bones have not yet been found or recognized, and one or more of them might be more directly ancestral to us than most or even any of the species so far defined.

FIGURE 3.16
Teeth tell the story of a significant difference in the diets of the gracile and robust australopithecines. A photo-micrograph of an africanus *molar (top) provides evidence of a diet of soft foods, perhaps roots and meat. A photo-micrograph of a* robustus *molar (bottom) shows clear evidence of a diet rich in such foods as hard seeds and nuts.* (Courtesy of F. E. Grine)

FIGURE 3.17
This phylogeny shows the chronological relationships among the fossil hominids discussed in this chapter.

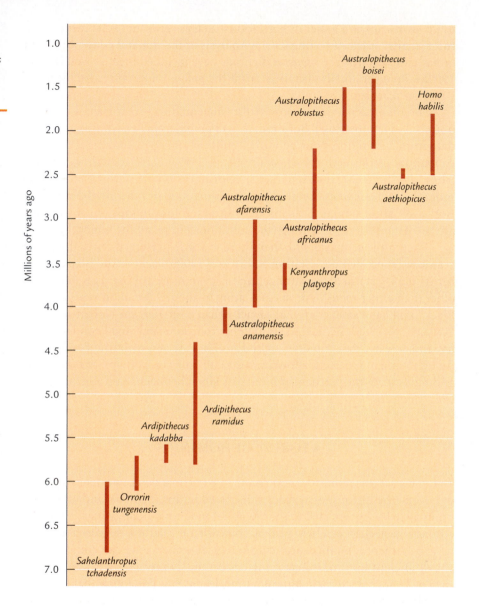

With all that is uncertain, a number of elements of the early story of the human family do seem clear. It appears that a number of somewhat different forms of upright-walking creatures with chimp-sized heads, a mix of human-like and apelike teeth but with tantalizing evidence of a humanlike way of walking on two feet, existed beginning about 6 million years ago. They lived in a variety of environments and seem to have flourished where there was a mosaic of different habitats including forest and grassland. Their ability to walk on two feet and, perhaps, climb trees seems to have provided them with

an adaptive advantage over many of the Miocene apes whose forests they shared. Some of these upright walkers that we call hominids also shared the fate of many of the Miocene apes and became extinct. But one of these hominids was a winner in the evolutionary saga. Its progeny are the focus of the rest of this chapter.

A DIFFERENT PATH—*HOMO HABILIS*

Soon after 2.5 million years ago, and just as the **australopithecines** were experiencing great changes in their evolutionary pathway, another hominid seems to have branched off from the main line of the *Australopithecus* genus (see Figure 3.17). This breakaway group followed a different evolutionary route, one in which its survival on the African savanna was not the result of an increasingly specialized diet but, instead, was due to an increase in intelligence made possible by an expanding brain. This creature first appears in the fossil record about 2.4 million years ago (Bower 1993b,c; Hill et al. 1992; Schrenk et al. 1993), a little before *africanus* became extinct, which makes it a contemporary of *Australopithecus robustus* and *aethiopicus.* But this new form cannot be mistaken for any variety or form of *Australopithecus.* With a much flatter face, a steeper forehead, and a larger brain—a mean size close to 700 cc, larger than any ape brain and just about one-half the modern human mean—this clearly is a new and different hominid. It is called *Homo habilis* (Figure 3.18).

Assigning them to the same genus as modern humans means that *Homo habilis* was much more like us than were any of the australopithecines.

FIGURE 3.18

The cranial capacity of this fragmentary cranium of Homo habilis *shows that* habilis *possessed a brain larger than any ape's. Dated at 2.4 million years ago,* habilis *represents the first hominid with an expanded brain.* (© National Museums of Kenya)

Whereas taxonomically *Homo sapiens* might live in the same general neighborhood as the australopithecines, we live on the same street as *Homo habilis.*

The skull of *Homo habilis* was not just larger than that of the australopithecines but was shaped differently as well, with significantly less prognathism, a taller, steeper forehead, and a more rounded profile. All of these features seem to presage modern human beings.

Once again, however, this "new and improved" hominid retained some pongid features in its postcranial skeleton. Though postcranial remains of *habilis* are scanty, what have been found show that from the neck down the members of this species can be safely characterized as upright. Unlike some earlier australopithecines, their arms are still long and the legs short in proportion to each other, much like an ape's but unlike a human's short arms and long legs (Johanson et al. 1987).

The Ability to Make Stone Tools

The species we label *Homo habilis* on the basis of its skeletal characteristics exhibits another key feature not previously seen in the archaeological record: Its members made stone tools. We do not know whether any of the australopithecines made tools out of soft material such as wood or animal hide that would have decayed long ago. Modern chimps are known to manufacture tools by stripping the bark off of twigs, which they then poke into termite mounds (Goodall 1986). The termites adhere to the sticky residue on the stripped wood. The chimps pull out the twigs after a suitable wait and then feast on termites. Some chimps use stones to hammer open nutshells to get at the nutmeat within, even placing the nuts on stone anvils to magnify the effect. There is no reason to believe that *Australopithecus* was not capable of similar work.

It also is possible that at least some of the later australopithecines were physically capable of making stone tools. Researcher Randall Susman (1994) compared the hand bones of specimens of *Australopithecus afarensis, Australopithecus robustus, Homo erectus* (see Chapter 4), *Homo sapiens neanderthalensis* (see Chapter 5), and modern humans. Whereas the *Australopithecus afarensis* hand Susman examined was similar to that of a chimp, all of the other specimens examined, including that from *Australopithecus robustus,* were more similar to a modern human's hand.

The first appearance of the oldest stone tools closely coincides with the earliest appearance of *Homo habilis.* As archaeologists Kathy Schick and Nicholas Toth (1993:103) point out, the relatively small brain of the robust australopithecines and the small number of presumed stone tools found at their sites argue against their being proficient toolmakers. The massive cranial architecture of *Australopithecus* further suggests to these researchers that they didn't need a cultural assist in the form of stone tools to process food in the first place. Although the question of exactly who made the first stone tools—and who did not—is still open to debate, it is certain that *Homo habilis* pos-

FIGURE 3.19
Ancient hominids began crafting stone tools— the technology is called Oldowan—about 2.5 million years ago. Thin, sharp stone flakes struck off cores like this one were used for cutting and scraping, while the remaining cores could be used as chopping tools.
(© Institute of Human Origins)

sessed both the hand anatomy and the increased intelligence needed to carry out the sophisticated process of forethought and action in the production of permanent tools.

Oldowan Technology

These oldest stone tools date back to about 2.6 million years ago at Gona, Ethiopia (Quade et al. 2004; Semaw et al. 1997). Tools like these were first recognized, defined, and described by the famous paleoanthropologist team of Louis and Mary Leakey (Leakey 1971). They called the tools **Oldowan,** after the place where they were first found and where the Leakeys had devoted so much of their research energy, Olduvai Gorge in Tanzania (Figure 3.19).

The Leakeys originally defined Oldowan tools as a series of specifically shaped, sharpened rocks that served as chopping tools. Mary Leakey (1971) classified Oldowan choppers into a number of types based on shape and inferred function—cutting, chopping, scraping, and so forth. More recent work,

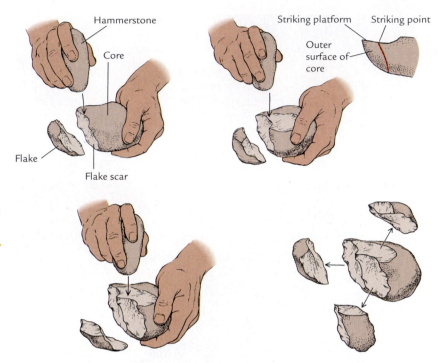

however, by Nicholas Toth (1985) and Kathy Schick (Schick and Toth 1993) shows clearly that, though some of the "Oldowan choppers" may have been used as tools, the vast majority functioned as **cores** from which **flake** tools were produced.

The maker of the tool, or the **knapper,** begins with a more or less spherical nodule of stone. Holding this **object piece** in one hand, the knapper strikes it with a **hammerstone,** usually a fortuitously shaped harder rock (or just one less likely to break as a result of its particular geometry). Without much trouble, the knapper can knock a flake off the stone (Figure 3.20). Then the knapper turns the object piece around in his or her hand so the interior surface of the rock that was just exposed with the first hammerstone blow is facing up. Next, using that surface as a **striking platform,** the knapper strikes down on it with the hammerstone, thereby removing a stone flake from the opposite side of the object piece. Repeating this several times can produce a number of sharp, relatively straight-edged flakes useful for cutting, scraping, sawing, chopping, and the like. Microscopic analysis of a large collection of Oldowan flakes shows that many were used for these purposes (Keeley and Toth 1981; Toth 1985). The flakes exhibit a polish on their edges that is typically caused by cutting plant material, butchering animals, and woodworking.

Stone flakes are sharper, stronger, and more durable than the teeth or nails nature provided our ancestors. Although one doesn't need to be a genius to figure out how to make stone tools, it does take what researcher John

Gowlett calls an "appreciation of the properties of stone" (1986:251). The production of Oldowan tools took some knowledge of the characteristics of different rocks, an understanding of their breakage patterns, forethought in planning the sequence of blows, a bit of hand–eye coordination, and flexibility to change the planned sequence when problems cropped up. More fundamentally, this process takes enough intelligence to recognize that a round, dull rock can be transformed into a large number of straight, thin, sharp pieces of rock suitable for many different uses. Clearly, this is the thought process of an intelligent being.

I am certain that most of us would not know what kinds of rock would be useful in toolmaking, and we wouldn't know where to find any of it even if we did know the kinds that work best. In the experimental archaeology course I teach in which students learn about stone-tool technology by attempting to actually replicate stone tools, I instruct them to go off into the wilds of Connecticut and collect stones from which they think they might be able to produce sharp-edged stone blades. We won't talk about the one student who actually bought rocks at a local rock shop (the price tag was still on one of them). Most students return to the class with sandstone and schist and other rock types common in our region but that shatter or crumble when struck, producing no usable tools. The point is, it takes knowledge and experience to recognize rocks with the best qualities for making tools. There is a lithic learning curve, and *Homo habilis* was pretty far along on that curve.

The hominids at Gona selected the best stone in their territory, rock that fractures readily and regularly to produce sharp, thin flakes. Flaking was not random but done according to a sensible pattern of removal from a core. In fact, the Gona researchers propose that the 2.6-million-year-old tools found there almost certainly do not represent the first or even a very early attempt by these hominids to make stone tools. These researchers suggest that further study may likely reveal evidence of even older toolmaking, more representative of the initial experimentation performed by our ancestors as they literally invented stone toolmaking (Semaw et al. 1997).

To Schick and Toth (1993), the archaeological record at *Homo habilis* sites suggests quite a bit of forethought and planning in the manufacture of stone tools. In their view, Oldowan was not a simple and "expedient" technology in which tools were made only to fill an immediate need from whatever happened to be available. If this had been the case, then flakes and the cores from which they originated would all be found together where they were made and used, and they would have been produced from raw materials found nearby.

Instead, the archaeological record shows that cores were transported, sometimes several kilometers from their point of origin. *Homo habilis* was willing to travel some distance for a source of stone known to be superior for the production of sharp, durable tools. The cores themselves appear to have been moved around to wherever flakes were needed; it is common to find flakes but not their source cores at a site. The cores, apparently, were carried to the next place tools might be needed. This process shows a high level of planning and intelligence. As Schick and Toth maintain, "This is a much more complicated pattern than many would have suspected from this remote period of time. It bespeaks to us an elevated degree of planning among these early hominids than is presently seen among modern nonhuman primates" (1993:128).

The Fate of Homo habilis

The existence of *Homo habilis* was rather short in evolutionary terms: Occurring first in deposits that are about 2.4 million years old, their remains disappear entirely sometime after about 1.8 million years ago. But the evidence does not imply that *Homo habilis* simply became extinct, leaving no evolutionary descendants. In fact, *habilis* appears to have evolved into another hominid species. This evolutionary jump and the new species that resulted are the focus of the next chapter.

ISSUES AND DEBATES

WHAT WERE THE FIRST STEPS IN HOMINID EVOLUTION?

The evidence regarding how the hominid family began is unequivocal. The first hominids were, fundamentally, bipedal apes; the first steps of our evolution were literally "first steps." The physical evidence shows that creatures dating to at least 6 million years ago had a skeletal anatomy, reflected in the morphology of their femurs as well as the positioning of their skulls on their vertebral columns, suitable for walking on two feet, in a manner similar to the way modern human beings walk. At the same time, these creatures possessed brains of a size and configuration virtually indistinguishable from those of some species of fossil and modern apes (Figure 3.21). The consensus on this is clear.

This scenario of the origin of the human line, based on locomotor patterns rather than growth in brain size and intelligence, was not what most nineteenth-century evolutionary scientists expected and may seem to contradict common sense even today. After all, the hallmark of our species, the characteristic that seems to distinguish us the most from other animals, including the apes, is our great intelligence. Chimps and bonobos, for all their great intelligence, their inventiveness, and even their capacity for communication, have brains less than one-third the size of the modern human brain (about 450 cc compared to about 1,450 cc). In other words, our brains are a quantum leap larger in volume, more than three times larger than those of chimps and bonobos.

We might expect, therefore, that the human brain has been evolving the longest and was the first characteristic that differentiated us from the other primates—and that its growth is what initiated the split between the pongid and hominid families. In fact, many scientists held this view in the late nineteenth and early twentieth centuries. For example, Grafton Elliot Smith, a

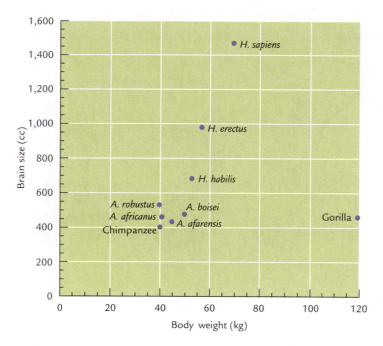

FIGURE 3.21
A comparison of brain size and body weight in a number of different ape and hominid species.

renowned British scientist who published extensively on human evolution, expressed the perspective of many others when he characterized the then hypothetical earliest human ancestor as "merely an ape with an overgrown brain" (1927:105–6). The belief that the fossil record should provide specimens that looked like apes with "overgrown" brains made many people susceptible to a hoax. The famous fossil found at Piltdown in southern England seemed to be that big-brained early ancestor. Many scientists suspended their usual skepticism and accepted the Piltdown finding. But the fossil turned out to be a modern human skull planted with an ape jaw that was doctored so as to appear to belong to the skull (see Feder 2007).

HOW DO WE KNOW THE HOMINIDS WERE UPRIGHT?

The configuration of the skeleton is quite different for creatures who walk quadrupedally and for those who are habitual bipeds. The most important part of the skeleton in this regard is the pelvis, made up of a left and a right **innominate bone** (Figure 3.22). The innominate bones of a primate quadruped—for example, a chimpanzee—have a long and narrow top blade (the **ilium**) that connects to the base of the pelvic bone (the **ischium**), creating a flat plane. A human innominate, on the other hand, has an ilium that is short and broad and, when compared to a chimp's, flares out at the top and seems twisted to the side, producing a complex curve away from the plane of its ischium (Lovejoy 1988).

FIGURE 3.22

A comparison of the pelvis of a gorilla, an Australopithecus, *and a modern human. Despite some differences, the pelvises of the extinct and the modern hominid are far more similar to each other than either is to that of the ape. This is because the pelvis determines the configuration of the muscles that attach to the upper leg, which, in turn, determines how an animal walks: Apes are quadrupeds;* Australopithecus *and modern human beings are bipeds.*

(From "The Antiquity of Human Walking" by John Napier. Copyright © April 1967 by *Scientific American*, Inc. All rights reserved; drawing © Enid Kotschnig)

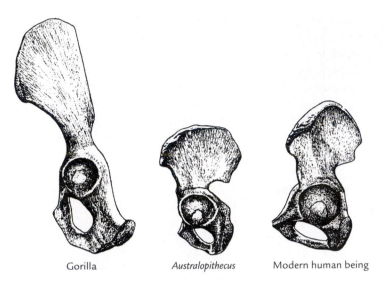

Gorilla   *Australopithecus*   Modern human being

The configuration of the innominate bone in an animal determines the position of the large gluteal muscles, which in turn determines how the creature could most easily get around. Thus, the position of the ilium on the innominate bone of an extinct animal allows us, with some accuracy, to deduce how that creature walked—in other words, whether it got around on four legs or two.

There really is very little argument about the pelvis of *Australopithecus afarensis* as well as that of the other australopithecines with preserved pelvises; they have an innominate bone very similar to that of a modern human being (Lovejoy 1988; Lovejoy, Heiple, and Burnstein 1973; see Figure 3.22). Scientists who have examined the bones disagree about whether *afarensis* differed in some of the particulars of walking; for example, Stern and Susman (1983) suggest that, though bipedal on the ground, *afarensis* shuffled more in the way a chimp does. However, most of these scientists maintain that *afarensis* walked much in the way we do (Lovejoy 1988).

IS THERE OTHER EVIDENCE FOR BIPEDALITY?

Though the pelvis is the best place to look for evidence of locomotion, fossil discoveries are not made to order and we don't always find this skeletal element. Other parts of early hominid anatomy, however, are also useful to assess a creature's locomotor pattern. For example, the femur of *Orrorin* has characteristics that indicate bipedality 6 million years ago. The toe bone of *Ardipithecus* conforms to the foot of an upright walker. The Laetoli footprints (see Figure 3.1) are virtually indistinguishable from footprints of a modern human; individually they exhibit the typical pattern of a human foot, and together they match the human stride (Charteris, Wall, and Nottrodt 1981; Day and Wickens 1980; T. White 1980; White and Suwa 1987). The prints display a humanlike arch and lack any hint of the divergent big toe that characterizes the apes.

As we saw earlier, the location of the foramen magnum determines the position of the vertebral column, which in turn indicates whether a species is quadrupedal or bipedal. Fossil hominid crania as far back as *Sahelanthropus,* dating to 6 million years ago, possess a foramen magnum located at the base of the cranium, in nearly the same position as in modern human beings, who, of course, are bipedal.

Fragments of the **femur** (upper leg) and **tibia** (lower leg) of *afarensis* show clearly that its upper and lower leg joined at an angle more like that in modern human beings than that in apes (Johanson and Shreeve 1989). The preserved foot bones of *afarensis* are longer and more curved than the modern human form, but, like the footprints, they exhibit a modern arrangement of the big toe. In fact, when the large, well-preserved foot from the site of Hadar (see the "Case Study Close-Up" in this chapter) is scaled down to the size of the Laetoli prints, it is a perfect match (Johanson and Shreeve 1989:197).

WHY BIPEDALISM?

As anatomist Owen Lovejoy (1984) points out, we can't explain the success of bipedalism on the basis of its current utility. The question must be asked in an evolutionary framework and placed within the context of natural selection: If you are an ape, what is it about walking on two feet in the savanna that increases your likelihood of survival and, in turn, the probability that you will reproduce and pass on the genetic disposition for bipedal locomotion to another generation, for whom greater proficiency for that mode can be further acted on by natural selection?

Seventeenth-century natural historian John Ray, who we mentioned in Chapter 1, believed that upright walking was an endowment from God, giving human beings a unique advantage, enabling them to see for greater distances—to spot resources as well as dangers—and to carry objects.

Modern explanations of why this ability was the key selective factor in early hominid evolution are a bit more complex, though they often build on Ray's assertions. Modern hypotheses elaborate on how the ability to walk on two feet allowed our ancestors to survive at the end of the Miocene when so many other ape species became extinct and why it continued to be the central adaptive trait of the hominids until brain expansion took over more than 3.5 million years later.

The Upright Provider

Consider the hypothesis proposed by Owen Lovejoy (1981, 1984), who suggests that the key advantage to bipedal locomotion was that it freed the hands to carry things. Specifically, it freed the hands of males to carry food back to a camp or village where females and their offspring could be provisioned.

Among modern primates, chimp females raise their children alone. They are often good mothers, devoting much time and energy to the health and well-being of their offspring. From an evolutionary perspective, they are doing all they can to ensure that these children—individuals carrying half their genes—will survive to reproduce and pass on those genes. Male chimps, on the other hand, generally have little to do with infants. Because chimp society is sexually promiscuous, the males don't know which, if any, infants they have sired. So from an evolutionary perspective, why should they waste time providing for offspring that probably do not carry their genes?

Obviously, for a female the more offspring she gives birth to, the greater the likelihood that one or more will survive to adulthood and continue passing on her genes. But there's a trade-off in a species like chimps (and especially humans), where offspring are dependent on their mothers for extended periods (chimps commonly stay with their mothers for 8 to 10 years): With each new baby, the female can spend less and less time caring for older children, which may lower their chances for survival. Any help she can get, especially if she has more than one young child, will improve the likelihood of survival of all of her children. It makes sense for her to solicit assistance from a concerned adult male.

But how can she convince a male to do this? In Lovejoy's view, she must assure him that the offspring are his and that, by helping them, he ensures that half his genes get passed along as well. Only a pattern of sexual fidelity— in other words, monogamy—can do this. Basically, it's a trade: Females increase the likelihood their children will survive by remaining sexually faithful to one male. The male receives exclusive sexual access to a female and an increased probability that he will father offspring. All he has to do is faithfully provision the female and the children he has sired with her. This ability to bring food and other resources back to the female and the young is made feasible, in Lovejoy's view, by the freeing of the hands—which, in turn, is made possible by walking on two feet.

Remember, individual animals are not making a conscious choice to enhance their contribution to the evolutionary gene pool. Females merely are choosing to associate with males who help them care for their children, and males help females who provide them with sex. These behaviors increase the probability that offspring survive to adulthood. In terms of natural selection, it should be apparent that those late Miocene apes who acted in a way that increased the likelihood of their offspring's survival were more successful than those who did not: Their population increased while other groups became extinct. Because the provisioning behavior was made possible by upright walking, that ability would be strongly selected for.

Lovejoy's hypothesis explains bipedality, sexuality, and the development of monogamous family structure all at the same time. However, it has been criticized for being male-oriented and generally mistaken about modern primate behavior and the prevalence (or actual lack) of monogamy in modern human foraging societies (Tanner 1981; Zihlman 1979). There is at least one glaring problem here: When a male is away gathering food, what is to prevent a female from copulating with other males? In fact, such behavior may be to her advantage because it would increase the number of males willing to provision her and her offspring. Sex is used in many of the social primates to make alliances and maintain friendships. In such a scenario, sexual fidelity might even be disadvantageous, particularly if the male doesn't do a good job of provisioning. Ultimately, it is difficult to understand how a more rigid pattern demanding sexual fidelity actually could have been maintained in ancient hominid societies.

The Upright Scavenger

Anthropologist Pat Shipman (1984, 1986) has proposed another hypothesis. Using the scanning electron microscope, Shipman has examined the remains of animal bones recovered at early hominid sites. She found microscopic evidence of tooth marks from predators and scavengers, as well as cut marks from stone tools, made when hominids removed the meat. In some instances she found carnivore and stone-tool marks on the same bones, either with the tool marks superimposed on the carnivore tooth marks or with the tool marks made first. In other words, sometimes the hominids got at the bones after carnivores had already chewed on them (indicating hominid scavenging behavior), and sometimes carnivores had access to the bones only after the hominids had processed them (indicating hominid hunting behavior). There are too few marks, however, to come to any conclusion regarding the relative contribution of hunted versus scavenged meat.

As we will discuss later in this chapter, archaeologist Lewis Binford (1987a) has shown that the animal bones found at ancient hominid sites usually are from meat-poor parts of the carcass. This finding suggests to Binford, as well as to Shipman, that the early hominids largely were scavengers of meat, chasing off large carnivores after a kill or simply waiting for them to leave after they had filled their stomachs.

Walking on two feet was highly advantageous to hominids who were opportunistic scavengers rather than habitual hunters. Hunters need to run, and an animal can run faster on four feet than on two. Scavengers, however, don't need to run; their prey isn't going anywhere. But scavengers still need to find their quarry, and that means walking great distances and scanning a broad territory for evidence of a predator kill. Bipedalism is highly energy-efficient, in part because it involves only two limbs and yields greater endurance for walking long distances.

In addition, because scavengers always need to be wary of the return of the predator who did the killing in the first place, as well as of other large, aggressive scavengers—like hyenas or jackals, who might compete for the same kill—it is wise to get in and out quickly: Cut the meat off the bone as fast as possible and carry it back to a safe place to eat. The free hands of a bipedal hominid can carry both the tools for extracting the meat from the carcass and the meat.

The Efficient Walker

Primatologist Peter Rodman and anthropologist Henry McHenry (Johanson, Johanson, and Edgar 1994) have proposed what may be the simplest and most elegant hypothesis of all. After analyzing the energy expended by chimps when they walk quadrupedally and by humans with their upright gait, Rodman and McHenry determined that human locomotion was simply more efficient than chimp locomotion, meaning we expend less energy to accomplish the same task. As the Miocene forest shrunk, some ape species may have thrived by exploiting the resources of the growing savanna, where food resources were more dispersed. An efficient way of moving across increasing distances in the search for food became adaptively advantageous. The ability to walk efficiently on two feet may have provided that advantage.

All of the accumulated evidence of twentieth-century paleoanthropology basically brings us back to John Ray's seventeenth-century suggestions for the advantages of bipedalism. Though the modern hypotheses are more elaborate, they all suggest that the ability to carry things, to move around in a more energy-efficient way, and perhaps to see across greater distances was crucial in the selection process. Hominids, who could walk upright, had advantages that afforded them a better chance of survival in their diverse habitat.

The Endurance Runner

The Olympic marathon race (26 mi, 285 yd; 42.195 km) is run to commemorate a legendary marathon run by a Greek herald 2,500 years ago. The story begins with the invasion of Greece by the Persians in the fifth century B.C. The Persians landed a huge military force at the town of Marathon, in Greece, prepared to march on and then defeat the much smaller Athenian army. Against all odds, however, the Athenians were able to defeat the Persians. A Greek herald named Phidippides ran the approximately 26-mi route from Marathon to Athens to announce the stunning victory, and then promptly dropped dead.

More recently, marathon running has become extremely popular (mostly without the dying part); the 1996 record contingent of runners in the Boston Marathon, for instance, included over 36,000 who completed the run. Thousands more compete in marathons all over the world, and many more than that train for long-distance running, though they will never actually compete.

Not being a runner, I can scarcely comprehend the attraction of what, to me, seems like a particularly agonizing way to spend your time. Nevertheless, I do understand that in the human ability to run for great distances—not necessarily quickly when compared to the sprinting abilities of, for example, a horse or a cheetah, but consistently, over the course of many hours—we are unique among the primates. No monkey or ape species can run, bipedally or quadrupedally, for great distances. In fact, as experts in the field of biomechanics, Dennis Bramble and Daniel Lieberman (2004) point out, human physiology seems supremely well adapted to running. As they indicate, running is not just ramped-up walking; it is a very different manner of locomotion made possible by a unique combination of skeletal morphology, muscle configuration, and tendon placement (Zimmer 2004). For example, our tendons are arranged in a manner very different from those of chimps; they act like springs, allowing our legs to store energy with each stride. Our legs are proportionally much longer than those of the apes, allowing for longer strides and a faster pace, without expending the additional energy required to run faster by moving shorter legs more quickly. Running produces a pounding on our joints with each stride, but our skeletons are adapted to this as well. The surfaces where our leg bones meet—their **articular surfaces**—are proportionally broader in humans than in apes, allowing the great impacts of running to be dampened by spreading them out over a larger area. Bipedal running can be an unsteady way of moving about, and here too humans seem uniquely well-adapted to maintain stability, especially with a pelvic configuration that allows for large and powerful gluteal muscles that work to keep us upright.

Bramble and Lieberman point out that the skeletal features that adapt us so well for running are absent even in the demonstrably bipedal australopithecines, appearing first in *Homo habilis*. They suggest that the ability to run would have been highly advantageous both in hunting and in scavenging. Particularly before the development of long-distance weaponry—things like bows and arrows, developed much later—the need to catch up to prey, to get close enough to hurl rocks or other projectiles, provided good long-distance runners with a decided advantage (Carrier 1984). Scavengers too benefit from endurance running; based on clues provided by smell and the presence of circling vultures, wild dogs and hyenas regularly run great distances to exploit carcasses (Bramble and Lieberman 2004:351). Hominids who could run great distances would be able to better compete with these other scavengers for access to those carcasses.

So, the next time you compete in a marathon, of just watch one on TV, consider the possibility that the pounding, the agony, and the relentless pushing it takes to accomplish the run may be made possible because of evolutionary forces that enabled our ancestors on the plains of Africa more than 2 million years ago to successfully compete with animals larger, stronger, and faster than us.

WERE THE EARLY HOMINIDS HUNTERS?

It was once a popular belief that our most ancient ancestors were "killer apes" and that their evolutionary success resulted from their ferocity and savagery in the hunt (Ardrey 1961). That same theory posited that we are still "killer apes," if a bit more evolved, and that this explains everything from the territoriality of youth gangs, high murder rates, internecine violence, and our species' propensity for war.

We humans may be a uniquely violent species, but we cannot blame it on our Miocene heritage. There simply is no evidence that killing animals was the dominant mode of subsistence among our most ancient ancestors. For example, dental morphology shows that *Ardipithecus* and *Orrorin* were browsers who consumed soft fruit and leaves, not carnivores who concentrated on animal flesh (Gibbons 2002). The preserved teeth of *Australopithecus afarensis* imply a diet of mostly fruits, leaves, roots, insects, and small mammals. The habitat in which *Australopithecus anamensis* lived implies a diet of fruit, insects, and small mammals.

Even for the toolmaking *Homo habilis*, there is no evidence that hunting dominated the subsistence quest. Neither the Oldowan choppers nor the used flakes would have been handy as spearpoints. Moreover, a detailed **taphonomic** analysis conducted by archaeologist Lewis Binford (1987a) has shown that animal bones found at early hominid sites typically are not those we would expect to find at the hunting camps of proficient hunters. The animal skeletal elements found are not those that would have been associated with the best cuts of meat, such as upper limbs. Binford determined that the excavated animal bones were mostly lower limbs and parts of skulls and mandibles, among the least meaty of animal parts. Moreover, many of the tools found at *Homo habilis* sites would have been more suitable for extracting marrow than for removing meat from bones; marrow inside the shafts of long bones, typically left behind by carnivores, is a staple for many scavengers. Binford's analysis indicated that early hominids were probably not proficient hunters at all but, instead, opportunistic scavengers of the carcasses of animals killed by large carnivores.

Electron microscope analysis conducted by Pat Shipman (1983, 1984, 1986) along with Richard Potts (Potts and Shipman 1981), which we discussed in connection with the origins of bipedality, further supports the hypothesis that scavenging played a major role in the diet of early hominids. For example, the cut marks on animal bones Shipman examined from *habilis* sites in Olduvai Gorge in Tanzania tend to be near the midshaft of the bones (Shipman 1983). For later groups known to be butchering entire carcasses rather than just scavenging them, the cut marks are almost always located near the joints, where the best meat is available. The location of the cut marks on the Olduvai animal bones seems to conform better to a scavenging than a hunting mode of subsistence.

Though scavenging might seem an unreliable mode of subsistence, under certain circumstances it is a reasonably low-risk strategy that yields an abundance of food. Using as a model modern ecosystems broadly similar to those in which the early hominids found themselves, a number of analyses have shown scavenging to be a productive subsistence strategy (Blumenschine 1989; Blumenschine and Masao 1991). Hyenas are virtually the perfect scavenger; they are powerful and intelligent, and they prowl their territory looking for fresh kills in organized social groups. A large group of hyenas can run a pride of lions off their kill, and they would have provided fierce competition for any other species, including hominids, that might have relied on scavenging. On the other hand, where hyenas occurred in small numbers and posed little threat, it may have made sense for hominids to wait for large predators such as lions to make their kills and then take advantage of what they left behind—or even run them off and "steal" the meat in what is called "confrontational scavenging." In fact, a decrease in the number of hyenas seems to coincide with the appearance of *Homo habilis* (Blumenschine 1987).

Though scavenging clearly was important in the early hominid quest for food, other research shows that hunting also was a part of early hominid subsistence. Anthropologists Henry Bunn and Ellen Kroll (1986) analyzed stone flakes and bones from the 1.8-million-year-old FLK site in Olduvai Gorge and found substantial evidence for reliance on meat; bones representing the meatiest parts of animals bore ample evidence of stone-tool cut marks. The evidence for hunting seems a bit stronger for small animals, with a pattern of scavenging but also some hunting of larger animals.

If animals are being scavenged, the scavenger grabs whatever portion of the killed animal can be obtained and takes it to a secure place. The archaeological sites that develop in such secure places produce lots of small portions of animals, bones reflecting whatever pieces of the animals the scavenger was able to grab. On the other hand, hunters carry most, if not all, of an animal back to a place where the food can be shared; they have complete control of the animal from the time of its killing to the time of its being eaten. At the FLK site, large sections of animals were found, suggesting that hunting was a primary mode of subsistence there.

It is possible that ancient hominids used another food resource in their subsistence quest beyond plants and hunted or scavenged animals: termites. Though it might not occur to most of the people who would read this book that termites are a viable selection on the human menu, many modern human foragers eat termites and, in fact, view them as a delicious treat. Yum. This modern practice can be traced back for nearly 2 million years. Researchers Lucinda R. Blackwell and Francesco d'Errico (2001) examined close to 90 bone tools from the Swartkrans Cave site in South Africa, occupied between 1.8 and 1.0 million years ago. The wear patterns on the bone consisted of a series of scratch marks and gouges, which when looked at microscopically did not match bones gnawed on by hyenas, walked on by animals, or tumbled in a river. The researchers produced experimental replicas, which they proceeded to use to dig up roots, scrape animal hides, and excavate in termite mounds. Only the wear produced by the termite-mound probing looked like the wear seen on the actual ancient bone tools. On this basis, the researchers concluded that the inhabitants of Swartkrans included termites in their diet. There is no indication in their report whether they carried the experiment to its logical conclusion and actually ate the termites their experimental tools provided.

We needn't be too concerned about the finer points of early hominid subsistence. All researchers would probably agree that hunting was not predominant in the subsistence base of the australopithecines or in *Homo habilis.* Though we have to be careful when generalizing from nonhuman primates, we do know that chimpanzees in the wild occasionally engage in cooperative hunts (Goodall 1986). As paleoanthropologist Daniel Stiles (1991) has pointed out, there is no reason to believe our hominid ancestors were less capable than chimps in their ability to plan, coordinate, and carry out a hunt. The first hominids were not born killers, but they probably did rely on meat to a certain degree, some of it scavenged, some from hunting. The early hominids probably were opportunistic foragers, taking whatever food they could, whenever the opportunity presented itself.

WHERE DID THE IDEA FOR STONE TOOLS COME FROM?

It is not intuitively obvious that a more or less spherical, relatively small, single nodule of stone can be transformed into a large number of consistently contoured stone flakes that cumulatively provide several feet of sharp tool edge. It takes some amount of reflection, study, and deliberation to figure out that stones with certain properties, when struck in the right way, at the right place, with just the right amount of force, and at the right angle can produce useful tools that can cut, pierce, or scrape far more effectively and efficiently than our teeth and nails. That *Homo habilis* was able to figure this all out is implied by the archaeological record of Oldowan tools. The question remains, then, "What might have inspired our first tool-using ancestors in this intellectual process?"

Though chimps in the wild have never been observed modifying stone to make tools, they do use rocks to crack open hard-shelled nuts. Chimps in the Taï Forest of the African nation of Côte d'Ivoire, for example, use extremely hard igneous rocks that they have to collect from outcrops and then transport to the location of the nut-producing *Panda* trees (Mercader, Panger, and Boesch 2002). The chimps position the nuts on bedrock outcrops or exposed tree roots that serve as anvils and then crack the nuts open by striking them with the igneous hammers (Figure 3.23). Occasionally, slices of these hammers accidentally flake off, unintentionally producing sharp-edged stone flakes. This got the researcher of the chimp behavior thinking.

Nuts are a nutritious and abundant food source. When *Panda* nuts are in season in the Taï Forest, chimps have been calculated to obtain more than 3,000 calories of food per day from this food source (Mercader, Panger, and Boesch 2002:1452). The researchers of chimp nut-cracking sensibly suggest the possibility that some Miocene apes and early hominids could have exploited the same or similar nut foods in their subsistence pursuit. The only viable way to access the rich meat of some species of nuts is to strike the nuts with a hard hammer. Certainly, Miocene hominids might have practiced the

FIGURE 3.23
Chimpanzees living in the Taï Forest of the African nation of Côte d'Ivoire use rock hammers and root and stone anvils to pound open nutshells to extract the rich and nutritious nutmeats. In this process, chimps may accidentally break the stones, producing, again accidentally, sharp-edged flakes of stone that litter the surroundings of their nut-processing stations. It is possible that our human ancestors used stones to perform the same task, producing flakes that they realized were, themselves, a valuable by-product of the activity, usable as tools. It may then have been a short intellectual leap for our ancestors to then intentionally and directly produce stone tools by knocking two stones together. (© Michael Nichols/ National Geographic Society Image Collection)

same nut-cracking behavior as the chimps in the Taï Forest. These same researchers have proposed that nut-cracking hominids might have been inspired by accidentally breaking their stone hammers and unintentionally producing sharp flakes that could be used as tools. Perhaps they recognized the utility of the sharp flakes and then set about the process of trying to figure out how to intentionally and consistently produce sharp stone flakes—for butchering an animal, cutting fiber, and so on. It is interesting to consider the possibility that the invention of stone tools ultimately was the by-product of an accident.

WHAT DO WE KNOW ABOUT THE EARLY HOMINID BRAIN?

Under the very best of circumstances, paleoanthropologists are limited to the direct study of the hard parts of a hominid's anatomy—those that lend themselves to preservation: teeth (which are the hardest parts of our bodies and so the most abundantly preserved ancient hominid remains) and bones (which, though not as hard as teeth, under the right circumstances will fossilize and be preserved for millions of years). But if we want to know about early hominid intelligence, we are usually limited to hypothesizing on the basis of brain size as determined from the volume of the preserved skull.

The cranium is the vessel in which the brain resides. Where the cranium is well preserved, we can measure its volume to determine the size of an early hominid brain—in some cases, using sophisticated computer imaging technology (Conroy et al. 1998). Most of the early hominid brains turn out to be about the size of a chimpanzee's. The mean size of a chimp brain is about 400 cc. Compare this to the mean size of a modern human brain, about 1,450 cc. Though we do not have enough cranial fragments to accurately assess the size of the *Ardipithecus* or *Australopithecus anamensis* brain, the *afarensis* brain can be measured; its mean is about 413 cc, marginally larger than a chimp's. *Australopithecus africanus* possessed a brain about 440 cc in size, and the distorted cranium of *Kenyanthropus* suggests a similar size. The more robust and larger australopithecines had brains that were closer to 500 cc in size. *Homo habilis,* the first member of our genus, possessed a brain with a mean size of close to 650 cc, still less than half the size of the modern human brain.

The brain itself is soft tissue and quickly decays, usually leaving no trace. However, under rare circumstances a cast of the brain, showing features of its exterior surface, can survive when minerals replace the brain as it decays, filling the skull like Jell-O in a mold. Called **endocasts,** these natural models of ancient brains can show us what the exterior surface of an ancient brain looked like.

Anthropologist Dean Falk (1984) has examined the seven known cranial endocasts of *Australopithecus africanus.* The exterior surfaces of all these casts are virtually indistinguishable from the exterior surfaces of the brains of modern apes. They display none of the characteristics of the exterior of the human brain that distinguish it from that of an ape's brain. Specifically, the brains of the australopithecines are symmetrical: The left and right halves appear to be mirror images of each other. Modern human brains are decidedly asymmetrical: The left and right halves look different and actually are associated with different functions. Considering our view of the australopithecines as a series of bipedal apes, we should expect them to lack this feature of the human brain.

Where nature has not provided endocasts, they can be manufactured by coating the inside of a fossil skull with liquid latex or a similar material that, when dry, can be peeled off. This artificial endocast reflects the form of the interior surface of the skull and, it is hoped, shows features of the exterior of the brain with which the skull was in constant contact for an individual's lifetime. The artificial endocast of a *Homo habilis* specimen (ER 1470) shows a far more humanlike, asymmetrical morphology, providing further evidence of the ancestral connection this species shares with us.

WHAT CAUSED THE PROLIFERATION OF HOMINID SPECIES?

Paleoecological evidence collected in association with the earliest hominids shows that our ancestors were not restricted to living in the grassland. *Sahelanthropus, Orrorin, Ardipithecus, Australopithecus anamensis, Australopithecus afarensis,* and *Kenyanthropus* have been shown to have lived in diverse environments with both savanna and open woodlands in their territories. Paleoanthropologist Richard Potts (1996) suggests that rather than adapting to one specific set of ecological circumstances, our ancestors seem to have proliferated and prospered in environments characterized as **mosaic**—a diverse mixture of habitats. Perhaps it was their adaptive flexibility that gave them an evolutionary advantage in the diverse and inconstant world of 3 to 6 million years ago. An animal that could both readily climb trees *and* walk on two feet in the expanding grasslands might have possessed a significant adaptive advantage over those species that could only climb trees. It makes sense and it establishes a pattern we will see throughout later human biological and cultural evolution: The flexibility to adjust to a diverse and uncertain environment has long been the hallmark of the hominid family.

RATES OF CHANGE IN EVOLUTION

As paleontologist Stephen Jay Gould (1994) pointed out, most people think that evolution proceeds along a steady, even course, with small, incremental changes leading to large changes across the vast expanse of time. Yet, when we look at the evidence for the fossil species *Australopithecus afarensis,* we see something quite different. The oldest commonly accepted *afarensis* specimen is the Belohdelie frontal bone from a skull dated to 3.9 million years ago. The youngest is the nearly complete Hadar cranium, A.L. 444-2, dated to 3 million years ago. Separated by nearly 1 million years, these two specimens are remarkably similar, where comparisons can be made. They imply fundamental stability in the species during this period, not accretional change.

Gould and his colleague Niles Eldredge proposed a perspective on evolution called **punctuated equilibrium** (Eldredge and Gould 1972). In this view, species tend to remain stable for long periods of time before undergoing—perhaps in response to a dramatic change in their environment—a period of relatively rapid change ("rapid" in geological time is still rather slow by human standards). Long periods of stability—"equilibrium"—marked by rapid bursts of change—"punctuations"—seem to characterize the history of many species, including our own. If Gould is right then the extinction of *afarensis* and the proliferation of a number of new hominid forms after 3 million years ago are directly connected.

Hadar, located in the Afar triangle of northeastern Ethiopia, is one of the most spectacular fossil hominid sites ever excavated. All by itself, the Hadar site disproves the notion that the pronouncements of paleontologists are based on a tiny handful of unrecognizable bone fragments or indistinguishable teeth. This one site produced 250 hominid fossil bones representing 14 individual members of the species *Australopithecus afarensis* (Johanson and Shreeve 1989:21). Perhaps most significantly, Hadar produced Lucy.

**CASE STUDY
CLOSE-UP**

The remains of the fossil that her discoverers named Lucy were found in 1974. Close to one-half of her skeleton was recovered, including parts of the skull, the lower jaw, ribs, vertebrae, arm bones, left innominate, left femur (upper leg), and parts of the lower right leg (see Figure 3.11). The following year, fragmentary remains of 13 more individuals were found, including 9 adults and 4 children. Dubbed "the First Family," all these individuals were deposited at the same time and seem to have died together.

The Hadar fossils provided the name for this hominid species, *Australopithecus afarensis,* after the Afar region of Ethiopia, where the site is located. Lucy and the First Family fossils constitute solid support for the interpretation presented in this chapter: Dating to more than 3.18 million years ago, these early hominids were, essentially, bipedal apes.

Lucy has received most of the attention as a result of her remarkable degree of preservation, but her size is not typical of the group found at Hadar. Lucy, an adult, was tiny by modern standards, standing only a little over 110 cm (3½ ft) tall, with an estimated weight of about 30 kg (65 lb), small even by *afarensis* standards. But Lucy is a female in a species that exhibits a large measure of **sexual dimorphism**—that is, a big difference between males and females. For example, among gorillas—a species with strong dimorphism—males are commonly twice the size of females. An analysis by Henry McHenry (1991) shows that sexual dimorphism among the known *afarensis* specimens is less than that exhibited by gorillas and orangutans but more than in chimpanzees and much more than in modern human beings. Lucy falls within the broad range of sizes represented in the First Family fossils. Though she is a small female, she is clearly a female.

The Hadar specimens show what these ancient hominids looked like: They were bipedal. Their arms were proportionally longer than those of modern humans, with hands quite modern in appearance except for fingers that curled more like an ape's fingers. Their jaws were an amalgam of ape and human. They had ape-sized brains housed in skulls that exhibited large, ape-like bony ridges above the eyes and a highly prognathous profile.

Hadar presents an astonishing picture of more than a dozen individuals who probably knew each other and perished together in the dim mists of our own beginnings. Like the footprints at Laetoli, they have achieved a kind of immortality as a result of the lucky accident of the preservation of their bones. And like the Laetoli prints, that lucky accident affords us, 150,000 generations later, the luxury to contemplate where and how we began.

 VISITING THE PAST

Unfortunately, most of you reading this book will probably not be able to visit Africa anytime soon, so you won't be visiting any of the fossil localities discussed here. Even if you were able to, most of the sites are nondescript, without any on-site museum or display. The Laetoli footprints, for example, were left in place and, after casts of the individual hominid prints were made, were covered up. The footprints have since been stabilized and covered in an attempt to preserve them for the future. The site is not open to visitors (Agnew and Demas 1998). Some of the sites are in areas where tourists are not welcome. For example, Donald Johanson, Lucy's excavator, was unable to return to Hadar for some time because of political turmoil in that part of Ethiopia (Johanson and Shreeve 1989).

Most of the significant early hominid fossils are housed in museums, particularly the National Museum of Tanzania in Dar es Salaam and the National Museum of Kenya in Nairobi, in eastern Africa, and in various museums in southern Africa. However, very few of the actual original specimens are on display. Almost all are locked away, to preserve them for future research as new techniques of analysis are developed—for example, the extraction and analysis of minute quantities of DNA left in fossil bone.

The good news is that many natural history and science museums, especially those in big cities in the United States and Canada, have displays showing casts of some of the original fossils, replicas of the Laetoli pathway, dioramas showing artists' reconstructions of ancient hominids, and even some actual stone tools. Many of these exhibits are quite well done and certainly worth a visit. The Hall of Human Biology and Evolution at the American Museum of Natural History in New York City is a fantastic museum exhibit, with casts of many of the most important human ancestor fossils, replicas of Upper Paleolithic artwork, and four incredibly realistic, life-sized dioramas. These tableaux present re-creations of imagined moments in time in the lives of our hominid ancestors, including a depiction of two australopithecines walking on a bed of volcanic dust, leaving behind the Laetoli footprints discussed at the beginning of this chapter.

SUMMARY

Humanity began its evolutionary journey in Africa more than 6 million years ago as an "upright ape." Bipedal locomotion—not brain size or intelligence, the things that *most* distinguish us from the other animals—was what *first* differentiated us, the hominids, from the apes. *Sahelanthropus, Ardipithecus,* and *Orrorin* are among the candidates for the designation "oldest hominid," all dating to about 6 million years ago. By 4.2 million years ago, *Australopithecus anamensis* certainly was upright and may have been ancestral to all later forms of hominids. The ability to walk on two feet was advantageous in many ways: Hominids could travel with greater energy efficiency, which assisted in scavenging. Hominids seem uniquely adapted for long-distance running, and this ability to cover great distances may have been highly advantageous. With the hands freed, they could carry tools to where they were needed and bring back food to provision the young.

Around 2.5 million years ago, an environmental change in Africa, sparked by worldwide cooling, induced a burst of evolution in the hominid family. A number of varied species branched off from *Australopithecus afarensis* after this time. One branch, *Homo habilis,* had a brain size larger than any ape's.

With its larger brain, *Homo habilis* was able to produce the first stone tools—simple but revealing a level of planning and forethought that reflects the great intelligence of this first member of our genus.

TO LEARN MORE

Technical Summaries

For detailed discussions of the Miocene fossil apes, see John Fleagle's *Primate Adaptation and Evolution* (1988) and F. Szalay and Eric Delson's *Evolutionary History of the Primates* (1979). For a broad presentation about the modern apes, see J. R. Napier and P. H. Napier's *A Handbook of Living Primates* (1967).

Popular Summaries

For a terrific summary of current thinking about the evolution of the apes, see David Begun's (2003) Planet of the Apes in *Scientific American*. For very well written, less technical, and broad discussions of the paleoanthropology and archaeology of the first hominids, books written by some of the best-known scientists in the field are good choices: Donald Johanson and Maitland Edey's *Lucy: The Beginnings of Humankind* (1981), Donald Johanson and James Shreeve's *Lucy's Child: The Discovery of a Human Ancestor* (1989), and Richard Leakey and Roger Lewin's *Origins Reconsidered: In Search of What Makes Us Human* (1992). Donald Johanson, Lenora Johanson, and Blake Edgar's book, *Ancestors: In Search of Human Origins* (1994), is quite good. It brings the reader up-to-date on the latest discoveries in Africa and beyond and covers the entire story of human evolution. The book was a companion to a series on PBS with the same name. The videos are available at many university libraries and anthropology departments. For a broad, all-encompassing, popular treatment of human evolution, see the beautiful coffee-table book written by Donald Johanson and Blake Edgar called *From Lucy to Language* (1996). There is no better source for artistic photographs of fossil hominid remains (taken by well-known photographer of paleoanthropological specimens David Brill).

National Geographic magazine has remained very current on the latest hominid discoveries and newest interpretations in an ongoing series titled "The Dawn of Humans" that has appeared in many individual issues over the past few years. Look through back issues of the magazine starting with September 1995 for well-presented information—and, of course, fantastic graphics—on any of the periods of human evolution discussed in this book.

Some authors outside of paleoanthropology have chronicled the search for and analysis of the earliest hominids—and exposed the humanity behind the scientists involved in the search. See Delta Willis's *The Hominid Gang: Behind the Scenes in the Search for Human Origins* (1989) and noted science writer Roger Lewin's *Bones of Contention: Controversies in the Search for Human Origins* (1987).

On the Web

For a remarkable, interactive presentation about human evolution, visit the Web site of the Institute of Human Origins to see their Web-based documentary *Becoming Human* (http://www.becominghuman.org/). It is absolutely incredible, detailed, informative, stunning, and fun. For a page with links to a number of sites focusing on human evolution, try Biozone's http://www.biozone.co.uk/biolinks/HUMAN_ EVOLUTION.html. For a very helpful index of fossil hominids with short descriptions, visit David Kreger's *A Look at Modern Human Origins* at http://www.modern humanorigins.com/hominids.html. The Smithsonian Institution has a very well done online exhibit titled the *Human Origins Program* (http://www.mnh.si.edu/anthro/ humanorigins/). You can look at 360-degree Quicktime movies of important skulls and read the details of important fossil discoveries.

Online Learning Center: www.mhhe.com/feder4

The Online Learning Center (OLC) Web companion to *The Past in Perspective* features a variety of supplemental study aids. For each chapter, this free Web site includes

ONLINE LEARNING CENTER

- Self-Quizzes to take as pretests prior to exams
- Interactive Timeline Study Guides for additional review and reinforcement of key information
- Learning Objectives
- Chapter Site links with Web addresses for many of the fossil and archaeological sites mentioned in the text

KEY TERMS

arboreal, 87
articular surfaces, 105
australopithecine, 93
bipedal locomotion, 79
brachiating, 76
core, 96
cranium, 83
diastema, 88
endocast, 110
femur, 101
flake, 96
foramen magnum, 82
genera, 75
hammerstone, 96
hominid, 73

humerus, 87
ilium, 99
innominate bone, 99
ischium, 99
isotope, 77
knapper, 96
mandible, 88
maxilla, 88
Miocene, 75
mosaic, 111
niche, 75
object piece, 96
Oldowan, 95
paleoecological, 110
phylogeny, 77

Pliocene, 77
pongid, 91
postcranial, 86
prognathous, 87
punctuated
    equilibrium, 111
sagittal crest, 90
savanna, 77
sexual dimorphism, 112
striking platform, 96
taphonomic, 106
tibia, 101
ulna, 87

4

The Human Lineage

CHAPTER OVERVIEW

A bit before 1.8 million years ago another great change is seen in the fossil record of Africa. A new hominid makes its appearance on the evolutionary stage—*Homo erectus*. *Homo erectus* possessed a brain larger than that of *Homo habilis*, from which it evolved; the *Homo erectus* brain is, on average, two-thirds the size of a modern human's.

Homo erectus exhibits increasing intelligence as well as a greater reliance on cultural adaptations. Though born in an African nursery and possessing an anatomy best suited to life in the tropics, culture allowed *Homo erectus* to expand into other regions with very different climates soon after it first appeared in Africa. Tools found in Israel and bones found in the Republic of Georgia reflect the existence of a likely corridor of hominid expansion beyond Africa beginning soon after 1.8 million years ago. Remarkably, *Homo erectus* fossils found far to the east, on the island of Java, date to nearly the same time. *Homo erectus* appears not to have entered into Europe until after 1 million years ago.

A sophisticated stone tool technology, cooperative hunting, the controlled use of fire, clothing, and the possible construction of shelters were all a part of the *Homo erectus* adaptation. A reliance on culture is a hallmark of this human ancestor.

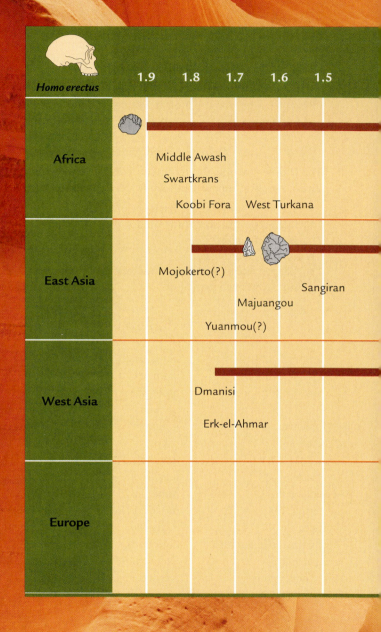

Homo erectus

	1.9	1.8	1.7	1.6	1.5
Africa		Middle Awash			
		Swartkrans			
		Koobi Fora	West Turkana		
East Asia	Mojokerto(?)			Sangiran	
			Majuangou		
		Yuanmou(?)			
West Asia		Dmanisi			
		Erk-el-Ahmar			
Europe					

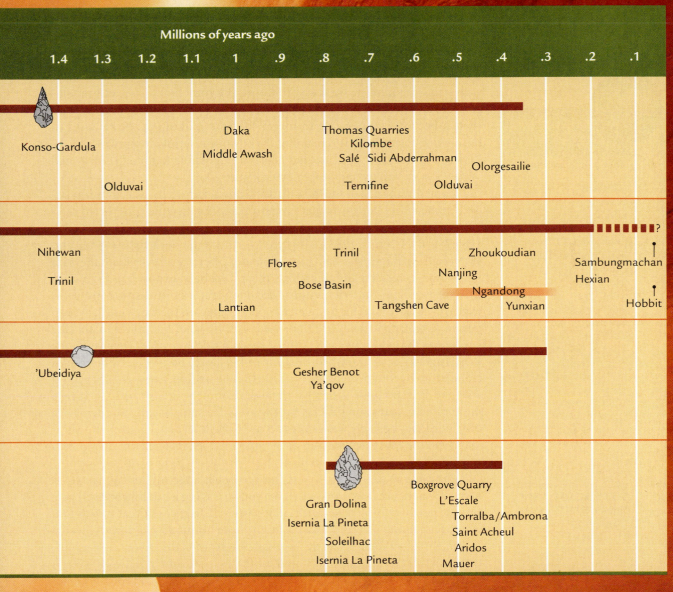

Millions of years ago

1.4	1.3	1.2	1.1	1	.9	.8	.7	.6	.5	.4	.3	.2	.1

Konso-Gardula

Daka
Middle Awash

Thomas Quarries
Kilombe
Salé Sidi Abderrahman
Olorgesailie

Olduvai

Ternifine

Olduvai

Nihewan

Trinil

Trinil

Flores

Bose Basin

Lantian

Zhoukoudian

Nanjing

Ngandong

Tangshen Cave

Yunxian

Sambungmachan
Hexian

Hobbit
?

'Ubeidiya

Gesher Benot
Ya'qov

Gran Dolina

Isernia La Pineta

Soleilhac

Isernia La Pineta

Boxgrove Quarry
L'Escale
Torralba/Ambrona
Saint Acheul
Aridos
Mauer

Go to **www.mhhe.com/feder4** for an
interactive study guide version of this timeline.

ONLINE
LEARNING
CENTER

117

PRELUDE

CHAPTER SITES

As famed paleoanthropologist Richard Leakey (Leakey and Lewin 1992) admits, it sometimes is easy to forget that the bits and fragments, shards and slivers of fossilized bone paleoanthropologists hold in their hands, place under their microscopes, and mount in museum displays were connected to actual, thinking, feeling beings. Perhaps such small fragments make it easy to forget. But sometimes paleoanthropologists get lucky and recover the nearly complete skeleton of an individual—then it becomes impossible to forget they are looking at the remains of once-living creatures. The remains of the boy from Nariokotome, west of Lake Turkana, in Kenya, is one case that makes it impossible to forget (Leakey and Walker 1985a; Walker and Leakey 1993; Figure 4.1).

Ironically, the age of the West Turkana boy is judged by paleoanthropologists in much the same way that modern parents gauge the progress of their young children's physical development, by looking at his teeth (Brown et al. 1985:789; B. H. Smith 1993). All of the West Turkana boy's first (6-year) and second (12-year) molars had erupted; that is, they are above where the gum line would have been and, therefore, must have been exposed in his mouth when he was alive. Both of his upper deciduous canines (these are baby teeth) were still in place, and his permanent upper canine on the right side had been poised to replace its baby-tooth predecessor. None of his third molars (the wisdom teeth that erupt at 18 years of age in modern people) were yet in the West Turkana boy's mouth at the time of his death. So if he were a modern child, an archaeologist would conclude that he had been about 12 years old when he died. Because of other skeletal development indicators suggesting a more rapid maturation process for the West Turkana boy, researchers have concluded that he likely was closer to 9 or 10 when he died (Walker and Shipman 1996:188). A recent analysis of the amount of enamel growth on his teeth suggests that he was closer to 8 than 12.

The cause of death of the West Turkana boy is a sad mystery. What we do know is that he was struck down in his youth, leaving a remarkably well preserved, nearly complete skeleton that shows little except great health and vigor. Forget any stereotypes you might have about short, broad-chested "cavemen." Alan Walker, one of the fossil's excavators, describes the Nariokotome boy as a "strapping youth" and estimates his height at between 5 feet 4 inches and 5 feet 8 inches (Leakey and Lewin 1992). That is considerably taller than a modern human boy of the same age in most populations. In a mixed population in the United States, for example, the mean height of 8-year-old boys is 4 feet 3 inches, and 10-year-old boys are only about 4 feet 8 inches.

The West Turkana boy died on the edge of a lagoon near a lake. Except for some evidence of infection where he had lost a deciduous tooth, there is no sign of pathology on the skeleton, no evidence of disease, and no indication of trauma. The position of his bones indicates that his body floated face down in the shallow water after he died. Fortunately, no scavengers picked at his corpse as it decayed, so most of the body remained pretty much in place, if not intact. Animals coming to the lagoon for a drink may have walked on the body, breaking one of the legs and scattering the rest of the bones as the flesh, muscle, and tissue that had once been a boy were washed away. After the soft parts had decayed, a gentle current dispersed the bones across a linear distance of about 7 m (slightly more than 21 ft). The bones were then covered in the mucky lake bottom by waterborne silt and ash from a nearby volcano, where they rested for close to 1.6 million years.

In August 1984, Kenyan paleontologist Kamoya Kimeu was scouting for fossils in Nariokotome, in an area that is now a dry lake bed. Kimeu was looking for fossils on his day off before the camp of paleontologists moved to

CHAPTER SITES

www.mhhe.com/feder4

EAST ASIA: CHINA
Yuanmou, *126*
Yunxian, 136
Zhoukoudian, 135

EUROPE
Ambrona, 143
Aridos (1 & 2), 143
Boxgrove Quarry, 137
Gran Dolina, 136
Isernia La Pineta, 137
L'Escale, *126*
Mauer, 137
Soleilhac, 137
Saint-Acheul, 139
Torralba, 143

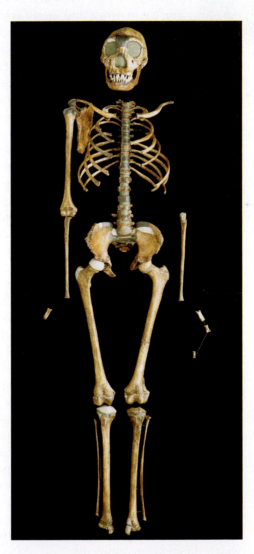

FIGURE 4.1
One of the most complete fossil hominid skeletons ever found: WKT-15000, the 9-year-old Homo erectus *boy from Nariokotome.*
(© David L. Brill)

another locality as planned because so little of importance had been found in the area. Within a short time, he spotted a skull fragment, and an excavation was initiated. Soon the nearly complete skeletal remains of a boy were uncovered, revealing, with unprecedented clarity, an enormously ancient ancestor.

It is ironic that by dying in the right place at the right time, a young boy achieved an immortality that likely none of us will attain. Even 1.6 million years after he lived, in a time and world we can barely imagine, people still ponder his life. We place him in the taxonomic category *Homo erectus,* and his people are the focus of this chapter.

CHRONICLE

As indicated by a series of new fossil specimens, soon after 1.8 million B.P. in Africa, and nearly as long ago in Asia and somewhat later in Europe, an acceleration of human evolution took place. The new fossils are different enough from *Homo habilis* to warrant a new name or names for the reasons enumerated in our discussion of species designation in Chapter 3. The new specimens have skeletal anatomies so different from that of *habilis* that they cannot reasonably be placed in the same group. But what to name the new fossils, and should they all be placed together in the same group?

Many paleoanthropologists believe that all of the hominids that follow *Homo habilis* and predate *Homo sapiens*—from after 1.8 million B.P. until about 400,000 B.P. or even later—belong to a single species: *Homo erectus* (Potts et al. 2004). When the sample of specimens recovered for this group was small and anatomical variation seemed quite limited among those fossils found from Africa all the way to east Asia, this assumption was reasonable. A recent spate of discoveries has convinced others, however, based on highly technical analyses of the morphology of the various specimens, that this period of human evolution instead presents us with a number of related but more or less geographically separate species (Schwartz 2004): *Homo ergaster* in Africa, *Homo erectus* in central and east Asia, and *Homo antecessor* in Europe. In other words, a population of fossils that had all been placed within a single species is now seen by some to exhibit enough variation to separate them into three. The jury is still out on this taxonomic realignment.

For the sake of clarity and to make this part of the human story more straightforward, we will take the simpler approach here, labeling all of the specimens to be discussed in this chapter *Homo erectus.* (Figure 4.2 presents two different phylogenies, one based on the simpler view followed here and one on the multispecies model.) Of course, the number of hominid species alive at any given time is of enormous importance. But for our purposes, it is not as important as understanding that—one species, two, three, or more—during the period from 1.8 million to after 400,000 B.P., populations of intelligent hominids, relying on cultural adaptations, spread throughout much of the Old World, using their intelligence to successfully adjust to a series of widely different environments.

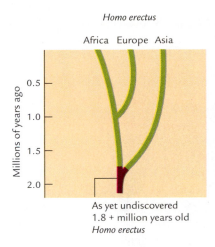

As yet undiscovered
1.8 + million years old
Homo erectus

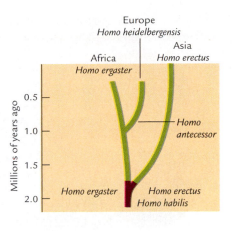

FIGURE 4.2
*Two competing models for
the number of species, evolution, and spread of hominids after 2 million years
ago (mya). In the more
traditional model (left),*
Homo habilis *gave rise to*
Homo erectus *in Africa
sometime after 2 mya. From
there,* Homo erectus *populations quickly spread into
Asia and, later, western
Europe. In the competing
model (right),* Homo
habilis *gave rise to* Homo
ergaster *in Africa sometime
after 2 mya.* Homo habilis
*or a descendant also spread
into Asia soon after 2 mya,
where it evolved into* Homo
erectus. Homo ergaster *may
have spread into Europe,
where it gave rise to yet
another hominid species,*
Homo antecessor, *which
later evolved into* Homo
heidelbergensis.

HOMO ERECTUS

Soon after 1.8 million B.P., a new form of hominid appeared in the fossil record of eastern Africa. The West Turkana boy is an example of one of these new hominids. Potassium/argon dating has placed the oldest specimen—a skull labeled ER 3733 (Figure 4.3) from a rich fossil locality called Koobi Fora, east of Lake Turkana (Leakey and Walker 1985b)—at about 1.78 million years ago (Feibel, Brown, and McDougal 1989). The species is given the name *Homo erectus*. Physically and culturally, *Homo erectus* is recognizably human, yet it is intriguingly different from us.

The cranium of this new member of the human lineage was quite different from that of its evolutionary antecedent, *Homo habilis* (Figure 4.4). To begin with, its skull, and by implication its brain, was significantly larger. Most specimens have cranial volumes in excess of 800 cc, and the species as a whole has a mean cranial capacity of about 960 cc (Table 4.1). This is an increase of more than 37% over *Homo habilis,* whose cranial capacity was only about 700 cc. The Nariokotome boy's cranial capacity was 880 cc; it is estimated that his brain size, had he lived to adulthood, would have been a little over 900 cc (Begun and Walker 1993:346). The largest members of the species have skulls with volumes of over 1,200 cc. This measurement places the brain size of the species far above that of *Homo habilis* and within the lower range of the size of the modern human brain.

The skull of *erectus* was not just larger than that of *habilis,* but it was also differently configured and differently proportioned in ways that signify a shift toward a more modern human appearance. For example, the forehead of *erectus* is somewhat flatter and less sloping than that of *habilis,* a bit more similar to the modern, virtually vertical human forehead. The back, or **occipital,** portion of the *erectus* skull is rounder than that of *habilis,* with a much larger

FIGURE 4.3
This fossil cranium designated ER 3733, at nearly 1.8 million years of age, is the oldest known specimen of the fossil species Homo erectus. (© National Museums of Kenya)

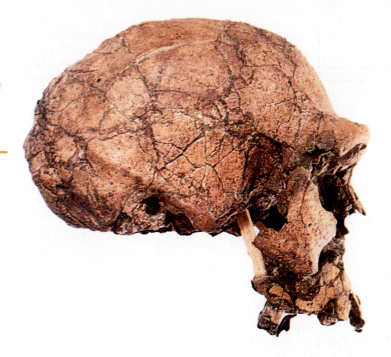

FIGURE 4.4
In this comparison of the skulls of Homo habilis *and* Homo erectus, *the skull of* erectus *is seen to be larger and more modern (less apelike) than that of* habilis.

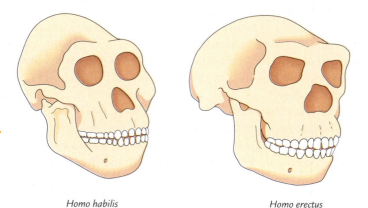

Homo habilis   *Homo erectus*

area for muscle attachment. Larger and stronger muscles were needed to support its much larger, heavier skull.

Analysis of cranial endocasts (see Chapter 3) of a number of *Homo erectus* specimens (Holloway 1980, 1981) shows intriguing similarities to the modern human brain. Most significantly, anthropologist Ralph Holloway discovered hemispheric asymmetry in the *erectus* brain, similar to that seen in modern human beings. The different halves, or hemispheres, of the human brain regulate different tasks; in particular, human speech is ordinarily controlled by the left hemisphere. As a result, the two halves of a human brain are

TABLE 4.1

Major Homo erectus Fossils Discussed in Chapter 4

COUNTRY	LOCALITY	FOSSILS	CRANIA	AGE	BRAIN SIZE (CC, SUB-ADULTS IN ITALICS)
Kenya	East Turkana	Cranial and postcranial fragments including mandibles and pelvis and long bone fragments	KNM-ER 3733	1.78 million yrs	850
			KNM-ER 3883	1.57 million yrs	800
	West Turkana	Nearly complete juvenile individual	KNM-WT 15000	1.6 million yrs	*880*
	Olorgesailie	Cranial fragments	KNM-OL 45500	0.97–0.90 million yrs	<800
Tanzania	Olduvai	Cranial and postcranial fragments including mandibles and pelvis and long bone fragments	OH 9	1.25 million yrs	1,060
			OH 12	0.6–0.8 million yrs	800
Ethiopia	Daka	Cranium		1 million yrs	995
Algeria	Ternifine	Three mandibles and a skull fragment		0.5–0.7 million yrs	
Morocco	Thomas Quarries	Mandible and skull fragments			
	Sidi Abderrahman	Two mandible fragments			
	Salé	Skull fragments	Salé	0.4 million	880
Java	Trinil	Skull cap, femur	"Java Man"	<1 million yrs	940
	Sangiran	Cranial and postcranial fragments from ~40 individuals	S-2	0.7–1.6 million yrs	800
			S-4	0.7–1.6 million yrs	900
			S-10	0.7–1.6 million yrs	850
			S-12	0.7–1.6 million yrs	1,050
			S-17	0.7–1.6 million yrs	1,000
			1993 Cranium	1.1–1.4 million yrs	856
	Ngandong	Cranial and postcranial fragments from >1 dozen individuals	N-1	<1 million yrs	1,170
			N-6	<1 million yrs	1,250
			N-11	<1 million yrs	1,230
			N-12	<1 million yrs	1,090
	Sambungmachan	Three partial crania	Sm3	<.5 million yrs	917
	Mojokerto	Child's cranium		1.8 million yrs?	*663*
Flores	Flores	Cranium, mandible, femur, tibia, pelvis, vertebrae, feet, hands	LB1 or "Hobbit"	18,000 yrs	417

(continued)

TABLE 4.1 *continued*

COUNTRY	LOCALITY	FOSSILS	CRANIA	AGE	BRAIN SIZE (CC, SUB-ADULTS IN ITALICS)
China	Zhoukoudian	Cranial and postcranial remains of >40 individuals	II	<0.46 million yrs	1,030
			III	<0.46 million yrs	915
			VI	<0.46 million yrs	850
			X	<0.46 million yrs	1,225
			XI	<0.46 million yrs	1,015
			XII	<0.46 million yrs	1,030
			Locality 13	0.7 million yrs	
	Hexian (Lontandong)	Partial skull	"Hexian Man"	0.27 million yrs?	1,000
	Lantian (Gongwangling)	Cranial fragments and mandible	"Lantian Man"	1.15 million yrs	800
	Yunxian	Two crania		>0.35 million yrs	
	Tangshan Cave	Parts of two crania	"Nanjing Man"	>0.60 million yrs	
Georgia	Dmanisi	Three crania	Young male	1.75 million yrs	775
			Female teen	1.75 million yrs	*650*
			Young female	1.75 million yrs	*600*
		Mandible fragment and 16 teeth			
Spain	Gran Dolina	Remains of six individuals	Partial skull of child	.8 million yrs	
England	Boxgrove Quarry	Tibia		0.48–0.51 million yrs	
				Mean (excluding sub-adults and "Hobbit")	960
				Mean (excluding sub-adults but including "Hobbit")	941
				Standard Deviation (excluding sub-adults and "Hobbit")	142
				Standard Deviation (excluding sub-adults but including "Hobbit")	268

Data from Asfaw et al. (2002); Gabunia et al. (2000); Holloway (1980, 1981); Rightmire (1990); Vekua et al. (2002).

of slightly different shape, proportion, and size. Whether the asymmetry in the endocasts of the *erectus* brain means they were capable of humanlike speech cannot be determined. But the configuration of the *erectus* brain was definitely more like that of modern human beings and different from that of the chimp, gorilla, orangutan, australopithecine, and *habilis* specimens to which Holloway compared them.

Beneath the intriguingly humanlike brain, the *erectus* face itself is somewhat flatter, projecting less than the *habilis* face, though it still is far more **prognathous** than that of a modern human. Above the eye orbits, *Homo erectus* crania display a ridge of bone called a **supraorbital torus.** This "brow ridge" is present in the skulls of all ape species and is generally absent in the modern human form, though some people, especially males, exhibit relatively smaller but discernible ridges above their eyes.

From the front, the *erectus* skull presents a flattened trapezoidal shape as opposed to the corresponding very round appearance of a modern human skull. The sides of the *erectus* skull begin nearly parallel at the base and then angle inward toward the top. This provides a keel, but not a bony crest, at the apex of the skull. Also, preserved nasal bones indicate that *erectus* was the first of our ancestors to possess the modern human form of a projecting nose rather than the inset nostrils that characterize the living apes and earlier hominids (Franciscus and Trinkaus 1988).

Below the skull, the bones of *Homo erectus* bear witness to a creature that indisputably walked upright, in a manner similar, if not identical, to that of modern human beings. To be sure, the West Turkana boy and other, more fragmentary postcranial remains exhibit a skeletal architecture indicative of great muscularity and strength, probably outside the range of modern human beings. Nonetheless, as more than one paleoanthropologist has stated, you would not be alarmed if a *Homo erectus,* with a cap pulled down low over his or her forehead and face and appropriately dressed, were to sit down next to you in class.

The Evolutionary Position of Homo erectus

The oldest *erectus* fossils are found in Africa, often in the same areas where *habilis* remains have been recovered (Figure 4.5). Current consensus, therefore, is that *Homo erectus* is the direct evolutionary descendant of the African hominid species *Homo habilis.* Fossils such as the Nariokotome boy (officially designated KNM-WT 15000), ER 3733, ER 3833, and OH 9 share the standard suite of *erectus* cranial characteristics and date to between 1.78 million years ago and 1.25 million years ago (Rightmire 1979a, 1990). Dated to about 1 million years ago, the Daka remains from the Middle Awash in Ethiopia include some postcranial remains and most of a cranium that closely resembles older African forms of *Homo erectus* (Asfaw et al. 2002). It is a little smaller than OH9 and has an estimated cranial capacity of 995 cc.

Homo erectus cranial fragments, designated KNM-OL 45500, have recently been found at the Olorgesailie site in Kenya (Potts et al. 2004). The

FIGURE 4.5
Fossil localities of Homo erectus.

stratigraphic layer in which the fragments were recovered has been dated by the Argon/Argon method to some time between 970,000 and 900,000 years ago. An abundance of stone tools called Acheulean were found in the same stratum. As we will discuss later in this chapter, Acheulean tools are typically found with *Homo erectus* remains in Africa, Europe, and west Asia.

KNM-OL 45500's head was small by *Homo erectus* standards—its cranial capacity, while difficult to determine because of the highly fragmentary and incomplete nature of the remains, has been estimated to be less than 800 cc. Nevertheless, based upon its morphology—its double-arched supraorbital torus, the degree of slope of the front of the cranium—researchers have designated its species as *Homo erectus*.

Later African *erectus* remains, dating from 500,000 to 800,000 years ago, include the OH 12 **calvarium** from Olduvai Gorge in Tanzania, a skull fragment and three mandibles from Ternifine (now called Tighenif) in Algeria, and skull and mandible fragments at Thomas Quarries, a braincase from Salé, and two mandibles from Sidi Abderrahman, all in Morocco. These later fossils are quite similar, where comparisons can be made, to the older African material.

HOMINIDS CONQUER THE WORLD

Homo erectus, like its hominid predecessors, evolved in Africa. Unlike its fore-bears, however, *Homo erectus,* or perhaps an immediate evolutionary descen-dant, was not restricted to that continent. Fossils similar to the *erectus* specimens found in Africa have been found in Asia and date to soon after their initial appearance 1.8 million years ago. Though we cannot yet trace the expansion of *Homo erectus* with a trail of sites leading beyond the borders of Africa to the rest of the Old World, we are able to sketch out in broad terms the path-way hominids took in their extension into and across Europe and Asia.

If you look at a map or globe, it is easy to see that Africa is physically con-nected to the rest of its hemisphere in only one place: at its northeastern apex where it borders onto southwest Asia, the place we today call the Middle East. Of course, we cannot entirely rule out the possibility that *Homo erectus* may have managed to enter Europe by crossing the Mediterranean, especially at its narrowest point at the Strait of Gibraltar, but at this point there is no evidence that they did so. In fact, some of the oldest hominid sites outside of Africa have been found exactly where they might have been expected, where Africa is connected by land to southwest Asia and nearby in the southern section of Eurasia—a broad zone where Europe and Asia come together (Figure 4.6).

For example, at Erk-el-Ahmar in Israel an assemblage of choppers and flake tools have been excavated in a stratigraphic level bracketed between lev-els dated to 1.7 and 2.0 million years ago based on **paleomagnetism** (Holden 2002b). Just a few kilometers north is another, somewhat younger, hominid site dating to 1.4 million years ago. Called 'Ubeidiya, it has produced a hand-ful of choppers, picks, and flakes along with some very fragmentary remains of hominids (Belfer-Cohen and Goren-Inbar 1994).

Although it is farther to the north, beyond the Middle East, in Eurasia, an extremely important site that relates precisely to the issue of the spread of hominids beyond Africa is located at Dmanisi near the shore of the Black Sea in the Republic of Georgia in what used to be the Soviet Union. Two mandibles, three relatively complete crania, a **tibia**, a **talus** (ankle bone), and a **metatarsel** (foot bone) have now been unearthed there from a deposit that has been dated to about 1.75 million years ago (Gabunia et al. 2000; Holden 2003a; Vekua et al. 2002). The first two Dmanisi crania were recovered in 1999 and are those of a young adult male and an adolescent female (Figure 4.6). The adult male's cranial capacity was approximately 775 cc, while that of the young female was smaller, about 650 cc. The third cranium was found in 2002 and is even smaller, with a cranial capacity of about 600 cc (Vekua et al. 2002). All three crania are small by African *Homo erectus* standards—all of them fall closer to the mean cranial capacity of *Homo habilis* than to that of *Homo erectus*.

FIGURE 4.6

Found near the intersection of three continents—Africa, Asia, and Europe—the Dmanisi specimens likely represent the remains of some of the earliest Homo erectus *migrants out of Africa.* (Photo by Gouram Tsibakhashvili. Courtesy Professor Dr. David Lordkipanidze, Deputy Director, Georgian State Museum.)

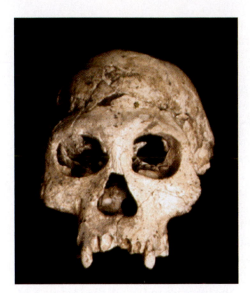

Nevertheless, this may be explained by the fact that at Dmanisi we have the remains only of young individuals, whose heads had not reached their fully adult size. Also, there is at least one small female—and possibly two—in the sample. Except for their size, the Dmanisi crania otherwise look remarkably like African crania dating to the same time period. When Pat Shipman, who had co-directed the excavation of the Nariokotome boy, first saw the Dmanisi mandible, her reaction was one of amazement; the jaws were not just similar, but could have come from twins (Shipman 2000:491).

The tool kit of the Dmanisi hominids is another piece of evidence that links them to an African hominid heritage. Only simple chopping and flake tools have been found at the site. These tools clearly belong to the Oldowan tradition seen at *Homo habilis* and early *Homo erectus* sites in Africa. In other words, there is no evidence of a great leap forward in stone-tool technology that might explain the achievement of expansion beyond Africa. In fact, the tools found in Africa and in Eurasia at this early date are identical. As researcher Susan Antón states it: "If we are right about when hominids left Africa, it is biology, not new tools, that prompted their dispersal. As soon as you get larger body sizes and brains, you see shifts in what they eat and how far they range that ultimately led them out of Africa" (as quoted in Balter and Gibbons 2000:950).

East Asia

It is a long way from Africa to the shore of the Black Sea, where the Dmanisi site is located, but it is not nearly the end of our journey or that of the hominid species *Homo erectus*. The next set of ancient sites we will visit are literally half a world away, at the other end of our planet's largest continent.

FIGURE 4.7
The first Homo erectus *skull fragment found was this skullcap recovered in Java in the late nineteenth century by Dutch scientist Eugene Dubois.* (© National Museum of Natural History)

East Asia is the farthest point in the Old World from the African source for *Homo erectus* populations; it is at the end of the migration pipeline. Ironically, however, *Homo erectus* specimens were found there before they were found in Africa. Dating indicates that some of the east Asian *Homo erectus* specimens rival in age even the oldest *Homo erectus* fossils in Africa.

The fact that *Homo erectus* fossils were found first in east Asia—Java, to be more specific—is no mystery. It is simply a factor of where a scientist first looked. In a remarkable instance of intuition, Dutch physician Eugene Dubois (1894) traveled to the island of Java in the western Pacific in the late nineteenth century expressly to seek out evidence of human origins in the Asian tropics. In 1891, along the Solo River in the vicinity of the town of Trinil, he came upon a calvarium that looked not quite human but not quite apelike (Figure 4.7). It possessed large brow ridges like those of apes. But the cranial capacity, as best as could be judged at the time, was far larger than an ape's while still smaller than a modern human's. Dubois labeled the find *Pithecanthropus erectus,* meaning "upright ape-man." Still popularly referred to as "Java Man," we now include Dubois's discovery in the *Homo erectus* species. Its estimated cranial capacity of 940 cc and its age (still uncertain but probably about 1 million years old) place it firmly in the *erectus* species. Though Java today is an island, during periods of lowered sea level it was part of the mainland of Southeast Asia, enabling *Homo erectus* to arrive there on foot.

Also along the Solo River, northeast of Trinil, is the site of Ngandong. About a dozen crania were found here in the 1930s (Bartstra, Soegondho, and Wijk 1988; Santa Luca 1980). Though their skulls are quite large when compared to those of the other *Homo erectus* specimens, paleoanthropologist Philip Rightmire (1990) in his summary monograph on the species provides a detailed analysis that indicates the Ngandong fossils belong in the same taxonomic group.

Just 65 km (40 mi) east of Trinil, another important fossil locality, called Sangiran, was found in 1937. The cranial remains of about 40 individuals have been recovered (Figure 4.8). Some of the crania are more complete than the Trinil calvarium and share its form and size (Holloway 1981).

FIGURE 4.8
Crania of Homo erectus
from Sangiran, Java (top),
and Zhoukoudian in China
(bottom). (*Top:* Courtesy of
Ralph L. Holloway; *bottom:* The
Human Origins Program,
Smithsonian Institution)

Most of the Javanese hominid remains were found more than 50 years ago—primarily by local farmers and other workers, not in controlled archaeological excavations. As a result, dating the specimens is problematic, for it is difficult to be certain in which geological deposit, and precisely where in the deposit, the material originated.

Geologists have gone back into the deposits in which the Java hominids were found and have applied newly developed procedures in an attempt to nail down an accurate chronology for the expansion of *Homo erectus* into east Asia. For example, recent dating by the argon/argon technique of the Bapang geological formation in which the Sangiran fossils were recovered indicates that all of the Sangiran *Homo erectus* remains date to more than 1.0 million years ago. Some of the fossils are older and can be shown to date to 1.5 million years ago, and at least one cranial fragment was found below the layer that produced the date of 1.5 million years ago and is therefore older still (Larick et al. 2001).

Redating of three *Homo erectus* crania from Java, one found in 1936 (the Mojokerto child) and two at Sangiran in 1974, has excited everyone in the field. The dates (determined by the $^{40}Ar/^{39}Ar$ technique) are 1.8 million years for the Mojokerto child's skull and 1.6 million years for the Sangiran crania (Swisher et al. 1994).

Not only redating deposits but also discovering additional hominids has helped solidify the dating of *Homo erectus* in Java to more than 1.5 million years ago. Paleoanthropologist Donald Tyler has identified another skull unearthed by farmers at Sangiran (Rose 1993). It is clearly a *Homo erectus,* with a cranial capacity of 856 cc. Tyler has been able to associate the skull with a specific geological deposit more precisely than was possible with the earlier Sangiran discoveries. He has dated the age of the deposit to between 1.1 million and 1.4 million years ago.

The data just presented include the oldest dates derived for *Homo erectus* in east Asia. At the other end of the chronological spectrum are some remarkably recent dates for hominid specimens that are anatomically quite similar to those ancient examples of *Homo erectus* just discussed. Again on Java, *Homo erectus* fossils recovered at the Ngandong and Sambungmachan sites have recently been redated to sometime between just 27,000 and 53,000 years ago (Swisher et al., 1996).

Who Was the Hobbit?

I saw the MSNBC report of the discovery of what researchers (Brown et al. 2004; Morwood et al. 2004) were calling *Homo floresiensis* soon after watching the DVD of the third movie in the *Lord of the Rings trilogy.* I suppose that is why it struck me as mildly hilarious that some were referring to the diminutive female hominid recovered on the Indonesian island of Flores as a "hobbit." With an adult height of not even 1 m (less than 3 ft) and a probable weight of about 20 kg (44 lbs)—essentially the size of a four-year-old modern human child—indeed it was hobbit-sized. Brain size initially was estimated to be about 380 cc (it is now computed to have been about 417 cc); that's a bit less than the mean size of a chimp and equivalent to the brain size of a newborn modern human baby (Figure 4.9). Small though their brains may have been, these hobbit-sized hominids appear to have been quite intelligent; a variety of well-made stone flake tools were found alongside the fossil.

It isn't all that often that a paleoanthropological discovery is covered by the networks, every major cable news channel, and newspapers as well. The hobbit hook helped; and the Flores fossil—consisting of a cranium, mandible, the right half of the pelvis, the right femur and tibia, additional fragmented

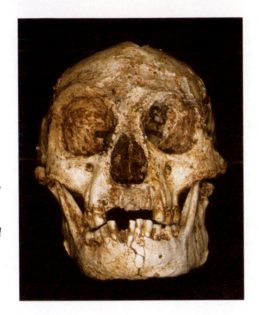

The tiny skull of a diminutive hominid, found on the island of Flores in the western Pacific, caught the attention of the public when it was discovered in 2004, not only because it immediately was likened to a Hobbit. Called by its discoverers Homo floresiensis, *the very-small-brained hominid produced sophisticated stone tools and lived only 18,000 years ago, long after similar creatures had become extinct.* (© The Human Origins Program, Smithsonian Institution)

bones of the left leg, both hands and feet, and the vertebral column—was one of those rare instances that generated a tremendous amount of interest among scientists and nonscientists alike for a number of reasons beyond any Lord of the Rings allusions (Figure 4.10).

Though the discoverers applied a new species name to the fossil, in many ways it resembles a highly miniaturized *Homo erectus.* But how and why would an adult *Homo erectus* be so tiny? Some suggested that *Homo floresiensis* was, in fact, merely an exceptional *Homo erectus* individual, one afflicted by some rare genetic growth disorder. Others still proposed that what the discoverers were calling *Homo floresiensis* was an anatomically modern human being, but one reflecting a pathology called **microcephaly,** a condition marked by a small head enclosing a small brain, usually resulting in severe mental retardation. Others suggested that the small size might be an example of the well-known biological phenomenon of island dwarfing. As biologist Jared Diamond (2004) points out, there are many examples of nature selecting for smaller versions of animals who have colonized remote islands. So conceivably, *Homo erectus* ancestors arrived on Flores by way of a very difficult and unlikely journey and managed to survive on the island for a long period. In fact, stone tools have been found on Flores dating to a much earlier period, indicating the arrival there of hominids at least 900,000 years ago (Morwood et al. 1998). In this scenario, small individuals among those early arrivals were at an adaptive advantage, perhaps because they could survive on less food and water than their larger companions. Over time, natural selection for smaller individuals resulted in an entire population of very small hominids. Support for this hypothesis has been revealed in new excavations at the site. Along with the right arm bones from the original "Hobbit," researchers recovered

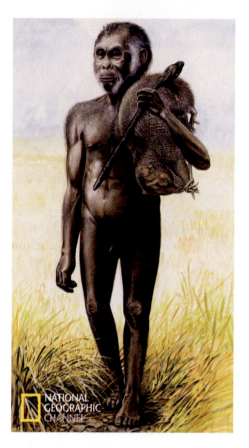

FIGURE 4.10
An artist's conception of what a living example of Homo florensiesis *might have looked like; or, if you prefer, what a real Hobbit looks like.* (© AP/Wide World Photo)

another mandible, a vertebra, a shoulder blade, as well as a mix of arm, leg, finger, and toe bones from as many as nine additional individuals, all about the same size as the first discovery (Morwood et. al 2005).

To assess the place of the Hobbit, researchers have analyzed the interior of the recovered cranium using **three-dimensional computed tomography,** a process by which theye were able to produce what amounts to a "virtual brain," or, at least, a virtual image of the surface of the Hobbit's brain (Falk et al. 2005). They compared their results to those obtained by applying the same technology to a sample of other crania, including those belonging to various hominid and pongid species, including *Australopithecus, Homo erectus, Homo sapiens* (including a modern human pygmy and a modern microcephalic), gorilla, and chimpanzee.

The results of this research indicate that the Flores cranium is not a perfect match for any of the specimens to which it was compared. However, it was absolutely clear that the Hobbit was neither an ape nor a modern human with microcephaly. Equally clearly, the Hobbit was not a modern human pygmy. In fact, though the ratio of its brain size to its body size is similar to what is seen for *Australopithecus,* the virtual brain of *Homo floresiensis* actually was a pretty good match for that of *Homo erectus*, leading some researchers to conclude that, though not of the same species, *Homo floresiensis* shares a common ancestor with *Homo erectus*. The tiny size of the brain and the association with complex stone tools astonishes everybody and is leading to a reassessment of the significance of overall brain size in the evolution of intelligence in the hominid family.

Just as astonishing as the creature's small size and chimp-sized brain was the date researchers determined for the stratigraphic layer in which she was found. Luminescence dating bracketed the sediments above and below the skeleton to a period between 35,000 and 14,000 years ago, and charcoal from the layer of the bones produced a date of 18,000 years ago, suggesting that the Flores fossil is even younger than the remarkably young specimens from Ngandong and Sambungmachan. All three sites have produced amazingly recent dates for an extinct version of a human ancestor, but there are precedents for the continued existence on an isolated island of a remnant population of a species extinct everywhere else. This supports the possibility already mentioned that even after the evolution of anatomically modern human beings, other, older versions of human beings, in this case, *Homo erectus* or, at least, something very similar to *Homo erectus,* continued to survive in other places until fairly recently.

Homo erectus: *Ocean Explorer?*

The appearance of hominids on the island of Flores brings up one additional point. As distant as all other *Homo erectus* sites are from their ultimate source in Africa, all of these places are within "walking distance" of their point of origin—at least over many generations of wandering and expansion. Remember, even the island of Java was, when *Homo erectus* arrived, connected to the Southeast Asian mainland as the result of lowered sea level. However, for *Homo erectus* or members of any other ancient hominid group to get to Flores, they had to travel at least in part by sea. Flores is separated from the nearest land by a deep, natural underwater trench. Even during periods of lowered sea level, Flores would still have been separated from lands to the west by approximately 19 km (12 mi) of open sea. It was previously assumed that only anatomically modern human beings were capable of crossing open ocean. The Flores evidence shows that as much as 900,000 years ago *Homo erectus* too possessed at least some nautical skills.

Robert G. Bednarik is so interested in the seafaring capability of *Homo erectus* that he has been willing to risk his reputation and even his life on its study. He has twice constructed bamboo rafts, which he has then taken to sea with hardy crews, attempting to show the seaworthiness of watercraft so elementary that perhaps *Homo erectus* would have been capable of making and sailing them (Bower 2003a). Through trial and error—his first attempt at crossing the 48-km (30-mi) sea gap between the Indonesian islands of Bali and Lombok (they are in the same chain of islands as Flores) was abandoned after six fruitless hours of rowing—in 2000 Bednarik and his crew barely, but safely, crossed between those two islands in about 12 hours. Like all replicative archaeological experiments, this proves only that such a trip is possible, not that *Homo erectus* had actually been capable of building and then sailing a similar craft. Nevertheless, we do know that *Homo erectus* made it to Flores, and Bednarik has provided and successfully tested one possible way in which this may have happened.

China

The oldest evidence for the presence of hominids in China has been found in the form of chert, sandstone, quartz, and andesite cores and flakes at the Majuangou site in the Nihewan River basin (Zhu et al. 2004). This site presents researchers with another example of how quickly *Homo erectus* must have spread across the face of Asia once expanding beyond its place of origin in Africa. The Nihewan is located in north-central China, and the lowest stratigraphic layer at the site that has produced stone artifacts has been dated to 1.66 million years ago. Remember that the oldest *Homo erectus* find outside of Africa dates to 1.78 million years ago at Dmanisi, located at the other side of the Asian continent from Majuangou. This implies that it took *Homo erectus* just a little more than 200,000 years to spread across several thousand miles of territory. It is also important to point out that Majuangou is situated at 40° N latitude. Hominids living there would have been faced with a climate far different from that of Africa, where they evolved. Their ability to adapt to the very different environmental conditions of northern China is a testament to their reliance upon and the effectiveness of their cultural adaptation.

The oldest hominid fossils in China with confirmed dates are all somewhat younger than this. The Lantian skull from Gongwangling Hill of Shensi Province in east-central China is now believed to date to about 1.15 million years ago (Chen and Zhang 1991; Zhu et al. 2001). The Lantian cranium had a capacity of about 800 cc (Woo 1966). Its large brow ridges and broad face are very close in appearance to those of the Zhoukoudian fossils.

Other hominid fossils found in China have been dated to the period before 500,000 years ago. These include the fossils of "Nanjing Man," found in Tangshen Cave near the city of Nanjing. Nanjing Man may be representative of a *Homo erectus* population living in central eastern China more than 600,000 years ago (Hanson 2001).

One of the most important *Homo erectus* sites ever discovered in China—and certainly the most widely known hominid locality—is in the village of Zhoukoudian, about 50 km (35 mi) southwest of Beijing. The cave at the site and the surrounding area produced the remains of about 45 *Homo erectus* individuals in a region possessing a continental climate (typified by hot summers and cold winters with ample precipitation spread more or less evenly throughout the year), then and now, not unlike that in the northern United States—obviously a far cry from the climate of tropical Africa, where the species originated. Occupation of the main site (Locality 1) by "Peking Man" has been dated through thermoluminescence, electron spin resonance, uranium series, and fission track dating to between about 600,000 and 230,000 years ago, though a maximum date of 462,000 years ago is considered more accurate for the earliest occupation of the site (Pope 1992). Another site, located about 1 km south of the original Peking Man cave site, Locality 13, has been dated to 700,000 years ago (Jia and Huang 1990).

More details concerning the site, its discovery, and its significance—and the tragic mystery of the disappearance of the fossils more than 60 years ago—are provided in this chapter's "Case Study Close-Up" (see Figure 4.8).

The remains of at least three individuals, including the nearly complete calvarium of a young male, were found near the village of Longtandong in Hexian County, Anhui Province, in eastern China. The calvarium has an estimated cranial capacity of about 1,000 cc (Wu and Xingren 1982). The Hexian material seems to include the youngest *Homo erectus* specimens yet discovered in China; thermoluminescence and uranium series dating place the specimen at somewhere between 150,000 and 270,000 years old (Pope 1992). This late date, if it holds up, indicates that late populations of *Homo erectus* were contemporary with early groups of *Homo sapiens* in China as well as in Java (see Chapter 5).

Also found in China are the crania of two individuals excavated in Yunxian in Hubei Province in the east-central part of the country (Li and Etler 1992). These crania are quite large and complete, though very distorted. The researchers estimate a minimum age of 350,000 years for the two crania, which present an interesting mix of features similar to those of both the Zhoukoudian material and later, more modern-looking human ancestors. Much work needs to be done restoring these very important fossils before their significance can be fully assessed.

Europe

The oldest unequivocal hominid remains found in western Europe were recovered at the site called Gran Dolina in the Atapuerca Mountains in Spain (Carbonell et al. 1995). The Gran Dolina finds show that humans were present in western Europe by at least about 800,000 years ago and perhaps as much as 1 million years ago (Parés and Pérez-González 1995).

The Gran Dolina hominid fossils include the remains of at least six individuals, including two adults, one teenager, and one 10–12-year-old child. The preserved lower portion of the child's body is entirely modern in its morphology and therefore quite different from that seen in *Homo erectus* fossils dating to the same period. As a result, the Gran Dolina researchers have assigned these fossils to a new species, *Homo antecessor* (Bermúdez de Castro et al. 1997). As a result of the mosaic of primitive and modern traits of the Gran Dolina fossils, the researchers suggest that *antecessor* represents a descendant of *Homo erectus* (see Figure 4.2). Whether *antecessor* possesses features sufficiently different from those of *erectus* to justify the naming of a new hominid species becomes an argument between the lumpers and the splitters again, and the details need not concern us here. Following the practice established at the beginning of this chapter, we will label these specimens as *Homo erectus*. Whatever we call them, it is reasonable to say that African hominids first entered Europe by at least 800,000 years ago. Why they arrived to colonize Europe so long after they had spread into Asia as far as the island of Java (1.75 million years ago) and northern China (1.66 million years ago) will be addressed in "Issues and Debates."

Other hominid fossils in Europe are more recent. At Boxgrove Quarry, in England, a hominid tibia has been dated to about 515,000 years ago (Bahn 1994). Of similar age is the so-called Mauer mandible, found in Heidelberg, Germany, in 1907. It has been less firmly dated to about 500,000 years ago.

There also are at least a few middle Pleistocene sites in Europe where artifacts—but no hominid bones—have been found. One of the oldest of these sites is Isernia La Pineta, in central Italy. Here a stone-tool industry of limestone choppers and unmodified flint flakes was found in association with the remains of bison, deer, elephant, rhinoceros, and hippopotamus (Coltorti et al. 1982). The site was found under a volcanic deposit K/Ar-dated to 730,000 years ago. At Soleilhac, in France, artifacts and faunal remains have been dated to 800,000 years ago (Weaver 1985).

THE AGE OF ICE

In 1991 one of the largest volcanic eruptions of the twentieth century occurred on Mt. Pinatubo in the Philippines. The eruption had an impact on worldwide climate as tons of fine ash wafted into the upper atmosphere and circled the globe. The ash cloud blocked out sufficient sunlight to drop the earth's temperature by a few degrees, enough to be the probable cause of the long, cold winter experienced in the northern hemisphere after the eruption.

As significant as the eruption of Mt. Pinatubo was and as serious as its climatic impact may have been, it pales in comparison to the change in worldwide climate, the first impacts of which were felt about 3.2 million years ago (see Chapter 3) and accelerated after 2.5 million and then again at about 1.6 million or 1.7 million years ago (Shackleton et al. 1984). For reasons that are still uncertain, beginning at this time the earth became a significantly colder place, particularly after about 900,000 years ago, with northern latitudes and higher elevations becoming covered by huge, expanding ice fields called **glaciers** (Shackleton and Opdyke 1973, 1976; Figure 4.11). Some of the proposed explanations blame the descent into colder temperatures on a decrease in solar output, interplanetary dust, or a change in the earth's orbit.

This colder period of time is called the **Pleistocene epoch** (see Figure 3.3 for a time chart placing the Pleistocene chronologically in the history of the earth). By convention, its inception is marked at 1.7–1.6 million years ago. Researchers mark the end of the Pleistocene at 10,000 years ago, when

FIGURE 4.11

Worldwide glacial coverage during the peak periods of glaciation in the Pleistocene epoch.

worldwide temperature rose and glaciers shrunk. The modern period is called the **Holocene epoch.** Many climate experts believe that the Holocene is simply a relatively warm period that is destined to end in only a few thousand years, with glacial conditions nearly certain to return.

Though initially conceptualized and still commonly thought of as an "Ice Age" of unremitting cold, the Pleistocene actually was an epoch of fluctuating climate, with periods called **glacials** much colder than the present. These glacials were characterized by widespread ice and snow cover—imagine most of the central and northern United States and Canada and much of northern Europe looking and feeling like Greenland. But within the glacials themselves were colder and warmer periods, with attendant glacial advances (**stadials**) and retreats (**interstadials**). Between the glacials were relatively long **interglacial** periods, during which temperature often approached, sometimes equaled, and rarely may even have exceeded the modern level.

Analysis of a lengthy ice core taken from the permanent ice fields of Antarctica shows in great detail the cycle of glacials and interglacials over the past 740,000 years (EPICA 2004). One of the interglacials reflected in the ice core appears to have lasted for 28,000 years. Considering that the Holocene has lasted for about 10,000 years, there may be another 18,000 years left in the current interglacial, so there's lots of time for those of us who live in northern latitudes to stock up on warm clothes.

The pattern of temperature fluctuation and glacial advance and retreat can be studied in a number of ways. Glaciers leave significant and recognizable features as they cover the land. If you live in the northern third of the United States or virtually anywhere in Canada, then you can still see the effects of the huge, moving continental sheets and rivers of ice, some a few kilometers thick, as they rode over everything in their path. Glacial geologists can read a landscape for its glacial deposits, which can then be dated to develop a chronology of glaciation, as each subsequent expansion of ice overrode the previous one. (See Richard Foster Flint's *Glacial and Quaternary Geology,* 1971, for the classic work on the New World Pleistocene.)

The Oxygen Isotope Curve

The curve representing the relative proportion of ^{16}O:^{18}O has been determined by Shackleton and Opdyke (1973, 1976; and see Chapter 2). Their results are presented in Figure 4.12. Covering the last 780,000 years, a bit less than the last half of the Pleistocene, the Shackleton and Opdyke chronology exhibits 10 periods of drops in ^{16}O and therefore significantly colder temperatures and greater ice cover on the earth's surface. Further research has indicated at least 10 additional such periods in the first half of the Pleistocene.

All of this climatic instability must have affected our hominid ancestors. Though *Homo erectus* did not penetrate into areas where there were large continental ice sheets after 1.7 million years ago, all of the earth was influenced during the Pleistocene. Sea level dropped substantially, perhaps by as much as 125 m (more than 400 ft), during glacial maxima. Such a drop altered the configuration of most of the world's coasts, exposing as dry land thousands of square kilometers that previously were and presently are under water. Lowered sea levels would have made the colonization of islands like Flores easier by lessening the distance between them and the nearest mainland. The climate of areas even far south of the farthest extent of the glaciers changed, as low-pressure systems altered their usual flow patterns. These changes certainly altered the conditions to which *Homo erectus* needed to adapt. Adaptive flexibility seems to have been a hallmark of the members of this species. Their ability to inhabit new regions with environmental conditions far different from their tropical source, as well as their ability to change as their surroundings altered, bear witness to their great intelligence and in fact their humanity (see "Issues and Debates").

HOMO ERECTUS: THE TOOLMAKER

The great advance in toolmaking represented by *Homo erectus* as compared to *Homo habilis* is made clear by the following anecdote.

In a class I teach called "Experimental Archaeology," we spend a lot of time trying to replicate, as authentically as possible, various stone tools made by prehistoric people. We follow a chronological, evolutionary sequence, first replicating the Oldowan tools of *Homo habilis* and then making copies of the **Acheulean handaxe** (named for the French site of Saint-Acheul, where they were first identified) that typifies *Homo erectus,* at least in Africa and Europe

FIGURE 4.12

The Shackleton and Opdyke curve of ^{18}O concentration in fossil foraminifera is an indirect reflection of glacial expansion and contraction during the past 780,000 years.

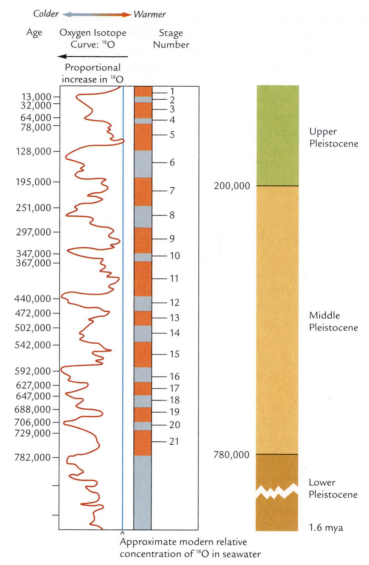

Colder ⟵⟶ Warmer

Age	Oxygen Isotope Curve: ^{18}O	Stage Number

Proportional increase in ^{18}O

13,000 — 1
32,000 — 2
64,000 — 3
78,000 — 4
— 5
128,000 — 6
195,000 — 7
251,000 — 8
297,000 — 9
347,000 — 10
367,000 — 11
440,000 — 12
472,000 — 13
502,000 — 14
542,000 — 15
592,000 — 16
627,000 — 17
647,000 — 18
688,000 — 19
706,000 — 20
729,000 — 21
782,000

^ Approximate modern relative concentration of ^{18}O in seawater

Upper Pleistocene

200,000

Middle Pleistocene

780,000

Lower Pleistocene

1.6 mya

Odd-numbered stages (in orange) = warmer periods, less glacial ice cover
Even-numbered stages (in blue) = colder periods, more glacial ice cover

(Figure 4.13). The earliest and simplest handaxes have been found in Africa and can be dated to about 1.4 million years ago. Earlier tools (prior to 1.4 million years ago) made by *Homo erectus* give the appearance of advanced Oldowan choppers. There seems to have been a slow development of the far more complex handaxe from the simpler Oldowan chopper after the first appearance of *erectus* in Africa sometime after 1.8 million B.P.

Students generally have little trouble making impressive versions of Oldowan choppers and flake tools—with a little elbow grease and after mas-

FIGURE 4.13
A finely chipped, symmetrical Lower Paleolithic handaxe. First occurring in the archaeological record nearly 1.5 million years ago, handaxes were sophisticated, multipurpose tools made by Homo erectus *in Africa, Europe, and western Asia.* (© Boltin Picture Library/Bridgeman Art Library)

tering the proper striking angle of hammerstone on core. This is not the case, however, for the *Homo erectus* handaxe, which is not easy to make, at least not without lots of practice, knowledge, and time. Very few of my students ever develop proficiency in handaxe production.

This comes as no surprise. To produce an Oldowan tool takes very few steps, and the process affords wide latitude for variation: With only three or four blows from a hammerstone and little precision in placing the blows, you can make such a tool. A handaxe is another thing entirely. Handaxes are symmetrical, finely flaked, and often aesthetically exquisite (see Figure 4.13). Dozens of flakes are removed from the core, not just a few (Figure 4.14). Even quite simple handaxes, such as the earliest known examples, from the site of Konso-Gardula in Ethiopia (Asfaw et al. 1992) and dated to 1.4 million B.P., can take 25 individual hammer strikes. The best-made examples, which date to after 1 million B.P., in Africa and more recently in Europe, took nearly three times that number (Constable 1973:128). Each flake blow must be located precisely in order to allow for the proper positioning of the next strike. The stone must be turned over again and again between hammer strikes to maintain symmetry and to keep the edge of the tool straight. All—or, at least, most—of the exterior rind, or **cortex,** of the object piece was removed in

FIGURE 4.14
Through a process of bifacial flaking, a symmetrical, finely made handaxe was produced. Compare this to the process for producing Oldowan tools (see Figure 3.19). (Noel G. Coonce)

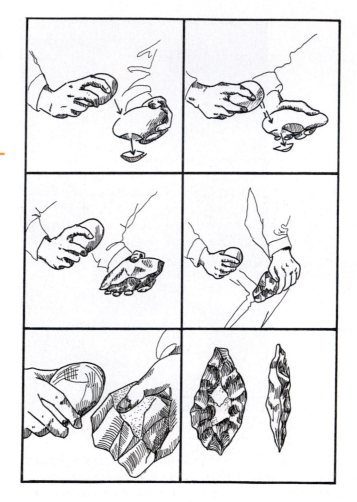

order to keep the tool relatively thin and light, so flakes needed to shoot across the face of the axe at the same time that the edge was being maintained. This takes great skill, precision, and strength.

Experimental archaeologist Mark Newcomer (1971) has replicated handaxes, determining that at least some were made in three separate steps. First, a blank, or **preform,** was roughed out with a stone hammer into the general shape of the desired end product. Then the preform was refined via a second stage of percussion with a softer stone or even a piece of antler used in thinning the tool. Finally, the edges were straightened and sharpened in one last application of percussion. All the work was worth it: For the same mass of stone, a handaxe produces about four times more cutting edge than an Oldowan chopper and, at the same time, yields far more usable, sharp flakes. During the production of a single handaxe, Newcomer produced more than 50 flakes usable for cutting or scraping.

The handaxe appears to have been an all-purpose tool (a colleague of mine calls them the "Swiss Army rocks" of the Pleistocene). Its sharp tip was used for piercing, the thin edges for cutting, and the steeper-angled edges toward the butt of the tool for scraping or chopping.

SUBSISTENCE

Remember one major issue concerning the subsistence base of *Homo habilis:* Did the members of this species hunt big game or merely scavenge remnants of kills left by carnivores? As a whole, the evidence supports the view that *Homo habilis* had a broad and opportunistic subsistence strategy: Big-game hunting was probably not preeminent, but hunting, scavenging, and gathering wild plants together provided subsistence for *Homo habilis.*

The evidence regarding the hunting abilities of later hominids is far stronger than for *Homo habilis.* For example, at the 1.0-million-year-old Daka site in Ethiopia, the butchered remains of ancient horses, hippos, and wild cattle were found together with the remains of *Homo erectus* (Asfaw et al. 2002).

Further evidence for *Homo erectus* hunting comes from Europe at the sites of Torralba and Ambrona in Spain, which date to about 350,000 years ago. The sites are located on two hills overlooking a valley that served as a natural pass for large game animals on their seasonal migrations during the Pleistocene. Though no hominid remains were found at the site, lots of tools and the remains of 55 elephants, 26 horses, 25 deer, 10 wild cattle, and 6 rhinoceroses were recovered (Freeman 1973).

It seems clear from the evidence of tools as well as cut marks on the bones (Shipman and Rose 1983) that hominids were present at the site and cut some meat off the animal carcasses. However, because the bones themselves were so badly weathered, it cannot be concluded that the animals were hunted, killed, and then systematically butchered by the hominids (Binford 1987b).

Better evidence, at least of butchery, comes from the nearby sites of Aridos 1 and 2, 18 km (11 mi) southeast of Madrid, Spain (Villa 1990). Both sites produced an apparently butchered elephant, dating to probably about 350,000 years ago. Mixed in with the bones were the tools used to cut off the meat, as well as the waste flakes produced in sharpening the cutting and scraping tools.

While there is no evidence of hunting at either Aridos site—no spearpoints were found, for example—there also is no evidence that *Homo erectus* gained access to the carcasses after carnivores had their fill—there are no tooth or gnaw marks on the bones.

That the flint serving as the raw material for the tools at Aridos came from deposits at 3 km distance and that much of the toolmaking occurred away from the butchery site, with mostly sharpening conducted on-site, offer evidence for what researcher Paola Villa calls "planning depth." In other words, the hominids who butchered the elephant carcasses at Aridos knew that elephants roamed the area and that there was always a chance one or more of them might die at any given time—the Aridos 1 elephant was a juvenile and Aridos 2 was an old male, both part of subpopulations with high natural mortality rates. The *Homo erectus* population in the area seems to have planned for the lucky occasions when a carcass became available by collecting the raw material and making the tools in advance. Planning ahead for a future eventuality is a human behavior, and the evidence at Aridos suggests that *Homo erectus* was capable of such behavior.

Evidence for the hunting abilities of the earliest European hominids is clear at Boxgrove Quarry. The remains of four butchered rhinoceroses found there show cut marks made by stone tools. The researchers at Boxgrove have demonstrated that these butchering marks were made on the animals' vertebrae, just where you would expect for the most efficient dismembering of the animal (Bower 1997b).

That the *Homo erectus* diet consisted of much more than meat is shown at the 800,000-year-old Gesher Benot Ya'aqov site (GBY) in Israel (Goren-Inbar et al. 2002). Among the artifacts researchers recovered at the site were chunks of stone, including cores, blocks, slabs, and flakes of hard, volcanic rock. Fifty-four of these chunks exhibited a peculiar pitting. Experimental replication indicates that the pits on these stones (and on those found at other ancient sites) are produced by using them as hammers to break open nuts. Remember our discussion in Chapter 3 of chimpanzee nut-cracking behavior in the Taï Forest of the African nation of Côte d'Ivoire. It seems that *Homo erectus* was exploiting a similar set of resources at GBY. Because of waterlogged conditions at the site, organic preservation was quite high. The site's researchers were able to recover the remains of seven separate species of plants that produce hard-shelled edible seeds or nuts that would have required hard hammering to break open to gain access to their nutritious kernels.

ISSUES AND DEBATES

DID THE PLEISTOCENE CAUSE THE EVOLUTION OF *HOMO ERECTUS*?

We saw in the case of the earliest split between pongid and hominid at the end of the Miocene, between 5 and 7 million years ago, that a significant change in climate predated and may have inspired the evolution of our ancestors. It is tempting to suggest that the changes produced by the Pleistocene are at the root of the apparently rapid divergence of *Homo erectus* from *Homo habilis* sometime soon after 2 million years ago. However, the timing of the climate changes during the Pleistocene seems to rule out this possibility. Though the first appearance of *erectus* and the accepted beginning of the Pleistocene epoch are roughly contemporaneous, significant global cooling and the growth of continental ice sheets predate the appearance of *erectus* as well as its expansion into Asia and Europe. This conclusion may change if older specimens of *Homo erectus* are found.

Even if the Pleistocene is not at the root of the development of *erectus* as a new species of hominid, it remains an important consideration in our reconstruction of *Homo erectus*'s intelligence and cultural capability. *Homo erectus* whose origin we can trace to the tropics was able to thrive and expand geographically despite the unsettled climatic and geographic conditions produced by the Pleistocene. Its adaptability and flexibility are hallmarks of the human cultural adaptation and show how similar to us members of this different species must have been.

WHAT ENABLED THE GEOGRAPHIC EXPANSION OF *HOMO ERECTUS*?

The spread of members of *Homo erectus* out of Africa into new habitats with different climates, resources, and challenges was not made possible by or accompanied by any change in their physical adaptation. The earliest hominids in Asia or Europe were not a cold-adapted version of African *Homo erectus*.

Intelligence

It seems clear that what enabled *Homo erectus* to survive where human ancestors had not previously been able to penetrate was intelligence and the ability to invent new adaptations as needed. Whereas *Homo habilis* was a cultural creature, as shown by its invention, manufacture, and use of stone tools, *Homo erectus* seems to have been the first human ancestor to rely for survival on the invented, learned, and passed-down adaptations of culture. In the use of sophisticated tools and ultimately in the taming of fire (see the next section), *Homo erectus* exhibits how similar the species was to us.

Consider the diversity of environments with which this one hominid species was associated across its enormous geographic range. Certainly, *Homo erectus* began its evolutionary journey in the warm and humid tropics of Africa at least 1.8 million years ago and likely possessed physical adaptations for that environment. The rapid expansion of this species across much of southern Asia may indicate a natural affinity for a tropical or subtropical climate. But physical adaptations and natural affinities cannot explain *Homo erectus* thriving in northern China more than 1.6 million years ago where the climate was cold and dry (Zhu et al. 2001). The vast extent of the longitudinal (east-west) range of *Homo erectus* evidences its ability to spread quickly from Africa to easternmost Asia. The vast extent of its latitudinal range (north-south) and the wide diversity of climates in which *Homo erectus* survived are indications of a flexibility and adaptability made possible by culture. Possession of the intelligence to invent new adaptations virtually instantaneously when the need presents itself is usually considered a uniquely human trait. This kind of intelligence and a reliance on the cultural adaptation define what it means to be a human being and are the most important things we modern humans share with our evolutionary kin, *Homo erectus.*

Control of Fire

There is something very compelling, even to us twenty-first-century humans, about a simple open flame: the smell of wood smoke, the crackling and popping of dry tinder, the warmth of the fire. For countless generations of our human ancestors, fire was more than just a diversion; it meant warmth and light, power and strength—in fact, survival itself. When did the first human ancestors make the great leap from fearing this elemental natural force to understanding and controlling it?

The best available evidence indicates that *Homo erectus* was our first ancestor able to control fire. The timing of the earliest use of controlled fire, however, is a point of contention within paleoanthropology; see James (1989) for a skeptic's perspective.

An analysis performed by paleoanthropologists Andrew Sillen and C. K. Brain (1990) at the site of Swartkrans in South Africa, for example, shows that controlled fire may have been present as long ago as 1.3 million years. That there was fire at Swartkrans is indisputable: There is evidence of burned bones, though there are no hearths. But fire can be produced naturally, by lightning or by extremely hot, dry conditions. Sillen and Brain have shown, through experimentally burning bone to different temperatures, that the bones at Swartkrans had been heated to a temperature of perhaps 800°C, far higher than expected for a natural grass fire and more in keeping with an artificially produced and maintained flame. The jury is still out on their conclusion, though the possibility is intriguing.

It had long been thought that Zhoukoudian presented the best evidence for the use of fire by *Homo erectus.* Fire certainly would have been a valuable asset in the long, cold winters of northern China. The most recent analysis, however, shows no confirming evidence for this supposition (Weiner et al. 1998). In fact, though some of the animal bones found in the same level as the oldest *Homo erectus* remains recovered at Zhoukoudian do show evidence of burning, there is no direct evidence of a fire in the cave itself. No hearths nor ash or even charcoal remains have been found in the cave. So, though it would seem reasonable to suggest that the control of fire would have been a significant cultural achievement and might have enabled hominid expansion outside the tropics, evidence is equivocal about exactly where or when control of fire was achieved—and even which of our ancestors was responsible for this development.

The so-called **Levantine Corridor** gets its name for being a natural geographic passageway of low-lying land hugging the eastern margin of the

Mediterranean, linking Africa, Asia, and Eurasia. When African-born hominids expanded beyond the margins of the continent on which they evolved, they almost certainly traveled the Levantine Corridor. The nearly 800,000-year-old site, Gesher Benot Ya'aqov, in Israel, is located along that corridor and exhibits strong evidence for the controlled use of fire by *Homo erectus* (Goren-Inbar et al. 2004).

Though it is often easy to recognize the presence of burning in the archaeological record, it is just as often difficult to distinguish naturally started fires from those that might have been started and maintained by our hominid ancestors. At Gesher Benot Ya'aqov, bits of burned seeds and wood, along with burned flint were found in discrete clusters. Excavators of the site argued that if a wildfire had been the cause of the fire, for example, one set by a lightning strike, the evidence for burning would have been widespread, not in small pockets. They interpret the individual pockets of burning as simple hearths.

The controlled use of fire may have been the key cultural adaptation that enabled members of this tropically derived and adapted species to survive outside the tropics (Balter 2004b). Fire gives warmth and protection from animals and enables cooking, which renders meat more digestible and makes it safer by killing bacteria. Fire also produces light and therefore probably played an important role in extending the usable part of the day for members of a species who, like us and most other primates, relied primarily on vision for their sensory input but who, also like us, did not see well in the dark.

THE "ART" OF MAKING TOOLS

An important point should be made about the handaxes we discussed previously: They were better made than they had to be. That is to say, the Acheulean handaxes—at least many of the later ones—have a symmetry, balance, precision, and beauty that took a lot of work, but work that was not absolutely necessary from a utilitarian perspective (see Figure 4.13). A high level of consistency in handaxe form can be found within sites, as if the makers were adhering to a particular standard. For example, paleoanthropologist John Gowlett (1984) found a remarkable consistency and uniformity in the ratios among length, width, and thickness of the handaxes he studied from the 700,000-year-old Kilombe site in Kenya.

That such extra care was taken in their production implies that their makers were interested in more than simple utility. *Homo erectus* toolmakers must have been producing beautiful objects for the sake of displaying their great skill or for the sheer pleasure of producing a thing of symmetry and beauty. Though the first true art is usually associated with anatomically modern humans of a much later period—the cave paintings of the European Upper Paleolithic (see Chapter 6) are clearly recognizable as art—for producing stone tools more artfully than they needed to, some of our much earlier

FIGURE 4.15

The Movius line reflects an interesting but not yet fully explained aspect of the distribution of handaxe technology: Handaxes are common in Homo erectus *sites in Africa, Europe, and West Asia but rare in Asia east of India.* (From Kenneth Feder and Michael Park, *Human Antiquity: An Introduction to Physical Anthropology and Archaeology,* Fourth Edition, Mayfield Publishing Company, 2001. Reprinted with permission from The McGraw-Hill Companies.)

ancestors may well deserve the credit, if not for being the first true artists, then at least for being the world's first craftspeople (Gowlett 1984). They produced useful tools in a manner so artful, we recognize the "art" in their craft as much as 1.4 million years after they made them.

THE MYSTERY OF THE MISSING HANDAXES

Beginning about 1.4 million years ago, handaxes become ubiquitous at *Homo erectus* sites in Africa. These symmetrical, sometimes exquisitely flaked tools turn up in Europe with the arrival of *Homo erectus* on that continent after 800,000 years ago. Though seemingly a key element in the species' tool kit, handaxes are, mysteriously, extremely rare or more commonly entirely absent from *Homo erectus* sites in Asia east of the Indian subcontinent where generally nonsymmetrical, less morphologically consistent, chipped stone tools made from stone nodules predominate. This geographic division poses an interesting puzzle: Why would a tool so common as to be diagnostic of *Homo erectus* stone-tool technology in Africa and Europe be absent—or nearly so—in east Asia? This geographically based, technological dichotomy even has a designation. The so-called **Movius line,** named for paleoanthropologist Hallam Movius, who first articulated it, separates the sites to the west of the line where handaxes are found from those where they do not occur to its east (Figure 4.15).

The Movius line is not viewed as having been an absolute barrier. There are some sites far to the east of the line where bifacially flaked tools that resemble handaxes have been found: for example, in the Bose Basin of southern China (Yamei et al. 2000). Such examples, however, are exceptional, and the line still seems to demarcate a genuine, though not absolute, distinction between tool technologies to the west and east. So the question remains: Why?

The answer to this puzzle may lie in the nature and timing of *Homo erectus* expansion beyond the confines of the African continent. Based on the very early timing of *Homo erectus* migration to west and east Asia and their altogether rather late movement into Europe, it seems that *Homo erectus* populations in Africa first expanded into Asia *before* they had developed Acheulean technology with its emblematic handaxe. Remember that the early stone-tool technologies at Erk-el-Ahmar in Israel, Dmanisi in the Republic of Georgia, and the Nihewan Basin sites in northern China all look a lot like the Oldowan technology in Africa as practiced by, first, *Homo habilis*, and later, the early representatives of *Homo erectus*. But *Homo erectus* did not penetrate Europe until after 1 million years ago, well after African populations of the species had already developed handaxes. When they expanded into Europe, and when they sustained subsequent population movements into southwest Asia and Eurasia, these African migrants brought the new stone-tool technology with them. That the technology did not pass to the east, beyond the Movius line, later on is still a mystery. It may have been due to the fact that handaxes were superfluous in east Asia, their tasks already being carried out with the use of bamboo tools (Pope 1989).

RAISING *HOMO ERECTUS*

My understanding of the care necessary for raising human babies as compared to the young of other species has been forged on the anvil of experience: I've got two kids and have raised five cats, and there simply is no comparison. We adopted the various cats when they were between 7 and 12 weeks old and ready to leave their mothers. They all could walk, could feed themselves, were litter-box trained, knew how to manipulate human beings to get anything they wanted, and were fierce hunters of blowing leaves and dust bunnies. My kids, like all baby humans, are another story. Immediately following birth and for an extended period thereafter, my kids were capable of crying, filling their diapers, sleeping, and little else.

Whereas after just several weeks of life, animals such as cats attain a reasonable level of competence at moving around, eating, and defending themselves, human children are utterly dependent on adults to satisfy all their needs for a very long time—usually years, even decades. Some specialists characterize even full-term human babies (9 months of gestation) as inherently premature and little more than embryos living outside the womb. The term **altricial** is used to characterize baby birds who are completely dependent on their parents for fulfilling their needs. Intellectually, human babies are

FIGURE 4.16

The birth canals of apes and modern human beings and the fossil pelvises of extinct hominids allow for a comparison in the birth process of these three kinds of creatures. (Courtesy of Robert Tague)

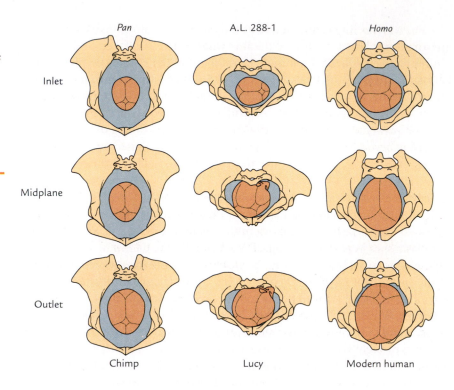

anything but altricial; almost from birth they begin to gather and process sensory information, and they are quickly insatiably curious and experimental about their world. Physically, however, they are born at an earlier stage of development and remain immature for longer than the offspring of other species; human babies are said to be **secondarily altricial.**

There are a number of reasons why evolution would have selected for a seemingly dangerous situation in which human children are born at an early stage of physical development. A reconfiguration of the human pelvis was necessary to allow our first hominid ancestors to stand up. This change in pelvic form provided for a change in muscle positioning and shape necessary for bipedal locomotion. It also had an incidental effect: It greatly narrowed the pelvic outlet in females, making it far more difficult for a baby's body to pass through the birth canal. This difficulty can be shown by a simple statistic: Average birth labor time for a chimpanzee is about 2 hours; for a human mother it is more than 14 hours (Rosenberg 1992:99; see this study for an informative discussion of the evolution of human childbirth).

A detailed comparison by anthropologists Robert Tague and Owen Lovejoy (1986) of the reconstructed pelvis of the fossil Lucy (*Australopithecus afarensis*) with the pelvises of a chimpanzee and a modern human female indicates that, though bipedality probably complicated birth for *Australopithecus* females, it still was not as problematic as it is for modern human women (Figure 4.16). The brains of the various *Australopithecus* species were still quite small, so while there may have been a tighter fit at birth, this probably presented little problem because their heads were still no bigger than those of chimp babies.

However, as natural selection began to favor greater intelligence in the hominids—made possible by an increase in brain and therefore head size—a problem did develop: A smaller pelvic outlet was forced to accommodate an increasingly large head at birth. Nature's solution, still hardly perfect, as witnessed by the often difficult time women have in childbirth, was twofold. The first strategy was to maximize pelvic outlet size in females by fine-tuning the configuration of the pelvis. Male and female human pelvises became readily distinguishable because the pelvis exhibits sexual dimorphism.

The second strategy of natural selection was timing the birth of human babies at an earlier stage in fetal development, when the head, though large, was still small enough to pass through the birth canal. Today this timing is reflected in the fact that the human newborn has a smaller head, proportional to its ultimate adult size, than do any of the living apes. A human newborn's brain is less than 25% of its ultimate adult size (Jordaan 1976:274). Compare this to the great apes, in whom a newborn's brain is more than 40% of its adult size or to a typical monkey, the macaque, whose brain at birth is 70% of its adult volume.

Most human brain growth occurs outside the womb, after birth. This is fundamentally different from the situation for all the apes. For example, whereas the rate of brain growth declines dramatically in chimpanzees immediately after birth, human babies maintain what is essentially a relatively fast fetal rate of brain growth for an entire year after they are born (Martin 1989; Rosenberg 1992:106). The proportionally small size of the human baby's head at birth is what enables the baby to be born at all, given the constraints of pelvic outlet size necessitated by upright walking. But this situation presents problems, for the less developed a newborn of any species is, the more susceptible it is to trauma, infection, cold, and death.

Unfortunately, there is only one well-preserved cranium of a *Homo erectus* child, the Mojokerto fossil found on the island of Java. The volume of that cranium as determined through a computerized tomography (CT) scan is 663 cc (Coquenugniot et al. 2004), making the Mojokerto child's brain size about 70% of the mean calculated on Table 4.1 (using a somewhat different sample, Coquenugniot et al. figure it at between 72% and 84% of the adult *Homo erectus* volume). The other variable in the equation, the age at death of the Mojokerto child, is far more difficult to determine than cranial volume. Estimates range from 1 to 8 years. If closer to the lower estimate, the Mojokerto child's pattern of brain growth is more similar to that of an ape than a modern human being. If closer to the higher estimate, the Mojokerto child's pattern of brain growth is quite similar to that of a modern human child. Until the child's age at death can be determined, its pattern of brain growth cannot be fully assessed.

Birth at an early stage of development for an organism with a large and complex brain has some advantages. Stimulation and learning begin earlier, while the brain is still experiencing rapid growth, and bonding between parents and children is, of necessity, stronger. This timing can be advantageous in a species that depends for its survival so thoroughly on learned behavior and social relations. It is beneficial for humans to be born at an immature stage of development and to have an extended childhood; the learning curve is simply a lot steeper and longer for us than it is for cows, cats, or even other primates.

An additional hypothesis holds that one of the key changes that characterized ancient hominids from *Homo habilis* onward is **neoteny,** or the "holding on" to features that are typical of newborn apes (Gould 1977). And modern human adults resemble baby chimps more than they resemble adult chimpanzees. Our lack of body hair, rounded skulls, flat faces, and even the point of articulation between the base of our skull and backbone are all things we share with fetal or newborn, but not adult, chimpanzees.

This brings us back to the boy from West Turkana. Though his cranial capacity and that of his species was substantially larger than that of *Homo habilis,* the size of the *Homo erectus* skull—and therefore the size of the brain—in proportion to the size of its body was really no different from the proportion for *Homo habilis* (Walker and Shipman 1996:215–216). In other words, the *Homo erectus* brain was larger to control a larger body, but it falls right in line with what would have been expected based on the brain-size to body-size ratio for *habilis.* There was no great, disproportionate increase in brain size for *Homo erectus.* As paleoanthropologists Alan Walker and Pat Shipman (1996:212) point out, if you want an impression of what the Nariokotome boy looked like at the age of 8 or 9 years, picture a 15-year-old modern human boy (based on the Nariokotome boy's height) with the head of a 1-year-old modern human child (based on cranial capacity)! Recognizably human but alien indeed.

Nevertheless, when the pelvis of *Homo erectus* is reconstructed, it is clear that the size of the birth canal had been so diminished to accommodate upright locomotion that even the proportional increase in *Homo erectus*'s brain size would have seriously compromised an infant's ability to pass through the mother's body. During birth, the Nariokotome boy's head size surely challenged the size of his mother's birth canal. Almost certainly, natural selection was already at work, favoring survival of infants born at an earlier stage of fetal development. This selective process, however, would work only if adults—particularly mothers but potentially fathers and other adults—could spend an enormous amount of time caring for the newborns. This must have been the case for the West Turkana boy.

The physical immaturity of a *Homo erectus* child at birth can be added to another human characteristic exhibited by the West Turkana boy: an extended period of physical development and delayed maturation. An 8- or 9-year-old cat is an older adult, and even an 8- or 9-year-old chimp is close to being an adult. But the 8- or 9-year-old West Turkana boy was still physically immature, as evidenced by his dental development and the development of the bones of his arms, legs, hands, and feet—none of the **epiphyses** (see Chapter 2) of the West Turkana boy had yet fused at the time of his death. He was, indeed, just a boy.

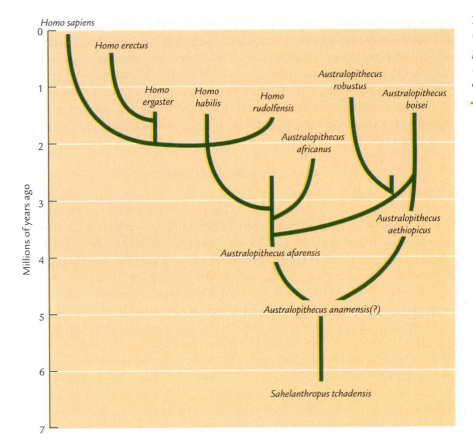

FIGURE 4.17
*One alternative phylogeny
proposed for the fossil
hominids.* (Based partially
on Bernard Wood 1992a,b)

As paleoanthropologists Frank Brown et al. (1985) point out, the West Turkana boy shows clear evidence of an extended period of immaturity that is characteristic of modern human beings. This long period of childhood allowed him, 1.6 million years ago, and all *Homo erectus* children to learn what they needed to know. A long period of learning is emblematic of the human species.

WHEN DID *HOMO ERECTUS* BECOME EXTINCT?

It should be clear by this point that human evolution was not a simple, progressive process with each species thriving during its time and then giving way to the next in line, repeating this process as a series of steps leading directly to modern human beings. The human story is, instead, far more complex, characterized until fairly recently by geographically separated, multiple contemporary hominids (Figure 4.17).

We will begin the next chapter talking about a new, more modern-looking hominid species that can be dated to about 400,000 years ago. The appearance of this new species does not mean that all older species conveniently disappeared from the scene at that time. In fact, in the scenario presented in this book, only one of the *Homo erectus* populations—that in Africa—is directly ancestral to us. That African *Homo erectus* line evolved into another hominid that looked and behaved more like modern humans, while other branches of *Homo erectus,* particularly those in Europe and Asia, almost certainly continued on more or less the same as they always had perhaps into the recent past as implied by the Ngandong, Sambungmachan, and Flores fossils.

STABILITY OR CHANGE?

How much change is exhibited in *Homo erectus* fossils included in the species but separated by an extraordinarily long time span? Lasting from 1.78 million years ago to 0.4 million years ago, *Homo erectus* is one of the longest-lived of the hominid species. If evolution is thought of as a gradual, steady process (see the discussion of punctuated equilibrium in Chapter 3), then we might expect *erectus*, if it was the direct ancestor of humanity, to exhibit such steady evolution toward the anatomically modern condition over its lengthy existence on the planet. As evidence for this view, some researchers point to certain changes through time within the *Homo erectus* species: The back teeth get smaller, and the anatomical structure of the face and lower jaw decrease (Wolpoff 1984).

On the other hand, paleoanthropologist Philip Rightmire (1981, 1985, 1990) argues that such changes are extremely minor and that, especially when considering the enormous amount of time involved and the geographical breadth of *Homo erectus,* the evidence is overwhelming for great stability within the species over its entire existence. As Rightmire points out, all of the *Homo erectus* specimens, from the very oldest to the most recent, are "built on a common plan" (1990:190).

Even brain size within the species can be shown to be fundamentally stable through time: There is no significant increase in cranial capacity within *erectus* from its earliest appearance in Africa 1.78 million years ago until it is replaced by *Homo sapiens* sometime after 400,000 years ago (Figure 4.18). Rightmire (1981, 1990) applies the statistical procedure of regression analysis to the data and finds no statistically significant temporal trend in brain size. Though researcher Steven Leigh (1992) disputes this result, maintaining that, at least within the Asian subsample of *erectus,* the increase in brain size through time is statistically significant, that increase is extremely small. As Figure 4.18 shows, statistical significance issues aside, there appears to be little change in cranial capacity through time until about 400,000 years ago.

Interestingly, this period of relative stability in brain size is also a period of great cultural stability regarding stone tools. The handaxes made by *Homo erectus* change only slightly from 1.4 million to 400,000 years ago. One million years of relatively little change in a technology is in stark contrast to the modern situation, in which technologies change virtually overnight. That sta-

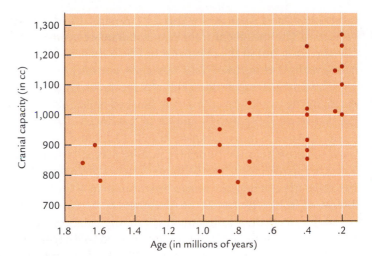

FIGURE 4.18
This graph of the trend in Homo erectus *brain size through time shows a rather remarkable stability from the first appearance of the species some 1.8 million years ago to the most recent specimens, dating to 400,000 years ago.*

bility lends further support to the notion of *Homo erectus* as a fundamentally unchanging species representing a long period of evolutionary equilibrium. At about 400,000 years ago, however, a steep increase in brain size over a short interval is seen. This jump in brain size, in fact, is how the earliest appearance of members of our species is identified.

So it seems that *Homo erectus,* like *Australopithecus afarensis* (see Chapter 3), was a stable, long-lived species. The fossil evidence again supports the evolutionary model of punctuated equilibrium—with *Homo erectus* representing a long period of equilibrium in the hominid line. Major changes in brain size and cranial morphology did not occur until around 400,000 years ago. Those changes produced and defined the first *Homo sapiens* in what is seen here as being a punctuational event (see Chapter 5).

CASE STUDY CLOSE-UP

In 1918 a fossil locality southwest of Beijing, China, was explored by Swedish geologist Johan Gunnar Andersson. Andersson took advantage of a local Chinese belief that fossil bones were actually the remnants of dragons and that powder made from ground-up "dragon bones" was a cure-all. Many local druggists collected such bones for use in their medicines. Even today, paleontologists rely on local druggists for leads in their search for fossil ("dragon") bones (Jian and Rice 1990).

In 1918 Andersson was directed by a druggist to a hill called Jigushan (Chicken Bone Hill) near the village of Zhoukoudian (Jia and Huang 1990). Convinced there was a rich array of fossil bones in the surrounding region, he began excavating on another hill, called Longgoshan—Dragon Bone Hill. In 1926 two humanlike teeth were recovered; in 1929, with the dig now led by British scientist Davidson Black, a nearly intact skull was encountered in a cave at the top of the hill (Locality 1). The fossil was recognizably different from almost everything that had been found previously, with the possible exception of Java Man. A new species was named and defined: *Sinanthropus pekinensis.* The specimens from Zhoukoudian are now included in the species *Homo erectus,* but in the popular mind both then and now, they may forever be known as "Peking Man" (see Figure 4.8, bottom).

The cave at Dragon Bone Hill was spectacularly productive by any standards. By the time excavations were finished at Zhoukoudian, the expedition had recovered, along with thousands of specimens of ancient animals, 15 fragmentary skulls, 6 more complete crania, 13 fragmentary mandibles, 3 upper jaws, some postcranial bones (including pieces of femur, upper arms, toe bones, numerous teeth), and a single vertebra of Peking Man (Jia and Huang 1990:161–62). All told, the remains of more than 40 hominid individuals were recovered from deposits in the cave dated to between 462,000 and 200,000 years ago (according to fission-track dating as reported by Jia and Huang 1990:111). Being so numerous and discovered so early in our thinking about human evolution, the Peking Man fossils played an important historical role in the scientific conceptualization of human evolution and in interpretations of the culture of ancient human beings.

Tragically, the Zhoukoudian hominid assemblage was lost during World War II when the fossils were being removed from China by U.S. Marines in an attempt to keep them away from Japanese invaders, coincidentally on the same day that Pearl Harbor was attacked. The Marines were captured and imprisoned, and to this day no one knows what became of their precious fossil cargo. (It may have been destroyed by Japanese troops or simply lost, or it may have been found later by Chinese druggists who ground the bones up for medicine. There is even a very slight possibility that some are still hidden away in China, Japan, or the United States.)

 VISITING THE PAST

Just as with the fossils and sites related to *Australopithecus* and *Homo habilis* discussed in the previous chapter, you need to travel a great distance to visit the *Homo erectus* sites discussed here. Even then, the important fossil remains usually are unavailable for viewing by all but researchers in the field. Again, however, most large museums in major American cities have displays on human evolution that cover some of the important discoveries and issues dealt with in this chapter.

China has a fine museum display at Zhoukoudian. The museum is devoted to the finds made at the Peking Man site as well as the area surrounding Zhoukoudian. Though, unfortunately, the original fossils are all missing, the museum does have casts of the skulls on display as well as some of the tools and the bones of animals killed and eaten by the ancient inhabitants of the locality; there is also a general display on human evolution. The caves where the fossils were found are accessible from the museum. Zhoukoudian, being close to Beijing, is reasonably accessible to tourists.

In Kenya the Olorgesailie sites, containing a number of excavated localities, are open to tourists. The sites date to after 400,000 years ago; numerous, sometimes finely made handaxes have been left exactly where they were found by the excavators (including Louis and Mary Leakey) and, presumably, where they were left by *Homo erectus.* The monograph by archaeologist Glynn Isaac (1977) provides details on the excavation and analysis of the Olorgesailie sites.

One of the most interesting of the Olorgesailie localities is Site B. The remains of many stone tools and the smashed bones of an extinct species of baboon were found there; some have been left in place for viewing. The bones appear to have been broken for marrow extraction. Because so many of the stone tools have been left in place, the visitor can gain a unique insight into the appearance of a 400,000-year-old *Homo erectus* site as it was discovered by the archaeologists who excavated it.

SUMMARY

Sometime after 1.8 million years ago, *Homo habilis* was replaced by a new hominid species, *Homo erectus. Erectus* possessed a larger brain than *habilis;* its mean brain size of just under 1,000 cc is two-thirds the modern human mean. With its larger brain and attendant greater intelligence, *Homo erectus* was able to adapt to the changing environmental conditions posed by the Pleistocene epoch.

Homo erectus was the first ancestral human being to expand beyond the borders of our hominid family's African birthplace and nursery. Following the most reasonable trail beyond the borders of Africa, *Homo erectus* fossils and their tools are found in southwest Asia and Eurasia more than 1.7 million years ago, very soon after they first appeared in Africa. For reasons that are still debated, these African migrants did not enter into western Europe until much later, perhaps no more than 800,000 years ago.

It was intelligence and not any physical adaptation that enabled *Homo erectus* to adapt to the diversity of habitats offered throughout Asia. New and more sophisticated tools, new methods of hunting, and the use of fire were all part of the *Homo erectus* behavioral repertoire.

Homo erectus was a stable and long-lived species. Fossils from Africa to east Asia show a consistent morphology from close to 1.8 million to 400,000 years ago. After 400,000 years ago, brain size, relatively stable during the existence of *erectus,* exhibits a rapid increase, signifying the evolution of the first *Homo sapiens* from an *erectus* base.

TO LEARN MORE

Technical Summaries

The definitive work on the Nariokotome *Homo erectus* boy has been edited by two of its excavators, Alan Walker and Richard Leakey: *The Nariokotome* Homo erectus *Skeleton* (1993). A good, very descriptive, general technical work on *Homo erectus* is G. Philip Rightmire's *The Evolution of* Homo erectus: *Comparative Anatomical Studies of an Extinct Human Species* (1990).

Popular Summaries

Richard Leakey and Roger Lewin's (1992) *Origins Reconsidered: In Search of What Makes Us Human* discusses the discovery, excavation, and interpretation of the Nariokotome skeleton. Much information about *Homo erectus* is offered in *Ancestors: In Search of Human Origins* by Don and Lenora Johanson and Blake Edgar (1994). A very helpful, popular summary of evolution with quite a bit of information on the Lower Paleolithic is provided in Alan Walker and Pat Shipman's *The Wisdom of the Bones* (1996).

There are two great summary chapters devoted to *Homo erectus* (and fossils here called *Homo erectus* but labeled *Homo ergaster* by the authors) in the book *Extinct Humans* by paleoanthropologists Ian Tattersall and Jeffrey Schwartz (2000). Paleoanthropologist Harry Shapiro's *Peking Man* (1974) provides a riveting account of the discovery and loss of Peking Man. See *The Search for Peking Man,* by Christopher Janus and William Brashler (1975), for an interesting, if unreliable, account of an attempt to track down the present whereabouts of the bones, replete with stories of clandestine meetings atop the Empire State Building and multimillion-dollar ransom demands. Also, see *The Story of Peking Man* (1990), by Jia Lanpo and Huang Weiwen, for a detailed telling of the story of Peking Man by one of its excavators (Jia Lanpo).

The best popular books on science present the story of scientific discovery within the personal and cultural context of the individuals involved in those breakthroughs. Paleoanthropologist Pat Shipman (2001) has accomplished just this in her book *The Man Who Found the Missing Link: Eugene Dubois and His Lifelong Quest to Prove Darwin Right.* It is a great read about the initial discovery of a fossil we would come to label *Homo erectus.* Another useful book using the Java hominid discoveries both as a jumping-off point to discuss human evolution and to provide the personal contexts of scientists involved in this analysis is *Java Man: How Two Geologists Changed the History of Human Evolution* by Carl Swisher, Garniss Curtis, and Roger Lewin (2000).

On the Web

Unlike the Neandertals, one of the fossil populations we will be discussing in the next chapter, there aren't really any pages devoted just to *Homo erectus.* However, there's plenty of information about *Homo erectus* sites and specimens on the Internet included within Web pages on the broader topic of human evolution. For example, for details on selected *Homo erectus* fossils and sites, see the pages devoted to this fossil species on the Smithsonian Institution's *Human Origins Program* Web site at http://www.mnh.si.edu/anthro/humanorigins/ha/erec.html. You will find a brief discussion and lots of photos of *Homo erectus* fossils on David Kreger's page titled *A Look at Modern Human Origins* at http://www.modernhumanorigins.com/hominids.html (follow the hominids link). On the PBS page *The Origins of Humankind,* you can find an interactive timeline that provides some chronological context for *Homo erectus* (http://www.pbs.org/wgbh/evolution/humans/humankind/index. html). You can take a QuickTime spin with one of the crania from Zhoukoudian at http://www.unipv.it/webbio/dfpaleoa.htm#H.ERECTUS.

ONLINE
LEARNING
CENTER

Online Learning Center: www.mhhe.com/feder4

The Online Learning Center (OLC) Web companion to *The Past in Perspective* features a variety of supplemental study aids. For each chapter, this free Web site includes

- Self-Quizzes to take as pretests prior to exams
- Interactive Timeline Study Guides for additional review and reinforcement of key information
- Learning Objectives
- Chapter Site links with Web addresses for many of the fossil and archaeological sites mentioned in the text

KEY TERMS

altricial, 149

Acheulean handaxe, 139

calvarium, 126

cortex, 141

epiphysis, 152

glacial, 138

glacier, 137

Holocene epoch, 137

interglacial, 138

interstadial, 138

Levantine Corridor, 146

metatarsal, 127

microcephaly, 132

Movius line, 148

neoteny, 152

occipital, 121

paleomagnetism, 127

Pleistocene epoch, 137

preform, 142

prognathous, 125

secondarily altricial, 150

stadial, 138

supraorbital torus, 125

talus, 127

three-dimensional computed tomography, 132

tibia, 127

5

The First Humans:

THE EVOLUTION OF *HOMO SAPIENS*

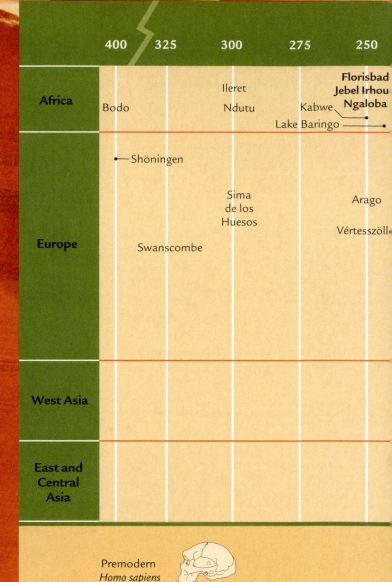

	400	325	300	275	250
Africa	Bodo		Ileret Ndutu	Kabwe Lake Baringo	**Florisbad Jebel Irhou Ngaloba**
Europe		•—Shöningen Swanscombe	Sima de los Huesos		Arago Vértesszöll
West Asia					
East and Central Asia					

Premodern
Homo sapiens

CHAPTER OVERVIEW

Beginning about 400,000 years ago, a great change is seen in the fossil hominid record. Brain size expanded, and the fossils look so much more modern that they are categorized as *Homo sapiens*, though of a type classified as "premodern." The best known of the premoderns are the Neandertals. They appear to have been physically highly specialized to life in the arctic cold of Pleistocene (Ice Age) Europe and west Asia.

Anatomically modern human beings appear in the fossil record of Africa at 195,000 years ago. The question must be posed: "How did these first anatomically modern human beings arise?" Two competing models—the multiregional approach and the replacement hypothesis—have been proposed. In the multiregional model, modern human beings evolved from their premodern antecedents in various world areas more or less simultane-

ously. In the replacement model, modern humans evolved from a premodern variety just once, in one place—in all likelihood, Africa—and spread out from there. In this scenario, anatomically modern human beings replaced premodern humans wherever the two came in contact. A deductive test of the evidence using skeletal, artifactual, and genetic evidence is applied in this chapter. The results lend support to the replacement view.

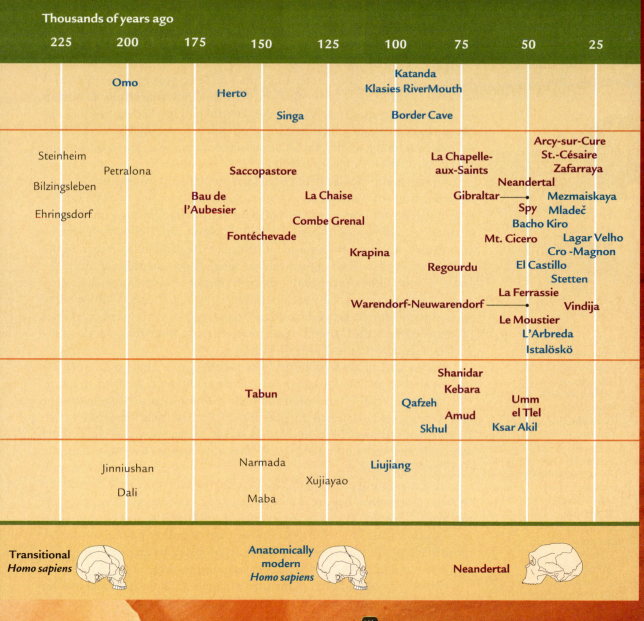

Thousands of years ago

225 200 175 150 125 100 75 50 25

Transitional Homo sapiens (top row, blue):
Omo, Herto, Singa, Katanda, Klasies RiverMouth, Border Cave

Neandertal (middle section, dark red):
Steinheim, Bilzingsleben, Ehringsdorf, Petralona, Saccopastore, Bau de l'Aubesier, Fontéchevade, La Chaise, Combe Grenal, Krapina, La Chapelle-aux-Saints, Regourdu, Warendorf-Neuwarendorf, Arcy-sur-Cure, St.-Césaire, Zafarraya, Neandertal, Gibraltar, Mezmaiskaya, Spy, Mladeč, Bacho Kiro, Mt. Cicero, Lagar Velho, Cro-Magnon, El Castillo, Stetten, La Ferrassie, Vindija, Le Moustier, L'Arbreda, Istalöskö

(lower section, dark red):
Tabun, Shanidar, Kebara, Qafzeh, Amud, Skhul, Umm el Tlel, Ksar Akil

Anatomically modern Homo sapiens (bottom section, mixed):
Jinniushan, Dali, Narmada, Maba, Xujiayao, Liujiang

Transitional *Homo sapiens*   **Anatomically modern** *Homo sapiens*   **Neandertal**

Go to www.mhhe.com/feder4 for an interactive study guide version of this timeline.

ONLINE LEARNING CENTER

Science consistently has shown that, though *individual* human beings may differ in terms of their athletic propensities, math and writing skills, or musical and artistic talents, collectively all human *groups* share equally in these physical and intellectual abilities. All categories of humanity, whether these are defined by national borders, ethnic designations, religious affiliations, or racial determinations, are in fact equally smart, talented, and athletically gifted.

Now imagine what the world would have been like, if instead, two or more different kinds of human beings with *unequal* abilities had evolved side by side in the ancient world and then actually survived into the present. This fascinating possibility was the basis for the 1953 novel *You Shall Know Them*, by Jean Bruller, a French author who wrote under the pen name Vercors. In the novel, a group of explorers investigates a secluded, pristine valley in the highlands of New Guinea in the mid–twentieth century. The explorers discover a population of a presumedly extinct variety of human beings—*living* hominids, more advanced than Peking Man (*Homo erectus*) yet less advanced than modern people. Called "tropis," these creatures make stone tools, speak a simple language, have fire, and bury their dead.

In actuality, all modern human beings belong to a single species, *Homo sapiens sapiens*, and all of us are more alike than different. But this situation was not inevitable. There could today be different, coexisting species of human beings with different physical and intellectual capacities, just as there are different species of bear, antelope, elephant, and camel—and just as there were different, contemporaneous, and coexisting species of hominids in the past (see Chapter 3).

In Vercors's novel, the primitive people discovered in New Guinea are treated quite badly. They are essentially enslaved. On the one hand, they are not legally "people," so no law prevents their exploitation (just as there is no law against harnessing a horse to a plow). On the other hand, they are far more intelligent than any other nonhuman animal and can be trained to do things modern humans can do but find degrading, boring, or dangerous.

Considering the amount of mistrust and hatred that exists today among the empirically minimally different individuals of our single species, it is frightening to consider what the world would be like if there were truly different, coexisting species of human beings. In a broad sense, however, this might have been.

The Neandertals to be discussed in this chapter are an extinct variety of human beings that come chronologically closer to the modern era than do any other nonmodern hominid; they became extinct less than 30,000 years ago, a mere tick on the evolutionary clock. In fact, there was an overlap of tens of millennia during the waning years of the Neandertals and the ascendance of the earliest anatomically modern human beings.

The Neandertals were not only similar to us in many ways but also quite different. Though often depicted as apelike or subhuman, they managed to

survive for tens of thousands of years during an extremely harsh period of the Pleistocene, or Ice Age. They did so through their great intelligence, inventing sophisticated stone tools for hunting, producing clothing and shelter, and using fire. Neandertals are also noted for another behavior that contradicts their modern stereotype: They buried their dead. In recognizing the enormity of death and in ceremonially disposing of the mortal remains of their comrades, they exhibited a behavior that shows their close kinship to us. Despite this, Neandertals were surely quite different from us both in how they looked and, almost certainly, in their intellectual capabilities. Considering how badly we humans treat one another—and that we are more similar to one another in how we look and how we think than we would be to living Neandertals—the Neandertals probably would have ended up like the primitive hominids in Vercors's book, doomed by us to lives of confinement, drudgery, and pain (Gould 1988).

As we saw in Chapter 4, after about 1 million B.P., the tapestry of human evolution seems to have been characterized by

CHRONICLE

a single primary thread made up of three generally similar strands in Africa, Asia, and Europe. Then, beginning as much as 600,000 years ago, there was a burst of change, with new hominid varieties appearing on the evolutionary stage. Though regional differences are maintained among the fossils seen in Africa, Asia, and Europe, these hominids all appear to have been more modern in appearance than previous hominid species, so much more modern in cranial capacity and shape that some researchers call these new hominids **premodern,** or **archaic,** Homo sapiens (Figure 5.1).

These premodern humans shared a bigger, more modern brain than previous hominids had. The mean cranial capacity of the premoderns (excluding the Neandertals, who will be treated separately) was a little over 1,200 cc—more than 20% larger than that of their evolutionary antecedents (see Table 5.1 on p. 168). Most of the premodern fossil specimens still possess large brow ridges. But more like the modern form, they also exhibit steeper foreheads, generally (though not universally) thinner cranial bones, and flatter faces than *erectus.* However, there is a lot of variation among the premodern *sapiens* specimens: Some have relatively thin cranial bones, others thick; some have nearly vertical foreheads, while others' foreheads slope back more severely.

PREMODERN HUMANS: FOSSIL EVIDENCE

Versions of premodern *Homo sapiens* are known from Africa, Asia, and Europe, where they appear to have evolved in place from previous indigenous populations of hominids.

CHAPTER SITES

www.mhhe.com/feder4

**EUROPE
(Neandertals)**
La Chappelle-aux-
   Saints, 180
La Ferrassie, 180
Le Piage, 207
Le Moustier, 180
Les Furtins, 212
Mt. Circeo, 180
Neandertal, 171
Regourdu, 212
Saccopastore, 180
Saône-et-Loire, 212
Spy, 180
Vindija, 182
Warendorf-
   Neuwarendorf, 202

**WEST ASIA
(Neandertals)**
Amud, 180
Kebara, 180
Kobeh, 181
Shanidar, 180
Tabun, 180
Teshik-Tash, 184
Umm el Tlel, 181

**AFRICA
(Transitional)**
Florisbad, 164
Jebel Irhoud, 164
Ngaloba, 164

**AFRICA
(Anatomically modern
homo sapiens)**
Border Cave, 188
Herto, 187
Katanda, 204
Klasies River Mouth, 187

Africa

The oldest premodern human remains have been found in Africa. Three specimens from East Africa—Bodo, Ileret, and Ndutu—are representative of the African premoderns. Bodo, from Ethiopia, exhibits a round cranial profile and dates to as much as 600,000 years ago. The cranial capacity of the Ileret specimen, found in Kenya, may be as much as 1,400 cc, which is entirely modern in brain size, though it dates to about 300,000 years ago (Bräuer et al. 1997). It also exhibits large brow ridges, like other archaic specimens. The Ndutu cranium, from Tanzania, has a brain size of over 1,100 cc and exhibits a more rounded profile than that seen in earlier *Homo erectus* skulls (Clarke 1990). It is likely more than 200,000 years old.

Other ancient premodern *Homo sapiens* remains found in Africa and dating to more than 200,000 years ago include the Jebel Irhoud remains found in Morocco, the Florisbad remains in southern Africa (with a pretty firm date of 259,000 years old; Grün et al. 1996), and Ngaloba from Tanzania.

The Kabwe, or Broken Hill, cranium from Zambia is round in profile, like a modern human's, with a capacity of 1,280 cc, well within the modern human range (Figure 5.2). Its brow ridges, however, are huge, larger, in fact, than what is seen in most *Homo erectus* specimens. Unfortunately, the age of Kabwe is uncertain, but likely is about 250,000 years old.

FIGURE 5.1
Fossil localities of premodern Homo sapiens.

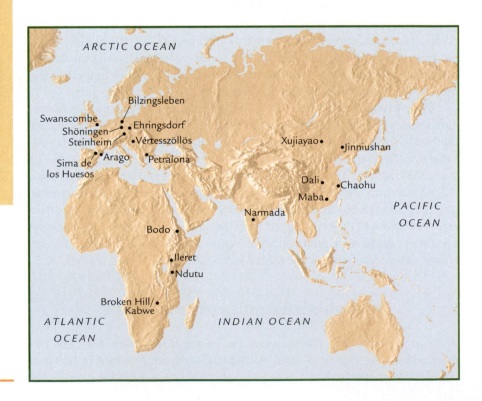

Asia

In Asia a number of fossils can be placed within the premodern category. From central India comes the Narmada hominid, with its cranial capacity of 1,200–1,400 cc and a morphology reminiscent of the African premoderns (Kennedy et al. 1991). Dating is unclear, though artifacts associated with the skull are probably no more than 150,000 years old. The Narmada cranium, though distinctive, has more in common with the just-described premoderns from Africa than it does with *Homo erectus.*

A growing list of sites in eastern Asia is providing testimony for the presence there of premodern *Homo sapiens* (Brooks and Wood 1990; Chen and Zhang 1991; Pope 1992). Perhaps of greatest interest because of its antiquity and the relative completeness of the skeleton is the so-called Jinniushan Man from Yingkou County, Liaoning Province (Figure 5.3; Lu 1987). The cranial capacity, estimated at about 1,330–1,390 cc, is large for a premodern *Homo sapiens,* and the cranial bones are very thin, like a modern human's and unlike the thick cranial bones of other premoderns. Its general shape and form, however, are a mixture of primitive and modern; it doesn't look quite like anything from anywhere else. Animal teeth found in the same cave and from the same layer as the hominid have been dated by electron spin resonance to about 165,000–195,000 years ago and by uranium series to 200,000 years ago (Chen, Yang, and Wu 1994).

Other archaic or premodern *Homo sapiens* from China include the Dali cranium from northern Shaanxi Province. Its cranial capacity has been estimated

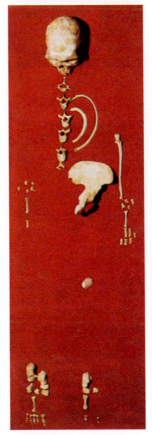

FIGURE 5.3

Premodern Homo sapiens *from Asia include this specimen from Yingkou in the Jinniushan Mountains, one of the most complete premodern human fossils outside of Europe.* (© China Pictorial Photo Service)

at 1,120 cc; its form has been described as intermediate between that of *erectus* and that of modern *sapiens* (Pope 1992). The site has produced a uranium series date of about 200,000 years old.

Europe

The earth is often stingy in giving up the remains of our ancestors. Paleoanthropologists usually feel themselves lucky to find the remains of even a single ancient individual. They are understandably ecstatic when, as was the case at the site where Lucy was recovered, more than a dozen individuals are found (Chapter 3). With this in mind, the excavators of Sima de los Huesos (the "Pit of the Bones") in the Atapuerca Mountains in northern Spain must view themselves as among the most fortunate paleoanthropologists to have ever put a spade in the ground (Arsuaga et al. 1993; Bahn 1996). The 1,600 bones they have recovered represent the remains of more than 30 and perhaps more than 50 ancient people (Figure 5.4).

The fossils were recovered beneath a stratum that has been dated to more than 300,000 years ago; the bones must be at least that old. Volumes have been measured at 1,125 and 1,390 cc for the two adult crania recovered and 1,200 cc for the juvenile cranium, all within the range of the premodern humans we have already discussed from Africa and Asia.

Other European examples of premodern *Homo sapiens* include the Steinheim cranium from Germany (Ikeya 1982; Figure 5.5), the Swanscombe cranial fragments found in England (Howell 1960; Ovey 1964), the Petralona cranium from Greece (Poulianos 1970–72), Vérességzöllös in Hungary (Gamble 1986), Arago in France (Cook et al. 1982), and cranial fragments in Bilzingsleben and Ehringsdorf, Germany. All date to a period sometime between 200,000 and 400,000 years ago. All of the crania present a more rounded profile than seen in *Homo erectus* and capacities of at least 1,200 cc (see Table 5.1).

PREMODERN HUMANS: CULTURAL EVIDENCE

There is no great cultural break or jump seen in the archaeological record of the archaic humans. Handaxes similar to those manufactured by *Homo erectus* are common at premodern *Homo sapiens* sites in Europe and Africa; east Asia shows continuity in the stone-toolmaking tradition as well. In fact, it was not until about 200,000 years ago that a new and more efficient industry developed.

When we begin replicating stone tools in my experimental archaeology course, it is the tendency of many students simply to grab hold of a couple of random rocks, placing one in each hand. Next, they close their eyes (behind the required safety goggles), wind up with their dominant hand, say a prayer, and viciously smash down on the rock they were hoping to break. This approach involves a level of serendipity that our ancient ancestors left behind

FIGURE 5.4
Cranium of one of the more complete premodern Homo sapiens *specimens from Sima de los Huesos (the Pit of Bones) in the Atapuerca Mountains, Spain. The Sima de los Huesos hominids have been dated to 300,000 years ago and have been shown to possess many of the same anatomical features as the later, so-called classic Neandertals.*
(© Javier Trueba/Madrid Scientific Films)

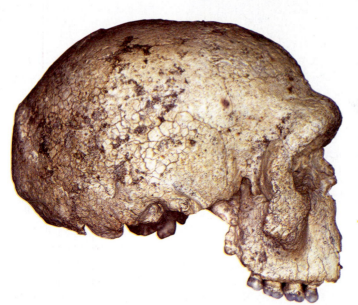

FIGURE 5.5
The Steinheim cranium from Germany, one of the most complete premodern Homo sapiens *specimens found in Europe, falls within the lower range of cranial capacity of modern humans. The form of the skull, however, is far from modern in appearance.*
(Courtesy Milford Wolpoff)

more than 2.5 million years ago. Sure, using my students' initial approach, you may produce, by sheer luck and determination, some usable, sharp-edged flakes. But this is a wasteful strategy, and much of the good stone my students worked so hard to find and transport back to the lab ends up as battered, shattered chunks of useless rock. Stone toolmaking, as my students soon learn, is not a random, but a highly controlled process, often designed to get the most sharp-edged flakes of a consistent size and shape as is possible from

TABLE 5.1
Major Premodern Homo sapiens *Fossils (Exclusive of the Neandertals)*

COUNTRY	LOCALITY	FOSSILS	AGE (YEARS)	BRAIN SIZE (CC)
Germany	Steinhem	Cranium	200,000–240,000	1,200
	Bilzingsleben	Cranial fragments	228,000	
	Ehringsdorf	Cranial fragments	225,000	
	Mauer	Mandible	<450,000	
England	Swanscombe	Occipital cranium	225,000	1,325
Greece	Petralona	Cranium	160,000–240,000	1,400
France	Arago	Cranium and fragmentary remains of 7 individuals	250,000	1,200
Spain	Atapuerca	Remains of at least 30 individuals	>300,000	1125
			>300,000	1390
			>300,000	1220
Hungary	Vértesszöllös	Occipital fragments	200,000	1,250
Zambia	Kabwe (Broken Hill)	Cranium, additional cranial and postcranial remains of several individuals	>125,000	1,280
Tanzania	Ndutu (Olduvai)	Cranium	200,000–400,000	1,100
Kenya	Ileret	Cranium	300,000	1,400
Ethiopia	Bodo	Cranium	200,000–400,000	
South Africa	Elandsfontein	Cranium		
India	Narmada	Cranium	150,000?	1,300
China	Jinniushan	Nearly complete skeleton	200,000	1,350
	Dali	Cranium	200,000	1,120
	Maba	Cranium	130,000–170,000	
	Xujiayao	Fragments of 11 individuals	100,000–125,000	
			Mean	1,261.43
			Standard Deviation	87.86

Data from Arsuaga et al. (1993); Day (1986); Pope (1992); Rightmire (1990).

a stone nodule. The **Levallois** stone-tool industry that typifies premodern *Homo sapiens* does just this.

The new industry involved a shift in emphasis from the production of core tools to the production of flake tools. Instead of sculpting a large, multi-purpose tool from a stone nodule and using only the waste flakes that fortu-

Side views

Top views

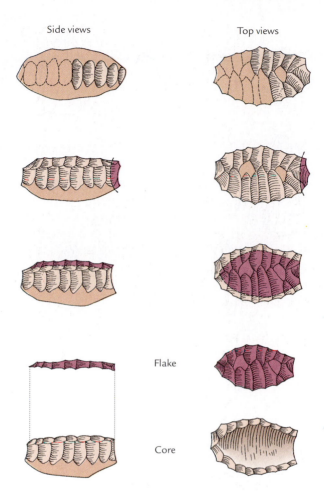

Flake

Core

FIGURE 5.6
In the toolmaking technology called Levallois, a stone core was prepared so as to produce flakes of a consistent size and form. (After J. Bordaz 1970)

itously fit a given need, emphasis now shifted to the flakes themselves, whose form and size were controlled by careful preparation of the core (Figure 5.6). The stone nodule, or core, was no longer the object to be shaped into a tool but instead became the source from which flakes of given sizes and shapes were produced. The flakes were used as blanks to be refined into tools intended for specific tasks. The Levallois technique enabled flakes of predetermined size and form to be produced (Figure 5.7).

Modern experts in stone-tool replication often perform the following remarkable feat: They take a stone nodule in hand and draw an outline directly on it in the precise shape of the flake they want to remove by striking the core with a hammerstone. A good knapper can remove a flake whose edges closely approximate the drawn outline. The key is knowing how a particular rock type breaks and preparing the rock beforehand in order to control how it will break when struck. The Levallois technique involves this kind of careful preparation of the stone core for patterned and predictable flake removal.

FIGURE 5.7
These triangular Levallois flakes from sites in Israel may have been used as stone tips on wooden spear shafts.
(Courtesy of John Shea)

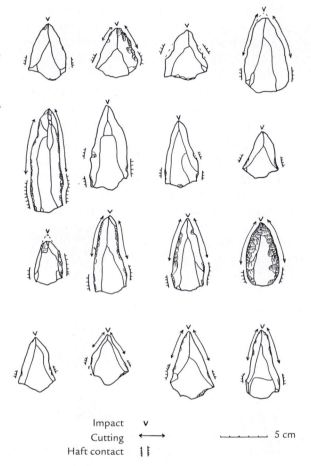

Impact	v	
Cutting	⟷	
Haft contact	∤∤	

5 cm

Preparing the core allowed premodern humans finer control of flake removal than had previously been possible. The right shape for tools with particular functions like cutting, piercing, or perforating could be ensured. The technique was also far more efficient in its use of stone than either Oldowan or Acheulean. A greater amount of sharp, usable edge is produced per unit weight of core. A replicative study by Bruce Bradley (Gamble 1986) showed that four or five consistently shaped flakes could be removed from a single Levallois core.

We often think of ancient people as having been restricted to the use of stone in the raw materials from which they made their tools. After all, we designate much of the human past as "the stone age." But this fallacy results from the fact that stone tools preserve over an enormous period of time and other raw materials simply don't last. Under extraordinary conditions, however, raw materials other than stone do hold up and we can get a glimpse of the broader repertoire of raw materials used by ancient humans to manufacture their tools and weapons. An example of this comes from a coal mine in Schöningen, Germany, where three remarkably well-preserved wooden spears were recovered (Thieme 1997). Found in a well-understood stratigraphic sequence, the spears are approximately 400,000 years old and range in size from 1.82 to 2.30 m (about 6 to 7.5 ft) in length (Figure 5.8). These artifacts are thought to be spears, in part, on the basis of gross morphology (they have sharpened tips and certainly resemble more recent spears). Beyond this, all three spears were made the same way; each was produced from a spruce sapling with the harder, denser, and heavier wood from the base of the tree used for the spear tip, which was sharpened. The butt ends of the spears taper gently, and the balance point of each spear is located about one-third the spear length from the tip, just as it is in a modern javelin. Their form seems a clear indication that the spears were meant to be thrown, and their size implies that large game animals were the target.

THE NEANDERTALS

You know that an extinct variety of human being has become a cultural icon when it's used in a national television advertising campaign by a major corporation. Perhaps you have seen the commercial. The ad begins inside what appears to be a television studio where the crew is, in fact, filming a commercial. The mellifluously voiced spokesperson, commenting on the advantages of the product he is shilling for, states: "It's so easy, even a caveman can do it." At that point, the camera swings rapidly to the crew member holding the boom mike. Though dressed normally and casually in a long-sleeved shirt and shorts, he is, rather stereotypically, a caveman, apparently a Neandertal,* hairy and unkempt, with huge brow ridges and a prognathous face. The Neandertal, clearly offended by the ad copy, throws down the mike, points an accusing finger at the actor and spits out, in perfect diction, "Not cool!" and storms out of the studio. Later in the real commercial, we see the interior of a rather chic apartment, tastefully appointed and nicely decorated, and in which, it is apparent, three Neandertals are living. One of the individuals in the apartment, though looking like a stereotypical caveman, is exhibiting a behavior that belies his appearance; he is playing a lovely tune on a grand

FIGURE 5.8
This 400,000-year-old throwing spear was one of three found at the Schöningen site in Germany. These spears are evidence of hunting on the part of their makers and represent a hint of the role organic materials—which preserve only under extraordinary circumstances—played in ancient tool technology.

---

*You will sometimes find *Neandertal* spelled *Neanderthal*. The original German spelling included an *h*, though it was (and is) pronounced as if no *h* were present. Modern German spelling has removed the *h*, so it is not used in this text. To complicate matters further, according to the rules of biological nomenclature, under most circumstances the original name given to a species cannot be changed. Because the Neandertals were originally given the species name *neanderthalensis*, with the silent *h*, we are obliged to leave the *h* when using the taxonomic name.

FIGURE 5.9

This artist's conception of a Neandertal, first published in the French magazine L'Illustration *in 1909, was not the result purely of artistic speculation. The illustrator, Kupka, produced this image under the watchful eye of paleoanthropologists who were working on Neandertal skeletons. This drawing set the precedent for many subsequent depictions of Neandertals as animal-like and bestial.*
(*Illustrated London News,* March 6, 1909. Artist: Kupka)

piano. While he is playing, the aforementioned "offensive to cavemen" ad appears on a large-screen plasma television in the apartment. When the offensive line is spoken in the commercial within the commercial, one caveman says, "What's that supposed to mean?" and a third Neandertal looks up from the laptop on which he is working and says, "That is *really* condescending."

Neandertals have always been caricatured as primitive beasts. The first artistic reconstruction of a Neandertal in a natural setting, ostensibly based on a Neandertal skeleton, appeared in 1909 in the French magazine *L'Illustration* (Figure 5.9). The image is a grotesque caricature of a hairy ape-man. Neandertals have been the archetype of "cavemen" ever since: ugly, apelike, violent, brutish, and stupid (Hager 1994). The television ad is funny precisely because it works against the stereotype, depicting Neandertals as just funny-looking "regular guys" who, in fact, are quite sensitive about being pigeonholed in this way.

In reality the Neandertals were just another group of premodern human beings. They happen to be better known because of a number of historical accidents. For example, they were abundant in Europe (Figure 5.10), and most early paleoanthropological research was undertaken there because most of the world's paleoanthropologists have come from Europe. Also, Neandertals used caves extensively, and archaeological remains are better preserved in cave settings. The Neandertals deserve an in-depth look, if only because so much is known about them by both paleoanthropologists and the general public.

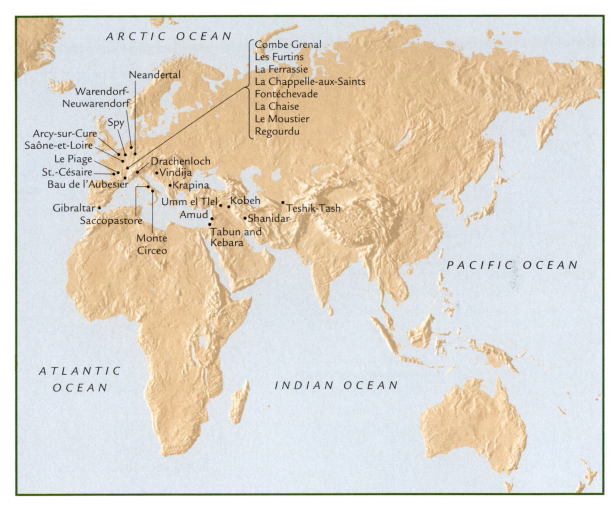

FIGURE 5.10
Fossil localities of Neandertals.

In many ways the Neandertals were similar to us. Their brain size was equal to or even larger than our own (Table 5.2). But the heads that housed these large brains were differently shaped than are those of modern human beings. Viewed from the side, the modern human head presents a globular profile. As science writer Michael Balter (2002) puts it, the human head in profile looks like a volleyball. Balter points out that, in contrast, the Neandertal cranial profile is more of a flattened circle, like a football. The configuration of the Neandertal brain was different from ours, with less in the front and more to the rear. Their skulls were marked with huge brow ridges like those of older hominid species, their faces protruded in an apelike fashion, and there was an enormous mass of bone at the rear (occipital) portion of the skull, where large muscles were attached that enabled the Neandertals to

TABLE 5.2
Major Neandertal Specimens Discussed in Chapter 5

COUNTRY	LOCALITY	FOSSILS	CRANIA	AGE (YEARS)	BRAIN SIZE (CC)
Germany	Neandertal	Skullcap			1,250
France	La Chapelle	Skeleton	"Old Man"		1,620
	Fontéchevade	Cranial fragments of several individuals		100,000	1,500
	La Ferrassie	8 skeletons		>38,000	1,680
	La Chaise	Cranium		126,000	
	St.-Césaire	Skeleton		36,000	
Belgium	Spy	Cranium			
Italy	Mt. Circeo	Cranium			
	Saccopastore	Cranium			1,350
Yugoslavia	Krapina	Cranial and postcranial fragments of >45 individuals		Isotope stage 5	1,300
Israel	Tabun	Skeleton, mandible, postcranial fragments		60,000	1,270
	Amud	Skeleton		70,000	1,740
	Kebara	Postcranial skeleton		60,000	
Iraq	Shanidar	9 partial skeletons		70,000	1,600
				Mean	1,478.89
				Standard Deviation	165.68

Data from Day (1986).

balance their large, heavy heads. They were physically far more powerful than modern human beings, and their pelvises were configured differently.

The Neandertal name comes from the Neander Valley in Germany, where, in 1856, not the first such fossil was found, but the one that first caught the attention of the scientific community (see Chapter 1; Figure 5.11). The recovered skull exhibited both modern human and primitive, nonhuman features. Though it was big, indicating a brain size at least as large as that of a modern human being, the shape was all wrong, with protruding, apelike bony ridges above the eyes, a face that projected forward like that of an ape, and a flattened profile rather than the rounded profile of a modern human skull.

Researchers of the time had difficulty explaining the Neandertal skull. (One scholar even suggested that its peculiar appearance was the result of

FIGURE 5.11
This skullcap of the specimen that gave the Neandertals their name was discovered in the Neander Valley in Germany in 1856.
(© Landschaftsverband Rheinland)

"stupendous blows" with a heavy instrument sustained during the individual's lifetime.) However, as more Neandertal specimens—as all such similar fossils were labeled—were discovered in Europe, it became clear that the Neandertal skull form represented a distinct and extinct variety of humanity.

In the attempt to assess the precise relationship between the Neandertals and modern humans, a major error crept into the discussion. In 1913 French scientist Marcellin Boule produced a reconstruction of the entire Neandertal skeleton that was rife with error (Boule and Vallois 1923). Assuming, on the basis of the form of the skull, that the Neandertals were apelike, Boule's reconstruction showed a bent-over, splayed-toe, apelike creature.

It probably didn't help that the specimen Boule chose to focus on had had a bad case of arthritis that may have caused the individual to bend over when walking. As Erik Trinkaus (1985) points out, however, Boule had two other, perfectly normal Neandertal specimens in his lab at the time, and the disease present in the one he chose to work on did not justify the apelike appearance Boule imparted. Most likely, Boule made the reconstruction apelike from the neck down because it fit his preconception of what it would have looked like based on its appearance from the neck up.

But who were the Neandertals, really? The evidence now is quite extensive that they were not club-toting caricatures; neither, as Erik Trinkaus and Pat Shipman put it, were they "simply funny-looking humans" (1993:385). They were a distinctive, now-extinct variety of premodern human beings, in some ways like us and in some ways very different (Figure 5.12). Most paleoanthropologists apply the taxonomic label *Homo sapiens neanderthalensis* to them, though some believe that they were sufficiently different from anatomically modern human beings that they are not directly ancestral to us and warrant a separate species classification, *Homo neanderthalensis*.

Their roots in Europe can now be traced back to more than 300,000 years ago, an age equivalent to that of some of the other European premoderns

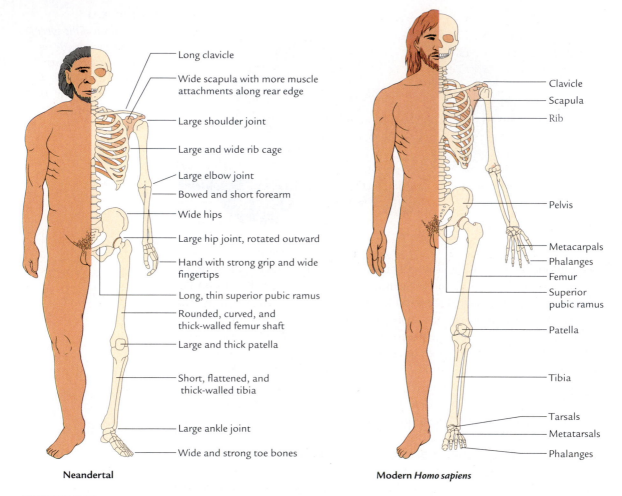

Neandertal — Long clavicle; Wide scapula with more muscle attachments along rear edge; Large shoulder joint; Large and wide rib cage; Large elbow joint; Bowed and short forearm; Wide hips; Large hip joint, rotated outward; Hand with strong grip and wide fingertips; Long, thin superior pubic ramus; Rounded, curved, and thick-walled femur shaft; Large and thick patella; Short, flattened, and thick-walled tibia; Large ankle joint; Wide and strong toe bones

Neandertal

Modern *Homo sapiens* — Clavicle; Scapula; Rib; Pelvis; Metacarpals; Phalanges; Femur; Superior pubic ramus; Patella; Tibia; Tarsals; Metatarsals; Phalanges

Modern *Homo sapiens*

FIGURE 5.12

In this comparison of the skeletons of a modern human being and a Neandertal, the so-called musculoskeletal hypertrophy of the Neandertals is readily apparent. (After Stringer and Gamble 1993)

already mentioned (Arsuaga et al. 1993; Stringer 1993). However, true, or "classic," Neandertals possessing all the typical traits (to be discussed) were confined to Europe and west Asia and date from about 130,000 to 30,000 years ago.

Morphological Evidence

Though we now recognize the Neandertals as being closely related to modern humanity, controversy persists concerning the precise place of the Neandertals in the human family: Were they our evolutionary grandparents or just distant cousins? (See Trinkaus 1983a,b, 1986, 1989; Trinkaus and Shipman 1993; Wolpoff 1989b; and especially F. Smith 1991.) On this issue, paleoanthropologists seem to suffer from the ironic disadvantage of a wealth of data:

Whereas other fossil species are represented by samples of just a few to a dozen or so, more than 400 separate Neandertal individuals have been excavated and are represented by thousands of bones. A limited database presents less to argue about than does a more substantial body of evidence.

Cranial Morphology   Neandertal brain size often surpassed that of modern human beings. Cranial capacities range from about 1,300 cc to more than 1,600 cc, with a mean of nearly 1,480 cc (see Table 5.2); modern human mean cranial capacity is about 1,450 cc. This is, in a sense, just a little misleading; larger bodies ordinarily require larger brains to control them, and Neandertals did have more massive bodies than anatomically modern human beings. When we allow for this and look at the ratio of brain to body size, modern humans do have a proportionally larger brain, but not by that much (Balter 2002).

The configuration of the Neandertal cranium—long and low in profile, with a steeply sloping forehead—is far different from the round, high profile of a modern human with its virtually vertical forehead. The Neandertal face was large, with the lower portion far forward of the eyes and brows. The Neandertal nasal bridge was wide and flaring, and Neandertals lacked the thin, pointy chin that typifies modern human beings. The robust features and flat profile of the Neandertal head can be seen even in young Neandertals, including a 3-year-old Neandertal child from Gibraltar (Dean, Stringer, and Bromage 1986), an infant possibly as young as 6 months old from Amud Cave in Israel (Ponce de Léon and Zollikofer 2001), and even a neonate estimated to have been no more than 4 months old when he or she died (Maureille 2002).

From the Neck Down: Designed for Cold   Contrary to Boule's reconstruction, below the head the Neandertal skeleton is essentially modern in appearance but with some crucial differences. One morphological pattern is consistent with a physical adaptation to cold: Neandertals were big—relatively wide with broad, squat torsos and short extremities (see Figure 5.12; Ruff et al. 1993; Trinkaus 1983a), a body form associated in modern humans with cold environments because it retains heat better than does a body with a small torso and long limbs. Anthropologist Christopher Ruff (1993) compares the Neandertal body to that of a modern Inuit (Eskimo). This adaptation probably reflects the fact that the Neandertals flourished during isotope stage 4 (see Figure 4.12), a glacial maxima in Ice Age Europe. Another likely adaptation to cold was the Neandertal's large, projecting nose, beyond the size range of the modern human nose, valuable in cold, dry climates for conserving moisture during vigorous physical activity (Trinkaus 1989). In the architecture of the nasal cavity itself, Neandertals possessed a feature not present in modern human beings: triangular peninsulas of bone projecting into the nasal opening from both sides of the nasal margin. Researchers have suggested that these bony knobs may have provided additional surface area for mucus-producing nasal membranes, which, in turn, may have aided in warming and humidifying the cold, dry air of the Neandertal environment (Menon 1997).

Science writer Michael Balter (2004a) has reported on the research of paleoanthropologist Leslie Aiello and physiologist Peter Wheeler modeling Neandertal and modern human metabolism. Based on Neandertal body shape and proportions, they found that what is called the "lower critical temperature"—the air temperature at which an organism needs to begin eating more in order to maintain its core temperature—likely was about a degree Celsius (1.8 degrees Fahrenheit) lower for Neandertals than for anatomically modern humans. Even that small differential reflects an important distinction, triggering a need for additional food among human beings whose bodies reflected a modern configuration at a temperature when Neandertals could get by with proportionally less.

From the Neck Down: Built for Strength   Not all skeletal features of the Neandertals are directly related to their adaptation to life in a cold climate. A suite of characteristics seems to reflect their enormous strength and endurance and shows them to be strikingly different from modern humans.

In about every area on the skeleton where researchers have looked, the Neandertals exhibit what is called **musculoskeletal hypertrophy.** For example, the Neandertals were generally short and stocky when compared to modern humans, and the bones of their lower legs reflect this build (Gibbons 1996a). The breadth of their scapulae (shoulder blades) and the length of their clavicles (collar bones), along with the robustness of areas of muscle attachment on those bones, are indicative of broad, powerful shoulders (Churchill and Trinkaus 1990).

The great size and robustness of their upper arm bones (Ben-Itzhak, Smith, and Bloom 1988) and the large areas for muscle attachment on their forearms (Trinkaus 1983a) are clear indications that the Neandertals had tremendous upper-body strength. Trinkaus and co-worker Christopher Ruff X-rayed and performed computerized tomography on the fossil bones of Neandertals and anatomically modern human beings (Gibbons 1996a). The upper arms of the Neandertals had more bone and reflected far greater strength than did those of anatomically modern humans who lived at the same time as the Neandertals. Also, in their ribs, vertebrae, and fingers, Neandertal bones show areas for muscle attachment far larger than what is seen in modern humans.

The bones of the Neandertal hand are indicative of an extremely powerful grip (Trinkaus and Villemeur 1991). Researcher Wesley Niewoehner (2001) conducted an intensive analysis of Neandertal hand and finger bones, comparing them in detail to those of anatomically modern human beings. He found that Neandertal hand bones denote a size and strength of musculature beyond that seen in modern people. Additionally, he found that Neandertal fingertips were extremely broad and has suggested that the unique orientation of some of the joints in the fingers and hands further contributed to a level of strength greater than that seen in modern people. Niewoehner concludes that Neandertal hand anatomy indicates that they were capable of an enormously strong "power grip" in which objects are held in the palm with the fleshy part of the base of the thumb serving as a brace. In other words, if you were to shake a Neandertal's hand, you would need to be prepared to get yours crushed.

Paleoanthropologist Fred Smith has succinctly summarized the anatomical data in this way: "Neandertals seem to represent the high-water mark for the genus *Homo* in favoring the brawn approach to environmental adaptation" (1991:225). Put another way, a spear-wielding Neandertal would have been an imposing adversary.

Fossil Evidence

Neandertal Origins   The hominids mentioned earlier in this chapter whose remains were recovered at Sima de los Huesos in the Atapuerca Mountains of northern Spain are more than twice as old as the so-called classic Neandertals. Nevertheless, the researchers characterize the morphology of the crania of the two adults and one child thus far recovered as "Neandertal-like" and as anticipating the Neandertal cranial form (Arsuaga et al. 1993:535). Preliminary analysis by paleoanthropologist Christopher Stringer (1993) indicates that of 15 typically Neandertal cranial and postcranial characteristics, the Atapuerca hominids exhibited 10, or two-thirds. They had less in common with either *Homo erectus* or modern *Homo sapiens.*

These pre-Neandertals from northern Spain shared some features in common with the other premodern *Homo sapiens* from Europe already listed. Stringer (1993) proposes that the Atapuerca specimens and most, if not all, of the other European premoderns represent a single, variable group of hominids, whose differences are the result of geographic distance and time. The excavators propose that the morphology of the Atapuerca fossils implies a gradual evolution in Europe through time.

"Classic" Neandertals   Whereas these oldest pre-Neandertal fossils can now be dated to more than 300,000 years ago, "classic" Neandertals are less than half that age. The site of La Chaise, France, has produced typical Neandertal remains dating to 126,000 years ago (Cook et al. 1982), and the site of Fontéchevade, also in France, is probably more than 100,000 years old (Gamble 1986). Because the earliest Neandertal sites are in Europe, and because their physical characteristics originated in an environment marked by the ice and cold of the Pleistocene, it seems clear this marks their origin. They spread into southwest Asia only later, retaining their unsuitable (for the Middle East) physical adaptation to a cold climate.

The great florescence of the Neandertals in Europe and southwest Asia occurred between 80,000 and 40,000 years ago. Sites that have produced important Neandertal remains that are closely similar in morphology (Figure 5.13)

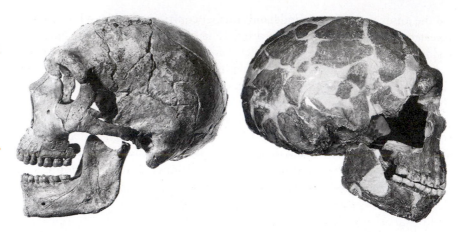

include Le Moustier, La Chapelle-aux-Saints, and La Ferrassie in France; Spy in Belgium; Saccopastore and Mt. Circeo in Italy; Krapina in Yugoslavia; Amud, Kebara, and Tabun in Israel; and Shanidar in Iraq.

NEANDERTAL CULTURE

Stone Tools

Named for the French Neandertal site of Le Moustier, the **Mousterian** tool-making tradition of the Neandertals represents not a replacement of the Levallois technique but rather a refinement. Mousterian flakes were smaller and more precisely made than the earlier Levallois flakes: The Neandertals were capable of producing flakes whose size and shape matched more precisely the form needed for a predesignated purpose. Instead of a single all-purpose tool like a handaxe or a few particular kinds of tools as in the earlier Levallois industry, dozens of different task-specific, standardized Mousterian tool types are recognized. Archaeologist François Bordes (1972) defined 63 specific Mousterian tool types for cutting, slicing, piercing, scraping, sawing, and pounding (Figure 5.14). Archaeologists disagree about how to interpret these types. Bordes broke them down into five groupings that he interpreted as representing five separate, coexisting European Neandertal cultures. Lewis Binford and Sally Binford (1966; S. Binford 1968) viewed the five groupings of tools as five different sets of **tool kits** made and used at different sites by the same, not different, groups. Archaeologist Harold Dibble (1987) considers both of these views incorrect, suggesting that Bordes's groupings represent only different stages in the use-life of the tools; that is, they look different as they wear out and are resharpened. Whatever the case, the complexity of the Neandertal stone-tool assemblage clearly is the result of the complexity of what the Neandertals were doing with those tools.

Each Mousterian flake received more precise treatment once it was removed from the core. Whereas an Acheulean handaxe may have required as many as 65 blows of a hammerstone, the production of a highly specialized Mousterian tool required an additional hundred or more blows to shape and sharpen the edge once the flake was removed from its core (Constable 1973).

Subsistence

Though we cannot provide anything like a detailed breakdown of the Neandertal diet, there is some direct, if general, evidence of what items were on the menu. For example, investigators at Kebara Cave in Israel (Bar-Yosef et al. 1992) found evidence of an abundance of gazelle and fallow deer in the Neandertal diet. Evidence of burning and cut marks on their bones, as well as on those of elephant, horse, and several other mammalian species, shows the breadth of the animal subsistence base of the cave inhabitants. An abundance of carbonized seeds of wild peas found in the fireplaces is a direct indicator that the Kebara Neandertals also ate locally available vegetable foods.

Meticulous work conducted by archaeologists Curtis Marean and Soo Yeum Kim (1998) at Kobeh Cave in Iran shows that many of the bones found are the upper and lower limbs of wild goats. These limb bones are meat-rich portions of the creatures, unlikely to have been left behind by predators for Neandertals to scavenge. Further, few of these limb bones showed animal bite marks, again supporting the notion that the animals were killed by people, not by lions or other predators. The bones do exhibit much evidence of cut marks made by stone tools precisely where one would expect them if hunters had been cutting off the best cuts of meat. In addition, there are plenty of percussion marks on the limb bones, most likely representing blows from stone hammers in the process of removing protein-rich marrow. Evidence seems clear here that Neandertals had first crack at the meat on these bones, that they were hunters of the meat, not scavengers. Marean and Kim conclude that the Neandertals were capable hunters, at least at this site.

Though a single kill may not give us a statistical measure of the contribution of hunting to the Neandertal diet, it can at least provide dramatic evidence that hunting was a part of the Neandertal behavioral repertoire. At the 50,000-year-old Umm el Tlel site in Syria, researchers found a shattered stone point still embedded in one of the cervical vertebrae (neck bones) of a wild ass (Boëda et al. 1999). Apparently, the stone had been hafted onto a shaft, likely of wood, and had been thrust so powerfully into the animal's neck that the stone weapon had shattered in two places, at its tip and base.

Archaeologist John Shea (1998) has examined stone spearpoints found at 58 cave sites in the Middle East. Some of these sites are known to have been occupied by Neandertals, others by contemporary, anatomically modern human beings. The stone tips made by the Neandertals and those by the anatomically modern humans were technologically similar and likely had been hafted onto wooden shafts by both groups of humans.

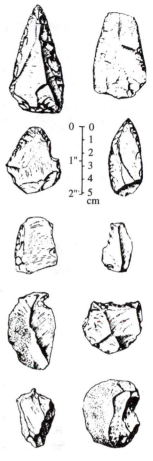

FIGURE 5.14
These typical Mousterian tools are produced by a core-and-flake technology practiced by the Neandertals. (Reprinted with permission from F. Bordes. 1961. Mousterian cultures in France. *Science* 134:803–10. Copyright © 1961 American Association for the Advancement of Science)

An isotope analysis of Neandertal bones further points to the importance of meat in their diet. The ratios of stable isotopes of carbon and nitrogen in the bones of carnivores and herbivores are demonstrably different and can be used as a relative measure of the proportion of meat and plant foods in the diet. When Neandertal bones recovered at the Vindija Cave site in Croatia were analyzed in this way, their carbon-to-nitrogen proportions were similar to those determined for contemporary carnivores, in particular, saber-toothed cats, and quite different from that same calculation performed on herbivores (Richards et al. 2000).

Based on their analysis, the researchers at this site concluded that the Neandertals behaved as "top-level carnivores," satisfying most of their dietary needs with meat (Richards et al. 2000:7663).

Archaeologist Lewis Binford has been an important researcher in the field of **ethnoarchaeology,** in which anthropologists residing with living groups of people study them from an archaeological perspective. One focus of ethnoarchaeology is to examine how behavior is transformed into what we find in the archaeological record. By investigating the data's journey from behavior to archaeological evidence, anthropologists hope that insights will be gained on how to interpret backward from archaeological evidence to behavior.

Lewis Binford's (1978) classic study among the Nunamiut, a living Inuit (Eskimo) group in Alaska, focused on patterns of hunting, butchering, preparing, and disposing of animal resources. Binford has used what he learned among the Nunamiut to interpret the archaeological record at the Neandertal site of Combe Grenal in France (Binford 1987a). In examining the remains of animals processed by the Neandertal inhabitants of the site, he recognized butchering patterns in the cut marks preserved on the bones he had seen in the fresh kills of the Nunamiut. Cut marks similar to those made by the Nunamiut on caribou jaws to extract the tongue, for example, were seen by Binford on the mandibles of horse, reindeer, and aurochs (wild cattle) at Combe Grenal. From his comparisons he concluded that the Neandertals had a similar pattern of behavior designed to extract the tasty delicacy of tongue meat.

The extent of the faunal deposits at some Neandertal sites clearly indicates that these premodern human beings were proficient at obtaining meat for their diet. That they likely were successful hunters should not be surprising considering the enormous skeletal and muscular strength that would have provided Neandertal hunters the stamina necessary to walk great distances in tracking animals—and in Pleistocene Europe, in the snow and cold. Their ability to track down animals across great distances, their great physical strength, and their sophisticated tool kit would have made them formidable hunters indeed.

Compassion

It is often said that a society can be judged by how it treats its sick or injured. Ironically, evidence shows that the Neandertals, whose intelligence is so often maligned and who are used as a symbol for brutality, may actually have been compassionate and caring. This suggestion stems from evidence of the survival of Neandertal individuals who had significant health problems or who had suffered severe trauma sometime during their lives. Some of these individuals had been in such bad shape that they probably could have survived only with the help of comrades.

For example, the excavators of the French rockshelter Bau de l'Aubesier characterize the Neandertal lower jaw they recovered there as reflecting the worst dental health of any ancient human ancestor yet found (Lebel et al. 2001). You don't need to be a dentist to see what a mess this individual's mouth was more than 169,000 years ago. Yet the person survived for some time with this condition; there is even wear on what must have been exposed tooth roots. So many teeth were missing or worn down to their nubs, it is unlikely that this individual could have eaten anything tougher than stuff the consistency of modern baby food. The researchers at this site suggest that this, effectively, is how the person survived, with his or her comrades providing only soft foods like fruits and perhaps actually pounding other foods into the consistency of a puree. The survival of this individual would likely have been impossible without the cooperation and care of his or her family and friends.

The Neandertal male who lived in Shanidar Cave in Iraq lived a rather eventful life, to judge by his skeleton, which showed several serious but healed bone factures (Solecki 1971; Trinkaus 1983b). There was evidence of severe trauma to the left side of the head: The left eye orbit had been fractured so badly that it is likely the blow blinded his eye. His right arm had been so severely smashed that the lower part had been amputated (perhaps by the blow, perhaps intentionally in an early example of surgical amputation). The right leg showed signs of disease and possible trauma.

It is clear this individual had sustained a heavy trauma at some time in his life and that rather remarkably he had survived. Such survival would have been impossible without the help and care of his companions. As anthropologist K. A. Dettwyler (1991) points out, he still could have made a significant contribution to his society, so we should not interpret his and other remains as indicating absolutely selfless acts of compassion; he was not an individual who, once healed, necessarily would have been a physical "burden" to society. Nevertheless, the survival of Shanidar I does show a level of care, at least during the healing process, that is usually associated only with modern human beings. That the Neandertals may have cared for the sick and wounded merely shows how similar they may have been to us.

Symbolic Expression

The creative or artistic impulse and the desire to use symbols in expressing that impulse might seem to be uniquely human traits. Did the Neandertals have that same desire?

Examples of grooved or perforated bones, perforated animal teeth, polished ivory, and even geometrically incised bone and ivory found at Neandertal

FIGURE 5.15

Though they are commonly viewed as unintelligent brutes, the archaeological record of the Neandertals belies this mischaracteri-zation. These artifacts from the French site of Arcy-sur-Cure are tiny works of art, carvings that may have served as items of adorn-ment made and worn by these significantly different but fully human creatures.
(© Jean-Jacques Hublin)

sites are the closest things yet found that could reflect an artistic impulse on the part of the Neandertals (Bahn 1998; Chase and Dibble 1987; Simek 1992). At one site in France, Arcy-sur-Cure, there are more than 142 such objects (Hublin et al. 1996). Some of these, especially the perforated objects, may have been used in personal ornamentation—for example, as pendants (Figure 5.15).

What might the use of such ornamentation tell us about the Neandertals? Even today, along with simply providing beautiful decoration, our jewelry may be intended to convey messages to others concerning our marital status, our economic position, our membership in a particular social group, or even our religion. It is an intriguing possibility that in wearing items of personal adornment, Neandertals may also have been conveying messages like these in a symbolic way.

Burial of the Dead

In at least one essential area, Neandertals behaved much as we do: They buried their dead. At sites such as Le Moustier, La Chapelle-aux-Saints, and La Ferrassie in France; Teshik-Tash in Uzbekistan; Shanidar in Iraq; and Amud, Tabun, and Kebara in Israel, the evidence indicates that Neandertals interred their dead in the ground, most often in an intentionally flexed position, knees drawn up toward the chest, and even with some simple items such as stone or bone implements, ochre, or unmodified animal bone (Figure 5.16; Harrold 1980).

Archaeologists Anna Belfer-Cohen and Erella Hovers (1992) surveyed burial data for the Middle Paleolithic period of the Neandertals and counted

FIGURE 5.16
This intentional burial site found at La Ferrassie in France shows the Neandertals' affinity with the modern human practice of burying their dead.
(© Musée de l'Homme, Paris. M. Lucas, photographer)

59 intentional burials. They point out that these burials make no sense as a mere hygienic way to dispose of a dead body. Why put that much time into digging a hole if a dead body can be far more unceremoniously dumped in the woods, allowing scavengers to do the work? They conclude that the Neandertals were burying their dead in recognition of the significance of death.

More than that is difficult to tell. It is impossible to know, for example, if Neandertals regarded the tightly flexed position of many of the bodies in the way some modern people have, as mimicking a fetus in the womb. Archaeologist Frank Harrold (1980:200) found that 14 of 20 bodies examined (70%)

were in this flexed position. Did the Neandertals use the fetal position to symbolize death as the end of the circle of life? Were the bodies tied into this flexed position to confine the spirit to the grave? Or was such a position simply most convenient because it minimized the size of the hole that had to be dug? Were grave goods intended for use in a perceived afterlife? Or were they remembrances for a dead friend? We simply do not know the answers.

We should not conclude that Neandertals were just like us—had funerals, memorial services, and formalized cemeteries; Lewis Binford (1987a) and Robert Gargett (1989) debunk some of the more fanciful reconstructions of Neandertal burial ceremonialism. But the questions raised by the intentional disposal of the dead practiced by the Neandertals are more important than the answers we might suggest. Clearly, Neandertals understood the significance of death and recognized it through burial. Here again, these very different human ancestors exhibit their kinship to us.

ANATOMICALLY MODERN *HOMO SAPIENS*

Between 400,000 and 150,000 years ago, the hominid family appears to have been a complex tapestry with multiple threads represented by several significantly different regional variants of premodern humans. As we have just seen, by about 300,000 years ago, one of those threads began to differentiate, eventually evolving into the classic Neandertal form by about 125,000 years ago. It now appears that around the same time that the classical Neandertals were becoming established in Europe, and maybe a little before, another one of those hominid threads also had differentiated. This thread eventually developed a morphology that we can all examine directly, simply by looking in the mirror. It is us.

An African Source

New discoveries in archaeology and paleoanthropology are always welcome, but archaeologists and paleoanthropologists also recognize that new analytical procedures applied to specimens discovered long ago may add equally to our understanding of the human past. Precisely this has occurred in the case of the Omo hominid remains (Figure 5.17). Two crania, labeled Omo I and Omo II, were discovered along the Omo River in southern Ethiopia in 1967 (Day 1969). The crania were recovered from an ancient layer (specifically Member I) of what geologists call the **Kibish Formation,** but, at the time, more precise dating was unavailable for the deposit.

Omo I was immediately recognized as anatomically modern, or nearly so, while Omo II appeared to retain a more archaic appearance (Day 1969). Though the two Omo crania possessed a different morphology, they were thought to be of similar age, having been recovered from the same geological stratum.

FIGURE 5.17
The Omo I cranium. Round in profile and lacking a major bony protuberance in the rear (the occipital region), the Omo I cranium indicates a modern morphology. Recent redating of the sediments in which Omo I was recovered indicate that, at an age of 195,000 years, it is the oldest anatomically modern human fossil remain yet discovered. (Courtesy of M. H. Day)

A recent reexamination of the stratigraphic context in which the Omo remains were found in 1967 supports the original belief that the specimens are of similar antiquity. The new analysis has determined a chronometric age for the remains. Applying the Argon/Argon procedure (Chapter 2), Member I of the Kibish Formation and, by association, the Omo crania, are now firmly dated to 195,000 years ago (McDougall, Brown, and Fleagle 2005). This represents the oldest date yet derived for a specimen, Omo I, that appears to have been anatomically modern.

In 1997 a team led by paleoanthropologist Tim White recovered the remains of three human crania representing two adults and one child at the Herto site in the Middle Awash, Ethiopia (White et al. 2003). The layer in which the crania were found has been Ar/Ar dated to 160,000 years ago (Clark et al. 2003). The best-preserved of the crania is estimated to have had a capacity of 1,450 cc, by some measures precisely the modern human mean. Along with sharing a common brain size with modern humans, in profile, the Herto crania are tall and round, to a degree virtually indistinguishable from a modern human, with a flat face quite unlike those of the Neandertals or other premoderns. To be sure, the brow ridges are fairly large by modern human standards, and overall the crania can be fairly characterized as robust. Nevertheless, the crania are very close to the modern human form. Tim White (White et al. 2003:745) and his colleagues point out that the Herto crania fall very close to the modern end of a morphological continuum between the premodern African fossils mentioned earlier in this chapter (Bodo and Kabwe, for example) and the entirely modern looking individuals from Klasies River Mouth and Qafzeh (to be discussed in more detail later). Thus, the Omo and Herto crania together show that, just like the first hominids (Chapter 3), the first

FIGURE 5.18

This nearly complete skull from Border Cave in South Africa has a suggested date of 70,000 to 80,000 B.P. *If this is correct, the Border Cave hominid is an early anatomically modern human being.* (Courtesy of Professor P. V. Tobias, University of the Witwatersrand, Johannesburg, South Africa)

members of the genus *Homo* (Chapter 3), the first *Homo erectus* specimens (Chapter 4), and the earliest representatives of the premodern humans (this chapter), the earliest morphologically modern human beings have been found in Africa.

Following this, the paleoanthropological record in Africa shows the shift to the entirely modern form known as **anatomically modern *Homo sapiens.*** The Border Cave site, for example, produced the remains of four hominids from different layers in the cave deposit: a complete mandible, a partial mandible, a fragmentary infant skeleton, and a fairly complete cranium (Figure 5.18). The cranium looks quite modern (Rightmire 1979b): It has a modern cranial capacity and no appreciable brow ridges; it is round in profile; and the face is flat (Beaumont, de Villiers, and Vogel 1978; Bräuer 1984). Electron spin resonance (ESR) dates on animal teeth found in association with the hominid remains indicate that the cranium and partial mandible are probably more than 70,000–80,000 and less than 90,000 years old; the complete mandible is 50,000–65,000 years old; and the infant skeleton is 70,000–80,000 years old (Grün, Beaumont, and Stringer 1990). Unfortunately, the cranium was not excavated professionally, so precisely where it came from in the cave is not certain and therefore the date may not apply.

At Klasies River Mouth (KRM; see Figure 5.30), the hominid material can be assigned more confidently to a stratigraphic layer and therefore to a date; but the bones are more broken up and, as a result, more difficult to assign to a particular taxonomic category. The site itself was meticulously exca-

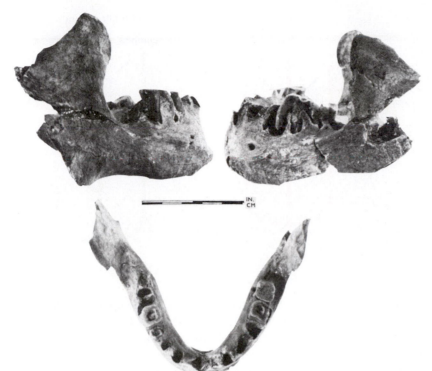

FIGURE 5.19
This mandible from Klasies River Mouth, though fragmentary, is rather lightly built and therefore relatively modern in appearance. The hominids found at this site are firmly dated to around 90,000 years ago. (From *The Middle Stone Age at Klasies River Mouth, South Africa*, by Ronald Singer and John Wymer, University of Chicago Press, 1982)

vated in 1966–68 and produced thousands of artifacts and several fragmentary human remains (Figure 5.19; Singer and Wymer 1982). The bones, including several lower jaws and some cranial fragments, were analyzed by their excavators as well as by paleoanthropologist Philip Rightmire (1984). They agreed that the Klasies River Mouth fossils were essentially modern in appearance. A modern human chin was clearly apparent in at least one of the mandibles, and the bits of cranial bones, though large and robust by modern standards, nevertheless looked more modern than premodern. For example, there is no evidence of a brow ridge. The hominid remains were firmly dated to nearly 100,000 years ago by reference to stratigraphy.

Along with their skeletal remains, some of these ancient, anatomically modern people also left a short path of footprints that, like the Laetoli trail discussed in Chapter 3, has luckily been preserved. Dating to about 117,000 years ago, the trail, found in South Africa, was originally made in soft sand that hardened to rock over the millennia (Bower 1997a). Not unexpectedly, the footprints reflect an anatomy and pattern of walking that is indistinguishable from that of a modern human being.

Research has served to confirm both the identification of the hominid material at KRM as modern and the great antiquity of the site. Fragments of two upper jaws, some individual teeth, and a broken lower arm bone (ulna)

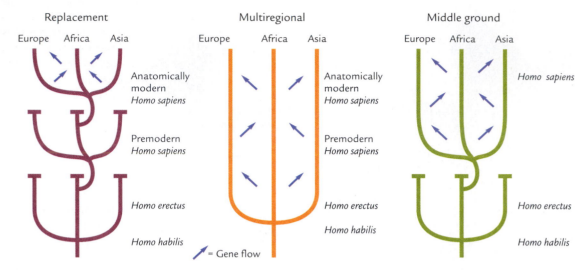

FIGURE 5.20
Schematic depiction of replacement, multiregional, and middle ground models of the evolution of anatomically modern Homo sapiens.

were recovered in 1984–89. Detailed analyses of the upper jaws indicate that they are quite modern (Bräuer, Deacon, and Zipfel 1992). Additional analyses of these newer finds and the original discoveries at KRM provide further confirmation of the modern aspects of the material (Deacon and Shuurman 1992; Rightmire 1991a). Finally, ESR dating of animal teeth found in the same layer as the hominid fossils places the age of the specimens at about 90,000 years (Grün, Shackleton, and Deacon 1990).

EXPLAINING THE EVOLUTION OF US

Clearly, there were several geographic variants of premodern *Homo sapiens* in antiquity, but there is only one fundamental version of human being in the present. How did that happen? How did we avoid the hypothetical scenario (some might call it a nightmare) presented at the beginning of this chapter with multiple versions of human beings in the present, each type possessed of different aptitudes, levels of intelligence, and abilities? In other words, how did a situation characterized in antiquity by the jumble of premodern human types found in Africa, Asia, and Europe and discussed in this chapter become the modern condition of one variety of human being?

There are fundamentally two scenarios that have been proposed to explain the evolution of anatomically modern human beings: the "replacement" and the "multiregional" models (Figure 5.20). Certainly, though there are a fair number of researchers who support the multiregional explanation and, at the same time, some who support a middle ground in this debate, it is fair to state that there is a growing consensus behind the replacement model, though the case has in no way been closed. Let's look at both of these models and assess the data that have been marshaled in their support.

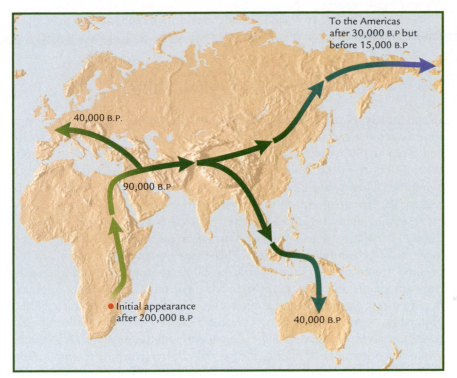

FIGURE 5.21
The geography of the evolution of modern humans implied by the replacement model.

THE REPLACEMENT MODEL

In the **replacement model,** whose chief proponent is British paleoanthropologist Christopher B. Stringer (1990, 1992a,b, 1994; Stringer and Andrews 1988), nearly all of the fossils of premodern humans described in this chapter (at least those from Europe and Asia) represent extinct forms of human beings that contributed very little to the evolution of modern humanity. Instead, the evolution of anatomically modern human beings is considered to have occurred just once, in one place—Africa—and fairly recently, between 100,000 and 200,000 years ago.

In this view, the first anatomically modern human beings spread out from their African homeland, first into southwest Asia and then east to the rest of Asia and north and west to Europe (Figure 5.21). There, these African-originating modern humans encountered populations of premodern humans—including remnant groups of *Homo erectus.* For a time they were contemporaries, perhaps living virtually next door to each other. The anatomically modern humans possessed some fundamental advantage, as yet poorly understood, over their premodern neighbors—perhaps they were smarter and could communicate more effectively, a result of their differently configured brains. The modern-looking humans replaced premoderns wherever they came into contact. Premoderns could not successfully compete for resources with the modern humans and so became extinct, leaving no genetic endowment to modern humanity.

THE MULTIREGIONAL MODEL

In the **multiregional** (or **regional continuity**) **model,** whose champion is American paleoanthropologist Milford Wolpoff (Frayer et al. 1993; Thorne and Wolpoff 1992; Wolpoff 1989a, 1992; Wolpoff and Caspari 1997; Wolpoff, Wu, and Thorne 1984; Wolpoff et al. 1994), the evolution of modern human beings was a geographically broad process, not an event restricted to a single region. Various geographically separated groups of premodern humans—representing many regions—together evolved toward the modern form. Enough contact between groups in Africa, Europe, and Asia was maintained to allow for **gene flow** among them. This gene flow was sufficient to keep the premoderns as a single, variable species. Through migration and intermarriage among the different groups, new, advantageous modern traits, originating in various places and among different archaic groups, rippled through the population of premodern humans (Wolpoff et al. 1994:178). Together and simultaneously, not separately and independently, all these groups evolved into the modern form while maintaining some relatively minor regional traits traceable to their premodern ancestors. Gene flow among groups was not so great as to wipe out such local, regional, or "racial" characteristics. So *Homo erectus* and premodern *Homo sapiens* in east Asia evolved into the modern people of Asia. In this view, the Neandertals of Europe and west Asia evolved into modern Europeans and west Asians and the premodern humans of Africa evolved into the modern people of Africa. All groups remained part of the human species, yet all maintained their own unique physical features.

A MIDDLE GROUND

The replacement and multiregional views have been tempered by scholars searching for a middle ground in this debate. This approach is sometimes labeled "weak replacement" because it still requires some level of replacement, of genes if not entire populations. Günter Bräuer (1992), for example, agrees with Stringer that Africa was the source of modern humanity at a fairly late date but does not accept the notion of complete replacement. He believes that as the first anatomically modern human beings spread from Africa, they did not simply replace the premoderns they encountered; instead, they mated with them, producing hybrid populations that, ultimately, were pulled along to modernity. Also falling somewhere in between is paleoanthropologist Fred Smith (1991, 1992), who holds that modern human traits developed in a single population (maybe Africa, maybe someplace else) and then spread primarily through gene flow (as opposed to migration) into premodern groups.

Biologist Alan Templeton (2002) expresses an opinion similar to Fred Smith's, seeing major traits that characterize modern human skeletal anatomy as having originated in Africa and then having spread by a population movement from there to Europe and Asia more than 90,000 years ago. However, Templeton also views anatomical traits that characterize earlier, local premodern populations in Europe and Asia as surviving even after the spread of the African moderns. He interprets this fact as supporting the hypothesis that the early African modern migrants mated with, rather than replaced, local human groups when they encountered them.

Because there is so much debate on the issue of the evolution of modern human beings, this "Chronicle" must end here. Because virtually all data are interpreted differently depending on which model is being used, the evidence for both models will be presented in "Issues and Debates." As yet there are no definitive answers to the questions to be raised. The issues are complex and the debate is unresolved, which makes this part of the human story both exasperating and exciting.

REPLACEMENT OR CONTINUITY?

ISSUES AND DEBATES

As both Christopher Stringer and Milford Wolpoff agree, the competing views of modern human evolution must be tested deductively with data. Here we will lay out the predictions of the replacement, multiregional, and middle ground models—those things we expect to find in the fossil and genetic records if one or the other hypothesis is correct—and then examine the record to see how well it matches those predictions. The predictions are taken largely from Stringer and Andrews (1988), Wolpoff (1992), and Wolpoff et al. (1994).

What We Would Expect on the Basis of the Replacement Model

If the replacement model is correct—if early anatomically modern humans evolved in Africa from earlier archaic roots and then spread from there, replacing indigenous hominids in Europe and Asia—then the fossil record should show the following:

1. The oldest anatomically modern human fossils should be found in Africa and nowhere else.
2. There should be anatomical continuity only in Africa. That is to say, fossil forms intermediate between premoderns and moderns should be found only in Africa.
3. Outside of Africa, the emigrant moderns should be contemporaries of indigenous premoderns until the nonmodern humans become extinct.
4. The first anatomically modern humans in Europe and Asia should look like the early anatomically modern humans in Africa because that is where they originated. The earliest modern-looking humans in Europe

and Asia should exhibit no specific skeletal continuities with the pre-modern human fossils of their regions.

5. Anatomically modern humans should be genetically distinct from pre-moderns. Modern human DNA should be quite similar to DNA recovered from the bones of ancient, anatomically modern-looking humans. DNA recovered from the bones of premodern humans should be significantly different from that of their anatomically modern-looking contemporaries as well as from the DNA of living people.

6. The archaeological record is expected to show the sudden appearance of nonlocal, African-originating artifact types in Europe and Asia as the early anatomically modern African population spread from its place of origin.

What We Would Expect on the Basis of the Multiregional Model

If the multiregional hypothesis is to be upheld, then the following, quite different predictions can be made about the fossil record:

1. Early versions of anatomically modern *Homo sapiens* should be found in many different regions. No one region should have anatomically modern fossils substantially older than any other region.

2. Intermediate forms—advanced premoderns—should be found in each region because evolution from premodern to modern occurred everywhere.

3. Because local premoderns are everywhere ancestral to modern humans in their regions, there should be no or very little chronological overlap between the premodern and modern forms.

4. Local skeletal traits should show continuity between premodern and modern humans because in each region local premoderns evolved into modern people.

5. DNA recovered from the bones of ancient, archaic-looking human beings should be as similar to the DNA of modern humans as is the DNA recovered from the bones of ancient, modern-looking individuals.

6. The archaeological record should show a continuity in regional artifact types. As local premodern humans evolved physically into modern humans, their archaic toolmaking traditions evolved into more sophisticated modern traditions.

What We Would Expect on the Basis of the Middle Ground

If the middle ground is to be upheld, then the following predictions can be made about the fossil record:

1. The oldest anatomically modern human fossils should be found in Africa and nowhere else.

2. Outside of Africa, at least in some areas, there should be chronological overlap between indigenous premodern humans and emigrant moderns.

3. Premodern morphology will grade into modern forms everywhere that hybridization occurred as modern genes slowly replaced premodern genes.

4. There should be continuity of regional physical traits seen in local premodern groups wherever they mated with bearers of modern human genes. Local characteristics seen in modern human regional populations can be traced back to the premodern of these regions.

5. DNA recovered from the bones of premoderns should show a gradual transformation into the modern form. DNA recovered from older premodern bones found outside of Africa should be different from that of modern human beings, but more recent premodern bones found outside of Africa should have increasingly modern DNA to reflect the fact that archaic-looking Europeans and Asians mated with modern-looking Africans.

6. Cultural remains in Europe and Asia should show a gradual shift to more modern forms as local people adopted the more sophisticated technologies of anatomically modern *Homo sapiens*.

Testing the Implications of Replacement and Continuity

1. Are the oldest anatomically modern human fossils found in Africa and nowhere else, or are early versions of anatomically modern Homo sapiens *found in many different regions?*

The oldest anatomically modern human skeletal remains yet found are those mentioned earlier in this chapter, found at the Omo site in Ethiopia (Figure 5.22). At an age of 195,000 years, the Omo remains are older, by far, than any anatomically modern or near-modern remains found anywhere in Asia or Europe. The earliest modern human remains in east Asia (specifically, in China) date to about 100,000 years ago at the Liujiang site (Pope 1992). The oldest anatomically modern humans in southwest Asia (in Israel) date to between 90,000 and 100,000 years ago at the sites of Skhul and Qafzeh (Stringer 1988; Stringer et al. 1989). The oldest modern human remains found in Europe are younger still, dating to no more than 43,000 years ago at the Bacho Kiro site in Bulgaria (Churchill and Smith 2000). Currently, the early modern human fossil record supports the prediction derived from the replacement model; the older modern humans appear in Africa before they show up anywhere else.

2. Is there continuity only in Africa, or are forms intermediate between premodern and modern humans found in many regions?

Supporters of the replacement model maintain that Africa is the only continent that has produced fossils intermediate in form between its earliest modern specimens and older premodern humans. Multiregionalists and middle ground advocates see intermediate forms in other places.

As mentioned previously in this chapter, African fossils like Bodo (600,000 years ago), Ileret (300,000 years ago), Ndutu (more than 200,000

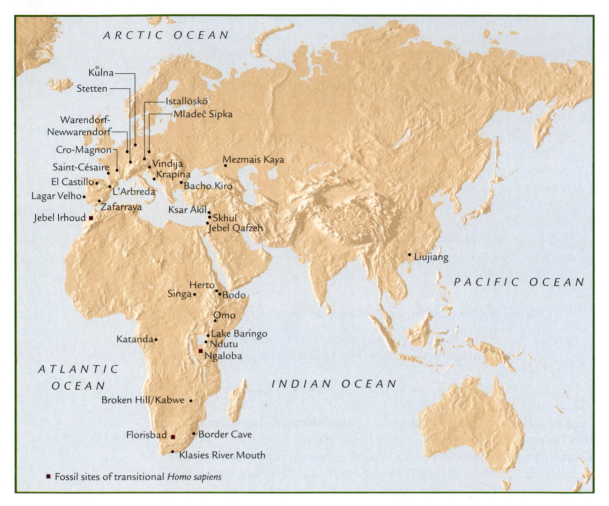

ARCTIC OCEAN

Kůlna
Stetten
Istallöskö
Mladeč Sipka
Warendorf-
Newwarendorf
Cro-Magnon
Saint-Césaire
Vindija
Krapina
Mezmais Kaya
El Castillo
Bacho Kiro
Lagar Velho
L'Arbreda
Zafarraya
Ksar Akil
Jebel Irhoud
Skhul
Jebel Qafzeh

Liujiang

PACIFIC OCEAN

Herto
Singa
Bodo
Omo
Lake Baringo
Katanda
Ndutu
Ngaloba

ATLANTIC
OCEAN

INDIAN OCEAN

Broken Hill/Kabwe

Florisbad
Border Cave
Klasies River Mouth

■ Fossil sites of transitional *Homo sapiens*

FIGURE 5.22

Fossil localities of early anatomically modern Homo sapiens *and late, near-modern transitional forms.*

years ago), and Kabwe possess a suite of archaic features, while the Omo I remains in Ethiopia, at 195,000 years ago, look modern or very nearly so. The replacement hypothesis predicts that there should be forms intermediate between the premodern and modern humans in one place, Africa, and that prediction seems to be borne out by the evidence. The Florisbad (South Africa), Ngaloba (Laetoli hominid 18, in Tanzania), and Jebel Irhoud (Morocco; Figure 5.23) crania all appear to represent forms transitional between the premoderns listed above and the modern-looking Omo remains. Together this evidence shows that African fossils reflect a continuum of human forms from archaic to modern.

Some researchers interpret the fossil remains from several eastern European sites—including Kůlna, Sipka, and especially the bones recovered at Vindija—as transitional forms between one variety of premodern humans, the Neandertals, and anatomically modern Europeans (F. Smith 1994). These

FIGURE 5.23

This cranium from Jebel Irhoud in north Africa has been interpreted as representing a form intermediate between premodern and modern Homo sapiens. *Some researchers contend that such intermediate forms are found only in Africa, lending support to the replacement model (see Figure 5.20).* (© Musée de l'Homme, Paris)

crania are lighter and less robust than those of classic Neandertals. If these Neandertals represent such a transition, multiregionalism might be supported; the evolution of modern people from premoderns would have taken place in both Africa and Europe.

Though recognizing the less robust form of these fossils, many researchers dispute both of these interpretations. Certainly not all Neandertal skulls must fit the stereotype; some are more robust, some less so without implying an evolution toward modern humans. As paleoanthropologist Ian Tattersall (1998:158) states, these supposedly transitional specimens are still "distinctively Neandertal." Although brow ridges in some populations like that of Vindija are smaller, the crania more rounded, and the face less prognathous, the bones below the head retain the typical suite of robust Neandertal features. Though we must recognize some degree of variability within the Neandertals, it is difficult to conclude that these eastern European Neandertals represent an overall transition to the modern form. These specimens do not supply good evidence for the multiregional model. Truly transitional forms from premodern to modern *Homo sapiens* are, as yet, confined to Africa.

An interesting alternative hypothesis has been suggested by paleoanthropologist Günter Bräuer (1992) to explain the less robust morphology of fossils at sites like Vindija. He suggests that these less robust forms represent hybrids between local Neandertals and immigrant (from southwest Asia) anatomically modern humans.

This fascinating possibility of intermating between Neandertals and anatomically modern humans who lived in the same regions at the same time has also been suggested by the excavators of a 24,500-year-old fossil from the

Lagar Velho site near Lisbon, Portugal (Duarte et al. 1999; Zilhão and Trinkaus 2003). The bones are those of a 4½-year-old boy. The cranium was crushed, but the mandible was only somewhat damaged and looks like the lower jaw of a modern human child, much as one might expect for the given date. Furthermore, the boy had been carefully buried in a manner typical of modern human beings in Spain and Portugal dating from the period around 25,000 years ago. However, a careful analysis of the postcranial skeleton revealed that the young boy had an extremely robust body, with a wide, barrel chest and proportionally short arms and legs. In other words, the bodily proportions, along with some detailed skeletal characteristics, of the Velho child were Neandertal-like. The paleoanthorpologists who analyzed the remains describe the skeleton as a "morphological mosaic" and believe that the mixture of modern and Neandertal traits seen in the child's skeleton are the result of a long-term pattern of interbreeding between contemporary anatomically modern human beings and Neandertals (Duarte et al. 1999:7608).

Although this is a fascinating possibility—and science writers had great fun with the "make love, not war" angle between Neandertals and modern-looking human beings—other paleoanthropologists remain unconvinced that the young boy's remains prove interbreeding at all, much less a pattern of it. The boy may simply have been a stout, modern human. Researchers Ian Tattersall and Jeffrey Schwartz (1999:7118) are particularly skeptical that the single, somewhat broken up skeleton suggests "a population that had been hybridizing for many centuries." So it is unclear at this point how significant the Velho child is in this debate. The analysis of his skeleton doesn't seem to lend support to the multiregional model, and, at best, it may indicate that while the modern morphology was replacing the premodern one in Europe, the replacers had time for dalliances with the replaced, a situation that seems to conform to the weak replacement model.

3. Were premodern and anatomically modern human beings contemporaries?
The replacement and middle ground models predict that outside of Africa, fossil evidence will show the contemporaneity of locally evolved premodern humans and immigrant groups of African moderns; southwest Asia is pointed to as verification. There, in caves that are sometimes in close proximity to each other, the remains of Neandertals and anatomically modern humans have been found. Dating techniques place the premodern and modern humans in their respective caves during the same periods and may even indicate that the modern humans are *older* than some of the Neandertals.

For example, classic Neandertals have been excavated at Kebara Cave, as well as at the sites of Amud and Tabun (see Figure 5.13), in Israel. With their large, heavy skulls, large brow ridges, flattened occipitals, sloping foreheads, and prognathism, their form is unmistakably Neandertal. The Kebara site dates to 60,000, Amud is closer to 70,000, and Tabun has now been dated to about 100,000 years ago (McDermott et al. 1993).

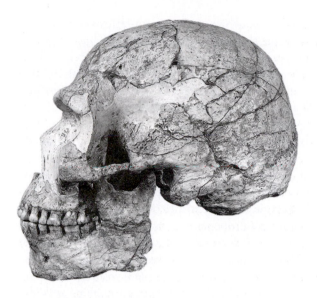

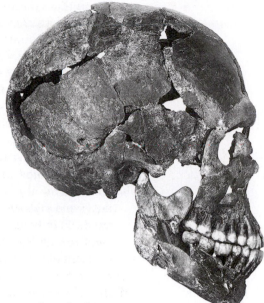

As previously mentioned, robust but otherwise rather modern-looking specimens have been excavated at the sites of Skhul and Qafzeh, also in Israel. Skhul, on Mount Carmel, is not even 100 m (300 ft) from Tabun, with its Neandertal fossils, and Qafzeh is less than 30 km (18 mi) east of those two cave sites. Kebara Cave is also close by, about 10 km (6 mi) south of Mount Carmel. It is remarkable that such different-looking, generally contemporaneous hominids have been found in such a restricted area (see Figures 5.10 and 5.22).

The 10 or so individuals represented in the fossil record at Skhul and the 20 hominids at Qafzeh are generally categorized as anatomically modern or near modern. The crania present round profiles, nearly vertical foreheads, and flatter faces than do the Neandertals, though their brow ridges, small by Neandertal standards, are quite marked when compared to those of most modern humans (Figure 5.24). A detailed comparison of 82 fossil hominids from Africa, southwest Asia, and Europe, including Neandertals as well as the Skhul and Qafzeh materials, showed that the latter were primarily anatomically modern, with certain specimens from these sites showing some similarities to Neandertals (Bräuer and Rimbach 1990:805).

The Skhul and Qafzeh sites are now judged to be broadly contemporaneous with the new date for Tabun. Thermoluminescence conducted on burned flints at Qafzeh has produced a date of 92,000 years ago (Valladas et al. 1988), ESR produced an age of more than 90,000 years (Stringer 1988), and a uranium series date further confirms this with a range of 85,000–110,000 years ago (McDermott et al. 1993). Skhul has been dated with ESR to between 81,000 years ago and 101,000 years ago (Stringer et al. 1989) and more recently by uranium series to about 80,000 years ago (McDermott et al. 1993).

FIGURE 5.24
The Skhul (left) and Qafzeh (right) skulls from Israel are quite modern in appearance and are clearly dated to the period of about 90,000 years ago. Neandertals lived in Israel at the same time, supporting the replacement models. (*Left:* © Peabody Museum, Harvard University. Photo by Hillel Burger; *right:* Laboratory of Vertebrate and Human Paleontology, Paris, Bernard Vandermeersch)

In the replacement scenario, southwest Asian populations of anatomically modern *Homo sapiens,* like those at Skhul and Qafzeh, had migrated from Africa about 100,000 years ago. These migrants were descendants of modern humans who had originally evolved in Africa as much at 195,000 years ago, like those represented at the Omo site. These modern migrants into southwest Asia had moved into a region in which another, premodern kind of human being, the Neandertals, was already living. The widely different appearance of the moderns and Neandertals, along with their contemporaneity and geographic overlap is congruent with the replacement hypothesis.

As shown earlier in this chapter, the oldest Neandertal-like fossils are found in Europe and date to 300,000 years ago. The oldest of the classic Neandertals are also found in Europe and date to 125,000 years ago. The last of the Neandertals again are found in Europe with remains at Saint-Césaire (Figure 5.25) in France dating to 36,000 years ago (Mercier et al. 1991; Stringer and Grün 1991), Zafarraya in Spain dating to 33,400 years ago (Rose 1995), and the latest of the Vindija remains in Croatia dating to 28,000 years ago (F. Smith et al. 1999). The oldest of the anatomically modern human remains are older than these youngest Neandertals; as mentioned earlier, the Bacho Kiro remains from Bulgaria are as much as 43,000 years old (Churchill and Smith 2000). This temporal overlap between Neandertals and anatomically modern humans in Europe is congruent with the replacement hypothesis.

4. Is there a break in the form of premodern and modern human fossils outside of Africa, or do local skeletal traits show continuity between premodern and modern humans in each region?

If anatomically modern humans evolved in Africa and spread from there, replacing premoderns in all regions, locally derived, region-specific anatomical traits should have disappeared in each area as the indigenous premoderns became extinct. The modern in-migrants in Europe and Asia should have looked like the earliest anatomically modern Africans and not at all like the local premoderns they were replacing. Local traits presently seen among modern people (skeletal features that are the equivalent of "racial" characteristics) would have evolved only very recently, after the replacement occurred.

If, instead, there was regional continuity in Africa, Europe, and Asia, then region-specific traits of the skeleton might be expected to be maintained within populations evolving from premodern to modern. In other words, skeletal traits specific to a particular region would show continuity from *Homo erectus* through premodern *Homo sapiens,* through the earliest anatomically modern humans, right up to the population of human beings living in an area today (at least among those individuals who can trace their ancestry back deeply in the area).

Remember our discussion of Neandertal skeletal anatomy earlier in this chapter. There we said that the Neandertals were built for strength and for cold, with broad chests and short, thick arms and legs. The oldest skeletons of anatomically modern human beings found in Europe date to between 25,000

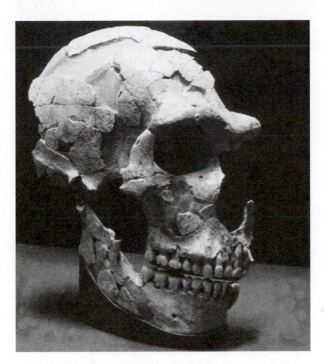

FIGURE 5.25
This Neandertal skull from Saint-Césaire, France, is among the more recent of the Neandertal specimens, dating to about 36,000 years ago, which is long after anatomically modern Homo sapiens *evolved, making problematic any hypothesis that modern humans evolved from the Neandertals.* (Transparency # A11, courtesy of Department of Library Services, American Museum of Natural History)

and 40,000 years ago and don't look anything like this. Tall and thin, with long extremities, they looked, as Christopher Stringer has said, "as if they walked straight out of Africa" (as quoted in Ross 1991:47).

5. Are anatomically modern humans genetically distinct from premoderns? In the replacement model, modern human DNA should be quite similar to DNA recovered from the bones of ancient, anatomically modern humans. DNA recovered from the bones of premodern humans should be significantly different from that of contemporary, anatomically modern humans, as well as from the DNA of living people.

Nuclear DNA, the so-called double helix of two parallel, connected strands of chemicals, looking much like a twisted ladder, serves as the blueprint for an individual and a species and is present in most cells of an organism. Most cells also contain another kind of DNA called **mitochondrial DNA (mtDNA).** Mitochondria (*sing.,* mitochondrion) are usually referred to as the cells' energy factories.

In tracking the genetic heritage of a species, biologists tend to rely on mtDNA for a number of reasons. To begin with, mitochondrial DNA consists of a much shorter set of genetic instructions than does nuclear DNA. For example, instead of the human nuclear DNA's double helix, coding for more than 100,000 genes, human mitochondrial DNA comes in small, two-strand rings and codes for only 37 genes that control the mitochondrion (Wilson and Cann 1992).

Furthermore, although the DNA contained within the mitochondria of an organism's cells is unique to that individual and species, it plays little if any role in coding for the characteristics of the individual. The appearance of the mtDNA within a population is largely the result of accumulated accidents that otherwise have little impact. Observation indicates that mutations (changes) or errors build up at a relatively rapid and constant rate in the mtDNA when compared to nuclear DNA. MtDNA can be viewed, therefore, as a clock, whereby the number of mutations from a previous state is primarily a function of time. This aspect of mitochondrial DNA has enabled its use in the investigation of the nature and timing of the evolution of modern human beings.

Another advantage of using mtDNA in assessing evolutionary connections rests in the fact that it is inherited only through the female line. As a result, it is less complicated to use as an evolutionary marker. You do not get mixing of the mtDNA of two different individuals in each generation, so it is much easier to trace back through generations than is ever-recombining nuclear DNA. MtDNA evolutionary analysis is analogous to genealogically tracing a family name that remains pretty much the same as far back as you go, with only random, regular changes in the spelling occurring through time. Using nuclear DNA for the same purpose would be like trying to trace back a lineage of people where in each generation the family name changes to a random combination of letters in the mother's and father's names.

Researchers were very lucky, indeed, when they were able to recover mitochondrial DNA from one of the bones found at the site that provided the Neandertal name (Krings et al. 1997). When the small, preserved mtDNA segment (technically, 379 base pairs of a total mtDNA length of 16,500 base pairs in humans) was compared to that same segment in modern human mtDNA, a large number of differences were found. When you compare this same section of mtDNA between any two modern human beings, you will find a mean of about 8 differences. The Neandertal mtDNA exhibited more than three times the number of differences (27) when compared to the same mtDNA segment in a modern human being.

Another sample of Neandertal mtDNA—this time, a 345-base-pair segment—was recovered from a 29,000-year-old bone taken from the skeleton of an infant found at Mezmaiskaya Cave in the northern Caucasus in Russia (Ovchinnikov et al. 2000). This second sample allows us to again compare Neandertal to modern mtDNA and also to compare mtDNA within the Neandertals. The Russian Neandertal mtDNA exhibited 22 differences when compared to the same mtDNA segment in modern human beings. When the two Neandertal mtDNA segments were compared to each other, about 12 differences were seen.

DNA from the nucleus of cells has also been recovered from two Neandertal bones, one in Germany (the Warendorf-Neuwarendorf site) and one in Croatia (the Krapina site) (Scholz et al. 2000), as well as from the bone of an ancient, anatomically modern human being found in the Stetten site, in Germany. When researchers analyzed this material, it was clear that the DNA of ancient, anatomically modern human beings was much more similar to the DNA of living people than was the Neandertal DNA.

We shed our DNA, including our mtDNA, all of the time, leaving our distinct genetic fingerprint on everything we have ever touched, including on ancient bones handled long before it was realized that such unprotected treatment might contaminate them. In a work-around, researchers analyzed a sample of Neandertal and early modern human bones looking not for modern human mtDNA, which they expected to find on all of them, at least in part as the result of modern contamination, but for mtDNA that matched the distinctly Neandertal fingerprint recognized from the research just described (Serre et al. 2004). The results are compelling; all of the Neandertal bones in the sample from which mtDNA was recoverable produced mtDNA that was a good match for the material previously recovered from Neandertal bones. None of the anatomically modern human bones produced mtDNA that matched the material found in the Neandertal bones. In sum, mtDNA in Neandertals on the one hand and in their contemporary early modern humans on the other is significantly different and distinct. This appears to support the assertion that these two kinds of human beings were, in fact, different and distinct. This conclusion, again, lends support to the replacement hypothesis.

6. Does the archaeological record show the sudden appearance of nonlocal, African-originating artifact types in Europe and Asia as the early anatomically modern African population spread out from its place of origin, or is there continuity in regional artifact types as local premodern humans evolved into modern ones?

Assessing the sophistication of a stone-tool technology can be a bit subjective. It may be difficult to state, categorically, that one technology is "more advanced" or "more sophisticated" than another. Ordinarily, a technology that (1) requires a greater number of steps and more forethought in preparing a stone core, (2) results in greater efficiency (less wasted stone), and (3) produces tools that simply do the job better because they are sharper or more aerodynamic is considered to be more advanced or sophisticated.

A technology that produces **blade** tools fits these criteria for increased sophistication. The production of long, thin, sharp blades of a consistent size and shape ordinarily requires more preparation of the stone core from which the blades are struck, results in a more efficient use of the stone, and produces proportionally more cutting edge from the same amount of stone than in the Mousterian technology. And, in fact, when we look to Africa, we see evidence of the production of blade tools long before they turn up in Europe or Asia.

The oldest stone tools indicating a blade technology have been found in Kenya by paleoanthropologist Sally McBrearty (Gutin 1995). She found these stone blades at a site near Lake Baringo, and they show careful core preparation that resulted in consistently sized and shaped stone blades (Figure 5.26). These tools predate the appearance of anatomically modern human beings in Africa; they are about 240,000 years old. There also is evidence for blade tools

FIGURE 5.26

Blade tools represent a technological advance over flake tools, reflecting a more efficient use of lithic raw materials, producing more usable edge from a stone core. The oldest evidence of a blade technology—the pictured tools are examples—has been found at Lake Baringo in Kenya, dating to 240,000 years ago. (Courtesy Sally McBrearty)

at Klasies River Mouth (Figure 5.27; see this chapter's "Case Study Close-Up"). The tools are quite consistent in size and shape. KRM dates to about 90,000 years ago.

Evidence—not in stone, but in bone—for increased technological complexity associated with early anatomically modern human beings in Africa has been found at three sites at Katanda in eastern Zaire. Dating to about 90,000 years ago, the lithics recovered at these sites reflect a fairly typical Middle Stone Age assemblage and, as such, are similar to European Mousterian industries (Yellen et al. 1995). The excavators of these sites also recovered very sophisticated bone tools, including barbed and unbarbed points and a dagger-shaped object of unknown function (Figure 5.28). They suggest that the technological sophistication of these bone tools indicates "modern behavioral capabilities" of the early anatomically modern inhabitants of Africa, distinct from the capabilities of contemporaneous premodern humans of Europe (Yellen et al. 1995:555). This evidence is the first clear artifactual support for the notion that human beings possessing a modern level of intelligence evolved in Africa first, as much as 90,000 years ago.

These Middle Stone Age African blade and bone tools do not appear to have accompanied their makers on their migration to Asia. In fact, there is no archaeological evidence in the form of an alien or invasive tool technology in Asia that might mark the arrival of immigrant, anatomically modern Africans. The earliest modern-looking hominids in southwest and east Asia practiced the same stone-toolmaking tradition as the local, indigenous archaic-looking people. The stone-tool assemblages from Skhul and Qafzeh, with their modern-looking fossils, and nearby Tabun, with its contemporary, archaic-looking fossils, exhibit the same stone-tool tradition: The people at these sites were all making Mousterian tools (Shea 1990; Thorne and Wolpoff 1992).

The situation in Europe, on the other hand, is quite different. Though African blades are not found at the earliest modern human sites, there is,

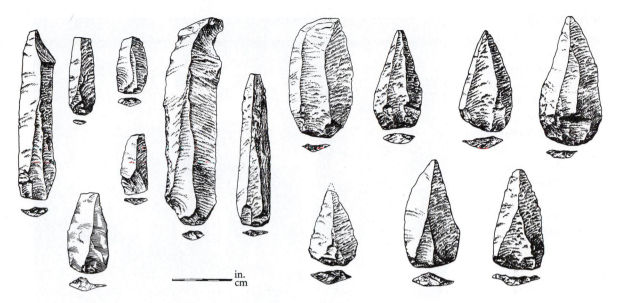

FIGURE 5.27
These long blade tools dating to close to 90,000 years ago from the site of Klasies River Mouth, South Africa, were associated with fragmentary remains of anatomically modern human beings (see Figure 5.19).
(From *The Middle Stone Age at Klasies River Mouth, South Africa,* by Ronald Singer and John Wymer, University of Chicago Press, 1982)

as archaeologist Francis Harrold (1992) points out, a close correspondence between different-looking hominids and tool traditions on that continent: Neandertals in Europe are almost always associated with tools of the Mousterian tradition, while the first anatomically modern humans in Europe are associated with the more sophisticated Aurignacian tradition (to be described in detail in Chapter 6).

The earliest sites exhibiting the Aurignacian tradition in Europe include L'Arbreda Cave in eastern Spain, El Castillo Cave in northern Spain, Istallöskö in Hungary, and Bacho Kiro Cave in Bulgaria (Straus 1989). As mentioned previously, the Spanish sites date to about 38,000 years ago (Bischoff et al. 1989; Valdes and Bischoff 1989); the Hungarian and Bulgarian sites date to as much as 43,000 years ago. Archaeologist James Bischoff and his colleagues, who analyzed the Spanish sites, characterize the appearance of Aurignacian tools in the Spanish caves, as well as the other European sites mentioned, as "abrupt" (Bischoff et al. 1989:573). The Mousterian and Aurignacian technologies are quite different, and, in the case of the Spanish sites, the raw materials used are different: The Mousterian flakes are almost all made of locally available quartz and quartzite, whereas the Aurignacian tools are almost all made of a more distantly available flint. There is no evidence there of a slow, steady transition from a Mousterian to an Aurignacian tradition, no sign of an evolution of the simpler Mousterian tradition of the Neandertals to the more sophisticated Aurignacian tradition of the first anatomically modern humans in Europe. Bischoff and his colleagues take this to support the replacement model; when a new toolmaking tradition appears abruptly in the

FIGURE 5.28

Barbed bone artifacts found in Katanda, Zaire. These sophisticated implements date to more than 90,000 years ago and may reflect the greater intelligence and technological sophistication of the first anatomically modern Homo sapiens *when compared to pre-modern members of our species. (Chapter 6).*
© Alison Brooks, George Washington University

archaeological record, with no evidence of its having evolved from an earlier way of doing things, it is often concluded that the new tradition arrived from the outside, the product of a new group's migration into the area.

Researcher Paul Mellars (2004) also points out that the dates derived for Aurignacian sites across Europe implies a wave of population expansion from east to west. In other words, the first Aurignacian sites, generally, are oldest in the Middle East, a bit more recent in eastern Europe, and successively younger as one moves to the west. This is exactly the pattern we would expect if the bearers of that technology were migrants from the Middle East, expanding their territory westward across Europe through time.

In a few cases, early Aurignacian artifacts have been found in association with anatomically modern human skeletal remains (Mellars, 2004); specifically at Ksar Akil in Lebanon (40,000 years ago), Les Rois in France (32,000–35,000 years ago), and Mladeč in the Czech Republic (the level dated to about 34,000 years ago). Neandertal remains have never been found with Aurignacian tools, and this provides additional evidence that they were culturally separate from the anatomically modern humans who entered Europe and coexisted with them for a period of time.

Soon after the blade-based Aurignacian tradition arrived in Europe along with anatomically modern people, rather interestingly the Mousterian tradition of the resident Neandertals began to change. The Neandertals began to produce tools that look more like the blades being produced by the incoming anatomically modern humans. It appears as though the native Neandertals and the anatomically modern migrants were, at least, aware of each other, and

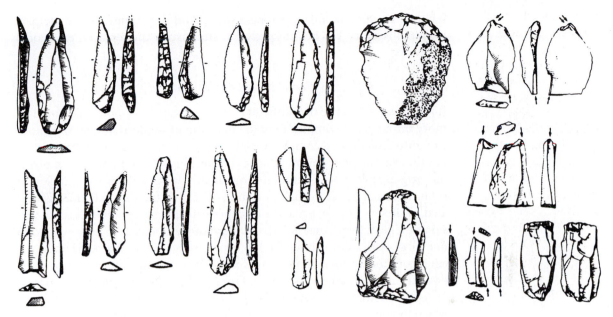

FIGURE 5.29
Tools of the Châtelperronian tradition, such as these, were found with the Saint-Césaire Neandertal. This tradition may represent a cultural blending of the Neandertal Mousterian and the anatomically modern human tradition called Aurignacian. (Adapted from Bordes and Labrot 1967)

the Neandertals appear to have been picking up some of the toolmaking practices of the newcomers.

The best known of these apparently hybridized technologies is the **Châtelperronian,** in France, seen at Neandertal sites like Saint-Césaire and Arcy-sur-Cure (Figure 5.29). This technological tradition has much in common with Mousterian and differs only in the addition of long, thin blade tools, exactly the kind of tools that characterize the Aurignacian tradition. Elsewhere in Europe the situation may have been repeated, and other "hybrid" tool traditions are suggested for Italy, Greece, and central Europe (Gibbons 2001). This suggests a fascinating scenario of contact between two fundamentally different kinds of human beings in Europe after 40,000 years ago. We cannot prove, as some researchers have suggested, that they shared genes (see the discussion earlier in this chapter), but it does appear that at least they did share ideas.

A careful analysis of the Châtelperronian blades shows that their production was somewhat different from Aurignacian blades. In other words, Neandertals had not simply watched anatomically modern humans produce blade tools and then unquestioningly copied each of the steps (Bahn 1998).

Châtelperronian is rather short-lived, dated between about 36,000 and 33,000 years ago. Châtelperronian artifacts are sometimes found in the same sites as Aurignacian but separated stratigraphically; they are sometimes even interdigitated, with Châtelperronian tools in layers sometimes above Aurignacian tools, sometimes below (and sometimes both), such as at Le Piage in France (Simek 1992). This indicates fairly clearly that they were produced by separate groups who inhabited these sites at different times. The Châtelper-ronian, therefore, can be interpreted as supporting the replacement model in Europe.

Replacement or Continuity?

It is the way of science that difficult and complex issues—and what could be more difficult and complex than the question of modern human origins—generate difficult and complex debates. There certainly is no unanimity of opinion among paleoanthropologists concerning which model best explains our origin: replacement, continuity, or something in between. Nevertheless, it is fair to conclude, following our testing of each of the six predictions generated by these hypotheses, that the evidence gathered so far supports some version of replacement. Anatomically modern humans appear to have evolved in one place, Africa, something like 195,000 years ago. From that African homeland, our modern-looking ancestors spread, likely through the Levantine corridor, settling first in the Middle East. From there, to the east, all of the vastness of Asia lay before our ancestors. To the west, Europe offered more territory in which to settle. As they spread into these new worlds, they encountered already-established, indigenous populations of hominids, human beings, to be sure, but with a nonmodern or premodern morphology. In each case, that contact resulted in the extinction of the indigenous population.

WHY WERE THE NEANDERTALS REPLACED?

The Neandertals and other premodern humans are extinct, having been re-placed by anatomically modern human beings. In the view presented in this book, the Neandertals were not the immediate ancestors of modern people but rather a side branch of human evolution, at least partially overlapping in time with anatomically modern human beings. What significant advantages did the early anatomically modern humans have over the premoderns that led to the survival of the modern humans and the extinction of the premod-erns? The European fossil record may shed light on this question.

Some evidence indicates that the Neandertals were having a rough time in Pleistocene Europe. For one thing, the Neandertals were rather short-lived as compared to even ancient anatomically modern humans. Erik Trinkaus and D. D. Thompson (1987:126) have shown that in a sample of 246 Neander-tals, 4 out of 10 died before reaching adulthood. And of those that survived childhood, less than 10% were more than 40 years old at death (1987:127). Paleoanthropologist Olga Soffer (1992:252; 1994:103–4) has shown that in her Neandertal sample of about 200, 43% died at less than 12 years of age, whereas less than 30% of early modern humans in a similar-size skeletal sample (about 150) died that early in life.

As alluded to in Chapter 2, the human skeleton preserves a record of dietary deficiencies suffered during its developmental years. For example, **Harris lines,** cracks on the ends of long bones (arm and leg) that result from dietary deficiency during the developing years, and **enamel hypoplasia,** zones of thin tooth enamel that result from unmet nutritional needs during early childhood, are present to a far greater degree in Neandertal remains than in the remains of early anatomically modern human beings. Marsha Oglivie, Bryan Curran, and Erik Trinkaus (1989), for example, found evidence of hypoplasia in the enamel of 36% of 669 Neandertal teeth, reflecting an estimated incidence of 75% in the individuals represented. This is more than double the incidence in nutritionally stressed recent human samples (Oglivie, Curran, and Trinkaus 1989:30). Other studies have produced similar results (M. Brennan 1991; Molnar and Molnar 1985). As Olga Soffer (1994) points out, this paleopathological evidence indicates that Neandertal children suffered far more physical stress than did their anatomically modern contemporaries.

Together this evidence has been interpreted as indicating that the Neandertals were, perhaps, too highly specialized in their physical, genetically determined adaptations to the harsh climates of the Ice Age and in their great size and strength. That may sound like a contradiction; Neandertals became extinct because they were too well adapted? But, in fact, that may have been the case. When a species becomes exquisitely adapted to a very particular set of environmental conditions, its members may thrive, but only as long as those conditions are maintained. Environmental change, especially if it is rapid and intense—as suggested by the analysis of cores taken from ancient ice layers in Greenland (Stringer and Davies 2001)—may place an enormous burden of stress on a species that has an adaptation to the previous set of circumstances. Stated succinctly by paleoanthropologist Ian Tattersall, "Adaptation to specific conditions is a passport to extinction" (as quoted in Balter 2001).

Moreover, anatomically modern humans may have possessed better cultural buffers against the climate of the Pleistocene. According to archaeologist Richard Klein (1994), when compared to the cultures of Middle Paleolithic Neandertals, anatomically modern humans produced more complex tools with a greater number of types, obtained better raw materials from greater distances to make those tools, used bone as a source of raw material for tool manufacture, built more complex structures, buried their dead in more complex graves, and produced indisputable works of art. As Klein puts it, a "very substantial behavioral gulf" separates the Neandertals from anatomically modern humans (1994:11).

Archaeologist Mary Stiner (1994) has determined that anatomically modern humans were more adept than the Neandertals at wringing every last bit of nutrition out of those foods that were available in Pleistocene Europe. Neandertals broke open animal bones to extract the rich protein of the marrow, whereas anatomically modern humans boiled the bones to get at the same food source. Stiner estimates that you can extract twice as much fat out of a bone by boiling it (as cited in Balter 2001).

Furthermore, and importantly, rather than having to burn calories to keep warm, anatomically modern humans could more efficiently burn wood than could their Neandertal cousins. As pointed out by Klein (1994), Neandertal hearths were simple and did not exhibit the more sophisticated design and better heat retention of fireplaces constructed by anatomically modern human beings. At Kebara Cave, for instance, Neandertal hearths were round or oval and used no stone and therefore had no banking of the heat as was typically found in the hearths of early modern humans. Additionally, paleoanthropologist Arthur Jelinek (1994) suggests that some of the artifacts made by modern human beings—but not by Neandertals—were part of a tool kit for the manufacture of more effectively tailored cold-weather clothing; Jelinek calls this clothing "personal insulation" (1994:83). Because cultural adaptations are faster, more flexible, and often less energy-expensive than physical adaptations that accomplish the same thing, anatomically modern humans would have had an enormous advantage over the Neandertals.

This superiority of the cultural adaptation of the early anatomically modern human beings appears to have been the key to their success. Even though the Neandertals appear to have been biologically better adapted than anatomically modern human beings to the cold, through the invention and application of a superior cultural buffer that may have included warmer, tailored clothing, superior hearths, and so on, anatomically modern humans were actually better able to survive the cold than the Neandertals. Through reconstruction of local climate conditions where the archaeological sites of Neandertals and anatomically moderns have been found in Europe, researchers Leslie Aiello and Peter Wheeler have shown that the locations where anatomically modern humans lived had median temperatures (specifically, windchills) that were between 4 and 7 degrees Celsius *colder* than the Neandertal sites (Balter 2004a).

Our anatomically modern human ancestors were not precisely adapted to the environmental conditions of late Pleistocene Europe as were the Neandertals, and this likely contributed to their survival. They were not locked into a particular set of environmental circumstances, and when those conditions changed dramatically, they simply were not affected as severely. The essence of the modern adaptation is cultural flexibility, the ability to respond, even to rapid and dramatic environmental changes, by inventing new technologies and approaches to subsistence, housing, clothing, heating, and so on. The key behavioral advantage of modern human beings is our flexibility, our ability to adapt to a wide range of conditions, and this may have meant the difference between survival and extinction in the late Pleistocene.

Statistical models based on these probable advantages indicate just how easily the extinction of the Neandertal could have been accomplished. Ezra Zubrow (1989), a mathematician turned archaeologist, has determined that under certain circumstances, when Neandertal mortality exceeds that of anatomically modern humans by between only 1% and 2%, the complete extinction of the Neandertals can occur in only 30 generations—less than 1,000 years. So it is ironic: The very physical features that allowed Neandertals to survive and even thrive for a time under the harsh conditions of Pleistocene Europe ultimately led to their extinction. They appear to have become too massively built, too specialized, for life in the cold. This specialization put them at a distinct disadvantage when conditions changed and food became harder to obtain.

NEANDERTAL NATION

This chapter began with a startling possibility: Imagine the modern world with not one, but two or more distinctly different kinds of human beings. We have now seen that this scenario nearly occurred, with anatomically modern human beings and Neandertals living in the same regions, at the same time, not even 28,000 years ago. We have shown in this chapter that Neandertals and our direct ancestors have separate, parallel histories, but their extinction does not render them any less interesting. As our evolutionary cousins, they have much to tell us about the human condition.

Could Neandertals Talk?

This question may appear to be almost impossible to answer. After all, sound does not fossilize, and the next best source of information about oral communication—the muscles and tissues that make up the human vocal tract—leave no direct physical trace. Fortunately, however, such muscles and tissues are connected to bone, in particular at the base of a hominid's cranium. Analysis of the **basicranium** may give us information about an extinct hominid's ability to speak.

The work of researchers Philip Lieberman (1984; Lieberman et al. 1992) and Edmund Crelin (1987), both separately and together (Lieberman, Crelin, and Klatt 1972), has served as a lightning rod in the debate about Neandertal speech. Based on their analysis of the basicranium of Neandertal, they reconstructed the soft parts of Neandertal vocal anatomy and then used a computer to simulate the sounds a Neandertal might have been capable of making and the speed with which they could be made. In their reconstruction of Neandertal vocal tract anatomy as implied by the morphology of the base of the skull, the larynx was positioned high up in the throat and the pharynx lacked the sharp bend that typifies modern humans. In fact, the reconstructed Neandertal vocal tract resembled that of a chimpanzee or a newborn human more than that of an adult human being. They concluded that although the Neandertals could make sounds, they were incapable of producing anything close to the range of sounds that characterizes human speech.

Many, if not most, paleoanthropologists are highly critical of Lieberman and Crelin's conclusions. Even if the Neandertals were physically incapable of producing the complete range of sounds we are capable of making, no modern human language requires all those sounds anyway. Neandertal brains are so large and their culture so complex, it is difficult to believe that their linguistic abilities were as elementary as some researchers have suggested. In addition, the recent discovery of a very modern-looking hyoid bone (a horseshoe-shaped bone in the throat) at Kebara Cave (Arensburg et al. 1990) has led some researchers to conclude that the Neandertals were physically capable of fully human speech. There this debate stands.

Did Neandertals Worship Cave Bears?

You may still find in popular literature the claim that the archaeological record shows that the Neandertals regularly killed the large species of European Ice Age bear, *Ursus spelaeus,* and then built shrines for the skulls of these huge beasts.

Unfortunately, the notion of bear-worshipping Neandertals simply doesn't hold up under careful taphonomic analysis. As shown by paleontologist and cave bear expert Björn Kurtén (1976), the supposed archaeological features used to support this notion—a stone chest filled with bear skulls at the site of Drachenloch, Switzerland; a stone cubicle with 20 skulls at Regourdu in France; and other accumulations of cave bear skulls at Les Furtins and Saône-et-Loire—were more in the minds of the excavators than in reality. Kurtén has shown in these and other cases that key data concerning the positioning of the bones are contradictory in the various sketches made by the excavators and further contradict some of their notes on the discoveries. Moreover, if Neandertals cut up the bear carcasses with stone tools, they were very neat about it; no stone tools have been found in association with the bear remains, and no cut marks have been found on the bear bones.

The bears likely died natural deaths in the caves, where there is clear evidence of their having lived. Scavengers then came in, removing some of the body along with some of the bones. Commonly in such a situation, the large skull is left in place. Any other bear who subsequently moves into the cave simply pushes the skull against a wall, out of the way. After a time, a group of skulls can accumulate. It might appear to be intentional and cultural, but it is not. It can be explained as the result of taphonomic processes that involve no human agency. And the stone chests the researchers reported were nothing more than piled-up rock, fallen from the roof of the caves, covering the bones of the bears who lived and died there. The image of the lone hunter, with nothing more than a spear in hand, facing off against an angry bear well over 10 feet tall when on its hind legs, hoping to claim its cave home and then to propitiate its dead spirit, is evocative indeed. The extant evidence, however, simply does not support this romantic image.

FIGURE 5.30

The area around the caves at Klasies River Mouth, South Africa. (From *The Middle Stone Age at Klasies River Mouth, South Africa,* by Ronald Singer and John Wymer, University of Chicago Press, 1982)

Looking out from the Klasies River Mouth caves, you can see the huge expanse of the Indian Ocean. Inside the cave, looking with the mind's eye back through the ancient layers deposited at your feet, you can see the story of the earliest beginnings of modern humanity (Figure 5.30).

CASE STUDY
CLOSE-UP

The caves near where the Klasies River empties into the Indian Ocean may have been first explored scientifically in 1923 during a survey of caves and rock shelters along the South African coast. The geological, paleontological, paleoanthropological, and archaeological work accomplished at the cave in the major excavations of 1966–68 are reported in Ronald Singer and John Wymer's (1982) *The Middle Stone Age at Klasies River Mouth in South Africa.* Because of the caves' significance to questions of the origins of anatomically modern human beings, additional excavations were carried out there in 1984–89. The human remains recovered at Klasies River Mouth (KRM) have already been discussed in this chapter, so the focus here will be on the stone-tool assemblage and the faunal remains.

An extensive array of stone tools was recovered at KRM. The vast majority of the tools were made from locally available beach cobble quartzite. Cobbles used by the cave's inhabitants to make tools were available virtually at the doorstep of the Klasies River Mouth caves.

The technology represented at KRM is, in the vernacular of African archaeology, a Middle Stone Age (MSA) industry, which means that it is essentially Mousterian in its technology. For the duration of the Late Middle Stone Age occupation of the caves, the inhabitants were removing flakes of various shapes and sizes from carefully prepared nodules of stone in a manner not unlike that of their European contemporaries.

Compared to European Mousterian industries, however, KRM technology exhibits a number of more finely made long flakes, called blades, with parallel or slightly subparallel (gently converging) sides (see Figure 5.27). Some blades with converging edges had been further flaked, after removal from their cores, into apparent spearpoints. Some of these tools seem, in a general way, to anticipate later, more advanced Late Stone Age industries in Africa and even the Aurignacian industry of the European Upper Paleolithic, to be discussed in Chapter 6. It is probably not coincidental that these more advanced-looking tools are found associated with modern-looking humans.

Faunal analysis of the bone assemblage at KRM supports the notion that hunting played a major role in the inhabitants' subsistence. We know that the inhabitants of KRM and other Middle Stone Age sites in coastal South Africa were among the first people in the world to exploit aquatic resources, including shellfish, seals, penguins, fish, and sea birds (Klein 1977).

A detailed analysis by Richard G. Milo of the Klasies River Mouth faunal assemblage shows that the inhabitants were active hunters of large game animals (Bower 1997c). About 20% of the 5,400 animal bones examined showed signs of butchery, often in areas that indicate the humans at Klasies were extracting prime cuts of meat, not just scavenging what carnivores had left behind (there are few signs of carnivores gnawing on the bones). Beyond this, a stone spearpoint was found embedded in the cervical vertebrae of a giant buffalo. Milo's analysis indicates that anatomically modern human beings were hunting in a behaviorally modern way by 100,000 years ago in South Africa.

VISITING THE PAST

The site at Sima de los Huesos in the Atapuerca mountains of northern Spain is one of the most important paleoanthropological sites in the world. Though you cannot go spelunking in the cave yourself, you can conduct a virtual visit to the location where "pre-Neandertals" were found by going to http://www.ucm.es/info/paleo/ata/english/. Although most large natural history museums present displays on human evolution in which the fossils and time period covered in this chapter are touched on, few fossil species can boast that there are entire museums devoted to them. This, however, is precisely the case for the Neandertals. The Neandertal Museum opened in 1996 and is located in Mettman, Germany, near Feldhofer Cave where the fossil skullcap that gave the Neandertals their name was found. A series of themed exhibits present the story of the discovery of the Neandertals, the world in which they lived, the tools they used, and their adaptation to life in the Pleistocene. You can engage in a virtual visit to the museum at http://www.neandertal.de.

Virtually any large natural history museum will have displays on the origin of anatomically modern human beings. The American Museum of Natural History in New York City presents an excellent exhibit where the vexing question of modern human origins is touched on. The important sites discussed here are located all across the face of the earth. The key fossils are housed in various museums and research facilities.

SUMMARY

Beginning as much as 600,000 years ago, existing hominids gave way to more modern-looking hominid forms. With a mean cranial capacity exceeding 1,220 cc, the brain size of these premodern humans falls well within the modern human range. One sort of premodern human, the Neandertal, is the best known of these. Present in large numbers in Europe and southwest Asia, Neandertals were successful and intelligent hominids. There is evidence that they cared for their sick, buried their dead, and were the first human ancestor to produce art. The preponderance of evidence seems to indicate that the Neandertals were physically specialized to life in Ice Age Europe and represent an extinct side-branch of human evolution.

Two different models, and a middle ground combining elements of both, have been proposed to explain the evolution from premodern to anatomically modern human beings. The replacement model maintains that anatomically modern people evolved just once from a population of premodern *Homo sapiens* living in Africa, sometime between close to 200,000 years ago. After 100,000 years ago, these first anatomically modern humans expanded beyond the boundaries of Africa, encountering and replacing indigenous groups of premodern *Homo sapiens* and even, possibly, *Homo erectus,* which had reached Europe and Asia during a previous period of hominid expansion out of Africa. The multiregional model proposes that anatomically modern humans evolved as a group across all of Africa, Europe, and Asia, together and simultaneously. Gene flow resulting from mating was sufficient to move newly evolved modern traits throughout the many premodern populations but was not sufficient to swamp local physical features, which have been maintained into the present era as so-called racial characteristics. In the middle ground approach, it is proposed that anatomically modern human beings evolved in one place, likely Africa. These first anatomically modern people expanded their population into Europe and Asia where, rather than replacing indigenous groups of premodern humans, they mated with them, incorporating their genes and at least some of their anatomically characteristics into what became modern humanity. The data discussed in this chapter, consisting of skeletal evidence, artifacts, and genetics, seem to lend more support to the replacement model. The question of modern human origins, however, continues to be a source of debate among paleoanthropologists and geneticists.

TO LEARN MORE

Technical Summaries

A richly detailed summary of the Neandertals has been provided by Paul Mellars in *The Neanderthal Legacy* (1996). Mary Stiner's *Honor Among Thieves: A Zooarchaeological Study of Neandertal Ecology* (1994) presents an interesting perspective on Neandertal subsistence strategies. A recent technical synthesis of Neandertal archaeology is O. Bar Yosef and D. Pilbeam's (2000) *The Geography of Neandertals and Modern Humans in Europe and the Greater Mediterranean.*

If you wish more information about current thinking regarding the origins of anatomically modern people, the citations contained here are a good place to start. There also are a couple of very nice summary articles that qualify as midway between technical and popular summaries. They neatly, succinctly, and even-handedly present the story of our current thinking about the evolution of anatomically modern people and their relationship with anatomically premodern humans, especially the Neandertals. See the piece by science writer Ann Gibbons titled "The Riddle of Coexistence" in the journal *Science* (March 2, 2001). Also in *Science,* there is a terrific updating of this issue by science writer Michael Balter titled "What Made Humans Modern?" (February 15, 2002). Paul Mellars (2004) has provided about the best recent summary of the relationship between the Neandertals and first anatomically modern human beings in Europe in his article, "Neandertals and the Modern Human Colonization of Europe," in *Nature.*

Popular Summaries

Who the Neandertals were—and what happened to them—are mysteries that have captured the popular imagination. As a result, there is no shortage of popular articles and books focusing on these extinct members of the human lineage. For example, Erik Trinkaus and Pat Shipman's *The Neandertals: Changing Images of Mankind* (1993) is an enormously informative and well-written history of the discovery and interpretation of the Neandertals. Paleoanthropologist Christopher Stringer and archaeologist Clive Gamble have written *In Search of the Neanderthals* (1993), a terrific book on the modern arguments and consensus regarding the significance of the Neandertals and their role in the evolution of anatomically modern people. One of the best popular treatments of the Neandertals is paleoanthropologist Ian Tattersall's *The Last Neanderthal* (1995). Science writer James Shreeve's (1995) *Neanderthal Enigma* is another good popular treatment. Paul Jordan (2001) has produced a wonderfully written book on the Neandertal question. Another terrific recent book is *The Neanderthal's Necklace: In Search of the Fast Thinkers,* written by Juan Luis Arsuaga (2002), one of the excavators of the Atapuerca pre-Neandertals.

African Exodus (1996), written by Christopher Stringer and R. McKie, is a forceful and convincing defense of the replacement model (with a little wiggle room left for some genetic admixture between anatomically modern and premodern humans). One can always expect a fascinating read from paleoanthropologist Ian Tattersall, and in this case you have two: *The Fossil Trail: How Do We Know What We Know About Human Evolution?* (1995) and *Becoming Human: Evolution and Human Uniqueness* (1999). Both books cast a wide net and deal with the entire story of human evolution, but both are especially useful on the topic of modern human origins. There also is a wonderful and dramatic piece of speculative fiction, *Dance of the Tiger,* by paleontologist Bjorn Kurten (1980), focusing on the shared world of Neandertals and anatomically modern human beings.

On the Web

NOVA produced a documentary focused on the Neandertals in 2002, called *Neanderthals on Trial.* There is also a companion Web site: http://www.pbs.org/wgbh/nova/neanderthals/. It's a terrific resource and provides the kind of interactive learning experience the Web is so good for. You can examine a Neandertal and ancient anatomically modern human skull, rotate them, and see for yourself their essential distinctions. Very cool. For additional information concerning the Neandertal and anatomically modern humans who lived at the same time in the Middle East, read John Shea's article at http://www.athenapub.com/8shea1.htm.

I also highly recommend a couple of Web sites for their very detailed presentations on the two models of modern human evolution. Michael Roberts of the Department of Biology at Linfield College in Oregon has put up a very informative site comparing the replacement and multiregional models (http://www.linfield.edu/~mrobert/origins.html). Equally valuable is a site developed by Patrick Quinney at the University of Liverpool in England discussing the evolutionary relationship between Neandertals and anatomically modern human beings (http://www.sciencenet.org.uk/articlesfeatures/archpal/neaderthal.html).

Online Learning Center: www.mhhe.com/feder4

The Online Learning Center (OLC) Web companion to *The Past in Perspective* features a variety of supplemental study aids. For each chapter, this free Web site includes:

- Self-Quizzes to take as pretests prior to exams
- Interactive Timeline Study Guides for additional review and reinforcement of key information
- Learning Objectives
- Chapter Site links with Web addresses for many of the fossil and archaeological sites mentioned in this text

ONLINE
LEARNING
CENTER

KEY TERMS

anatomically modern *Homo sapiens,* 188
archaic *Homo sapiens,* 163
basicranium, 211
blade, 203
Châtelperronian, 207
enamel hypoplasia, 208
ethnoarchaeology, 182
gene flow, 192

Harris lines, 208
Kibish Formation, 186
Levallois, 168
mitochondrial DNA (mtDNA), 201
Mousterian, 180
multiregional (regional continuity) model, 192

musculoskeletal hypertrophy, 178
nuclear DNA, 201
premodern *Homo sapiens,* 163
replacement model, 191
tool kit, 180

6

Expanding Intellectual Horizons

ART AND IDEAS IN THE UPPER PALEOLITHIC AND LATE STONE AGE

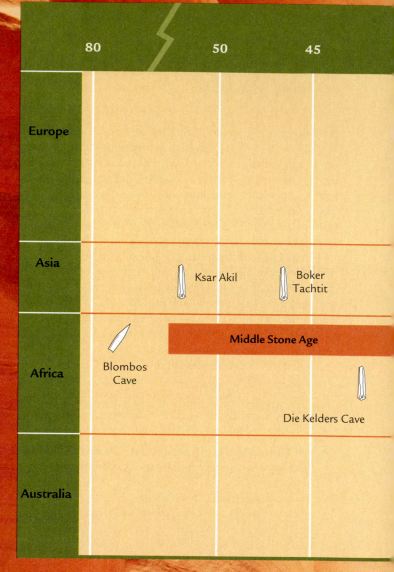

	80	50	45
Europe			
Asia		Ksar Akil	Boker Tachtit
Africa	Blombos Cave	Middle Stone Age	Die Kelders Cave
Australia			

CHAPTER OVERVIEW

The Upper Paleolithic of Europe and Asia and the Late Stone Age of Africa are marked by dramatic changes in human culture. Some of these changes seem to be rooted in developments seen among the earliest anatomically modern human beings of Africa. The 90,000-year-old stone blade tools of Katanda, in Zaire, and the 77,000-year-old polished bone tools and incised ochre objects found in Blombos Cave, in South Africa, seem to presage an explosion in stone and bone technology and in the artistic impulse. After 50,000 years ago, we see a dra-

matic shift toward a lithic technology based on the production of blade tools; an expansion in the subsistence quest; an increase in site size; use of raw materials like bone, shell, and antler; the production of nonutilitarian objects; the use of exotic materials; the elaboration of burials; and the production of true art in the form of cave paintings and portable sculptures. The tools and art of the Upper Paleolithic and the Late Stone Age are recognizably the product of a modern level of human intelligence.

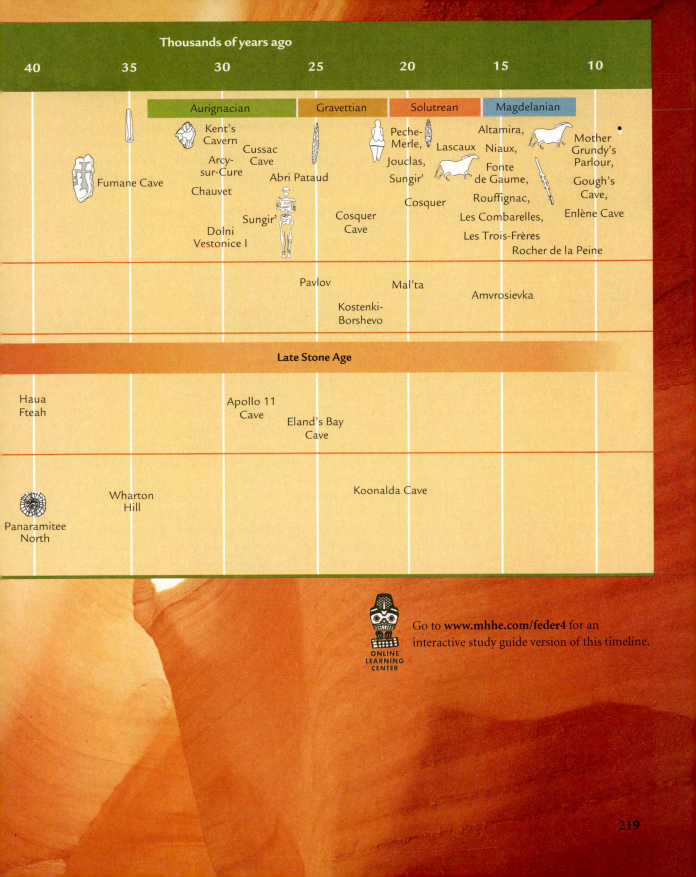

Thousands of years ago

| 40 | 35 | 30 | 25 | 20 | 15 | 10 |

Aurignacian · Gravettian · Solutrean · Magdelanian

Kent's Cavern

Cussac Cave

Arcy-sur-Cure

Abri Pataud

Fumane Cave

Chauvet

Peche-Merle, Jouclas, Sungir'

Lascaux

Altamira, Niaux, Fonte de Gaume, Rouffignac, Les Combarelles, Les Trois-Frères

Mother Grundy's Parlour, Gough's Cave, Enlène Cave

Cosquer

Sungir'

Cosquer Cave

Dolni Vestonice I

Rocher de la Peine

Pavlov

Mal'ta

Amvrosievka

Kostenki-Borshevo

Late Stone Age

Haua Fteah

Apollo 11 Cave

Eland's Bay Cave

Wharton Hill

Koonalda Cave

Panaramitee North

Go to **www.mhhe.com/feder4** for an interactive study guide version of this timeline.

ONLINE LEARNING CENTER

Across all of North America and possibly other parts of the world as well, the broad, blank, metal panels along the fronts and sides of our refrigerators serve as personal art galleries on which we display the creative work of our kids. On canvases of construction paper, photocopier paper, and recycled computer printouts, their boldly colored images in crayon, pencil, ink, paint, chalk, and marker gaily decorate our kitchen appliances.

Who could deny the obvious talent of these young artists?

More to the point, who could deny their humanity? Although there have been some silly attempts to get zoo animals to produce works of art (chimpanzees and elephants, at last count), which then sell for ridiculous sums (at least they raise money for financially strapped zoos), only human beings possess the desire, the ability, and perhaps even the *need* to produce art.

Educational psychologists have long pondered the significance of the universal and unique human behavior of producing art, which manifests itself even when we are quite young (DiLeo 1970; Gardner 1980; Thomas and Silk 1990). For Freud (1976), children's drawings represent a safety valve, allowing them to express deep, largely unconscious fears by safely reliving them on paper. According to Freud, art also provides a way for children to express unconscious wishes. For the best-known child development researcher, Jean Piaget (Piaget and Inhelder 1969), drawings reflect the developmental stages a child's intellect passes through on the road to adulthood.

Other researchers have emphasized the sensory pleasure (both motor and visual) of producing a picture; still others (Arnheim 1956) have suggested that drawing and painting are simply "universally satisfying." Ultimately, however, as psychologists Glyn V. Thomas and Angèle M. J. Silk (1990:70) point out: "It is not easy to give a totally convincing answer to the question of why children draw. . . . While all these proposed motivations [those just listed] seem plausible, it is rare to find independent evidence for their validity."

I am certain that most of you passed through the well-established stages of symbolic/artistic achievement, unaware of the arguments among psychologists over the significance of your accomplishments. Each of you has been a link in a long chain of human beings—first as children, later as adults—who have applied pigment to metaphorical canvases and produced something that was initially just in their heads but now resides outside them. This chain begins perhaps more than 70,000 years ago with our anatomically modern ancestors and continues to the present. The periods when we see the explosion of uniquely modern human capacities like artistic, symbolic expression—the Upper Paleolithic and Late Stone Age—are the focus of this chapter.

CHRONICLE

Did Neandertals produce art and make music? The answer is a somewhat equivocal "sort of." There is some evidence that Neandertals adorned themselves with pendants or maybe simple necklaces (at Arcy-sur-Cure, in France, for example; see Figure 5.15), and this is taken as evidence of a behavior they shared, at least in part, with modern human beings. They weren't dumb oafs. Perhaps they appreciated beauty and made objects other than purely utilitarian tools, stuff that simply looked nice with which they could adorn themselves.

That makes them like us; however, we did not see any direct evidence of the Neandertals using symbols, that is, depicting images that are intended to symbolize something, either concrete—like a realistic drawing of an animal—or abstract—like a tally count tabulating days. Artistic expression, defined broadly, is certainly a uniquely human capability and practice. Although, as seen in the previous chapter, anatomically modern skeletal morphology can be traced back to more than 190,000 years ago; the oldest evidence for the practice of art and symbol is more recent than this. Perhaps the first glimmerings of artistic expression can be seen in Qafzeh Cave, Israel, dating to 90,000 years ago. Along with skeletons of anatomically modern human beings (see Chapter 5), researchers have found concentrations of red ochre in the cave (Hovers et al. 2003). Red ochre is a form of hematite, a mineral consisting of iron oxide, actually ranging in color from near black through various shades of red and orange. Ground up into a powder and mixed with a binder (animal grease, egg white, or even saliva), ochre has been used by people all over the world to produce red-hued paint.

Natural deposits of red ochre are not found in Qafzeh Cave, so the 71 lumps recovered there must have been brought in from nearby sources. The Qafzeh ochre was found near the human skeletons excavated in the cave and, in fact, appears to have been used intentionally to impart a red stain to some of the stone tools found there. It is difficult to call this art, but it is also difficult not to speculate about the possibility that the residents of Qafzeh were using the red ochre in a symbolic way, replicating the color of blood as part of a ceremony to memorialize the comrades whose remains they buried in the cave.

Incised ochre fragments recovered at Blombos Cave in southern Africa represent unequivocal evidence of symbolic expression by at least 77,000 years ago.

CHAPTER SITES

www.mhhe.com/feder4

EUROPE
Lascaux, 239
Les Combarelles, 239
Les Trois-Frères, 239
Mother Grundy's
  Parlour, 226
Niaux, 239
Pavlov, 226
Peche-Merle, 239
Rocher de la Peine, 231
Rouffignac, 240
Sungir', 229

AUSTRALIA
Panaramitee North, 237
Wharton Hill, 236

AN INTELLECTUAL GREAT LEAP FORWARD: THE LATE STONE AGE AND UPPER PALEOLITHIC

The use of red ochre by the inhabitants of Qafzeh as well as the incised ochre lumps at Blombos appear to represent the initial steps taken by our anatomically modern human ancestors toward the practice of symbolic and figurative expression. Those preliminary steps led to an explosion of artistic expression, an intellectual great leap forward in the Late Stone Age of Africa and the Upper Paleolithic of Europe and Asia.

Blombos overlooks the Indian Ocean at South Africa's southern tip. The cave shows evidence of repeated human occupation over the last 100,000 years or so (Henshilwood et al. 2002). Throughout the cave's human occupation, there is evidence of a subsistence focus on the rich resources of the ocean. Cave inhabitants ate fish and shellfish, as well as meat they obtained by hunting marine and terrestrial mammals. Along with the subsistence evidence,

FIGURE 6.1

Among the 8,000 fragments of ochre recovered at Blombos Cave, South Africa, from a habitation level dated to more than 70,000 years ago, was this intentionally incised piece with regular crosshatching. The marking may reflect abstract thinking and symbolic notation by the ancient human beings who inhabited the cave. (Photograph courtesy of Chris Henshilwood. Photo by Francesco d'Errico)

researchers excavating the cave found more than 8,000 pieces of red ochre. Two of the larger chunks of the ochre recovered at Blombos, and possibly several more, had regularly spaced incised markings in the form of crosshatching across their lengths, intersected at a right angle by another set of incised, parallel lines (Figure 6.1). The ochre artifacts were found in the same layer as bifacially flaked spearpoints; spearpoints of similar style have been found elsewhere in South Africa at sites dating to before 65,000 years ago. Thermoluminescence dating on burned flints found in the same stratigraphic layer as the marked ochre artifacts produced a date of 77,000 B.P.

The authors of the study admit that it is not possible to determine what the crosshatching means, but they maintain that it is not simple doodling—though that, in and of itself, would be interesting evidence of another kind of modern human practice. They suggest that the markings follow convention; are abstract, unrelated to any real or natural images (the maker was not simply depicting something seen in nature); and may be symbolic—in other words, the markings are symbols that had a certain meaning that could have been "read" by anyone familiar with the arbitrary code on which the symbols were based. It is not surprising that human beings are capable of this. We do this all the time. What is surprising is that ancient humans may have been doing this 77,000 years ago.

Archaeologist Randall White (1982) has contrasted specifically the cultures of the Middle and Upper Paleolithic; his listing also applies when comparing the Middle and Late Stone Age of Africa. Using as guides his list and the lists of archaeologist Richard Klein (1989) and Heidi Knecht, Anne Pike-Tay, and Randall White (1993), we can examine the following cultural evolutionary "disconformities," or breaks, between the Middle and Upper Paleolithic:

- A dramatic shift in stone-tool technology, from a reliance on flake tools to the production of stone blades
- A broadening of the subsistence base to include a greater range of animal and plant species in the quest for subsistence

- Much larger sites
- A dramatic increase in the production of bone, antler, ivory, and shell tools
- A shift from very few nonutilitarian items to an abundance of them
- A greater use of imported, "exotic" goods—raw materials obtainable only from sources at great distances from habitation sites
- Much more elaborate burials
- A shift from virtually no works of art to the highly characteristic use of symbol and the production of art

We will now discuss in detail each of these changes from Middle Paleolithic to Upper Paleolithic culture.

Blade Technology

As discussed in the previous chapter, compared to a stone-tool technology based on the production of flakes, one based on the production of blades is seen as more advanced or sophisticated because it results in a more efficient use of the raw material and allows for the mass production of consistently sized and shaped blanks that then can be made into final tool forms. We also saw in that chapter that the earliest evidence for a blade-based stone-tool technology was found at the sites of anatomically modern human beings in Africa, especially 100,000 years ago at Klasies River Mouth (see the "Case Study Close-Up" in Chapter 5). An explosion in the elaboration of blade-based toolmaking occurs after 50,000 years ago with the development of the Aurignacian tradition.

Aurignacian blade technology dates back to before 40,000 years ago (Figure 6.2). In the Near East, for example, at the sites of Boker Tachtit in Israel (Marks 1990, 1993) and Ksar Akil in Lebanon (Ohnuma and Bergman 1990), the shift from Levallois technology (prepared core and flake; see Chapter 5) to a stone-tool technology based on the production of elongated blades occurred by at least 45,000 years ago at Boker Tachtit and perhaps as much as 52,000 years ago at Ksar Akil (Marks 1993:12). In Africa, Late Stone Age sites like Haua Fteah Cave show this shift to have occurred by about 40,000 B.P. (Van Peer and Vermeersch 1990). In central and southeastern Europe, the shift from Mousterian flake to Upper Paleolithic blade production occurred before 40,000 B.P. (Svoboda 1993); in western Europe, the shift seems to have occurred a bit later, about 38,000 B.P. (Allsworth-Jones 1990).

In reconstructing stone-core reduction sequences at these and other sites, researchers have concluded that whereas removal of just a few flakes would exhaust a Levallois core, removal of blades was more efficient—many more blades could be removed from the same core, producing far more cutting edge from the same mass of stone. The Aurignacian tradition represents a far more efficient use of stone, with more than five times the amount of usable edge generated from the same quantity of stone than when regular flakes were being produced.

FIGURE 6.2

These stone blades from the site of Ksar Akil in Lebanon date back to before 40,000 years ago and may be as old as 52,000 years. (Reprinted from Paul Mellars, ed.: *The Emergence of Modern Humans: An Archaeological Perspective.* Copyright © Edinburgh University Press. Used by permission of the publisher, Cornell University Press)

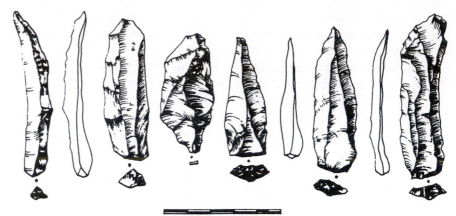

FIGURE 6.3

The stone-tool technology of the Upper Paleolithic included the production of beautifully flaked, symmetrical, spearpoints shaped like a willow leaf. Solutrean spearpoints like these, made more than 18,000 years ago, represent, in an aesthetic sense, some of the finest stone tools ever made.
(K. L. Feder)

The blade technologies of the Upper Paleolithic are short-lived, and change is greatly accelerated. In western Europe, for example, the Aurignacian tradition consisted of a specific set of tools that included retouched blades, engraving tools called burins, and stone scrapers, and it is dated to between 34,000 B.P. and 27,000 B.P. From 27,000 B.P. to 21,000 B.P., the **Gravettian** tradition developed, with its emphasis on smaller blades and denticulate knives. The **Solutrean** tradition, dated from 21,000 B.P. to 16,000 B.P., is the most striking of all, characterized by finely made, bifacially flaked, symmetrical, leaf-shaped projectile points. Solutrean points are among the most finely made stone tools ever found (Figure 6.3). The Solutrean was followed by the **Magdelanian,** from 16,000 B.P. to 11,000 B.P., when the emphasis was not on stone tools at all but rather on bone and antler, with the attendant production of microblades.

Together, artifacts from these various industries of the Upper Paleolithic reveal two very important facts. First, lithic technology had become more complex and elaborate, with a number of different manufacturing techniques that used stone more efficiently; produced more effective tools for cutting, scraping, piercing, and so on; and yielded objects far more symmetrical, balanced, and aerodynamic than those of the Middle Paleolithic. From our twenty-first-century vantage point (or, perhaps, bias), Upper Paleolithic and Late Stone Age industries produced tools that are more aesthetically pleasing, more artfully rendered, than those of earlier traditions.

Second, and equally as important, the profusion of specific tool-tradition names points to one of the most salient differences between the Middle and Upper Paleolithic: Whereas Middle Paleolithic technology was marked by relative homogeneity temporally and geographically, Upper Paleolithic technology was characterized by an explosion of toolmaking diversity marked by relatively rapid change and far greater geographic variability.

Broadening the Subsistence Base

Undeniably, the hunting of big game—**megafauna**—made a significant contribution to the subsistence of Upper Paleolithic people. In central and eastern Europe, for example, sites dating between 28,000 B.P. and 10,000 B.P. reflect the major role of the woolly mammoth in the subsistence base of Upper Paleolithic people. At a single site, Dolni Vestonice I, researchers have identified the remains of more than 100 mammoths butchered by the inhabitants (Soffer 1993). At this same site, butchering marks have been located on the remains of horse and reindeer as well. Also in Europe are the Kostenki-Borshevo sites located along the Don River in the eastern part of European Russia. The list of game animals present at these Upper Paleolithic sites is extensive; included in archaeologist Richard Klein's (1969:64) enumeration are mammoth, woolly rhinoceros, horse, cattle, musk ox, red deer, elk, reindeer, and saiga antelope, among others. Klein also points out the extensive presence of the butchered bones of carnivores such as brown bear, arctic fox, lynx, and wolf and suggests that they are significant not so much for food but for the rich, warm fur they would have provided for people living in a cold, tundra environment.

The situation is much the same in Africa and western Europe, where Upper Paleolithic and Late Stone Age inhabitants exploited local large game animals. In Siberia, the site of Mal'ta near Irkutsk shows extensive hunting of woolly mammoth and reindeer. In South Africa, at Late Stone Age sites such as Die Kelders Cave and Eland's Bay Cave, remains of eland (a large antelope) are abundant and there is evidence of the hunting of the Cape buffalo, a far more dangerous animal and one avoided during the Middle Stone Age (Klein 1983). In the Upper Paleolithic of western Europe, at sites such as Abri Pataud in France, excavators found the bones of reindeer, elephant, horse, and wild cattle (R. White 1982). At Mother Grundy's Parlour, a cave occupation site in Great Britain dating to about 12,000 B.P., the remains of woolly rhinoceros and mammoth, reindeer, and wild horse were found (C. Smith 1992). Also in Great Britain, Gough's Cave shows extensive use of wild horse and red deer more than 12,200 years ago (C. Smith 1992).

Following the pattern established at a few Middle Stone Age sites of anatomically modern humans in Africa, most notably Klasies River Mouth, Die Kelders, and Blombos Cave, the remains of fish have been found at Late Stone Age sites. The same South African sites just mentioned, for example, show evidence of the extensive reliance on seals, penguins, dolphins, mollusks, and flying shorebirds (Klein 1983:43). The bones or shells of these organisms have been found, along with grooved-stone net weights used in fishing and possible early fishhooks (called "gorges") that were baited and attached to lines.

Small mammals also contributed to the food quest. At one of the mammoth hunting sites mentioned, Dolni Vestonice I, and at the nearby site of Pavlov, there is indirect evidence of the use of nets in hunting small game (Pringle 1997). Fragments of netting made by the inhabitants of these sites, dating from between 29,000 and 22,000 years ago, had accidentally been pressed into the clay floors of the inhabitants' houses. In a few cases, those houses burned and the impressions of the netting were preserved in the baked clay.

The nets were sophisticated, indicating a probable long tradition of net weaving (Adovasio, Soffer, and Klima 1996). The netting mesh was too fine to have been used to capture large animals, but there are plenty of bones of smaller creatures, including hare and fox, at these sites. A large hare can produce 6 pounds of meat and a pelt. Driving small mammals like hares into nets is an efficient hunting technique that all members of a social group can participate in—the very young and the aged, pregnant or nursing females, and, of course, strong males in their prime. It seems likely, therefore, that net hunting played a substantial role in subsistence at these and other sites that date to the same period (Pringle 1998a).

Human beings are omnivores, not carnivores. As much as some of us may like to eat meat, we cannot survive on meat alone; fruits, vegetables, and grains make up important components of our human diet. Unfortunately, seeds, fruit pits, and starchy roots usually do not preserve as well as large animal bones. As a result, the role of big-game hunting in Upper Paleolithic subsistence has most likely been exaggerated. Furthermore, archaeologists often don't find what they are not looking for. Unfortunately, there has been a self-fulfilling prophecy at work here. Archaeologists have focused on the search for animal bones, and they have found them, reinforcing the notion that big-game hunting was the key form of subsistence in the Upper Paleolithic. At the same time, many researchers assumed that plant foods were not as important—and wouldn't have preserved anyway—so they didn't look for these remains, at least not very closely.

Researchers are beginning to remedy this omission by applying intensive techniques for recovering and analyzing plant remains; and, not surprisingly, now that they are looking for them, they are finding these kinds of food remnants. For example, researcher Sarah Mason has found the burned residue of edible taproots in hearths at Dolni Vestonice I (Pringle 1998a). And berries have been found in hearths at other Upper Paleolithic sites.

It is highly unlikely that Upper Paleolithic people overlooked important sources of protein, carbohydrates, or vitamins available in their territories. Portrayals of ancient hunters fighting a daily duel to the death with huge, aggressive beasts may offer us a romantic image, but it seems an unlikely strategy for survival. It is far more likely that the people of the Upper Paleolithic subsisted on a broad spectrum of foods, including the meat from animals both large and small, birds, fish, seeds, nuts, berries, and starchy roots. Archaeological evidence is finally beginning to support this sensible reconstruction.

Larger Sites of Aggregation

Middle Paleolithic sites tend to be small, representative of the encampments of nomadic, **opportunistic foragers,** who took whatever resources they could wherever they became available, without much planning in advance (Binford 1984). Though Upper Paleolithic sites include similarly small foraging camps, much larger sites also date to the Upper Paleolithic. Randall White (1982) interprets these as places of aggregation, localities where numerous small bands of people would come together seasonally. The site of Mal'ta, in Siberia, for example, covers an area of some 600 m^2 (about 6,500 ft^2; Chard 1974:20); it includes the remains of numerous dwellings whose frames were made from the large bones of woolly mammoth (Figure 6.4). This size is far larger than that of the standard Middle Paleolithic site.

The **settlement pattern** of the Middle Paleolithic reflects a strategy of opportunistic foraging within a pattern of unrestricted wandering. Here, the nomadic band moves in no particular pattern, following resources wherever they might become available. The pattern of subsistence in the Upper Paleolithic appears to be different, at least in part. During the Upper Paleolithic, the settlement pattern seems to indicate a shift to a fixed seasonal round as part of a strategy of **logistical collecting** (Binford 1984). People still lived in nomadic bands, but the movement of the band was no longer unrestricted, instead following a fixed yearly pattern where at least some seasonally occupied sites were returned to each year, perhaps by members of several bands. Subsistence and movements were planned out in advance as people gained a detailed knowledge of their territory, seasonality, and the behavior and shifting locations of the plants and animals on which they subsisted.

Some sites were continually visited by aggregations of related people during fixed and known times of the year when resources may have been particularly abundant at these places—for example, at a topographic bottleneck on a migration route for large animals. Some of these sites, perhaps, became

FIGURE 6.4

This reconstruction of a dwelling made of mammoth bone is evidence that in the Upper Paleolithic in Siberia, trees were not generally available for construction but the bones of large game animals were. (Negative no. 69368fr15, courtesy of Department of Library Services, American Museum of Natural History)

ritually sanctified through the use of artwork to denote the significance of a particular place to the members of the group. This possibility will be discussed in the section on the appearance of artwork in the Upper Paleolithic and in "Issues and Debates."

Branching Out in Raw Materials

We begin to see a branching out in the use of raw materials by anatomically modern people in the African Middle Stone Age. In the same Middle Stone Age layers at Blombos Cave dating to 77,000 years ago in which incised ochre rods were recovered (see the beginning of this chapter), researchers found 28 precisely crafted bone tools (Henshilwood et al. 2001; Figure 6.5). Inhabitants of the cave made bone awls and apparent spearpoints in a way that implies a strict adherence to a sequence of steps throughout the toolmaking process. As the formal and consistent fashioning of bone tools is not seen at the sites of premodern humans, the Blombos researchers conclude that this is one indicator of the technological sophistication of the anatomically modern humans who inhabited the cave, more than 25,000 years before the inception of the Late Stone Age in Africa and the Upper Paleolithic in Europe and Asia.

Although the use of bone tools after 50,000 years ago may not have been absolutely innovative, the use of bone, as well as ivory, antler, and shell for the production of tools used in sewing—for example, awls, punches and needles—and for hunting equipment—for example, spear tips—is a virtual hallmark of the Upper Paleolithic. For example, along the Dnestr River in Russia, Upper Paleolithic sites have produced slotted daggers of reindeer antler. At the Kosoutsy site in this same region, reindeer antler was also

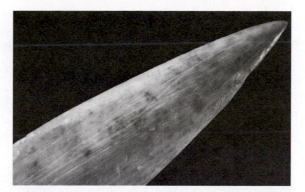

FIGURE 6.5

This finely sharpened awl is one among 28 precisely crafted, technologically sophisticated bone tools recovered at Blombos Cave, South Africa, dating to more than 70,000 years ago. (Photograph courtesy of Chris Henshilwood, African Heritage Research Institute, Cape Town)

used as a raw material to manufacture spearpoints for use in the hunt, and thin slivers of reindeer bone were used in the production of eyed needles (Borziyak 1993).

Eyed needles are indirect evidence of sewing and the inferred production of sewn clothing during the Upper Paleolithic. More direct evidence of the production of tailored clothing comes from the 22,000-year-old site of Sungir', just north of Moscow, in Russia. Beads used for fastening were found in a pattern in the ground, outlining what appears to have been pants, a shirt or jacket, a cap, and shoes (Klein 1989; R. White 1993).

Eyed needles of ivory have been found at Jouclas, in France, dating to 21,000 years ago (Dennell 1986). Eyed needles allowed for more precisely tailored and sewn clothing. The production of protective outergarments that were, at least to a degree, windproof and waterproof, with seams stitched tightly through the use of such needles, would have been extremely important as people spread into colder climates, fundamentally inhospitable to our tropically evolved and adapted ancestors. In no small measure, tight, weatherproof seams enabled by thin, eyed needles made expansion into places like the Arctic a more reasonable possibility for ancient humans.

Long, pointed bone spearpoints with inserts of small, sharp flint blades have been reconstructed at the Amvrosievka sites in eastern Europe (Krotova and Belan 1993). Barbed bone harpoons (like those from Kent's Cavern in Great Britain; C. Smith 1992), antler hammers, wrenchlike bone "shaft-straighteners" (like the one recovered at Gough's Cave in Great Britain and often called *bâtons de commandement*), and bone awls all have been found in Upper Paleolithic sites from western Europe to east Asia.

The **spear-thrower** was an innovation of the Upper Paleolithic and Late Stone Age. This tool is an elongated, hooked handle that attaches to the butt of a spear and effectively increases the length of the arm of the person throwing the spear. A longer arm increases the contact time between the inception of the throw and the release, allowing for greater accuracy, speed, and distance; it works for the same reason a baseball pitcher with a long arm can often throw the ball harder and faster than can someone with a shorter pitching arm.

FIGURE 6.6
Two ibexes wrestle on this fragment of a spear-thrower. The fine carving of this artifact is diagnostic of the Upper Paleolithic and is an example of the great skill and artistic abilities of this period. (© Musée de l'Homme. Photo by D. Destable)

The spear-thrower is a remarkable example of applied physics practiced by ancient humans. By artificially extending the arm—and by exploiting the stored energy in the bending shaft of the dart as it is thrown—our ancestors were able to dramatically increase the accuracy as well as the power with which they could launch a spear in the quest for food.

Recent experiments have compared the force of various methods of propelling a projectile. The force of a dart thrown with a spear-thrower far exceeds that generated by a hand-thrown spear, a traditional bow, or even a modern compound bow (Karl and Bruchert 1997). Spears propelled by a spear-throwing device have been clocked at more than 100 mph, and a computer-designed spear-thrower recently produced a record throw of 250 m (over 800 ft)!

Spear-throwers date back to as much as 30,000 years ago. The bearers of this technology certainly had an advantage in the hunt over those who needed to get much closer to large, dangerous animals in order to successfully spear them.

A 13,000-year-old spear-thrower from Enlène Cave, France, was carved from reindeer antler (Dennell 1986). Along with being a useful tool, this spear-thrower is far more beautiful than it had to be; the handle was finely carved into the image of two ibexes (mountain goats) locked in combat (Figure 6.6).

Clearly, the Upper Paleolithic and Late Stone Age represent periods when our human ancestors perfected technologies that previously they had barely experimented with, branching out into the use of raw materials other than stone for the unique benefits and special qualities afforded by bone, ivory, and antler.

Abundance of Nonutilitarian Objects

In my classes I see many students, men and women, wearing nonutilitarian items of personal adornment: necklaces, earrings, nose rings, tongue studs, ear cuffs, finger rings, bracelets, anklets, hairpins. Some have gold and silver draping every extremity and dangling from a multitude of pierced body parts.

All our bodies look basically the same, built along one of two fundamental models: male or female. But we have invented numerous ways of decorating ourselves—defining, identifying, and distinguishing ourselves—with objects of adornment.

Artifacts interpretable as items of personal adornment are rare at the sites of premodern humans. The Neandertal site of Arcy-sur-Cure is one of the very few places where multiple objects of personal adornment have been found associated with premoderns (see Figure 5.15). For the most part, stone, bone, antler, shell, or ivory jewelry is restricted to the sites of anatomically modern human beings.

One of the oldest sites where such items of adornment have been found is Blombos Cave in South Africa. There, dating to 75,000 years ago in the same stratigraphic level in which red ochre was recovered (discussed earlier in this chapter), researchers have found 41 perforated mollusk shell beads (Henshilwood et al. 2004). The perforation appears at the same spot on 36 of the shells—on the back near the lip (Figure 6.7). Mollusk shells can become perforated naturally, but the location of the holes in the Blombos shells is rarely seen in nature and clearly seems to have been intentional, perhaps to hang the beads in a necklace.

The Blombos beads date to the African Middle Stone Age, but it is in the Late Stone Age and Upper Paleolithic when there appears to be an explosion in the production of items of personal adornment and other nonutilitarian objects. For example, a handful of 40,000-year-old sites in Africa, west Asia, and Europe have produced shell beads or perforated teeth, likely intended to be suspended from a necklace. Dating to 15,000 B.P., Mal'ta, in central Asia (Chard 1974) has produced a wealth of items of adornment. A small child was found buried at Mal'ta with a necklace made of bone and antler beads (Figure 6.8). Also found were schematic carvings of birds, a carved bone plaque with designs consisting of dots and wavy lines etched or punched into the surface of the bone, and depictions of human beings (Figure 6.9).

A spectacular necklace was recovered from Rocher de la Peine in France. There, 13,000 years ago, an Upper Paleolithic jewelry maker strung together beads of dentalium shell, three large bear teeth, and one tooth from a Late Pleistocene European lion (Dennell 1986). The shells came from the coast, about 160 km (100 mi) from the site.

FIGURE 6.7
These perforated shell beads found in Blombos Cave, South Africa, date to 75,000 years ago. They are among the earliest non-utilitarian artifacts yet found by archaeologists and reflect both the capacity and the desire to produce decorative art at this early date. (Courtesy of Chris Henshilwood and Centre for Development Studies, University of Bergen)

As Randall White (1982) points out, the appearance of items of personal adornment that were often painstakingly made, frequently out of exotic material that must have been difficult to obtain—and therefore "expensive" in terms of time and effort to obtain it—is significant. In White's view, such objects imply increasing awareness and importance of individual identity in Upper Paleolithic society.

Archaeologists Heidi Knecht and Anne Pike-Tay, writing along with Randall White (1993:3), have suggested that the use of personalized ornaments may signify the existence of hierarchical social systems in the Upper Paleolithic, with such ornamentation symbolizing the social position and role of the wearer. Whatever the significance of the development of items of personal adornment, it seems clear that people in the Upper Paleolithic were much like ourselves.

Use of Exotic Raw Materials

The ability to obtain raw materials and manufactured goods from great distances might seem to be a feature strictly of modern societies. Look around your house and try counting the goods that originated in other countries—

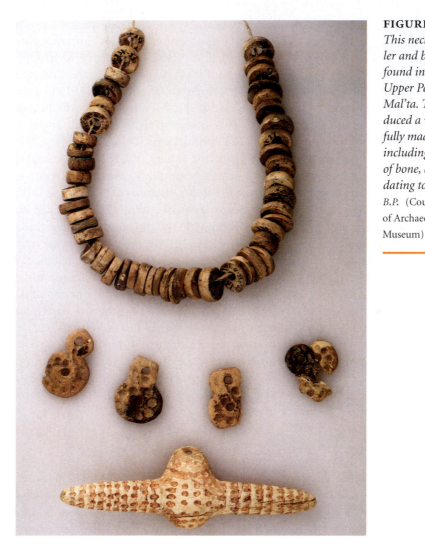

FIGURE 6.8
*This necklace, made of ant-
ler and bone beads, was
found in Siberia at the
Upper Paleolithic site of
Mal'ta. The site has pro-
duced a wealth of beauti-
fully made pieces of artwork,
including sculpted pieces
of bone, antler, and ivory,
dating to around 15,000*
B.P. (Courtesy of Department
of Archaeology, The Hermitage
Museum)

stereo equipment and camera manufactured in Japan, clothing made in China
or the Philippines, car from Germany, dishware from Great Britain, backpack
from India, wristwatch from Switzerland, calculator from Singapore, and on
and on.

But the expansion of economic systems to connect places at great distances from each other actually has a long history. As far back as the Upper
Paleolithic, the expansion of the geography of economies can be seen, as raw
materials and manufactured goods began traveling far greater distances than
in the Lower or Middle Paleolithic.

Whereas Middle Paleolithic people relied on raw materials whose source
was close to their habitations, in the Upper Paleolithic we see far more extensive use of raw materials available only at great distances from living sites. For

example, at the Kostenki-Borshevo sites in Russia, inhabitants used local lithic materials (quartzite and brown and yellow flint) in making stone tools. Also used, however, was a black flint that possessed superior chipping qualities (it chipped more regularly) but was not available in the Kostenki-Borshevo region. Its nearest possible source was about 150 km (93 mi) away. Analysis of the raw materials recovered at the site suggests that the flint obtained by the inhabitants of the Kostenki-Borshevo region for their artifacts actually came from a source 300 km (186 mi) distant (Klein 1969:227).

The situation is much the same throughout the geographic extent of Upper Paleolithic cultures. For example, in Moravia, in south-central Europe, flint commonly was moved across distances of 100 km (62 mi) from its source (Oliva 1993:52). In rare instances, apparently highly valued material like obsidian (volcanic glass) from Hungary is found in Paleolithic sites up to 500 km (310 mi) away (Oliva 1993:52). Even where quite serviceable stone was available locally, material obtainable only from great distances was often used. Archaeologist Martin Oliva (1993) suggests that maintaining long-distance contacts through trade seems to have been more important than the specific qualities of the lithics themselves and that the stone and its trade took on more of a ritual meaning than just a utilitarian significance.

The use of raw materials from great distances away by Upper Paleolithic peoples implies a greater reliance on trade with distant groups and perhaps also implies broader social networks (hypothetically maintained by seasonal get-togethers evidenced at the aggregation sites) than anything seen in Middle Paleolithic contexts.

More Elaborate Burials

If the modern folktale is true, a woman in California (sometimes the story has it in Florida) was buried in a nightgown, seated at the wheel of her brand new Jaguar (or Porsche, take your pick). Other modern examples include the burying of married people wearing their wedding bands or the burying of devout Christians with a cross around their neck. Burying the dead with treasured personal items is a long-standing human tradition. Egyptian pharaohs were buried with food, jewelry, furniture—even other people (see Chapter 11). The emperors of imperial China were buried with chariots and entire life-size ceramic armies of soldiers and horses (see Chapter 12). We see this pattern repeated over and over. Whether because it is believed that the deceased will need such items in the afterlife or simply because of the desire to place some items of personal identification with a departed friend, the practice of burying the dead with objects that were meaningful to them and their loved ones seems nearly universal.

Clearly, the first human burials are associated with Middle Paleolithic archaic humans—that is, European and southwest Asian Neandertals (see Chapter 5). However, fundamental differences exist between Middle and

Upper Paleolithic burials. For example, archaeologist Frank Harrold (1980) has compared a series of 36 Middle Paleolithic Neandertal burials with 96 Upper Paleolithic burials of anatomically modern humans. Only about 40% of the Neandertal burials included **grave goods,** objects intentionally buried with the dead (as objects of remembrance or, perhaps, as needed in an after-life). Virtually all such objects were simple tools or animal bones. On the other hand, about 90% of the Upper Paleolithic burials contained grave goods, and these items were far more elaborate than the material included with the Middle Paleolithic interments.

In another analysis, this time of the remains of 77 Middle and Upper Paleolithic skeletons excavated in Europe and southwest Asia (Riel-Salvatore and Clark 2001), there was clear evidence of the practice of ceremonially disposing of the dead among anatomically premodern humans. Though the authors of this study argue that there was no great disconformity or break in the burial behavior of Middle and Upper Paleolithic people (Neandertals and anatomically modern *Homo sapiens*), it was clear in their sample that the modern humans (32 burials in the sample) exhibited far more elaborate interment practices, with grave goods found in a greater proportion of their graves. Upper Paleolithic burials in both of the studies cited here exhibited some of the same items of personal adornment mentioned previously: necklaces, bracelets, and stone and bone tools (see the "Case Study Close-Up" in this chapter).

Production of Art

We can imagine many compelling scenes from the human past—for example, australopithecines walking side by side on an African ash bed (Chapter 3) or Neandertals mourning over the remains of a fallen comrade placed in a crudely dug grave. But perhaps none of these is more evocative than an imagined scene of two cave painters from the Upper Paleolithic.

In the dark and distant recesses of a cave's narrow passageway, a flickering oil lamp smears dancing shadows on a flat rock wall. A young woman, tall and muscular, her arms coated with a thin layer of grime and sweat, carefully places a dark slurry in her mouth. Next, she holds a hollow reed to her lips and places her other hand palm down on the rock face. Aiming the reed at the area around her hand, she begins puffing up her cheeks, spraying a fine mist of pigment out of the end of the reed. Some of the paint thinly coats her hand, but much of it covers the cave wall immediately around the area hidden by her palm and fingers. After a few puffs through the reed, she removes her hand from the cave wall, and we see in our mind's eye her remarkable artistic creation: a negative image of her own hand, a signature some 20,000 years old calling out across time.

By her side, a tall and broad young man with a deeply lined face belying his years dips a frayed twig into a thick red paste. Using skills of observation and artistry developed during his short life, he conjures up a vision held in a part of his memory as deep as where he now labors breathlessly in the cave: The horse, wild and free, runs across his mind, her legs leaving the ground as she gallops in her desperate but doomed attempt to flee from the hunters. A deep red gash on her belly where a stone-tipped spear pierced her hide leaks her lifeblood. Soon, he remembers, very soon, she falls, and his comrades are upon her, thrusting their spears deep into her viscera. Then, at last, she is quiet and still. He shudders, thinking of her spirit now returned to the sky. Then he remembers the taste of her flesh in his mouth. Her life lost, the life of his people maintained. It is the way of life and death in the world he knows.

Now long dead and no longer of this life but of another world, a world of stories and magic, the mare lives again in a creation of pigment, memory, awe, and sorcery. Once a creature of blood and bone, of sinew and muscle, she is now a creature of color and binder. No longer running across the plains of western Europe, she now runs and bellows on a flat sheet of rock, straining against her fate and bleeding eternally in the deep recesses of a dark cave. In this incarnation, she has lived for 20,000 years now; and in her life of pigment and memory and magic, she will live forever.

A REVOLUTION OF INTELLECT: THE MEANING OF UPPER PALEOLITHIC ART

Symbolic expression is a uniquely human ability. Only humans are capable of converting ideas into images that we then can recognize and understand as expressions of those specific ideas. Stick-figure renderings of animals and Michelangelo's paintings on the ceiling of the Sistine Chapel; crude tally marks on sticks of ochre and complex mathematical formulas; geometric patterns etched into cave walls and the words printed on the pages of anthropology textbooks; all of these involve the use of symbols, some abstract, some realistic. The ability to create and then "read" symbols virtually defines the human mind.

Dating to 77,000 years ago, in the African Middle Stone Age, the engraved ochre artifacts recovered at Blombos Cave appear to be early examples of this uniquely human trait (see Figure 6.1). But artifacts exhibiting the use of symbols are rare in the Middle Stone Age and the Middle Paleolithic. In fact, it is not until after 50,000 years ago that the archaeological record shows an explosion of artistic and symbolic expression by our anatomically modern human ancestors (Conkey 1978:74; Pfeiffer 1982) (Figure 6.10). It is to this art that we now turn our attention.

The Earliest Art: Australia and Africa

Though we may not know what the images and objects mean, many artifacts dated to the period beginning about 40,000 years ago clearly denote the use of symbol and the production of art (Figure 6.11). For example, at Wharton Hill in Australia, more than 36,000 years ago, an aborigine etched an oval

FIGURE 6.10

This image of a human handprint from the cave wall of Peche-Merle in France is an eternal signature of a human being who lived more than 20,000 years ago. (© Musée de l'Homme. B. G. Dellue)

shape into the abutting rock face (Bednarik 1993:5; see Chapter 7 for a discussion of the human presence in Australia). To derive a radiocarbon date, archaeologists recovered organic material from inside the groove. Encased in the rock varnish (a weathering rind of rock that builds up on an exposed surface) of the **petroglyph** (literally, "rock-writing"), the organic deposit could have gotten into the groove only after the groove was made, providing, therefore, a minimum possible age for the carved oval shape. At the nearby site of Panaramitee North, a curvilinear petroglyph has been dated via the same technique to 43,000 B.P. (Bednarik 1993:6). These dates, if correct, render the Australian petroglyphs the earliest evidence of art in the world.

The first African art has been dated to as early as 28,000 B.P. (Phillipson 1993). Stone slabs with painted and engraved images of animals have been excavated from deposits dating to this time at the Apollo 11 Cave site in southern Namibia (see Figure 6.11; Wendt 1976). The images are naturalistic renderings of the fauna of southern Africa for the time period of their production.

FIGURE 6.11
Upper Paleolithic/Late Stone Age sites in Australia, Africa, Asia, and Europe.

Upper Paleolithic Art in Europe

The artwork of late Pleistocene Europe is far better known than the Australian or the African artwork, partly as a result of geography—it is found in an area where extensive archaeology has been conducted—and partly because of placement—its location in caves has kept it better preserved. In the cave paintings (**parietal art**) and in carved statues and inscribed bone, antler, and ivory (**mobiliary art**), Upper Paleolithic Europeans produced an astounding amount of art (see Figure 6.11). Some of the paintings and inscribed artifacts incorporate geometric designs and abstract images whose meanings are difficult to interpret. In many of the paintings and carvings, though we may never

FIGURE 6.12

The so-called Chinese Horse from Lascaux Cave, France, is one of the best-known and most beautiful of the Upper Paleolithic cave paintings. Viewing these pieces of art allows us, at least in a small way, to look at the Upper Paleolithic world through the eyes of those who lived in it.

(© Art Resource, NY)

be certain of the artist's intent (see "Issues and Debates"), we cannot help but recognize the images they were producing. Cave walls in France and Spain especially, but also others scattered throughout Europe, are adorned with realistic depictions of the animals of the Upper Paleolithic. Images of prehistoric horse and bison, woolly mammoth and rhinoceros, reindeer and wild cattle flow across cave-wall canvases at places like Lascaux and Altamira, Les Combarelles, Niaux, Les Trois-Frères, Peche-Merle, and Fonte de Gaume (see Figures 6.12 and 6.13; Leroi-Gourhan 1982). Southwestern Europe alone has more than 200 caves with Paleolithic artwork, and more caves are found fairly regularly.

To assess the origins and evolution of cave paintings, it is important to obtain accurate dates for when Paleolithic artists created their truly timeless masterpieces. Though dating cave art presents unique challenges, researchers can derive absolute dates from cave paintings in a number of ways (Valladas et al. 2001). For example, when organic material was used in the production of the pigment or binder, small samples can be retrieved and radiocarbon dating applied. In other cases, if a part of a painting sloughed off of a cave wall and then became inserted into a stratigraphic sequence on the floor of

FIGURE 6.13

Though one of the oldest, Chauvet has some of the most sophisticated artwork found in the Paleolithic painted cave sites. Here, a grouping of rhinoceroses (woolly rhinos, known to have inhabited Europe during the Pleistocene) have been juxtaposed (not to scale) with two master-fully rendered lions.

(AP/Wide World Photos)

the cave, a chronometric date derived for the stratum from which the fragment of art was recovered can be applied to the art itself. This latter technique was used to date a red-ochre drawing found on a rock slab recovered from Fumane Cave, near Verona, Italy. One of the slabs presented the depiction of an unidentified animal, the other appeared to be a strange hybrid creature. The hybrid figure is upright and two-legged, like a human, but appears to have horns or antlers. The Fumane Cave researchers refer to the image as a "sorcerer," inferring that the painting is of a human being wearing an animal mask or a headdress, participating, perhaps, in a ceremony of some kind (as cited in Balter 2000). The date derived for the slab is between 32,000 and 36,500 years ago, making this drawing one of the oldest or, if the upper date proves correct, the oldest example yet found of cave art in Europe.

The most exciting find in the last 10 years, Chauvet Cave (Hughes 1995), near Avignon, France, contains an amazing array of paintings. Most people who have seen them consider them some of the most beautiful examples of Paleolithic artwork ever discovered (see Figure 6.13). The dates derived for the artwork at Chauvet are stunning: The two oldest dates of the eight derived from carbon samples taken from the paintings were earlier than 31,000 B.P. (Chauvet, Deschamps, and Hillaire 1996).

In their paintings, produced from 32,000 years ago to 10,000 years ago, the artists of the Upper Paleolithic have willed to us evocative images of their natural surroundings and, at the same time, whispered to us of their intellectual world. At Niaux, in France, a prehistoric bison with two spears still hanging from its belly lies dying on a cave wall, recalling for eternity a life and a death that transpired nearly 20,000 years ago. At Rouffignac, also in France, two woolly mammoths confront each other, frozen in an apparent dance for dominance that a human being likely witnessed and then, in art, immortalized. At Chauvet, a group of overlapping, stiff-maned horses, rendered with a degree of realism that can only be described as breathtaking, relax on the cave wall surface as they have for 30,000 years. At Lascaux, a badly injured bison, its viscera hanging from its wounded belly, is facing its human attacker in a final, defiant act of confrontation that can never end. It is a marvelous legacy of art and intellect, one that fascinates us today, tens of thousands of years after the drawings were produced.

Upper Paleolithic artists also depicted themselves, though commonly more schematically and less realistically (Figure 6.14). One of the oldest of these human portraits was found in 2000 at Cussac Cave, located in the Dordogne Valley in France. More than one hundred incised, rather than painted, images of animals including mammoth, rhinoceros, deer, horse, and bison were found on the cave wall. Along with the animals drawn by the Paleolithic artists was the outline of a human female. The skeletal remains of seven people were found in the cave. Radiocarbon dating of their bones provided a date of more than 25,000 years ago, and it is assumed that this is also the date of the images in the cave (Balter 2001).

What might the human depictions mean? Researchers Patricia Rice and Ann Paterson (1988) analyzed more than 100 human images from 32 caves in western Europe. Their statistics are provocative: More than three-quarters of the images are men, who tend to be depicted singly, in an active mode—running, walking, throwing spears. Females tend to be portrayed at rest and in close proximity to other females. What does this mean in terms of the roles of males and females in Paleolithic society? This glimpse into the sexual division of labor in societies that existed more than 15,000 years ago simply is not based on a sample large enough to allow us to draw any conclusions.

Though largely enigmatic in the meaning of their images, these caves were clearly not art galleries. In the more than 150 mostly western European caves where significant numbers of paintings have been found, some images overlap and the strange juxtapositioning of the animals—some floating above others, some upside down in relation to others—shows quite clearly that individual paintings and panels were not intended as part of a single tableau.

The relative frequency of species depicted and their locations are not random. Carnivores, for example, are often placed in the least accessible parts of the caves, and the herbivores seem to be depicted in proportion to their significance in the diet of the people who painted them (see "Issues and Debates"). Whereas at some caves animal species that served as food for Paleolithic hunters predominate, Chauvet Cave has quite a few paintings of carnivores: three cave lions, a panther, and a bear. Chauvet also presents us with the single largest concentration of paintings of woolly rhinoceroses—50 of them.

FIGURE 6.14
Interestingly, though they were accomplished artists and rendered animals with great accuracy, only infrequently did Upper Paleolithic artists depict human beings and these portrayals are often vague and schematic. An example can be seen in the engraved outline of a human female in Cussac Cave, in France.
(© CNP/Min. Cuture/Corbis Sygma)

Figurines

The art of the Late Stone Age and Upper Paleolithic includes sculptural as well as painted work. Like two-dimensional cave paintings, whose artists often focused on the animal world, many of the early three-dimensional, carved pieces depicted animals. Among the oldest are two ivory carvings found in excavations in Hohle Fels Cave in southwestern Germany and dated to between 33,000 and 30,000 years ago. The figurines depict, respectively, a graceful waterfowl in flight and the head of what appears to be a wild horse (Conrad 2003). Another series of animal carvings in Germany includes depictions of bears, lions, and mammoths (Sinclair 2003).

It is not so surprising that people whose lives depended on an understanding of the animal life with which they shared the planet painted and carved their representations. Some of the animals depicted are the prey of ancient human hunters, but a preponderance are impressive, dangerous, aggressive predators, fierce and intelligent hunters who were likely viewed by ancient people with a mixture of fear and respect; they were creatures whose characteristics ancient humans might have hoped to emulate (Conrad 2003; Sinclair 2003).

Perhaps the most famous of the sculptural art pieces are not of animals but of people, especially women. Among these are the so-called **Venus figurines.** Most of them, across much of Europe, date to the period between 25,000 and 23,000 years ago—some were made nearly 27,000 years ago, and a few date to 20,000 years ago (Gamble 1986). One group, but by no means all, of these statuettes depicts obese females, usually without faces but with enlarged breasts and buttocks (Figure 6.15). This particular variety of the female figurines has become the stereotype of this class of artifacts, perhaps, as archaeologist Patricia Rice (1981) points out, because these are the ones most often depicted in books on prehistoric art. Many researchers have suggested that they were fertility symbols, realistic depictions of pregnant females, or portrayals of women with various medical conditions.

However, these suggestions are difficult to support when large samples are examined. Rice (1981) looked at a group of 188 Venus figurines and found their shape, size, and form to be quite varied. There were depictions of thin and fat women, women with large breasts and women with small breasts, pregnant and not pregnant women, and women who were, by Rice's estimation, old, middle-aged, and young (based on the depiction of physical appearance, especially the presence or absence of lines in their faces and in how flat or saggy breasts, stomachs, hips, and buttocks looked).

Rice (1981:408) proposes that the deduced age spread of the Upper Paleolithic female figurines in her large sample was remarkably similar to the actual age distribution in historical hunter-gatherer populations. So in her view, the Venus figurines depict women of all shapes and sizes, all ages, and all states of fertility. More recently, prehistorian Jean-Pierre Duhard (1993) has examined Upper Paleolithic depictions of human beings. While he questions some of Rice's methodology, he agrees with her most general conclusion: "The women depicted display every variation and accurately reproduce the forms encountered among living people" (Duhard 1993:87). Duhard also points out

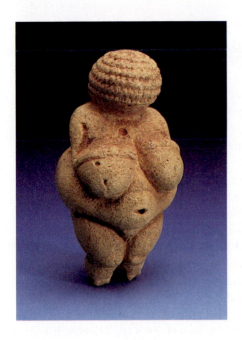 

FIGURE 6.15
These two examples of the so-called Venus figurines— the famous Venus of Willendorf (left) and a relief carving from a cave in France (right)—fit the common stereotype of such figurines: broad hips, large breasts, fat bellies, and vague faces. (*Left:* Naturhistorisches Museum, Wien, Neg. # 9075F. *Right:* © Musée de l'Homme. D. Ponsard)

that some males are depicted among the figurines, although most are female and many of the females are pregnant.

As beautifully rendered as some of the ancient sculptures just discussed may have been, another set of figurines may be even more significant in terms of the insights they provide us into the intellectual and even spiritual lives of ancient people. These carvings are not depictions of animals or even of people but of strange chimeras, beasts that appear to be part human, part animal. Two such sculptures excavated in Germany and dating to about 30,000 years ago appear to display the body of a human and the head of a lion (Sinclair 2003). Again from Hohle Fels Cave in Germany, along with the above-mentioned water bird and horse, is an upright figure that seems to be a human being from the neck down, but a lion from the neck up. Another statue, the Vogelherd "lion man" may be a bit younger, but even more clearly shows a human, standing on two legs, although with a very obvious lion's head. The meaning of carvings like these is unclear, but perhaps we are seeing in them some element of the spiritual world of ancient people, a world inhabited by beasts hosting spirits of both people and the animals whose courage and ferocity they hoped to emulate.

The precise meaning of the cave paintings, as well as of the figurines, is elusive. But what is key here is that in painting their images in caves, in engraving designs on antler, and in sculpting depictions of women, the artists of the Upper Paleolithic were doing something that we recognize as human behavior: They were creating images from their memory, filtered through the lens of their imagination. In doing this, they left us wonderful works to ponder.

IS THERE A GAP BETWEEN THE EVOLUTION OF ANATOMICALLY MODERN HUMANS AND THE DEVELOPMENT OF MODERN INTELLIGENCE?

At the beginning of this chapter, I characterized the period beginning 50,000 years ago, the Upper Paleolithic, as representing an "intellectual leap forward." When you look at the magnificent cave paintings, the artfully rendered sculptures, and even the beautifully symmetrical stone tools in the photographs provided in this book, it is easy to view this period as exhibiting a steep step up by our ancestors in art and intellect.

Therein lies a puzzle. As shown in Chapter 5, anatomically modern human beings have been identified in Africa dating to more than 190,000 years ago. If they were so much more intelligent than their premodern contemporaries—and if, as a result of that intelligence, they were able to outcompete those anatomically and, it is assumed, intellectually archaic humans with whom they shared the evolutionary stage for tens of thousands of years—why did it take those first anatomically modern humans 140,000 years to develop a material culture that we can recognize as reflecting a modern level of intelligence and sophistication? Why don't cave paintings, sophisticated burials, beautifully symmetrical blade tools, and the like show up with those first anatomically modern humans?

This apparent 140,000-year gap has long troubled prehistorians. One leading archaeologist, Richard Klein (1989, 1993), has even suggested that though we call them anatomically modern *Homo sapiens* on the basis of skeletal features, perhaps the hominids represented at Omo, Herto, Border Cave, Klasies River Mouth, Skhul, and Qafzeh (see Chapter 5) were only superficially modern, retaining a fundamentally archaic neuroanatomy. In other words, though we can't prove it archaeologically, perhaps their modern-looking skulls housed brains that were not yet modern and so they were not yet intellectually capable of producing the material culture that characterizes the Upper Paleolithic. Klein suggests that what amounts to a rewiring of the human brain occurred sometime between 40,000 and 50,000 years ago, allowing for a great leap to modern intelligence.

How real is this gap? In a thought-provoking article, paleoanthropologists Sally McBrearty and Alison Brooks (2000) suggest that the perception of a lengthy break between anatomically modern humans and intellectually modern behavior results from an overreliance on the archaeological record of the European Upper Paleolithic. In fact, McBrearty and Brooks (2000:491) see virtually all of the elements listed previously in this chapter as distinguishing the Middle from the Upper Paleolithic as doing so, perhaps, in Europe but not in Africa, where the archaeological record of the Middle Stone Age at sites like Klasies River Mouth, Kantanda, and Blombos already exhibits features like formal bone tools; technologically complex stone-blade production sequences; bifacially flaked, symmetrical tools reflecting great geographic diversity; long-distance connections for obtaining raw materials; a subsistence reliance on marine resources where available; the production of nonutilitarian objects; and the use of symbols in art.

According to McBrearty and Brooks, there was no revolution, no great leap forward in intellect and behavior at the boundary between the Middle and Upper Paleolithic or the Middle and Late Stone Age. It only looks that way in Europe because it was a geographic backwater, the end point into which anatomically modern humans arrived relatively late in the sequence with fully formed, modern behaviors. Their argument is strong that when the "great leap" is looked at closely in Africa, the geographic source of anatomically modern human beings, it appears to have been the end product of a complex mosaic of small steps taken at different times and in different places.

McBrearty and Brooks show that there is no genuinely mysterious gap of tens of thousands of years between anatomical and behavioral modernity that ends abruptly with the European Upper Paleolithic. Nevertheless, perhaps we can conclude that when all of these little steps taken in Africa came together, an intellectual critical mass was reached that produced the truly spectacular societies that characterize the Upper Paleolithic and Late Stone Age of the period after 50,000 years ago.

WHAT DOES THE ART OF THE UPPER PALEOLITHIC MEAN?

It is difficult not to be moved by the images that adorn the cave walls of ancient Europe and elsewhere. With twenty-first-century-A.D. eyes, we can appreciate the glorious beauty and movement of the artwork. But what did these works mean to the twentieth- and thirtieth- millennium-B.P. eyes of their creators? And why did they create them?

There are as many answers to these questions as researchers who have contemplated them. Some have argued that the art of the Upper Paleolithic explains itself: It is (and was) beautiful and, just like modern art, was produced for the simple joy of creating something of beauty and power. It was "art for art's sake" (Halvorson 1987).

Most researchers, though, eschew such an explanation as no explanation at all and have sought deeper meaning in the art. There has long been a "just-so" explanation, proposing that when a hunting people depict animals in their artwork, they are necessarily practicing what is called sympathetic magic. The hunters paint the animals and show them being speared or captured in the magical, symbolic realm to ensure their capture and slaughter in the real world.

French researcher André Leroi-Gourhan (1968) championed a popular hypothesis that the cave art was filled with sexual symbolism, with phallic spears piercing vulva-like wounds on the animals. So the animal depictions of the Upper Paleolithic were not about animals or hunting at all; instead, they were about sex and gender.

Other researchers have suggested that cave paintings depicted actual historical events, hunts symbolically and artistically recorded for posterity. And still others have likened the paintings to mounted animal-head trophies hung on walls by their modern hunters.

Researchers hoping to delve more deeply into the minds of humanity's first artists interpret the artwork as part of a system of communication of ideas—a system that uses animals and geometric patterns as symbols, the specific meaning of which may be lost forever. For example, archaeologist Meg Conkey (1980) views the 1,200 bones engraved with abstract geometric patterns at Altamira Cave, Spain, as the identifying symbols—the "flags"—of different groups of people who came together at the cave during periods of population aggregation. Anthropologist Michael Jochim views the cave paintings of northern Spain and southern France—the so-called Franco-Cantabrian region—as symbols marking territory. Social stresses that accompanied population influx into the region during the period after 25,000 B.P. may have resulted in the need to mark territory with symbols of ownership. Painting animals—probably the most important resources of a territory—within a sacred place in the territory like a cave might have served to announce to all interlopers the rightful ownership of the surrounding lands. Prehistorian Clive Gamble (1982, 1986) views the Venus figurines as a symbolic social glue, helping to maintain social connections between geographically distant groups through a common religion and art style.

Researchers Patricia Rice and Ann Paterson (1985, 1986) have returned to a more economic perspective. Their statistical analysis of the numbers and kinds of animals seen on cave walls in the European Upper Paleolithic shows interesting correlations with the faunal assemblages of habitation sites in Spain and France. Small, nonaggressive animals such as reindeer and red deer were important in the diet of the cave painters and seem to have been depicted on cave walls in proportion to their economic importance. On the other hand, animals less often seen in faunal assemblages but impressive, dangerous, and productive of large quantities of meat when they were successfully procured also were commonly included in the artwork. However, Chauvet Cave contradicts this pattern, with its stunning depictions of animals not known to have been exploited for food by Paleolithic Europeans, including carnivores like lions, bears, and panthers, as well as woolly rhinoceroses.

A fascinating neuropsychological approach has been applied by researchers J. D. Lewis-Williams and T. A. Dowson (1988) to explain at least some of the less naturalistic cave art. They note that there are six basic geometric forms that people who are placed into an altered state of consciousness under experimental conditions report seeing: dots, wavy lines, zigzags, crosshatching or grids, concentric circles or U-shaped lines, and parallel lines (Bower 1996). Interestingly, these geometric forms are precisely those seen in some ancient cave art dating to more than 30,000 years ago.

Lewis-Williams and Dowson's approach is cross-cultural. In other words, they surveyed a wide variety of historical and archaeological cultures, finding common images in artwork all over the world. Lewis-Williams and Dowson point out ethnographic records of shamans or priests who, in an attempt to communicate with spirits or to see into other worlds, induce a trancelike state by fasting, dancing, hyperventilating, going into isolation in absolute darkness, undergoing sleep deprivation, or even ingesting natural hallucinogens. When these shamans produce an artistic representation of what they have seen in their trances, they often include the geometric shapes induced in modern experimental subjects that also are seen in Upper Paleolithic artwork.

These trance-induced images are not culturally controlled but result, in part, from the structure of the optic system itself and are therefore universal. Perhaps through sleep deprivation, staring at a flickering fire, or ingesting drugs, ancient shamans or priests induced these images in their own optic systems. They then translated these images to cave walls as part of religious rituals.

The art of the Upper Paleolithic has been depressingly resistant to any comprehensive explanation for its existence. That we cannot even fathom the reason for our own children's scribblings (see this chapter's "Prelude") does not bode well for our attempt to illuminate the motives for and meanings of the artwork of our Upper Paleolithic ancestors. Perhaps we are destined merely to enjoy the cave paintings and Venus figurines, much as we delight in those crayon, pencil, and paint images we attach with magnets to our refrigerators. That would not be so terrible, so great is the aesthetic enjoyment we might derive from them. Then again, there are insights yet to be extracted from these beautiful puzzles that when solved will tell us much about what it means to be a human being.

WAS THE PALEOLITHIC "A MAN'S WORLD"?

On many levels, gender issues are part of our ideas about human behavior, both in the past and in the present (Gero and Conkey 1990; Spencer-Wood 1991). For example, the discussion of the origins of upright walking in Chapter 3's "Issues and Debates" presented the hypothesis of Owen Lovejoy that bipedalism arose to enable males to provision females. Issues of sex roles, monogamy, and paternity—for *Australopithecus* as well as for their modern descendants—are bound up in his hypothesis.

Issues of gender and sex are just as pertinent to our discussion of the Upper Paleolithic. Consider cave art. I intentionally tried to surprise you in the "Chronicle" section's vignette of two Paleolithic artists: One of them was female. Many people think, on the basis of virtually no data, that men were the ancient artists of the Paleolithic. But why?

Archaeologist Diane Gifford-Gonzalez (1993) points out that in most popular reconstructions of ancient life, virtually all of the important and exciting behaviors reflected in the archaeological record have been ascribed only to ancient males. Surveying the work of 88 modern artists, Gifford-Gonzalez determined the proportions of Paleolithic males and females depicted performing a number of different tasks (Figure 6.16). Her results are truly amazing.

FIGURE 6.16

In this graph, archaeologist Diane Gifford-Gonzalez shows the kind of sex-role stereotyping modern artists have engaged in when depicting Paleolithic people. Women are commonly shown caring for children and working animal hides; men are shown hunting, using tools, carrying game, performing rituals, and producing art. (Adapted with permission from Diane Gifford-Gonzalez 1993)

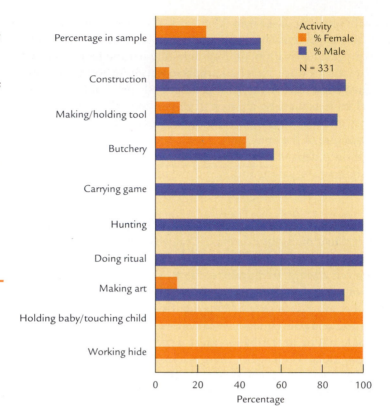

For example, in her sample of 331 images of individual ancient people, all of the individuals depicted performing a ritual, hunting, or carrying game were males. And 90% of those depicted producing Paleolithic artwork were males. In the same sample, not one male was shown holding a baby or touching a child.

From illustrations in coffee-table books to diorama kits for kids to professionally produced museum dioramas, images abound of ancient men hunting, creating art, and performing ceremonies, while women are shown in the background with children, performing drudge work like scraping hides or cooking. So it is not surprising that many people assume the role of ancient women focused on cooking food, making clothing, and, of course, bearing and raising children. These same people assume it was men who, by wit, sinew, and intelligence, fed their families by tracking, killing, and bringing animals back to the cave. Then, though exhausted from providing sustenance for their families, they worked the evenings away, producing great works of art, as fresh and vibrant today as they must have been 25,000 years ago when they were painted. In this view, men were involved in all of the exciting, intellectually stimulating, and physically challenging activities, while women got to clean up.

In truth, we must admit our ignorance; we don't know who produced the cave art in the Upper Paleolithic or who performed rituals. We must not allow our twenty-first-century preconceptions about the sexual division of labor to bias our view of the ancient past. It could have been women as easily as men who applied those remarkable images onto the cave walls, carved the figurines, and held positions of ritual importance. At the same time, we should not presume that Paleolithic men played out a 1950s-style fatherhood: stiff, distant, and uninvolved. It is far more likely that survival during the Pleistocene required all members of a group to contribute in many different ways; Paleolithic people probably could not have afforded to restrict the contributions of individuals on the basis of sex. Perhaps at some point we might recognize the same thing.

THE IMPORTANCE OF LIVING LONG: THE GRANDMOTHER EFFECT

I grew up and even entered into my teen years in the enviable and not all that uncommon position of knowing all four of my grandparents. My father's parents lived not too far away, and I remember how much I enjoyed our frequent visits. My mother's parents lived even closer, just across the hall in the same multifamily house. They served as surrogate parents when my own were at work or away—for example, when my mother was in the hospital giving birth to my sister. My two children have not been quite so lucky; my wife's father passed away several months before our second child was born. Nevertheless, our folks have always spent as much time as they could with their grandkids, doting on them, and they have always been generous with their advice, help, time, and resources.

Clearly my kids have benefited in ways both tangible and intangible by having grandparents around, and so have my wife and I. We especially appreciated the help our parents provided when our first child was born. We were pretty comfortable as parents of a newborn, but, admittedly, we were doing it all for the first time. I freely admit that, at least occasionally, I was concerned that I might break the kid. Grandparents can be and were for us a tremendous help—yes, sometimes that help can be a source of friction—but emotionally drained, physically exhausted, and psychically spent new parents can use all the help they can get.

Statistics show that the existence of grandparents and the help they can provide to their own children in raising their kids is more than simply a convenience; it actually increases the likelihood that the kids will survive and thrive. In a survey of mortality statistics in eighteenth- and nineteenth-century Finland and Canada, researchers showed that the presence of a grandmother in the household increased both the number of children born to her children and the proportion of those grandchildren who survived to adulthood (Lahdenpera et al. 2004). In other words, a surviving grandmother present in a household contributed a significant benefit to the reproductive success of her daughters and daughters-in-law as well as the longevity of her grandchildren.

It now appears that the "grandmother effect" may be traced back to no more than about 30,000 years ago. Rachel Caspari and Sang-Hee Lee (2004) assessed the age at death of ancient hominids by examining teeth, including those that belonged to *Australopithecus, Homo erectus,* premodern human beings including Neandertals, and anatomically modern *Homo sapiens* from the European Upper Paleolithic. Caspari and Lee found that within the context of a slight apparent increase through time in individual longevity among the hominids, there was a significant and substantial longevity leap between the premoderns and anatomically modern humans only in the Upper Paleolithic. In fact, within their sample, for the first time, at about 30,000 years ago, there was a major change in the human population pyramid; for the first time, there appear to have been a greater number of older adults than younger adults among the hominids.

So, the existence of doting, generous, helpful, and knowledgeable grandparents seems to have been a rather recent development in human evolution. The presence of grandparents, an older generation of people with experiences and memories that track back to a previous time—grandparents are, in fact, a living library—likely had a significant impact in the transmission of cultural memories and knowledge.

CASE STUDY CLOSE-UP

The site of Sungir' is located about 150 km (93 mi) northeast of Moscow, in Russia (R. White 1993). To date, nine burials have been excavated at the 28,000-year-old site. The better-preserved remains have been identified as a 60-year-old male; a female skull; a headless adult; an adult, probably male; a 7–9-year-old girl; and a 13-year-old boy.

The Sungir' graves are loaded with grave goods, primarily items of adornment (all data on the Sungir' graves are taken from R. White 1993:287–96). The older male was adorned with nearly 3,000 finely worked ivory beads; some apparently were part of a beaded cap, and the rest were positioned in strands around his body (Figure 6.17). A flat stone pendant was located on his neck. On his arms were 25 finely carved bracelets made from the ivory of a woolly mammoth. The adolescent boy's body was surrounded with more than 4,900 ivory beads. A carved ivory pendant had been placed on his chest. He wore a belt decorated with 250 polar fox teeth. There was an ivory pin at his throat, an ivory lance and carved ivory disk at his side, an ivory sculpture of a woolly mammoth under his shoulder, and by his left side a human femur (not his own) whose cavity was filled with red ochre. Next to the adolescent boy lay the young girl, buried with more than 5,200 strung beads, an ivory pin at her throat (perhaps a clasp for a garment long since decayed away), small ivory lances, and three ivory disks carved with intricate latticework.

An enormous amount of time must have been invested in preparing these items for burial. Replication of the beads has indicated that 45 minutes to an hour was needed to make just *one* of the ivory beads in the Sungir' burials (R. White 1993:296). If this estimate is accurate, more than 2,000 hours of

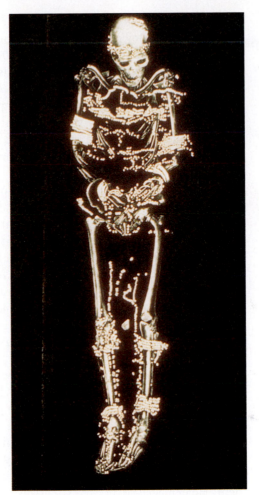

FIGURE 6.17
This skeleton of an older man who lived more than 25,000 years ago is one of nine burials excavated at the Upper Paleolithic site of Sungir' near Moscow. More than 3,000 ivory beads were sewn into his burial garments. (© Musée de l'Homme. O. Bader)

work were needed just for the beads in the older man's burial, and more than 3,500 hours per child were needed for their beadwork.

The children's burials at Sungir', therefore, actually took more time and effort than did those of the adults, and therein lies an interesting thought. Paleoanthropologist Randall White notes that in most hunting and gathering societies, status is earned and not ascribed. A lifetime of work and achievement results in elevated status, and this earns an individual respect that is eventually manifested in an elaborate burial with all the trappings—like the finely made objects that accompanied the 60-year-old male at Sungir'. But children have not lived long enough to achieve status or wealth. As White suggests, children buried with high-status goods must have been afforded their high status not because of what they had accomplished in life but rather on the basis of who they were related to. White goes on to suggest that the situation at Sungir' implies the existence of a complex social system in which status was passed down from one generation to the next.

Certainly, the burials imply that 28,000 years ago, the people at Sungir' were much like us, viewing their children as their most precious and beloved possessions. The tragedy of the early death of a child required significant symbols to mark her or his passing. Twenty-eight thousand years after they were secreted in their graves, the beads, pendants, pins, lances, and sculptures interred with the children of Sungir' resonate with what can only be interpreted as the love those left behind felt for the young ones who had died.

VISITING THE PAST

Of all the site visits suggested so far in this book, none is as dramatic as the painted caves of Paleolithic Europe. Unfortunately, many of the best-known sites are now closed to the public. One noteworthy exception to this (at least as of this writing) is Peche Merle in the Dordogne region of southwest France. To keep deterioration to a minimum, the number of daily visitors is restricted—no more than 700 are allowed into the cave each day—so it is best to call ahead if you plan to visit. Unfortunately, years of tourist visits have taken their toll on the artwork when the caves are open to visitors. Lights and especially the increased humidity produced by breathing and perspiring have harmed many of the precious painted images.

Sadly, even in instances where only a very small number of visitors have been allowed into caves to view the artwork, significant deterioration is occurring. For example, only about 20 people per day are escorted into Altamira Cave in Spain. If you hope to be one of the 20, you better have a great deal of patience; Altamira tours currently are booked up for three years. Even here, presumably as a result of artificial lighting and moisture brought in by this small number of visitors, bacteria are growing on the paintings and damaging them (Holden 2002a).

Spain and France have come up with a different solution to this problem: Replicas of some image groups from Altamira and Lascaux Caves have been produced. The actual contours of the ceiling of Altamira Cave were measured and copied in an artificial material. The cave paintings were then copied on this surface. The artificial cave with its replica artwork is on display at the Archaeological Museum in Madrid.

At Lascaux, a new cave has been constructed to the exact measurements of the original. Modeled concrete precisely replicates the cave surfaces, and teams of artists have produced perfect copies of the originals. Lascaux II recreates two of the main galleries of Lascaux I, artificially placing most of the major paintings together. Hundreds of thousands of tourists have visited Lascaux II since it opened in 1984, providing a wonderful opportunity to visit the past, even when the original is off-limits.

Art conservators are attacking the problem of deterioration of the cave paintings, but it is uncertain if this will ever lead to the reopening of caves like Lascaux. It has been shown, for example, that the bacterial growth that results from the application of artificial lighting can be slowed down considerably when wavelengths are chosen that cannot be absorbed by the bacteria (Castellani 2005). But for now, archaelogical tourists will have to settle for replicas and those few examples of painted caves still open to the public.

SUMMARY

Glimmerings of enormous change emanate from the Middle Stone Age and the Middle Paleolithic. Incised ochre rods, shell beads, and simple pendants provide just a faint hint of what is to come in the explosion of change that transforms the intellectual landscape of a time called the Upper Paleolithic and Late Stone Age. The cultures of the period are characterized by the production of blade tools; a broadening of the subsistence base; an increase in the size of some sites (implying a practice of temporary population aggregation); the use of bone, antler, ivory, and shell in toolmaking; the production of nonutilitarian items, some of which served as items of personal adornment; the extensive use of nonlocal, exotic raw materials; the regular placement of elaborate grave goods in burials—including items of personal adornment; and the first appearance of artwork, in the form of naturalistic paintings, fanciful sculptures, and engraved bone and antler. In their use of symbol, whether realistic in the case of animals painted on cave walls or abstract in the form of geometric patterns etched into bone or carved into rock, the artists of the Upper Paleolithic and Late Stone Age were practicing a behavior that is one of the hallmarks of the modern human intellect. In these elements of their culture, we see a recognizably "modern" human pattern.

TO LEARN MORE

Technical Summaries

Many useful works detail the significant changes seen at the boundary between the Middle and Upper Paleolithic. For technical reports, see many of the individual articles in *The Emergence of Modern Humans: An Archaeological Perspective,* edited by Paul Mellars (1990). For a book-length treatment that attempts to understand the nature and meaning of the art of the Upper Paleolithic, see *The Dawn of Belief: Religion in the Upper Paleolithic of Southwestern Europe,* by Bruce Dickson (1990).

Popular Summaries

Informative, densely illustrated, coffee-table books have been published on several of the major cave painting sites. For Lascaux, there is Mario Ruspoli's *The Cave of Lascaux: The Final Photographs* (1986), a virtual encyclopedia of the major art panels in the cave, with the last photos taken before the cave was closed to ensure its preservation. Chauvet Cave has its own book as well, titled *Dawn of Art: The Chauvet Cave* (1996), by Jean-Marie Chauvet, Éliette Brunel Deschamps, and Christian Hillaire. On the Spanish cave Altamira, there is *The Cave of Altamira,* by Pedro A. Saura Ramos (1998). Finally, for Cosquer Cave there is *The Cave Beneath the Sea: Paleolithic Images at Cosquer,* by Jean Clottes and Jean Courtin (1996). The format of these books is pretty similar with detailed discussions of the discovery of the caves, their archaeological contexts, dating, and, of course, the art. The photographs are the primary draw of these books, and the imagery is truly mind-boggling.

There also are a number of books that cover the cave art more broadly, examining and comparing styles and methods at different sites, including, but not limited to, the major caves that are the focus of the books just listed. One of the best of these is *Journey Through the Ice Age,* by Paul Bahn and Jean Vertut (1997), a comprehensive guide to cave art. Another general book that attempts to explain the art as the result of shamanism is *The Shamans of Prehistory: Trance and Magic in the Painted Caves,* by Jean Clottes and David Lewis-Williams (1998). If all you do is look at the photographs in any of these books, it will have been time well spent, and you likely will want to read the text to learn more about humanity's first artistic explosion.

On the Web

As just mentioned in "Visiting the Past," few of the painted caves are open for tourist visits, and those that are severely restrict the numbers of visitors. Nevertheless, the Internet gives all of us the opportunity for virtual visits to the painted caves. Through the magic of your computer, you can explore any of the following cave sites and see the spectacular works of art produced by our human ancestors:

http://www.culture.gouv.fr:80/culture/arcnat/lascaux/en/ (Lascaux)
http://www.culture/gouv.fr:80/culture/arcnat/chauvet/en/ (Chauvet)
http://www.culture/gouv.fr:80/culture/archeosm/en/fr-cosqu1.htm (Cosquer)
http://www.quercy.net/pechmerle (Peche Merle)
http://www.turcantabria.com/Datos/Historia-Arte/Cuevas/Cuevas%20Altamira/altamira-i.htm (Altamira)

For broad presentations about the earliest human art in Europe, Asia, and Africa, visit the Web site of the Bradshaw Foundation (http://www.bradshawfoundation.com /); check out the link labeled "Paleolithic Art in France" for a great summary article by researcher Jean Clottes. Click the link labeled "Chauvet Cave" and from there click "Other French Caves" for lots of images from an array of the painted caves of the European Upper Paleolithic. Don't miss the spectacular photographs of early rock art in Africa (links labeled "African Rock Art," "North Central Tanzania," and "Western Central Africa") and Australia (link labeled "Bradshaw Paintings").

Wonder at the remarkable world we live in where the products of 30,000-year-old human imaginations are made accessible by a technology made possible by the modern human imagination.

Online Learning Center: *www.mhhe.com/feder4*

ONLINE LEARNING CENTER

The Online Learning Center (OLC) Web companion to *The Past in Perspective* features a variety of supplemental study aids. For each chapter, this free Web site includes

- Self-Quizzes to take as pretests prior to exams
- Interactive Timeline Study Guides for additional review and reinforcement of key information
- Learning Objectives
- Chapter Site links with Web addresses for many of the fossil and archaeological sites mentioned in the text

KEY TERMS

Aurignacian blade, 223
grave goods, 235
Gravettian, 224
logistical collecting, 227
Magdelanian, 224

megafauna, 225
mobiliary art, 238
opportunistic foragers, 227
parietal art, 238
petroglyph, 237

settlement pattern, 227
Solutrean, 224
spear-thrower, 229
Venus figurines, 242

7
Expanding Geographic Horizons

NEW WORLDS

	45	40	35
Sunda		Niah Cave Lang Rongrien	Lene Hara
New Guinea		Huon Bobongara Hill	
Australia	Panaramitee North	SwanRiver Carpenter's Gap Keilor Lake Mungo Malakunanja	Mammoth Cave Devil's Lair Wharton Hill Ngarrabulgan
Tasmania			Wareen Cave
Pacific Islands			
Northeast Asia		Mamontovaya Kurya Ikhine	Lake Baikal

Go to www.mhhe.com/feder4 for an interactive study guide version of this timeline.

CHAPTER OVERVIEW

After 50,000 years ago, human population expanded beyond the mainlands of Africa, Europe, and Asia and into the rest of the habitable world. Sahul (Australia/New Guinea/Tasmania) exhibits clear evidence of human occupation by at least 40,000 years ago. The islands of western Melanesia were populated beginning about 35,000 years ago. Micronesia and Polynesia also show evidence of occupation after 3,500 years ago as human population expanded eastward into the Pacific.

An enormous body of land called Beringia, joining northeast Asia and northwest North America, was exposed during periods of lowered sea level that accompanied the expansion of glacial ice during the Pleistocene. Inhabitants of northeast Asia expanded into the interior and along the coast of Beringia and, ultimately, into the New World, probably by about 20,000 years ago. Some migrants may have traveled along the coast reaching as far south as Chile by 13,000 years ago. Others seem to have migrated through the interior, reaching the American southeast perhaps as early as 18,000 years ago. Though the dates of the earliest sites in the New World are controversial, the archaeological record provides unequivocal evidence of a highly successful human adaptation to the late Pleistocene world of the Western Hemisphere at least as early as about 12,000 years ago.

Thousands of years ago

30	25	20	15	10	5	Present

Leang Burung — Timor

Kuk — Nombe, Kosipe

Willandra Lakes 50 — Mandu-Mandu, Hamersley, Koonalda — Puritjarra — Nullarbor — Kow Swamp

ORS7, Acheron, Bone, Nunamira — Cave Bay Cave — Kutikina, Beginner's Luck

Solomon Islands — Society, Cook, Samoa — Fiji — Easter Island, Hawaii, New Zealand

Yana RHS — Dyuktai — Ushki

NEW WORLD

Oldest human remains
Luzia — Midland — Spirit Cave
Kennewick
Tepexpán, Marmes, Pelican Rapids
Arlington — On Your Knees Cave

Pre-Clovis
Cactus Hill — Meadowcroft
Bluefish Caves
? Topper — Topper — Monte Verde

Nenana
Dry Creek I
Moose Creek
Walker Road

Denali
Dry Creek II
Usibelli, Slate Creek,
Donnelly Ridge, Campus Site,
Healy Lake, Teklanika River,
Panguingue Creek II

Clovis contemporaries
Mesa
Quebrada Jaguay — Onion Portage
Quebrada Tacahuay

Clovis
Templeton
Debert
Naco —
Murray Springs,
Dent, Lehner
Clovis, Richey,
Colby, Domebo,
Vail

Folsom
Casper
Olsen-Chubbuck
Folsom
Lindenmeier

South America
Caverna da Pedra
El Inga
Fell's Cave
Los Toldos — Palli Aike
Taima Taima

Sunday, July 20, 1969, was a momentous day in human history: For the first time in the existence of our species, a human being walked on the soil of another world. On that day, American astronaut Neil Armstrong left the relative safety of the lunar lander, climbed down the ladder, took a final step off, and became the citizen—if only temporarily—of another world.

NASA, leaving nothing to chance, had scripted a weighty but succinct statement to be intoned by the first human to walk on the moon. Armstrong actually flubbed his line as he jumped off the lander onto the lunar surface, saying: "That's one small step for man, one giant leap for mankind." But that's redundant; "man," and "mankind" are the same thing in this context. He was supposed to say, "That's one small step for *a* man, one giant leap for mankind." In other words, though the step off the lunar lander was literally a "small step" for an individual, it represented a giant metaphorical leap forward for the human species.

The literal and figurative step Armstrong took that day was a significant one, but really just one stride in the great march of human history—a history marked by uncounted steps, both small and big, and leaps, both modest and great. From our literal first steps in Africa to Armstrong's first step onto the lunar surface, human history has been filled with small steps that collectively have added up to giant leaps. One thing that surely characterizes our species is the desire to take those steps and to explore both new vistas of the imagination and actual vistas of new lands. This chapter focuses on the exploration of such new horizons by our anatomically modern ancestors as they spread into the new worlds of Australia, the islands of the Pacific, and the Americas.

CHRONICLE

When British explorer Captain James Cook's ship made landfall on the east coast of Australia in 1770, he had no professional speechwriters to help commemorate the occasion. The record of his first impressions on encountering native Australians is more mundane than Neil Armstrong's remarks: "Sunday 29th April. Saw as we came in on both points of the bay Several of the natives and a few hutts. Men, women and children on the south shore abreast of the Ship, to which place I went in the boats in hopes of speaking with them" (as quoted in Price 1971:65).

When the first British settlement of the Australian continent was established at Sydney harbor in 1778, the colonists also arrived by oceangoing vessels, as had Cook. Cook and those who followed found a land populated by more than a quarter million and perhaps as many as three-quarters of a million people (Mulvaney and Kamminga 1999:69). Those natives were the descendants of settlers who had also arrived by sea. Lacking a written language, the original settlers left no record of their reaction to their "giant leap" to a new continent. Only the archaeological record speaks to us about how they survived as a people in their new world.

THE SETTLEMENT OF GREATER AUSTRALIA

The original Australians, called Aborigines, were an enigma to the European colonizers. In the Europeans' myopic view, the Aborigines seemed primitive in their material culture, a Stone Age people with few material advances, throwbacks to a distant time in human history. Yet what these people lacked in things, they more than made up for in ideas. They possessed a range of sophisticated social systems; the individual Aborigine had a far denser web of relations and was far more knowledgeable of his or her social connections than was the average European. These supposedly primitive people also had a richly detailed mythology and oral history and a sophisticated knowledge of their natural surroundings. Australian Aborigines also produced a richly textured artistic tradition, painting fantastical images of the animals they encountered in their environment, as well as the ancestors, heroes, and spirits that inhabited their spirit world (Gray 1996; Mulvaney and Kamminga 1999).

As different as they were from the European settlers, these native Australians shared at least one thing with the newcomers; as already mentioned, they had arrived by watercraft (Birdsell 1977; Jones 1989:1992; J. White and O'Connell 1982). Their voyages of exploration and migration—a series of small steps adding up to one giant leap to a new world—occurred at least 40,000 years before the arrival of the Europeans.

Paleogeography in the Western Pacific

During the height of the Pleistocene, ice covered much of the northern latitudes and higher elevations of the world, locking up a prodigious quantity of the earth's water in permanent ice fields—so much water that sea level was lowered by at least 100 m (about 325 ft) and perhaps as much as 135 m (about 440 ft). During glacial maxima, the islands of Java, Sumatra, Bali, and Borneo were connected to each other in a single landmass called **Sunda** (or **Sundaland**) (Figure 7.1). Sunda, in turn, was connected to mainland southeast Asia. The oceans separating these islands from one another, as well as from Asia proper, are not as deep as the amount by which sea level was depressed during glacial maxima. Wide swaths of land connecting these territories, now many meters under the ocean's surface, were exposed during periods of lowered sea level.

During these same periods of depressed sea levels, Australia, New Guinea, and Tasmania were similarly connected as a single landmass, called **Sahul,** or "Greater Australia" (see Figure 7.1). Unlike Sunda, however, Sahul was never connected to mainland Asia. Even when the Pleistocene glaciers were at their most extensive and sea level was at its lowest, Sahul was still separated from Asia by a water barrier. In fact, Greater Australia has been separated from Asia since the two were separated through continental drift more than 100 million years ago. This long-standing isolation of Australia has resulted in that continent's unique native fauna of kangaroos, wallabies, wombats, and koala

bears—which are marsupials (primitive mammals that give birth to very immature young that complete their gestation in pouches)—and platypuses, echidnas, and spiny anteaters—which are monotremes (egg-laying mammals). Only a very small number of Asian placental animals, including some rodents (rats and mice) and bats, were able to cross the gap and populate Australia in prehistory (Diamond 1987a). Bats flew across the water, and rodents were probably washed out to sea from Asia on matted vegetation, which fortuitously washed up on the shores of Sahul.

The **Wallace Trench,** located between New Guinea–Australia and Java–Borneo, is an enormous undersea chasm, nearly 7,500 m (25,000 ft) deep. Though the distance between the shores of Sunda and Sahul lessened as sea level became depressed during glacial maxima at 65,000 years ago, then 53,000 years ago, and again at 35,000 years ago, the islands never coalesced, kept apart by the deep waters of **Wallacea,** the sea over the Wallace Trench (Glover 1993).

The Road to Sahul

Oceanic islands in Wallacea, like Timor and Sulawesi (formerly called the Celebes), would have served as stepping-stones between Asia and Australia during the Pleistocene. Anthropologist Joseph Birdsell (1977) has suggested a series of possible routes from Sunda to Sahul during periods of lowered sea level (see Figure 7.1). During glacial maxima and the concomitant lowering of sea level, one viable route starts on the eastern shore of contemporary Borneo,

FIGURE 7.1

The current coastlines of Australia, New Guinea, and southeast Asia, as well as the coastline during glacial maxima. Arrows show proposed migration routes from Sunda (the combined landmass of the islands of southeast Asia) to Sahul (Greater Australia).

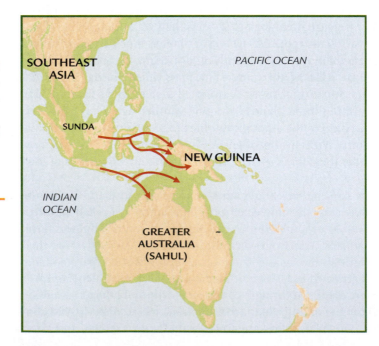

continues east through Sulawesi, and includes several island hops to north-west New Guinea. The longest inter-island gap would be about 70 km (43 mi); the mean of the eight gaps in this route is only about 28 km (17 mi) (Birdsell 1977:127). An alternate route suggested by Birdsell is more southerly, beginning in Java, traversing the Indonesian archipelago, crossing south to Timor and then south to Australia proper. This route also contains eight ocean crossings, with a maximum of 87 km (54 mi) and a mean of a little more than 19 km (12 mi) between landfalls (Birdsell 1977:127). When sea level is not as low as the proposed maximum, the distances become greater and the trip more difficult.

As Birdsell points out, this voyage likely did not take place all at once but transpired, perhaps, over several generations, as people with a marine adaptation explored the islands in their vicinity and discovered more distant islands accidentally by being blown off course during storms. These people might then have settled on some of the islands, and the process would have been repeated, pushing the limits of their world ever farther out along its edges.

The Discovery of Greater Australia

The timing of the original human discovery and settlement of Greater Australia has long been disputed. It cannot have preceded a human presence on coastal southeast Asia (which is the most logical source for the native Australian population), and it must have followed the development of a coastal adaptation and the invention of seaworthy watercraft.

As we saw in Chapter 4, stone tools dating to as much as 900,000 years ago have been found on the island of Flores, located at the eastern end of the Indonesian archipelago (Morwood et al. 1998). With the lowered sea level of that time period, Flores was separated from the mainland by only about 19 km (12 mi) of open water. Nevertheless, this indicates that even at this early date, hominids were capable of surviving deepwater crossings.

It should come as no surprise, therefore, that anatomically modern humans were capable of crossing the wide stretches of open ocean separating Greater Australia from Sunda at 40,000 years ago. Unfortunately, however, only a very few archaeological sites have been found thus far at the most logical points along the presumed island pathway (Figure 7.2).

For example, one of the older sites in southeast Asia is located in Niah Cave on the island of Borneo. The lowest levels in the cave produced stone flakes, bone tools, and the remains of several animal species, including tapir, pig, monkey, deer, and porcupine (Jones 1989). One of the larger stone tools recovered at the site exhibits a distinct notching or grooving around its middle—in essence, a "waist." This form turns up again on the other side of Wallacea, in New Guinea and Australia, and may indicate a cultural connection between the peoples who made this tool form on both sides of the Wallace Trench. Radiocarbon dates place the earliest occupation of Niah Cave at around 40,000 years ago. A fully modern, lightly constructed human skull was recovered from this same level in the cave.

FIGURE 7.2

Sites representing the earliest occupation of Greater Australia.

Most of the rest of the sites in southeast Asia date to after 40,000 B.P. For example, Lang Rongrien, in Thailand, dates to 37,000 years ago (O'Connell and Allen 1998). The oceanic island of Sulawesi in Wallacea has produced archaeological evidence of human occupation dating to 31,000 years ago at the Leang Burung Cave site (Jones 1992).

The oldest evidence for the occupation of the island of Timor, located east of Flores in the Indonesian archipelago, was found in Lene Hara Cave. More than 400 pieces of chipped stone as well as shell beads were found by excavators in association with charcoal that has been radiocarbon-dated to at least 35,000 B.P. (Holden 2001).

The archaeological evidence found on these Indonesian islands supports the idea that they served as stepping-stones in a wave of human population east from southeast Asia into the western Pacific. Even farther east and toward the north lay the planet's largest ocean, with widely scattered, fertile bits of land, many of which would also be settled in antiquity by human voyagers (see the discussion later in this chapter). To the east and south, however, lay the biggest real-estate prize of all: the landmass of Greater Australia. It is on the settlement of this region that we next focus our attention.

THE EARLIEST OCCUPATION OF GREATER AUSTRALIA

The Archaeology of Sahul

The earliest-known settlement of New Guinea, then a part of Greater Australia, was located on an ancient, exposed coral reef on Bobongara Hill on the north coast of Papua New Guinea, at the southeastern terminus of the Huon Peninsula. The site has been dated by thermoluminescence to 40,000 B.P. (Groube et al. 1986). Recovered from the site were a number of axe heads with a distinct narrowing or notching toward their middles (thus the name "waisted axes" and the similarity to the waisted tool found at Niah Cave in Borneo), a couple of stone cores for making flake tools, and a small number of flakes. Waisted axes have been found in archaeological contexts elsewhere in New Guinea, most notably at the Kosipe site, dating to 26,000 years ago, and at Nombe, dating to 25,000 years ago (J. White and O'Connell 1982). The waist was probably produced to aid in hafting the stone axe onto a wooden handle. Les Groube et al. (1986) suggest that these axes were used in forest clearing, an activity that, according to Rhys Jones (1989:764), would have encouraged the growth of wild foods like yams, taro, and sugarcane by opening up the thick forest canopy and allowing more sunlight to reach the ground. The Kuk site in the New Guinea highlands, consisting of some carbon and **fire-cracked rocks,** is dated to a little before Kosipe and Nombe and may be as old as 30,000 years.

The timing of the first human settlement of Australia is a contentious issue among archaeologists, geologists, and geneticists (Brown 2000). One school of thought places the earliest human movement on the island continent at around 60,000 or more years ago. For example, at a meeting of specialists in Australian prehistory held in late 2003, geneticist Rosalind Harding argued that analysis of the mitochondrial DNA of Australian Aborigines shows that they have been genetically isolated from the rest of the world for no less than 60,000 years (as quoted in Dayton: 2003).

Some archaeologists argue that physical evidence for this early arrival date has been discovered at the Malakunanja II site in northwestern Australia, where more than 1,500 artifacts have been found including stone flakes, a grindstone, and pieces of ground hematite and ochre. Optically stimulated luminescence dating suggests that Malakunanja II was occupied at least 45,000 and perhaps as many as 60,000 years ago (Roberts, Jones, and Smith 1990:154).

Paleoecological data have also been cited to support an early date for initial human settlement. At the aforementioned meeting held in 2003, ecologist Peter Kershaw reported on his analysis of a number of deep stratigraphic cores in Australia in which he consistently found a significant peak in charcoal dating to about 45,000 years ago (Dayton 2003). He interprets the peak as having been the result of a substantial population of human beings in Australia tending hearths and using fire in hunting. In Kershaw's view, for there to have been a human population large enough to produce a charcoal peak at 45,000 years ago, they must have arrived in small numbers substantially before this. It should be pointed out, however, that Kershaw also found a charcoal peak at 130,000 years ago, which he suggests might be due to naturally started fires. Perhaps the 45,000-year-old charcoal peak has a similar, noncultural explanation.

Ultimately, archaeological evidence is required to support the claim of a 60,000-year-old migration to Australia, and that evidence is not terribly strong. Archaeologists J. F. O'Connell and J. Allen (1998) are particularly skeptical of Australian sites alleged to be more than 40,000 years old, strongly questioning the appropriateness of the dating techniques applied and, in some cases, the validity of the artifacts themselves. Remember, anything much older than 40,000 years stretches beyond the reliable range of radiocarbon dating but is far too young for potassium/argon and related techniques (see Chapter 2). The older Australian dates, including the date derived from Malakunanja II, have been determined by using techniques like electron spin resonance and optically stimulated luminescence (see Chapter 2) that, while of great potential, can be problematic in their application and interpretation.

Crucial in the debate about the timing of the earliest human settlement of Australia is the Lake Mungo 3 skeleton, the remains of an anatomically modern human being. Lake Mungo is one of a number of dry lake beds located in the Willandra Lakes region of western New South Wales in southeastern Australia (Figure 7.3). Found in 1974, the geological deposit in which the burial was encountered was initially dated to no more than about 43,000 years ago (Brown 2000). Others date the stratum in which the burial was located to between 28,000 and 32,000 B.P. (Mulvaney and Kammiga 1999:162). If that date of the geological deposit is correct, this would represent an absolute maximum age for the skeleton whose grave, rather obviously, could only be placed in a deposit sometime after that deposit was laid down (Bowler and Magee 2000). Nevertheless, in 1999 a team of researchers led by archaeologist Alan Thorne, using three separate techniques, redated sediments nearby the Lake Mungo 3 skeleton to about 62,000 years ago. Thorne subsequently applied that new date to the bones themselves (Thorne et al. 1999).

This early date attracted quite a bit of attention—and also a fair amount of skepticism—when it was published. The dates were derived from sediments about 300 m (330 yd) away from the skeleton, and it has been suggested that the very old dates do not accurately reflect the age of the human remains (Bowler et al. 2003:840). The ensuing debate about the ancient date inspired more work, reanalysis, and redating of the sediments in which Lake Mungo 3 was placed. This newest analysis lends strong support for the original dating of about 40,000 years ago (Bowler et al. 2003).

A second burial, Lake Mungo 1 was located just 450 m (about 500 yd) away from Lake Mungo 3 (Bowler, Thorne, and Polach 1972). The Lake Mungo 1 skeleton is that of a cremated female. After her death, her body was

FIGURE 7.3
*Willandra Lakes, the fossil
lake region of southeast
Australia, have produced
some of the oldest skeletal
evidence of a human
presence on the continent.*
(© Institute of Human
Origins. Donald Johanson,
photographer)

burned, her bones were pulverized, and then she was interred. About 25% of
the Lake Mungo 1 skeleton was recovered, and enough recognizable cranial
fragments were found to partially reconstruct the skull. Much like the Lake
Mungo 3 remains, the young woman was fully anatomically modern and
rather **gracile** physiologically, lacking the large brow ridges or heavy buttress-
ing bone typical of modern Australian natives (Bowler et al. 1970). Lake
Mungo 1 has dated by radiocarbon to 24,710 years ago.

Though the redating of Lake Mungo 1 and 3 places these remains at a
time period of not more than 40,000 years ago, the story of the dating of the
earliest human settlement of Australia does not end there. Interestingly, stratigraphic analysis indicates that the Lake Mungo 1 and 3 burials do not represent the earliest human occupation of the area around the lake. Bowler and
his colleagues also reported the discovery of 11 chipped stone flakes that were
almost certainly produced as a result of human toolmaking. These flakes were
found in a stratigraphic layer at Lake Mungo that was above a separate level
dated to about 50,000 years ago and below another level dated to 46,000 years

ago (Bowler et al. 2003:839). The stratigraphic bracketing of these artifacts indicates a date of between 46,000 and 50,000 years ago.

Though there is no consensus among Australian archaeologists about sites dating to before 40,000 years ago, there is broad agreement that there are many sites on the Australian continent that date to soon after this time (O'Connell and Allen 1998).

For example, the Upper Swan Bridge site in the southwestern part of the country has produced radiocarbon dates of 39,500 B.P., 37,100 B.P., and 35,000 B.P. in association with about 200 artifacts, including stone chips, worked flakes, and flakes with edges exhibiting wear patterns (Jones 1992). The chert used to make some of the Swan River artifacts was available only during the Pleistocene, when sea level was low enough to allow access to the source. Also in southwest Australia is Devil's Lair, with a series of hearths, stone and bone artifacts, and the remains of kangaroos that had been killed, butchered, and eaten by the cave's human inhabitants. Radiocarbon dates place occupation of the cave at before 32,000 years ago and perhaps as much as 38,000 years ago (Jones 1992). Eleven kilometers (7 mi) northwest of Devil's Lair is Mammoth Cave, where burned bones, possible stone artifacts, and charcoal have been dated to between 31,000 years ago and 37,000 years ago. The Keilor site, near the city of Melbourne in southeastern Australia, has produced some quartzite flakes that were intentionally struck off a core. The soil layer in which the artifacts were recovered is estimated to be between 36,000 and 45,000 years old (J. White and O'Connell 1982). Radiocarbon and OSL procedures mutually support a date of about 37,000 B.P. for the earliest artifact-bearing strata at Ngarrabulgan Cave in north Queensland in eastern Australia (David et al. 1997). Carpenter's Gap Rockshelter, located in Kimberly in the northwestern part of the continent, has produced a radiocarbon date of 39,700 B.P. (O'Connor 1995).

Willandra Lakes

Just north of Lake Mungo, the Willandra Lakes skeleton was recovered. Dating to between 20,000 and 30,000 years ago, Willandra Lakes 50 (as the skeletal remains are designated) is far different in appearance from either Lake Mungo 1 or 3, exhibiting enormously thick cranial bones (some seven times thicker than the Lake Mungo remains). As Australian archaeologist Rhys Jones (1992) has pointed out, in these three specimens (Mungo 1 and 3 and the Willandra Lakes 50 cranium) from sites just a few miles apart, there is a greater difference in cranial bone thickness than within and among all modern human populations! For Jones, such a difference is not possible within a single population. He sees two biologically distinct populations inhabiting the same region of Australia at different times. However, as archaeologists J. Peter White and James O'Connell (1982) point out, this conclusion is difficult to support with such a small sample of crania for an entire continent and with so many differing habitats that people adapted to over such an extensive period of time. In their view, variations in cranial form merely reflect regional differentiation among native Australians, who can be derived from a single population wave from Asia more than 40,000 years ago.

THE SPREAD THROUGH AUSTRALIA

The Australian sites discussed so far are located in a ring around the perimeter of the continent (see Figure 7.2). As archaeologist Sandra Bowdler (1977, 1990) points out, the initial human population entered Australia from the north and then spread primarily east and to a lesser degree west along the coast, focusing on those areas with tropical coastal environments most like those of the source areas from which it migrated. When the migrants moved inland, they always did so along major river systems, enabling a shift in their subsistence foods from marine to riverine resources.

This pattern makes sense when you consider that the first inhabitants of Australia were almost certainly a coastally adapted people. This coastal adaptation, including the use of watercraft, enabled their discovery of Sahul and their migration onto its landmass in the first place. People with a history of coastal subsistence would have been wise to spread along the coast of their newly found home. And, as shown, the oldest human sites in Australia are located along the modern coastal rim or in formerly wetter interiors drained by rivers or dotted with lakes (the Lake Mungo area, for example).

The Australian Interior

The earliest inhabitants of Australia seem to have avoided, at least initially, the vast, harsh, dry interior of the continent (J. White 1993). Not until 20,000–25,000 years ago did human groups begin to penetrate the dry core of central Australia. Evidence from the Puritjarra Rockshelter in the Cleland Hills of central Australia shows that the cave was occupied intermittently between 22,000 and 12,000 years ago (M. A. Smith 1987). The stone-tool assemblage included primarily large flake tools but also some small flakes and cores. Other interior sites of similar antiquity include two rockshelter sites from the Hamersley Plateau in western Australia—dated at 21,000 B.P. and 26,000 B.P., respectively—and evidence of flint mining in the Nullarbor Plain dated to 20,000 years ago (Jones 1987).

TASMANIA

Tasmania is the last "new world" in Sahul to be occupied by human beings. A human population first entered what is today the island of Tasmania when it was still connected to the Australian continent. The earliest people of Tasmania lived farther south and closer to Antarctica than did any other human group to that point. The environment was entirely different from any faced previously by Australian Aborigines—a frozen tundra not unlike that of Upper Paleolithic Europe (see Chapter 6).

Tasmania shows archaeological evidence of occupation as early as 35,000 years ago at Wareen Cave and 30,000 years ago at the ORS7 site as well as at Acheron, Bone, Bluff, and Nunamira Caves in south-central Tasmania (Cosgrove, Allen, and Marshall 1990). Archaeologists Richard Cosgrove, Jim Allen, and Brendan Marshall (1990) conducted a survey of south-central Tasmania, locating 41 sites occupied between 30,000 and 11,000 years ago. Sites like Cave Bay Cave, located on Hunter Island off the northwest coast of Tasmania, date to about 23,000 B.P. (Bowdler 1974). On Tasmania proper there is Beginner's Luck Cave and Kutikina Cave (formerly Fraser Cave), both initially occupied at 20,000 years ago. Kutikina is extraordinarily rich, with over 75,000 stone flakes and tools recovered from less than a 1% sample of the site (Kiernan, Jones, and Ranson 1983). Most of the tools are steep-edged scrapers, similar in appearance to those recovered at Lake Mungo. The faunal assemblage is dominated by the remains of the large wallaby, which is a member of the kangaroo family, and the wombat, a sizable, heavyset, burrowing marsupial (Kiernan, Jones, and Ranson 1983:30). Interestingly, there are no remains of the larger, now extinct animals that typified the Pleistocene of Australia. This Australian Pleistocene megafauna probably was already extinct by the time humans first penetrated Tasmania.

GREATER AUSTRALIA: A BROAD RANGE OF ADAPTATIONS

In the stereotype, the Australian Aborigines were a homogeneous group, possessed of a simple technology, barely eking out a living in the great arid desert of central Australia. In this view, they had become stuck in time, holdovers from a primitive Stone Age society, forever limited by their harsh environment. But the archaeological record shows clearly that such a stereotype is inadequate to characterize Aboriginal culture. Rather, the ancestors of the native people of Australia arrived by watercraft by about 40,000 years ago in what had to have been, at least in part, a planned, intentional migration. Beginning with an adaptation to a tropical, coastal environment, they managed by 20,000 years ago to have adapted to the myriad habitats of Greater Australia. Coastal people maintained many of their original maritime adaptations, but others adjusted to the temperate regions of the interior, and some even developed cultural strategies for coping with environments as diverse as the Great Sandy Desert in the interior—one of the hottest, driest places on earth—and the sub-Antarctic tundra of south-central Tasmania. And the lives of these people extended far beyond the quest for subsistence. In Koonalda Cave, located near Australia's south-central coast, is some fascinating, ancient artwork, a series of meandering lines made by human fingers as much as 24,000 years ago—a sort of finger painting in the soft limestone of the cave's ceiling (Johanson, Johanson, and Edgar 1994). As mentioned in Chapter 6, potentially even older art has been dated at Wharton Hill and Panaramitee North, where microscopic vegetable matter recovered from within the grooves of petroglyphs of geometric figures has been dated to 36,000 B.P. and 43,000 B.P., respectively (Bednarik 1993).

The lesson of the earliest settlement of Australia is not one of the persistence of a primitive, backward people but of the nearly infinite capacity of human groups for adaptive flexibility. It is a lesson we will see repeated in the initial discovery of and migration to the Americas.

EAST INTO THE PACIFIC

As mentioned earlier in this chapter, as population expanded from southeast Asia to the east, a more southerly route brought human beings to the enormous landmass of Greater Australia. A more northerly route brought migrants out into the vast unexplored world of the Pacific Ocean. Covering more than one-third of the earth's surface, the Pacific stretches 15,500 km (9,600 mi) from north to south and 20,000 km (more than 12,000 mi) from east to west (Figure 7.4). Its total area is about 180 million km^2 (70 million mi^2).

Europeans, considered relative latecomers, did not cross the Pacific until Ferdinand Magellan's circumnavigation of the globe in A.D. 1519–22. Close to a thousand of the 25,000 islands scattered across the ocean were already inhabited by people—and had been for a few thousand years—by the time of Magellan's voyage.

A Pacific Islander "Age of Exploration"

The fascinating story of the initial exploration and settlement of the Pacific belies the cultural conceit that the "age of exploration" began and ended in the European Renaissance. The successful exploration and colonization of Pacific islands by a people without some of the technological advantages of European explorers (such as quadrants, sextants, compasses) is all the more remarkable when you consider the following: The total landmass of the 25,000 Pacific islands represents only 0.7% of the total area of the ocean, and average island size is only about 10 km by 6 km (6 mi by 4 mi) (Terrell 1986:14). Some of the inhabited islands are far smaller. Though many of these islands are geographically clustered and "intervisible" (visible one from the other), the individual clusters are often separated by hundreds, even thousands, of kilometers. Simply finding such island clusters while sailing a small canoe required great skill and not just a little luck. Finding one's way home and then returning to settle the newly discovered island was nothing short of miraculous.

Yet, discover, explore, and colonize many of those islands is precisely what settlers from southeast Asia and New Guinea did. And they accomplished this largely as the result of intentional geographic expansion. Certainly, serendipity

FIGURE 7.4

Modern Polynesians use traditional navigational techniques to travel hundreds of miles across the open ocean, much as their ancestors did when they initially explored and settled the Pacific islands.

(Transparency K6306, courtesy of Department of Library Services, American Museum of Natural History)

played a role in the peopling of the Pacific. Though countless sailors must have been blown off course and died before making it to safe haven, some lucky ones may have made accidental landfall on uninhabited islands and become their permanent settlers. But this cannot be the primary way in which Pacific islands were colonized. Just as Europeans in the fifteenth century began deliberately to explore the oceans, the southeast Asians and New Guineans must have been doing the same many years before. As archaeologist Geoffrey Irwin (1993:7) points out, "We know colonisation was deliberate, because explorers took with them the plants and animals, women and men necessary to establish viable settlements." In other words, colonization of the Pacific was largely planned, and colonists brought with them the people and things necessary for the successful establishment of new communities (see Figure 7.4).

Geoffrey Irwin (1993) has, with his colleagues S. H. Bickler and P. Quirke (1990), conducted computer simulations of exploration and colonization strategies in the Pacific. They have shown that under the right conditions and when the right search strategies are applied, even Pacific islands at great distance from each other can be safely and successfully explored and colonized, with return trips possible to the original homes of the migrants. They have shown graphically and mathematically that, as archaeologist John Terrell (1986:72) has suggested, to the highly skilled navigators and sailors of ancient

Polynesia, "the sea must have been more an enticing highway than an encompassing barrier."

Pacific Geography

The Pacific islands are usually divided into three groupings: **Melanesia**—the so-called black islands of New Guinea and smaller islands to the east, including the Solomon Islands, the Bismarck Archipelago, Santa Cruz, New Caledonia, Vanuatu, and Fiji; **Micronesia**—the "small islands" north of Melanesia; and **Polynesia**—"many islands," including a broad triangle of islands demarcated at its points by Hawaii to the north, Easter Island to the southeast, and New Zealand to the southwest.

Pacific Archaeology

Some of the larger islands of Melanesia, including New Britain and New Ireland in the Bismarck Archipelago, were settled by seafaring explorers from Australia by at least 35,000 years ago, not that long after the initial settlement of the island continent (O'Connell and Allen 1998). Even farther to the east, Buka, in the Solomon Island chain, was discovered and settled no less than 28,000 years ago. At a distance of 180 km (110 mi) from the Bismarck Archipelago, the initial settlement of the Solomons is proof of sophisticated navigational skills on the part of the settlers. The Melanesian islands farther to the east and in deeper water, as well as all the islands of Micronesia and Polynesia, were settled much later in a second wave of exploration and migration beginning probably little more than 3,500 years ago (Irwin 1993).

We know from the ethnographic record that the native peoples of the Pacific were brilliant navigators. They built up a substantial reservoir of knowledge about currents and wind patterns. Even without navigational devices, the native navigators of the Pacific could reckon by the stars, were familiar with cloud patterns indicating that land was nearby, possessed a detailed knowledge of bird flight paths from island to island, and constructed seaworthy ships capable of journeys across wide stretches of open ocean.

The spread of people through east Melanesia and Polynesia was accompanied by a common culture. Because they were a maritime people, fishing played a significant role in their food quest. They also were food producers, who brought non-native agricultural staples with them as they colonized islands; these staples included pig, as a major source of animal protein, and domesticated root crops, especially yams. They also brought a common pottery style, called **Lapita** (Figure 7.5). In fact, the earliest occurrence of a human population on the inhabited islands of Polynesia is invariably marked by the appearance of Lapita pottery. The Lapita designation is now applied to the entire cultural complex of Polynesia and includes a maritime adaptation, the raising of pigs, the growing of certain root crops and fruit trees, the use of shell in producing tools and ornaments, and the manufacture of Lapita pottery.

FIGURE 7.5
*Lapita pottery is found
virtually everywhere that
Polynesians explored and
settled after 3500 B.P.*
(Courtesy of Dr. Richard
Shutler, Jr. and Dr. Mary
Elizabeth Shutler)

The Lapita complex is absent from Australia or the islands of Micronesia. It appears first in the archaeological record of the Bismarck Archipelago and, perhaps, Fiji a little more than 3,500 years ago (Irwin 1993:39). Expansion proceeded eastward, with large island groups like Tonga at 2,800 years ago (Burley and Dickinson 2001) and Samoa, the Cook Islands, and the Society Islands being settled in turn, after about 2,500 years ago. The Hawaiian Islands, far to the north, were settled by about 1600 B.P. (about A.D. 400); Easter Island, at the eastern limit of Polynesia, was settled at about the same time. New Zealand, though much closer to the Australian coast, was settled not by natives of that continent but by Polynesians. The earliest evidence for a human presence on New Zealand dates to about A.D. 1000.

Why the Pacific Islands Were Settled

Geoffrey Irwin (1993:211–12) lists some of the possible motives for the expansion into the vast and previously uncharted Pacific: curiosity about what lay beyond the horizon, a desire to find areas suitable for habitation and rich in

FIGURE 7.6
Altogether there are more than 800 of these stone sculptures in various conditions and positions on Easter Island. (© Royalty-Free/Corbis)

resources, and the need to find new land as a result of overpopulation or warfare. As Irwin points out, motives are not testable archaeologically. And, as John Terrell (1986) indicates, the motives to move out into the Pacific were likely as mixed and as varied as those of Europeans in their own age of exploration.

Whatever the reasons, the many inhabited islands of the Pacific, populated initially by people possessing very few, rather homogeneous cultures, produced a wide array of adaptations once they were settled. Settlers exploited the most valuable resources, developing their own unique adaptations to each island or island chain. On New Zealand, the moa—a large flightless bird unique to that nation—became a major component in the diet of a hunting society. Powerful and complex agricultural societies arose on Hawaii and Tonga (Kirch 1984). The fascinating people of Easter Island developed great skills at organizing their own labor, which enabled the quarrying, carving, transportation, and erection of the hundreds of enormous stone sculptures that have generated such interest and speculation (Figure 7.6). All of today's enormous diversity developed from those first courageous voyages across the vast Pacific Ocean a few thousand years ago.

COMING TO AMERICA

On Thursday, October 11, 1492, a sea voyager had an encounter that forever affected the trajectory of human history—another one of those small steps that resulted in a giant leap in the march of human history. Documenting the ship's arrival, the journal of the captain of that momentous voyage reads: "When we stepped ashore we saw fine green trees, streams everywhere and different kinds of fruit. . . . Soon many of the islanders gathered around us. I could see that they were people who would be more easily converted to our Holy Faith by love than by coercion" (Cummins 1992:94). Thus begins Christopher Columbus's narrative of the first contact between Europeans and American natives since the series of short-lived, brutal incidents on Newfoundland in Canada that were recorded in the Viking sagas about 1,000 years ago (Magnusson and Paulsson 1965).

Thinking he had discovered a series of islands off the coast of Asia, Columbus called the people he encountered *los Indios,* or Indians. After his initial voyage, Columbus returned three more times, always expecting that the Asian continent lay just beyond the limits of his previous exploration. Though Columbus never accepted it, most European scholars concluded that he had happened on not a cluster of islands immediately off the coast of south Asia but, as Amerigo Vespucci was to characterize it in 1503, a "new world," populated by peoples unknown to and not even conceived of by Europeans.

This New World consisted of two entire continents that make up almost 28.5% of the world's land surface, with a native population estimated to have been in the tens of millions and speaking more than 1,500 different languages and dialects. Over centuries and millennia, descendants of the small bands of hunters and gatherers who initially entered into the New World developed successful adaptations to nearly all of the countless habitats of the Western Hemisphere, from frigid arctic tundra to arid sandy deserts, from luxuriant tropical rain forests to temperate woodlands, from seacoasts to mountains, from river valleys to plateaus. And they lived ways of life as varied as did people inhabiting the "known" continents: hunters and gatherers in small, nomadic bands foraging for food in a seasonal round; fisherfolk in established villages, harvesting the plentiful natural resources of river and shore; farmers in huge adobe apartment complexes, tending the kinds of crops that even today feed the population of the planet. There were great kingdoms with impressive cities, splendid monuments of pyramids and palaces, and powerful hereditary rulers, not unlike King Ferdinand and Queen Isabella of Spain, the monarchs who had funded Columbus's expedition.

THE SOURCE OF *LOS INDIOS*

Almost as soon as it was recognized that Columbus had "discovered" a new world with people unknown to his benefactors, questions were raised concerning the origins of those "new" people. True to the spirit of the period, the answers had to conform to biblical interpretation: American natives had to be derived, ultimately, from Adam and Eve and then more recently from those few people who had survived Noah's flood.

Despite broad speculation concerning the source of the Native American population (see Feder 2007 and Williams 1991), quite early on some scholars recognized a connection between the natives of the New World and the people of Asia. As early as 1524, Giovanni de Verrazzano, an Italian navigator sailing for France, noticed a physical similarity between the native people of the New World and certain groups in the Old World. Verrazzano made landfall at what is today the border of North and South Carolina, sailing north, looking for a sea route to the west and, it was hoped, a way past the New World and to Asia. He entered Delaware Bay and the mouth of the Hudson River, sailed along Connecticut's coast, entered and explored Narragansett Bay in Rhode Island, and followed the shore of Cape Cod on his way home, unsuccessful in his attempt to find a passage to the west. Verrazzano spent several weeks exploring the interior of Rhode Island and had an opportunity to examine local natives closely. In his report, Verrazzano noted that in the color and texture of their hair and in the shape of their eyes, the people he encountered looked like the people of Asia.

Jesuit missionary Friar Joseph de Acosta (Huddleston 1967) used the Bible to come up with a precociously accurate hypothesis concerning the geographic origins of Native Americans. Acosta pointed out in 1590 that all animals on earth except those on board Noah's ark had been killed in the great flood. After their annihilation in the flood, the world's animal communities were reconstituted by descendants of those saved on board the ark. Acosta reasoned that for this to have occurred, the animals must have been able to walk from the landing place of the ark—according to the Bible, someplace in southwest Asia on "the mountains of Ararat"—to their new homes. That process must have included the New World. In other words, animals native to the New World must have arrived there after the flood by walking into the Americas from the landing place of Noah's ark. Acosta argued that what animals could accomplish, people could have done as well.

Thus, there must have been a land connection between the Old and the New Worlds to allow animals descended from those saved on the ark to walk into the Western Hemisphere, Acosta argued. He knew where such a connection could *not* have been, based on sixteenth-century exploration of the American coastline. By a process of elimination, he suggested that the Old World and the New World were probably joined somewhere in northwestern North America and northeastern Asia. That is, the first Americans must have come from Asia, having walked into the New World from the Old World at a point where they were joined. It was not until about 50 years after Acosta's hypothesis that Russian trader Semyon Dezhnyov became the first Russian to travel through the region, and it wasn't until 1732 that two more Russian traders, Ivan Fyodorov and Mikhail Gvozdev, crossed the strait that separated the Old World from the New World and recognized how close Russia and America actually were. In fact, the Old World and the New World are separated by only about 85 km (53 mi) of sea, called the Bering Strait (Figure 7.7).

Today the Bering Strait is only 30–50 m (100–165 ft) deep. But during periods of glacial maxima in the Pleistocene, sea level was depressed by far

FIGURE 7.7

The modern coastlines of northeast Asia and northwest North America as well as the projected coastline of Beringia during glacial maxima.

more than this, by as much as 135 m (440 ft) exposing a platform of land connecting Russia and Alaska that was as wide, perhaps, as 1,500 km (1,000 mi) from north to south, a land area of more than 2 million km² (770,000 mi²). During long periods in the Pleistocene, people in northeast Asia could have walked into the New World across the body of land today called **Beringia,** or the **Bering Land Bridge** (see Figure 7.7).

Early thinkers like Acosta were correct. Geographically, a northeastern Asian origin for Native Americans makes sense. Gross anatomical characteristics such as those cited by Verrazzano have long shown the biological connection between Asians and Native Americans. Modern analysis of the mitochondrial DNA of Native Americans also supports the idea that the aboriginal human population of the New World was derived from Asia (Derenko et al. 2001; Gibbons 1993; Stone and Stoneking 1993; Wallace, Garrison, and Knowler 1985).

WHEN DID THE FIRST MIGRANTS ARRIVE?

Though most anthropologists accept a Beringian route for America's first human settlers, there is still great controversy over the timing of their arrival. To find out when people first entered the Americas from Siberia, we need to know three things:

1. When was Beringia exposed and open for travel?
2. When was eastern Siberia first inhabited (the source population for New World migrants)?
3. What is the age of the earliest New World sites?

When Was Beringia Exposed and Open for Travel?

If Australia's first settlers could have populated that "new world" more than 40,000 years ago (remember, there was no land bridge between Sunda and Sahul; they had no choice but to arrive by boat), then northeast Asians might have done the same thing during periods when no land bridge was present between Asia and North America. And even without a land bridge, during periods of extreme cold the Bering Strait would have frozen, producing an ice bridge between the two hemispheres.

Nonetheless, a 1,500 km-wide land connection between the two continents certainly would have facilitated the movement of animals and people either through the interior of northeast Asia, then through the middle of the exposed land bridge, and then into the interior of Alaska, or else along the Pacific coast of northeast Asia, then along the southern Beringian coast, and finally south along the coast of northwest North America (see Figure 7.7).

Beringia was exposed several times during the Pleistocene and was above water more or less continuously from the period beginning about 35,000 years ago. Analysis of submarine sediments in the area where the land bridge was located indicates a peak in glacial conditions between 22,000 and 19,000 years ago (Yokoyama et al. 2000). Sea level was at a low point for a few hundred years sometime during this period, and Beringia would have been at its most extensive. By inference, during this period Beringia would have presented the most extensive pathway to the New World from the Old for both animals and the people who hunted them. Radiocarbon dating of peat deposits that now reside beneath the Bering Sea but that must have been produced on dry land shows that the land bridge was still exposed, at least in part, until shortly after 11,000 years ago and possibly even until 10,500 years ago (Elias et al. 1996). So, in fact, the land bridge was available for the movement of animal and people for much of the time between about 35,000 and 11,000 years ago.

When Was Eastern Siberia First Inhabited?

Just as the most likely source area for the original migration of people into Australia is poorly known archaeologically, so too is the most likely source area for the original migration of people into the New World. Eastern Siberia is a difficult place to do archaeology, and relatively little work has been done there. Archaeologist David Meltzer (1989) points out that we simply do not know when it was first inhabited.

Of course, in order for human beings in antiquity to have survived in Siberia, they must have acclimatized themselves to life in the Arctic, one of the last of the world's environmental zones to which human beings developed an adaptation (Figure 7.8).

The Beringian connection between the Old and New Worlds was located in the far north. Its northern component was located north of the Arctic Circle (latitude of 66° 33′ N) and the rest of the land bridge was located in

FIGURE 7.8

The locations of a number of important localities in Russia mentioned in the text that may provide important information related to the migration of human beings from the Old World to the New in the late Pleistocene.

the sub-Arctic (a broad band of land between 50° N and the Arctic Circle). Beringia was accessible, therefore, to people in the Old World only through the Arctic and sub-Arctic of northeast Asia, and the endpoint for migrants through the land bridge was the Arctic and sub-Arctic of North America. Clearly, anyone entering the New World from the Old through Beringia must have possessed an adaptation to the extreme climate of the region in which it was located. The timing of the earliest human adaptation to the Arctic and sub-Arctic, therefore, serves as a limiting factor in our discussion of the timing of human movement into and across Beringia. This cannot have occurred before humans had developed the highly specialized adaptation necessary to survive the rigors of life in the far north.

The oldest archaeological evidence of a human presence in the Arctic has been found far from Beringia, at the Mamontovaya Kurya site in the northeasternmost section of European Russia (Pavlov, Svendsen, and Indrelid 2001). Here, at a latitude of 66° 34′ humans subsisted in the harsh climate of the Arctic by hunting mammoth, horse, reindeer, and wolf close to 40,000 years ago. Moving east, sites in the Arctic are younger than this. The Yana RHS site provides the oldest evidence of human occupation of the Arctic in eastern Siberia (Pitulko et al. 2004). Here, people living along the banks of the Yana River at 70° N latitude, subsisted primarily by hunting large game animals like reindeer, bison, woolly mammoth, and musk-ox 27,000 years ago.

Further south, radiocarbon dates indicate that central Siberia, for example, around the area of Lake Baikal, was occupied no earlier than about 34,000 years ago. Dyuktai Cave, located near the Aldan River in central Siberia, was

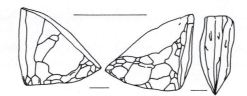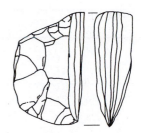

0   5 cm

FIGURE 7.9

These stone tools from the Dyuktai culture, eastern Russia (about 18,000 B.P.), exhibit a preponderance of so-called wedge-shaped cores, small stone cores of the implied shape from which sharp microblades were removed. (From "The Dyuktai Culture and New World Origins" by Seon-bonk Yi and Geoffrey Clark, University of Chicago Press, 1985)

occupied 18,000 years ago (Figure 7.9 and Table 7.1). The **wedge-shaped cores** from which the inhabitants produced blades there are similar in appearance to cores found in Denali Complex sites in Alaska dating to 10,700 years ago and discussed later in this chapter. (See Figure 7.15 and compare it to Figure 7.9.)

Moving east, Siberian sites were occupied successively more recently. In far eastern Siberia, the lowest stratigraphic levels at sites like those around Ushki Lake on the Kamchatka Peninsula have now been dated to about 11,300 B.P. (Goebel, Waters, and Dikova, 2003). The stone-tool industry seen in the oldest Ushki Lake component included small, finely made, stemmed, bifacially flaked spearpoints. Bifacial points are also a hallmark of the Clovis culture found in the New World, discussed later in this chapter.

Though none of these Siberian sites can be interpreted as having tool technologies that can be proven to have served as prototypes for the stone tools found at the oldest sites in the New World, it is clear that people were living in Siberia, on the western edge of Beringia, practicing stone-tool technologies that at least could be ancestral to those first technologies seen at the other end of the land bridge between Asia and the New World. Considering the age of the oldest Siberian sites, it seems likely that the movement of people into the New World from Siberia occurred probably no more than about 20,000 years ago. This time period, you will remember, represents a glacial maximum, with attendant maximum sea-level decline, during which the land bridge was at its largest.

What Is the Age of the Earliest New World Sites?

When Beringia became exposed as sea level fell, people adapted to the interior habitats of northeast Asia would have been able to expand their territories by moving east through the interior of the land bridge and then into the interior of northwestern North America. At the same time, people living along the Pacific coast of northeast Asia could have moved along the coast of the land bridge as it became exposed. As sea level continued to fall, the growing coasts of northeast Asia and northwest North America finally coalesced, creating a single coast from northeast Asia, across the newly exposed land

TABLE 7.1

Sample of Sites in Russia Occupied at Times of Possible
Human Population Movement into North America

SITE NAME	LOCATION	AGE	ARTIFACTS
Berelekh	Lower Indigirka Valley	12,000–13,000 years ago	Bifaces
Ushki Lake	Kamchatka	11,300 years ago	Bifaces, burins, microblades, unifaces
Ust'-Mil II	Central Siberia	11,500–35,000 years ago	Wedge-shaped cores
Dyuktai Cave	Central Siberia	After 18,000 years ago	Wedge-shaped cores, bifaces
Ikhine	Southern Siberia	31,000–34,000 years ago	Burins, cores
Ezhantsy	Central Siberia	35,000 years ago	Wedge-shaped cores, biface fragments
Mamontovaya Kurya	Arctic Russia, Ural Mountains	40,000 years ago	Mammoth, horse, reindeer, and wolf bones; unmodified flakes; bifaces
Yana RHS	Yana River	27,000 years ago	Stone flakes, rhino horn

bridge coast, and then along the coast of northwestern North America. Over several generations, northeast Asians expanding east along this coast would have found themselves in the New World, where they might have continued the process of expansion south along its coast. These migrants, moving through the interior as well as along the coast, would have had no sense that they were moving into a "new world": They merely would have been taking advantage of additional territory (Figure 7.10).

THE FIRST HUMAN SETTLEMENT OF AMERICA

The legend of the midnight ride of Paul Revere tells us that one or two lamp-lights placed in the window of the Old North Church steeple would signal the mode of the British attack on Boston: "One if by land and two if by sea." Regarding the first "invasion" of America by human beings, there also are two possible modes of movement: The first migrants may have been an interior-adapted people taking an interior land route, or they may have been a coastally adapted people taking a sea route along the coast. Obviously, to assess which of these is correct—or whether both routes were used simultaneously by different groups—we need to locate the oldest sites in the New World.

It would be convenient if the oldest sites in the New World were located near the point of entry, either in the interior of Alaska for a group arriving by

land or along the Alaskan coast for a group arriving by sea. Unfortunately, the Alaskan interior can be a very inhospitable place to conduct archaeology, and many places along the coast that might have provided shelter for a people living and moving within sight of the sea have been inundated by sea-level rise after the last glacial period.

One If by Land

A few ancient sites in northwestern North America have provided evidence of an interior adaptation. The inhabitants of these sites may represent the descendants of people who came from the interior of northeast Asia and then crossed through the interior of the land bridge. For example, Bluefish Caves in western Canada, reasonably close to the Beringian point of entry, has produced artifacts in a level that has been dated to between 15,000 and 12,000 years ago (Cinq-Mars 1978).

Most of the evidence for the late Pleistocene occupation of the interior of the New World, however, has been found far to the south of Alaska. Before we can bring the transplanted Asians from Alaska, south into the rest of the New World, there is an additional environmental issue that must be considered. During the Pleistocene, there were two primary centers of glacial expansion: the **Laurentide** ice sheet in northeastern North America, which spread south, east, and west and covered much of the northern latitudes of this continent, and the **Cordilleran** ice sheet, whose center was in the Rocky Mountains. During glacial maxima, when sea level was at its lowest and the land bridge at its largest, the Laurentide continental glacier reached its western limit and the Cordilleran mountain glacier reached its eastern limit. Though the two major ice bodies did not wax and wane in synchrony (Catto and Mandryk 1990), it is likely that they coalesced, at least in some places, for periods of time as they simultaneously expanded. We know, for example, that at about 18,000 B.P. the two major ice fields coalesced near the present border of British Columbia and Alberta, Canada, across a linear distance of close to 1,200 km (750 mi; Wright 1991).

In other words, the periods when it was easiest for human groups to migrate into Alaska from northeast Asia may have coincided with the periods when it was impossible for them to spread farther south because their way was blocked by an impenetrable ice barrier a few kilometers high.

We do know that during the late Pleistocene, a pathway opened up episodically between the Cordilleran and Laurentide ice fields that would have allowed movement southward (Figure 7.11). The reason people might have migrated south, through the cold, likely windswept pathway between the glaciers, called the **ice-free corridor,** or **McKenzie corridor,** would have been to follow migrating herds of animals whose meat and hides provided the necessities of life. However, the bones of large mammals dating to between 21,000 and 11,600 years ago are notably lacking in the area where the ice-free corridor would have been (Burns 1996). Pollen studies indicate that when an ice-free corridor was available for travel, vegetation was too poor to support large populations of animals (Mandryk 1990). Based on this sort of negative evidence, the ice-free corridor would not seem to have been a very appealing place for ancient hunters. And, in fact, there is no archaeological evidence for the presence of human beings in the corridor much before 11,000 years ago (Burns 1990).

The challenges that must have accompanied any attempt to move south of the ice sheets make interpreting the occupation of the Meadowcroft Rockshelter so difficult. Located in western Pennsylvania, south of the ice sheets and thousands of miles from Beringia, it is one of the oldest and most deeply

FIGURE 7.11

The proposed boundaries of the Cordilleran and Laurentide ice sheets of North America. Though the two may have coalesced in some localized areas during glacial maxima, for long periods an ice-free corridor may have existed by which people south of Alaska could have migrated into North America south of the ice sheets. (Courtesy of David Meltzer)

stratified archaeological sites ever excavated in North America. Within the natural rock enclosure, human beings made tools, cooked food, and threw away trash, taking advantage of the natural protection the small cave afforded. Moving back in time, the excavators of Meadowcroft have chronicled the human occupation of western Pennsylvania, covering a time span of thousands of years (Adovasio et al. 1979–80a,b; Adovasio, Donahue, and Stuckenrath 1990; Carlisle and Adovasio 1984). And at the base of the sequence brought to light by these researchers is one of the oldest radiocarbon dates associated with human-made material south of Alaska. Six dates earlier than 12,800 B.P. have been associated with stone tools near the base of the Meadowcroft sequence. Sealed beneath a rockfall from the roof of the shelter dated to 12,000 B.P. were some 400 lithic artifacts, including blades, knives with retouched edges, and an unfluted, bifacial projectile point (Figure 7.12).

To the south of Meadowcroft, a pair of sites at least as old and possibly older have been discovered in Virginia and South Carolina. At the Topper site in South Carolina, so-called Clovis artifacts (see the discussion of Clovis later in this chapter) datable to about 11,000 years ago were encountered in a discrete stratigraphic level by archaeologist Albert Goodyear (1999) and his team. Though Clovis has long been considered the earliest culture in North America, Goodyear continued excavating beneath the level of their discovery

FIGURE 7.12

The stone point at the far left was recovered from the earliest indisputable cultural layer at the Meadowcroft Rockshelter in western Pennsylvania. The layer in which this tool was found dates to more than 12,800 years ago. (Courtesy of James Adovasio, Mercyhurst Archaeological Institute)

at Topper. If Clovis tools really represent the technology of the first people in the New World, there should have been no cultural remains in lower stratigraphic layers. Needless to say, Goodyear was enormously surprised when he found chipped stone flakes that appear to have been cutting tools in the soil level beneath the Clovis artifacts (Figure 7.13). Though no datable material was found in association with these stone flakes, the layer immediately beneath them did provide a date of about 20,000 years ago. So the Topper artifacts must be older than 11,000 years and could be close to 20,000 years old. More recently, things have gotten even more interesting at Topper. In the 2004 summer field season, in another part of the site, Goodyear and his students found a deep stratum sprinkled with chipped stone flakes (Wilford 2004). Some of these pieces of stone may be tools; others may be fragments discarded in the tool-making process. One of Goodyear's students recovered flecks of charcoal in the same soil level. The archaeological community was stunned when in late 2004 Goodyear announced the results of radiocarbon dating of this charcoal: 50,000 years. This date is an extreme outlier to the dates derived from even the other pre-Clovis sites. As a result, many are skeptical while, at the same time, eagerly awaiting publication of the details of the site and of its extraordinary date.

The stratigraphy at the Cactus Hill site in Virginia also indicates the presence of an ancient settlement of the American southeast. Here, a stone-scraping tool, stone blades, and the core from which the blades were struck were found by archaeologist Joseph McAvoy and his group in an undisturbed soil layer 15 cm (nearly 6 in.) below a stratum in which Clovis-type artifacts were found (Stokstad 2000; see Figure 7.13). Of course, this discovery shows pretty conclusively that the points in question are older than Clovis. When specialists have examined the Cactus Hill blades, they note substantial similarities with

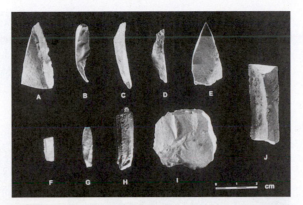

FIGURE 7.13

Artifacts from two sites in eastern North America, Topper in South Carolina and Cactus Hill in Virginia. The Topper artifacts (top)—chipped-stone cutting tools—were found in a stratigraphic layer below one containing Clovis artifacts and dated to 11,000 years ago and above a culturally sterile layer dated to 20,000 years ago. The Cactus Hill artifacts (bottom)—including a stone scraping tool, stone blades, and a stone core—were found in an undisturbed layer 15 cm (6 in.) below one in which Clovis artifacts were found. (Top: SCIAA photo by Daryl P. Miller; *bottom:* © Kenneth Garrett/National Geographic Society Image Collection)

the tools recovered at the oldest levels at Meadowcroft Rockshelter (Bonnichsen and Schneider 2001–02).

At Cactus Hill researchers were able to recover enough organic material for a date. The remarkable result: The pre-Clovis layer has been radiocarbon-dated to about 15,000 years ago (Bower 2000b) (though there is some question whether the date was derived from older charcoal that had mixed with a younger archaeological deposit).

As you know, western Pennsylvania, Virginia, and South Carolina aren't anywhere close to Beringia. Because the inhabitants of these sites could not have parachuted into their habitation, the necessary implication is that we should be able to find an extensive archaeological trail of sites successively older still, leading from their locations back to Beringia, reflecting the movement of people through an ice-free corridor, south of the glaciers, and then east—but such a trail simply does not exist. Perhaps we simply haven't looked in the right places, or the sites are barely visible archaeologically. Maybe we have it all wrong and the first Americans didn't come from northeast Asia via

FIGURE 7.14

These stone tools and possible tent pegs from Monte Verde, in Chile, date to as early as 12,500 B.P. (Courtesy of Tom Dillehay)

Beringia but instead arrived first in northeast North America from Europe (see "Issues and Debates" in this chapter). The other possibility, of course, is that we have found no trail of sites leading from Beringia to eastern North America because there is none, suggesting that Meadowcroft, Topper, and Cactus Hill are younger than we think.

Two If by Sea

The Monte Verde site in Chile is located on Chinchihuapa Creek and exhibits a remarkable degree of preservation (Dillehay 1987, 1989, 1997a,b; Dillehay and Collins 1988). In addition to finding hundreds of stone artifacts, including long, slender spearpoints and cutting and scraping tools, the excavators of the site, led by archaeologist Tom Dillehay, found wooden lances and stakes that likely held down the bases of the inhabitants' hide-covered tents (Figure 7.14). The wet peat that covered the site produced an environment in which the bones of animals killed and butchered at the site, and even pieces of meat and skin tissue (identified as mastodon) and fragments of almost 70 different plant species, were preserved. Thirty radiocarbon dates firmly date the site to 12,500 years ago.

Located near the coast, Monte Verde might best be explained as the remains of a community whose distant ancestors had entered the New World along the Beringian coast, obviously long before 12,500 B.P. Archaeologist David Meltzer suggests that the age of the Monte Verde site implies a time of entry into the New World along the Beringian coast before 20,000 B.P. (1997: 755). These coastal migrants traveled south along the Pacific coast of the New World—virtually all of their sites would have been submerged by rising sea level and cannot be found. Eventually, these people reached the southern coast of South America, where they then moved into the interior, leaving the remains at Monte Verde.

How likely is such a scenario? Would it have been possible for a maritime people to have skirted the huge tongues of ice from the Cordilleran glacier as they calved into the Pacific? Would these people have found a sufficient number of safe harbors to sustain themselves as they expanded southward along the coast until they bypassed the glaciers and could have established a more permanent presence on the North and then South American continents?

Recent work on Prince of Wales Island in Alaska supports this possibility (Dixon 1999). Paleontologist Timothy Heaton found substantial evidence of plant and animal life in the ancient layers of On Your Knees Cave, specifically in strata that dated to the late Pleistocene. This discovery indicates that even with glaciers all around it, there were places where human beings could have found sufficient resources for survival. And, in fact, at On Your Knees Cave there is direct evidence for that, at least late in this story. A human skeleton was found in the cave and dated to about 10,500 years ago. Isotope analysis of the bones indicated the individual's diet consisted almost entirely of marine foods; in fact, the isotope calculations performed on this person's bones were similar to the same calculations performed on the bones of marine mammal carnivores like ringed seal and sea otter (Dixon 1999:118). The point is, even in Alaska, it seems that there were havens for a maritime people and that the coastal route may have offered a feasible pathway into the New World.

Far to the south, new and very important data from the South American coast offer further evidence for ancient, coastally adapted settlers of the New World (Pringle 1998b). At one section of the southern Peruvian coast, the floor of the sea slopes away sharply from the shore. As a result, and unlike most stretches of the coast, when sea level rose at the end of the Pleistocene, the shoreline did not move much. Two archaeological teams, working independently, have located two sites—Quebrada Jaguay (Sandweiss et al. 1998) and Quebrada Tacahuay (Keefer et al. 1998)—that are among the oldest sites found in South America.

Dating to 11,100 B.P., Quebrada Jaguay presents clear evidence of a maritime adaptation by its occupants. Hunting was not a significant contributor to the diet at Quebrada Jaguay, and the remains of very few terrestrial mammals have been found. On the other hand, the bones of numerous, small drumfish, most likely caught by nets, and a large assemblage of the shells of wedge clams indicate that the inhabitants of the site depended on the sea for subsistence. At 10,700-year-old Quebrada Tacahuay, the sea was the major source for subsistence. Close to 100% of the bones recovered at the site were those of marine creatures, with a focus on anchovies and cormorants (a seabird).

Though both of these sites are substantially younger than Monte Verde, they are clear indications of an early coastal occupation of the New World. Their ancestors—and the ancestors of the inhabitants of Monte Verde—were most likely coastally adapted northeast Asians who took a coastal route across the Bering Land Bridge into the New World.

ALASKA

Back in Alaska, close to the Beringian point of entry, are a number of sites dating to before 11,000 B.P. As archaeologists William Powers and John Hoffecker (1989) point out, it is now clear that there was a widespread tradition of producing small blades from wedge-shaped cores in northeast Asia and northwest North America at the end of the Pleistocene. Sites with wedge-shaped cores and **microblades** have been excavated in Siberia, China, Japan, and Mongolia, as well as in Alaska and northwestern Canada (Morlan 1970). These sites are older in the Old World than in the New World, and a "genetic" connection between the industries of western and eastern Beringia seems clear. Conceivably, these sites may represent a separate wave of population movement from the Old World to the New.

Denali and Nenana

Sites exhibiting tools of the locally designated **Denali Complex** of wedge-shaped cores, microblades, bifacial knives, and **burins** have been excavated in the Nenana Valley, about 100 km (62.5 mi) southwest of Fairbanks, in east-central Alaska (Figure 7.15; Powers and Hoffecker 1989). Sites such as Dry Creek (Component II), Panguingue Creek (Component II), Usibelli, and Slate Creek in the Nenana Valley are assigned to the Denali Complex; Dry Creek has produced a radiocarbon date of about 10,700 B.P. (Powers and Hamilton 1978). Denali Complex sites outside of the Nenana Valley include Donnelly Ridge in central Alaska, the Campus site near Fairbanks, the Teklanika River sites in Mt. McKinley National Park, and Healy Lake (West 1967). These all date to around 10,000 years ago (West 1975). A very different-looking industry of microblades and cores has been found in the earliest levels at the Onion Portage site (Akmak) in western Alaska, also dating to around 10,000 B.P. (Anderson 1968, 1970).

All of this seems to provide a very neat and simple answer to questions surrounding the first human settlement of the Americas: Beginning some 18,000 years ago, microblade-making northeast Asians like those at the Dyuktai site slowly made their way across Beringia, ending up in Alaska by about 10,700 years ago or a few hundred years earlier. The problem is that Denali Complex sites are not the oldest in the New World; they're not even the oldest in Alaska. There is a cultural level at Dry Creek (Component I) earlier than the Denali level at the same site, and the Moose Creek and Walker Road sites have produced radiocarbon dates ranging between 11,000 B.P. and 11,800 B.P. in their lowest levels. The stone-tool assemblages at these sites—classified as the **Nenana Complex**—show no evidence of Denali Complex wedge-shaped cores and look very little like the stone-tool assemblage at Dyuktai. Instead, these assemblages include bifacially flaked spearpoints (Figure 7.16).

The stone tools representative of the Nenana Complex bear a general resemblance to those found in the lowest stratigraphic level at Ushki Lake, in

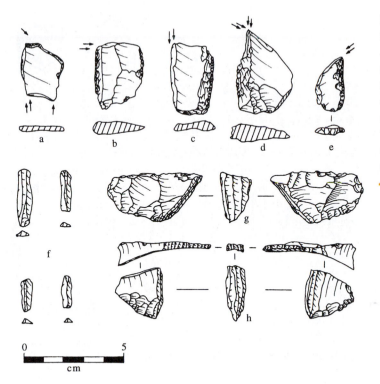

FIGURE 7.15
These stone tools from the Denali Complex of Alaska, dating to after 11,000 B.P., include some wedge-shaped cores (g and h), suggesting a derivation from the older wedge-shaped cores in Asia (see Figure 7.9). (Courtesy of William Powers)

Kamchatka, mentioned previously. Both the Nenana and Ushki Lake (Component 7) industries consist of small, bifacially worked knives and unifacially retouched flakes and blades; both lack microblades (Dikov 1978; Goebel, Waters, and Dikova 2003). Interestingly, Component 6 at Ushki Lake, dating to 10,000 B.P. has a stone-tool industry quite similar to Denali; both are characterized by the presence of microblades (Goebel, Waters, and DiKova 2003).

The Nenana Complex may be derived from the industry seen at Ushki in Kamchatka, representing an early movement of Asians (about 12,000 B.P.) across the Bering Land Bridge into the New World. Following the hypothesis of West (1981), Powers and Hoffecker (1989) suggest that the Siberian microblade industry seen at sites like Dyuktai and Ushki Component 6 may be at least indirectly ancestral to the later Denali Complex (dated to about 11,000 B.P.) and other early New World microblade industries. Denali, in this view, represents a migration subsequent to an earlier movement of Siberians with a bifacial industry like that seen at the Ushki and Nenana Complex sites.

As Powers and Hoffecker see it, the Denali Complex was restricted to the far north. However, in their view, possessors of the earlier Nenana stone-tool tradition were able to expand to the south. Archaeologists Ted Goebel, Roger Powers, and Nancy Bigelow (1991) point out that with the exception of fluted spearpoints (to be discussed shortly), the Nenana stone-tool assemblage is virtually identical to that seen to the south and associated with these points. Descendants of these people, Powers and Hoffecker argue, made a small technological

FIGURE 7.16

In these stone tools from the Nenana Complex of Alaska, dating to 11,800 B.P., the lack of wedge-shaped cores, the presence of bifacially flaked tools, and dates that are older than those associated with the Denali Complex suggest a different and older migration of northeast Asians into the New World. (Courtesy of William Powers)

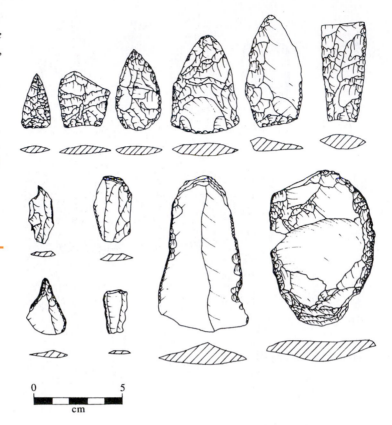

step in spearpoint form—the so-called **fluted point**—that allowed for an enormous adaptive leap and the successful occupation of two continents.

CLOVIS

Sometimes called **Clovis,** for the site in New Mexico where the distinctive spearpoints that characterize the tool assemblage were first recognized, **Paleoindian** sites number in the hundreds and are found throughout the continental United States. Where dates have been derived through ^{14}C, almost all Clovis sites fit into a narrow range, between 11,200 B.P. and 10,500 B.P., appearing virtually simultaneously across much of the New World (Haynes 1982, 1987, 1992). The actual "calendar" ages of these sites may be even a bit greater. Variations in some of the conditions affecting radiocarbon dating (for example, the amount of ^{14}C in the atmosphere) during the late Pleistocene suggest that these sites (and all other sites worldwide dated by radiocarbon to the same time period) are actually about 2,000 years older than their radiocarbon dates; in other words, the oldest Paleoindian sites are actually 13,200 years old (Fiedel 1999). For the sake of consistency and to avoid

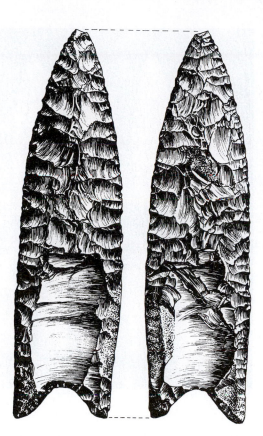

FIGURE 7.17
The flutes, or channels, on both faces of this Paleo-indian Clovis projectile point from the Lamb site in western New York State extend less than halfway up the point. Clovis dates to between 11,200 and 10,500 B.P. (Courtesy of Michael Gramly, Great Lakes Artifact Repository; drawn by Val Waldorf)

additional confusion, we will continue to refer to the radiocarbon ages of sites; you simply need to keep in mind that these radiocarbon ages do not necessarily translate directly into actual calendar dates.

Clovis Technology

Clovis spearpoints are distinctive in having a channel, or flute, on both faces (Figures 7.17 and 7.18). The channel, made by removing (usually) a single broad flake from both faces of the point, originating at the base and ordinarily extending one-quarter to one-third of the way toward the tip, is assumed to have been an aid in hafting the stone point onto a wooden shaft. As mentioned previously, this small technological step seems to have resulted in an adaptive leap that allowed for the rapid expansion of human groups across the New World. This great leap forward is strictly an American invention. It was not part of any western Beringian technology, nor is it present in the Nenana Complex in Alaska. The Mesa site in northern Alaska has produced about 50 bifacially flaked spearpoints, none of which possesses a channel. The Mesa site's 13 radiocarbon dates range from 9700 B.P. to 11,700 B.P. (Bower 1993a) and may be contemporary with fluted points farther south. Michael Kunz, the excavator of the Mesa site, maintains that the points there are not

FIGURE 7.18

An array of finely flaked fluted points from the Richey Clovis Cache discovered in Washington State and dating to 11,200 years ago. Fluted points, exhibiting distinctive "flutes," or channels, were hafted onto wooden shafts and used by Paleoindians to prey on the abundant populations of large game animals at the end of the Pleistocene. (© R. M. Gramly/Great Lakes Artifact Repository)

directly related to fluted points and represent yet another separate and distinct early stone-tool industry in northwestern North America (Bower 1993a:215).

Interestingly, in an undated but ancient deposit at the Cactus Hill site, researchers recovered two rather crude fluted points. They suggest that these points are examples of a very early stage in the development of Clovis technology; other researchers have called the points "proto-Clovis," implying that they may represent a form ancestral to Clovis (Marshall 2001).

The rapid, almost simultaneous appearance of fluted points throughout much of the New World is striking. Whereas there are either no sites or, at best, very few sites in America dated to before 12,000 years ago (see "Issues and Debates"), there is a virtual explosion of Clovis sites in the American Southwest and beyond dating to after 11,200 B.P. (Haynes 1992). Stratified sites such as Clovis, Lehner, Murray Springs, Dent, Colby, and Domebo, all in the Southwest, produced fluted spearpoints and dates in that time range (Haynes 1982).

But Clovis points are also found throughout Canada, the continental United States, and Mexico. In the Northwest, the spectacular Richey Clovis Cache in central Washington State (see Figure 7.18), an apparent ceremonial interment of huge fluted points as much as 23.25 cm (a bit more than 9 in.) in length, has been dated at 11,200 B.P. (Gramly 1993; Mehringer and Foit

1990). In the American Northeast and Southeast, thousands of fluted points have been recovered from hundreds of sites (Anderson 1990). Sites may be younger in the East—but not much: The Vail site in Maine has produced radiocarbon dates of 10,300 B.P. and 11,120 B.P. (Gramly 1982); the mean radiocarbon age of the Debert fluted-point site in Nova Scotia is 10,600 B.P. (MacDonald 1985); and Templeton (6LF21) in Connecticut has been dated to 10,190 B.P. (Moeller 1980).

Even at the most distant New World spot imaginable from Beringia, Fell's Cave at the southern tip of South America (Tierra del Fuego), a fluted point in association with the bones of extinct horse and sloth has been recovered from a site dated to 10,000 years ago (Bruhns 1994). Nonfluted fishtail points were also found in Fell's Cave and in other sites dating to this time in South America at sites such as Palli Aike, also in Tierra del Fuego, Los Toldos in Patagonia, and El Inga in northern Ecuador. Long, leaf-shaped El Jobo points were found at Taima Taima in Venezuela, also dating to the late Pleistocene.

The Clovis Advantage

It is not entirely clear what it was about the Clovis adaptation that allowed its bearers to spread so quickly across two continents. The Americas south of the ice sheets must have been a treasure trove for a people whose subsistence depended, at least in part, on hunting (Haynes 1964, 1980). Ecologist Paul S. Martin (1987) has jokingly referred to the New World, with its abundant big-game resources, as "Clovisia, the Beautiful." Imagine a continent teeming with animals—animals that had never seen a human hunter, with no fear of this puny, two-legged beast. There were mammoths, mastodons, bison, horses, caribou, musk ox, ground sloths, giant beavers, tapirs, and more, all ripe for the taking by efficient hunters who had very little competition (Martin and Guilday 1967). A new hunting technology such as the fluted spear may have been a key factor in the success of the culture. Even a small initial population, given a reasonably high birth rate, could have moved out in a rapid wave of population expansion, resulting in the narrow range of the Clovis radiocarbon dates (Martin 1973; Mosimann and Martin 1975).

Clovis Subsistence

The megafauna (big-game) hunting component of Paleoindian subsistence has been exaggerated in the past. Kill sites tend to be highly visible archaeologically, with their large complement of bones, broken weapons, and butchering equipment (see the "Case Study Close-Up"). Though the image of Paleoindians risking life and limb to track down and kill a two-ton, hairy elephant is more romantic, they most probably relied on root grubbing, seed gathering, and small-mammal trapping, at least some of the time (Johnson 1991; Meltzer 1993a). Still, some Paleoindians, like the Inuit people (Eskimos), must have relied on hunting because little else was available in their territories. During some parts of the year, most Paleoindian groups relied on

FIGURE 7.19

Folsom points are younger and generally smaller than Clovis points, and the flute extends nearly the entire length of the point. This is a Paleoindian fluted Folsom point from the Johnson site, Colorado. (Courtesy of Michael Gramly, Great Lakes Artifact Repository; drawn by Val Waldorf)

hunting for survival. But once past the glacial and periglacial north and onto the American plains, they could find and exploit many other foods, including seeds, nuts, berries, fish, and small mammals. Away from the glacial front, where animals may have been the only consistent source of food—for example, in the woodlands of eastern North America—Paleoindians were probably "generalist foragers" who not only took big game when the opportunity presented itself but also exploited smaller game and plant foods in their territories (Dincauze 1993).

Nonetheless, large game animals played a part in the Paleoindian economy. Geologist C. Vance Haynes points out that the remains of the two varieties of extinct North American elephants, the woolly mammoth and the mastodon, have been recovered from the majority of Clovis sites in the American West, where animal bones have been preserved (1982:390). When these elephants became extinct around 11,000 years ago, the Paleoindians in the western United States shifted their hunting focus to bison. The technology changed, producing shorter spearpoints, but with channels extending almost to the tip. These so-called **Folsom** points (Figures 7.19 and 7.20) are of the culture that bears the same name.

Though the makers of the fluted points may have been the bearers of the first widely successful New World culture, it would be a mistake to consider all of the earliest inhabitants of the Americas as Clovis hunters. Paleoindians lived and thrived in diverse habitats, including the tropical rain forest to the south. One site in South America displaying the great range of Paleoindian adaptation has been excavated by a team of researchers led by archaeologist Anna C. Roosevelt (Roosevelt et al. 1996). The Caverna da Pedra Pintada site is located in the Amazon basin in Brazil. The researchers recovered more than 30,000 stone flakes and 24 formal tools, including triangular, stemmed bifacial points, from a layer in the cave that has been radiocarbon-dated to between 10,000 and 11,200 years ago. Paleoenvironmental evidence recovered at the cave—in particular, preserved remains of plants and animals used by the inhabitants—shows quite clearly that when the site was occupied, the area was, as it is today, a tropical rain forest. Big game was only a part of the diet; abundant remnants of tree fruits, fish, mollusks, and birds, as well as small game, attest to the broad food base of the cave's occupants.

In the same layer as the Paleoindian artifacts, hundreds of lumps and drops of red pigment and two spalls of painted cave wall were found. The chemistry of the drops of red pigment match that of painted images found on the cave wall, implying a similar age for the paintings. The Pedra Pintada paintings, therefore, may be the oldest known examples of cave art in the New World.

First Skeletons

Altogether, the remains of fewer than 40 individual people have been found in the New World dating to more than 8,000 years ago; most are not even close to being complete skeletons, and some are extremely fragmentary, making a definitive analysis difficult at best (Bonnichsen and Schneider 2001–02).

The oldest human skeletons yet found in the New World date to no more than about 13,000 years ago. The Arlington bones from Santa Rosa Island in California (Owen 1984) have recently produced a date of 13,000 B.P., making them among the oldest human remains in the New World. The cranium called "Luzia" was found in Brazil, north of Rio De Janeiro, and has a proposed age of slightly more than 13,000 years. The female skeleton from Midland, Texas (originally called "Midland Man" but now known to have been a female), has been dated by uranium series to 11,600 years ago (Hoppe 1992). A small number of other human remains have been dated, with varying degrees of certainty, to the period between about 11,500 and 10,500 years ago: the Tepexpán skeleton from Mexico; the Pelican Rapids find (known as "Minnesota Man," another misidentified female); the Marmes skull from Washington State; and Wilsall (Anzick) skeleton in Montana.

Somewhat more recent are the remains of Spirit Cave Man in Nevada, dating to about 9,400 years ago, and the remains of Kennewick Man in Washington State, dating to about 9,300 years ago.

Much has been made of the fact that these oldest human remains found in the New World do not match the morphology of modern Native Americans. Before a proper date was obtained, Kennewick Man was initially identified as a white settler, largely because of the shape of his skull. The female Luzia appears to have more in common morphologically with the crania of native Africans or even Australians than she does with modern Native Americans (Parfit 2000). Modern Native Americans tend to have short, broad skulls with tall, wide faces and broad cheekbones. The oldest crania in the New World simply look different: Their crania exhibit a longer and narrower cranial vault. The overall look is less robust or rugged than modern Indians, and their faces aren't as broad.

Does this mean that the people who left behind the oldest skeletal remains in the New World are not the ancestors of modern Native Americans and that the ancestors of modern natives represent a different, later migration to the New World? Not really. In fact, comparison of gross cranial morphology—**craniometrics**—is proving to be a very poor way to trace America's first inhabitants. For example, researchers in 2003 examined 33 historical crania of a Native American group (the Pericú) who inhabited the southern tip of the Baja peninsula in Mexico (González-José et al. 2003). The skulls of the Pericú were long and narrow, wholly unlike those of modern American Indians or Northeast Asians, all of whom tend toward broad crania. The overall shape of the Pericú crania was, instead, similar to those of modern southern Asians and Australian Aborigines. A long head is also a common feature of the oldest human crania found in the New World. These data led the researchers to suggest that the Pericú represented a genetic isolate, a remnant of a coastal migration to the New World of a people who originated in south Asia, not

FIGURE 7.20

Folsom is another variety of fluted spearpoint. Folsom points tend to be smaller than Clovis, their flutes or channels occupy a greater proportion of their lengths, and they are younger than Clovis. When found in association with animal remains, it is clear that they were used to hunt bison; they are not found with the remains of mammoth or mastodon. (Courtesy R. M. Gramly, American Society for Amateur Archaeology, artifact courtesy Dr. Douglas Sirkin)

northeast Asia. They further suggested that most modern Native Americans were the descendants of a later, separate Beringian migration of northeast Asians to the New World.

It was an interesting and thought-provoking piece of reasoning, but it was, after all, based only on cranial morphology. The researchers recognized that the next step in testing their hypothesis of at least two separate migrations to the New World would require DNA analysis. That work is ongoing, but the results seem clear enough. Pericú skulls may look like those of south Asians and Australians and unlike those of modern Native Americans and northeast Asians, but their mitochondrial DNA turns out to be a very close match to modern Indians and Siberians (Dalton 2005). Head shape simply seems not to matter all that much in tracing populations. Skeletal morphology, including cranial shape, can change from one generation to the next as a result of changes in diet and behavior. DNA is the key, and DNA supports the model of a single migration to the New World from northeast Asia through Beringia.

People have been in the New World for more than 13,000 years. They have been adapting to the many habitats of the Americas during this entire time. It is expected that the processes of evolution would have altered their appearance to varying degrees in that lengthy period. Though the research is still in its initial stages, and though the sample size is quite small, skeletal morphology still indicates that, indeed, the first human migrants to the New World came from Asia, but at a time before the entire stereotypical suite of modern Asian skeletal features had developed on the west side of Beringia.

ISSUES AND DEBATES

WHAT OTHER KINDS OF DATA CAN CONTRIBUTE TO SOLVING THE RIDDLE OF THE FIRST AMERICANS?

Linguistic Diversity

Were the coastal-living ancestors of Monte Verde's inhabitants the first Americans? How about the ancestors of Meadowcroft Rockshelter's, Topper's, and Cactus Hill's interior-dwelling residents? Did the first northeast Asians cross through the interior of the Bering Land Bridge or along its coast? Did the initial migration occur about 20,000 years ago or even earlier? Or are the dates from Monte Verde and Meadowcroft somehow incorrect? Did the first people to populate the New World enter at about 13,000 or even only 12,000 years ago and soon thereafter develop the fluted Clovis spearpoint? Unfortunately, at this point in time, the archaeological record is unclear on all of these questions.

A consensus has been growing among linguists that the number and diversity of Native American languages would have required far more than 12,000 years to develop. Linguists have devised a number of crude methods for measuring change in languages—how long it takes for languages to diverge, first becoming different dialects and then becoming mutually unintelligible languages. No one believes these linguistic clocks are entirely accurate;

but assuming they are in the right ballpark, linguists such as Johanna Nichols (1990) maintain that 22,000 years is the minimum amount of time it would have taken for a small initial group of migrants to spread throughout North and South America and develop the astonishing array of languages spoken by native people here. In fact, 30,000 or even 40,000 years are reasonable estimates of the time depth implied by the degree of diversity present in American Indian languages (Gibbons 1998).

Genetic Diversity

The mitochondrial DNA of modern people points to a northeast Asian population source for Native Americans. Specifically, geneticists recognize five distinct mtDNA clusters called **haplogroups** among Native Americans and label them A, B, C, D, and X (Gibbons 1993; Stone and Stoneking 1993). The great majority of Native Americans exhibit one of these clusters, and the clusters are present in northeast Asia as well. By and large, however, these haplogroups are not found in Australia, Africa, or Europe.

All five of the mitochondrial haplogroups seen among Native Americans have also been found among the Altatians, a native group living southeast and southwest of Lake Baikal in Siberia (Derenko et al. 2001). Some researchers have suggested that the Altatians—living in a part of Siberia where excavation of archaeological sites dating close to 20,000 years ago has produced artifacts similar to some of the earliest stone tools found in the New World—is the population genetically most closely related to Native Americans. As of now, the people of central Siberia seem to represent our best guess for the source of the native people of the New World. A European team of geneticists has looked at the mtDNA data and has suggested that the amount of genetic variation in Native Americans, when compared to that of native northeast Asians, suggests a separation of 20,000 to 25,000 years (Gibbons 1996b).

Unfortunately, linguistic and genetic clocks cannot yet be precisely calibrated. They provide us with some tantalizing clues about the timing of the first migration into the New World, but they cannot prove when it occurred—at least not yet. The most reliable clock we now have for dating the earliest migration of people into the New World is that of radiocarbon-dated material in precise stratigraphic context at undisturbed archaeological sites left behind by those first Americans. Archaeologists will, of necessity, continue to search for the material remains of those people—and they will almost certainly succeed.

COULD NATIVE AMERICANS REALLY HAVE COME FROM EUROPE INSTEAD OF ASIA?

It can often be a good thing to step back from the "facts" that we all know to be true and consider, at least the possibility, that everything we know is instead wrong. This happened recently when it was proposed that the native people of the New World may have arrived during the late Pleistocene, not from Asia through Beringia but instead by boat from Europe along the margin of the ice-covered waters of the northern Atlantic. This scenario fundamentally calls into question all of our current models of the settlement of the New World based on archaeology, linguistics, biological anthropology, and genetics, but it's still worth a look.

The argument presented by archaeologists Dennis Stanford and Bruce Bradley (2000) is based on perceived detailed and deep technological and morphological similarities between Clovis technology and that of the Solutrean tradition of the European Upper Paleolithic (see Chapter 6). Stanford is an archaeologist at the Smithsonian, and I don't think there is a human being on the planet who knows more about lithic technology than Bradley. Nevertheless, the hypothesis has little to recommend it.

Archaeologist Lawrence Guy Straus (2000) has provided a detailed response to Stanford and Bradley's proposal, providing the perspective of an expert on the Solutrean. Straus rejects the suggestion of a Solutrean/Clovis connection completely, calling the Solutrean an "impossible candidate" as the source for Clovis. As Straus points out, perhaps the biggest problem in attempting to trace Clovis technology to the Solutrean lies in timing. On the one hand, the Solutrean is a short-lived technological tradition that essentially disappeared from Europe by 17,000 years ago. Clovis, on the other hand, didn't develop in North America until nearly 5,000 years later. Attempting to prove a connection between the makers of stone-tool technologies whose homelands are separated by 5,000 km (about 3,100 mi) of ocean is difficult enough. Connecting two peoples separated by 5,000 years seems quite impossible.

Straus also points out the lack of any evidence of maritime abilities on the part of the Solutrean toolmakers that might have made a trans-Atlantic crossing by them feasible, even through a series of island-to-island hops. Furthermore, the Solutrean toolmakers didn't live in the far north of Europe, where movement along the ice-covered Atlantic might have been an option for a maritime people.

Straus's argument against a connection between Solutrean and Clovis seems definitive. The hypothesis of a European source for the indigenous people of the Americas, at least those responsible for Clovis, is not supported by the evidence at hand.

WHO—OR WHAT—KILLED THE AMERICAN AND AUSTRALIAN MEGAFAUNA?

Archaeologists, historians, and paleoecologists have long been aware of the curious, apparent correlation between the first arrival of human groups in Australia and in the New World and the massive extinction of large game animals that occurred in these two regions. In Australia, 23 of the 24 animal genera whose individual members weighed more than 45 kg (about 100 lb) became extinct by about 46,000 years ago (Roberts et al. 2001), and in North America, 35 large mammalian genera disappeared soon after 11,000 years ago (Grayson 1987:8). Both of these dates are close enough to the timing of either the first appearance of human beings in Australia or the age of the first widespread and successful adaptation to North America (Clovis) to raise the obvious question: Were the human migrants in some way responsible for these events?

Ecologist Paul S. Martin's "Pleistocene overkill" hypothesis (Martin 1967; and see Martin and Wright 1967) involves a compelling scenario: The first human migrants to the American heartland find a flourishing bestiary that would put any modern African game park to shame. The seemingly limitless food source allows these paleohunters to expand their population at a rapid rate, ultimately filling two continents. Yet the seeds of their destruction are planted in the magnitude of their success. Large game animals, their populations already stressed by the changing climate at the end of the Pleistocene, are overhunted and ultimately suffer extinction. The human hunters at the root cause of this disaster go on to shift their adaptive strategies to other resources, having little choice but to drastically restructure their subsistence and their culture.

Although climate changed at the end of the Pleistocene, warming trends had happened before (see Figure 4.12). A period of massive extinction of large mammals like that seen about 46,000 years ago in Australia and 11,000 years ago in North America had not occurred during the previous 400,000 years, despite those changes (Guthrie 1990). The only apparently significant difference in Australia after 46,000 years ago and in the Americas after 11,000 years ago was the presence of human hunters of these large mammals. Was this coincidence or cause-and-effect?

We do not know. Paul Martin has championed the model that associates the extinction of large mammals at the end of the Pleistocene with human predation. He has co-authored a work (Mosimann and Martin 1975) in which a computer simulation showed that in around 300 years, given the right conditions, a small influx of hunters into eastern Beringia 12,000 years ago could have spread across the New World in a wave and wiped out game animals in a "blitzkrieg" (their term) to feed their burgeoning population.

The researchers ran the simulation several ways, always beginning with a population of 100 humans in Edmonton, Alberta, Canada, at 11,500 years ago. Assuming different initial North American big-game-animal populations (75–150 million animals), different population growth rates for the human settlers (0.65%–3.5%), and varying kill rates, Mosimann and Martin (1975:314) derived figures of between 279 and 1,157 years from initial contact to big-game extinction.

A more detailed version of a late Pleistocene extinction model has been rendered by evolutionary biologist John Alroy (2001). Beginning with a population of human hunters in the northwestern region of North America at about 13,000 years ago, Alroy found that in virtually any scenario you could model, when you plugged in even very conservative values for parameters like hunting success rates, speed of population expansion, prey competition, and levels of meat-eating by people, the growing human population in the New World wiped out the large game animals in less than 1,640 and as little as 801 years (Alroy 2001). Alroy (2001:1893) concludes that a "realistically scaled burst of human population growth" could have resulted in the number of extinctions that occurred in North America at the end of the Pleistocene.

Many scholars continue to support this scenario. For example, geologist Larry Agenbroad (1988) has mapped the locations of dated Clovis sites alongside the distribution of dated sites where the remains of woolly mammoths have been found (in both archaeological and purely paleontological contexts). These distributions show remarkable synchronicity (Agenbroad 1988:71). The species hardest hit in the extinction wave were large animals who would have been precisely those preferred by hunters, slow breeders who would have been most affected by overhunting. At the same time, animal species that survived the extinction wave tended to be nocturnal and/or tree, mountain, or deep forest dwellers, precisely the kinds of animals that might not be on the human menu because they are difficult to find (Barnosky et al. 2004).

At the other end of the world, in Australia, rapid or severe climate change did not contribute to the extinction of large animals because the two events—the end of the Pleistocene and the burst of extinction—didn't happen at the same time. As noted, the massive extinction event in Australia occurred about 45,000 years ago and was accompanied by no substantial climate change. Australian extinction, however, was contemporary with the earliest human settlement of the continent. Was this a coincidence or did the presence of humans contribute to this extinction?

In a fascinating recent analysis, Gifford Miller and his colleagues (2005) examined the concentration of the ^{13}C carbon isotope in a substantial sample of preserved eggshells of two kinds of large flightless birds, emus and the even larger but extinct *Genyornis newtoni*. The eggshells were dated to the period between 140,000 years ago and the present.

In both species, the carbon isotope ratios in the eggs evidence an abrupt and significant change at about 45,000 years ago. Before that time, the shells of both indicate a varied diet, with significant contribution by both C4 plants (grasses with their higher ^{13}C concentrations) and C3 plants (trees and shrubs with their lesser amounts of ^{13}C). At 45,000 years ago, the emu eggs show a significant and abrupt decline in their ^{13}C concentration, indicating a sharp spike in the contribution of C3 plants to the diet. *Genyornis* eggs disappear completely at this time as the species became extinct. In other words, it appears that the available plant foods shifted dramatically at 45,000 years ago in Australia, with trees and shrubs replacing tropical grasses. Emus adjusted to this change by altering their diets. *Genyornis* reacted to this change by becoming extinct.

Though the Australian flora seems to have changed substantially at 45,000 years ago, there is no accompanying evidence of a climatic change to explain this. The authors of the study propose, instead, a human agency. They suggest that when the first people arrived in Australia, they engaged in the practice of burning off grassland to aid in hunting and to promote the growth of certain plants that were of economic use to them (Miller et al. 2005:287–90). This had the unintended effect of so altering the foods avavilable to emus and *Genyornis* that one changed its diet and other, apparently unable to do so, died off. In this scenario, it is not overkill that caused the extinction, but ecological change wrought by human activity. This sounds remarkably like the modern world where endangered species are threatencd, not so much because people hunt them, but because people have altered their habitats.

There are, however, many problems with the overkill hypothesis, at least in North America. Significantly, though a few sites are quite impressive (see the "Case Study Close-Up"), there really is very little archaeological evidence to support it. Writing in 1982, Paul Martin himself admitted to the paucity of evidence; for example, at that point the butchered remains of only 38 individual mammoths had been found at Clovis sites (Martin 1982:403). In the years since, few additional mammoths have been added to the list. Surveying the data in 2002, Donald Grayson and David Meltzer came up with only 12 sites in all of North America with convincing evidence of woolly mammoth hunting and 2 sites with credible evidence that mastodons were hunted. There is no compelling evidence of the hunting of any of the other 33 Pleistocene genera that became extinct at the end of that epoch (Holliday 2003).

Though Martin claims the lack of evidence actually supports his model (the evidence is sparse because the spread of humans and extinction of animals occurred so quickly), this argument seems weak. And how could we ever disprove it? As archaeologist Donald Grayson (1987) points out, in other cases where extinction resulted from the quick spread of human hunters—for example, the extinction of the moa, the large flightless bird of New Zealand mentioned earlier—archaeological evidence in the form of butchered remains is abundant. Grayson (1991) has also shown that the evidence is not so clear that all or even most of the large herbivores in late Pleistocene America became extinct after the appearance of Clovis. Of the 35 extinct genera, only 8 can be confidently assigned an extinction date of between 12,000 and 10,000 years ago (Grayson 1991:209). Many of the other genera, Grayson argues, may have succumbed before 12,000 B.P., at least half a century *before* Clovis showed up in the American West. Recent analysis of ancient DNA recovered from 442 specimens indicates that the bison population of Beringia and North America may have been falling rapidly beginning as much as 37,000 years ago, far too early a date to have been caused by human predation (Shapiro et al. 2004).

Ultimately, environmental change at the end of the Pleistocene may have played a significant role in the widespread extinctions that occurred at this time with human predation, perhaps, providing the coup de grâce—the nail in the coffin—for these species. Biologist R. Dale Guthrie (1990) suggests that the Pleistocene–Holocene boundary was unlike previous periods of warming and resulted in far more drastic consequences for large herbivores hunted by humans and also for small rodents and other species not part of Clovis subsistence. Geologist Ernest Lundelius (1988) proposes that the end of the Pleistocene produced climates that displayed greater seasonality—more seasonal differences in temperature and precipitation. As climate became more seasonal, biotic diversity decreased because extreme seasonal conditions made large areas uninhabitable for many species. This, Lundelius maintains, was the primary cause of late Pleistocene extinction.

As of this moment, which factors were key and which were incidental in the extinction of megafauna at the end of the Pleistocene is unclear. As most researchers admit, it will take years of research to solve this puzzle.

CASE STUDY CLOSE-UP

At the Naco site in Arizona, a single mammoth was slaughtered by Paleoindian hunters more than 11,000 years ago. Eight large fluted points were found resting in the skeleton of the dead prehistoric elephant.

At the Lehner site, also in Arizona, 13 elephants were killed by Clovis hunters brandishing spears tipped with fluted points (Haury, Sales, and Wasley 1959). The age profile of the Lehner mammoths is catastrophic. In other words, the age spread of the mammoths killed at the site (from 2 to 30 years) is similar to the age spread in a living group of elephants. This suggests to archaeologist J. Saunders (1977) that the Lehner mammoths do not represent 13 individual, random kills of elephants in nearly the same spot over an extended period. Instead, it suggests that an entire small family group of adult, adolescent, and juvenile elephants was killed at the same time. Though some archaeologists have questioned whether Clovis hunters equipped with only stone-tipped spears could have killed so many elephants at one time (Haynes 1982), the age profile is significant.

The hunting skills of the Paleoindian hunters at the Casper site in Wyoming have been questioned by no one (Frison 1974a,b). Though they ordinarily lived in small hunting bands for much of the year, several bands coalesced in a larger encampment during the late summer and fall, when the bison were traveling in larger groups and were relatively easy to herd. The bringing together of small bands for communal hunts also allowed for the reinforcement of social connections and trade and gave young people an opportunity to find suitable mates in other bands.

A bit more than 10,000 years ago, a small group of bison approached the dune field at what is today the Casper archaeological site. Using whatever natural cover was available, perhaps camouflaging themselves with brush and even smearing themselves with bison dung to mask their human smell, the hunters quietly surrounded the beasts—members of an extinct subspecies (*Bison bison antiquus*) of today's American buffalo (*Bison bison bison*). As the

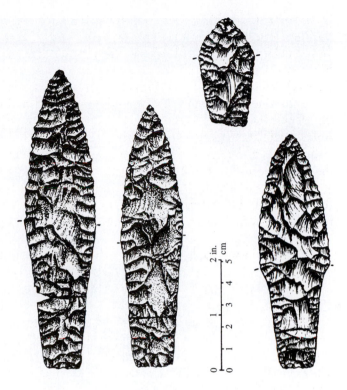

FIGURE 7.21
These projectile points from the Casper site in Wyoming were probably used to kill bison who were stampeded into the leeward side of a parabolic sand dune about 10,000 years ago. (Courtesy of George Frison)

bison approached the edge of the sand dune, the hunters burst from their hiding places, creating an enormous amount of noise and commotion.

Heeding their instinct to flee when threatened, the beasts rushed head-long into what appeared to be the only safe avenue, where no hunters were in their way. But instead of escape, the bison found a natural trap as they stampeded into the sandy hollow on the leeward side of the parabolic dune, precisely where the hunters had intended them to go. The animals quickly became mired in the soft sand. They panicked as they dimly perceived their predicament and then quickly exhausted themselves, trying helplessly to extricate their huge bulks on hooves intended for long treks across the hard ground of the plains, not the soft footing of sand. They became easy targets for human hunters wielding stone-tipped spears (an unfluted variety called "Hell Gap"; Figure 7.21). Nearly 80 bison were caught, killed, butchered, and eaten by the Paleoindians at Casper (Figure 7.22). After eating their fill and then drying and preserving the huge quantity of meat left over, the various bands went their separate ways, perhaps to meet again in another year and another place where the bison could be hunted yet again.

FIGURE 7.22
This is part of the bison bone bed at the 10,000-year-old Casper site in Wyoming. The animals were trapped in the sand by the ancient hunters and then killed with projectile points like those shown in Figure 7.21. (Courtesy of George Frison)

VISITING THE PAST

Most larger natural history and university museums in the United States have displays on the earliest human settlement of the New World and information regarding Paleoindians. In the Southwest, the Blackwater Draw Museum, located between Clovis and Portales, New Mexico, devotes part of its display to the nearby Blackwater Draw Paleoindian site. The Alaska Museum of Natural History in Eagle River has an exhibit devoted to the Broken Mammoth site, an 11,800-year-old Paleoindian occupation of the central Tanana valley of interior Alaska.

SUMMARY

In the late Pleistocene, expanding human populations intruded into new territories and ultimately migrated into three previously uninhabited continents: Australia, North America, and South America. Australia was populated by coastally adapted southeast Asians. Using watercraft, by accident and perhaps through intentional exploration, they moved out into the western Pacific, inhabited the oceanic islands of Borneo, Sulawesi, and Timor, and eventually made landfall on Greater Australia: New Guinea, Tasmania, and Australia proper. Archaeological evidence offers a date for this habitation of 40,000 years ago—possibly more—during a period of lowered sea level, when the trip by watercraft would have been easier than it is today. The first settlers maintained a tropical/coastal orientation to their economy, initially turning inland only along major rivers. The dry interior of the continent was settled about 20,000 years later.

During the Pleistocene, the New World was intermittently connected to the Old World by a vast land bridge, making it possible for interior-dwelling people in northeast Asia to travel through the interior of the land bridge into the interior of northwest America and for coastal people in northeast Asia to travel along the southern Beringian coast onto the coast of northwestern North America and from there south.

Sites as distant from the land bridge as Monte Verde in Chile (dated to 12,500 B.P.), Meadowcroft Rockshelter in western Pennsylvania (dated to 12,800 B.P.), Topper in Virginia (occupied before 11,000 B.P.), and Cactus Hill (15,000 B.P.) imply a much earlier time of entry onto the land bridge—20,000 years ago or possibly more—but no definitive archaeological evidence of sites this old in the New World has yet been found. Many sites that would have been evidence of migrants taking a coastal route to the south were long ago inundated by rising sea level at the end of the Pleistocene. Interior sites may be so ephemeral that finding them could be almost impossible.

Several early sites in Alaska and the Canadian Yukon date to the period immediately after 12,000 years ago and bear lithic industries analogous to those in Siberia. Some of the early settlers moved south, perhaps through an ice-free corridor, into the American West, where they invented a new projectile-point technology. These fluted projectile points allowed these settlers to expand across two continents. These Clovis people may not have been the first arrivals; some sites in both North and South America may be older. But Clovis represents the first broadly successful occupation of the New World.

TO LEARN MORE

Technical Summaries

For a detailed overview of Australia's past, see John Mulvaney and Johan Kamminga's *Prehistory of Australia* (1999). For the best recent summary of the controversy over the timing of the earliest settlement of Australia, see James F. O'Connell and Jim Allen's 1998 piece, "When Did Humans First Arrive in Greater Australia and Why Is It Important to Know?" in the journal *Evolutionary Anthropology* (volume 6, issue 4). Two excellent sources on the colonization of the Pacific are John Terrell's *Prehistory in the Pacific Islands* (1986) and Geoffrey Irwin's *The Prehistoric Exploration and Colonisation of the Pacific* (1993).

Frederick Hadleigh West's *American Beginnings: The Prehistory and Paleoecology of Beringia* (1996) is a useful source on the connection between Siberia and the first settlement of the New World. For an evenhanded treatment of the controversy over the earliest settlement of the Americas, read David Meltzer's 1993 article, "Pleistocene Peopling of the Americas," in the journal *Evolutionary Anthropology.* For a personal perspective on the controversies concerning the acceptance of the early date for the Monte Verde site in Chile, see "The Battle of Monte Verde," by that site's principal researcher, Tom Dillehay, in the journal *The Sciences* (January–February 1997).

For detailed information about the Paleoindian adaptation to the Americas, see the numerous articles in *Clovis: Origins and Adaptations,* edited by Rob Bonnichsen and K. L. Turnmire (1991). For a review of the data concerning the role played by human hunters in the extinction of megafauna at the end of the Pleistocene, read the article by Barnosky et al. titled "Assessing the Cause of Late Pleistocene Extinctions on the Continents," in the October 1, 2004, issue of *Science.*

Popular Summaries

For a nontechnical discussion of the archaeology of the first Australians, see Josephine Flood's *Archaeology of the Dreamtime* (1990).

David Meltzer's *Search for the First Americans* (1993), in the Smithsonian's series Exploring the Ancient World, remains one of the most thorough and best-written examinations of who the first Americans were and when they got here. Meltzer's short article in the weekly magazine *Science,* "Monte Verde and the Pleistocene Peopling of America" (1997), provides the current archaeological consensus on the significance of that site.

Always a good read, archaeologist E. James Dixon's *Bones, Boats, and Bison* (1999) presents a thoughtful summary of our current thinking about the earliest settlement of North America. A well-written and predictably wonderfully illustrated article written by Michael Parfit, "The Hunt for the First Americans," was published in the December 2000 issue of *National Geographic.* That issue contained a spectacular map showing the locations of the many ancient sites so far discovered in this search in North and South America. An articulate defense of the pre-Clovis model has been written by Rob Bonnichsen and Alan Schneider (2001–02) in their article, "The Case for a Pre-Clovis People," appearing in the popular magazine *American Archaeology. The Settlement of the Americas: A New Prehistory* is a terrific popular account of the many issues involved in solving the mystery of the first Americans written by one of the archaeologists on the front lines: Tom Dillehay (2000), the excavator of Monte Verde in Chile.

On the Web

For a terrific site on the peopling of the New World, there is no better place to start than National Geographic's *Who Were the First Americans?* Web page at http://www.nationalgeographic.com/ngm/0012/feature3/index.html. Another excellent Internet resource on the topic of the initial human migration into the New World has been provided by The Center for the Study of the First Americans (CSFA). The information on this organization's Web site allows you to see the various controversies about the timing and geography of the first human settlement of the Americas unfold. CSFA's home page can be found at http://www.centerfirstamericans.com. Electronic versions of The Center's newsletter, *The Mammoth Trumpet,* can be found at http://www.centerfirstamericans.com/mt.html/.

Check out an online animation of the configuration of the Bering Land Bridge at http://instaar.colorado.edu/QGISL/bering_land-bridge/downloads/beringlandbridge11.mov. The movie begins at 21,000 years ago and follows the course of Beringia in thousand-year increments to 1,000 years ago.

A great Internet source on the prehistory of Australia is located at http://arts.anu.edu.au/arcworld/resources/resource.htm. It offers links to a wealth of information on Australian and Pacific archaeology. Concerning the archaeology of the Pacific islands, visit the University of Otago (New Zealand) Web site at http://www. otago.ac.nz/Anthropology/Pacific.

Online Learning Center: www.mhhe.com/feder4

The Online Learning Center (OLC) Web companion to *The Past in Perspective* features a variety of supplemental study aids. For each chapter, this free Web site includes

ONLINE LEARNING CENTER

- Self-Quizzes to take as pretests prior to exams
- Interactive Timeline Study Guides for additional review and reinforcement of key information
- Learning Objectives
- Chapter Site links with Web addresses for many of the fossil and archaeological sites mentioned in the text

KEY TERMS

Beringia (or Bering Land Bridge), 276
burin, 288
Clovis, 290
Cordilleran, 282
craniometrics, 295
Denali Complex, 288
fire-cracked rock, 263
fluted point, 290
Folsom, 294

gracile, 265
haplogroup, 297
ice-free corridor (or McKenzie corridor), 282
Lapita, 271
Laurentide, 282
Melanesia, 271
microblade, 288
Micronesia, 271

Nenana Complex, 288
Paleoindian, 290
Polynesia, 271
Sahul, 259
Sunda (or Sundaland), 259
Wallacea, 260
Wallace Trench, 260
wedge-shaped core, 279

8

After the Ice

CULTURAL CHANGE IN THE POST-PLEISTOCENE

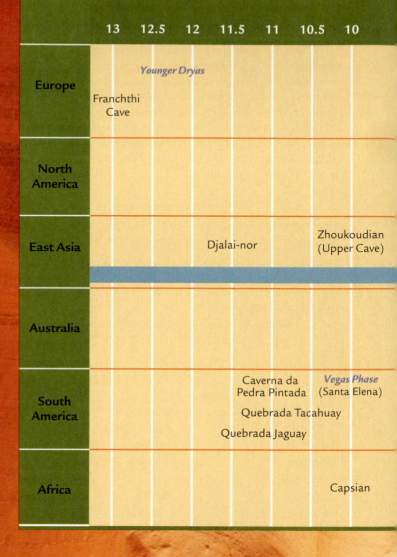

	13	12.5	12	11.5	11	10.5	10
Europe		*Younger Dryas*					
	Franchthi Cave						
North America							
East Asia				Djalai-nor		Zhoukoudian (Upper Cave)	
Australia							
South America				Caverna da Pedra Pintada	*Vegas Phase* (Santa Elena)		
				Quebrada Tacahuay			
				Quebrada Jaguay			
Africa						Capsian	

CHAPTER OVERVIEW

The end of the Pleistocene is marked by massive, long-term climate change. Human beings throughout the world were faced with the challenge of adapting to the new environments being established in the early Holocene.

Not surprisingly, as the post-Pleistocene environment became more diverse, many areas were marked by increasing cultural diversity during what is called the Mesolithic period in the Old World and the Archaic in the New World. Different societies responded in myriad and diverse ways to post-Pleistocene changes. In many areas, subsistence shifted necessarily when plant and animal species became locally extinct due to climate change. Small mammals and plant foods increased in economic importance in some regions. Some human groups expanded their resource base and practiced a broad subsistence strategy. Others intensified the subsistence quest, focusing on a small number of particularly rich resources. Some groups continued a nomadic pattern, moving to exploit the seasonal shift in resource availability. Other groups became more sedentary, investing their subsistence labors in a particular place.

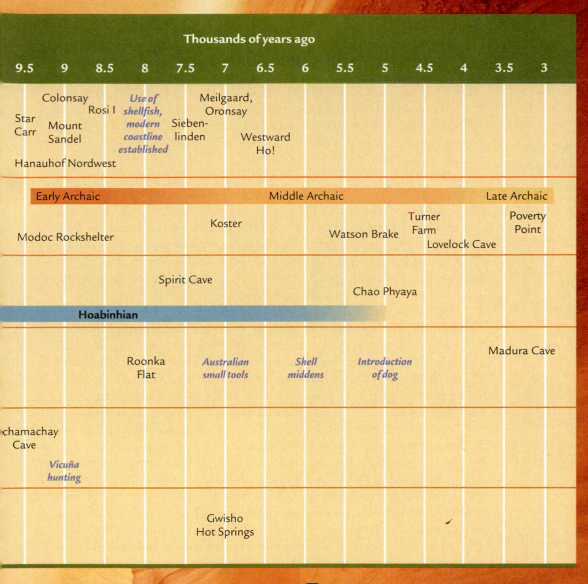

Thousands of years ago

9.5	9	8.5	8	7.5	7	6.5	6	5.5	5	4.5	4	3.5	3

Star Carr

Colonsay

Mount Sandel

Rosi I

Hanauhof Nordwest

Use of shellfish, modern coastline established

Sieben-linden

Meilgaard, Oronsay

Westward Ho!

Early Archaic — **Middle Archaic** — **Late Archaic**

Modoc Rockshelter

Koster

Watson Brake

Turner Farm

Lovelock Cave

Poverty Point

Spirit Cave

Chao Phyaya

Hoabinhian

Roonka Flat

Australian small tools

Shell middens

Introduction of dog

Madura Cave

chamachay Cave

Vicuña hunting

Gwisho Hot Springs

Go to **www.mhhe.com/feder4** for an interactive study guide version of this timeline.

ONLINE LEARNING CENTER

We tend to think of the Pleistocene as enormously distant in time from us. The Ice Age isn't *our* age; it's a time when conditions were much colder and glaciers covered large portions of the earth that today are home to tens of millions of people. We blithely refer to the period after 10,000 years ago as the **Holocene** (recent) epoch, as if giving it a separate name ensures that our time is different and our climate more pleasant and constant than that of times past.

But this pleasant view is almost certainly false. In Figure 4.12, we saw variations in the ^{18}O content of seawater and, by inference, the amount of glacial coverage on land. That figure shows a series of other breaks from cold climate—long **interglacials** and shorter **interstadials**—other remissions from glaciation during the Pleistocene. The current, relatively ice-free period most likely is simply another break in Arctic-like conditions over much of the higher elevations and higher latitudes, an interglacial inevitably to be followed by another descent into glacial conditions.

Deep cores taken in the Greenland ice cap, where ice formed in strata that can be analyzed for air temperature during each period of formation, indicate that we are in the most recent of a series of relatively warm periods punctuating the last 90,000 years (Monastersky 1994a). The previous interglacial lasted about 20,000 years (from 135,000 to 115,000 years ago), and at least one of the ice cores taken in Greenland indicates wild swings of climate even within that relatively warmer period (Monastersky 1994b). With that as our guide, then, perhaps we are only about halfway into an interglacial and glacial conditions are poised to return in 10,000 years.

Even when we look back into the recent past, we see relatively short-lived, minor "blips" in the warm trend that has characterized the earth's climate for the last 10,000 years. In fact, the climate from the mid-twelfth to the mid-nineteenth centuries has been characterized as a "Little Ice Age." Historical records make it clear that this short relapse into glacial conditions had a significant impact on the agricultural patterns and lives of millions of Europeans and Americans (Grove 1988).

For example, historical records as well as paleoclimatological data indicate a significant, though brief, cooling trend between A.D. 1150 and 1400. The Vikings were forced to abandon their western Greenland colony by A.D. 1345 as expanding pack ice and a sharp increase in the number of North Atlantic icebergs made the voyage between the colony and Scandinavia treacherous and as life on Greenland became increasingly harsh.

Things warmed up between A.D. 1400 and 1550 but then cooled off again for another three centuries. In the mid-nineteenth century, when another warming trend commenced—a trend we probably are still in (but for how long?)—people were once again forced to respond and readapt to the new climatic conditions.

But any adaptations developed in response to such short-term, small-scale environmental changes pale in comparison to what it must have been like at the end of the Pleistocene, between 12,000 and 10,000 years ago, when enormous, fundamental, and sometimes quite abrupt changes in climate occurred—changes so vast that they often rendered previous human subsistence systems untenable. Certainly, human groups needed to adjust their way of life in response to those changes if they were to survive. Adding to the challenge, the end of the Pleistocene cannot be described as just an overall, measured, steady warming trend that human groups might readily adjust to. Conditions were in a far more severe state of flux, with the climate oscillating between the new warmer temperatures and previous colder temperatures. This set of circumstances was far less stable and, in fact, more difficult for human groups to adapt to. For example, evidence from tree rings and air bubbles trapped in permanent ice fields in Greenland indicate that a dramatic and sudden cold snap hit the earth about 10,300 years ago, right in the middle of a long-term warming trend at the end of the Pleistocene (Bjorck 2001). This sharp decline in worldwide temperature lasted for nearly two centuries whereupon the planet recommenced a trend of temperature increase that marked the beginning of the modern, Holocene epoch. During some episodes of climatic oscillation, abrupt and severe climate changes occurred in an even narrower time frame, sometimes at the time scale of a few human generations—or even a single one (Stager and Mayewski 1997).

Clearly the late Pleistocene and early Holocene was a period marked by a level of climatic volatility that tested the ability of human beings to adapt in response to their changing, unstable world. From the cave painters of Upper Paleolithic Europe to the mammoth hunters of central Asia, from the Paleo-indian hunters of Pleistocene megafauna in the New World to the reindeer hunters of northern Europe, from the lakeside dwellers of southeast Australia to the lake dwellers of central Africa—people were faced with massive and rapid changes in their accustomed environments. Temperatures rose, ice sheets melted, coastlines were inundated and reconfigured, large herbivores became extinct, new game and unfamiliar plant life invaded home territories, lakes dried up, and weather patterns changed. The old ways of living no longer meshed with changed climates, altered habitats, and different floral and faunal populations.

Human beings had little choice but to adapt, move, or die. Where they could, some groups shifted territories, trying to follow conditions with which they were most familiar. Others may have seen their cultures wither and die as conditions changed more rapidly than they could or were willing to respond to. Many groups, however, changed their ways of life by adapting to the new conditions of the Holocene. Their cultural response to the changes wrought by the end of the Pleistocene is the focus of this chapter.

The key characteristic of the cultures of the early Holocene is adaptive change, reflected in the following features:

- In most places, the archaeological record shows that human groups quickly shifted their subsistence focus as the animals and plants

CHAPTER SITES

www.mhhe.com/feder4

SOUTH AMERICA
Caverna da Pedra
  Pintada, 333
Pachamachay Cave, 334
Quebrada Jaguay, 333
Quebrada Tacahuay, 333
Santa Elena, 334

AUSTRALIA
Madura Cave, 331
Roonka Flat, 332

CHRONICLE

FIGURE 8.1

Sites of the early post-Pleistocene.

on which they previously had relied became extinct or unavailable in their home regions.

- In some regions, the post-Pleistocene subsistence base changed from megafauna to smaller animals, fish, shellfish, and birds and included a greater reliance on plant foods previously absent or rare during glacial conditions.
- In other regions, rather than a broadening, the subsistence shift involved more intensive exploitation of some uniquely productive elements in the food quest. More intense exploitation means there was a focus on a small number of highly productive resources in those areas where such resources existed—for example, wild cereal grasses in the Middle East.
- In some areas, the focus on certain abundant resources encouraged a shift from a nomadic existence to a more sedentary one.
- A broad and rich diversity characterizes the cultural adaptations developed by people all over the world in response to the new, modern climatic regimes that are ultimately established in the Holocene. This diversity is reflected in a proliferation of subsistence strategies, artifact assemblages, and settlement patterns as seen in the archaeological record (Figure 8.1).

Unfortunately, while vast regions during the Paleolithic can be readily characterized in terms of cultural adaptations, that cannot be done for the cultures of the Holocene. After the Pleistocene, the cultural situation becomes far more complicated and an increasing number of distinct adaptations evolved in many different regions. The picture is so complex that only a brief description of some of the best-known adaptations to life "after the ice" will be presented. The discussion will now turn to how various world regions reflected these cultural changes.

EUROPE

A warming trend can be deduced from the pollen record of Europe for the period after 16,000 B.P. This trend was sufficient to render even Scandinavia ice-free just 3,000 years later, by about 13,000 B.P. This warming was interrupted at least once by a rapid and severe shift back to glacial conditions. This so-called **Younger Dryas** interval began soon after 13,000 years ago and appears to have lasted for about 1,400 years, until about 11,600 years ago (Severinghaus et al. 1998). Paleoclimatologists studying air trapped in bubbles in Greenland's ancient ice have estimated that at the peak of the return to glacial conditions during the Younger Dryas, mean air temperature at the summit of Greenland may have been as much as 15°C (27°F) cooler than it is today—and that huge drop in mean temperature occurred during the course of only about a decade (Severinghaus et al. 1998). Mean air temperature in Europe would have been similarly depressed when compared to modern, interglacial conditions.

The Younger Dryas was, nevertheless, a relatively minor deviation from a trend that would result in near-modern conditions across much of Europe by 8500 B.P. (Gamble 1986; Price 1991; C. Smith 1992). Sea level was rising, too, breaking the connection between Great Britain and the continent by 8,000 years ago and establishing modern coastlines relatively soon thereafter (Figure 8.2; Megaw and Simpson 1979; C. Smith 1992).

Though the northernmost reaches of the continent retained their Arctic-like characteristics, the Pleistocene tundra and its suite of large game animals, including woolly mammoth and rhinoceros, wild cattle, horse, and reindeer, was gone throughout most of Europe after 9000 B.P. The cold-loving grasses and sedges of the tundra on which those large herbivores subsisted were replaced first by birch and pine trees and later by elm and oak to the south. The gregarious megafauna whose huge migratory herds were accommodated by the treeless expanse of the tundra could not exist in or migrate through the expanding, dense woodlands. These large animals were replaced by smaller, less mobile, forest-dwelling animal species, including red deer, roe deer, and wild pig, along with even smaller fur-bearing animals such as marten, beaver, otter, and wolf (Price 1991). As archaeologist T. Douglas Price (1991:190) points out, the key characteristic of the environment of Holocene Europe when compared to that of the Pleistocene was the vast array of plants and animals available for exploitation. Thus, the most salient feature of the food resource base of post-Pleistocene Europe was its diversity.

It was to the extremely diverse mixture of plants and animals establishing themselves in post-Pleistocene Europe that human groups adjusted

FIGURE 8.2

As this map of the coastline of Europe during the early Holocene shows, broad areas that were dry land 9,500 years ago are today under the sea. (Courtesy of T. Douglas Price)

themselves. This diversity, both within and between regions, helps explain the cultural record of Europe after the ice. The European **Mesolithic**—the cultural period that follows the Paleolithic in Europe and precedes the appearance of farming cultures—was marked by many of the features of post-Pleistocene cultures (see earlier list).

Mesolithic Subsistence Patterns

Archaeologist Christopher Meiklejohn (1978) points out the greater diversity of species exploited by Mesolithic Europeans than by their Paleolithic forebears. In a survey of seven Mesolithic sites in Great Britain and France, 11 different large-animal species were reported, with an average of 4 different species at each site (Meiklejohn 1978:67). Upper Paleolithic sites in northern Europe commonly have only a single large mammal species represented.

Sites of the **Maglemosian** culture of the Mesolithic exemplify the broadening of the subsistence quest as well as the spread of a sedentary way of life made possible by the establishment of productive Holocene habitats. Maglemosian people built sizable semipermanent villages on the margins of large, post-Pleistocene lakes in northern Europe (see the "Case Study Close-Up").

The Irish site of Mount Sandel shows evidence of the use of seasonally available resources that together span the entire year, beginning 9,000 years ago (Price 1987:250). This, along with the size of the substantial residential structures—circular buildings about 6 m (20 ft) in diameter—argues for a degree of permanence of occupation not seen previously.

In the cold climate of post-Pleistocene northern Europe, hunting was a significant element in the subsistence quest. Mesolithic sites ordinarily produce a wide array of animal food species, including red deer, roe deer, elk, wild ox, wild sheep, goat, pig, and rabbit. Small fur-bearing mammals such as wolf, fox, badger, beaver, marten, squirrel, and hare were used by these Mesolithic people, almost certainly for their warm pelts.

Charred seeds provide evidence for the significance of plant foods in the Mesolithic diet. Hazelnut shells are commonly found in Mesolithic sites in northern Europe, and the hazelnut and other nut foods, along with water lily and wild apple, probably made a significant seasonal contribution to the diet (Price 1987). For example, near Scotland, on the island of Colonsay, in the Hebrides, an enormous pit was found containing thousands of roasted hazelnut shells (Denison 1995). The hazelnuts likely were being processed in the pit, perhaps to render the nutmeats suitable for grinding into a flour. Radiocarbon dates on the shells indicate that this occurred close to 9,000 years ago, early in the Mesolithic. At Mesolithic sites in southern France, a wider array of plant-food remains have been recovered, including vetch, lentils, and chickpeas (Price 1987).

In his survey of archaeological sites located in southwest Germany, Michael Jochim (1998:67) noted a significant increase in subsistence diversity between the Late Paleolithic and Early Mesolithic. For example, he provides a lengthy list of animal species that contributed to the diet of the human inhabitants of the 8,500-year-old Rosi I site near Rottenberg, including large game animals, such as red and roe deer, wild boar and aurochs, and reindeer, and small game, such as red fox, beaver, and squirrel. Also on the menu at Rosi I were birds, wild raspberries, wild apples, cabbage, and, the most abundant of the wild plant foods at the site, hazelnuts. Jochim (1998:202) found that among the Mesolithic sites excavated in southwest Germany, archaeologists have recovered the remains of 8 different large game animal species (with red deer, roe deer, and wild boar topping the list), 10 different small game species (with beaver, hare, fox, and wildcat being the most abundant in archaeological assemblages), and several species of fish, shellfish, and birds. Jochim also found that plant foods made a significant contribution to the diet of Germans in the Mesolithic, with hazelnuts being the most important element of the plant assemblage.

Occupied in the period between 8700 and 6900 B.P., the Siebenlinden Mesolithic sites in southern Germany reflect the wide range of animal and plant species exploited by the inhabitants of the region (Kind 2001). The site's investigator refers to the approach of Mesolithic Germans as "opportunistic," and the lengthy list of animal and plant species exploited by the inhabitants bears this out. For example, the bones of large mammals like aurochs (wild cattle), red deer, roe deer, elk, and wild boar were abundant in site hearths. Also, the bones of animals probably not killed for their meat but for their pelts were found at the sites. The fur-bearing species recovered include beaver, red fox, marten, and wild cat. Plant foods also contributed to the food quest with the apparent Mesolithic staple, hazelnut, found at the sites, along with raspberry, wild apple, and weedy, seed-bearing plants: knot weed and common lamb's quarters.

Although rising post-Pleistocene sea levels have inundated most Mesolithic coastal sites and many ancient lakes have become dry land (see Figure 8.2), there still is evidence of the extensive use of lake and coastal resources during the Mesolithic. Modern dredging in the English Channel and the North Sea to facilitate ship traffic has brought up Mesolithic bone and antler artifacts from sites now located many meters underwater (Price 1987). Where local topography has preserved the ancient coast, Mesolithic sites are numerous. Excavation of such sites has shown an extensive reliance on coastal resources. Of greatest significance was the pike, a saltwater fish that enters inland channels and inlets to spawn. But the bones of cod, ling, perch, bream, eel, and haddock have also been recovered (Clark 1980). Marine mammals are also found in Mesolithic contexts. Species that were hunted include ringed, harp, and gray seals. The remains of hunted or beached whales and porpoises are also found. Birds also contributed to the subsistence quest; 55 different species have been found in Mesolithic sites. For example, at Mount Sandel in Ireland, the remains of duck, pigeon, dove, grouse, goshawk, and capercaillie were excavated (Price 1987:248).

Shellfish also made an important contribution to the diet in coastal localities. For example, at the Danish site of Meilgaard, a shell **midden** with a volume of 2,000 m^3 (21,000 ft^3) was made up of millions of mollusk shells (Bailey 1978). In Portugal, coastal middens consisting primarily of mollusk shell are common for the period after 7400 B.P. Mesolithic shell middens dot the island of Oronsay, 30 km (20 mi) off the west coast of Scotland (Mellars 1978). Crab and limpet shells, along with the bones of seal, fish, and 30 species of birds, were found among the food remains (Price 1987). At Westward Ho! in north Devon, England, Mesolithic kitchen middens of oyster, winkle, mussel, and limpet shells have been dated to more than 6,500 years ago (Price 1987).

Diversity and Regionalization

Regionalization is another process seen clearly in European Mesolithic sites. Whereas a single lithic tradition characterized the Middle Paleolithic across much of Europe, and only a few geographically demarcated, different, but related traditions were present there in the Upper Paleolithic, the Mesolithic period in Europe was marked by a far more diverse cultural pattern.

For example, the **Hamburgian** cultural tradition of the northern European Upper Paleolithic was quite homogeneous throughout northern Europe.

Whereas at most 3 geographically separate and distinct stone-tool traditions within the Hamburgian have been recognized, archaeologist T. Douglas Price (1991:199) counts at least 15 different regional stone-toolmaking patterns by the end of the Mesolithic.

Cultural regions of the European Upper Paleolithic—as determined by the geographic extent of archaeological sites where similar tool styles and types are found—have been estimated to encompass as much as 100,000 km^2 (38,610 mi^2). During the Mesolithic, defining cultural regions or territories the same way results in a far greater number of much smaller territories, more on the order of 1,000 km^2 (386 mi^2) each (Price 1991:200).

It seems clear that various groups settled into their own distinct regions in Europe after the Pleistocene, evolved their own adaptations to their unique set of local postglacial environmental conditions, and developed their own tool assemblages and their own distinctive patterns of subsistence and settlement.

Trade in the European Mesolithic

Mesolithic trade networks expanded, but in a pattern different from that established during the Upper Paleolithic (Price 1987). Whereas trading networks actually extended over longer distances in the Upper Paleolithic (see Chapter 6), trade during the Mesolithic was more intraregional. Lithic raw materials were exchanged in greater amounts, but trading was generally restricted to within smaller cultural regions. In other words, materials didn't move as far as they had in the Upper Paleolithic, but more of them were moving through the more geographically restricted regional systems.

For example, obsidian from the Mediterranean island of Melos is found abundantly in Mesolithic levels of Franchthi Cave on the Greek mainland. English Portland chert was traded, but only within England and not more than 240 km (150 mi) from its source. Brown quartzite from Wommersom in Belgium and the southern Netherlands has been found spread across a restricted area in northern Europe, at Mesolithic sites no more than 120 km (75 mi) from the source (Clark 1980) and almost always within an area about 250 km by 200 km (155 mi by 125 mi; Figure 8.3; Price 1991:200). A kind of banded chert, valued perhaps for its great beauty as well as its more functional characteristics, is found at Mesolithic sites in southwest Germany, many miles from its source in Bavaria. For example, at the Hanauhof Nordwest site, located on the shore of a large lake, the Federsee, more than 98% of the lithic assemblage consisted of locally available materials including a plain chert, radiolarite, and a variety of coarse-grained material. Between 1 and 2% of the stone tools found at the site were made of a type of banded chert available only far to the east, in Bavaria (Jochim 1998:159).

Innovation in the Mesolithic

The European Mesolithic was also a time of great innovation. Early evidence of the manufacture of canoes is dated to the Mesolithic. The use of bow and

arrow actually may predate the Mesolithic, going back perhaps more than 15,000 years to the Upper Paleolithic. The earliest evidence for the use of the bow in Europe, however, dates to between 8000 B.P. and 9000 B.P. in northern Europe. In addition, the bones of wolflike animals have been found at Star Carr (see the "Case Study Close-Up"), dating to before 9000 B.P. These animals had not been used for food; and based on their relatively small size and the crowded nature of their teeth, they seem to have been removed from a purely wild state. In fact, the wolflike bones at Star Carr and many other Mesolithic sites are examples of domesticated wolves—that is, dogs (Clark 1980).

NORTH AMERICA

Though the post-Pleistocene prehistory of the New World is distinct from that of the Old World, parallel patterns are apparent in the human response to the end of the Ice Age in both hemispheres. As in Europe, with deglaciation and the extinction of large herbivores that accompanied the end of the Pleistocene, the archaeological record bears witness to a dramatic shift in culture in North America after 10,000 B.P. Whether purely a result of climate change, overhunting, or some combination of the two (see Chapter 7), the massive disappearance of large game animals necessitated dramatic changes in the cultures of the Native Americans of the early post-Pleistocene.

New World prehistorians have recognized the great cultural changes that accompanied the end of the Pleistocene by bestowing a different name on the cultures of this period. In Europe, the Upper Paleolithic is followed by the Mesolithic; in America the Paleoindian period is followed by the **Archaic,** lasting from about 9,000 to 3,000 years ago. The Archaic represents a complex

FIGURE 8.4
Lake Forest Archaic people exploited the shores of the Great Lakes and other large inland bodies of water. Chipped-stone spearpoints are typical artifacts of this culture. (Photo by K. L. Feder; artifact drawings from *A Typology and Nomenclature for New York State Projectile Points,* by William A. Ritchie, 1971, reprinted with the permission of the New York State Museum and Science Service)

era when specific adaptations to the different climatic and environmental regimes became established across North America.

Regionalism in the New World Archaic

Archaic cultures of North America traditionally have been divided geographically, reflecting adaptations to the post-Pleistocene habitats that characterized the continent. Post-Pleistocene cultures named for the regions to which people adapted include the Desert Archaic of the Great Basin, the Southwestern Archaic, the Shell Mound Archaic of the Southeast, the Eastern Archaic, the Central Archaic, and the Western Archaic, as well as the **Paleo-Arctic tradition** (Willey 1966). In other words, various prehistoric people in North America began following their own regionally focused adaptive pathways in the face of the new conditions being established at the end of the Pleistocene.

Even this geographic breakdown masks the diversity within these regions. As in Europe, regionalization is the hallmark of the post-Pleistocene of North America. For example, archaeologist Dean Snow (1980), in his synthesis work on the archaeology of New England and New York State, further breaks down the Archaic cultures based on region, subsistence focus, and other behavioral characteristics. Snow describes a **Lake Forest Archaic** tradition (northern New England west of Maine and western New York), which apparently developed as a response to the unique conditions of the areas adjacent to the Great Lakes and the lake region of western New England. The material culture shows a heavy reliance on **lacustrine** (lake) resources, with a settlement pattern of home bases on lakeshores occupied in the spring and seasonal winter and summer hunting in the uplands surrounding the lakes (Figure 8.4).

FIGURE 8.5

The Maritime Archaic people developed an adaptation that focused on resources of the Atlantic coast (the southern coast of Maine is shown here). Ground-stone artifacts are typical of this culture. (Artifact drawing from C. C. Willoughby's *Antiquities of the New England Indians,* 1935; photo by K. L. Feder)

Snow's **Maritime Archaic** is situated on New England's North Atlantic coast—primarily in Maine but also extending north into New Brunswick. Sites such as Turner Farm in Maine, dating to 4,600 years ago, show a clear subsistence focus on sea resources. Bone fishhooks, net weights and plummets, and faunal remains indicate that fish was a major component of the diet; even **pelagic** (open ocean as opposed to coastal) creatures like swordfish were hunted from open boats in the deep sea. Human burials were filled with finely crafted objects such as long slate knives and carvings of whales and dolphins (Figure 8.5). The human remains were powdered with red ochre (a mineral), giving the name "the Red Paint People" to these Archaic inhabitants of coastal Maine. The rich maritime resources allowed for sedentary coastal home bases.

Snow also defines a **Mast Forest Archaic** for most of southern New England. The term "mast" refers to the acorns and other nut foods from trees (hickory, beechnut, chestnut, walnut) that accumulate on the ground of the forest and serve as food for animals. These Mast Forest Indians focused on the rich resources of the river-drained woodlands of New England. They hunted deer and trapped small animals, fished in the rivers using nets and weirs as well as hooks and lines, collected acorn, hickory, walnut, and chestnut in the fall and the seeds, leaves, and roots of wild plants in the spring (Figure 8.6).

Although deep-sea fishing and marine mammal hunting in New England seem to have been the exclusive province of the Maritime Archaic tradition, the use of shore resources was not confined to them. The Mast Forest Archaic also has a coastal component, with a heavy reliance on shellfish such as oyster,

FIGURE 8.6
The Mast Forest Archaic cultural pattern is centered in the thickly wooded valleys of southern New England (a Connecticut woodland with a treeless bog in its center is shown here). Chipped-stone spearpoints are typical of Mast Forest Archaic artifacts. (Photo by K. L. Feder; artifact drawings from *A Typology and Nomenclature for New York State Projectile Points,* by William A. Ritchie, 1971, reprinted with the permission of the New York State Museum and Science Service)

scallop, soft-shell clam, and quahog. Before development in shoreline communities destroyed them, large shellfish middens were common in Mast Forest Archaic coastal sites in Connecticut and Massachusetts.

The same pattern of cultural regionalization in the Archaic is repeated elsewhere in North America. Piñon nuts were a major component of the diet throughout much of the desert West. The Archaic occupation of the desert shows a subsistence focus on desert lakes that are now dry, low-lying areas called sinks. For example, at Lovelock Cave, in Nevada, paleofeces provide direct evidence for the diet of its Archaic inhabitants. The cave was located near a desert lake (now the dry Humboldt Sink). Virtually all of the food remains retrieved from the preserved human feces in the cave came from the lake and its immediate environs (Heizer and Napton 1970) and included duck, mudhen, chub fish, and plant foods like cattail and wetland grasses.

In the Midwest is Modoc Rockshelter, located less than 15 km (9.3 mi) from the Mississippi River in Illinois. Modoc was successively occupied from the early Holocene, beginning close to 9000 B.P. and continuing through the Archaic period and into the subsequent Woodland period (Ahler 1993; Fowler 1959). Melvin Fowler, the principal investigator of the site, was able to trace the evolution of subsistence strategies on the part of the inhabitants of the rockshelter from the Early through the Middle and into the Late Archaic. Fowler deduced that the initial occupants of Modoc were generalists, subsisting on whatever foods were available in their early Holocene environment in the broad region of the rockshelter. Later, the site's inhabitants began to

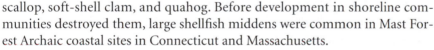

tighten their subsistence approach, intensifying the food quest by focusing on a smaller number of productive, locally available food resources.

In the Arctic, the resources of the coast were heavily exploited by the Holocene inhabitants, with evidence of seal, sea lion, walrus, and puffin as major elements in the diet. In the Far West, nut foods became key elements in the diet, establishing a subsistence pattern that would continue into the historic period.

In yet another example of regionalism, the Shell Mound Archaic has been defined for the American Southeast, in particular at sites marked by extensive and deep piles of freshwater shells located along the Tennessee River in Tennessee and the Green River in Kentucky. Sites located in South Carolina, Georgia, West Virginia, and Florida, similarly characterized by substantial accumulations of freshwater, particularly mussel shells, are also included in the Shell Mound Archaic.

Clearly, the people of the Shell Mound Archaic greatly relied on freshwater shellfish for their subsistence, and the mounds themselves have been interpreted as the accumulations of food remains of dense and sedentary, or nearly so, people living in the American Southeast—their population density and degree of sedentism, it has been suggested, were made possible by the rich and abundant food resource of freshwater shellfish.

As archaeologist Cheryl Claassen (1996) points out, the mounds also appear to have been focal points for human interments with associated grave goods, which suggests that they were more than simply trash piles. Claassen argues that the mounds were, in fact, intentionally constructed as important ceremonial or ritual locations.

Differences in the quantity of goods interred with individuals buried in the shell mounds—which, in some cases, includes finely made shell bead necklaces and copper objects made from a raw material available only at very great distances from the sites—are indicators of the differentiation of economic and social status among those buried. Some folks were buried with lots of valuable stuff—in the sense that the raw material was hard to come by and that a substantial amount of work went into producing the objects—and some folks were buried with little of value. This implies a more complex social pattern than is usually assumed for most Archaic period cultures, with at least an incipient level of social differentiation, some based on sex, some based on age, and some, perhaps, based on family ties.

The construction of large-scale or even monumental features by ancient people is often the gauge by which social and political complexity is measured by archaeologists. When features are found in the archaeological record whose monumental scale implies the coordinated labor of a well-organized workforce—a workforce of those giving orders and those following the orders— it is deduced that a complex social system must have developed in order to facilitate such complex construction projects. Some of the Southeast shell mounds may reflect at least early evidence of that kind of complexity.

It is during the Archaic in the Southeast that indisputable evidence of this complexity can be found in the archaeological record: in the existence of large-scale projects of earthen-mound building at the Watson Brake site in Louisiana (Russo 1996; Saunders et al. 1997). Beginning soon after 5,200 years ago, the inhabitants of the site constructed 11 distinct earthen mounds and connecting ridges that together form an oval enclosure of mounded soil about 280 m (more than 900 ft) along its long axis (Frink 1997). The tallest of the mounds at Watson Brake is about 7.5 m (about 25 ft) high.

Clearly, moving the amount of earth necessary to produce the monuments at Watson Brake required the kind of large, coordinated labor force that is a hallmark of cultural complexity. It is interesting to point out that, in this instance, the requisite complexity evolved without agriculture. Fish played the dominant role in subsistence at the site; 175,000 animal bones were found there, the majority representing various species of freshwater fish. Also found in the trash midden were the bones of deer, raccoon, opossum, squirrel, rabbit, and dog (Saunders et al. 1997:1798). Also key to the subsistence base at Watson Brake were two of the wild plant species that were to become key components in the independent Neolithic Revolution seen among the native people of the American Mid-South and Southeast (see Chapter 9); the charred seeds of goosefoot and knotweed were recovered in excavation of the site. The rich food base of local, wild seed plants, medium and large mammals, and, especially, abundant aquatic resources made the area of Watson Brake so economically rich that the social and political complexity needed to construct the earthworks seen there developed in the absence of an agricultural food base.

The much larger and more impressive mound complex at the Poverty Point site, also in Louisiana, dates to before 3200 B.P. Located adjacent to the Macon Bayou and the broad, rich floodplain of the Mississippi River, the Poverty Point earthworks are truly monumental in scale (Figure 8.7). The site consists of a series of six segmented, concentric earth ridges, enclosing a rough semicircle with a radius of 0.65 km (0.4 mi; the distance from its center to the edge of the outermost ridge). The ridge tops were living surfaces; archaeologists have found evidence of construction along their tops, along with hearths and trash pits. Each of the six segmented ridges is about 24 m (80 ft) wide, 3.5 m (10 ft) tall, and separated from adjacent ridges by about 45 m (150 ft). The outermost ridge is about 2 km (1.25 mi) long; altogether there are 9.7 km (6 mi) of these ridges in the Poverty Point earthwork surrounding a flat central plaza of 37 acres. If the soil to produce Poverty Point had been mounded up in 23-kg (50-lb) basket loads, it would have taken 30 million such loads to complete the monument (Kopper 1986). Also part of the complex, outside of the ridge enclosure, was another monumental earthwork, a bird-shaped mound of dirt 21 m (about 70 ft) high, covering an area of nearly 13 acres.

Just as at Watson Brake, but on a substantially larger scale, the construction of the Poverty Point earthworks implies the existence of a large labor

FIGURE 8.7

Depiction of the massive, semicircular earthworks at Poverty Point, Louisiana. An enormous amount of labor, perhaps coordinated by some central authority, was needed for the construction of this earthwork. (© Jon Gibson, State of Louisiana Division of Archaeology)

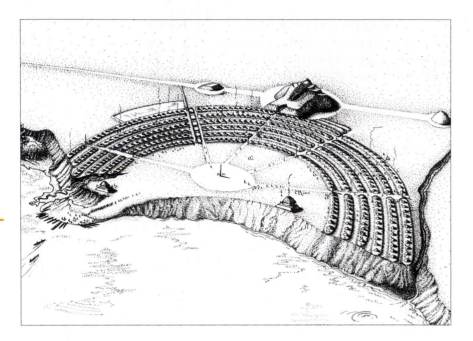

force coordinated through a complex social and political structure. The inhabitants of Poverty Point also were engaged in a broad trading network that enabled them to obtain raw materials, including hematite, slate, and lead ore, as well as good stone for making sharp-edged tools. The presence of these materials also implies that some people were freed from subsistence pursuits to obtain these precious resources not available in their local territory.

Once again, as at Watson Brake, the natural abundance of the surrounding territory seems to have been the key to subsistence at Poverty Point and the factor that allowed for the production of a food surplus, freeing the labor of hundreds of people for the construction of the earthworks. At Poverty Point there is evidence of domesticated squash; but wild foods, especially fish and other aquatic resources, again seem to have been the mainstays of the Poverty Point diet. Watson Brake and Poverty Point are clear indicators that although the rich and abundant surplus made possible by an agricultural way of life may be the more likely precursor to cultural complexity, it is not the only pathway to such complexity.

Koster: Emblem of the Archaic

Perhaps no site in the American Midwest exemplifies better the Archaic period than the Koster site in Illinois (Struever and Holton 2000). Adjacent to the Illinois River, the site is the location of a series of villages dated from soon after the end of the Pleistocene. The inhabitants of all periods exploited the rich and seasonally varied habitat. In fact, the environs of the site were so economically rich from the standpoint of subsistence that as early as 7,000 years

FIGURE 8.8

The Koster site excavation in Illinois revealed a series of overlapping habitations dating from the early post-Pleistocene, illuminating the evolving adaptations to the area around the Illinois River during the Archaic period of North American prehistory. (Courtesy of Northwestern University)

ago the inhabitants were cutting down sizable trees and constructing permanent houses. This was far earlier than for the permanent villages that appeared in most of ancient North America, usually only after the introduction of an agricultural way of life (Figure 8.8).

The Archaic people of Koster hunted deer, small mammals, and migratory fowl, including ducks and geese. The carbonized seeds of wild smartweed, sunflower, goosefoot, pigweed, and marsh elder were found at the site and were major contributors to the diet (see the discussion of the domestication of these crops in Chapter 9). Fish and freshwater shellfish were collected in the river, and nut foods such as hickory, hazelnut, and acorn were harvested seasonally in the uplands around the river valley. Groundnuts, wild duck potatoes, cattail shoots, pecans, pawpaws, persimmons, and sassafras root rounded out the broad subsistence base at Koster.

FIGURE 8.9

All pet owners and animal lovers whose beloved companion has died can relate to this image of one of the dog burials at the Koster site. No mere hygienic disposal of a dead body, 5,000 years ago someone put an old friend to rest, laying the dog on its side and then curling it up, just as if it were asleep.
(© Center for American Archaeology, Kampsville)

Three Middle Archaic human burials dating to nearly 6000 B.P. were recovered at Koster and, like those seen in the Shell Mound Archaic further to the south and east, there were differences in the amounts and kinds of grave goods interred with the deceased, implying some degree of social differentiation.

Also as at Koster, there was another type of burial, not of people, but of dogs. These interments appear to be not the mere hygienic disposal of dead animals, but the ritual entombment of creatures important to those interring them (Figure 8.9). The three buried dogs excavated at Koster were consistently laid out in shallow pits with their legs turned in and their heads set in toward their bodies, affecting the appearance of animals merely asleep. The dogs did not look like their wild ancestor, the wolf, but had proportionally large heads and short legs. At a calculated height of 45–50 cm (18–20 in.), the Koster dogs were the approximate height of modern fox terriers (Struever and Holton 2000:38). In fact, they likely looked very much like the *techichi*, a domesticated breed described by chroniclers of the Native Americans separated from the Koster dogs by more than 5,000 years.

The presence of domesticated dogs at Koster is highly significant and likely resulted from the intentional breeding of wild animals with characteristics deemed advantageous by those who controlled them; perhaps they were less aggressive, more submissive to humans, loyal, strong, and more willing to help their human masters in exchange for food and affection than were their wild cousins. The domestication of plants and animals is the major focus of the next chapter, and the taming and domestication of the dog by people in the post-Pleistocene provides a model for the revolution to come in the relationship between human beings and plants and animals.

A Diverse Set of Adaptations

The focus on locally available foods and the development of highly specialized and localized economies is the most characteristic feature of the Archaic in North America. Evidence is provided by the foods eaten, the types of settlements people lived in, and the material culture seen in archaeological excavations. No longer is a single artifact style with a small number of regional and temporal variants the rule, as it was with the fluted-point tradition during Paleoindian times. We now see a complex, diverse pattern of stone-tool technologies spread across North America, much as was seen in the European Mesolithic, a pattern discernible across virtually all of the inhabited world in the post-Pleistocene.

ASIA

The Asian Mesolithic is less well known than that of Europe, but what is known follows the pattern established there. Archaeologist Kwang-Chih Chang's (1986) synthesis work on the archaeology of China describes different Mesolithic adaptations to China's distinct post-Pleistocene habitats. He begins by dividing the country geographically and culturally into north and south. In the north, Chang recognizes two major Mesolithic groupings on the basis of stone tools: a blade-and-flake industry in the forests of Manchuria and a microblade industry in the riverine and lake habitats that constituted oases in the deserts of Mongolia (Figure 8.10).

The regions of Mongolia inhabited by the **microblade** manufacturers are analogous to the region inhabited by the Desert Archaic culture of North America: Their sites are on the margins of dry, shallow depressions that were small lakes during early post-Pleistocene times. Spearpoints and arrow points are few at these sites, probably indicating the marginality of hunting in the north. The most common faunal remain is ostrich shell fragments, and people almost certainly relied on the fish available in the lakes around which they settled.

Evidence at sites like Djalai-nor and Ku-hsiang-t'un, in the woodlands of Manchuria, indicates that hunting was more important than in the lakeside habitations. Spearpoints are more common, as are bone and antler tools. At sites like the Upper Cave at Zhoukoudian, a Mesolithic occupation of north China near where *Homo erectus* remains were discovered (see Chapter 4), the faunal remains of wapiti (elk) and ostrich have been found. Whereas these were hunted for food, smaller mammals such as badger, fox, wildcat, and tiger were hunted for their thick, warm fur and their teeth, which the Mesolithic occupants of the Upper Cave site perforated to make items of personal adornment. Zhoukoudian is located some distance from the Chinese coast, yet also

FIGURE 8.10
Artifacts from the post-Pleistocene culture in Manchuria, northern China. (From *The Archaeology of Ancient China*, by K. C. Chang, Yale University Press, with permission)

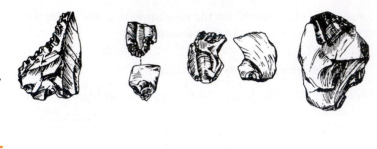

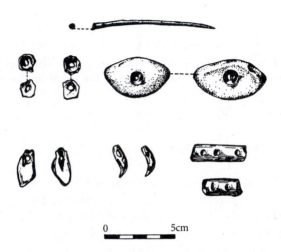

0   5cm

found in abundance in the Upper Cave Mesolithic deposits were the remains of marine shellfish, which were traded for and then used to manufacture beads and other nonutilitarian items found at the site.

In southern China, another distinct set of Mesolithic adaptations evolved in response to the end-of-Pleistocene conditions. Environmental change was not as dramatic here, and there is great continuity with the Upper Paleolithic cultures of the region. The tradition of making stone tools from chipped pebbles is called **Hoabinhian** and marks the southern Chinese Mesolithic. Sites such as Hei-ching-lung imply a subsistence base that included wapiti, wild cattle, other small game, mollusks, and wild plant foods.

A similar pattern of regionalization can be seen farther south in mainland southeast Asia (Higham 1989). Along with a great diversity of archaeological cultures dated to the Mesolithic, an increasingly sedentary way of life is also seen in some particularly rich areas. The broad range of foods available in Thailand at the Spirit Cave site, occupied more than 7,500 years ago, apparently allowed for a settling into and focusing on the territory immediately surrounding the cave. The Khong stream at the base of the cliff face where the cave was located provided fish and freshwater crab. The surrounding forest provided otter, several monkey species (including langur and macaque), bamboo rat, badger, porcupine, and the sambar and pig deer, the bones of which have all been found in the Spirit Cave excavations (Gorman 1972). Along with animal foods, the remains of 22 genera of plants have been recovered in the cave, including bamboo, betel nut (a stimulant), butternut, and assorted tropical fruits (Higham 1989:53).

Spirit Cave and other upland sites in north Thailand not only share their own unique set of adaptations but also exhibit the same pattern seen in many other ecologically distinct regions of southeast Asia: the Red River Delta region of northern Vietnam, the Vietnamese coast, the Chao Phraya plains of southern Thailand, and the Gulf of Siam coast. Each region has produced vastly different yet contemporaneous archaeological cultures dating to the Mesolithic. In each case, local people developed distinctive adaptations to their own rather narrowly circumscribed regions. In this way, the Asian cultures of the Mesolithic exhibit the same pattern seen in Europe and North America: cultural diversity evolving as a result of the developing ecological diversity of the post-Pleistocene.

In western Asia, hunter-gatherers also were adapting to the changing environment that characterized the end of the Pleistocene. Their adaptation would include a new and innovative approach to subsistence—the cultivation of plants and the domestication of animals—an adaptation that ultimately was to make the modern world possible. We will pick up their story in the next chapter.

AUSTRALIA

As a result of its geography, Australia experienced no drastic environmental changes at the end of the Pleistocene. This is not to say that there were no impacts. A drying in the southeast of the country resulted in the disappearance of most inland lakes there by 16,000 B.P. The northern coast, on the other hand, saw an increase in rainfall as storm tracks changed. But because there had been no extensive glaciation in Australia during the Pleistocene, we find no deglaciation and attendant warming like that seen in northern Europe and North America.

Though climate change in Australia at the end of the Pleistocene was not as dramatic as that seen in the higher latitudes of Europe and America, conditions did alter significantly. Mean temperatures rose beginning about 8,700 years ago in the period called the **Holocene Warm Maximum.** Depending on your location in Australia, temperatures were between 0.5°C (0.9°F) and 3°C (5.4°F) higher than they are currently (Mulvaney and Kamminga 1999:226). Outside of the drier southeast, rainfall appears to have increased during this period by 20 to 50%; lakes were full and even the dry interior of the continent was a bit wetter (Mulvaney and Kamminga 1999:226). The Holocene Warm Maximum ended, and the cooler and drier conditions of modern Australia were established by about 4,500 years ago.

Aboriginal culture changed during this period; for example, ground stone hatchets and flaked stone adzes make their appearance during the Holocene

FIGURE 8.11
*Stone hatchets and flaked
adzes from the post-
Pleistocene culture of
Australia.* (From *A Prehistory
of Australia, New Guinea, and
Sahul,* by J. Peter White and
James F. O'Connell, Academic
Press, with permission)

Warm Maximum (Figure 8.11). Also, archaeologists have identified what they have labeled the **Australian Small Tool Phase,** which began around 6,000 years ago and became widespread within about a thousand years. The phase is marked by the production of blade tools, reflecting a more efficient use of stone than in earlier technologies. As mentioned in Chapter 5, long, narrow stone flakes (i.e., blades) produce proportionally more edge for the same mass of stone than do flakes of other configurations. The Small Tool Phase also included the production of extremely finely made, unifacially and bifacially retouched spearpoints, the aesthetic equal to anything seen in the European Upper Paleolithic or among the Paleoindians of the New World (Figure 8.12).

As John Mulvaney and Johan Kamminga (1999) state in their synthesis of Australian archaeology, the toolmaking reflected in the Australian Small Tool Phase was not a reflection of the merely expedient use of stone flakes as was seen earlier in Australian prehistory. The tools manufactured in the small tool phase did not result from the simple process of "rock knocking" and hoping for the best—in other words, hoping that, by chance, some flakes produced by striking a core of stone with a rock hammer would result in a shape that happened to make them useful. Instead, careful core preparation allowed the Australian Small Tool Phase stoneworker to produce predictably shaped and sized flakes. These flakes served as tool blanks. Fine retouch work on the blanks enabled the toolmaker to fashion the tool into a precisely controlled, predetermined form. The Australian Small Tool Phase involved innovations in lithic technology, including the application of far more challenging techniques that would have required great skill and a steep learning curve for the apprentice toolmaker.

The inhabitants of Australia seem to have maintained a relatively stable subsistence adaptation through the late Pleistocene and Holocene and even into the modern era. Whereas shellfish were collected as much as 30,000 years ago at Lake Mungo (see Chapter 7), marine shellfish became a major component of the diet of Australia's coastal people only after 8,000 years ago, around the time that the modern coastal configuration was established. Large shell middens dating especially to after 6000 B.P. are common along the temperate southeast coast and to a lesser degree on the tropical north coast. Shellfish seems not to have been a significant food source along the southwest coast at any time in Australia's history; there are no shell middens, and ethnographic groups in the area were not reported to have been much interested in shellfish (J. White and O'Connell 1982).

The major period of cultural change in Holocene Australia dates to the period beginning about 5,000 years ago. In their synthesis of Australian prehistory, J. Peter White and James F. O'Connell (1982:104–5) point out that in this period the dingo is seen in archaeological contexts for the first time.

The dingo is nearly as emblematic of the wildlife of Australia as the kangaroo and the koala. A feral dog, the dingo is a nonmarsupial migrant, a descendant of domesticated dogs likely brought to Australia by travelers ultimately from southeast Asia who journeyed through the islands of the western Pacific

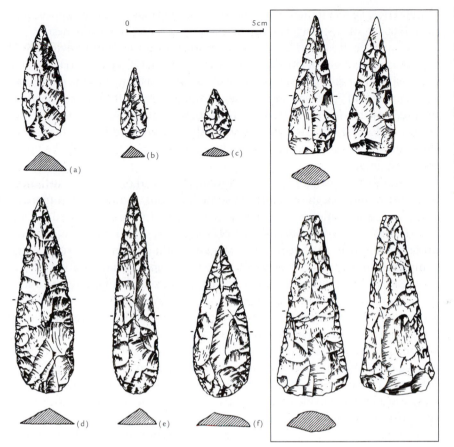

FIGURE 8.12
Beautifully flaked, precisely sharpened, leaf-shaped weapons—unifacially retouched points on the left and symmetrically bifacial points (in the box on the right)—of the Small Tool Phase in Australia. (From Mulvaney and Kamminga 1999)

(dog remains have been found on Borneo dating to 4,500 years ago) and who made landfall on Australia's northern coast.

By intention or accident, some of these traveler's dogs ended up stranded in Australia, where they managed to survive in the wild. Dingoes became a fixture around human settlements reverting to their tame condition, likely maintaining some degree of independence, but accompanying people on hunts, serving as guard dogs and companions. The earliest evidence for the presence of dingoes in Australia has been found at the Madura Cave site on the Nullarbor Plain in Western Australia, with a radiocarbon date of 3450 B.P. (Mulvaney and Kamminga 1999:259). Dingoes are intelligent, sturdy, and resilient animals and spread quickly across the continent. After 3,000 years ago, their remains are common at archaeological sites in Australia.

Also, macrozamia, an otherwise poisonous plant whose underground stem, when properly prepared, produces an edible starch, becomes an important food source after 5,000 years ago. There is also a substantial increase in site density in the eastern Australian highlands, made possible by the broadening of the subsistence quest to include new food sources and the development of new cooking techniques in southeast Australia (marked by the appearance after 4500 B.P. of a new style of hearth made from pieces of termite nest).

A few sites, Roonka Flat being the most impressive, exhibit evidence of an elaboration of burial ritual in Holocene Australia. Of the 82 burials located at this site, most date to recent times, but 12 can be assigned to the period between 4,000 and 7,000 years ago. A few of these were shaft tombs, vertical interments of the deceased. Most of the Roonka Flat burials contained grave goods, including the lower jaws of animals (with drilled holes for suspension), drilled shells, and bone pins. A few adults were buried with the bones of human infants.

A number of changes in the archaeological record of Australia, including an apparent increase in sedentism in some locations, a concomitant increase in site size, and evidence of social differentiation in burials, has led at least one researcher, Harry Lourandos (1997), to suggest that native Australians underwent a process of economic intensification and an increase in social complexity in the period after about 5,000 years ago. Lourandos notes the existence of an intricate and extensive cluster of ancient channels dug by native Australians in the southwest section of Victoria, the southeasternmost province of the island continent. Lourandos maintains that the channels were the product of communal labor, dug in order to connect a series of lakes and wetlands to enable the inhabitants to collect large quantities of seasonally migrating eels (Mulvaney and Kamminga 1999). The excavation of these channels would have required a cooperative effort on the part of a large cohort of people at a level not evidenced in older Australian sites. The resulting production of a food surplus allowed for an increase in sedentism, population growth, and, perhaps, social differentiation, with some individuals or families able to concentrate wealth and increase social status.

Some researchers have suggested that the increase in regional diversity of art styles seen in Holocene rock paintings (Figure 8.13) resulted from economic regionalization as geographically separated groups intensified the food quest, focusing on particularly rich resources in their own areas, as the native people did by intensifying their exploitation of eels in southwest Victoria (Mulvaney and Kamminga 1999). Whatever the cause, this diversity of styles is a clear indication of cultural heterogeneity in prehistoric Australia. A growth in cultural diversity is precisely what we have seen in the rest of the world during the Holocene epoch.

Australia is huge and has been occupied for 40,000 years. On the one hand, its material culture is easier to analyze than that of Europe, Asia, or North America because it is both more homogeneous and stable through time. On the other hand, there is a level of diversity apparent in subsistence data that more clearly follows the post-Pleistocene pattern seen in the rest of the world. As J. White and O'Connell (1982) maintain, the post-Pleistocene archaeological record of Australia reflects the significance of highly localized environmental factors in molding a settlement/subsistence pattern. Coastal, upland, desert, lake, and riverine foci all became established in different parts

FIGURE 8.13
The ancient people of Australia produced beautiful and artistically distinctive rock paintings across nearly their entire history. (© Archivo Icono-grafico, S. A./Corbis)

of the country. In that sense, Australia after the Pleistocene exhibits a pattern common to the one seen in the rest of the world.

SOUTH AMERICA

We saw in the previous chapter that great diversity characterized the subsistence patterns of the late Pleistocene inhabitants of South America. Certainly, as archaeologist Karen Olsen Bruhns (1994) states, some societies were largely dependent on big-game hunting. At the same time, the newly discovered sites of Quebrada Jaguay (Sandweiss et al. 1998) and Quebrada Tacahuay (Keefer et al. 1998; see Chapter 7) show that some South Americans had a maritime-based economy before 10,000 B.P. Also mentioned in Chapter 7, Anna C. Roosevelt's work (Roosevelt et al. 1996) at the Caverna da Pedra Pintada site in the Amazon basin in Brazil indicates that by about 11,000 years ago, in the late Pleistocene, some groups in South America had already developed an adaptation to the tropical rain forest habitat. A rich array of food remains at the site indicates a broad reliance by the inhabitants on tropical fruit and nut trees as well as on the animal life that abounds in the tropics, including fresh-water fish and mollusks, tortoises, turtles, snakes, birds, and small game.

The end of the Pleistocene wrought changes of climate in South America and attendant changes in the subsistence focus of the people living there. In some areas with a restricted community of edible plants and animals, human groups became highly specialized in exploiting individual species or a small number of species. For example, with the extinction of mastodon, horse, glyptodont (giant armadillo), megatherium (giant ground sloth), and many other Pleistocene species, some human groups who previously had at least partially relied on the hunting of these animals shifted focus to the single set of large game animals remaining after the Pleistocene—**camelids.** The South American camels included the wild guanaco and vicuña (llamas and alpacas are the domesticated versions of South American camels). For example, at Pachamachay Cave in the Peruvian Andes, a subsistence focus on vicuña hunting developed after 9000 B.P. (Bruhns 1994).

Elsewhere, a broadening of the subsistence quest is apparent. The Vegas complex, located in the Santa Elena Peninsula of Ecuador, shows an early (late Paleoindian) evolution of a maritime subsistence focus. This shift is ultimately seen in the coastal desert from northern Peru to southern Chile, where archaeological evidence shows early post-Pleistocene groups heavily exploiting resources like mollusks. This maritime, or **littoral,** tradition is seen, if a bit later, in coastal Colombia and Venezuela and also along the Caribbean Atlantic coasts of South America. Hunting remained important in some areas; some of the coastal sites are located near tar pits, natural traps where animals could have been killed once mired in the thick natural petroleum deposits. But maritime resources seem to have become most important to people living near the coast in post-Pleistocene South America. Some places even show signs of a population movement away from the interior and toward the coast. These post-Pleistocene coastal sites tend to be larger than earlier sites, more permanent, and with more elaborate burials. A sedentary way of life on the coast, made possible by the rich and reliable resources of the sea, seems to have set the stage, at least in part, for the great cultural changes that were to occur in South America (see Chapters 10 and 14).

AFRICA

Like Australia, the African continent was not affected as severely by climate change at the end of the Pleistocene as were Europe, Asia, and the Americas. Africa was not glaciated and suffered much less extinction of large mammals. And the kind of regionalization seen on the other continents in the early post-Pleistocene is seen in Africa in an earlier period. As indicated by archaeologist David W. Phillipson in his synthesis of African prehistory, the period of 100,000–8,000 years ago is characterized by the movement away from "broad cultural uniformity" and "towards the establishment of distinct regional traditions" (1993:60).

Typical among the regional cultures was that of the **Iberomaurusians** of northwest Africa (Klein 1993). At about 16,000 B.P., they inhabited the coastal plain and interior of what is today Tunisia and Morocco. They made small stone blade artifacts and used them as scraping and piercing tools—the former for scraping animal hides in clothing manufacture and the latter as arrow points or spearpoints for hunting. The animals that were the core of their subsistence strategy included wild cattle, gazelle, hartebeest, and Barbary sheep. Also important in their coastal habitat were marine mollusks, including snails. Though no plant food remains have been found in Iberomaurusian sites, grinding stones and digging-stick weights indicate some reliance on seeds, nuts, and roots.

Change accompanies the end of the Pleistocene, but there is no great cultural upheaval in Africa. After 10,000 B.P. in northwest Africa, the Iberomaurusian culture is replaced by another, called **Capsian;** as paleoanthropologist Richard Klein (1993) points out, this may have involved an actual migration of new people into the area, where they replaced the older inhabitants. Capsian subsistence is not very different from that of the preceding Iberomaurusians. The inhabitants continued to hunt wild sheep, collect shellfish and snails, dig for roots, and grind seeds and nuts. The Capsians set very small **microlith** blades into wooden or bone handles. These tools appear to have been used to harvest wild stands of grains; the microliths themselves exhibit a diagnostic kind of wear, or polish, called "sickle sheen" from repeated use in cutting the stalks of tall, grasslike plants.

The use of microlithic **backed blades** is all but ubiquitous in Holocene Africa. During the early post-Pleistocene of southern Africa, microlithic industries predominate at coastal locales where preservation is high; in dry caves and waterlogged sites such as Gwisho Hot Springs in Zambia, a broad array of artifacts was recovered, including bows and arrows, digging sticks, bark trays, and bags and clothing of leather. Plant foods were important in the diet within a seasonal round that saw winter settlement of the coast and summers spent inland.

South Africa also saw a proliferation of artwork, with an abundance of naturalistic rock paintings depicting animals and people (Figure 8.14). As Phillipson (1993:77) points out, the paintings almost certainly had a ritual significance. The eland—a large antelope—is depicted most frequently, but it is not the animal most commonly represented in the faunal assemblage at archaeological sites dated to the same period. Historically, however, the eland played an important role in the religions of some southern African people, and its abundance in ancient rock paintings may indicate that the ritual importance of the eland has a long history. Also, some of the paintings show people in positions and contexts that were common in historical times and related to trance. Again, as Phillipson (1993:77) points out, early Holocene rock paintings of people bent over or in a crouched position, often with blood apparently flowing from their noses, match the descriptions of trance experience of the San people living in southern Africa (Figure 8.15). The San describe their trances as riding on the backs of snakes, and people riding on the backs of enormous serpents or snakes are also found in the rock paintings.

Central, eastern, and western Africa also have produced archaeological evidence of microlithic tool industries as well as diversity and regionalization

FIGURE 8.14

Naturalistic engraving of a rhinoceros found in southern Africa and dating to the post-Pleistocene.
(From *African Archaeology,* by David W. Phillipson, p. 76, Fig. 4.8, Cambridge University Press, with permission)

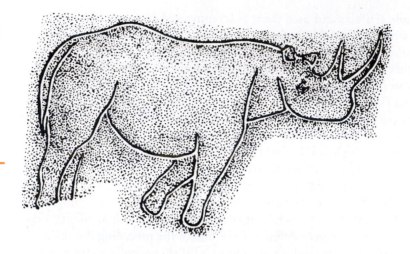

FIGURE 8.15

Rock paintings from southern Africa interpreted as representing two shamans in a trance. (From *African Archaeology,* by David W. Phillipson, p. 77, Fig. 4.10, Cambridge University Press, with permission)

of subsistence and settlement. In East Africa, on the shores of Lake Turkana, where so many key finds have been made related to human physical evolution (see Chapters 3 and 4), evidence of a specialized fishing adaptation has been recovered. In the dense forests of West Africa, a culture with a nonmicrolithic tool assemblage has been identified. Large stone hoes and axes predominate, with little evidence of hunting equipment. Subsistence may have been based on the abundant plant foods of the forest.

Africa, too, is marked by an explosion of cultural diversity as people became more specifically adapted to their own particular regions in the early Holocene. The stage is now set, here as elsewhere, for a revolution in human subsistence.

ISSUES AND DEBATES

WAS THE MESOLITHIC ONLY A "PRELUDE"?

For many scholars, the period immediately following the Pleistocene is not as intriguing as the periods before or a few thousand years after. It has not commanded as much attention in publications, for instance.

Grahame Clark's classic work on the European Mesolithic, *Mesolithic Prelude* (1980), implies, by its very title, that the significance of this period rests not so much in what transpired, but in what it led to: the Neolithic (see Chapter 9). Archaeologist T. Douglas Price (1987:227) points out that for many scientists, at least until fairly recently, the Mesolithic was marked by cultural "impoverishment." Remains were sparse, the artwork was unimpressive, and the period seemed less interesting than the more romantic Upper Paleolithic (with its images of bands of big-game-hunting artists) and less important than the Neolithic, with the inception of a sedentary, "civilized," farming way of life.

As Price points out, this view is no longer tenable. The Mesolithic in Europe—in fact, the early post-Pleistocene of much of the world—does not represent a chronological way station between Pleistocene big-game hunting and the inevitable shift to food production during the subsequent Neolithic period (Chapter 9). In fact, the Mesolithic and Archaic were periods during which human groups responded to one of the greatest environmental challenges humanity had yet faced. The evidence indicates that environmental changes at the end of the Pleistocene were substantial, rapid, and unpredictable. Mean temperature fluctuated widely over relatively short spans of time, and this had an enormous effect on human groups as well as the plant and animal species on which they relied for their subsistence. It took some time for conditions to become relatively stable and predictable, and this instability and unpredictability must have presented extraordinary challenges to human beings attempting to adjust their lifeways to the new circumstances. As Jochim (1998) points out, the archaeology of this period of time provides us with the opportunity to study how human beings react to environmental change, an issue of great importance to modern people contemplating our own future.

Study of the Mesolithic and Archaic reveals that humanity thrived by fairly quickly developing many varied cultural adaptations to the changing conditions. Although food resources, including shellfish, small mammals, and wild grains, were available to many groups in the Pleistocene, those who relied on big game had little reason to exploit these other possibilities. The end of the Pleistocene and the scaling back and even extinction of many of these big-game resources brought major change for these groups.

Wherever we look in the Old and New Worlds, human groups rose to the challenge of drastically changing environmental conditions, each in its own way. The ability of culture, with its enormous flexibility, to respond to such changes is the hallmark of our species and a reason for its great success—both then and now. Being able to invent, virtually instantly, new strategies for survival rather than having to wait for nature somehow to "come up with" a new adaptation and being able to adjust quickly to rapidly changing environmental conditions puts humanity at a tremendous advantage relative to other animal species. For human groups at the end of the Pleistocene, the only limitations were those of the imagination. And based on the diversity of the responses, this was hardly any limitation at all.

The post-Pleistocene also was the crucible in which was forged the adaptations that would lead to subsistence strategies that make modern life possible. It is hard to argue now with the characterization of the Mesolithic—and it could be applied to post-Pleistocene cultures the world over—by Russian archaeologist G. I. Mathyushin (Clark 1980:6; Price 1987:229) as "the most important epoch in history."

CASE STUDY CLOSE-UP

Beginning 10,700 years ago, and lasting for about 300 years, Mesolithic people intensively utilized a section of land jutting into an early postglacial lake located near the eastern coast of England (Clark 1971; Mellars and Dark 1998). The archaeological site that resulted from this occupation is called Star Carr and was excavated by British prehistorian J. G. D. Clark between 1949 and 1951 and subsequently by a number of researchers between 1975 and 1997.

More than 17,000 flint artifacts were recovered in the original excavation; many of these represented various steps in the manufacture of stone tools. Along with stone, a large assemblage of animal remains was recovered in the excavation. Many of the organic remains, including substantial quantities of bone and antler, ended up in the soft, wet mud along the lake's shoreline, where they became saturated in an environment hostile to the aerobic bacteria that ordinarily break down such remains. The result is a remarkable state of preservation, affording researchers a unique opportunity to reconstruct the diet of Star Carr's inhabitants. The bones of aurochs (wild cattle), elk, red deer, roe deer, and wild pig dominate the faunal assemblage, represent thousands of kilograms of food, and suggest a heavy reliance on the consumption of meat.

Smaller mammals also were used by the inhabitants: The bones of fur-bearing animals such as fox, wolf, badger, beaver, and hare were found at the site. The inhabitants also ate birds: The bones of duck, mergansers, grebes, and cranes were recovered. Surprisingly, despite the excellent level of preservation, no fish bones were found, perhaps indicating the inhabitants' lack of interest in that particular lake resource. Also, though the lakeside was home to a wide variety of plants, no direct evidence was collected at the site for the use of plant foods.

One category of tools found at the site could have been used for digging for roots—the elk antler **mattocks.** Flat sections of connected skull and antler were used as the digging blade, and a large hole was drilled through the base of the blade, into which a wooden handle was fastened. One of the mattocks found had a charred remnant of the wooden handle in place.

At least 80 red deer are represented in the antler assemblage; but, interestingly, the bones of most of these animals were not recovered at the site. The mystery of the missing bones can be solved in this way: The antlers most likely were collected, not by killing the deer but simply by picking them up after they had been naturally shed by the animals in the winter. The antlers likely were accumulated by the people who lived at Star Carr and carried to the site when they traveled there as part of their seasonal migrations.

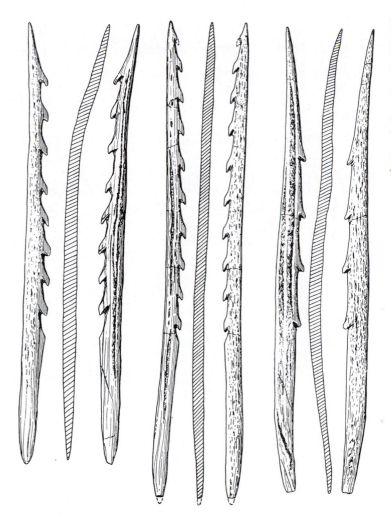

FIGURE 8.16
Sample of barbed antler harpoons from the Mesolithic site of Star Carr in England. (From *The Excavation at Star Carr,* by J. G. D. Clark, p. 139, Fig. 49, Cambridge University Press, with permission)

　　The antlers provided a valuable raw material to the inhabitants of the site. Using sharp, steep-edged stone tools, the community's toolmakers incised deep grooves into the antlers, enabling them to pry out long, narrow slivers of hard, dense material. These antler slivers were then worked into an extensive assemblage of deadly sharp weapons, vicious-looking things with a series of sharp, down-pointing barbs (Figure 8.16). Once in an animal, they would not fall out nor could they be pulled out without serious damage to the creature. These were highly effective hunting tools.

　　The ages of the animals that had been killed and used for food by the site's inhabitants as determined by a careful analysis of the development of their teeth indicates that the vast majority of them had been killed between March and April (Carter 1997). It seems likely, therefore, that the site was occupied during the spring and, perhaps, into the summer. The residents of Star Carr dealt with the thick growth of reeds along the edge of the lake by intentional

and regular burning. Archaeologists have found substantial deposits of charcoal along the lakeside. Well-preserved fragments of burned reed representing stages of early growth further support the notion of a spring occupation. To stabilize the wet surface around the lake and allow dry access to the waterside, the site's inhabitants laid down wooden planks, some of which have preserved because of the continuously waterlogged environment in which they were deposited.

Star Carr provides a rich picture of life in the Mesolithic (Figure 8.17). The preservation of so much organic material allows for a detailed look at the subsistence of this group of post-Pleistocene people. Though it is difficult to generalize about Mesolithic culture precisely because it represents a period of such great diversity, one impression left by Star Carr probably can be widely applied: The inhabitants exploited a broad range of resources in their subsistence quest. In this sense, the people of Star Carr are models of the Mesolithic and Late Archaic adaptations.

VISITING THE PAST

As a result of the common assumption that the early post-Pleistocene is a culturally uninteresting period, there are fewer places to visit that relate directly to this time in human antiquity. It is true that post-Pleistocene, pre-Neolithic sites produce less visually exciting artifacts and therefore are of less interest to casual tourists. You will find information on the pre-Neolithic in any museum that presents material on the origins of agriculture, at least as context for a display on the revolution in food production.

Perhaps one of the most important sites you can visit is that of Koster in Kampsville, Illinois. The Kampsville complex of research buildings is at the hub of the ambitious archaeological work of the Center for American Archaeology that has identified thousands of sites in the area. Though the Koster excavation itself has long been filled in, you'll find a visitor's center with displays focusing on the work of the Center, much of it related to the Archaic period (http://www.caa-archeology.org/).

Although most people are at least passingly familiar with the art of the Upper Paleolithic (Chapter 6), few are aware that the tradition of painting on cave walls did not cease at the end of the Pleistocene. You can conduct a virtual visit of some of the painted grottoes and open-air art sites of the Mesolithic at the Prehistoric Art Virtual Museum at http://vm.kemsu.ru/en/mezolith/.

SUMMARY

The common thread running through this chapter has been post-Pleistocene adaptation. Wherever we have looked in Europe, Asia, North and South America, Australia, and Africa, we have seen the same trends: intensification of food collection, increasing economic and social complexity, and a marked jump in regional, cultural diversity. After about 12,000 B.P., human beings were faced with fundamental changes in the Pleistocene environments to which they had become adapted. Land covered in ice became exposed, temperatures rose, and some areas became drier, others wetter. Land connections were breached, and coastal configurations rapidly changed. Animals on which some humans subsisted became extinct, and new, different animals took their place. Plants became available that were useful for food, in the form of nuts, seeds, fruits, leaves, or roots.

People were faced with many options in the rapidly changing post-Pleistocene world. Some broadened the subsistence quest to include a wide variety of plant and animal resources. Others intensified the subsistence quest, focusing on a single resource or very few particularly productive resources. Other human groups became increasingly sedentary as they adapted to rich Holocene environments. As a result of the diversity of the post-Pleistocene resource base, cultural diversity increased exponentially, with myriad cultures proliferating, each thriving in its own territory.

Some settlements became more permanent, and population grew. In a number of cases, the food quest was intensified further still as groups attempted to increase the productivity of the resources on which they depended. This intensification set the stage for what will be discussed in Chapter 9: the revolution in food production.

TO LEARN MORE

Technical Summaries

There are some excellent technical sources on regional post-Pleistocene adaptations. For Europe, Grahame Clark's classic book, *Mesolithic Prelude* (1980), is a good place to start. For a more up-to-date summary of the European Mesolithic, T. Douglas Price's 1987 article titled "The Mesolithic of Western Europe" in the *Journal of World Prehistory* is a good source. For North America, see Brian Fagan's *Ancient North America* (2000) for a detailed textbook treatment of post-Pleistocene adaptations. For an excellent source on this and other periods of South America's prehistory, see Karen Olsen Bruhns's *Ancient South America* (1994). Several chapters of John Mulvaney and Johan Kamminga's (1999) excellent overview, *Prehistory of Australia,* are devoted to a detailed discussion and analysis of post-Pleistocene adaptations to the island continent. For Asia, the general works by Kwang-Chih Chang—including *The Archaeology of Ancient China* (1986)—as well as Charles Higham's *The Archaeology of Mainland Southeast Asia* (1989) include considerable discussions of the post-Pleistocene. For Africa, see David W. Phillipson's *African Archaeology* (1993).

Popular Summaries

A new edition is available of a terrific popular book focusing on one of the best-known post-Pleistocene sites in North America, Stuart Struever and Felicia Holton's *Koster: Americans in Search of Their Prehistoric Past* (2000). The book is aimed at a popular audience; see especially the chapter titled "A Day at Koster in 3500 B.C."

On the Web

It cannot exactly be said that the Internet is burgeoning with sites dedicated to the Mesolithic or Archaic period in the Old and New Worlds. You can access a detailed discussion of a Mesolithic burial in Italy at http://web.unife.it/progetti/notes/emezzoc.htm. There is a very informative page about an ongoing project focused on Siebenlinden Mesolithic sites located near Tübingen, in southern Germany (http://www.landesdenkmalamt-bw.de/english/archaeol/siebenlinden/index.php). For North America, there is a summary page on the Koster site located at http://www.mnsu.edu/emuseum/archaeology/sites/northamerica/koster.html and you can visit the Web site devoted to the Archaic period that has been put up by the Cabrillo College Department of Anthropology: http://www.cabrillo.edu/~crsmith/noamer_archaic.html.

Online Learning Center: www.mhhe.com/feder4

ONLINE
LEARNING
CENTER

The Online Learning Center (OLC) Web companion to *The Past in Perspective* features a variety of supplemental study aids. For each chapter, this free Web site includes

- Self-Quizzes to take as pretests prior to exams
- Interactive Timeline Study Guides for additional review and reinforcement of key information
- Learning Objectives
- Chapter Site links with Web addresses for many of the fossil and archaeological sites mentioned in the text

KEY TERMS

Archaic, 318
Australian Small Tool
   Phase, 330
backed blade, 335
camelid, 334
Capsian, 335
Hamburgian, 316
Hoabinhian, 328
Holocene, 310
Holocene Warm
   Maximum, 329

Iberomaurusian, 334
interglacial, 310
interstadial, 310
lacustrine, 319
Lake Forest Archaic, 319
littoral, 334
Maglemosian, 314
Maritime Archaic, 320
Mast Forest Archaic,
   320
mattock, 338

Mesolithic, 314
microblade, 327
microlith, 335
midden, 316
Paleo-Arctic tradition,
   319
pelagic, 320
Younger Dryas, 313

9

The Food-Producing Revolution

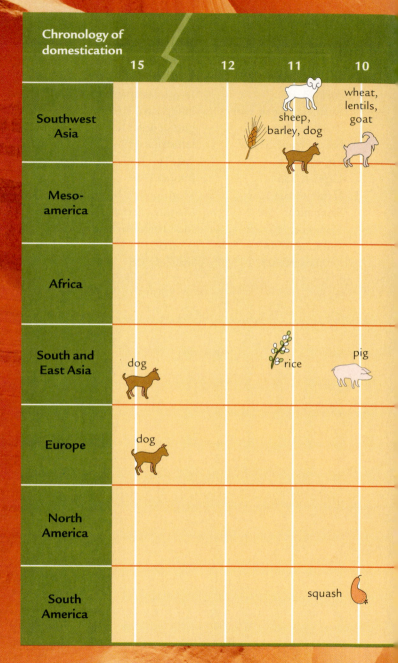

CHAPTER OVERVIEW

The Neolithic represents a revolution in subsistence. As the result of a complex process that began as much as 20,000 to soon after 12,000 years ago, some human groups began not just foraging for food—hunting wild animals, fishing, and collecting edible plants found in nature—but also actually producing it. A number of different human groups began the slow process referred to as "artificial selection," first by concentrating and tending plants and taming animals that were of economic importance and then by allowing only those individual animals or plants with characteristics desirable from a human subsistence standpoint—nonaggressive disposition among animals or large, easily harvestable seeds among plants—to survive and propagate. This shift to food production occurred independently in several places in the New and Old Worlds. Each of the several "agricultural revolutions" involved the manipulation of local wild plants and/or animals. Today, our diets reflect a wide array of foods, the majority of which were first domesticated by people many millennia ago. By 2,000 years ago, most human groups had adopted food production as their primary subsistence strategy.

Thousands of years ago

9	8	7	6	5	4	3	2	1

dog, cattle — cattle — camel

beans, chili peppers

squash — maize — sunflower

sorghum — millet — donkey

cattle — chickpea, barley, lentil, wheat, sheep, goat, cattle — yams — cat

chicken — millet, pig — cattle — banana

cattle — wheat, barley, legumes, sheep, goat, dog — millet, lentils

sumpweed — smartweed, knotweed, maygrass, little barley, goosefoot — maize

squash — sunflower

llama, alpaca, manioc, yams, arrowroot — beans, chili peppers, ulluco, potato, cotton, quinoa — oca, maca, yacon, jícama, arracacha, maize

ONLINE LEARNING CENTER

Go to **www.mhhe.com/feder4** for an interactive study guide version of this timeline.

345

Twenty-first-century anthropologists are not the first to ponder the human past and to imagine how humanity has changed and evolved over the millennia. Many people, often through myth or legend, have tried to explain their own past and to chronicle major changes they realize must have occurred in their societies over time.

Consider, for example, the ancient Chinese legend of Shen Nung, first written down close to 3,000 years ago (Chang 1968). According to this legend, Shen Nung was a wise and powerful emperor of ancient China. At the beginning of his reign, the people of China were nomadic, surviving on the wild plants and animals that nature provided. According to the story, "The ancient people ate meat of animals and birds. At the time of Shen Nung, there were so many people that the animals and birds became inadequate for people's wants, and therefore Shen Nung taught the people how to cultivate. . . . At the time of Shen Nung, millet rained down from Heaven. Shen Nung collected the grains and cultivated them" (Chang 1968:79). Shen Nung is also credited with inventing the plow to assist in the cultivation of crops.

The legend of Shen Nung represents a self-conscious attempt by the Chinese to explain what they understood as a fundamental change in their culture in past times—a shift from hunting and gathering to the cultivation of crops. Shen Nung gave the people the knowledge to plant, tend, and harvest crops, which, in turn, provided additional food. This rationale for the origins of agriculture actually sounds quite modern: the growth of human population beyond what hunting and gathering can support. We will see in this chapter's "Issues and Debates" that some twenty-first-century anthropologists have suggested much the same cause.

Like the Chinese of nearly 3,000 years ago, twenty-first-century anthropologists also recognize the significance of agriculture in making modern life possible and realize that humanity has not always had the knowledge of cultivation and animal husbandry. Like them, we seek to understand how and why we became agricultural. Our explanations do not rely on myth, but on scientific investigation of a period after the Pleistocene in many parts of the world when human groups began to change their relationship with their resource base. At this time, and in multiple locations, instead of simply collecting foods offered by nature, people began the process of actually altering the resources to fit their own needs. This period of change in how people fed themselves goes by several names. Some refer to it as the **Neolithic Revolution;** that name is a holdover from a time when researchers identified sites primarily on the basis of the kinds of stone tools that were found (Neolithic means literally "new stone," which distinguishes it from the Paleolithic, or "old stone," tool industries). Many prefer the more descriptive term the **Food-Producing Revolution** because it refers to precisely what is now viewed as the most significant aspect of what happened: People began the process of producing food rather than simply gathering the foods that nature offered. Other archaeologists and historians use the phrase **Agricultural Revolution** because the first steps of food production led to full-blown agriculture, the economic basis of modern existence. We will use these terms interchangeably here. The key point to remember is that this period marks a fundamental transformation of humanity as people became the managers, transformers, and masters of their food resources.

For most of human history, people have relied for their subsistence on **foraging**—hunting, fishing, and collect-

CHRONICLE

ing wild plant foods. As we saw in Chapter 8, the Mesolithic and Late Archaic periods are characterized by myriad combinations of hunting; trapping; line and net fishing; collecting shellfish; digging for roots; harvesting wild grains; collecting seeds, nuts, and fruits, and so on. Some groups had a broad resource base; others focused on a few highly productive resources. Some human groups were nomadic, continually traveling to wherever food could be found; others were more sedentary, staying in one place where a particularly abundant, reliable, and constant food source was available. Some groups in some regions adhered to a schedule of movement that coincided with seasonal changes in resource availability; other groups in other regions followed a less varied schedule, doing much the same work and relying on the same set of food sources year round.

What all these groups had in common, regardless of the particular plants or animals they relied on for food, was that those food sources were wild. For more than 99% of human prehistory, people have relied exclusively on the wild foods that nature provides (Figure 9.1). It is only very recently, within the past 12,000 years, that human groups began actively controlling their food sources by artificially producing conditions under which these sources could thrive and then, by manipulating them, altering them from a natural state.

HUMANS TAKING THE PLACE OF NATURE: ARTIFICIAL SELECTION

Though we refer to the shift from foraging to farming as a revolution, that term may be misleading. In fact, settled agricultural life represents not so much a rapid revolution as one step in a process stretched out along a lengthy continuum of change. The transition from food gathering to a total reliance on agriculture took thousands of years. Recent research at the Ohalo II site in Israel (Piperno et al. 2004) indicates that a heavy subsistence reliance on the seeds produced by some of the same wild grasses that would become—and that continue to be—staples in agricultural systems in the Middle East and, ultimately, all over the world (barley and emmer wheat) had already developed by 20,000 years ago, in the Upper Paleolithic. This is nearly 10,000 years before agriculture developed in the Middle East. In eastern North America, it took as much as 4,000 years for the shift to a fully agricultural way of life to

take place, and in Mexico as much as 5,000 or even 6,000 years passed between the first steps in plant domestication and the evolution of a fully agricultural people.

As archaeologist Naomi Miller (1992) lays out the continuum from foraging to farming, it begins with collecting wild foods and continues through a lengthy period of tending and encouraging wild plants or animals. In some instances, this may lead to manipulation of the reproduction of economically important plants or animals through **artificial selection**—that is, the directed breeding of plants and animals possessing characteristics deemed beneficial to human beings. At this stage, human beings (in a manner analogous to natural selection as defined by Charles Darwin—see Chapter 1) select for propagation only those individuals within a plant or animal species that possess some natural endowments useful to people. In describing the "art" of artificial selection, Darwin pointed out: "One of the most remarkable features in our domesticated races is that we see in them adaptations, not indeed to the animal's or plant's own good, but to man's use or fancy" (1859:47).

So both at the origins of agriculture and in our modern systems, humans protect and encourage only those individual plants that produce more, larger, or more readily digested seeds, only those individual animals within a species that exhibit less aggression and produce the most meat, milk, or wool, or only those trees that bear larger fruits. Selected animals in a wild species may be corralled and protected from predators. Certain individual plants within a wild species may be watered or weeded or planted near the village and then fenced in to prevent animals from eating them.

After many generations of such treatment, and as people have an increased opportunity to even more carefully select for propagation plants or animals with desirable characteristics, the cultivated plants and animals no longer resemble their wild ancestors or neighbors. They have been so altered through artificial selection that, again in a manner analogous to natural selection, they can no longer be considered the same species. They have, in essence, coevolved with their human overseers, no longer changing under entirely natural conditions but under the conditions established by people (Rindos 1984). Such plants and animals are said to be **domesticated.** Under extreme conditions of **domestication,** they cannot survive without human beings to attend to their needs and to propagate them. They are no longer adapted to a natural world but, rather, to a culturally constructed world of agriculture and animal husbandry. And in every case, the prehistoric record is clear: Wherever such a "revolution" occurred, it transpired over thousands of years. This chapter documents such a process for the Near East, Mesoamerica, Asia, Africa, Europe, North America, and South America.

WHY AGRICULTURE?

Many hypotheses have been put forth to explain why, more or less simultaneously, people over the world adopted an agricultural subsistence system. As archaeologist Mark Cohen (1977) has pointed out, under different environmental conditions and focusing on many kinds of plant and animal resources, between 11,000 and 2,000 years ago, most of the world's people either developed a domesticated food base independently or adopted the agricultural pattern of their neighbors. In other words, a slow-motion revolution occurred over 9,000 years and supplanted a pattern of foraging that had been successful for the hominid family for more than 6 million years.

That such a revolution took place is obvious. That there must have been some compelling human need behind it seems reasonable. What is not obvious, however, is *why* this shift took place at all.

Environmental Change

An environmental cause has often been suggested for this shift. This hypothesis proposes that the extinction at the end of the Pleistocene of plant and animal species on which some human groups depended for subsistence stimulated the development of agriculture to replace these extinct food sources. One specific version of the environmental-change explanation is British prehistorian V. Gordon Childe's (1942, 1951, 1953) "oasis hypothesis." Childe proposed that increasing post-Pleistocene aridity in the Near East forced surviving plants, animals, and people to congregate around permanent water sources. In Childe's view, people became more knowledgeable about the wild species now in close proximity to them and slowly tamed and molded the species to fill their needs.

Cultural Evolution

Other researchers have proposed that agriculture developed as the result of cultural evolution. This "readiness hypothesis," championed by archaeologist Robert Braidwood (1960, 1975), assumes that throughout the Paleolithic human groups accumulated knowledge about the wild plants and animals on which they depended and then discovered ways to increase the reliability, productivity, and usefulness of those species through selective breeding. In other words, here agriculture is viewed as the almost inevitable outcome of a people's increasing familiarity with the wild plants and animals on which they depend.

Population Growth

Some researchers have suggested that domestication resulted from the need to increase productivity to feed a growing population. In his provocative book, *The Food Crisis in Prehistory,* archaeologist Mark Cohen (1977) argues that only an overriding necessity could have induced human groups to shift to a subsistence pattern that involved fundamentally altering their way of life and adopting a far more labor-intensive pattern. Hunter-gatherers are known to work relatively short hours for their subsistence, especially compared to agriculturalists. The !Kung San people living in the Kalahari Desert in southern Africa, one of the least hospitable places on earth, work just 20 hours a week in subsistence activities (see Figure 9.1; Lee 1979). In Cohen's view, only the pressing need to feed an increasing number of mouths could compel people to abandon a more leisurely mode of life.

An Accident

Other researchers maintain that the domestication of plants and animals was not accomplished through conscious choice to improve the subsistence base but instead because human beings naturally alter the habitats they exploit. Humans change natural conditions simply by returning to the same place to collect foods seasonally, by killing or weeding out economically useless species, by disturbing the soil, by concentrating garbage, by moving plants or animals into areas outside of natural habitats, and by clearing out vegetation for villages (Anderson 1956). In this way, people unintentionally create better conditions for individual members of species that fortuitously thrive in a human-dominated and culturally altered and manipulated landscape. Species adapt to these new artificial conditions, while humans, in turn, culturally adapt to take full advantage of these species, all in a process that archaeologist David Rindos (1984) calls "co-evolution." In other words, the plants evolve in response to human behavior and human behavior evolves to better take advantage of, and to further amplify, the changes produced in the plant and animal species.

A Multitude of Reasons

There probably was no single "prime cause" for the development of agriculture in all the places that it occurred. Perhaps there was no one "Agricultural

Revolution," but many, each with its own explanation. As archaeologist Donald O. Henry (1989:236) points out, "given the complex ecological relationships that governed the transition from forager to food-producer," complexity and diversity in explaining these transitions is to be expected. And as archaeologist Ofer Bar-Yosef (1998) has pointed out, if there was a single, universal cause for the origins of plant and animal domestication, then nearly all foragers would have developed a subsistence system based on agriculture or animal husbandry when faced with the same or similar climatic or demographic conditions. That this universal adaptation did not occur is a clear indication that different cultural groups can and did respond differently to changes in the environment or in their population. It can be said no more clearly: Though several different groups at different times and places developed it, "There is no need to seek one single model to explain the origins of agriculture" (Bar-Yosef 1998:173).

However, significant patterns do exist in the record. A sedentary settlement pattern (evidenced by substantial and permanent architectural forms) *preceded* the appearance of domesticated foods. In other words, in the late Pleistocene/early Holocene, some human groups began to settle into regions so plentiful in food resources that people could stay in one place for much of the year and collect enough food to survive and even thrive. Population might have grown exponentially as the sedentary life may have lowered infant mortality and extended the length of life. During a long period of population growth, the food quest would have been intensified to feed the growing number of mouths. One step in this intensification would have been to artificially raise the productivity of the nearby wild plants by creating conditions that increased the yield of food: clearing forest, planting seedbeds, weeding, fencing in. At this point, the plant selection process changed: Whereas before plants were adapting to natural conditions, now they were adapting to conditions produced by the cultural manipulation of the environment. This was the first step toward domestication and, ultimately, a way of life dependent entirely on food production.

ARCHAEOLOGICAL EVIDENCE OF HUMAN CONTROL OF PLANT AND ANIMAL SPECIES

Because the shift from food gathering to food production was a process rather than an event, there really is no single point along that continuum of subsistence change marking *the* break between foraging and food production. We can, however, recognize aspects of that continuum of change in the archaeological record and thereby reveal the nature of the process that resulted ultimately in the development of an agricultural way of life.

Geography

For example, in the early steps in the path leading to full-blown agriculture, the plants and animals tended or encouraged by people in order to increase their yields will look just like their wild predecessors. Their remains as recovered in the archaeological record—seeds, nutshells, bones—will be indistinguishable from those of their truly wild forebears. However, though there may be no morphological difference that an archaeologist, botanist, or zoologist can recognize, there often is a difference in geography. As noted previously, in this early step in food production, human beings tend to take care of, protect, oversee, and encourage populations of wild plants or animals. As a strategy to increase the production of food, humans may attempt to expand the territory where economically important species grow by moving these plants and animals to habitats or regions where they do not thrive naturally. In fact, in many cases, these plants and animals brought into new territories will survive only through human care.

This scenario provides the archaeologist with concrete data concerning the relationship between ancient human beings and the plant and animal species on which they subsisted. When plant and animal remains appear abruptly in the archaeological record at sites located in territories where the plant and animal species represented are not known to have grown or lived naturally, it suggests human propagation or control. Even if the bones of the animals look just like those of wild members of their species, even if the seeds seem no different from those produced by wild plants, their appearance in locations where the wild versions of those plants and animals can't live implies that human beings were actively producing conditions—by watering plants, protecting seedlings from frost, providing food for animals—that allowed for the survival of these plants and animals. This level of human involvement can be a first step toward ultimate control of a species.

Size

The process of natural selection results in species that are adapted to natural conditions. The process of artificial selection in which human beings decide which members of a plant and animal species will be allowed to live and propagate results in species that are designed to meet human needs. For example, seeds produce the next generation of a plant species, and it may be advantageous for a plant to produce lots of little seeds that ripen over a long period of time to ensure that at least some of the seeds will end up in the ground when conditions are good for their survival through the winter and growth the following spring. However, for humans, seeds are not just the way a plant produces the next generation; they are a harvestable, nutritious commodity. A plant that produces lots of little seeds over the entire summer may not be desirable. It may be better, from a human perspective, to have a plant produce fewer but larger seeds—and therefore seeds with more food—and seeds that ripen all at once so that they can be efficiently harvested at the same time. Humans tending wild plants may intentionally kill off those individuals that produce the smaller seeds and then care for and encourage those plants left that have bigger ones that ripen at the same time. Those characteristics may actually be a disadvantage in a natural setting but ensure survival and propagation in a cultural setting. Where seed remains recovered at an archaeological site are significantly larger than seed size in the wild, it may be evidence of this level of human involvement in the plants (Figure 9.2).

The size of animals exploited by human beings may also be an indicator of human activity. To make use of a population of animals more efficient, human beings may capture a group of them and corral them or otherwise impede their movement. Larger, more aggressive animals that might thrive in the wild as dominant members of a herd now may be a liability, dangerous to their human captors in the close quarters produced by people, and these animals may be killed off. Only the less dangerous, perhaps smaller and less aggressive members of a population may be allowed to survive, and, in turn, these become the only members of the animal group that produce offspring that may also be smaller and less aggressive. Here again, though their individual bones found in an archaeological context may be no different in their form from those of wild members of their species, a significant decrease in size may be another early indication of human control of selection and breeding.

The Case of the Dog The initial domestication of the animal described by the cliché "man's best friend" is instructive here. Genetic analysis has shown that dogs are, essentially, domesticated wolves (Vilà et al. 1997). In one scenario for the transformation of wolf to dog, ancient people captured and raised wolf pups and then selectively bred less aggressive animals with small jaws and, presumably, less dangerous biting capabilities. People would have disposed of aggressive, dangerous wolves in captivity and allowed only those males and females to mate that were smaller, were less aggressive, and had smaller jaws. These features, desirable from a human perspective, would have been passed down to and reinforced in subsequent generations of the animals during the domestication process. The skeletons of even the earliest domesticated dogs are recognized by their smaller body size and their smaller jaws and crowded teeth (when compared to their wild wolf ancestors), as well as by their archaeological contexts, which suggest, even very early in the process, that they were human companions. Remember the remains of domesticated dogs found at the Koster site in Illinois and mentioned in Chapter 8 (Struever and Holton 2000). Dating to about 5,000 years ago, these animals had been intentionally buried, treated not as food but as friends. Beyond this, they were distinct from their wild wolf ancestors in terms of size: Gray wolves range in height (of their front shoulders) from 60 to 90 cm (24 to 35 in.) while the fully adult dogs at Koster were only between 45 and 50 cm (18–20 in.).

The archaeological record points to an initial domestication date for dogs of close to 14,000 years ago, making them the earliest example of domestication by human beings. Apparent dog remains, identified on the basis of their crowded teeth, have been found dating to about that long ago in Germany and central Europe. In Israel, archaeologists have even found the remains of a puppy in the eternal embrace of a human skeleton, seemingly cradled in the

FIGURE 9.2
Through artificial selection, people may encourage the survival of early-germinating and quick-growing plants produced by larger seeds. Researchers recognize such selection by ancient people when the seeds recovered in archaeological contexts are larger than those found in the wild and untended versions of the same species. See the three examples here: on the left, from top to bottom, are the wild seeds of marsh elder, sunflower, and squash; on the right, from top to bottom, are the significantly larger seeds of the domesticated versions of these crops.
(© Chip Clark 1995)

arms of a woman who died 12,000 years ago (Pennisi 2002). A man buried at the same site in Israel was accompanied by two small dogs as well.

Some researchers recently have conducted genetic analysis of a sample of 654 modern dogs and 38 wolves (Savolainen et al. 2002), and others have focused on DNA retrieved from the bones of some of the oldest dogs in the New World (Leonard et al. 2002). Their joint interpretation is that all modern dogs are the result of a domestication process that took place first in East Asia and that the descendants of these domesticated East Asian wolves spread throughout the Old World and accompanied people as they expanded into the Americas. The many and varied modern breeds of dogs, from the smallest Chihuahua to the massive mastiff, are all just variations on a theme, the result of a process of selective breeding that began more than 14 millennia ago. Though for the most part they were not bred for food, the process of selective breeding of wolves to produce a new kind of animal exemplifies the process at the heart of the Food-Producing Revolution wherein people controlled the breeding of a plant or animal species in order to amplify the characteristics most valuable to those people.

Seed Morphology

Along with size, other characteristics of seeds may be selected for differently by nature and people. For example, in many plant species, especially in temperate zones, the thickness of the protective, exterior seed coat may be important in determining whether or not the seed survives long enough to produce another plant. A thick seed coat may delay germination, protecting the enclosed seed during the winter and from late spring frosts. More of these thick-coated seeds survive, producing more thick-coated seeds when they grow into plants and mature. Thus, natural selection acts to produce more plants producing thick-coated seeds. However, where human beings plant the seeds and tend the seedlings, the delay in germination caused by a thick seed coat is no longer an advantage—people may be protecting seedlings from the cold—and may actually become disadvantageous. When a bunch of seeds are planted in a seed bed, the early germinators have a head start when it comes time to thin out the garden. Late germinators will be smaller and likely the first plants culled and discarded. Where people are consistently thinning out the seedlings growing from thick-coated seeds, only those members of a species that produce thin-coated seeds will grow. Where archaeological remains of seeds are recovered exhibiting seed coats significantly thinner than those produced by the same plant species in the wild, human control may be the cause.

There is another reason why people might intentionally select for plants that produce seeds with thinner seeds coats. Some wild plant species rely on animals for seed propagation. The animals, often birds, eat the seeds and then fly off. Some of the seeds are digested, but some pass through the animal intact and are excreted wherever the bird has flown off to or wherever the animal has wandered. The creature, unintentionally, serves as a propagator, moving the seeds to new areas where, once excreted, they may fall to the ground intact, germinate, and grow, thus spreading the plant species into a new area.

Plants that rely on animal propagation tend to have very thick seed coats to protect them in their journey through an animal's digestive tract. A thick seed coat, therefore, is highly adaptive to the plant and is strongly selected for in nature; only those seeds with thick coats survive the digestive tracts of the animals that have ingested them and therefore survive to germinate and grow. This characteristic, however, is not all that appealing to human beings because, to render the seeds more digestible, they must be processed, perhaps through grinding, and that means more work. However, there certainly will be variation in seed coat thickness within a population of plants, and people may end up selecting only those individual plants that produce thinner, more readily digestible seeds. Here, too, when the archaeological record shows a thinning of the seed coat, it may be the result of human beings intentionally choosing seeds whose characteristics might not be advantageous in nature, but that render their use more convenient to people.

There comes a point in the life cycle of a plant when the seeds it produces need to detach. All plants have developed mechanisms for the detachment and dispersal of seeds on the ground to produce the next generation of plants. The point of connection between a seed and its plant needs to become rather brittle at just the right time of ripening to allow a passing wind, a wandering animal, or a burst of rainfall to detach the seed.

This perfectly sensible feature of plants, however, produces a problem for human harvesters. The sharp blow of a sickle can harvest a plant but at the same time is more than adequate to detach and disperse on the ground most of the seeds that the sickle wielder is attempting to harvest. In fact, in what may at least initially be an entirely accidental result of harvesting practices, a disproportionate percentage of seeds that remain stubbornly attached to a plant stalk may make it back to the village, the seeds with a brittle attachment having already been detached in harvesting and transport. As a result, only the seeds ill-equipped to survive and that end up in the ground in the wild will be returned to the village where they may be planted nearby. In this way, subsequent generations of the plants near a settlement may produce a greater proportion of seed attachments that don't become brittle in the fall but, instead, will end up in the ground for propagation by their human overseers. Where the archaeological record shows the development of a predominance of nonbrittle attachments of seeds in plants harvested by an ancient people, this kind of unconscious selection may be at work.

Osteological Changes

It is as true in animals as it is in people: Degree and strenuousness of physical activity sculpts our bodies—our bones as well as our muscles. The bones of animals that are penned or corralled will not be as dense or as strongly built as the bones of their wild counterparts who roam freely where they experience

FIGURE 9.3

Sex and survivorship curves for male and female goats from Ganj Dareh in Iran. The graph shows that male goats were slaughtered at an earlier age than females. For example, at 28 months of age, 75% of female goats at this site are still alive but only 25% of males are. That pattern is typical in tended or domesticated animals; females are valuable for their production of milk and babies, so are kept alive longer than males. There is no reason to keep a large number of males alive, so they are slaughtered at an earlier age.

(From Zeder and Hesse 2000)

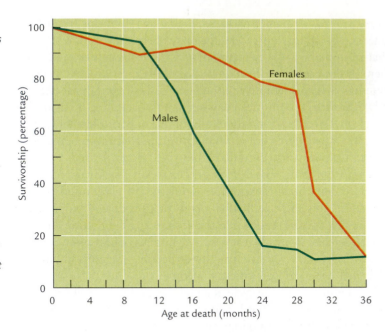

strenuous physical challenges on a regular basis. These differences between the bones of free-roaming and penned animals are apparent in zoo inhabitants and can be seen in bones recovered in the archaeological record. Lightly constructed bones of otherwise wild animals found in archaeological contexts may be interpreted as resulting from the animals having been penned by human controllers and protectors throughout their lives.

Population Characteristics

Bones found in an ancient fireplace or trash pile may not always indicate whether the animal was truly wild or instead tended by human overseers. However, sometimes the age and sex profile of an animal population can be used to determine the relationship between the people and the animals they utilized. This occurs because human hunters of wild animals have significantly less control over the age and sex of the animal they successfully harvest than does the human overseer of a captive population. A hungry hunter will kill whatever animal he or she has in his or her sights—young or old, male or female, it makes little difference. But in the case of a captive population, a human overseer can be far more selective. Knowing that adult males tend to be more dangerous and aggressive than adult females—and also aware that only a very few adult males are needed to impregnate a large herd of females—most males may be killed and eaten while they are still juveniles. It may make sense to keep females alive through their reproductive years as they are worth more as breeders and perhaps milk or wool producers than as food—and they will be eaten anyway when they become too old to produce offspring.

With a sufficiently large population represented by bones at an archaeological site, researchers can determine the age and sex profile of the animals being used by people. When an overabundance of the bones of subadult males is found at an archaeological site, this may indicate that people had a level of control over the population greater than what would be expected if they merely had been hunting free-roaming wild animals. This population characteristic implies that the people had corralled or penned the population of animals. This can lead to control of breeding by allowing only smaller, less aggressive, compliant males to live long enough to become breeders, which, in turn, may change the characteristics of the population animals under human control (Figure 9.3).

THE NEAR EAST

The name of the region in which many of the sites to be described here are located—the **Fertile Crescent**—is doubly descriptive. It is, indeed, shaped like a crescent, and it encompasses some of the richest and most fertile agricultural land in the Middle East. Beginning in Israel along the Mediterranean coast, the territory arcs to the northeast until it reaches its geographic apex—the top of the crescent—in Turkey and then bends to the south and east toward the Persian Gulf in Iran and Iraq (Figure 9.4). The late Pleistocene inhabitants of this region that now makes up parts of the nations of Israel, Jordan, Lebanon, Syria, Turkey, Iraq, and Iran long exploited wild varieties of **cereal** grasses, especially wheat and barley, that grow abundantly there (Figure 9.5).

Late Pleistocene Foragers in the Near East

Paleoclimatological data indicate that much of the Middle East was cold and dry during the late Pleistocene, but the hilly Mediterranean coast was wetter and thickly forested. People living in the region relied on hunting for part of their subsistence; the bones of wild boar, fallow deer, gazelle, and ibex have been found in sites dating to the period 20,000–14,500 B.P. (Bar-Yosef 1998). During this same period, wild plant foods were a significant part of the diet. At the 19,000-year-old Ohalo II site in Israel, a large number of the seeds and fruits of several different plant species have been found (Kislev and Carmi 1992).

At the 20,000-year-old occupation of the Ohalo II site mentioned earlier in this chapter, a team led by paleobotanist Dolores Piperno (Piperno et al. 2004) found evidence of the diet of the inhabitants. Along with the remains of gazelles, birds, fish, mollusks, and rats, the team also recovered charred seed remains of wild barley and emmer wheat. Also, **starch grains** identifiable as wild barley were recovered from the surface of a large basalt grinding stone

FIGURE 9.4
The Fertile Crescent in the Near East provided rich habitats for late Pleistocene and early Holocene hunter-gatherers where the wild ancestors of some of the earliest domesticated crops grew.

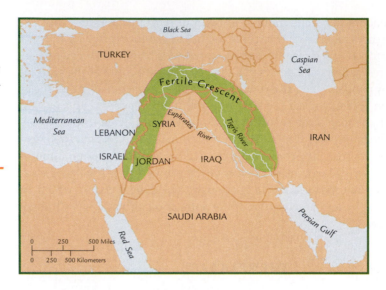

FIGURE 9.5
Archaeological sites in the Middle East where evidence of early food production has been found.

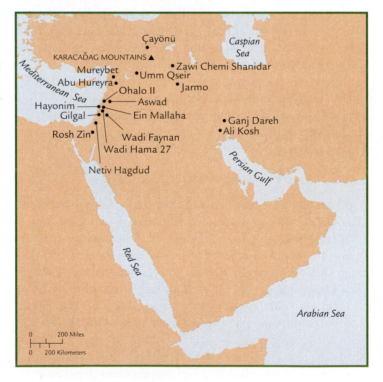

found at the site. As Piperno and her colleagues point out, stone tools for grinding or pounding seeds are first seen in the archaeological record of the Middle East at about 45,000 years ago and are abundant by 20,000 years ago. A subsistence reliance on seed grasses in the Middle East by 20,000 years ago, with specialized tools for processing those seeds, may set the stage for the development of an agricultural way of life ten millennia before it happened.

The period from 14,500 to 11,000 years ago is marked by increasing precipitation in the Middle East as the Pleistocene waned, and a number of cultures have been defined for this period of climatic improvement. For example, the **Geometric Kebaran,** beginning at about 14,500 B.P. and lasting until 12,500 B.P., is located in the moist Mediterranean woodlands of the central **Levant,** southward into the margins of the Negev and Sinai Deserts, and across southern Jordan (Henry 1989). The contemporary late Pleistocene **Mushabian** culture is located to the south in the steppe and arid zones of what today are the cores of the Negev and Sinai Deserts. Farther north, in the foothills of the Zagros Mountains, in northern Iraq, are the pre-Neolithic cultures of the **Zarzian** and **Karim Shahirian.**

As archaeologist Donald O. Henry (1989) indicates, the Mushabian sites seem to reflect the remains of small groups of highly mobile **simple foragers** with no particular focus on or commitment to any one food resource. Sites are small and impermanent, with direct evidence of the hunting of wild goats and gazelle. Dating to the same period as the Mushabian sites to the south, Kebaran sites vary more in size and complexity, indicating a pattern of population aggregation to take advantage of rich and seasonally available resources, particularly the wild cereal and nut foods available in the lowlands during spring and summer.

The Origins of a Sedentary Life: The Natufian

Following the Geometric Kebaran and the Mushabian is the **Natufian** culture, dating from 13,000 to 9,800 years ago. Natufian sites are located in the Mediterranean woodland zone, part of the same area occupied by the Kebaran from which it almost certainly developed. Along with the hunting of a broad array of animals, it is during the Natufian, at about 13,000 years ago, that we see a dramatic shift in subsistence from simple to **complex foraging** based on plant foods. In complex foraging, subsistence is focused on a few rich resources. These are collected intensively and stored, both requiring and allowing for more sedentary, denser human populations. This pattern is reflected in the archaeological record of the Natufian by the increasing number of grinding stones, large bedrock mortars and smaller, more portable mortars and pestles, food-storage pits, pits for roasting plant foods, and microblades of flint exhibiting sickle polish. The stone blades exhibit a sheen or polish that has been shown through replicative experiment to be the result of their use in cutting cereal plant stalks such as those of wheat, barley, millet, and sorghum (Unger-Hamilton 1989; Figure 9.6).

The Natufian culture homeland was located in the belt of woodland in the Levant. Here, wild cereal grasses offering human foragers protein and carbohydrate-rich seeds would have grown abundantly in open areas and as forest underbrush (Bar-Yosef 1998). Kernels and stalks of wild wheat and barley

FIGURE 9.6

In Kenya, this traditional harvest in which women use sickles is probably quite similar to how wheat was harvested thousands of years ago in the Near East, where it was first domesticated. (Food and Agriculture Organization, United Nations. Photo by Peyton Johnson)

have been found at several Natufian sites. For example, at Mureybet and Abu Hureyra, in Syria, wild einkorn wheat and vetch (a **legume**—a plant that produces pods with seeds) have been found in roasting pits dated to more than 11,000 years ago and as much as 13,000 years ago. These sites are located about 100 km (62 mi) from where wheat grows wild today. This may be an indication of intentional movement of the wild plant into a new territory by people consciously attempting to increase its geographic range. Carbonized kernels of wild barley, lentils, chickpeas, and field peas have been recovered at Wadi Hama 27 in Jordan, dated to 12,000 B.P.

Indirect evidence of the use of wild cereals by late Pleistocene people in the Near East includes heavy wear on human teeth (P. Smith 1972). This probably resulted from the ingestion of stone particles that became mixed into the meal or flour when wild cereals were processed with stone grinding tools. An increase in the strontium level of human bones seen at these sites may be the result of an increase in the use of cereal grains at this time; high levels of strontium are found in these cereals (Smith, Bar-Yosef, and Sillen 1985).

The intensive collection and storage of wild cereals necessitates a more sedentary way of life because the food source stays put and needs to be monitored regularly for the best time to harvest. At the same time, the abundant and dependable wild cereals, legumes, and nut foods allow for a sedentary life. As a result, Natufian sites exhibit a far more complex and sophisticated architectural pattern than do the Mushabian or Kebaran. Whereas Mushabian and Geometric Kebaran sites generally are small and impermanent, preagricultural Natufian sites show the distinctive architecture of permanent villages. At Ein Mallaha, Hayonim Cave, and Rosh Zin in Israel, the remains of substantial houses with stone foundations ranging in diameter from 2 to 9 m (about 6 to 30 ft) have been found (Henry 1989:211–12). Similarly substantial and permanent structures are known from Mureybet in Syria, where the preferred building materials were clay and wood, and Abu Hureyra, also in Syria, where the houses were built down into the earth. The amount of labor needed to build such domiciles is a clear indication that they were intended for long-term use.

Material culture, too, is far more complex and sophisticated at Natufian sites than at Mushabian or Kebaran sites. Bone, tooth, and shell beads and pendants are commonly found in burials. Dentalium shells, which were a favorite raw material, were available—often at great distances from the Natufian sites where they were found. Along with such items of personal adornment, other works of art have been recovered from Natufian sites, primarily carved stone statuettes of animals and people (Figure 9.7).

The First Agriculturalists

A return to colder and drier conditions in the Middle East between 11,000 and 10,000 years ago in all likelihood resulted in a decrease in the abundance of wild cereal crops there. Many of these cereals, especially barley and wheat, were the crops on which the Natufians had come to rely for their subsistence. Archaeologist Ofer Bar-Yosef (1998) suggests that it is during this period that Natufians initiated an attempt to artificially increase the abundance of these cereals, perhaps by planting and then tending the wild crops. In this scenario, as people gained some measure of control over these wild plants, selection shifted from natural to artificial. As people began imposing their will by encouraging those individual plants that possessed useful characteristics (they had larger seeds and were hardier), the population of tended plants changed from a wild pattern to a pattern determined by human selection.

Late Natufian and Karim Shahirian sites provide evidence of very early steps down the pathway of domestication, sometime around 11,000 years ago. At Netiv Hagdud and Gilgal in Israel and at Ganj Dareh in Iran, recovered barley kernels have been identified as an early domesticated version of that cereal. The size and morphology of the kernels distinguish them from wild barley, and they show features present in the domesticated grain. At Aswad in Syria and Çayönü in Turkey, domesticated wheats known as **emmer** and **einkorn** have been dated to more than 10,000 B.P. At both sites, lentils may also have been cultivated: At Aswad, 55% of the seeds of food plants recovered were from cultivated peas and lentils (Miller 1992:48).

FIGURE 9.7
Natufian artwork: a carved animal (top) and two carved sickle hafts. (From *From Foraging to Agriculture: The Levant at the End of the Ice Age,* by Donald O. Henry, University of Pennsylvania Press, with permission)

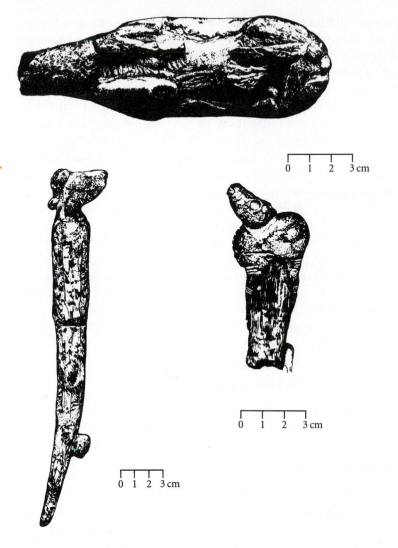

The evolution of dependence on domesticated plants can be traced at the site of Ali Kosh in southwestern Iran: More than 29,000 seeds from the Bus Mordeh phase at Ali Kosh, dated to earlier than 10,000 B.P., were recovered. The vast majority were from wild legumes and grasses, and only 10% were from domesticated emmer wheat and barley (Hole, Flannery, and Neely 1969:343). Forty percent of the seeds from the later Ali Kosh phase were from domesticated emmer wheat; in the subsequent Mohammed Jaffar phase, the seeds of legumes rose to prominence.

That the shift to an agricultural way of life was a revolution in slow motion is clearly shown at the Wadi Faynan 16 site in Jordan. Burned fragments of oak, juniper wood, willow, acacia, and fig have produced radiocarbon dates that range from between close to 9,900 and 9,400 years ago, at about the time when the seeds of domesticated cereal crops begin turning up in the archaeological record (Bower 2000a). The inhabitants of this site, however, were still reliant on a wide array of wild foods; the site's researchers found animal bones, the remains of marine shellfish, and seeds of wild legumes and fruits in their excavations. A single seed of barley was recovered as well, but it is unclear whether the barley represented was a wild or domesticated variety.

In the Zagros Mountains, in northern Iraq, the site of Zawi Chemi Shanidar has produced a substantial faunal assemblage of sheep bones dated to 10,600 B.P. (Wright 1971). The population structure of the archaeological sample of the sheep is unlike what would be derived from a group of hunted animals. Almost all were slaughtered when young. This kind of consistency in the population profile of an animal species implies a level of control over the animals usually possible only under conditions of corralling. The animals, though genetically the same as those roaming wild, were kept, controlled, and tended by people.

The bones of goats discarded by the inhabitants of Ganj Dareh in Iran 10,000 years ago look just like the bones of wild members of their species. The key difference lies, however, not in their morphology but in their population profile (see Figure 9.3). Researchers Melinda Zeder and Brian Hesse (2000) have shown that the site's inhabitants exhibited a level of population control over the goats that is unlikely the result of hunting wild, free-roaming animals. A disproportionate number of the goat remains are those of subadult males. As mentioned earlier in this chapter, when humans control a population of animals by penning or corralling them, they often kill off young males, allowing females and only a sufficient number of males to live to ensure the survival of the captive population. It is interesting to note that this level of herd management occurred 10,000 years ago in the Middle East. Genetic diversity in goats from this region suggests that domestication of the species occurred 10,000 years ago (Luikart et al. 2001).

This incipient stage in domestication likely enabled the human overseers to dispose of (and eat) those animals with undesirable characteristics and to allow only those with attractive features to survive and reproduce more generations like them. This practice led to intensive and rapid selection that soon altered the captive animal population, creating a group so different from the wild population that it no longer was of the same species.

A Model of the Shift to a Food-Producing Way of Life in Southwest Asia

Archaeologist Donald O. Henry (1989) has proposed an explanation for what happened in the Natufian period in the Near East that led to the origins of agriculture: When Natufians abandoned a mobile pattern of simple foraging and adopted a complex foraging strategy, they produced an inherently unstable subsistence system. Whereas simple foragers faced with a food shortage can move to where food is more abundant, complex foragers (who have adopted a sedentary mode to exploit locally abundant wild plant foods) can, under the right circumstances with the right kinds of plants, artificially raise the "resource ceiling" (Henry 1989:4) of their territory by tending and encouraging economically important wild crops. In other words, complex foragers respond to a food shortage by beginning artificial selection.

In Henry's model, the Natufian pattern of complex foraging that focused on wild cereals and nuts expanded geographically when the Mediterranean woodlands, where wild cereals were particularly abundant, expanded as the Pleistocene waned and as conditions became wetter. But by the onset of the Younger Dryas glacial re-advance in the north, 13,000 years ago, conditions had changed for the worse: By 10,500 B.P. the Mediterranean woodlands that had sustained an increasing Natufian population had shrunk to half the size they were at the beginning of the Natufian. Having committed their subsistence energies to wild cereals whose abundance was declining, the Natufians responded by more actively encouraging those plants. This response included tending the plants as well as artificially selecting those that had beneficial characteristics. These were the first shots fired in the Agricultural Revolution.

MESOAMERICA

Mesoamerica includes most of the modern nations located south of the United States and north of South America (including Mexico, Guatemala, Belize, El Salvador, the western regions of Honduras and Nicaragua, and northwestern Costa Rica). This area contributed many valuable agricultural crops to the world, none more important than maize (corn), beans, and squash, the triumvirate of plants that provided the subsistence base for indigenous New World civilizations (see Chapter 13). The shift to an agricultural mode of subsistence has been documented in only a few sites: Guilá Naquitz Cave (Flannery 1986), Tamaulipas, and Tehuacán (MacNeish 1964:1967). The Western Hemisphere's earliest evidence for the domestication of plants has been found in Mesoamerica (Figure 9.8).

The First Agriculturalists in the New World

Though maize (corn) is probably the first crop most people think of when asked to name the key agricultural crops domesticated by Native Americans, it was not the first wild plant they domesticated. The oldest evidence for domestication in the New World comes from Guilá Naquitz Cave in Oaxaca, Mexico, where squash seeds, rind fragments, and stems that are demonstrably different from those of wild squash have been recovered and dated to the period between 10,000 and 8,000 years ago (B. Smith 1997).

The seeds of the Guilá Naquitz squash are larger, the rinds thicker, and the stems bigger (likely implying larger fruits) than in wild specimens. Archaeologist Bruce Smith maintains that such increases result automatically when

FIGURE 9.8
Archaeological sites in Mesoamerica where evidence of early food production has been found.

people plant and tend initially wild crops as they thin out later-germinating, slower-growing individual sprouts in a process called **seedbed selection.**

Like all people who rely on wild plants, the ancient inhabitants of Guilá Naquitz Cave had a detailed knowledge of the characteristics of plants on which they depended and knew full well that seeds produce plants. They also were aware of the conditions necessary for the plants to flourish in seedbeds. Just like modern gardeners tending domesticated crops, ancient people would have tended these spring seedbeds carefully. As mentioned earlier in this chapter, there would have been a high level of unintentional artificial selection for plants that produced larger seeds: Where the endosperm is larger, food reserves for growth are greater and the plant grows faster. Slower-growing plants are normally weeded out of a patch to provide room for the larger and faster-growing varieties. In the same way, seeds with thinner seed coats sprout more quickly, again giving the young plants a jump on the competition in the seedbed. Later-germinating (thicker seed coats), slower-growing (smaller seeds) plants are at a distinct selective disadvantage under the culturally controlled conditions of a seedbed. After generations of encouraging the growth of those plants that produced larger seeds with thinner seed coats because they grew more quickly, plants were created that produced bigger seeds, which, in turn, produced larger squashes with larger stems. This process resulted in plants that had been so intensively manipulated by human action that they no longer resembled their wild antecedents. They had been, in fact, domesticated.

Though they may have domesticated squash first, when you think of the contribution made by the native people of the Americas to the diet of the modern world, maize is likely the first crop that springs to mind. Early steps in the transition of the small spikes of seeds on the wild **teosinte** plant from which the domesticated crop we call maize was derived, to the well-known, multirowed, large-kerneled cobs without which a summer barbeque would be incomplete, have now been traced to more than 7,000 years ago in Mexico.

Evidence of the early domestication of maize has been found at the San Andrés site located in Mexico's tropical Gulf of Mexico wetlands in the province of Tabasco (Pope et al. 2001). Here, pollen grains whose form and size allow their identification as teosinte have been found in levels dating to 7,100 years ago. Though teosinte is a wild crop, its occurrence in the region where the site is located is telling. As the authors of the study point out, teosinte is not native to the coastal wetlands of Tabasco (Pope et al. 2001:1373). The appearance of teosinte pollen at the site at the same time that evidence indicates the inhabitants were intentionally clearing off parts of the forest by burning may indicate that the residents of San Andrés were attempting to increase the productivity of what was still a wild crop by artificially extending its territory. As we have discussed, this sort of behavior may represent one of the preliminary steps taken by a people along the continuum toward domestication and a subsistence system based on agriculture.

It is not until about 7,000 years ago at San Andrés that at least some of the recovered pollen is recognizable as domesticated maize. Another three centuries passed here before the archaeological record indicates a substantial shift toward an agricultural way of life with a fundamental reliance on maize and large-scale clearing to produce agricultural fields. The San Andrés site also produced evidence of the earliest domestication of sunflowers in the Western Hemisphere dating to about 4,500 years ago (Pope et al. 2001).

Two multirowed mini-cobs producing tiny kernels of domesticated corn, looking quite different not only from the wild plant, teosinte, but also from the corn with which we are now familiar, have been found dating to 6,250 years ago at Guilá Naquitz Cave in the Oaxaca Valley in the southern highlands of Mexico. There is no evidence from earlier levels of this site of either teosinte or even more primitive early maize, so it is likely that earlier steps in maize domestication are yet to be found in the region.

Although it is likely that archaeologists at San Andrés and Guilá Naquitz Cave have revealed some of the early steps in maize domestication, researchers have not yet reached far enough back in time nor far enough back in the sequence to have revealed truly the first steps taken by the native people of the New World in their conversion of a wild crop into one of domesticated pillars that support modern subsistence the world over, and so their work continues.

The Tehuacán Valley

The **Tehuacán** Valley project, conducted in 1961–64 in Mexico by archaeologist Richard MacNeish and an international team of 50 scholars from many disciplines (MacNeish 1964, 1967), provided archaeologists with our most detailed picture of the process of maize domestication (Figure 9.9). The project also resulted in a sequence of archaeological cultures spanning the period from 12,000 to 500 years ago, from the late Pleistocene to the period of initial European contact (De Tapia 1992).

The Cultural Sequence at Tehuacán

MacNeish defined a series of stages, or periods, in the valley based on evidence gathered from a series of occupied caves. He began the sequence with the **Ajuereado phase,** dated from 12,000 to 9,000 years ago. Recovered food remains indicate that hunting was of primary significance in the seasons when the caves were occupied. Sites were small and impermanent, leading MacNeish to suggest that small family groups—**microbands** of fewer than 10 people each—wandered the valley, primarily hunting antelope and jackrabbit. Other, smaller fauna, such as turtles, rodents, gophers, and birds, were utilized, as were wild plant foods, including avocado, foxtail grass, and amaranth, a grain.

Toward the end of the Ajuereado phase, in the waning years of the Pleistocene, the Tehuacán Valley experienced a period of drying that eliminated some of the resources on which local groups depended. In MacNeish's view, the increased aridity led to a decrease in the importance of hunting and an increased reliance on wild plant foods. This can clearly be seen in the subsequent **El Riego phase,** dated from 9,000 to 7,000 years ago. Strong evidence for an increasing focus on wild plants at this time can be seen in the preserved remains of wild squash, beans, chili peppers, amaranth, and avocado. In MacNeish's construct, the previous pattern of year-round nomadic microbands was replaced during El Riego times with a more complex settlement system that included dry season fall/winter microbands but added larger macrobands during the wetter spring and summer months.

The settlement pattern of seasonal shifting from micro- to **macrobands** is continued in the **Coxcatlán phase,** dated from 7000 to 5400 B.P. The reliance on wild plant foods continued among those living in the caves. Later,

in the **Abejas phase** (5400–4300 B.P.), an increasingly sedentary pattern of central-based bands was established. Larger, semipermanent villages or home bases were settled, though a geographically broad strategy of wild-food collection continued. During this phase, domesticated plants first contributed to the diet; squash and maize date to this period in the valley. The oldest maize in the Tehuacán sequence (Figure 9.10) has been directly radiocarbon-dated to about 4,700 years ago (Fritz 1994; Long et al. 1989).

Much less is known about the **Purrón phase** (4300–3500 B.P.) than about previous or subsequent phases. Pottery was used for the first time by the inhabitants of the valley, but little else is known. In the following **Ajalpán phase,** dating from 3,500 to 2,850 years ago, diet was based on foraging for wild foods as well as on domesticated maize, beans, and squash. Ajalpán settlements continued to grow, and the degree of **sedentism** (remaining in one place) increased from the previous phase. Simple irrigation canals were built to water crops, a clear indication of the importance placed on agriculture and further confirmation of the abandonment of a nomadic way of life (construction of canals represents a long-term commitment to stay in one place).

Primitive Maize—But Not the First Maize

Though quite different from modern corn, the Tehuacán maize cannot have been the first domesticated version of that plant. The oldest examples from Tehuacán are only an inch or two long, with eight rows of six to nine kernels each. But even these oldest, tiny cobs from Tehuacán exhibit a morphology that is entirely inappropriate for life in the wild. The kernels of this maize were held tightly in place by long **glumes** (the casings in which individual kernels are enclosed). It took a human hand to remove the kernels from the glumes for eating or planting; the kernels would not have fallen out on their own, and so the crop could no longer have survived in the wild. Human beings must have already selected for this characteristic before the date of the Tehuacán corn, perhaps because it made the early maize easier to harvest and to process without losing kernels. Older, even more primitive maize almost certainly will be discovered, bringing us back further toward the origin of its domestication in Mesoamerica.

The Shift to Domesticated Foods Among the People of Tehuacán

The original analysis of dietary change through time at Tehuacán was based in part on the analysis of food remains in preserved fecal specimens recovered in archaeological strata in the excavated caves. A total of 116 preserved human fecal deposits were recovered in the valley. Researcher E. O. Callen (1967) was able to derive dietary percentages from the Tehuacán deposits. Unfortunately, those percentages necessarily reflect just a few meals of individual people, so Callen's statistics cannot be assumed to represent their diets over the long term. Moreover, if the caves were occupied only part of the year, then paleofeces and food remains recovered in middens or hearths reflect only those foods eaten when the caves were occupied. Because the caves were occupied during those seasons when wild plants were the subsistence focus, it stands to reason that the remains of wild plants would predominate in the archaeological record (Farnsworth et al. 1985:110) even if during the rest of the year other foods made significant contributions to the diet.

There is a way around this problem. An analysis of carbon isotopes has been successfully conducted on bones from 12 of the human skeletons recovered at Tehuacán, allowing for the reconstruction of the general diet of the inhabitants (Farnsworth et al. 1985). As discussed in Chapter 3, uptake of the ^{13}C isotope differs among plant groups. Those following the C4 photosynthesis pathway—chiefly grasses and sedges—use proportionally more ^{13}C than those following the C3 pathway—most trees, herbs, and shrubs. Animals (this includes people) incorporate into their bones proportions of ^{13}C that reflect the proportions in the plant foods they eat (or the proportions in the animals they eat, which reflect the proportions in the plant foods the animals eat). Because the carbon isotopes present in an individual's bones are the product of a lifetime's diet, seasonal changes or recent meals have little effect.

The isotope analysis of the Tehuacán material shows a clear jump in the reliance on C4 plants early in the Tehuacán sequence and then little change thereafter. Therefore, tropical grasses must have been mainstays of the diet of the people who produced the archaeological sites in the Tehuacán Valley. Based on the isotope analysis, their overall diet (meaning their reliance on C4 plants) did not change much for several millennia.

Combining MacNeish's reconstruction with the isotope data, it appears that the inhabitants of the valley went through a long period of increasing sedentism before adopting an agricultural way of life. This lengthy period of dietary reliance on C4-pathway tropical grasses—including, perhaps, the wild progenitor of maize, teosinte (see Figure 9.29)—is similar to the situation seen in the Near East. Archaeologist Paul Farnsworth and colleagues (1985:112) suggest that an extended period of reliance on wild plants and increasing sedentism in Tehuacán was "a Mesoamerican equivalent of the Natufian."

A Model of the Shift to a Food-Producing Way of Life in Mesoamerica

Archaeologist Kent Flannery (1968) has proposed a detailed explanation for the shift to an agricultural mode in Mesoamerica: The subsistence systems of late Pleistocene Mesoamerica were inherently stable. The seasonally restricted availability of certain resources and scheduling preferences for some resources over others available at the same time of year maintained a stable system in which no one resource was so intensively exploited that its abundance was threatened. Such a system can be said to be in "equilibrium."

In Flannery's view, however stable such a system might have been, it was susceptible to even a minor change in general conditions. For example, a mutation in teosinte that produced more easily harvested plants (see this chapter's "Issues and Debates") might have rendered this previously minor wild food more attractive. To take advantage of this more desirable form of teosinte, inhabitants of the region may have shifted other elements in the intricately balanced system. To encourage the growth of the new teosinte/wild maize, they may have changed their settlement pattern to allow more time in those places where teosinte grew, to encourage the new form. But this could have been accomplished only by changing the entire system of seasonal movement and scheduling. A pattern of larger and more sedentary groups may have developed to take advantage of the new teosinte. Overall population would have increased, necessitating a continual refinement through artificial selection of the new crop, to feed more mouths. Microbands would have become macrobands, and seasonal encampments semipermanent and then permanent villages.

In this way, the initial, casual, and almost accidental step of intensifying the exploitation of a crop could have thrown the entire system out of balance. The initial minor deviation from the established equilibrium would have become amplified as the culture tried to reestablish a new status quo. Other resources would have had to be granted less attention, resulting in the need to intensify further the use of the new crop. But intensification would have required a greater degree of sedentism, which would have meant even less time or opportunity for other resources. In Flannery's view, the intensification of the use of a particular food species can be the first step toward the inevitable destruction of a foraging subsistence system and the establishment of an entirely new equilibrium based on agriculture (Figure 9.11).

FIGURE 9.11
Agriculture established a new equilibrium for subsistence systems in Mesoamerica. Left: *In this traditional agricultural field in modern Mexico, the farmer is harvesting amaranth that is growing among the corn plants.* Right: *The same process is seen in an image from a Spanish source dating to the sixteenth century.*
(*Left:* Courtesy of Dan Early; *right:* Florentine Codex)

AFRICA

It cannot be said that there was a single agricultural revolution in Africa or even that there was a single point of origin for the African shift to a domesticated food base. Africa is enormous and has a broad range of climates and environments and a wide range of plant and animal communities. Myriad hunting-and-gathering cultures developed in Africa during postglacial times, each adapting in its own way to its region. And many different food-producing cultures developed in the African Neolithic, each devising its own adaptation through food production of the available plants and animals (Figure 9.12).

Neolithic Culture Complexes in Africa

Archaeologist Jack Harlan (1992) defines three distinct archaeological culture "complexes" of the African Neolithic: Savanna, Forest Margin, and Ethiopian. Savanna complex sites, located in the dry interior of central Africa, exhibit a reliance on pearl millet, a grain crop known for its resistance to drought.

FIGURE 9.12

Archaeological sites in Africa where evidence of early food production has been found.

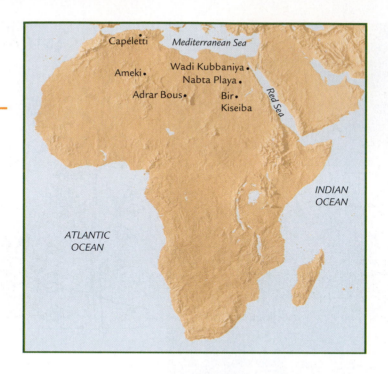

Watermelon was another important crop, not so much for its nutritive value but for its ability to store water and therefore to serve as a source of liquid. In the wetter, broad-leaved savanna, sorghum and African rice played major roles in subsistence. Other savanna plants contributing to the food quest were fonio (a cereal); Bambara groundnut; and kenaf, roselle, and tossa jute, all used as herbs in cooking.

In Harlan's Forest Margin complex, the focus is on forest resources combined with reliance on products of the savanna. Akee apples, Guinea millet, and kola nuts (best known as a component of cola beverages) formed a part of the subsistence base. Oil palm and cowpea also were important. Historically, the cultivation of yams, which grew wild on the forest edge, was one of the most important contributors to subsistence. Finally, in Harlan's Ethiopian complex, finger millet, teff (a cereal), enset (a relative of the banana), and noog (which produces an edible oil) were significant.

A Chronology of Food Production

The African reliance on wild plants extends well back into the late Pleistocene. At the Egyptian site of Wadi Kubbaniya, charred tubers of wild nutgrass have been dated to the period 18,000–17,000 years ago (Wendorf, Schild, and Close 1989; Wendorf et al. 1979). Heavily worn grindstones at the site were probably used to process the fat, starchy roots into flour. Stone blades inset into wooden or bone handles that served as sickles used in harvesting wild grains

FIGURE 9.13
Sorghum, used in the United States primarily to produce animal feed, has been an important food crop historically, particularly in Africa, where it was domesticated as early as 8,000 years ago. (Food and Agriculture Organization, United Nations. Photo by J. Chevalier)

and the grinding stones necessary to process the grains into flour are both dated to 15,000–11,000 years ago in southern Egypt in a culture called the **Qadan** (Phillipson 1993).

An 8,000-year-old site in the Sahara Desert of southern Egypt, Nabta Playa, supplies further evidence of early Holocene subsistence in Africa. Researchers excavated 1 storage pit, 14 hearths, and 122 cooking features (Wendorf et al. 1992). They recovered thousands of seeds, representing 40 different species of wild plants. Among the plants represented in the archaeological sample were sorghum and a number of varieties of millet. There are hundreds of varieties of sorghum; many produce edible grains, and others produce a sweet molasses or syrup. Millet and sorghum are commonly grown in modern, indigenous African agricultural systems (Figure 9.13). In fact, though not well known outside the semiarid tropics, millet and sorghum are the primary sources of protein in certain regions of the world.

Also found in the storage and cooking features at Nabta Playa were the remains of various legumes, fruits, tubers, and nut foods. There is even some suggestion that the sorghum at least was in an incipient stage of domestication at this site (Figure 9.14). To the eye, the sorghum looks like the wild plant, but the chemistry of the fats within the seeds is more like that of the modern domesticate. The identification of the sorghum from the site as a domesticate on this basis, however, is still far from clear. Nevertheless, as the site researchers point out, it is a "short step" (Wendorf et al. 1992:724) from the intensive use of sorghum and other wild plants to their domestication.

The earliest clear evidence of a shift from foraging to food production in Africa dates to about 7,000 years ago, in an area that today is the Sahara

FIGURE 9.14
Charred seeds recovered from Nabta Playa. Among the 40 or so plants identified in the archaeological sample were those of sorghum, in what has been identified chemically as an incipient stage of domestication. (Courtesy of Krystyna Wasylikowa)

Desert. A wet period, or **pluvial,** began about 8000 B.P., and lakes dotted areas that today are desert. Faunal evidence indicates that **pastoralists** raising sheep, goats, and cattle proliferated throughout the Sahara during this wet period. A thousand years later, by 7000 B.P., early agriculturalists were living along the Nile River in Egypt, raising sheep, goats, and cattle and planting barley, emmer, lentil, and chickpea for food and flax for linen.

The wild ancestors of domesticated sheep and goats are not native to Africa. These animals can be traced to the Middle East and Europe, where they lived in the wild and where domesticated versions appeared earlier than in Africa. Some of the crops were likewise introduced from the outside, but some may have been the result of indigenous experimentation.

To sort out the origins of domestic cattle in Africa, researchers have examined the genes of 50 separate breeds with long histories on the African continent (Bradley et al. 1998; Hanotte et al. 2002). For example, zebu cattle (*Bos indicus*), a common breed found in modern Africa, possess a hump on their backs directly behind the neck. Archaeological and genetic evidence allows us to trace the source of this breed to about 6,000 years ago in the Indus Valley in what is today Pakistan. It likely was introduced into eastern Africa sometime thereafter through trade and migration. However, the paleontological record along with early rock art shows that the oldest cattle in Africa were without the distinctive zebu hump (Figure 9.15). Humpless "taurine" cattle (*Bos taurus*) are also common in modern Africa, especially north of the Sahara Desert, and a humpless variety was first domesticated in the Middle East by about 8,000 years ago. Archaeological evidence suggests that this humpless variety was introduced into Africa by 6,500 years ago through trade and migration across a wide swath at the north of the continent.

According to animal researcher Olivier Hanotte et al.'s (2002) genetic analysis, along with the south Asian humped cattle and the Middle Eastern humpless varieties, there is a third, genetically distinctive group of domesti-

FIGURE 9.15
Ancient painting of an African cattle breed; note that these cattle lack the distinctive zebu hump that characterized Indian cattle. (© Erich Lessing/ Art Resource, NY)

cated bovines in Africa. This third cluster, today most commonly found in southern Africa, represents a group of cattle breeds whose most likely source is the indigenous African species *Bos primigenius*. This species was almost certainly domesticated by Africans in their own, independent episode of animal domestication that may have occurred as much as 10,000 years ago.

Another animal domesticated in Africa, likely not for food, but as a beast of burden, was the donkey. Archaeological evidence suggests that this occurred by about 5,000 years ago. Recently, researchers have compared the mtDNA of modern donkeys located in 52 separate countries across Asia, Africa, and Europe to that of wild asses in Africa and Asia (Beja-Pereira et al. 2004). All of the domesticated donkeys fell into two distinct mitochondrial groups, each of which was similar to one of two varieties of African wild asses. Neither of the two modern mitochondrial donkey groups was similar to Asian wild asses. Based on this, the authors of the study suggest that there may have been two independent domestications of donkeys from wild asses, both in Africa, with donkeys only later spreading from an African source into Asia and Europe.

Neolithic Cultures South of the Sahara

In Africa south of the Sahara, another set of largely independent agricultural revolutions took place, focusing on entirely indigenous tropical crops. Various millets (pearl, foxtail, finger, bullrush, broomcorn) were domesticated in tropical Africa. Domesticated pearl millet has been found dating to as early as 6,500 years ago—for example, at the Ameki site (Harlan 1992). Early sorghum domestication is seen at the Adrar Bous site dating to 4000 B.P. Yams, African rice, teff, fonio, groundnuts, enset, and noog are among other, entirely indigenous crops that were domesticated in sub-Saharan Africa in antiquity—all of which are unknown in the rest of the Neolithic world.

EAST ASIA

Most of us in the Western world think of rice as the agricultural food base of Asian peoples (Figure 9.16). As pointed out by archaeologist Gary Crawford (1992:8), however, there actually are 284 separate taxa of domesticated plants and animals known to have been used in east Asia.

Chronology of Food Production in China

The earliest evidence of plant or animal domestication in China from the Zengpiyan Cave site in Guilan dates to the period after 10,300 B.P. (Figure 9.17). A large proportion (85%) of the animal bones are those of young pigs, less than 2 years of age (Chang 1986:102–3). As was the case at Ganj Dareh in Iran and Zawi Chemi Shanidar in Iraq, this may indicate that the animals were not being hunted in the wild but instead were kept and tended. That the canine teeth are smaller than in a wild pig population may be explained by the artificial selection for the propagation of less dangerous animals with smaller teeth.

An analysis of a spate of new radiocarbon dates associated with the remains of rice grains, husks, and other rice-plant remains, as well as the impressions of rice grains on ceramics, shows that domesticated rice dates back to as much as 11,500 years ago along the middle Yangtze River in central China (Normille 1997). Ancient sites where early rice has been found both upstream and downstream of the middle Yangtze are younger, indicating that researcher Syuichi Toyama may have identified an early hearth for rice domestication in east Asia.

In northern China, the earliest Neolithic culture currently recognized is the **Peiligang,** as represented by sites such as Cishan, Peiligang, Laoguantai, Dadiwan, and Lixiatsun (Chang 1986). Dating to between 8,500 and 7,000 years ago, the Peiligang culture is centered in the deciduous forest zone of northern China. The evidence shows clearly that Peiligang sites do not represent the first steps toward settled life based on agriculture; Peiligang sites are already well-established farming villages, with hunting, fishing, and the gathering of wild plants also contributing to the food quest. Cultigens include foxtail millet, broomcorn millet, and Chinese cabbage. Domesticated animals include pig, dog, and chicken.

The better-known, later Neolithic culture of China is called the **Yang-shao.** Typified by the Banpo site near Xian, Yang-shao sites are five times larger than Peiligang sites, and the villages are not arranged as haphazardly; they appear to have been planned out before construction. Crops of the Yang-shao

FIGURE 9.16
Though a mainstay of agriculture in modern Asia, rice was not the first crop domesticated on that continent. (Top: Preparation of the seedbed for rice sowing.) Even long after its domestication about 11,500 years ago, rice remained a minor component of the diet. Today, along with wheat and corn, it is one of humanity's primary foods. (Bottom: a modern rice paddy.) (Both photographs, Food and Agriculture Organization, United Nations; *top:* photo by F. Botts, *bottom:* photo by Banoun/Caracciolo)

include foxtail millet, Chinese cabbage, and rice, though rice was a relatively minor component of the diet. Domesticated rice has been identified at the Hemudu site on the Yangtze River just south of Shanghai, with a radiocarbon date of 7000 B.P. (Crawford 1992:25).

The proportion of carbon isotopes in the human bones recovered at Yang-shao sites has been interpreted as indicating that nearly three-fifths of

FIGURE 9.17
Archaeological sites in east Asia where evidence of early food production has been found.

the diet was supplied by millet (An 1989). The various millets are grasses producing a large quantity of small seeds in long spikes. The seeds are ground into a flour and used in porridge and bread.

Food Production in Southeast and Northeast Asia

The situation is not as clear in the rest of east Asia. Spirit Cave in northeast Thailand (mentioned in Chapter 8) shows a clear reliance by about 12,000 B.P. on foods that were to become an integral part of the agricultural economies of later Neolithic peoples, including soybean, almond, cucumber, and water chestnut (Gorman 1972). A possibly early form of domesticated rice—at least rice that has been altered only slightly from its wild form—has been identified at Non Nok Tha in Thailand, dating to 5500 B.P. (Chang 1986). Indisputable evidence for domesticates in southeast Asia comes from excavations in the Chao Phraya Valley in northeast Thailand at sites dated to about 5,000 years ago (Higham 1989:80). The hunting and gathering of wild foods, along with the cultivation of rice, was the basis of this economy.

Data for Korea are sparse. Soils are very acidic, and few organic remains have been recovered in early archaeological contexts. We do know that by 3000 B.P., domesticated millet was used in a mixed economy that included hunting, fishing, gathering, and agriculture (Nelson 1993). Some archaeological evidence, in the form of increased sedentism, suggests that farming may have begun a couple of thousand years earlier.

There is far more information for Japan, but the sequence is not clear. The late Pleistocene/early Holocene **Jomon** culture had a foraging subsistence base, with an emphasis on resources of the sea. This productive resource base allowed for a sedentary settlement pattern, with dense populations, elaborate material culture, and some large, semipermanent villages at more than 10,000 years ago. Evidence of domesticates, including rice, soybean, adzuki bean, buckwheat, and pear, does not appear at Jomon sites but appears in the later Yayoi culture, dated to about 2400 B.P. Radiocarbon dating of food residue recovered from the interior surfaces of ceramic vessels in Japan may push that date back to about 3000 B.P. (Holden 2003b).

Because the preservation of organic remains is often quite low in tropical rain forests, archaeologists focus on subtle changes in local ecology in the search for the impacts of early food production. In New Guinea, for example, a marked shift in local plant communities, including a change from forest to open, grassy vegetation as early as 7800 B.P., is interpreted as a consequence of early steps in food production (Denham et al. 2003). Also, at the Kuk Swamp site in the New Guinea Highlands, artificially produced mounds and drainage channels have been dated to just after 7,000 years ago. Their likely purpose was to produce better-drained soils to improve conditions for tended plants. Dating to about the same period, researchers collected starch grains identified as **taro** from three stone tools. Taro is a common modern subsistence crop in New Guinea. The Kuk Swamp site is located in the highlands, an area outside of the current range of the crop. Its presence at Kuk Swamp, along with the culturally altered landscape to facilitate plant growth, is a likely indicator of the tending and possible domestication of plants soon after 7,000 years ago.

Additional direct evidence of food production and the domestication of local crops at Kuk Swamp comes in the form of preserved pollen grains and **phytoliths,** microscopic chunks of minerals that form in plants and that, ultimately, are released into the soil. Like pollen, phytolith morphology is species-specific; that is, each species of plant produces a unique suite of phytolith forms, recognizable and distinguishable from the phytoliths produced by other plant species. A high percentage at Kuk Swamp of phytoliths produced by banana trees in the period 4840–4440 B.P., found in an ecological context where researchers expected an abundance of grass phytoliths, is interpreted as evidence of the planting and domestication of banana at this time (Denham et al. 2003).

EUROPE

Europe is a diverse continent with a complex prehistory. Regarding the shift to an agricultural mode of subsistence, it can be argued that, as for Africa, there was not one revolution but several (Whittle 1985). Archaeologist Robin Dennell (1992) indicates that a series of parallel shifts to domesticated plants and animals occurred in southeast Europe, in central Europe, along the northern

FIGURE 9.18
Archaeological sites in Europe where evidence of early food production has been found.

Mediterranean coast, in the Alps, along the Atlantic coast, and in eastern and northeastern Europe. These agricultural revolutions, though not entirely independent of one another, occurred at different times, involved different crop and animal species, and had varying degrees of success (Figure 9.18).

For the most part, the Neolithic of Europe appears to have been imported from the south and east. Virtually all of the crops important in the European Neolithic, including einkorn, barley, bean, vetch, and lentils, are demonstrably Near Eastern in origin; there is little or no evidence for the existence of wild forms in Europe. The first appearance of these crops is in their domesticated form in the cultural contexts of archaeological sites dating to after 8000 B.P. Often these domesticated food sources seem to have been superimposed on an earlier, indigenous Mesolithic subsistence pattern (see Chapter 8) based on hunting animals and gathering acorns and hazelnuts (Dennell 1992). Certain crops—oats and some legumes—were probably domesticated independently by Europeans, but evidence so far indicates that the domestication occurred rather late in the Neolithic, after Near Eastern domesticates had already entered (via migrating farmers) and become important parts of the food base.

As was the case in southern Asia and Africa, domesticated cattle became an important element in the subsistence base of the European Neolithic. Unlike the situation in the Fertile Crescent, the Indus Valley, and Africa, however, Europeans seem not to have independently domesticated the cattle on which they came to rely. Genetic analysis of 392 living animals from the Middle East, Africa, and Europe and data derived from the bones of four members of an extinct wild European cattle species indicate that there was no in-place domestication of a native cattle breed in Europe. Instead, it seems that domestic cattle were brought into Europe primarily from the Middle East (Troy et al.

FIGURE 9.19
At Franchthi Cave in Greece, wild oats, barley, peas, and lentils were eaten by the inhabitants 13,000 years ago. (Courtesy Thomas W. Jacobsen)

2001). None of the living cattle tested, including those in Europe, were genetically similar to the wild European samples. In fact, the modern domesticated European cattle were all quite similar in their genetic makeup to the Middle Eastern *Bos taurus* individuals in the sample. The predominant mitochondrial haplogroup among the European cattle represents a variety also present in the Middle East. Further, the European cattle reflected the least genetic diversity of those in the sample, suggesting that they are the most recent of the breeds. Cattle, then, represent another example of a species initially domesticated elsewhere and then brought into Europe as part of the shift from foraging to food production.

The Shift to Agriculture in Southeast Europe

The earliest evidence of a shift toward agricultural life comes from southeast Europe. As seen elsewhere in the world, this shift is prefaced by an extended period during which the subsistence focus was on the wild ancestors of crops that would later become important domesticates. For example, Franchthi Cave in Greece (Figure 9.19) contains evidence of the exploitation of wild oats, barley, peas, and lentils by 13,000 years ago (Hansen 1981). Pear and pistachio also appear to have been used during the early occupation of the cave.

By about 7,500 years ago, the focus on wild plants seems to have evolved into at least a partial reliance on domesticated crops. At Nea Nicomedia, also in Greece, levels dated to this time produced evidence of domesticated varieties of wheat, barley, and legumes (Whittle 1985). Similar evidence was found at the sites of Azmak, Karanovo I, Chevdar, and Kazanlŭk in Bulgaria, where wheat, lentils, and grass-pea seem to have been the most important food crops (Dennell 1992:77).

The Shift to Agriculture in Southern Europe

We have noted throughout this chapter that the shift to food production was a revolution run in slow motion with an extended period of management or tending of wild plants and animals on which people depended for their subsistence. The situation in southern Europe is a bit different. As pointed out by researcher Joao Zilhao (2001), the earliest agricultural sites in this region do not show a slow development of the domestication of local plants or animals but instead appear fully formed rather quickly. In their spread across the European Mediterranean coast, the oldest agricultural sites do not exhibit a process of slow movement from east to west or west to east; rather, they show an almost instantaneous appearance from the eastern shore of Italy to Portugal at about 7,400 years ago. Zilhao suggests that instead of reflecting a process of independent evolution, adoption, and spread of food production in southern Europe, this pattern reflected the rapid colonization of this region by a maritime and agricultural people. The most likely geographic source for these people would be the Middle East, where agriculture precedes food production in Europe and where it clearly was an indigenous development. Zilhao suggests that an increasing population in the Middle East may have resulted in conflict that induced some seafaring farmers to leave their home territory in search of new lands to plant. Those who traveled along the European Mediterranean coast brought their domesticated plants and animals with them, finding rich new territories to settle.

The Shift to Agriculture in Western Europe

Throughout the rest of Europe, the shift to agriculture seems to have taken place later than in the southeast. For example, sites in the Swiss Alps exhibiting a reliance on domesticated crops, including emmer and bread wheat, lentils, peas, and millet, date to after 5500 B.P. In the central European, early Neolithic culture called **Linienbandkeramik (LBK),** a subsistence base that included emmer, barley, and pulses (grainlike legumes) has been traced back to about 6500 B.P. Along the Atlantic coast, in Great Britain, France, and Spain, evidence of the use of domesticates (a similar mixture of cereals and legumes) dates to no more than about 6,000 years ago.

British archaeologists Ian Simmons and John Innes have investigated the shift to an agricultural economy by the ancient inhabitants of northern Britain (Moore 1996). In an extremely detailed analysis of pollen found in stratigraphic layers in a peat deposit, these researchers were able to accurately reconstruct alterations in plant communities in the North York moors caused by changes in human adaptive strategies. Simmons and Innes discovered a dramatic drop in tree pollen, especially elm, probably indicating forest clearing by the human inhabitants of North York, sometime before 5400 B.P. There is no direct evidence for cultivation at this time, and Simmons and Innes suggest that the clearing was being done by hunters hoping to produce a habitat that would attract red deer, which had been an important food species to people in northern Europe since the Mesolithic. Following this time, an increasing proportion of weed pollen is evident, indicating the existence of cleared areas; and then, for the first time in the pollen sequence, there is evidence for the pollen of cereal plants, notably wheat, showing that agriculture had penetrated the northern half of Great Britain. For Simmons and Innes, the introduction of domesticated cereals in northern Britain was almost an afterthought, an add-on to an economic pattern that focused on producing a better hunting habitat.

As noted in Chapter 2, a person's life history, including—especially—trauma, disease, and diet, is encoded in his or her bones. Recognizing that fact, researchers in Great Britain have examined the skeletal remains of 183 individuals, 19 dating to the Mesolithic (between 9,000 and 5,200 years ago) and the other 164 to the early Neolithic (between 5,200 and 4,500 years ago; Richards et al. 2003), looking at their proportions of the stable isotopes of carbon. A diet rich in fish and marine mammals is also rich in ^{13}C and, not surprisingly, the bones of the great majority of the Mesolithic people represented in the bone sample, many of whom lived along the coast, had a high concentration of ^{13}C relative to ^{12}C. All of the Neolithic skeletal remains, however, reflected a proportionally much lower concentration or signal of ^{13}C, which implies a rapid change in diet beginning at about 5200 B.P. Though most grasses follow the C4 photosynthesis pathway with higher ^{13}C concentrations, wheat and oats are C3 pathway plants with a low concentration of the ^{13}C isotope. The authors of the study conclude that C3 pathway plants abruptly replaced marine resources in the diet of Britons beginning 5,200 years ago, marking the beginning of food production as the primary mode of subsistence there.

NORTH AMERICA

One of the most enduring images of the Indians of eastern North America is that of the natives helping the Pilgrims of seventeenth-century Plymouth, in Massachusetts, to survive their first winter in the New World. They brought the European settlers corn, beans, and squash and taught them how to plant and prepare these native agricultural foods.

Indeed, most historical native cultures in North America that were agricultural were dependent on these three crops. As we have seen earlier in this chapter, however, the wild ancestors of two of these crops—maize and beans—were tropically adapted plants, certainly not native to New England or the rest of North America. These crops were introduced into those areas north of Mexico in some unknown way—by trade, migration, indirect contact?

It is clear, however, that when maize penetrated the eastern woodlands of native America sometime after 1800 B.P., it did not replace an indigenous system of foraging for wild foods. Instead, maize initially supplemented an aboriginal pattern of hunting, collecting wild plants, and cultivating native squash and locally available seed plants. An independent, "pristine" pattern of indigenous domestication was established at about 4000 B.P., more than 2,000 years *before* the initial appearance of maize in the East (B. Smith 1989, 1992a, 1995).

Indigenous Domestication North of Mexico

The primary native crops domesticated by the Indians of the eastern woodlands were squash, sunflower, marsh elder, goosefoot, and lamb's-quarter (pigweed)—all producers of starchy or oil-rich seeds (Figures 9.20 and 9.21). At Napoleon Hollow in Illinois, for example, charred marsh elder seeds retrieved from a 4,000-year-old archaeological deposit are uniformly larger (by almost a third) than the seeds of wild marsh elder (Ford 1985). The oldest evidence of domesticated sunflower in North America has been dated to 4265 B.P., at the Hayes site in central Tennessee, where the seeds are substantially larger than those of wild varieties (B. Smith 1995:191). As noted previously in this chapter, the oldest direct evidence of domesticated sunflower has been recovered in Mexico, at the San Andrés site, predating by about 200 years the large seeds of a domesticated sunflower recovered at the Hayes site in Tennessee, which had produced a ^{14}C date of 4265 B.P. (B. Smith 1995:191). If domesticated sunflower is older in Mexico, was Mexico the source of domesticated sunflower for Native Americans living in the central and eastern United States? In fact, this was likely not the case. Recent genetic analysis of a number of varieties and populations of sunflower across the United States and Mexico provides strong evidence that eastern North America was the historical source for existing varieties of domesticated sunflower (Harter et al. 2004). This same genetic study indicates that Mexican sunflowers did not contribute to the modern domesticated sunflower stock. Whether there was a separate process of sunflower domestication in Mexico that did not contribute to the modern domesticate is a question that can be answered with additional archaeological data. Goosefoot seeds from Newt Kash Hollow and Cloudsplitter Rockshelter in Kentucky, though not larger, do have significantly thinner seed coats than do wild plants. These thinner coats are most likely the result of intentional human selection for plants that produced seeds with inedible coverings that were thinner and therefore easier to penetrate and remove. Both sites have been dated to about 3400 B.P.

Squash was domesticated in Mesoamerica as part of a triad of agricultural crops that also included maize and beans. Though squash was long thought to have moved into North America from Mexico, archaeological evidence now indicates that it was domesticated independently in eastern North America as well. Squash seeds recovered at the Phillips Spring site in Missouri, dating to 4500–4300 B.P., are significantly larger than their modern wild counterparts (B. Smith 1995). The date for the site places squash domestication in eastern North America at about the time of the domestication of some

FIGURE 9.20

A modern, many-headed form of sunflower. The sunflower was domesticated by the native inhabitants of eastern North America by about 4,200 years ago, at least 2,400 years before the introduction of Mesoamerican domesticates.

(K. L. Feder)

FIGURE 9.21
Archaeological sites in North America where evidence of early food production has been found.

of the seed crops mentioned earlier, further supporting a picture of a broad indigenous agricultural revolution in the East two millennia before the introduction of maize.

The degree of reliance on these native domesticates is difficult to determine. One important source of quantitative information comes from Salts Cave in Kentucky, dated to between 2600 and 2200 B.P. In the 119 paleofeces found in the cave, domesticated goosefoot, sunflower, and marsh elder seeds make up nearly two-thirds of the undigested food remains recovered (goosefoot 25%, sunflower 25%, marsh elder 14%; Yarnell 1974, 1977).

Farming communities based on these native domesticates proliferated in the eastern woodlands, specifically in the American Midwest and Midsouth, between 3,000 and 1,700 years ago. Along with goosefoot, pigweed, marsh elder, and sunflower, other crops that were used included knotweed, maygrass, squash, and a little barley. As archaeologist Bruce Smith (1992a) indicates, the representation of the remains of these plants varies across the Midwest and Midsouth during this period. Their overall significance varied in different times and places as these domesticates became incorporated into a "mosaic of regionally variable . . . food production systems" (B. Smith 1992a:109).

The Appearance of Maize in the Eastern Woodlands

Maize begins to turn up in the archaeological record by about 1800 B.P.; some of the earliest evidence in North America for use of this most significant New World domesticate has been found at the Icehouse Bottom site in eastern Tennessee, with a radiocarbon date of 1775 B.P. (Chapman and Crites 1987). The Holding site, east of St. Louis, also has produced maize and may be slightly

FIGURE 9.22
The dramatic jump in the level of ^{13}C concentration in the bones of prehistoric Native Americans around A.D. 1000 is taken to indicate an increase in the reliance on maize agriculture in eastern North America. (From *The Emergence of Agriculture*, by Bruce Smith. © 1995 Scientific American Library. Used with the permission of W. H. Freeman and Company)

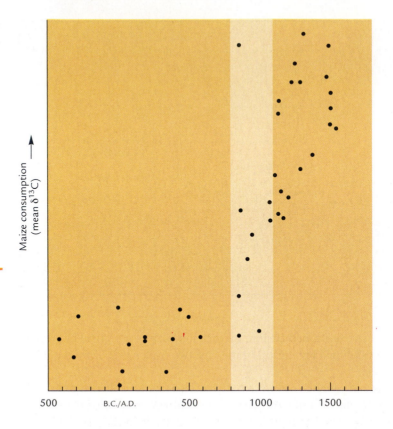

older (B. Smith 1995:191). For close to 1,000 years, however, maize continued to be a minor component of a broad subsistence system that still included hunting, fishing, collecting wild plants, and cultivating native seed crops.

All of the indigenously domesticated crops of eastern North America are treelike in following the C3 photosynthesis pathway; maize, however, is a C4-pathway plant. Analysis of the carbon-isotope chemistry of human bones recovered at archaeological sites in this region shows a shift away from C3- and toward C4-pathway plants just before A.D. 1000, preserving a chronicle in bone of the adoption of maize-based agriculture by the native peoples of eastern North America (Figure 9.22). This shift to maize enabled the evolution of the most complex archaeological culture north of Mexico, the Mississippian temple mound builders of the Midwest and Southeast (see Chapter 15).

The American Southwest

Unlike the situation in eastern North America, there is little evidence in the Southwest for the development of agricultural economies before the introduction of the Mesoamerican domesticates of maize, beans, and squash. These crops moved in and became part of the subsistence base of people who had not practiced agriculture previously.

The route taken by maize agriculture as it expanded north from its Mexican source can, in some measure, be traced archaeologically. For example, maize has been found at the Cerro Juanaqueña site in northern Mexico, very close to the border with New Mexico. The site is large, with a substantial commitment to agriculture; it dates to sometime soon after 3500 B.P. (Hard and Roney 1998).

On the U.S. side of the border, **accelerator mass spectrometry (AMS) dates** on maize from Bat Cave in western New Mexico and Tornillo Rockshelter in the southern part of that state show the crop to have been present by about 3200 B.P. (B. Smith 1995:202–3). A growing list of other sites shows the appearance of maize by 3,000 years ago or soon thereafter—for example, Milagro in Arizona and Tumamoc Hill and Jemez Cave in New Mexico (Minnis 1992). As Bruce Smith (1995) points out, it was during the four-century span between 3200 and 2800 B.P. that maize fully penetrated the American Southwest. Domesticated squash has been dated to about the same period at Sheep Camp Shelter (Simmons 1986), and beans appear to have come in 200 or 300 years later.

Though maize, squash, and beans originated as Mesoamerican crops, there was no movement of Mexican farmers northward, just the movement of the idea of domestication and the crops themselves, perhaps through trade. Most everything else in Southwest culture—tools, pots, habitations— remained more or less the same. Mesoamerican crops simply were grafted onto already existing lifeways. These new foods required only minor cultural adjustments, and the native people continued to exploit the wild plants and animals they always had.

Archaeologist Alan Simmons (1986:83–84) suggests that maize was initially a secondary and supplemental resource for otherwise nonagricultural people in the Southwest. Maize would have been planted in late spring and early summer and harvested in the late fall for use as a "survival food" in the leaner winter months. A little bit of extra work in preparing the soil and planting the crops provided extra food and perhaps greater subsistence stability. Archaeologist Paul Minnis (1992:122) calls it "casual agriculture."

This pattern was successful, continuing essentially unchanged for more than a thousand years. It was only around 2000 B.P. that southwestern cultures began to shift their subsistence drastically, relying ever more completely on domesticated crops.

SOUTH AMERICA

South America, like Africa, is enormous and contains a broad range of habitats with their attendant diverse plant and animal communities. As in Africa, geographic expanse and biological diversity mean human groups evolved many different regional cultural adaptations. And again, there was not just a single agricultural revolution in South America but several (Figure 9.23).

FIGURE 9.23
Archaeological sites in South America where evidence of early food production has been found.

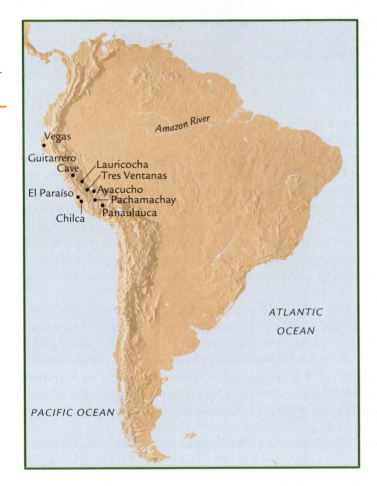

Three Regional Neolithics

Archaeologist Deborah Pearsall (1992) divides the South American Neolithic into three physiographic areas: low altitude, mid-altitude, and high altitude. Different plants growing wild in each of these divisions became the basis for distinct agricultural revolutions, with some crops from individual areas expanding into the others.

Sometime before 10,000 years ago in South America, the system of foraging for wild foods developed by Paleoindians was replaced by a more diverse and regionally specialized series of subsistence systems. In the Andes, hunters shifted from megafauna to small post-Pleistocene game such as deer and camelids (guanaco and vicuña). Elsewhere, subsistence shifted to a reliance on the abundant root crops of both the lowlands and the highlands; there is evidence in Chile for the use of a wild species of potato at Monte Verde by about 10,000 years ago (see Chapter 7 for a discussion of the earliest occupation of that site).

The earliest evidence for domesticated crops in South America appears not as seed fragments, rinds, or pollen but in the form of phytoliths. Researchers Dolores Piperno and Karen Stothert (2003) have determined that the phytoliths produced by wild and domesticated versions of the same plant type are distinguishable; the phytoliths of the domesticated varieties are significantly larger than those produced by their wild relatives.

Piperno and Stothert (2003) have recovered the phytoliths produced by the genus *Cucurbita* (squash and gourd) at a number of archaeological sites in coastal Ecuador. In stratigraphic layers dating to more than 10,000 years ago, these researchers recovered *Cucurbita* phytoliths already far larger than those produced by wild varieties of the plant. Piperno and Stothert conclude from this that the inhabitants of coastal Ecuador were exploiting the nutritious seeds of squash and gourds and, more than 10,000 years ago, were altering these plants through artificial selection. In other words, they were domesticating these plants and were engaged in a food-producing revolution.

Much of South America can be characterized as tropical. Historically, root crops like manioc, potato, and arrowroot were a part of the agricultural base of people living in the tropics. This presents a great challenge to researchers interested in identifying early evidence of domestication there. Roots are soft, not particularly durable, and unlikely to preserve in the wet, biologically active soil in which they grow. Researchers have long thought, in fact, that root crops have left little or no archaeological evidence that would enable the analysis of their early domestication.

Fortunately, however, when roots have been processed by use of a stone grinder, starch grains from the root may preserve in crevices in the stone. The shape and size of the grains are species-specific, and the grains of wild varieties of a plant are different and distinguishable from those produced by domesticated versions. And, in fact, the earliest definitive evidence of the use of domesticated plants south of Mexico has been found at the Aguadulce Shelter site in Panama by the recovery and analysis of starch grains on milling stones (Piperno et al. 2000). Dolores Piperno and her co-workers have identified the grains of domesticated manioc, yams, and arrowroot dating to nearly 7,000 years ago.

There is evidence of the domestication of common beans and chili peppers by 5,000 years ago at Guitarrero Cave in highland Peru, located in Pearsall's mid-altitude division (Kaplan, Lynch, and Smith 1973; Lynch et al. 1985). Also interpreted as an early domesticate at this site is the root crop ulluco, a source of brightly colored, carbohydrate-rich **tubers.** Ulluco is still popular as a delicacy in parts of South America. Dating to about the same time, in Holocene South America, is Tres Ventanas Cave. The inhabitants were eating domesticated potato, manioc (the root crop from which tapioca is made), and other root crops.

The use of domesticates was not restricted to the highlands of western South America. On the east coast, phytoliths and starch grains from domesticated varieties of squash (4190 B.P.), and beans (3050 B.P.) have been recovered

FIGURE 9.24

A stand of quinoa, a significant food crop in ancient South America that in higher altitudes surpassed maize as a staple in the native diet. (Courtesy of John F. McCamant)

from grinding stones found in the La Plata Basin of southeastern Uruguay (Iriarte et al. 2004).

Domesticated squash and gourds were recovered at Ayacucho Cave in the central Peruvian Highlands. Also at this site is some of the earliest evidence for the domestication of an extremely important crop in the agriculture of South America: quinoa (Figure 9.24). Quinoa is a species of the genus *Chenopodium.* North American goosefoot is another species in this genus. The earliest evidence of domesticated quinoa comes from Panaulauca Cave in Peru. Quinoa seeds with thinner seed coats than in wild specimens have been dated there to between 4000 and 5000 B.P. (B. Smith 1995:173). Quinoa plants produce particularly nutritious seeds, with a mix of amino acids superior to that of the better-known grains (see "Issues and Debates"). In some areas of South America, particularly the higher altitudes, quinoa exceeded maize in agricultural importance (McCamant 1992). Only the potato was more important in the diet of the inhabitants of high-altitude South America.

Cold-loving, high-altitude-adapted domesticated root crops, especially the potato, were the staples of much of upland South America. The potato, today a major component of European cuisine, was certainly South America's most significant agricultural contribution to Europe. Other important root crops, today unknown to most North Americans, also played important roles in the diet of ancient South America (Vietmeyer 1992). Oca, second in importance only to the potato, produced nutritious tubers at altitudes of up to 4,100 m (13,500 ft). The turniplike maca was cultivated at elevations of 4,300 m (14,000 ft), making it the only domesticated food crop able to be grown at that altitude. Other high-altitude roots domesticated and relied on as sources of food in the South American uplands were yacon, the legume jícama, ulluco, and arracacha. The 500-year-old Inca culture (to be discussed in Chapter 14), which occupied large portions of the western highlands of South

America, relied more heavily on root crops than did any other of the world's ancient civilizations.

At the previously mentioned Aguadulce Shelter site in Panama, starch remains from domesticated maize were recovered from grindstones dating to close to 7,000 years ago, about the time of maize's earliest appearance in Mexico (Piperno et al. 2000). The earliest appearance of maize in South America postdates this by more than two millennia. Evidence of maize in the form of phytoliths has been found adhering to the surfaces of pottery sherds recovered at sites dating to 4,200 years ago in coastal Ecuador (Brown 2001). Luckily, along with not thoroughly scrubbing their dishes, the inhabitants of these sites did not floss their teeth; maize remains have been found in the tartar of the teeth of two human skeletons excavated there. In the La Plata Basin of Uruguay, maize kernels have been found dating to 3600 B.P. and maize phytoliths and starch grains have been found adhering to grinding stones associated with a date of 3460 B.P. (Iriarte et al. 2004). Clearly, the advantages of maize were as apparent to ancient people in the New World as they were to become to Old World visitors who brought maize back to their hemisphere where it became an important food crop. Once domesticated in Mesoamerica, maize spread into North and South America, where it became a food staple for agricultural people.

Animal Domestication in South America

Unlike in the Old World, where domesticated animals were a major part of human diets, animal husbandry played a relatively minor role in the New World. Among the few New World species that were successfully domesticated were the guinea pig (used as a food), the turkey, the dog, and the Muscovy duck. By far the most significant animal domestication in the New World was in South America (Kent 1987).

As mentioned earlier, the wild camelid species, the guanaco and vicuña, were exploited by post-Pleistocene hunters in western South America. In the central Andes, camelids became increasingly important in the diet, replacing deer as the subsistence focus sometime after 8000 B.P. Though why this shift occurred remains unclear, the ratio of camelid to deer bones at archaeological sites increases dramatically as wild camels were exploited more intensively.

Vicuñas and guanacos are herd animals, with rigid dominance hierarchies. Their pattern of living in social groups and adhering to social hierarchies, along with their territoriality, rendered them attractive candidates for herding, controlling, taming, and then domesticating. Humans, placing themselves in the position of the most dominant members of the herd, could have exerted control over herds of wild camelids within their defined territory. Through artificial selection for animals more amenable to carrying heavy burdens and for animals that produced more meat and thicker wool, ancient South Americans produced domesticated llamas (as beasts of burden and for

FIGURE 9.25

Llamas and alpacas were the only large animal species domesticated in the New World. Llamas like this one were used as beasts of burden and for food.
(Food and Agriculture Organization, United Nations. Photo by F. Mattioli)

meat) and alpacas (for their wool and meat; Figure 9.25). Earliest evidence for this domestication has been found at Pachamachay and Lauricocha Caves in Peru, dating to as early as 6500 B.P. (Wing 1977).

Cotton

As was the case in the Near East, where flax was domesticated for use as a fiber at about 7000 B.P., a nonfood domesticate became an important element in the agricultural complex of South America. Domesticated cotton has been recovered at Ayacucho Cave dating to just after 5000 B.P.

Cotton has also been recovered at the El Paraíso site on the Peruvian coast, a large and permanent settlement that has been dated to between 3800 and 3500 B.P. (Quilter et al. 1991). Eight or nine large complexes of rooms, covering a broad area, demarcate the site. Evidence found there suggests a mixed and broad subsistence base. Remains of domesticated food crops were recovered, including squash, chili pepper, common and lima bean, jícama root, and fruits, especially guava. At least of equal importance in the food quest were the rich natural resources of the coast, including anchovies, mussels, and clams. Wild plant foods also contributed to the subsistence base.

Remains of domesticated cotton were far more abundant at the site than any of the domesticated foods. Cotton fiber was a major raw material for the production of fishing nets and lines as well as cloth. The authors of the El Paraíso Report maintain that the growth of this site is attributable to its loca-

EINKORN   EMMER

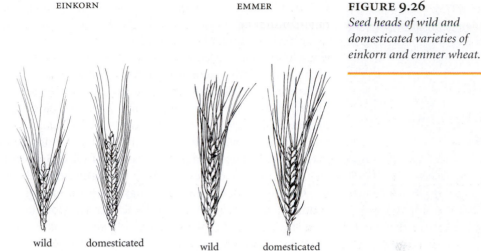

wild   domesticated   wild   domesticated

FIGURE 9.26
Seed heads of wild and domesticated varieties of einkorn and emmer wheat.

tion, perfect for the growing of cotton. Later, cotton became a major fiber for use in textiles of many cultures in South America.

HOW WAS DOMESTICATION ACCOMPLISHED?

ISSUES AND DEBATES

In the domestication of plants and animals, human beings take the place of nature in the selection process. We can examine how this may have occurred for a number of different crops: wheat, maize, and beans.

The Domestication of Wheat

The **rachis** of wild wheat—the area of attachment of the individual kernels of wheat—becomes quite brittle when the wheat ripens. A brittle rachis is a distinct advantage in nature. It promotes seed dispersal, which, in turn, promotes the growth of more wheat plants in the following growing season. When the kernels are ripe, a brittle rachis can be shattered by the wind, a rainstorm, or even an animal walking through a field (Figure 9.26).

Within any community of wild wheat plants today are individual plants that possess a combination of mutant genes for rachis form that results in a tougher, less brittle seed spike. Under conditions of natural selection, such forms are always in the minority, and they are at a clear disadvantage in terms of propagation: Their seeds are far less likely to disperse into the surrounding soil.

When humans enter the picture, however, the nature of selection changes drastically. Though preferred under wild conditions, a brittle rachis is *disadvantageous* for humans harvesting a wild crop, especially for those using a sickle to cut the plants off at the base. The impact of the tool is likely to

FIGURE 9.27
One of the many modern forms of wheat. (Food and Agriculture Organization, United Nations. Photo by the Kenya Information Office)

shatter a brittle rachis, widely disperse the seeds, and make harvesting quite time-consuming.

Either by accident or by design—and likely a combination of the two— when humans harvested wild wheat, a greater proportion of the mutant plants with a tough rachis were brought back to the village. Most of the seeds of the more abundant plants with brittle connections simply fell off and did not make it back to the settlement. Again either by accident or by design, more of the seeds of tough-rachis plants carrying the genetic instructions for that tough rachis became planted near human habitations. In this way, human beings fundamentally changed the process of selection, replacing a natural context with a human context to which the plants adapted (Figure 9.27).

Genetic evidence indicates that this process may first have occurred in southeast Turkey in the area of the Karacadağ Mountains. Researchers examined the DNA of 261 lines of wild wheat (einkorn), including 11 lines that grow abundantly in the Karacadağ Mountain region (Heun et al. 1997). Next, they compared the DNA of these strands of wild wheat to that of 68 lines of modern, domesticated einkorn wheat. They found that not only were the 11 lines of wheat from the Karacadağ Mountains the most genetically distinct of all the wild wheats, but of all the wild varieties sampled, the Karacadağ wheat was also the most genetically similar to the modern domesticated varieties examined. The presence of archaeological sites in the same region with evidence of the very early domestication of einkorn (for example, Abu Hureyra and Çayönü mentioned earlier in this chapter) lends further support to the hypothesis that the Karacadağ wild wheat was the ultimate source for the einkorn domesticated more than 10,000 years ago in southwest Asia.

From Teosinte to Maize

The wild maize, or teosinte plant, in some respects resembles the corn plant with which we are familiar. In fact, primitive varieties of maize are nearly identical to teosinte in cell form and genetic structure (Galinat 1992). However, teosinte produces not large cobs with rows of plump kernels but small seed spikes, each with a brittle rachis and tiny, thickly encased seeds (Figure 9.28). Teosinte seeds are nutritious and were exploited by ancient Mesoamericans. With their brittle rachis, however, they must have been difficult to harvest effectively. With their thick cases, teosinte seeds are well-adapted for survival in the gut of an animal that has ingested them, to be "planted" somewhere else when they pass through the creature's digestive system intact (Federoff 2003). As mentioned earlier in this chapter, however, this feature renders the seeds at least less convenient for people who need to process them in order to make them nutritionally more accessible.

Luckily, just a few genes control those features. Genetic analysis has shown that probably only about five genetic loci control the physical characteristics that distinguish maize from teosinte (Doebley, Stec, and Hubbard 1997; Jaenicke-Després et al. 2003; Raloff 1993), and maizelike teosinte mu-

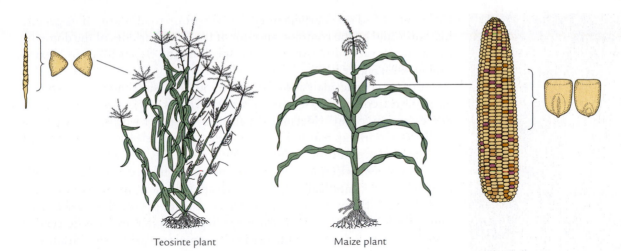

Teosinte plant   Maize plant

FIGURE 9.28
Teosinte plant, spike, and seeds and maize plant, cob, and kernels.

tants are produced in wild populations (Beadle 1977). For example, a mutation in a single gene changes the extremely tough and stony fruitcase that encapsulates each teosinte kernel into a far more easily processed, and much more readily digestible, exposed or naked kernel (Wang et al. 2005). In other words, a single genetic mistake can transform a nutritious but challenging plant food into a nutritious and far more easily used plant food. Other mutations produce a plant with a tougher rachis, a feature that is not advantageous in the wild but are preferred by humans. We also know that a single mutation on one teosinte chromosome doubles the number of rows of kernels, and another alters the standard pattern of single spikelets to paired, again greatly increasing seed yield (Galinat 1992). Still another mutation enlarges the individual kernels.

As maize researcher Walton C. Galinat (1992) points out, ancient users of teosinte would have recognized the desirable characteristics of some of the mutant forms of that plant. In the wild, these rare forms would remain rare because cross-pollination would be occurring with the overwhelming abundance of nonmutant forms. By isolating the mutants, however, ancient Mesoamericans could have ensured that plants with rare features, maladaptive in nature but desirable for humans, cross-bred only with mutants with the same or other desirable characteristics. As Galinat indicates, though ancient people lacked our knowledge of genetics, their powers of observation of the world around them were probably far better than our own—including, perhaps especially, their observation of the plant life on which they depended for survival. Applying the knowledge derived from such observation, they could have domesticated maize rather quickly. Once under human control, paleobotanical evidence shows consistent selection for larger cobs which exhibit a steady pattern of growth from 6250 B.P. to 4400 B.P. (Jaenicke-Deprés et al. 2003).

Genetic analysis of the hundreds of varieties of maize and the many different kinds of wild teosinte has been conducted by plant biologist John Doebley.

FIGURE 9.29

Teosinte is the wild ancestor of maize. This is a modern variety (Zea mays parviglumis), *from the Rio Balsas in Mexico, which may be the form from which domesticated maize is descended.* (Courtesy of Dolores Piperno, Smithsonian Tropical Research Institute)

He has identified one particular teosinte subgroup that, based on its genetic makeup, could be the common ancestor of the many varieties of the domesticated crop: a race of teosinte that grows along the Balsas River in Mexico (Raloff 1993; Figure 9.29).

A recent genetic analysis of 193 maize and 67 teosinte samples shows that all of the extremely diverse current maize varieties originated from a single domestication "event" (Matsuoka et al. 2002). In other words, native people of the New World appear to have, through artificial selection, domesticated teosinte just once, and all the myriad modern varieties of maize have resulted from subsequent selection that enabled the use of the crop across an incredibly broad and climatically diverse geographic region, from the southern reaches of South America to the northern reaches of North America. This same genetic analysis confirms Doebley's hypothesis that maize is descended from a single variety of teosinte (*Zea mays* spp *parviglumis*), specifically one that grows in the uplands of southwest Mexico, in the Balsas River drainage. Based on mutation rates known for maize, it has been estimated that teosinte was first genetically modified by ancient Americans as much as 9,000 years ago (Matsuoka et al. 2002:6083). Remember that the oldest archaeological maize specimens are close to 7,000 years old, making the domestication of maize another example of the evolutionary nature of the process that led to a revolution in subsistence and society.

Beans

Wild beans grow in twisted pods that become brittle when ripe, and the beans themselves are rather impermeable. People selected for mutant beans with straight, limp, nonshattering pods for easier harvesting and for more permeable varieties, which reduced the time needed for soaking in water before they could be cooked (De Tapia 1992; Kaplan 1981; Kaplan and Kaplan 1992). This process may have been repeated several times in Mesoamerica and South America, ultimately providing the world with four separate domesticated bean species: common, lima and sievas, scarlet runner, and tepary beans, and the many varieties of these various species, including kidney, lima, pinto, wax, and navy (Kaplan and Kaplan 1992:61; another commonly eaten bean, fava, is an Old World domesticate).

The Nature of Artificial Selection

Charles Darwin, who used artificial selection in agriculture as an analogy for natural selection in the wild, phrased it appropriately when, referring to horticulturists' ability to produce a spectacular array of plants and animals for human use, he stated: "The art is simple, and as far as the final result is concerned, has been followed almost unconsciously. It has consisted in always cultivating the best-known variety, sowing its seeds, and, when a slightly better variety chanced to appear, selecting it, and so onwards" (Diamond 1994:106). Much the same was true during the early post-Pleistocene.

THE REMARKABLY MODERN CUISINE
OF THE ANCIENT WORLD

You have probably tried and perhaps eat often the "ethnic" foods of different cultures that are widely available in the modern world. Virtually every city in North America has restaurants specializing in many kinds of foods: Chinese and Japanese food with their rice-based dishes, Mexican cuisine with its corn flour tortillas and tacos and beans, Middle Eastern food with wheat flour pita bread, Greek food with lamb, German food with beef and pork, the Native American turkey we eat on Thanksgiving, and so on—all part of our modern diet.

All of these foods—rice, wheat, potato, corn, beef, chicken, pork, turkey—form the basis for the diet of the world's burgeoning human population at the turn of the twenty-first century. And all were domesticated in antiquity. In fact, it is difficult to come up with any economically significant modern food sources that were not part of the food base thousands of years ago, during the Neolithic. Two exceptions are strawberries, which were not domesticated until the Middle Ages, and pecans, which were not domesticated until 1846 (Diamond 1994). Even chocolate, without which life itself would be impossible, was the result of an ancient process of domestication. Residue analysis of early Maya ceramic vessels recovered at the Rio Azul site in northeastern Guatemla, dating from A.D. 460–480, revealed the presence of a cacao-based beverage (Hurst et al. 2002). The researchers do not report the discovery of marshmallow residue.

So although we may think of ancient people as primitive, we have them to thank for virtually all the foods we rely on today. We have refined the work of the ancients by improving yield, increasing drought resistance, and accelerating ripening. But we have not added significantly to the inventory of domesticates. Statistics on year 2003 worldwide yields of modern agriculture show this to be the case (Table 9.1). Many of the crops in Table 9.1 were discussed in this chapter. Wheat, corn, rice, potato, barley, manioc, sweet potato, soybean, and sorghum are among the top modern crops, and all are ancient in origin. (Sugarcane surpasses their yields, but this is misleading because its weight is exaggerated as a result of water content.)

NEOLITHIC NUTRITION

Some of the plant foods domesticated by Neolithic people are high in protein. For example, on a scale comparing relative protein content of various foods (Table 9.2), where eggs represent a perfect score of 100 for their rich and complete complement of amino acids, wheat rates a 44, rice a 57, and corn a 41. Compare this to 69 for beef, 64 for chicken, and 70 for fish.

There is a serious problem, however, with relying on the cereals for protein: As Table 9.2 also shows, wheat, rice, and maize do not provide complete

TABLE 9.1

Worldwide Crop Production in Million Metric Tons for 2003

CROP	MILLION METRIC TONS[a]	CROP	MILLION METRIC TONS[a]
Sugarcane	1333.25	Plantains	32.97
Maize	638.04	Millet	29.81
Rice	589.13	Sunflower seeds	27.74
Wheat	556.35	Cantaloupes, etc.	26.75
Potatoes	310.81	Oats	26.27
Sugar beet	233.49	Carrot	23.32
Soybeans	189.23	Chilies and peppers	23.25
Manioc	189.1	Dry beans	19.04
Cassava	189.1	Squash, pumpkin, gourd	18.95
Barley	141.5	Olives	17.17
Sweet potatoes	121.85	Cauliflower	15.95
Tomatoes	113.31	Rye	14.85
Watermelons	91.79	Pineapple	14.61
Bananas	69.29	Dry peas	10.25
Cabbage	65.96	Taro	8.94
Oranges	60.05	Green peas	8.91
Sorghum	59.58	Chick peas	7.12
Onion	52.54	Green beans	5.93
Yams	39.91	Strawberries	3.20
Cucumbers	39.60	Lentils	3.09
Rape seed	36.15	Sesame seeds	2.94
Groundnuts	35.66	Linseed	2.09

Data compiled by the Food and Agriculture Organization of the United Nations (Year-book, Volume 57).
[a]*1 metric ton equals 1.1 American tons.*

proteins, for each lacks at least one of the eight essential amino acids necessary to sustain human life (isoleucine, leucine, lysine, methionine, phenylalanine, threonine, tryptophan, and valine). Wheat, rice, and maize, though high in protein, are each deficient in lysine. Quinoa, a significant South American domesticate, offers a more complete complement of amino acids, including lysine.

Remarkably, in the Near East, the Far East, and Mesoamerica, where wheat, rice, and maize, respectively, became the basis for a way of life, people also domesticated other wild crops that, though even less complete than wheat, rice, or maize in the amino acids they contain, are rich in lysine (Heiser 1990). In the Near East, it was a suite of legumes—including lentil, chickpea, and peas—that provided the amino acid missing in wheat. In the Far East, lentils provided the lysine missing in rice. In Mesoamerica, beans supplied the missing protein component.

TABLE 9.2
Amino Acid Content of Various Foods

FOOD	AMINO ACID[a]								PROTEIN SCORE[b]
	ISO-LEUCINE	LEUCINE	LYSINE	METHI-ONINE	PHENYL-ALANINE	THREO-NINE	TRYPTO-PHAN	VALINE	
Hen's egg	393	551	436	210	358	320	93	428	100
Beef	301	507	556	169	275	287	70	313	69
Cow's milk	295	596	487	157	336	278	88	362	60
Chicken	334	460	497	157	250	248	64	318	64
Fish	299	480	569	179	245	286	70	382	70
Maize	230	783	167	120	305	225	44	303	41
Wheat	204	417	179	94	282	183	68	276	44
Rice	238	514	237	145	322	244	78	344	57
Bean	262	476	450	66	326	248	63	287	34
Soybean	284	486	399	79	309	241	80	300	47
Potato	236	377	299	81	251	235	103	292	34
Manioc	175	247	259	83	156	165	72	204	41
Coconut	244	419	220	120	283	212	68	339	55

From Heiser (1990:31).
[a]*Measured in milligrams per gram of nitrogen.*
[b]*Each food's protein content is scored relative to that of the hen's egg, which, as the highest in protein, is given a score of 100.*

So without any knowledge of nutrition or biochemistry, prehistoric people in different parts of the world domesticated a range of plants that together provided the essential amino acids needed for them to survive and prosper.

WAS AGRICULTURE THE "WORST MISTAKE IN THE HISTORY OF THE HUMAN RACE"?

Scientist Jared Diamond (1987b) labeled agriculture the "worst mistake in the history of the human race" in the title of a provocative essay. His interesting idea is backed up by some impressive archaeological evidence. Clearly, agriculture can provide more food than can most foraging systems, and it can do so in a wide variety of habitats. In terms of caloric output, when agriculture works, it wins, hands down. At the same time, we have just seen that many of the world's ancient agricultural systems produced crops that complemented each other in amino acid content. So theoretically, not only can agriculture produce lots of food for lots of mouths, but it also can give a mixture of foods that together provide a healthy diet. Unfortunately, the evidence shows that this system often did not work in this way.

Biological anthropologists Mark Cohen and George Armelagos (1984) have summarized the evidence for the prevalence of paleopathology—ancient disease—coincident with the origins of agriculture in North, Central, and South America, the eastern Mediterranean, western Europe, the Middle East, southern Asia, and Nubia. When comparing parameters of health as revealed by prehistoric skeletons, in most instances older hunter-gatherer groups exhibited higher levels of health and nutrition than did the farmers who succeeded them. Specifically, there were higher levels of infection in farmers than in previous foragers in the same regions. Some early farming populations show increases in tubercular infections (Buikstra 1984); others show higher levels of gastrointestinal infections (seen in a survey of mummified humans in South America; Allison 1984). Many more farming groups show higher rates of infections of uncertain origin. Of course, agriculture itself doesn't cause disease; it merely establishes the conditions conducive for disease to spread: large, dense, sedentary populations.

Ironically, chronic malnutrition seems to be another major problem that accompanied the shift to an agricultural way of life. Although many people may stereotype hunter-gatherers as living hand-to-mouth, where every meal might be their last for some time, in most of the studies Cohen and Armelagos summarize, farmers show more evidence of malnutrition than do their foraging forebears. Nutritionally based anemia (as evidenced by porosity of the skull) was found to be severe in a number of farming groups in the American Midwest. Other evidence for poorer nutrition among some farming groups included an overall decline in stature. Episodes of severe malnutrition among farmers was further indicated by more incidences of enamel hypoplasia (see the discussion in Chapter 5 regarding the Neandertals and this condition).

Perhaps most remarkable of all, for the majority of cases reported in a symposium Cohen and Armelagos organized on this issue, where age at death was calculated for the archaeological samples, hunter-gatherers lived longer than did the farmers in the same regions. They conclude: "Taken as a whole, these indicators fairly clearly suggest an overall decline in the quality—and probably in the length—of human life associated with the adoption of agriculture" (1984:594).

However, not all data collected on this issue support the general hypothesis that the transition from a foraging to an agricultural way of life led to an increase in mortality and a decrease in longevity. A recent investigation by researchers in Israel indicates that the demographic pattern may be more complicated than that (Eshed et al. 2004). In their comparison of 217 Natufian and 262 Neolithic skeletons, they determined that there was an overall, though minor *increase* (about one year) in mean adult age at death among Neolithic food producers over Natufian food collectors in the southern Levant (mean adult age was defined as the age of death for individuals over 15 years of age, so the deaths of young children did not bring down the mean age of death).

Natufians in the sample died, on average, at the disturbingly low mean age of 31.2 years, whereas their Neolithic descendants died at a mean age of 32.1 years (Eshed et al. 2004:321). But here is where the demographic pattern actually gets more complex. In fact, it is only males who gained in longevity between the Natufian and Neolithic; females actually experienced a slight decrease in life expectancy. Male adult mean age at death increased from 32.2 years in the Natufian sites to 37.6 years in the Neolithic; female adult mean age at death decreased from 35.5 years in Natufian sites to 30.1 years in the Neolithic (Eshed et al. 2004:322).

How might this differing trend between males and females be explained? A more detailed look at the data suggests an explanation. Mortality among male and female adults aged 15–40 is very similar among the Natufians; male mortality is just a little higher in this age range. This changes dramatically at the Neolithic sites the authors examined, with a much higher portion of females than males dying in the 15–40-year range. As the authors of the study point out, these are the primary childbearing years, and this may explain the higher mortality/lower mean age of death for adult females in the Neolithic. New, consistent, and abundant food sources provided by an agricultural subsistence system may have increased and even prolonged female fertility, resulting in an increased number of pregnancies a woman might have during the course of her life and diminishing the spacing between those pregnancies. Pregnancy and childbirth can compromise the health of the mother—certainly more so than not being pregnant—and thus, a greater number of pregnancies increased the likelihood that a woman encountered a health- or even life-threatening issue. These new data indicate that, in terms of human longevity, the shift to an agricultural way of life was neither universally advantageous nor disadvantageous, and it was women who bore the brunt of the negative impact of the food-producing revolution on human longevity.

Another rather nasty result of a shift to an agricultural way of life seems to have been the institutionalization of warfare and violence. Direct evidence of personal violence is rare in Pleistocene archaeological contexts. Few skeletons exhibit traumatic wounds that might have resulted from interpersonal violence. In the Neolithic, however, such evidence becomes far more common within a context not of just one person killing another but of whole groups taking up arms against their neighbors. Perhaps the problems inherent in an agricultural way of life and the always present potential for a collapse of the subsistence base are at the heart of this phenomenon. Agriculture, though potentially of enormous benefit, is a fragile basis for subsistence. It allows for the existence of large and dense populations as long as it works; but when it doesn't work, there are a lot of hungry people. And when the neighbors of starving people have food, the hungry may become violent.

Maybe agriculture wasn't a mistake, but it had a fundamental drawback: Though it allowed more people to live, many did not live as well as their hunter-gatherer ancestors.

IMPLICATIONS OF THE NEOLITHIC: THE ROOTS OF SOCIAL COMPLEXITY

For most of human history, we have foraged for food. Small nomadic groups could easily supply the necessities for their families. No one needed more, and providing for more than one's needs made little sense. The organization of such societies could be rather simple, revolving around age and sex categories. Such societies likely were largely **egalitarian;** beyond the usual distinctions based on age and sex, virtually all people had equivalent rights, status, and access to resources.

Archaeologist Donald Henry (1989) suggests that the combination of a rich habitat and sedentism led to a dramatic increase in human population. In his view, nomadic, simple foragers have a relatively low level of fertility. Their high-protein, low-carbohydrate diets produce low proportions of body fat, and these low proportions are commonly associated with low fertility in women. High physical activity and long periods of nursing common among recent simple foragers also probably contributed to low levels of female fertility.

In Henry's view, the shift to complex foraging and a more sedentary existence would have contributed to higher fertility levels. A diet higher in wild cereals produces proportionally more body fat, leading to higher fertility among women. Cereals produce easily digested foods that would have supplemented and then replaced mother's milk as a primary food for older infants. Because lactation is a natural dampener of fertility, earlier weaning would have resulted in closer spacing of births and the potential for a greater number of live births for each woman. A more sedentary existence may also have lowered infant mortality and perhaps increased longevity among the aged. These more vulnerable members of society could safely stay in a fixed village rather than be forced regularly to move great distances as part of a nomadic existence with its greater risk of accident and trauma.

All of these factors may have resulted in a trend of increasing size among some local human populations in the Holocene. Given sufficient time, even in very rich habitats, human population size can reach **carrying capacity:** the maximum population an area can sustain within the context of a given subsistence system. And human population growth is like a runaway train: Once it picks up speed, it is difficult to control. So even after reaching an area's carrying capacity, Holocene human populations probably continued to grow in food-rich regions, overshooting the ability of the territory to feed the population, again within the context of the same subsistence strategy. In some areas, small changes in climate or minor changes in plant characteristics may have further destabilized local economies.

One possible response to surpassing the carrying capacity of a region is for a group to exploit adjoining land. However, good land may itself be limited—for example, to within the confines of a river valley. Where neighbors are in the same position, having filled up all the available desirable habitat in their home territories, expansion also is problematic. Impinging on the neighbors' territory can lead to conflict, especially when they too are up against the capacity of the land to provide enough food.

Another option is to stay put but shift and intensify the food quest in the same territory. The impulse to produce more food to feed a growing population was satisfied in some areas by the development of more complex subsistence strategies involving intensive labor and requiring more cooperation and greater coordination of increasing numbers of people. This development resulted in a change in the social and economic equations that defined those societies. Hierarchies that did not exist in earlier foraging groups but were helpful in structuring cooperative labor and in organizing more complex technologies probably became entrenched even before domestication and agriculture as pre-Neolithic societies reacted to population increase.

The results of this strategy of intensification of the exploitation of wild foods were, at least in some regions, even better than the participants could have anticipated. Not only were people able to increase their wild food base enough to feed a larger population, but they actually were also able to produce a food surplus by artificially selecting for propagation the most productive individuals in their wild food species. This food surplus changed the social and economic equations yet again, setting the stage for a dramatic increase in complexity in some human societies. The results of this increase are the focus of the next chapter.

CASE STUDY CLOSE-UP

The revolution that is the focus of this chapter was not an event but rather a slow process that only gradually changed the fundamental way people made a living. Analysis of this shift in the Khabur Basin in northeastern Syria is a perfect example (Zeder 1994a,b).

The area had been only sparsely occupied before 12,000 B.P. Beginning about 10,000 years ago, villages began turning up in the archaeological record with a subsistence base that included a variety of early domesticates, including wheat, lentils, peas, and beans. The bones of domesticated sheep and goats were found in early levels of these settlements, with pig and cattle remains showing up later.

A detailed analysis of one site in the Khabur Basin, Umm Qseir, clearly shows the evolutionary nature of the shift from foraging to farming. For example, after 8000 B.P., domesticated sheep, goat, and pig contributed to the diet in the settlement. But the Neolithic residents of Umm Qseir had not abandoned their earlier pattern of hunting and gathering. More than half the animal remains recovered at the site were of wild animals—gazelle, deer, wild cattle, hare, turtles, wild ass, birds, and freshwater clams (Zeder 1994b:5).

The use of both wild and domesticated sources of food seems to reflect a seasonal rhythm at Umm Qseir. Most animal species have a particular mating season and a fairly consistent gestational period, so most of the offspring are born within a narrow period of time during the year. Because the age of death of a juvenile animal can be estimated based on tooth eruption and bone development, archaeologists can often determine the time of year an animal was killed. In other words, if the young of a particular species tend to be born in the early spring and many of the younger animals at a site were slaughtered in their 15th month of life, just count 15 months from early spring to determine when they were slaughtered. In this hypothetical example, they were killed in the summer.

Pigs were slaughtered most commonly at Umm Qseir between August and October. The ages of sheep and goats killed at the site correspond to this same period, which actually extended until January. This is the arid summer and early rainy season, precisely when wild resources would have been at their leanest. So domestication did not supplant foraging in the subsistence system at Umm Qseir. Instead, domestication allowed for the permanent occupation of an area rich with seasonally available wild foods, even during seasons when those wild foods were not plentiful.

As archaeologist Melinda Zeder (1994b) points out, here and elsewhere the Neolithic was not a period during which all people marched down the path to a purely agricultural mode of subsistence. For a long time, domestication complemented foraging but did not replace it. Only much later did agriculture and animal husbandry become the primary sources of food for most of the world's people, setting the stage for the period of time to be described in Chapters 10–15.

VISITING THE PAST

In 1958, a museum was constructed right at the Chinese Neolithic site of Banpo in Shaanxi Province. The site has been dated to between 6,000 and 7,000 years ago. Site excavation revealed the remains of more than 40 houses and 200 storage pits in which excavators found remnants of the subsistence base of the inhabitants. Clearly, the people of Banpo had a diverse economy; on display are the remains of chestnuts, hazelnuts, hackberries, pine nuts, snails, antelopes, pigs, foxes, cattle, and many species of fish that have been found. Domesticated millet, Chinese cabbage, and leaf mustard were also found. Many artifacts unearthed at the site are on display, including tools for tilling the soil (stone spades and hoes) and ceramic jars for storing food. Part of the excavated site has been preserved at the museum, and visitors can also see reconstructed houses, or "cottages."

Five miles south of Areopolis, in Greece, is a museum dedicated to the archaeological remains excavated at Diros Caves. The Neolithic occupation of the area dates to after 7,000 and sometime before 5,000 years ago. Highlighted in the exhibit are some of the finer examples of the inhabitants' work in stone, bone, terra-cotta, and silver. These sites are instructive as object lessons in the enormous impacts of the Food-Producing Revolution in terms of the degree of sedentism implied, the size of the resident population, the specialization of labor, social stratification, and the construction of monuments.

SUMMARY

Archaeological evidence now shows that by as much as 20,000 years ago, some human groups had incorporated cereal grasses, including barley and emmer wheat in the Middle East, into their subsistence quest. These were wild crops, contributing to subsistence as part of an overall strategy of foraging that included hunting wild animals, fishing, and collecting plants. Then, beginning sometime after 12,000 B.P. and in a number of world areas, the archaeological record shows a subtle, barely perceptible shift in how people supplied their subsistence needs. Whereas humans previously had fed themselves, like all other animals, by foraging for wild foods, some groups began intentionally encouraging the growth of particular plants (by turning over soil, planting seeds, weeding, thinning out, and in other ways tending them) and herding and selectively culling herds of animals. Human beings replaced nature as the selective force operating on certain species. This "artificial selection" encouraged the growth of those individuals within plant and animal species that were not necessarily well adapted to a life in the wild but that had characteristics advantageous to their human caretakers. Over many generations of selection, human beings in the Near East, Europe, eastern Asia, Africa, New Guinea, and North and South America developed new species that were the product not of natural processes but of cultural requirements. This was the Food-Producing—or Neolithic or Agricultural—Revolution, which, while slow, would revolutionize the way people made a living and how they lived— and how we live in the modern world.

TO LEARN MORE

Technical Summaries

There are many detailed, technical works summarizing the shift from foraging to food production in a number of world areas. Among the best of these are *Last Hunters–First Farmers: New Perspectives on the Prehistoric Transition to Agriculture,* edited by T. Douglas Price and Birgitte Gebauer (1995). This book contains articles focusing on the development of an agricultural way of life in the Middle East, northern Europe, Southeast Asia, the New World, the tropics, and eastern North America. Another extremely helpful source is *Domestication of Plants in the Old World: The Origin and Spread of Cultivated Plants in West Asia, Europe, and the Nile Valley,* by Daniel Zohary and Maria Hopf (2001). Useful works discussing the food production revolution in individual regions or habitats are *Europe's First Farmers,* edited by T. Douglas Price (2000); *The Origins of Agriculture in the Lowland Neotropics,* by Dolores R. Piperno and Deborah M. Pearsall (1998); and *The Exploitation of Plant Resources in Ancient Africa,* edited by Marijke Van Der Veen (1999). For a succinct summary of the Neolithic of southwest Asia and the probable first plant and animal domestication in the world, see Ofer Bar-Yosef's 1998 article in *Evolutionary Anthropology* focusing on the Natufian culture of the Levant. An extremely detailed treatment of the origins of agriculture in the Near East is Donald O. Henry's *From Foraging to Agriculture: The Levant at the End of the Ice Age* (1989). See the volume edited by Bruce Smith, *Rivers of Change* (1992), for a series of discussions on the patterns and sequences of domestication in North America.

Popular Summaries

Archaeologist Bruce Smith's excellent synthesis titled *The Emergence of Agriculture* (1995) presents a broad, comparative survey of the origins of food production. His is the best detailed discussion of domestication written not just for other scientists but also for everybody interested in the topic. For a series of useful summaries of New World domestication, read the papers in *Chilies to Chocolate: Food the Americas Gave the World,* edited by Nelson Foster and Linda S. Cordell (1992). Archaeologist Brian Fagan (2002) has written a wonderful summary of the contribution of Native Americans to the cuisine of the modern world titled "Everything New Is Old Again" for the magazine *American Archaeology.* For a concise piece on the process of domestication, read Jared Diamond's "How to Tame a Wild Plant," in the September 1994 issue of *Discover* magazine. For a discussion of the health impacts of the agricultural revolution, see the article "Disease and Death at Dr. Dickson's Mound" (1985), by A. H. Goodman and George Armelagos in *Natural History* magazine.

On the Web

Mesa Community College provides a very thorough and detailed presentation on domestication at http://www.mc.maricopa.edu/dept/d10/asb/anthro2003/lifeways/hg_ag/where.html. The home page is a map of the world. Click on any world area and get transported to an inclusive listing of all of the crops and animals that were domesticated in the region. It's a great study tool. Check out the "crop of the day" links on the course companion site for Professor Paul Gepts's Evolution of Crop Plants, at the University of California, Davis (http://www.agronomy.ucdavis.edu/gepts/pb143/pb143.htm).

Online Learning Center: www.mhhe.com/feder4

ONLINE LEARNING CENTER

The Online Learning Center (OLC) Web companion to *The Past in Perspective* features a variety of supplemental study aids. For each chapter, this free Web site includes

- Self-Quizzes to take as pretests prior to exams
- Interactive Timeline Study Guides for additional review and reinforcement of key information
- Learning Objectives
- Chapter Site links with Web addresses for many of the fossil and archaeological sites mentioned in the text

KEY TERMS

Abejas phase, 368	Agricultural Revolution, 346	artificial selection, 348
accelerator mass spectrometry (AMS) dating, 387	Ajalpán phase, 368	carrying capacity, 402
	Ajuereado phase, 367	cereal, 357
		complex foraging, 359

10

The Roots of Complexity

THE ORIGINS OF CIVILIZATION

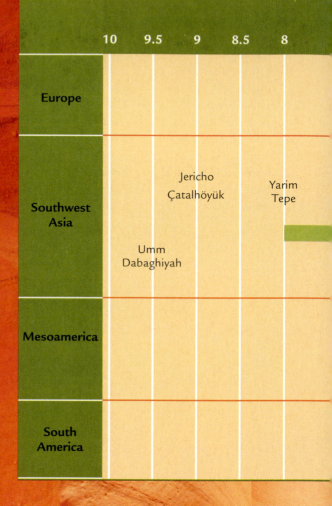

	10	9.5	9	8.5	8
Europe					
Southwest Asia			Jericho Çatalhöyük		Yarim Tepe
		Umm Dabaghiyah			
Mesoamerica					
South America					

CHAPTER OVERVIEW

For nearly all of the human past, societies were largely egalitarian with most decisions made at the level of the household, the family, or the local community. Populations were small and dispersed; and decisions were made, labor was divided, distributed, and organized; and wealth was apportioned on the basis of family relationships. Beginning in the Holocene, however, some societies in the Old and New Worlds became socially, politically, and economically more complex. In these complex societies, authority, work, and decision making were organized on the basis of a larger social group, not just the household or family. It is likely that complex social and political systems developed where the coordi- nated labor of a large group of people was needed to meet some immediate challenge or to exploit a unique opportunity. The great monuments that now dominate the archaeo- logical record of some ancient cultures and therefore occupy the time of so many archae- ologists are one result of the evolution of complex social, political, and economic sys- tems where the labor of the many can be harnessed, organized, and controlled.

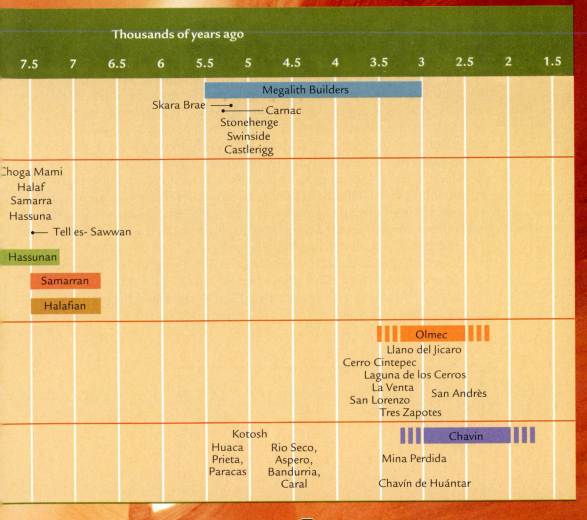

Thousands of years ago

| 7.5 | 7 | 6.5 | 6 | 5.5 | 5 | 4.5 | 4 | 3.5 | 3 | 2.5 | 2 | 1.5 |

Megalith Builders

Skara Brae — Carnac
Stonehenge
Swinside
Castlerigg

Choga Mami
Halaf
Samarra
Hassuna
• — Tell es- Sawwan

Hassunan

Samarran

Halafian

Olmec
Llano del Jicaro
Cerro Cintepec
Laguna de los Cerros
La Venta   San Andrès
San Lorenzo
Tres Zapotes

Kotosh   Chavin
Huaca   Rio Seco,
Prieta,   Aspero,   Mina Perdida
Paracas   Bandurria,
          Caral   Chavín de Huántar

ONLINE
LEARNING
CENTER

Go to **www.mhhe.com/feder4** for an
interactive study guide version of this timeline.

409

PRELUDE

Everyone reacts differently upon seeing Stonehenge for the first time (Figures 10.1 and 10.2). Surprisingly, for some the initial reaction is one of disappointment. Because visitors are often familiar with artists' conceptions of the site at its peak, the current ruin, with most of its component stones either missing or lying recumbent and sometimes in pieces, simply does not live up to their expectations. Anticipating an intact monument, instead they are confronted by a ruin. Further, the major highway that today transects the site certainly detracts from one's first impression of this 5,000-year-old monument. Controversial plans currently being discussed involve an ambitious reconfiguring of the roadway, placing it underground. Beginning the tunnel far enough away from the monument, however, so that it has a minimal visual impact and boring its pathway far enough underground to avoid any possibility of causing serious damage to Stonehenge would cost billions. Starting too close and digging the passage from the surface (and then covering it over) instead of boring from beneath, would save money but could result in the destruction of nearby associated archaeological remains and conceivably would make the visitor's experience significantly worse than it already can be. Current plans to construct only 20% of the length of the project by boring a tunnel under the site, leaving 80% of the length cut from ground level

FIGURE 10.1

The location of Stonehenge, which was an early chiefdom-level society in England.

with bulldozers, has concerned many who fear that such an approach will destroy the surroundings of one of the most important archaeological monuments in the world (http://www.savestonehenge.org.uk/).

For many of us, however, even in ruin and adjacent to a modern highway, Stonehenge is an ancient monument of uncommon beauty, majesty, and even mystery (Chippindale 1983). I was a teenager when my parents took my sister and me on a whirlwind trip to Europe—you know, the kind where you visit five different countries in two weeks. It wasn't quite *National Lampoon's European Vacation*, but it was close. I agreed to come along only if a visit to Stonehenge was on the itinerary, and my parents agreed.

The long bus trip from London was uneventful, and we finally arrived at the monument. I was speechless and, even now, more than 35 years later, find it difficult to find the right words to express my reaction. This was a time when tourists were still allowed to wander within the monument—it has been roped off for a couple of decades now to prevent damage—and I took full advantage of the opportunity, walking among the standing stones, touching them, making the kind of direct connection with an ancient people possible only through such a visit. I remember being overwhelmed by the remarkable, alien beauty of the enormous, unevenly and imperfectly carved stones. When I next visited Stonehenge it was in 1996, as an adult with a family. My otherwise laconic older son, just 11 at the time, approached me after about an hour of our walking along the rope circumnavigating the stones and said to me, "This is awesome." And indeed it was and indeed it is. Though the pyramids of ancient Egypt were built on a far grander scale (see Chapter 11), though the stone blocks that make up the city walls of the Inca were cut with much greater precision (Chapter 14), though the painted murals of the Maya may be more visually arresting (Chapter 13), and though the tombs of the ancient rulers of Mesopotamia may reflect greater wealth (Chapter 11), the Stonehenge ruin that can be seen today is every bit as compelling and impressive as these other works of the ancient world (Ruggles 1996).

FIGURE 10.2
Stonehenge is both massive and marvelous—a remarkable monument made possible by the development of a society in which the labor of many could be commanded by the few.
(K. L. Feder)

FIGURE 10.3

The small village of Skara Brae in the Orkney Islands, Scotland, was occupied at about the time Stonehenge was being built. Though the inhabitants of this village did not play a role in the construction of Stonehenge— they simply were too far away—it is likely that the populations of a large number of small villages like Skara Brae provided the labor that made Stonehenge possible. (K. L. Feder)

THE CONSTRUCTION OF STONEHENGE

Stonehenge was an enormously ambitious construction project, accomplished not by a sophisticated nation-state but rather by a people who otherwise appear to have been simple farmers (Figure 10.3; Castleden 1987). About 5,000 years ago, people living in the south of England in an area of low, undulating hills called the Salisbury Plain, began construction of Stonehenge by excavating a ditch, nearly perfectly circular and about 100 m (328 ft) in diameter. At first, this ditch was all that constituted Stonehenge. Then, by about 4,500 years ago, the people who built the monument began transporting dozens of volcanic stones (called bluestones for their slightly blue hue) from the Preseli Mountains in southwest Wales, a distance of about 200 km (125 mi) from the Salisbury Plain. The Stonehenge bluestones are a heavy, dense rock, each one weighing as much as 4,000 kg (more than 4.4 tons). They were arranged in a double half-circle located in the center of the area circumscribed by the circular ditch. Transporting stones weighing more than 8,800 lb more than 100 miles and then erecting them was no mean feat for an otherwise technologically unremarkable farming people with no machines or even draft animals. But even this impressive, early version of Stonehenge was a pale harbinger of what it was to become.

Barely a hundred years after erecting the bluestone semicircle, major construction commenced on the monumental Stonehenge we are familiar with today. Beginning around 4,400 years ago, the builders of Stonehenge began shaping and transporting 30 upright stones called **sarsens** from the area around the village of Avebury to the north, which is a distance of about 30 km

(18.6 mi). The sarsens dwarf the bluestones and are hard as iron; each sarsen is over 3 m (nearly 10 ft) tall and weighs 25,000 kg (55,000 lb). The 30 sarsens were erected in a circle 30 m (almost 100 ft) across, within and concentric with the older circular ditch.

The tops of each of the 30 roughly rectangular sarsens were precisely carved to produce two knobs, or tenons. Next, the builders of Stonehenge shaped 30 stone cap pieces, or **lintels,** of about 5,500 kg (more than 12,000 lb) each, sculpting two hollows, or mortises, on the bottom of each. Then, in an absolutely remarkable feat, they raised up these lintels and perched them on top of the sarsens, fitting the mortises on each lintel onto the tenons of two adjacent uprights (Figure 10.4). Each lintel had to be shaped precisely, curved on the exterior and interior surfaces to match the arc of the circle of the sarsens. Even a slight deviation in shape and size of any of the 30 lintels and any slight misalignment of the tenons on the sarsens or of the mortises on the lintels would have made completion of the monument impossible. What resulted was a smooth ring of massive stones, precisely positioned and joined together (Figure 10.5).

And there is more. Within the sarsen circle are five separate sets of three stones each—two uprights and one lintel. Arranged in a giant horseshoe shape, these **trilithon** uprights were the largest stones erected by the builders of Stonehenge. Each trilithon upright stands about 8 m (more than 26 ft) above the surface, with an additional 2 m (6.6 ft) of stone nestled in the chalky ground underlying the monument. The largest of the trilithon uprights weighs 45,000 kg (nearly 50 tons), and the associated lintel weighs 9,000 kg (10 tons); and remember—this 10-ton block had to be raised up to and perched precisely on the top of its 26-ft-high trilithon upright pair.

IMAGINING STONEHENGE

In a project replicating ancient technology sponsored by the PBS science series *Nova* (Page and Cort 1997), a series of experiments were conducted in an attempt to determine how Stonehenge and other ancient monuments could have been built. Two parallel sets of squared-off log beams were placed in the ground, producing a wooden trackway, and a cement trilithon upright weighing 50 tons was attached to a wooden sled that fit onto the trackway. After a bit of trial and error, a crew of about 200 volunteers was able to move the enormously heavy replica. With the help of some fundamental engineering principles reasonably within the capability of ancient people, the volunteers were able to erect the trilithon upright, setting it into a 6-ft-deep socket they had excavated in the chalky subsoil. Then, using staging, levers, counterweights, and human muscle power, they raised the 10-ton trilithon lintel up above a trilithon upright pair and positioned it firmly on top of them, attaching it by using the same mortise and tenon joinery employed by the builders of Stonehenge. Many mistakes were made along the way, but the participants

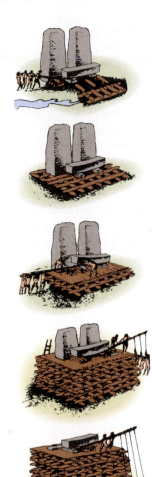

FIGURE 10.4
Artist's conception of the raising of the stone lintels that topped the sarsens and trilithons of Stonehenge by using wooden platforms.
(Department of the Environment, Crown Copyright Reserved. English Heritage.)

FIGURE 10.5

Depiction of an intact Stonehenge upon completion 4,000 years ago. Note the precision with which the enormous sarsens and trilithon uprights were connected to each other by their associated lintels.

(From Kenneth Feder, *Frauds, Myths, and Mysteries,* Fourth Edition, Mayfield Publishing Company, 2001. Reprinted with permission from The McGraw-Hill Companies.)

in this experiment showed that a group of people willing to work hard, a sensible division of labor, and an effective organization of that labor force could produce truly remarkable results in a relatively short period of time.

It could have been no different for the builders of Stonehenge and the hundreds of other stone monuments that can be found across much of Europe (Burl 1995), monuments whose primary features—being built of stone and tending to be massive—provide the name we apply to them: the **megaliths** (Figure 10.6). Consider Carnac, a less-well-known but equally impressive megalithic site located in Britanny, in northwestern France (Figure 10.7). As impressive as Stonehenge is, it consists of a total of a bit more than just 100 upright stones encompassed within a circle whose diameter is about 100 m. More than 5,000 years ago, the builders of Carnac, in contrast, constructed a far more expansive monument, positioning more than 3,000 upright stones in a series of about a dozen parallel rows, whose four primary segments together span a distance of more than 3 km (1.8 mi).

The labor involved in building Carnac is just as impressive as that which was needed in the case of Stonehenge and implies the existence of a social and political structure that could provide the organizational capacity to produce monumentally scaled construction projects and, at the same time, demanded that such projects were undertaken.

The builders of Stonehenge, Carnac, and the rest of the megalithic monuments are emblematic of a pattern we see throughout much of the world at various times after the beginning of the Neolithic. The roots of this new revolution in economic, social, and political complexity, evidenced in the archaeological record as monumental works, are the focus of this chapter.

CHRONICLE

Earlier in this book, archaeology was defined as the study of the material remains of human behavior. Most archaeologists focus on the material record—the stuff that people made and used—because these material remains are the only direct evidence we have of how people lived and what they accomplished during their lifetimes in the time

FIGURE 10.6
Stonehenge may be the best known, but it is only one of literally thousands of megalithic monuments located in western Europe. Two of the better preserved are shown here: Swinside (top) and Castlerigg (bottom), stone circles in the west of England. (K. L. Feder)

FIGURE 10.7
The megalithic site of Carnac is located on the southern coast of Brittany, in northwestern France. The site consists of four primary clusters of nearly 3,000 stones, some enormous, set in neatly parallel rows stretching across nearly 3 km (1.8 mi) of the French countryside. Clearly, the Carnac alignments required a large, coordinated, willing labor force and were far beyond what an individual family could achieve. (K. L. Feder)

before the invention of writing and the keeping of historical records. Ancient monuments such as Stonehenge and Carnac engage the archaeologist, at least in part, in the same way they engage everybody else: Very simply, they are beautiful and fascinating. Beyond this, however, anthropologists are drawn to ancient monuments not just because of their visual magnificence or enchantment but also for what they imply about the abilities of past peoples to conscript and organize the labor necessary to produce them.

SIMPLICITY AND COMPLEXITY

Most hunting-and-gathering societies organize their social, political, and economic lives at the level of the household or the family. Populations tend to be small and dispersed. Decisions are made; labor is divided, distributed, and organized; and wealth is apportioned on the basis of family relationships.

Many of you probably have been involved in a family or local community project. Perhaps you helped your parents build a storage shed for gardening tools, or maybe it was a deck added on to the back of your house; some of you may have helped set up a community garden in your neighborhood, or you assisted in cleaning up and renovating an abandoned house. The number of people involved in the project likely was small, the number of distinctly different chores or jobs in the overall project relatively few, and the task of coordinating the labor fairly straightforward. After all, organizing a labor party can be pretty simple when all the folks involved in the project are related to one another; it's usually pretty clear who the head or heads of a family are, and the task of organizing and overseeing the project usually falls to these elders.

The project becomes a little more complicated when the labor party consists of a small number of friends, acquaintances, close neighbors, or merely people who happen to live in the same community. Obviously, what's needed is some consensus about who will direct the project and which jobs will be done by whom and when. But consensus can be reached relatively easily when the group is small, the abilities of each individual are readily apparent, and there is a direct benefit for each person involved.

The project becomes far more complicated, however, when the group is large and there is no overall family or accepted community structure on which to base the coordination of a task. Remember the group of 200 volunteers who moved the single Stonehenge trilithon replica and who then raised the one lintel? They were not members of the same family or community. Of necessity, for the short period of time they participated, they had to accept the dictates of the people who organized the project. The project's organizers at least seemed to know what they were doing, and, therefore, their orders were followed. Now imagine the hundreds and even thousands of ancient farmers who built the real Stonehenge, Carnac, and the rest in fits and starts over the course of hundreds of years. In all likelihood, at any one time, many of the builders did not even know one another. There could have been no agreed-upon family head to coordinate the project, no clear sense of obligation based on kinship that convinced people to participate or follow the dictates of the family head; and there probably was not even an expectation of reciprocity, no prospect that one would get something tangible in return for participating in the project. For the decision to be made to build the monument in the first place and to conscript the labor force, to delegate tasks and coordinate all the many jobs that needed doing, there had to have been someone or, perhaps, a small group in charge. At the same time, there had to have been a social and political structure of command and an attendant process of decision making that transcended the individual household, family, or local community and that applied to the larger social group needed to accomplish the monumental task. Without such a structure, there likely would have been chaos. Chaos is the last thing needed when a large number of people are involved in a difficult and dangerous task requiring a great deal of precision.

The Origins of Complexity

In some instances, the food-producing revolution led to societies arranged in just such a way, where social, political, and economic systems were organized in a complex fashion. In these **complex societies,** authority, work, and decision making were organized not on a household or family basis but instead on the basis of a larger social group.

This shift to social, political, and economic complexity was not inevitable or universal; the archaeological record of Neolithic food producers does not reflect a pattern by which all peoples marched in lockstep toward such complexity. Instead, the ability to produce and control the production of a surplus of food, with few exceptions made possible exclusively by agriculture, made such complexity not certain but possible. In other words, where agricultural efficiency allowed just a few people to produce enough food to feed entire communities—and where these communities could greatly increase in size and density because agriculture allowed for the production of great amounts of food in a relatively small area—an enormous labor potential was released to accomplish other things, among them, construction of impressive monuments like Stonehenge. A television commercial for the agribusiness Archer Daniels Midland claimed that each American farmer in the 1990s produced enough food to feed 130 people, the vast majority of whom were free, therefore, to engage in other pursuits. On a smaller scale, some farmers of the ancient Neolithic, as a result of the agricultural richness of their region and the sophistication of their agricultural technology, similarly could feed masses of people whose labor, once appropriated and organized by an overseeing authority, could be directed to other tasks.

Why Complexity?

Why might a group of people take the road toward complexity? Why might individuals surrender some of their social, political, and economic independence and volunteer their labor to participate in a community project like the construction of a Stonehenge or a Carnac? In all likelihood, these monuments were *not* the cause of such complexity but an effect. Complex social, political, and economic structures did not develop explicitly so that people could build great and impressive monuments. It is far more probable that Neolithic people developed complex social and political structures to respond to more practical challenges where individuals gave up some of their independence and donated their labor, at least initially, to reap individual and practical benefits. For example, large-scale labor projects requiring coordination of the work of many people may have been made necessary by the need to increase agricultural output. The production of seedbeds or the construction of water-control structures (dams, canals, reservoirs) may have required complex social, political, and economic organization, at least more complex than what had sufficed previously. An external military threat may have required the organization of an army or of a construction gang to build defensive works—for example, a wall around a settlement. Even the discovery of an abundant source of an important raw material—for example, clay, stone, or metal—may have been seen as an opportunity to generate wealth or concentrate power if people organized their labor to quarry the raw material or devise ways of monopolizing it.

The notion here is that once a complex social or political structure develops to meet an immediate and practical need, that structure might not simply disappear once the threat is eliminated, the challenge answered, or the opportunity exploited. Such a structure might find other projects, not always practical ones, to devote its time to. The great monuments that dominate the archaeological record of some ancient cultures and therefore occupy the time of so many archaeologists are, in this interpretation, merely the incidental effects of the evolution of complex social, political, and economic structures that developed in response to more concrete challenges, threats, or opportunities.

A REVOLUTION IN SUBSISTENCE, A REVOLUTION IN SOCIETY

Society may become more complex when the labor of many must be organized—to prepare seedbeds, to clear forests, to control water, to build animal corrals, to construct a defensive wall—to meet the requirements of a growing population. Certain individuals, as a result of their competence or charisma, are given the authority to organize these group or communal activities. These individuals are able to organize the labor, assign tasks, divide responsibilities, direct actions, and oversee duties. Through their skills to persuade, bargain, marshal group opinion, and cajole, and even simply by the force of their will, they can get things done. They are invested not so much with power—there are no laws, police force, or army to coerce others to heed their directions—but with authority. They are good at organizing labor, keeping people happy, and successfully conducting projects that people recognize are for the good of the group. In Melanesia, such individuals are called "Big Men"; in anthropology that term is applied to individuals in any culture who perform such functions (Service 1975). When there are Big Men and some others below them who fill a limited number of specific roles in the society—in essence, people of higher status with differential access to resources—such a group is no longer egalitarian. Anthropologist Morton Fried (1967) labels these groups **rank societies.** Rather than everyone being more or less equal, a few socio-political "ranks" are filled by a relatively small number of people.

A Neolithic Base for Big Men

In some post-Pleistocene settings, the extra work involved in applying new, more intensive subsistence strategies, as organized by these newly developed leaders, substantially increased the food base. The additional labor invested in planting seedbeds, tending wild plants, or corralling wild animals created a new cultural environment in which natural selection was supplanted by artificial selection. The result was domesticated plants and animals that eventually produced far more food than was actually needed to feed even the growing Holocene human population in some areas.

Those who could control the new food surplus—redistribute it, save it for times of need, or even own it—possessed, for perhaps the first time in human history, wealth and power. To be able to redistribute excess food, reward some people and punish others, accumulate precious materials in trade, and distribute other resources—or withhold them—during lean times is to have power.

A food surplus poses the challenge of what to do with it all. To begin with, it needs to be stored. Village granaries are one solution, and their construction requires more communal labor. Once granaries are built and the grain is stored, the surplus must be protected from hungry animals, insects, and rot—not to mention greedy humans. So more communal projects are needed, more jobs are created for leaders to oversee, and there is more reinforcement for their position as leaders, as long as they are successful. Initially temporary, intended to last only until the task they were overseeing was complete, in some cases their leadership positions became permanent and even magnified.

It is expensive to build storage facilities and to protect the food. So why bother? The most obvious reason is that a surplus can help tide people over during lean times—during nongrowing seasons or during slim harvests. Plus, a food surplus can be distributed to individuals or families who have contributed significantly to the group, as a reward for hard work. Also, a food surplus can be used as wealth to obtain other valuable goods—or traded with the inhabitants of other regions for stone, metal, or other resources not locally available or accessible.

From Big Men to Chiefs

As long as such societies remain small, with Big Men managing only individual villages, the potential for complexity ordinarily is limited. As population grows, however, and as more importance is vested in the Big Man, that role may change. Anthropologist Elman Service (1975:71) refers to this as "the institutionalization of power": As the system expands geographically, group

FIGURE 10.8

Archaeological sites in western Asia where evidence of the evolution of chiefdom and early state-level societies has been found.

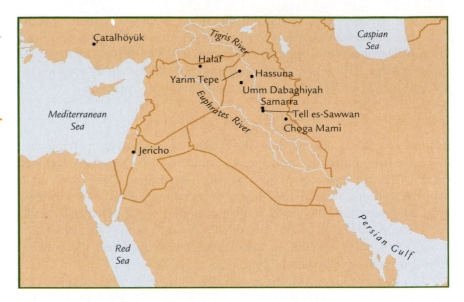

labor projects and the broader redistribution of food and other goods have a "politically integrative effect" (Service 1975:94). Social strata may develop, with the leader, or chief, and the chief's family at the top of the social pyramid. Chieftainship may be handed down from parent to child, further solidifying the position of the chief's family in the upper echelon of a stratified social system. A cadre of subordinate regional chiefs may also develop, each responsible for a local area and all reporting to the head chief. Most everyone else makes up the broad base of the social pyramid of these **chiefdoms,** giving at least some of the surplus they produce to the chiefs.

COMPLEXITY'S EARLIEST TRACES IN THE OLD WORLD

Though certainly a dramatic indicator of the capacity of chiefs to mobilize labor, Stonehenge, Carnac, and the other stone monuments of the European Neolithic are not the earliest archaeological evidence for the kind of complexity found in chiefdom societies; some archaeological evidence for nonegalitarian societies turns up soon after the development of agriculture.

Jericho

Some of the earliest evidence of large-scale communal construction and social stratification in the world can be seen deep in the sequence at a few sites in western Asia (Figure 10.8). For example, the archaeological site of Jericho, in Israel, was a village with a number of distinct features that at more than 10,000 years ago imply a movement away from the egalitarian pattern seen at other Neolithic sites (see Chapter 9). More than 9,000 years ago, the inhabi-

FIGURE 10.9
The wall at Jericho, probably built by members of an ancient chiefdom society beginning some 9,000 years ago, is among the earliest archaeological evidence in the world for construction on a monumental scale.
(© Fred Mayer/Magnum)

tants of Jericho—later memorialized in the Old Testament of the Bible—built a massive stone wall around their community (Kenyon 1954). Made of dry-laid stone, the wall was 2 m (6-1/2 ft) thick at the base and nearly 7 m (23 ft) high in places, with ramparts up to 9 m (nearly 30 ft) high (Figure 10.9). The construction of this wall required a level of coordination of labor not previously seen in the world.

Trade was an important element in the economy of early Jericho. Exotic raw materials, including Turkish obsidian, turquoise from the Sinai Peninsula, and cowrie shells from the Red Sea, are found at early levels of the site. The distribution of some of these exotic materials in human interments indicates a certain degree of social differentiation at Jericho: Whereas most burials were rather plain and undistinguished, one group of interments was set apart—the skulls were coated with a mask of clay, and the exotic cowrie shells were set into the eye sockets.

Çatalhöyük

Located in central Turkey, near the town of Çumra, the site of Çatalhöyük presents a fascinating enigma to archaeologists (Balter 1998; Hodder 2005; Mellaart 1965; Todd 1976). The oldest of the 18 occupation levels at the site dates to about 9,000 years ago, and the settlement persisted for 1,200 years. The site itself is about three times the size of Jericho, covering approximately 26 acres, and consists of what researchers have estimated to be about 2,000 densely compacted, interconnected homes within a huge, continuous structure (Figure 10.10). As Ian Hodder (2005), the director of archaeological research at the site points out, there were no streets or avenues at Çatalhöyük, and most of the houses had no ground-level entrances. Çatalhöyük's residents moved around in their community across the rooftops, and it was through openings in the roof that individuals gained entrance into their own and their neighbors' dwellings. First excavated between 1961 and 1965 by archaeologist James Mellaart, the site immediately drew worldwide attention, in part because of its scale and in part because of the fantastic works of art in the form of painted murals found on the walls of some of the excavated rooms.

Archaeology at the site recommended in 1993, led by British archaeologist Ian Hodder, and continues as an ongoing project with plans to excavate for 13 more years. The mission of these more recent excavations includes placing the site in a regional context, examining the changes in the natural environment and the domestication of plants and animals during the period between 13,000 and 7,000 years ago, investigating the ceremonial nature of the so-called shrines, and explaining the reasons why an early Neolithic complex culture developed here in the shadow of the Konya Mountains. Researchers hope that this planned 25-year project will shed light on the origins of cultural complexity in southwest Asia.

Herein rests one of the instructive enigmas of Çatalhöyük. The site is enormous; population is estimated to have been as high as 8,000 at its peak of occupation. Archaeologists initially expected that a large, dense, permanent community like Çatalhöyük could have been supported only by an intensive agricultural economy, yet archaeological evidence indicates that this dense accumulation of people was not reliant exclusively on agriculture for its subsistence. Though the inhabitants appear to have planted domesticated varieties of wheat and barley, and while they raised, primarily, sheep, goats and, to a lesser extent, cattle, much of their food was supplied by wild foods including assorted wild grasses and tubers, lentils, hackberries, acorns, and pistachios (Balter 1998) as well as wild animals including wild cattle, pigs, and horses (Hodder, 2005). Çatalhöyük seems to show us that the development of large, sedentary settlements at the end of the Pleistocene was not necessarily prefaced by the development of intensive agriculture.

Çatalhöyük was not a city but, as archaeologist Guillermo Algaze describes it, an "overgrown village" (as quoted in Balter 1998). For example, there is no public architecture, no evidence of municipal buildings, palaces, temples, or government structures; at least, none have been found in the 4% sample of the site excavated so far.

The community was architecturally undifferentiated. There were no mansions at the site, no middle-class neighborhoods, and no poor areas. In fact, all of the houses excavated to date at Çatalhöyük show very similar living quarters. Most of the rooms at the site are of a standard size: about 25 m^2 (269 ft^2). Ian Hodder suggests that the social unit at Çatalhöyük was the extended family living in four or five clusters of these rooms (Balter 1998:1443).

One of the most interesting elements at Çatalhöyük are what the original excavator thought made up a separate category he called "shrines" because of their elaborate paintings and sculptures. These have turned out, instead, to be rooms that were an integral part of family residences and in which ordinary activities like stone and bone toolmaking, as well as food preparation and consumption, and not just rituals, were carried out (Hodder and Cessford 2004). These rooms were decorated to varying degrees with paintings, often of men in leopard-skin pelts hunting animals, usually wild bulls and stags, as well as with images of leopards and vultures. Along with two-dimensional works of art, these ritual rooms were also decorated with three-dimensional sculptures affixed to the walls. These sculptures also depicted animals, most often rams and bulls. The fixation on images of wild bulls is so apparent, archaeologist Ian Hodder (2005:40) jokingly states that "in many dwellings one seems hardly able to move without facing a bull's head or painting." The bones of animals, again, especially wild bulls, are found in concentrations at Çatal-höyük, out of proportion to their likely overall contribution to the diet. These concentrations may be the remains of special, ritual feasts (Hodder 2005:40).

There is little evidence of labor specialization at the site. For example, a detailed analysis by Wendy Matthews of the mud bricks that make up the primary construction material of the community as well as the plaster used to coat the bricks shows tremendous variation (Balter 1998:1443). In other words, the evidence seems to indicate that family groups made these materials on their own; there were no specialist brick or plaster makers following standard recipes. Though many of the obsidian artifacts excavated at Çatal-höyük were very skillfully made, these too seem to have been the widespread work of families and not the products of specialist craftspeople. Hodder and his crew have found waste flakes that result from the manufacture of obsidian tools fairly evenly spread throughout the site in what they are interpreting as the family compounds represented by the clusters they have excavated (Balter 1998). This is likely an indication that lots of people, not just a handful of specialists, were making tools from the volcanic glass available locally in the Konya Mountains.

There is no separate burial ground at the site. Instead, men and women, boys and girls, were all buried beneath the floors of rooms in the village. In an extreme case, under the floor of one room located in Building 1, excavators uncovered the remains of more than 60 people. It seems likely that the inclusive demographic structure of those buried under the houses reflects a profile similar to that of those living in the houses. In other words, it seems likely that the burials were the equivalent of family plots where people related to the family who lived in the home were buried (Hodder and Cessford 2004).

Though no evidence of economic or social inequality is reflected in the burials—no large tombs or rich arrays of grave goods—one class of people was adorned to a slightly greater degree with jewelry in the form of bracelets, anklets, and necklaces of stone and bone beads. This "privileged class" was not a wealthy elite but rather babies and infants. Room burials tended to be spatially concentrated, and the wall nearest the burials was often decorated with a mural. These murals depicted various scenes: an erupting volcano, people hunting deer, headless men, leopards with women riding on their backs.

A few small sculptures have been found at Çatalhöyük. Probably the ones that have generated the most popular interest are those of what appear to be obese women, some apparently greatly pregnant and even in the process of childbirth (Figure 10.11). The original excavator, James Mellaart, labeled these fertility or mother goddesses, and though more recent analysts question this interpretation, the site has been embraced by some who believe that much of humanity went through a period in which people worshipped this goddess.

Çatalhöyük was, by all measures, a very successful village. It was home to thousands of people and endured for more than a millennium. It has long been thought that a large, dense, and long-lived community can survive only under a regime of social complexity, where there are people with the prestige,

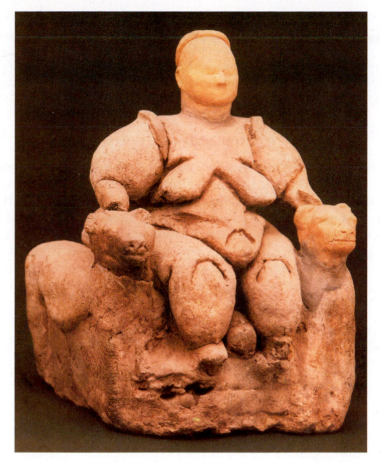

FIGURE 10.11
Called a mother goddess by some, the actual meaning of this sculpture of an obese, probably pregnant woman to the people of Çatalhöyük is unknown.

power, and position to regulate, rule, and control. But there is no archaeological evidence at Çatalhöyük for this kind of social, political, or economic differentiation: no wealthy people, no powerful individuals, no controlling group of folks who have bigger homes, who own better stuff, or who are treated differently in death. How does a very densely packed population of up to 8,000 people organize, coordinate, and regulate their activities; how does it deal with crowding, sanitation, economic necessities, and social realities without, apparently, any centralized authority, without a stratified social system with power invested in the few to maintain the orderly workings of the many? Ian Hodder and Craig Cessford (2004) recognize that this is one of the key issues that need to be addressed at Çatalhöyük.

Mesopotamia: Land Between the Rivers

The waters of the Tigris and Euphrates Rivers begin their journey to the Persian Gulf as a series of small streams in the modern nations of Turkey, Syria, Iraq, and Iran. Flowing southeast, the twin rivers are separated across their lengths by no more than about 200 km (125 mi) and commonly by less than 100 km (62 mi) until they meet and jointly flow into the Persian Gulf. Together their valleys demarcate the boundaries of the region called **Mesopotamia**— Greek for "the land between the rivers" (see Figure 10.8). These rivers played a fundamental role in producing the flat expanse of fertile soil in which the seeds of the world's first civilization were planted (see Chapter 11).

The Roots of Complexity in Southwest Asia

To the north, in the eastern horn of the Fertile Crescent, Neolithic villages had evolved in the early post-Pleistocene, where subsistence was based on wheat, barley, lentils, sheep, and goats (see Chapter 9). In northern Mesopotamia, this period is symbolized by the **Umm Dabaghiyah** culture. Villages were small, and the subsistence economy was mixed; some wheat and barley was planted, and sheep, goats, pigs, and cattle were raised (Lamberg-Karlovsky and Sabloff 1995). Of at least equal importance was the hunting of onager (wild ass); the bones of this animal made up more than two-thirds of the faunal assemblage at the site.

Beginning from this simple Neolithic base, by about 8,000 years ago, a subtle transformation toward social, political, and economic complexity is evident in the archaeological record. The sites of Hassuna, Samarra, and Halaf, each exhibiting distinctive pottery and architecture, lend their names to a chronological succession of three distinctive farming cultures (with substantial temporal overlap): **Hassunan, Samarran,** and **Halafian.**

Dating from 8000 to 7200 B.P., Hassunan sites are small, typically about 100 m (328 ft) in diameter, with populations estimated at a few hundred (Lamberg-Karlovsky and Sabloff 1995:96). These sites show clear evidence of the primacy of agriculture in the subsistence base. At the Hassunan site of Yarim Tepe, for example, there is evidence of the planting of einkorn, emmer, bread, and club wheat as well as barley, peas, and lentils (Merpert and Munchaev 1987). Although the hunting of wild animals persisted at Yarim Tepe, as evidenced by the appearance of the remains of fallow deer, gazelle, and onager, some 82% of the bones recovered archaeologically were from domesticated animals, including sheep, goat, pig, and especially cattle (Maisels 1990:112).

Though in most ways unremarkable Neolithic villages, Hassunan sites do exhibit just a few hints of what was to come in Mesopotamia in the form of architectural sophistication. There are multiroomed houses with courtyards, for example, at Yarim Tepe. But as archaeologists C. C. Lamberg-Karlovsky and Jeremy Sabloff (1995:97–98) point out, overall, Hassunan sites reflect a pattern of "rustic simplicity"; architecture was simple and homogeneous, there is no evidence of temples or palaces, few precious or luxurious items have been found, and there is no evidence of high-status burials reflective of status differentiation.

The site of Samarra and others included in the Samarran culture are located farther south, deep into the floodplain of the Tigris. These sites date to after 7500 B.P. The diets of the inhabitants of Samarran sites included the resources offered by the river, with archaeological evidence for the heavy use of fish and mussels. The inhabitants of the Samarran site of Tell es-Sawwan supplemented their diets by hunting gazelle and fallow deer, while they planted emmer and bread wheat, barley, and caper (a fruit-producing shrub; Helbaek 1965).

That agriculture was a significant part of the subsistence system at Samarra and related sites is itself informative. As pointed out by archaeologist Joan Oates (1973), here, in the central section of Mesopotamia, rainfall is meager, and an agricultural way of life would have been generally difficult and in some places impossible without the construction of irrigation canals. Direct evidence of this canal building has been found at the Samarran site of Choga Mami. Remember earlier in this chapter, when we discussed the reasons for the evolution of social, political, and economic complexity, one factor cited was the need, under certain conditions, to develop an organizational structure to conscript and coordinate labor at a level above the household, family, or local community. Control of water resources needed to expand agricultural production can be a powerful incentive for such an organizational structure to develop and an important factor in its perpetuation.

There is evidence for developing complexity in Samarran sites, including nonsubsistence-related large-scale works that would have required a level of cooperation and coordination of labor not previously seen. Tell es-Sawwan, for example, was surrounded by an enormous wall and a ditch that would have required the pooled labor of a large number of workers. Samarra has a large, buttressed fortification wall that similarly would have required a large regulated workforce.

At the same time, there is telling archaeological evidence at Samarran sites that differences in status between leaders and followers, between those giving the orders in large-scale construction projects and those following the orders, were being ritually legitimized. Some of the graves at Tell es-Sawwan are far more elaborate than those at Hassunan sites, and the differences among the burials are much greater. Although most Samarran burials are rather plain, some are filled with luxurious goods made of alabaster, turquoise, copper, greenstone, obsidian, carnelian (a lustrous, reddish-brown stone), and shell-bead necklaces and bracelets. Differences in grave wealth imply an increasing economic and social gulf among members of the society (Lamberg-Karlovsky and Sabloff 1995). Some of these raw materials must have been valuable because they were rare; required a great amount of work to locate, quarry, or work; or were available only at a great distance. Turquoise, carnelian, and obsidian, for example, are not locally available in the Samarran territory and must have been traded for by the inhabitants of Tell es-Sawwan.

It may be suggested that these more elaborate burials are the graves of a developing elite or upper class whose special treatment in death was made possible—or, perhaps, necessary—by their differentiation in life. These individuals may have been singled out to organize, coordinate, and lead large-scale construction projects such as the canals at Choga Mami or the walls at Samarra and Tell es-Sawwan. Socially, politically, and, perhaps, economically elevated in life because of the special and powerful role they played in the society, these people seem to have then been exalted in death as well through the elaboration of their graves.

A new architectural feature is also seen at Samarran sites. After about 7400 B.P., the inhabitants constructed T-shaped buildings that were used to house the community's grain. As Lamberg-Karlovsky and Sabloff (1995:100–1) point out, the communal storage of grain suggests a pooling of labor in both farming and the construction of the building where the grain was stored. Again, to accomplish the construction of communal granaries and to ensure the maintenance of the stored grain at the scale suggested by the archaeological data for Samarran sites, people needed to be organized beyond the level of the household or family, and a more complex social and political structure evolved to accomplish these tasks. This process portends what will happen a few centuries later, farther south into Mesopotamia.

Halafian sites, dating from 7500 to 6700 B.P., are not as well known as those of Hassuna or Samarra. Almost certainly the inhabitants were farmers. The residential architecture was simple, but in Halafian villages, a new architectural form is seen in nonresidential, round buildings (sometimes called **tholoi**). They seem initially to have served as communal storage buildings, like the T-shaped buildings of the Samarran culture. The round buildings at some sites contained human burials along with ceremonial objects, leading some researchers to suggest that these structures also served as burial places for important people.

These archaeological discoveries dated to the Mesopotamian Neolithic show a clearly evolutionary pattern of increasing sophistication and complexity in architecture and material culture. Communal projects and high-status burials imply the existence of chiefdoms at this point in the development of these societies. The existence of communal storage/ceremonial structures by the middle of the eighth millennium B.P. is intriguing, perhaps foreshadowing the key role of the temple in the first true civilization, the Sumerian city-states (see Chapter 11).

COMPLEXITY'S EARLIEST TRACES IN THE NEW WORLD

A pattern of increasing social, political, and economic complexity can also be seen in the New World after the development of agricultural economies. These more complex societies developed, almost certainly, completely independently from the sequence in the Old World, albeit usually at a later date (see "Issues and Debates" in this chapter). An agricultural economy that was based on the cultivation of corn, beans, and squash and included a host of other do-

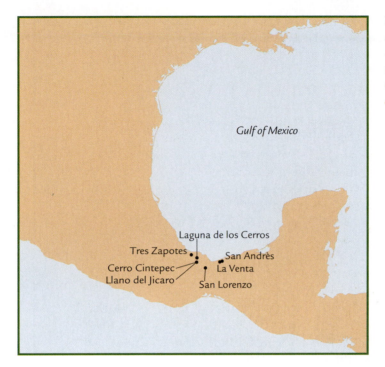

FIGURE 10.12
Archaeological sites in Mesoamerica where evidence of the development of complexity has been found.

mesticates was the key to the social, political, and economic complexity that developed in the New World as seen in Mesoamerica and South America (Figures 10.12 and 10.13).

The Olmec

Small agricultural communities had been developing in Mesoamerica since about 5,000 years ago (see Chapter 9). It seems as though a geographically expansive pattern of small, egalitarian, and independent farming villages located along the Gulf Coast tropical lowlands, particularly in the Mexican states of Tabasco and Veracruz, evolved into a pattern of more closely interconnected and complexly structured communities sometime after 3,250 years ago (Diehl 1989, 2004).

The complexity of the social, political, and economic order, as well as a pattern of a shared religious expression seen across a fairly broad geographic expanse, is reflected in the archaeological record by a constellation of common art motifs and monumental architectural patterns not previously seen in the New World. The motifs and patterns constitute what archaeologists label **Olmec** (Sharer and Grove 1989). The Olmec pattern includes several elements: depictions of a half-human, half-jaguar god; the production of jade sculptures; iron-ore mirrors; the construction of expansive platforms of

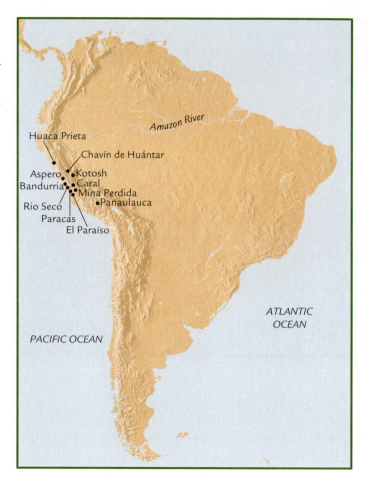

earth; the construction of earthen pyramids; and the carving of huge basalt boulders into the form of human heads—perhaps actual depictions of some of the regional chiefs.

The Evolution of Complexity   The Olmec heartland, located between the Tuxtla Mountains to the west and the tropical lowlands of the Chontalpa to the east, is a vast and richly varied region of uplands, estuaries, and floodplains. Population growth facilitated by the abundant and diverse habitats of the Olmec region may be part of the explanation for how and why complex societies developed here. Some places in the lowlands offered particularly rich farmland. In the tropical lowlands of the Mexican Gulf Coast, the richest agricultural lands can be found along the natural levees produced by rivers that flow through it. Archaeologist Richard Diehl (2004:29) characterizes the location of San Lorenzo, the earliest Olmec city, as "one of the best pieces of real estate in the Olmec world." As he points out, the main portion of the settlement is located on a high, dry terrace that would have remained so even during times of severe flooding in its flood-prone, tropical rainforest habitat. While protected from the ravages of flooding, the presence of freshwater springs high up on the terrace meant the residents would never be lacking for drinking water. At the same time, San Lorenzo is positioned close to extremely fertile, agriculturally productive river levee soils and a host of important resources including sandstone and limestone for construction. Furthermore, the location of the community in close proximity to the confluences of a number of watercourses would have allowed its residents to monitor and, perhaps, control the flow of traffic and attendant commerce throughout the central area of the Olmec heartland.

The richness of the farmland and the wealth of food sources available to the Olmec within their home territory is made clear in the archaeological record of the San Andrés site in the eastern portion of the Olmec realm. There, remains of agricultural produce, including maize, manioc, beans, sunflower, corozo palm nuts, and cacao, have been found (Diehl 2004:85). The remains of another domesticated food source was also recovered at San Andrés: dog. The bones of domesticated dog with clear evidence of butchery were recovered in abundance at the site. The diet of the inhabitants at San Andrés was further supplemented with wild foods, including clam, turtle, catfish, gar, snapper, crocodile, and deer.

Perhaps, as archaeologist Richard Diehl (1989) suggests, population grew in particularly rich areas like San Lorenzo and San Andrés, and an increasingly complex pattern of social organization and political control, of necessity, evolved to maintain order. An elite class that could control people, organize their labor, and dominate trade was the result. These developing elites—perhaps initially Big Men and then chiefs—could mobilize the large regional populations to produce monumental works that might further legitimize their elevated social and economic status (Lowe 1989). At the same time, the patchiness of resource distribution rendered other areas of the Olmec heartland uniquely attractive and valuable as well. The estuarine region provided rich coastal resources, while the mountains provided a valuable source of volcanic rock for toolmaking and monument construction (Grove 1996). People living in proximity to these resource-privileged areas may have been able to monopolize important resources and elevate their own status relative to the people who had to come to them for their supply of those valuable commodities.

Olmec Regal-Ritual Cities   Those initially small farming villages that were located on the best farmlands or in those areas most accessible to valuable resources became regionally significant as the residences of a developing elite class of people. Two such communities, La Venta in Tabasco and San Lorenzo in Veracruz, were settled initially nearly 3,650 years ago. A third, Laguna de los Cerros, also in Veracruz, was settled soon thereafter. These three villages became more than just farming settlements. Beginning first at San Lorenzo at about 3,200 years ago, by 2800 B.P. at La Venta, and then at Laguna de los Cerros, they became political, economic, social, and religious focal points and, in turn, the most powerful settlements in the realm of the Olmec.

San Lorenzo and La Venta have been characterized as **Regal-Ritual Centers** (Diehl 2004). At its peak, the center of San Lorenzo covered an area of about 7 km^2 (2.7 mi^2); La Venta was less than 30% the size of San Lorenzo, covering about 2 km^2 (a little more than 0.75 mi^2). Though often called "cities," these differed from our modern concept of an urban center primarily because they appear to have been only modestly populated. It is very difficult to suggest an actual size, but, in all likelihood, the populations of most Olmec centers did not exceed a thousand, including the ruler and his family, an elite class likely related to the ruler, artisans who served the elite, and a cohort of farmers. San Lorenzo, the largest Regal-Ritual Center, may have had a population of a few thousand. Most of what transpired in these Regal-Ritual Centers concerned the religious and political functions of the local polity.

Archaeologist David Grove (1996) points out that each of the Olmec Regal-Ritual Centers was uniquely positioned to exploit a particular set of natural resources and to, in turn, provide them to the rest of the Olmec domain. At the western edge of the Olmec heartland, Laguna de los Cerros is located next to the Tuxtla Mountains with their rich supply of the volcanic rock basalt at the Cerro Cintepec outcrop. In the center of the Olmec territory was San Lorenzo, located in a broad topographic basin with extraordinarily rich alluvial soil, crossed by the Coatzacoalcos River, through which raw materials and finished goods were traded across the Olmec realm. As noted previously the residents of San Lorenzo, therefore, were geographically positioned to control the flow of these materials through the Olmec heartland. La Venta, at the eastern margin, was located closest to the rich estuary habitat and its resources of rubber, salt, and cacao—the source for chocolate (Grove 1996).

The ability of the Olmec rulers to conscript and control the labor of a large population is evident in the archaeological record. For example, the Olmec moved enormous amounts of earth to construct platforms and pyramids and even to modify the landscape of their settlements. San Lorenzo is situated on a natural topographic eminence that had been added to and flattened by the inhabitants. It is estimated that the top 9 m (10 ft) of the plateau on which the community is located is artificial (Figure 10.14).

Perhaps the most striking of the Olmec sculpted works are the colossal boulders of basalt they carved into the representations of the heads of their rulers (Figure 10.15). Altogether, 17 of these enormous basalt sculptures have been found throughout the Olmec heartland. Ten of the heads were found at San Lorenzo and four at La Venta. Additionally, two were located at Tres Zapotes and one, the largest yet found, was found at La Cobata. They range in height from a little less than 1.5 m (5 ft) to more than 3.3 m (11 ft); the largest weighs more than 18,000 kg (40,000 lb). As David Grove indicates, these individualized depictions "glorified the rulers while they were alive, and commemorated them as revered ancestors after their death" (1996).

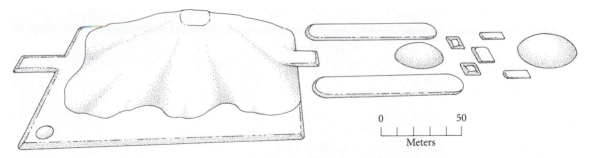

0   50

Meters

FIGURE 10.14
Layout of the Olmec capital of San Lorenzo with its major earthen mound and associated earthworks.

Monumental undertakings reflect the Olmec's growing ability to command and organize the labor of a large number of people, a characteristic typical of chiefdom societies. The artificial platform constructed at La Venta, for example, contained more than 2 million m^3 (70 million ft^3) of earth and is more than 32 m (105 ft) high. Many tons of basalt slabs were used to construct an elaborate water-supply system, now shown by excavations at San Lorenzo to have served as part of an aqueduct, providing drinking water to residents (Grove 1996). As indicated, the volcanic rock used to build the aqueduct as well as the raw material for the carved heads was obtained from the Tuxtla Mountains. A large quarry found at Llano del Jicaro, only about 7 km (4 mi) from Laguna de los Cerros, almost certainly was controlled by the elite at this Olmec center. This quarry is more than 80 km (50 mi) from San Lorenzo, yet large amounts of basalt were transported there, much of it by river. The movement of large quantities of this stone—and the enormous size of the boulders intended for the stone head sculptures—over such a great distance is another indicator of the ability of the Olmec chiefs to mobilize and manage the labor of a great mass of people.

The Olmec Regal-Ritual Centers were, effectively, the capitals of geographically broad regional polities that included communities which, together, possessed a population numbering in the thousands. Each Regal-Ritual Center was located at the hub of the religious, social, economic, and political activities of these people (Diehl 2004).

Archaeologists attempt to reveal the interconnectedness of communities in a region by tracing common artifact styles, shared ways of making things, raw materials, and collective patterns of behavior that translate into the material, archaeological record. The widespread appearance of ceramic types that originated at San Lorenzo suggests that it was the dominant player in an extensive network of dozens of communities within an area of more than 600 km^2 (more than 230 mi^2) (Figure 10.16). San Lorenzo was surrounded by and closely related to what appears to have been four smaller, secondary centers, each of which also contained ritual objects similar to, though not nearly as many nor as impressive as those found at San Lorenzo. Within the aforementioned 600-km^2 area were an additional 50 farming villages of various

FIGURE 10.15

This enormous basalt sculpture presents a portrait of an individual presumed to have been a ruler of the Olmec Regal-Ritual Center of La Venta. One of the larger of the 17 such sculptures found within the Olmec homeland, this example is a little less than 2 m (about 6 ft) tall and about 1.5 m (5 ft) across. The source for the basalt from which this sculpture was produced is located more than 80 km (50 mi) from La Venta.

(Danny Lehman/Corbis)

sizes, all of which appear to have been tied to San Lorenzo by a common pottery style and thus were also likely in the San Lorenzo orbit. Finally, in this same area, about 150 smaller-still agricultural hamlets and isolated farming homesteads have been located. The large, dispersed population in the villages and hamlets must have supplied most of the food for the political and religious elites living at San Lorenzo. This same population provided the labor necessary to construct the pyramids and platforms that mark the site, as well as the strong backs to transport the heavy building and sculptural raw material that so characterize San Lorenzo.

And San Lorenzo is characterized by a large number of deeply impressive works of art on a monumental as well as smaller scale. Archaeologists have recovered 124 massive stone sculptures at the site, ranging in mass from a few hundred to a stupendous 25,000 kg (about 28 tons).

Ninety smaller stone sculptures of various semiprecious stones have been found at La Venta. Each one is, by itself, a splendid work of art but, even more impressively, they were commonly found in clusters, ritual offerings depicting scenes of Olmec life. In one of the most famous such caches, the jade and serpentine sculptures of 16 men were found standing in a vaguely circular configuration, all facing toward a center point with six additional polished upright stones in a semicircle around them (Figure 10.17). The San Lorenzo and La Venta sculptures of whatever scale were certainly the works of true artists, specialists who produced them at the behest of the religious and ruling elite.

As seen with the evolution of complex societies in Mesopotamia, the growing authority of leaders in Olmec society is reflected in the archaeological record of their burials. At La Venta, for example, one ruler or chief was

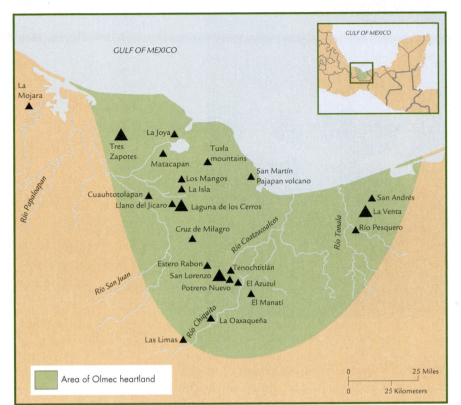

FIGURE 10.16
Locations of major Olmec sites, including the four recognized Regal-Ritual Centers: La Venta, Tres Zapotes, San Lorenzo, and Laguna de los Cerros. Sixteen of the seventeen known large basalt head ruler portraits (see Figure 10.15) were found in these Regal-Ritual Centers.

FIGURE 10.17
These splendid Olmec figurines found at La Venta were made of jade and serpentine. They were discovered just as displayed here, with a central figure carved in stone encircled by the other individuals. The figurines are between 15 and 25 cm (6 and 10 in.) in height. (© Boltin Picture Library/Bridgeman Art Library)

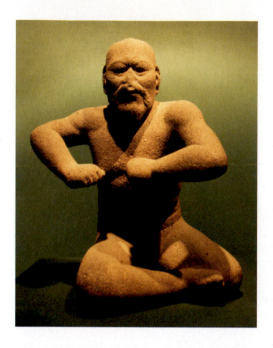

buried in a sandstone sarcophagus carved into an elaborate depiction of a caiman (a Central and South American crocodile). Most Olmec rulers were similarly interred, with many beautifully rendered artworks, including jewelry, sculptures, and celts, many of them carved of highly polished jade or greenstone (Figure 10.18).

What Was Olmec?   Olmec can be interpreted as a common religious iconography—a standardized set of visual images—that provided ideological and symbolic support for the sociopolitical system. The shared elements of Olmec religious iconography may have served to unify the large populations living around each of the ceremonial centers into politically unified chiefdoms.

This commonality of religious expression and artistic depiction integrating large populations into individual Olmec chiefdoms, however, apparently did not lead to the geographically broader political integration among the various Olmec centers (Diehl 1989). There is no evidence for a single, overarching Olmec "nation" or political unit. It appears, instead, that each of the largest and most elaborate Olmec sites especially San Lorenzo and La Venta represents the center of a separate chiefdom, politically autonomous but linked by a common iconography.

The spread of Olmec iconography across a wide swath of Mesoamerica can be seen between 3,000 and 2,800 years ago. At this time, Olmec-like imagery appeared in El Salvador, Honduras, Costa Rica, and Guatemala, as well as the highlands of Mexico (the Valley of Mexico and Oaxaca).

What does this spread imply about the impact of Olmec on the development of civilization in Mesoamerica as a whole? Michael Coe (1968) has referred to Olmec as the "mother culture" of Mesoamerica and in his current synthesis of the Olmec, Diehl (2004) largely agrees. Recent analysis of the primacy and subsequent spread of Olmec-style artifacts lends support to this notion. For example, San Lorenzo ceramics have been traced far beyond the confines of its local, 600-km^2 sphere of influence. Neutron activation analysis, a technique discussed in Chapter 2 that is useful in identifying the sources of raw materials from which artifacts were made, was applied to 725 Mesoamerican archaeological ceramics samples (Blomster et al. 2005). The researchers collected more than 600 raw clay samples from San Lorenzo, Oaxaca, and the Basin of Mexico and compared their elemental composition to the archaeological ceramics. The results were absolute and definitive; pottery bearing typical San Lorenzo Olmec motifs and made from clay traceable to San Lorenzo has been found throughout Mesoamerica, including ancient sites in the Basin of Mexico, Guerrero, the Valley of Oaxaca, Chiapas, as well as the Pacific coast. None of the ceramics from San Lorenzo were made from the clays found outside of its local area. The movement of clay and ideas about ceramic design all seem to have moved out from San Lorenzo. This lends strong support for Coe's and Diehl's view of Olmec as the original source of Mesoamerican civilization, to be discussed in more detail in Chapter 13.

Excavations in 1997 and 1998 at the Olmec site of San Andrés have revealed what may be the earliest evidence of writing in the New World (Pohl, Pope, and von Nagy 2002). Located just 5 km (a little more than 3 mi) from La Venta, archaeologists at San Andrés recovered fragments of a greenstone plaque with what appear to be simple **glyphs** of some kind. Even more impressive at the site was a carved stone cylinder depicting a bird. Markings found on the cylinder are similar enough to later Olmec glyphs to be read by those familiar with that language as a king's name—"King 3 Ajaw," which is also the date of his birth (Pohl, Pope, and von Nagy 2002:1986). The glyphs on the cylinder are connected to the bird's beak by two carved lines in what appears to be the Olmec equivalent of a comic strip thought balloon. In other words, it appears as if the Olmec at San Andrés were showing that the bird was speaking the name of a king. Both of the San Andrés artifacts with apparent writing were recovered from the same stratigraphic level at the site; that layer has been radiocarbon-dated to about 2,600 years ago.

South America

Until recently, the Norte Chico region of coastal Peru was not thought to have been a terribly fruitful place to investigate the origins of complexity in the New World (Mann 2005). After all, the oldest cities and first evidence of what is commonly called "civilization" in the Old World (Chapters 11 and 12), have been found in association with the extraordinarily productive habitats provided

FIGURE 10.19

This aerial view of Caral in Peru shows the monumental scale of pyramid construction undertaken by the inhabitants. The site's age of more than 4,500 years places it at the very beginning in the New World of monumental architecture and likely the complex society necessary for its construction. (© AP/Wide World Photos)

by major river valleys—the Nile, the Tigris and Euphrates, the Indus, and the Yang-tse. Norte Chico is marked by only a handful of relatively small rivers—Rio Fortaleza, Rio Pativilca, Rio Huaura, and Rio Supe—and, furthermore, is one of the driest places on earth, with a mean annual rainfall of no more than about 5 cm (2 in.). Agriculture is exceptionally difficult under these conditions and Old World evidence—as well as evidence from elsewhere in the New World—has long supported the idea that complexity develops where the environment allows for a rich agricultural subsistence base capable of producing an enormous food surplus. Nevertheless, a series of archaeological surveys have shown that Norte Chico river valleys produced what some are calling the oldest evidence of the development of complexity in the New World (Haas et al. 2004; Mann 2005). Located in Rio Supe, Caral is an example of the early development of complex societies in Norte Chico.

Caral   Seen from the air, Caral appears ancient and alien, a forbidden, almost extraterrestrial landscape of weathered pyramidal mounds, decayed house remains, and sunken circular plazas (Figure 10.19). Yet here, archaeologists have found the earliest material remnants in South America, and, in fact, in the New World, of cultural complexity—a complexity characterized by social stratification, economic inequality, and a level of monumental architecture possible only by the organization and coordination of a substantial labor force (Solis, Haas, and Creamer 2001).

Located in the Supe River Valley, about 23 km (14 mi) from the Pacific coast and 200 km (about 124 mi) north of Lima, the modern capital of Peru, Caral was the capital of a complex society that developed in western South America more than 4,500 years ago. The site covers more than 160 acres and includes an enormous earth and stone "truncated," or flat-topped, pyramid—the Pirámide Mayor—which stands more than 18 m (60 ft) tall, covers an area of about 24,000 m^2 (6 acres), and contains 200,000 m^3 (7 million ft^3) of river cobbles and cut stone fill, all moved and mounded up by human effort, one basket load at a time (Solis, Haas, and Creamer 2001:723). Imagine a structure 265 feet long, 265 feet wide, and nearly 100 feet tall, produced entirely by human effort, without mechanical assistance, and you have an idea of the monumental size of Pirámid Mayor at Caral.

Pirámide Mayor looms over the site, but it is not the only monumental structure produced by the inhabitants. Five other smaller pyramids demarcate the margins of a rectangular plaza, perhaps the social and spiritual center of the community. Alignments of numerous other smaller mounds and two large, circular plazas were also built by the site's inhabitants.

Residential complexes in which the individuals of the community lived provide evidence for a substantial population segregated by economic distinctions. The site's excavators have noted that each of the six major pyramids at the site are associated with elaborate complexes of finely constructed rooms made with substantial stone walls covered in plaster. Elsewhere at the site were other residential areas characterized by less substantially made structures of wooden poles, cane, and mud. The more elaborately made buildings were likely the residences of Caral's elite class; the wood and mud structures were the homes of the community's commoners (Pringle 2001).

Caral is ancient, impressive, and unexpected, but it is not alone. Jonathan Haas, Winifred Creamer, and Alvaro Ruiz (2004) have continued to investigate the river valleys of Norte Chico and have found substantial additional evidence of widespread cultural complexity dating to the period beginning about 5,200 years ago and reaching a peak between 4,500 and 4,000 years ago. Hass and his colleagues found 20 major sites in the Supe, Pativilca, and Fortaleza valleys. These sites reflect a common pattern of substantial populations; the construction of impressively large, stone structures; terraced, flat-topped pyramids that served as the bases for buildings; and expansive, sunken circular plazas as large as 40 m (131 ft) across. Though Pirámid Mayor at Caral is the largest of the Norte Chico structures, it is not the only monumentally scaled pyramid; the next largest has a volume of more than 100,000 m^3 (3 million ft^3).

The diet of the Norte Chico inhabitants was diverse and eclectic. Not surprisingly, agriculture made a significant contribution to subsistence. Excavators found evidence of a broad mix of domesticated plant foods including squash, beans, chili peppers, guava, lucuma (a round, green fruit), pacay (a sweet and smooth-textured legume), and camote (sweet potato) (Haas et al. 2004:1022). With no domesticated animals, Norte Chico residents obtained large quantities of shellfish, notably mussels and clams, from the coast, indicating that Norte Chico was not alone in its development but relied on contact and trade with populations on the coast who themselves would be developing increasingly complex social and political structures soon after.

To produce the monumental structures seen at Caral and the other Norte Chico sites, there must have been a large resident population, a complex social organization to coordinate and control the labor needed to produce the monuments, and a productive subsistence base to put food on the tables of those too involved in construction to produce food on their own. But the dry desert that has long characterized Norte Chico was not at all conducive to agriculture. There is no substantial plain subject to annual flooding and natural rejuvenation that would have rendered agriculture feasible at the scale necessary to feed a population large enough to have constructed the monuments at Caral. The site's researchers recognize that it would have been possible to produce enough food to feed all of Norte Chico residents only by the application of irrigation technology. Certainly, a labor force capable of building the pyramids seen in the Norte Chico sites would have been able to dig and maintain canals. In fact, the necessity of canal construction to expand the subsistence base to feed a growing population might have served as the overriding rationale for people to have worked cooperatively in the first place, subjugating themselves to an organizing authority and resulting, ultimately, in the social distinctions and economic inequality evidenced at Norte Chico.

The Push Toward Complexity   West of Caral, on the Pacific coast, complex societies were also developing. Between 5500 and 5000 B.P., coastal villages that had increased in size and subsistence expanded to include domesticates such as gourds, squash, and kidney and lima beans (Pineda 1988). At this time at sites like Huaca Prieta and Paracas, there is some evidence of increasing social complexity. While most residential buildings at these sites are quite similar in size and form, other structures are a bit larger and more ambitious. Small pyramids and platforms are included in this category.

After 5000 B.P., these specialized structures became increasingly large and sophisticated. Large pyramids were built, dominating the sites of Bandurria, Rio Seco, and Aspero (Pineda 1988:76). At these sites, there also is evidence of a developing pattern of social stratification in the form of differing house sizes. Aspero, for example, is a large site, covering 30 acres. There are seven large and six smaller ceremonial mounds at Aspero, on top of which were constructed small temples that contained human burials. Around the mounds were open plazas and artificial terraces. A large resident population exploited the rich resources of the coast.

The first evidence of the use of metals in South America dates to about 3100 B.P. Among a series of six early ceremonial centers with earthen pyramids and mounds located in Peru's Lurin Valley, Mina Perdida has produced gold and copper artifacts (Burger and Gordon 1998). No smelting or casting was done at this early date. Both the gold and copper had been found in a natural, nearly pure or "native" state and then hammered into thin foils. The existence of substantial earthworks along with fine metalwork at Mina Perdida is clear evidence of increasing complexity in the Andean region at this time. There is no obvious archaeological evidence before 3000 B.P. at these Lurin Valley sites for social stratification or wealth differentiation. The construction of large earthworks implies the existence of chiefs, but these chiefs were treated no differently—their residences were no larger and their graves no more elaborate—than those who followed them.

Though the precise process is not at all clear, it seems that the development of irrigation technology, population growth, and movement into the interior was accompanied by social differentiation. Some villages like Kotosh and Chavín de Huántar were strategically located along natural trade routes between the coast to the west and the uplands to the east, and trade seems to have played an important role in the developing social complexity at these sites. The focus on monumental architecture associated with ceremonial structures like pyramids is a good indication that the newly evolved social and economic power, perhaps as a result of trade, was focused on a religious elite class who could control the increasingly complex economy.

As long as this pattern of development was restricted to the rather small, individual river valley systems that cross Peru, sociopolitical differentiation could not become too marked. There simply were not enough resources and wealth for the developing elites to monopolize to enable them to attain the status of Egyptian pharaohs or Mesopotamian city-state kings (see Chapter 11). But sometime after 3000 B.P., populations started growing and their needs expanded beyond the narrow confines of their own particular river valleys. In the view of archaeologist Tom Patterson (1993), contact and competition among the political entities within individual valleys was a significant factor in the development of Andean civilization.

Cultural Convergence: Chavin   About 3,000 years ago, an apparently unifying religion with a distinct and striking art style began to spread across the previously highly regionalized valleys. Called **Chavin** and initially centered at the site of Chavín de Huántar, like Olmec it seems to have served to bring together a large and geographically broad population under the banner of a single religious, if not political, entity. Archaeologist Richard Burger (1988:111) calls Chavin an empire, but a "religious," not a political, one. The Chavin art style that accompanied the religion included the depiction of felines (possibly jaguars), raptorial birds, snakes, the caiman (a South American crocodile), and the so-called Staff God—a presumed deity holding two rods or staffs (Figure 10.20). Accompanying Chavin artistic and religious expression were several technological innovations that further served as unifying elements during this period of Peruvian prehistory. Beautiful and intricately woven textiles displaying common Chavin motifs were woven with the hairs of domesticated camelids. Across the broad and expanding region where Chavin motifs spread, hammered gold objects and three-dimensional objects made from joined sheets of gold are also found. Metallurgists producing Chavin motifs also used such production techniques as soldering and sweat welding as well as the decoration technique of repoussé. Silver-gold alloys, a hallmark of South American metallurgy, are first seen in Chavin artifacts.

Chavín de Huántar itself was strategically placed along a natural route of trade and transportation between the highland valleys, the Peruvian coast, and the interior tropical forest (Burger 1995). As a result, it likely was a magnet for excess wealth generated by trade. A unifying art-religion would certainly have

FIGURE 10.20
Some of the distinctive iconography of the Chavin art style is shown in this depiction of the staff god.
(Gordon Willey)

served to encourage this trade among previously very diverse groups. As archaeologist Karen Olsen Bruhns (1994) indicates, the site began about 3,000 years ago as a ceremonial center with a small population of residents, serving at least in part to facilitate trade between disparate groups living in different habitats, newly combined through a common mode of religious expression. By a little after 2500 B.P., however, this ceremonial center had grown to become one of the earliest urban centers in South America: a bustling town, with a large, dense population spread out across about 100 acres. Houses and neighborhoods were constructed according to a plan, a drainage system was in place, and temples and huge food-storage facilities served the residents.

Perhaps as river valleys filled up with population, the need to obtain resources from outside these valleys increased. Places like Chavín de Huántar that were propitiously placed took advantage of this increased need by regulating the trade that had to pass through their territories. The Chavin art style spreading a common and unifying religion initially simply served to facilitate trade among various groups, but it ultimately brought people closer together in all spheres, spreading technological innovations as well as new social patterns. Those in a position to control trade and information as it flowed through this coalescing system became the first members of a differentiated class of people who lived in larger houses, spent their time propitiating the Chavin gods, and monopolized certain key symbols of power in the developing civilization.

IS COMPLEXITY INEVITABLE?

ISSUES AND DEBATES

This chapter has focused on the development of social, political, and economic complexity in the Neolithic. Remember that the evolution of complex societies, though certainly facilitated by the development of food-producing economies, was not the inevitable outcome of this shift in subsistence. The capacity to produce a surplus of food and the attendant ability to free a proportion of the population from subsistence activities in no way guarantees that a society will elect to do so.

In some cases, the first steps along a pathway toward intensifying the food quest, organizing labor beyond the family or local community, and subjugating individual needs for the perceived needs of the group lead to an ever-intensifying spiral of escalating economic differentiation and inequality, increasing and solidifying social stratification, and growing distinctions in terms of the power wielded by individuals or families over everyone else. But this is not an inevitable trajectory. Food production and the surplus it makes possible merely open a door; other factors come into play in a society's determination whether or not to pass through that portal and follow a pathway that leads to a fundamental change in how the society is organized. In some cases, the decision to do so may be born of necessity. The need to produce more food to feed a burgeoning population or to respond to an external military

FIGURE 10.21

A ghoulish figure set into the wall of the Old Temple at the site of Chavín de Huántar is one of several that gaze down upon visitors to the site. To the rear of the heads were carved tenons that fit into sockets in the wall of the temple.
(Copyright © Ric Ergenbright/ Corbis)

threat may require the development of a new kind of societal structure in response. In other instances, the opportunity offered by a locally available resource may provide a source of wealth that can be more efficiently exploited by a complex social and political structure. The point is, the shift to complexity was neither universal nor inevitable.

**CASE STUDY
CLOSE-UP**

It must have been an imposing sight for pilgrims visiting Chavín de Huántar—and that almost certainly was the intention. The two major trails that led to the site along the Huachecsa and Mosna Rivers led not to the front entrance of the Old Temple but rather to the back sides of the monumental, U-shaped structure. At the end of either trail, visitors found themselves at the base of a massive, towering four-story wall of stone. Its setting and appearance were almost certainly intended as a message to all who saw it: Here is the seat of our power, the center of our might (Burger 1995).

The Old Temple was a mammoth construction project, with thousands upon thousands of granite, sandstone, and limestone blocks laid on each other in thin courses. The temple spread out across a broad area, covering more than 7,100 m² (nearly 77,000 ft²; more than 1.75 acres). Different segments of the temple differed somewhat in height; the top platform stood between 14 and 16 m (about 46 and 53 ft) above the surface. At about 10 m (33 ft) above the ground, at 3-m (10-ft.) intervals, the builders of the Old Temple had inserted a series of striking, carved anthropomorphic (humanlike) and zoomorphic (animal-like) stone heads (Figure 10.21). At the back of each of the heads, carvers had made tenons that fit into sockets made in the wall behind them. Twice the size of actual human heads, snarling, with exposed fangs

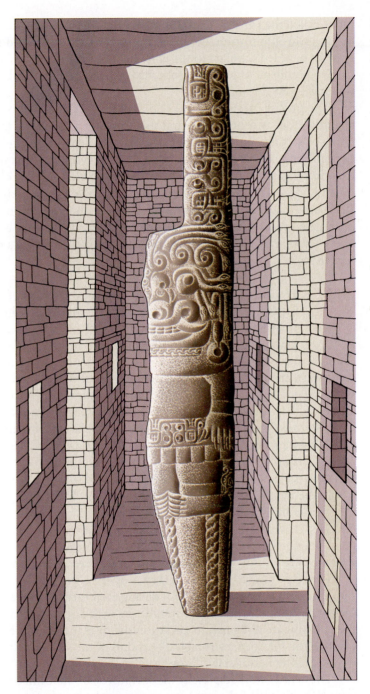

FIGURE 10.22
Deep within the Old Temple at the site of Chavín de Huántar is the famous Lanzón carving, a fantastic creature—perhaps the chief god of the Chavin pantheon—carved from a single piece of granite.
(From G. Willey. 1971. *Introduction to American Archaeology: South America.* Englewood Cliffs, N.J.: Prentice Hall. Reprinted with permission of the author)

and contorted faces, these stone heads seem to float in the air, gazing down on visitors, expressing the power and authority of the Chavin gods.

At the center of the Old Temple, ensconced in a tall chamber at the end of a dark corridor, stands a 4.5-m (almost 15-ft) tall upright monolith of granite today called the Lanzón. Onto the shaft of granite has been carved the shape of an anthropomorphic deity (Figure 10.22). The size and setting of the Lanzón have led scholars to the conclusion that this is the chief god in the Chavin pantheon of powerful supernatural beings, the god that the pilgrims may have come to worship.

The precise meaning of the Old Temple has been lost to us. Perhaps its alignment has astronomical significance, the open section of the U facing the rising or setting of an important set of stars. Maybe the shape and setting of the building conveyed some symbolic message to those who followed the Chavin religion, a message we may never be able to comprehend. But this much is clear: The Old Temple was made possible by the social and political structures that characterize complex societies; and at the same time, it communicated to all who saw it the power of the Chavin gods as well as those upon whom they looked down with favor. It must have been a powerful message indeed.

VISITING THE PAST

Precisely because one of the material correlates of complexity so often is monumental construction, some of the sites discussed in this chapter are, millennia after they were built, still impressive places to visit and investigate. There is no better example of this than the stone monuments of western Europe. Although Stonehenge is, in some ways, the most impressive of these, it is but one of literally hundreds of stone henges, circles, uprights, and **dolmens** (large stones raised up and balanced on three or more uprights) that can be seen throughout western Europe. To find them in westernmost Europe, one needs little more than some sturdy hiking boots and Aubrey Burl's (1995) *A Guide to the Stone Circles of Britain, Ireland, and Brittany,* with its photographs and detailed directions and even reviews of the various monuments and their settings.

In the massiveness of the component stones of Stonehenge and the other megalithic monuments and in the precision with which their stones were quarried, transported, erected, and, in some cases, conjoined, these monuments engage us in the present on an emotional level and convey in a visceral way a feeling for the kind of society that must have evolved to produce it.

The site of Çatalhöyük in Turkey is open to the public year-round. The site's researchers recommend a visit during their excavation season in the summer, and there is a visitor's center at the site with displays of artifacts recovered there. If you are not going to Turkey in the near future, you can visit the site through the Internet; a virtual walk-around of the site including a stop at the visitor's center is available at http://catal.arch.cam.ac.uk/visit/visitEN.html.

The artistic work, especially the sculptures, of the Olmec is tremendously impressive; many of the most impressive examples can be seen in museums located throughout Mexico. The Parque La Venta Olmec Museum at Villahermosa has a sculpture garden with 28 Olmec works, including a number of the large, carved heads. Other Olmec heads along with more of their finest artwork can be seen at the Xalapa Museum in Veracruz, Mexico.

SUMMARY

In several regions in both the Old and New Worlds, following the shift from a subsistence strategy based on wild, collected foods to one at least partially reliant on domesticated, produced foods, some societies began to shift from a simple social and political organization based on the household or family to a more complex framework. In some cases, the shift to complexity was fueled by the need to organize the labor of a large group of people to increase food production—for instance, to construct water-control facilities. In other instances, the development of a social and political structure to organize and coordinate monumental projects was necessitated by some external threat—for example, the construction of a defensive wall around a community. In still other cases, the evolution of an organizational framework beyond the household or family may have come about as the result of the unique opportunities offered by a particularly rich habitat or proximity to and monopolization of a valued resource.

Whatever the particular case, the results of this shift to more complex social, political, and economic life and the shift to rank societies and chiefdoms are evidenced in the archaeological record by the monumental works made possible by large groups of organized people—Stonehenge is but one example. In some cases, the shift to complexity and the creation of ranks or classes are also evidenced in the archaeological record by the appearance of burials differentiated by the inclusion of precious raw materials and finely made works of art.

The earliest examples of the development of complexity in the Old World are seen at Jericho in Israel and Çatalhöyük in Turkey. Soon thereafter, this complexity can be seen developing in Mesopotamia. The earliest example in Mesoamerica is seen along the Mexican Gulf Coast among the people called Olmec.

The earliest archaeological evidence for the development of complexity in South America is seen at about 4,500 years ago in Peru at the site of Caral, characterized by a cluster of enormous, flat-topped pyramids, plazas, and substantial residential complexes. By 3,000 years ago, the Chavin style developed as a regional iconography, a religious and artistic approach that served to unify a broad array of societies, setting the stage for the later development of regional states.

TO LEARN MORE

Technical Summaries

The best summary of the original archaeological work conducted at Çatalhöyük in the 1960s is James Mellaart's *Earliest Civilizations of the Near East* (1965). For a summary of the more recent work at the site, visit the official Çatalhöyük Web site discussed here under "On the Web." For the shift from the early Neolithic to complex farming communities in Mesopotamia, see Charles Maisels's *The Emergence of Civilization: From Hunting and Gathering to Agriculture, Cities, and the State in the Near East* (1990). To learn more about the Olmec, see Robert Sharer and David Grove's

Regional Perspectives on the Olmec (1989). For a series of articles on the Olmec, see *The Olmec World: Ritual and Rulership,* edited by Michael Coe (1996).

Popular Summaries

For an inclusive summary of how people through the centuries have viewed Stonehenge—and how they have been confused by the obvious sophistication exhibited by the monument in the context of an otherwise seemingly simple farming society—there is no better source than Christopher Chippindale's *Stonehenge Complete* (1983). A wonderful book on Stonehenge aimed at a popular audience is David Souden's *Stonehenge Revealed* (1997). For a broad look at the megaliths, see Aubrey Burl's (1999) handsome book, *Great Stone Circles.* For a beautifully photographed, eclectic, and just plain fun book on the stone monuments of Great Britain, don't miss musician Julian Cope's (1998) *The Modern Antiquarian* chronicling his odyssey across the British landscape and his atlas of more than 300 sites.

Çatalhöyük now has its own "biographer," science writer Michael Balter (2005), who has written a terrific summary of the work done at the site: *The Goddess and the Bull: Çatalhöyük: An Archaeological Journey to the Dawn of Civilization.*

For a thorough and thoroughly enjoyable discussion of the archaeology of the Olmec, there is no better source than Richard Diehl's (2004) book, *The Olmecs: America's First Civilization.* For a focus on the artwork of "America's first civilization," see Elizabeth Benson, Beatriz de la Fuente, and Marcia Castro (1996) catalog (*Olmec Art of Ancient Mexico*) of 120 pieces of Olmec art that were exhibited at the National Gallery of Art in Washington, D.C., in 1996.

On the Web

Stonehenge and associated megalithic monuments are well represented on the Internet. Some of the Web sites espouse New Age nonsense about Stonehenge, but many of the sites provide lots of valuable information and scads of great photographs. I especially like the Stone Pages site at http://stonepages.com and Andy Burnham's Megalithic Portal at http://www.stonehenge.uklinux.net/.

The Internet is the best place to read about original work and to get recent updates about the current research being conducted at Çatalhöyük. Go to http://catal.arch.cam.ac.uk/catal/catal.html for an intimate presentation by the researchers themselves; see photos of the excavations and artifacts, read excavation diaries, see artifact distribution maps, and read interim reports presenting preliminary conclusions about the nature of this important settlement. To have fun exploring the "mysteries" of Çatalhöyük, take a look at the Web site called, appropriately enough, Mysteries of Çatalhöyük at http://www.smm.org/catal/. There are comics, Quicktime clips of interviews with researchers, and lots of photographs.

For photographs and drawings of Olmec sculptures, go to the home page of the Xalapa Museum at http://www.dallas.net/~lalo/xala_mus.html.

Online Learning Center: www.mhhe.com/feder4

ONLINE LEARNING CENTER

The Online Learning Center (OLC) Web companion to *The Past in Perspective* features a variety of supplemental study aids. For each chapter, this free Web site includes

- Self-Quizzes to take as pretests prior to exams
- Interactive Timeline Study Guides for additional review and reinforcement of key information

- Learning Objectives
- Chapter Site links with Web addresses for many of the fossil and archaeological sites mentioned in the text

KEY TERMS

Chavin, 441
chiefdom, 420
complex society, 417
dolmen, 446
glyph, 437
Halafian, 426

Hassunan, 426
lintel, 413
megalith, 414
Mesopotamia, 426
Olmec, 429
rank society, 419

Regal-Ritual Centers, 432
Samarran, 426
sarsen, 412
tholoi, 428
trilithon, 413
Umm Dabaghiyah, 426

11

An Explosion of Complexity

THE FLOWERING OF CIVILIZATION IN THE OLD WORLD: MESOPOTAMIA, EGYPT, AND THE INDUS VALLEY

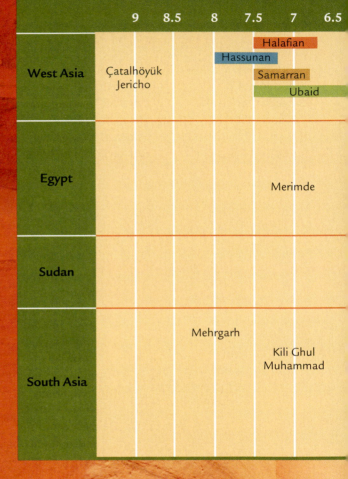

	9	8.5	8	7.5	7	6.5
West Asia	Çatalhöyük Jericho			Halafian / Hassunan	Samarran	Ubaid
Egypt					Merimde	
Sudan						
South Asia			Mehrgarh		Kili Ghul Muhammad	

CHAPTER OVERVIEW

A food surplus made possible by the agricultural revolution set the stage for the development of differential access to wealth, and with the concentration of wealth came the concentration of social and political power. "Civilization," characterized by the existence of a formal government, social stratification, large and dense settlements, monumental edifices, elaborate burials, large armies, full-time artisans, and a system of record keeping, developed in some parts of the Old World as fewer people were needed in the subsistence quest and as rulers attempted to legitimize, reinforce, and magnify their position of power and their level of wealth. Mesopotamia, Egypt, and the Indus Valley civilizations are discussed in this chapter.

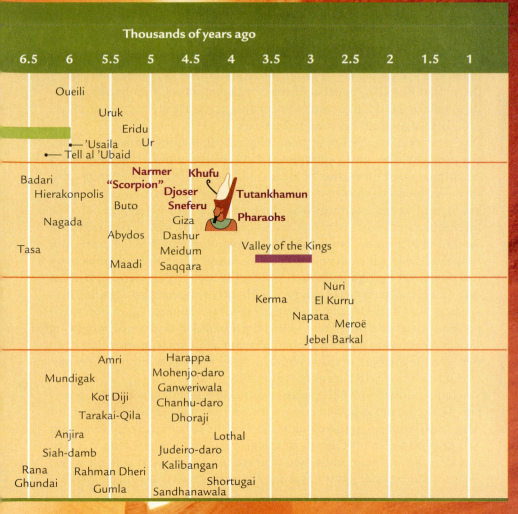

Thousands of years ago

6.5	6	5.5	5	4.5	4	3.5	3	2.5	2	1.5	1

Oueili

Uruk

Eridu

'Usaila   Ur

Tell al 'Ubaid

Badari   **Narmer**   **Khufu**

Hierakonpolis   **"Scorpion"**   **Djoser**   **Tutankhamun**

Buto   **Sneferu**

Nagada   Giza   **Pharaohs**

Abydos   Dashur

Tasa   Meidum   Valley of the Kings

Maadi   Saqqara

Nuri

Kerma   El Kurru

Napata

Meroë

Jebel Barkal

Amri   Harappa

Mundigak   Mohenjo-daro

Kot Diji   Ganweriwala

Tarakai-Qila   Chanhu-daro

Anjira   Dhoraji

Siah-damb   Lothal

Rana   Rahman Dheri   Judeiro-daro

Ghundai   Kalibangan

Gumla   Shortugai

Sandhanawala

ONLINE
LEARNING
CENTER

Go to **www.mhhe.com/feder4** for an
interactive study guide version of this timeline.

451

PRELUDE

By the summer of 1922, the wealthy British nobleman George Herbert, whose official title was the Earl of Carnarvon, had all but run out of patience. For 15 years, he had provided financial support for the work of archaeologist Howard Carter, who was digging in Egypt in the Valley of the Kings—the royal burial ground, or "necropolis," outside of the ancient Egyptian capital of Thebes. In all that time, Carter had found little to interest Lord Carnarvon or to enhance his benefactor's reputation as a sponsor of significant Egyptian archaeology.

In the peculiar practice of archaeological colonialism rampant throughout the eighteenth, nineteenth, and early twentieth centuries, wealthy Europeans purchased excavation "concessions" from foreign governments and then paid archaeologists to conduct investigations. Excavation concessions, put bluntly, were the equivalent of mining permits. The objects recovered by foreign archaeologists in places such as Egypt, Iraq, and Syria in the Old World and Mexico and Peru in the New World were considered to belong not to the nation in which the materials were found but to the individual who had purchased the right to dig and who had funded the excavations. In most cases, these benefactors had contracts with their archaeologists detailing how artifacts were to be distributed on their recovery. Sponsors commonly dispersed their portion to other wealthy friends and to museums, enhancing their reputations as supporters of important research; at the same time, they were divesting nations of their cultural heritage and rendering analysis of significant archaeological sites all but impossible.

In the summer of 1922, Carter returned to England to see Lord Carnarvon. Without any significant discoveries after 15 years, without any glory to bask in, without any archaeological treasures to distribute, Lord Carnarvon had decided to cut off Carter's support, and he informed Carter that this would be the final season he would fund archaeological research in the valley. Dejected, Carter returned to Egypt and commenced what he presumed would be his last digging for Carnarvon.

Carter knew there was not much time. His fieldwork season began in early November, and he would be forced to quit by mid-December, when the tourist season began. Excavation in the tiny piece of ground still unexamined by Carter—the only such piece left in the excavation concession purchased by Carnarvon from the Egyptian government—would block the entrance to the tomb of Pharaoh Rameses VI, the valley's most popular visitor destination.

Carter began work on November 1, 1922, and within three days his Egyptian workers had discovered the beginning of a staircase leading down into the ground. The staircase was slowly cleared of rock; at the bottom was a sealed door bearing the official symbol of the royal burial ground: jackals, symbolically protecting the king's tomb. It seemed possible that Carter at last had found a sealed tomb of an Egyptian king.

Carter was cautiously optimistic, but there had been false starts and false hopes before. Believing that this was his last chance, Carter took a gamble and telegrammed Lord Carnarvon in England: "At last have made wonderful discovery in the Valley. A magnificent tomb with seals intact. Recovered same for your arrival: congratulations" (Fagan 1994:205). Carter suggested that the earl travel to Egypt to witness the opening of what Carter fervently hoped was an unplundered tomb.

After a difficult trip, Lord Carnarvon arrived, with his daughter, Lady Evelyn Herbert. Carter provided a viewing area for Carnarvon and Lady Evelyn where, protected from the relentless Egyptian sun by an umbrella, they watched while workers opened the door at the bottom of the staircase. But instead of the hoped-for tomb, beyond the door was a rubble-filled corridor carved in the rock. Disappointed but intrigued, the workers began the laborious process of removing the rock and debris from the corridor, which extended an excruciating 25 feet. At the end lay yet another door.

The cleared second doorway stood before Carter and Carnarvon on November 26, a little more than two weeks before Carnarvon's patience and money—and Carter's time—were to run out. Carter drilled a hole through the door. Beyond was clearly an open space, a subterranean room. Carter widened the drilled hole just enough so he could put his head, one arm, and a candle through. Carter's own words to describe what he saw are some of the most famous in all archaeology:

> At first I could see nothing, the hot air escaping from the chamber causing the candle flame to flicker. But presently, as my eyes grew accustomed to the light, details of the room within emerged slowly from the mist, strange animals, statues, and gold—everywhere the glint of gold. For the moment—an eternity it must have seemed to the others standing by—I was struck dumb with amazement, and when Lord Carnarvon, unable to stand the suspense any longer, inquired anxiously, "Can you see anything?" it was all I could do to get out the words, "Yes, wonderful things!" (Buckley 1976:13)

Thus began the excavation of the fabulous tomb of the Egyptian "boy king," Tutankhamun (Figure 11.1). Though a relatively minor figure in Egyptian history, having served as pharaoh as a child from 1334 B.C. to 1325 B.C., Tutankhamun was to become the most famous of all ancient Egypt's rulers. His tomb had gone largely untouched since his death, and the spectacular array of burial goods in the tomb were to excite people everywhere (Figure 11.2).

We saw in Chapter 10 how in both the Old and New Worlds a handful of food-producing societies followed a pathway that led them to organize their social, political, and economic lives in ways that were more complex than in other Neolithic and most hunter-gatherer societies. The resulting cultures—called rank societies or chiefdoms—provide material evidence for the elevation of a proportion of a population to higher social, political, and often economic status. These elevated individuals achieved

CHRONICLE

FIGURE 11.1
An iconic moment of discovery; this photograph captures the opening of the tomb of Egyptian pharaoh Tutankhamun. Archaeologist Howard Carter (kneeling) points to objects in the tomb as co-workers look on in wonderment.
(Hulton-Deutsch Collection/ Corbis)

authority and accumulated wealth by becoming the heads of new social and political structures that developed out of a need to organize labor at a level beyond the household or the family. We see in the archaeological record the material manifestation of the end products of that organized labor—megalithic monuments like Stonehenge, Jericho's wall, Çatalhöyük's architecture, the Olmec heads, and Caral's pyramids—and in the ritual sanctification of the higher status of the leaders by their elevated treatment in death—in other words, their entombment in elaborate burials with precious grave goods.

In a few areas, the elaboration of social, political, and economic systems did not end here but continued to intensify, producing societies where the authority of a chief to *convince* others to follow his lead became the power of a pharaoh or king to *demand* obedience. With an exponentially greater degree of control combined with improved technology and a larger population, we see the development of a new kind of social order: the **state.**

The far greater concentration of power and control that characterizes and even defines the state allowed for the production of far larger and more impressive monuments and artwork, albeit made possible by the subjugation of a large class of people whose labor was devoted to the dictates of the ruler or rulers. Perhaps because in the present only the admittedly impressive ma-

FIGURE 11.2
Crafted from gold and lapis lazuli (the bands of dark-blue stone), the coffin lid of Egyptian pharaoh Tutankhamun is among the many splendid objects recovered from his tomb. The tomb symbolizes the wealth and power held by leaders of the world's ancient civilizations. (© Boltin Picture Library/Bridgeman Art Library)

terial manifestations of these early state societies are immediately apparent—and the toil and servitude of the workers and peasants whose backbreaking work produced them is hidden from our view—we refer to the evolution of state societies as the development of "civilization." The material achievements of these societies are impressive indeed, and we will devote much of this chapter to discussing them. As we do so, however, we need to remind ourselves that great pyramids, ziggurats, temples, and palaces come at a human price. For every King Tut buried in great splendor, there must have been hundreds and even thousands of peasants whose labor made possible the life the Boy King lived and whose toil provided Tut and his cohorts with an eternity surrounded by grandeur.

THE EVOLUTION OF THE STATE

Civilization is easier to recognize than to define. We know it when we see it, but find it a challenge to articulate what makes it so. Certainly, when we visit or see images of Egyptian pyramids or Mesopotamian temples (in this chapter) or ancient Maya cities or the palaces of the Inca (in Chapters 13 and 14), we know we are in the presence of the complex phenomenon called "civilization." But how can we formally define what we recognize intuitively?

A state is both quantitatively and qualitatively different from a chiefdom. States ordinarily are bigger and their material accomplishments more impressive. But they are more than simply big, impressive chiefdoms; states are true class societies, often rigidly stratified into social levels. The ruling class controls the populace not by consensus but by coercion and force. A state possesses a true government with formal laws and regulations—and formal penalties for those who disobey—and the ruling class in a state society runs the government. "Civilization" is most often used to characterize the recognizable material results of the development of state societies. Because archaeologists deal most directly with such material consequences, this discussion will use the terms "state" and "civilization" interchangeably.

THE CHARACTER OF CIVILIZATION

The most obvious material symbols of state societies are **monumental works.** The ruins of huge public buildings, tombs, temples, palaces, pyramids, and such are all the spoor of ancient civilizations. Works such as the Egyptian Sphinx, the Pyramid of the Sun at Teotihuacán in Mexico, the Citadel at Mohenjo-daro in Pakistan, and the great ziggurat at Ur in Iraq are the features by which we recognize ancient civilizations. However, while these monuments may represent the most obvious manifestation of state societies, they do not necessarily define them. How ancient people were able to coalesce their labor to build impressive monuments—and why they felt compelled to participate in their construction—are the key puzzles in our attempt to understand the evolution of ancient civilizations.

Food Surplus

There can be no monumental works without an available labor force, and there can be no available labor force without a food surplus. Like the chiefdoms and rank societies discussed in Chapter 10, but on a far larger scale, state societies engage in monumental construction projects; and such projects require a large number of workers. A large workforce can be made available only where a sizable proportion of the populace is freed from the day-to-day necessities of subsistence. As mentioned previously, the modern American farmer is said to produce enough food to feed 130 people, most of whose labor is therefore freed to engage in nonsubsistence pursuits.

Look around any of your classrooms and conduct a silent census of the distribution of the declared majors of your classmates. I'm sure there are some who are aiming for a degree in business, or perhaps in education, in one of the sciences, in computers, engineering, psychology, social work, maybe even anthropology. How many of your cohorts, do you think, are majoring in agriculture, how many hope to be farmers? I'll bet that, at least at most universities or colleges, the number will be very small. That fact is indicative of complex societies, ancient ones as well as our modern one. Civilizations rely absolutely on an agricultural base in which the few are able to feed the many, where only a relatively small proportion of the population needs to be engaged in full-time agricultural pursuits. Their production of a food surplus that then is distributed by a coordinating, overseeing authority allows for other members of the society to engage in other activities: to be soldiers, craftspeople, astronomers, traders, teachers, engineers, doctors, and even archaeologists.

Large, Dense Populations

Because without a sizable labor pool great monuments could never be built, a large population is a requirement of such societies, again supported by the evolving ability of farmers to produce increasing amounts of food. Increasingly efficient agricultural systems, along with the capacity to distribute food to non-producers, allow for increasingly large and dense communities, sometimes culminating in the development of urban centers—in other words, the city.

As a local population increases in size and density—in other words, as a growing population becomes packed into a relatively restricted area in the process of urbanization—a host of challenges are presented: How is order to be maintained among the many people now living virtually next door to each other? How are disputes among neighbors to be resolved? How are necessities—including food—produced outside of the urban area to be distributed among the populace? Issues of property ownership, transportation, and even practical concerns such as the disposal of human waste become greatly magnified when a large number of people are living in close proximity to one another, leading to a spiral of change amplifying the social and economic complexity of a group of people. Social and political structures need to be developed to deal with these and other problems. These structures fundamentally change the social and political lives of people living in urban centers by restricting behaviors that might be detrimental to the larger group.

Social Stratification

Monumental works and the fine art of ancient civilizations do not define those civilizations; they merely reflect their more fundamental features. Great pyramids, walls, palaces, irrigation networks, temples, and roads, as well as beautiful paintings, exquisite ceramics, gold statues, and fine linen—the "wonderful things" that Howard Carter saw in Tut's tomb—are the result of an increasingly complex, layered, or "stratified," socioeconomic system. **Social stratification** in a complex civilization is a division of society into levels, or strata, that one does not achieve but into which one is born (Figure 11.3). One's social level defines one's role in life, one's status, one's material wealth,

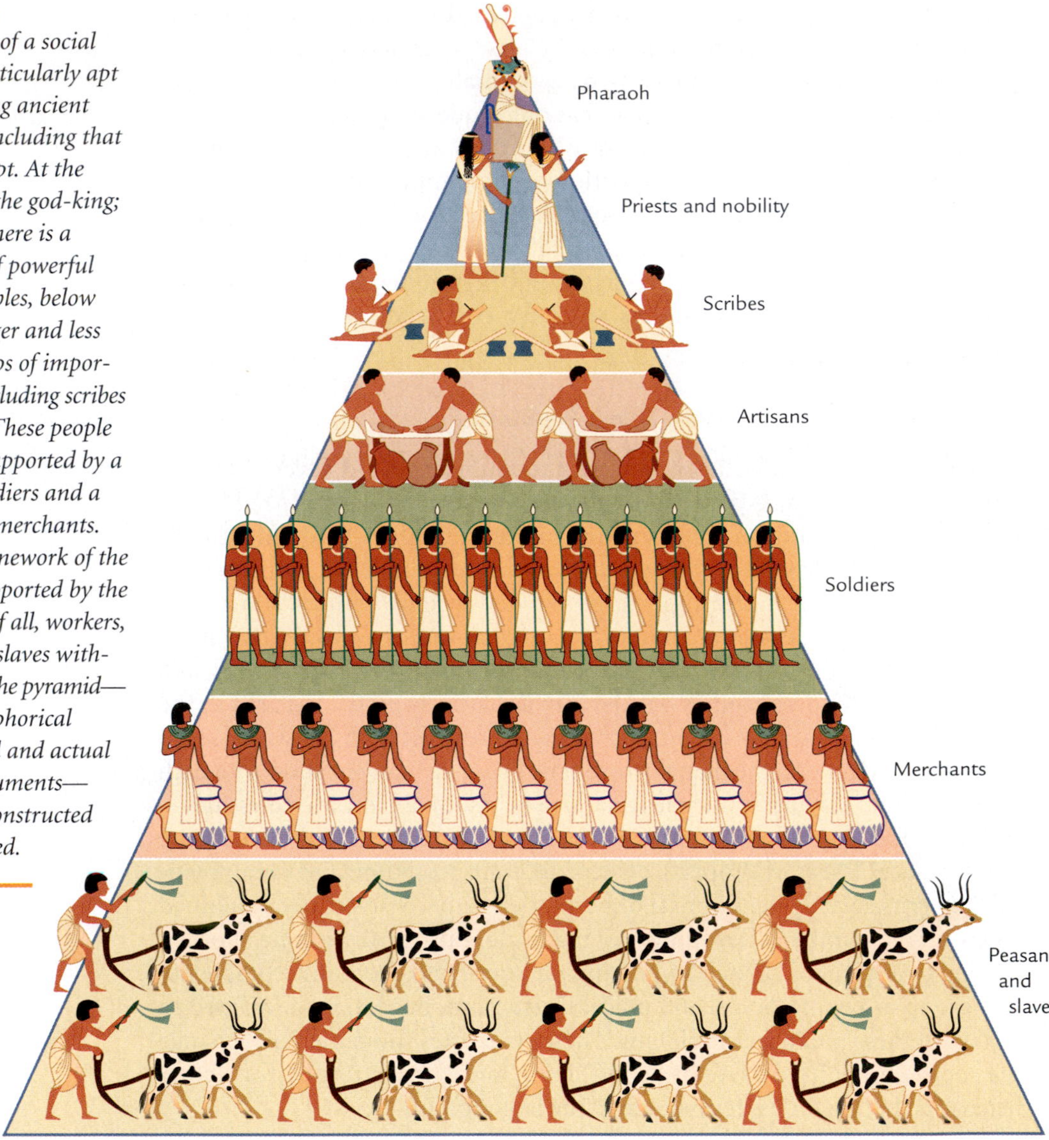

FIGURE 11.3

The metaphor of a social pyramid is particularly apt when discussing ancient civilizations, including that of ancient Egypt. At the pinnacle rests the god-king; beneath him there is a small coterie of powerful priests and nobles, below whom rest larger and less powerful groups of important people, including scribes and artisans. These people are, in turn, supported by a phalanx of soldiers and a population of merchants. The entire framework of the pyramid is supported by the largest group of all, workers, peasants, and slaves without whose toil the pyramid—both the metaphorical social pyramid and actual pyramid monuments—could not be constructed and maintained.

one's power (or degree of powerlessness)—in essence, one's destiny. Monuments and great art are only the material symbols of the powerful position of members of the elite social strata in these societies.

A Formal Government

Along with social stratification, a state possesses a true "government," defined by archaeologist Joseph Tainter (1988:26) as a "specialized decision-making organization with a monopoly of force, and with the power to draft for work, levy and collect taxes, and decree and enforce laws." The power of the state provided by its formal government is wielded by members of the upper social classes. Pharaohs, emperors, and kings, along with the nobles serving under them, are members of a permanently circumscribed social class of people ruling the great masses of people who make up a state society.

As shown in Chapter 10, complex societies are defined, in part, by the organization of society beyond the level of the household or family. Leadership accrues to those who are good at organizing the projects that need to be accomplished by a large labor force. Leaders in non-state complex societies achieve their status by their ability to convince other people to follow their commands and to marshal the opinion of the group. Chiefs and Big Men don't have laws, a police force, or an army to compel people to comply with their wishes. Chiefs do not have absolute power. They do, however, have authority—they are good at organizing labor, keeping people happy, and undertaking and conducting successful projects that people recognize are for the good of the group. Their leadership usually comes about as a result of their accomplishments and abilities. It is this earned respect that convinces people to listen and follow.

The kings, pharaohs, or emperors of state societies have much more than authority; they rule by more than simply the consensus of the populace. Instead, they have true power: the ability to make decisions, give commands, and then make sure those commands are carried out. Jail, enforced labor, banishment, and even the gallows await those who fail to heed the dictates of the ruler of a state society. The rulers of state societies sit atop a formal government with fixed laws. Leaders in such societies possess the ability to enforce those laws.

Labor Specialization

With the **specialization of labor,** certain individuals can devote all their time to perfecting skills in sophisticated and time-consuming specialties, such as technology, engineering, the arts, and crafts. Without the devotion of a lifetime's work, the level of skill exhibited in the great works associated with early civilizations, like the "wonderful things" in King Tut's tomb, could not have been achieved. Specialists can exist only in a society where enough food can be produced to feed all those people engaged in full-time specialist pursuits and where the social system provides a rationale for their existence. Such specialists are needed only in a society that demands their work by and for certain powerful people of an even higher class.

Record Keeping

Without some **system of record keeping** by which the elite could keep track of food surpluses and labor and, in essence, dictate history by recording it in a manner beneficial to them, it is unlikely that the entire system supporting the civilization could ever have developed. In modern America, for instance, how well would the Internal Revenue Service function—and how well would the country work—if there were no way to keep track of individual income and yearly tax contribution? On the other hand, a system of keeping records that can reinforce the legitimacy of the rule of the king—for instance, by demonstrating descent from previous rulers or even from the gods—is another important way the system justifies and maintains itself. As a result of the record keeping of civilizations, in this chapter and Chapter 12 we begin to breach the edge of history, reaching the end of the human story that is the focus of this book—that part of the human saga from the period before history.

Monumental Works

Finally, let us return to where we began this discussion, with the most obvious symbols of civilizations, the monumental works by which we recognize them in the archaeological record. Those monuments are made possible by the characteristics of the state just enumerated. A food surplus freeing the labor of a large labor force; a large, dense population; a stratified social system in which the many serve the dictates of the few; a formal government that enforces that social inequality; specialization; and a system of record keeping together make possible the production of the monumental works and great art that first command our attention when we are confronted by the remains of an ancient civilization.

Great monuments and art, therefore, are enabled by the social and political system of the state. The rulers in state societies have the power to cause the construction of fabulous tombs filled with splendid works of art. They can conscript armies, collect taxes, and call up workforces.

In a feedback process, such power, at the same time, adds compelling support for the existence of the state. In complex civilizations, the great mass of people must believe that there are individuals who can rightfully require their labor, time, and wealth. As archaeologist Joseph Tainter (1988) puts it, the early elites had to convince the great mass of society that their ruler was legitimate—in other words, "proper and valid"—and that the political world with a powerful elite commanding from on high and accumulating great wealth was "as it should be" (Tainter 1988:27). And, as the old saying goes, "nothing succeeds like success"; an awe-inspiring pyramid or temple may go a long way toward convincing the populace that the ruler who commanded that such a thing be built actually is as powerful as he is purported to be, and commands the attention of the gods, and that allegiance is due to him.

Pyramids, great tombs, huge palaces, and the like are the material symbols of the power of the state, both for those living within such systems and for those of us in the modern world who study them. In addition to being literal monuments to kings, gods, or generals, they also stand as symbolic monuments to the power of the state. They serve the role of providing, as Tainter characterizes it (1988:28), "sacred legitimization" for the power of the elite, and they reflect "the need to establish and constantly reinforce legitimacy" (Tainter 1988:27).

THE GEOGRAPHY OF CIVILIZATIONS

Perhaps most remarkably, these features of the world's first civilizations evolved from an earlier Neolithic base not once but several times, in both the Old and New Worlds: in southwest Asia and Egypt (this chapter); the Indus Valley of Pakistan, eastern China, and the island of Crete (Chapter 12); and in Mesoamerica (Chapter 13) and Peru (Chapter 14). These primary civilizations developed more or less independently, each following its own path. The next sections will present brief synopses of the evolution of each of the centers of early civilization in the Old World.

MESOPOTAMIA

In Chapter 10, we discussed the origins of one of the world's earliest complex societies in the land between the Tigris and Euphrates Rivers. We saw the evidence for complexity reflected in large-scale communal works such as granaries and defensive walls that surrounded entire villages. Southern Mesopotamia is also the place where archaeological evidence indicates that the world's first civilization developed.

Accelerating Change: The Ubaid

Not until after about 6300 B.P. did the area of southern Mesopotamia show substantial movement toward what we are here calling civilization. The culture of southern Mesopotamia during this period is called **Ubaid** and is reflected at the sites of Tell al 'Ubaid, Tell Oueili, Eridu, 'Usaila, and Ur (Figure 11.4).

Southern Mesopotamia is a land of sand dunes and marshes, a semiarid plain surrounded by a double river system prone to unpredictable, ferocious flooding. It is not an area in which the world's first civilization might be expected. Agriculture based on rainfall is impossible outside the marsh edges—the region receives as little as 15 cm (6 in.) of rain per year (Crawford 1991:8). Significantly, the construction of irrigation canals is an absolute necessity for farmers in southern Mesopotamia.

Beyond its rich floodplain soil, Mesopotamia proper has few other resources. As archaeologist Harriet Crawford (1991) points out, there are no sources for stone or metal in Mesopotamia and few areas with enough trees to provide wood for construction. It is not surprising, therefore, that Ubaid sites appear rather suddenly in this area, with no evidence of previous development. Much of the area simply was not immediately attractive to Neolithic farmers in the Middle East. Southern Mesopotamia was populated only after 6,300 years ago, when population growth, made possible by the settled life of the Neolithic, forced people to expand out onto the floodplain. Similarly, this area was populated only when the construction of a system of water control became technologically—and socially—feasible.

FIGURE 11.4

Archaeological sites in western Asia where evidence of the evolution of chiefdom and early state-level societies has been found.

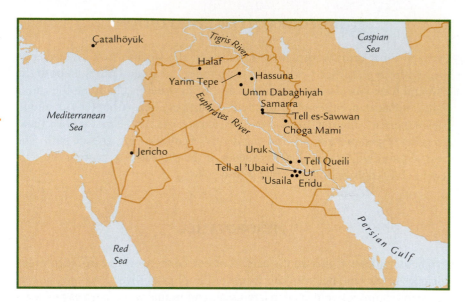

The Role of Irrigation

As archaeologist Charles Maisels (1990) points out, while the floodplain of the Tigris-Euphrates system is not an easy habitat to exploit, with the construction of irrigation canals to bring water to fields in the summer and to drain them after the spring floods, it becomes enormously productive farmland. Canal construction requires a large population whose labor can be organized. At the same time, an effective irrigation system allows for the production of even more food to support a larger and denser population. Maisels proposes that the deciding factors in the development of Mesopotamia's complex societies were (1) the need to concentrate population along the arable lands near the rivers, thereby increasing population locally, (2) the need to develop a complex social system that would allow the construction of canals, and (3) the ability of irrigation to produce a food surplus. In other words, the development of civilization was the result of dynamic feedback among population growth, the development of complex irrigation systems, and the attendant new social order necessary to organize and ultimately command the labor of the growing population.

Power Invested in the Temple

In early Mesopotamia, as elsewhere, no political or military structure was in place that could provide designers, builders, supervisors, maintainers, and controllers of the irrigation networks. Early Neolithic cultures were likely largely egalitarian or rank societies. But in Mesopotamia, again as elsewhere, one institution in society was set apart, and extraordinary powers resided

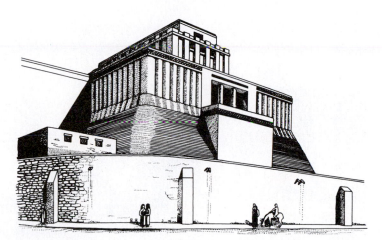

FIGURE 11.5
Artist's conception of the temple at the early Mesopotamian city of Eridu at around 5000 B.P. (From *The Art of the Ancient Near East* by Seton Lloyd, published by Thames & Hudson Ltd., 1961)

there even before social complexity increased. That institution was the temple (Figure 11.5). As seen in Chapter 10, religious shrines or temples date back to well before the Ubaid period in Mesopotamia. The familiar T-shaped northern Mesopotamian temple can be seen in prototype at Samarran sites and, perhaps, in the sense of a functional prototype, in the Halafian round storage buildings, which seem to have served as communal granaries and, at the same time, places of religious significance. In the view of archaeologists C. C. Lamberg-Karlovsky and Jeremy Sabloff (1995), when population grew and expanded onto the floodplain and when irrigation works became a necessity, a need developed for the evolution of an institution that could organize the labor necessary to build and maintain these works. In their view, the religious elite quickly filled the power vacuum and became the dominant political and social as well as religious force in Mesopotamian society. In other words, priests became chiefs. Control of the irrigation networks led to power, and with power came the ability to control the enormous food surplus that the evolving system produced.

Mesopotamia's First Cities: The Uruk Period

With the large and complex settlements of the Ubaid as a base, after 6000 B.P., dramatic changes occurred in southern Mesopotamia, and a number of communities became much larger. Between 5500 and 5200 B.P., the settlement at Uruk (also called Warka) became so large, with a population estimated to be more than 10,000, that we can reasonably call it a city—in fact, the world's first.

The growth of Uruk occurred, at least in part, through a process of population implosion. Archaeological evidence indicates that many of the smaller farming communities around Uruk were abandoned, with their populations congregating in the growing urban center. That this movement of population

Built more than 4,000 years ago, the impressive ziggurat at the Mesopotamian city of Ur is a testament to the ability of early state societies to conscript the labor of a large population to produce monumental public works. (© Dean Conger/ Corbis)

may have resulted from widespread warfare is supported by evidence at Uruk itself, where defensive fortifications were built at this time.

Another site, Eridu, became an urban center soon after Uruk, with an estimated population of 5,000; a large, finely built temple; and a neighborhood of larger houses with more impressive material culture, belonging to the newly evolved elite. By the Early Dynastic Period of the Sumerian civilization, dated from 4850 to 4600 B.P., there were more than 20 urban centers, or **city-states**—each with its own temple and territory consisting of a four-tiered hierarchy of settlement types, including the city and its associated towns, villages, and hamlets (Adams and Nissen 1972; Figure 11.6).

Along with monumental works such as great temples, palaces, and pyramids, state societies express in symbolic ways the social and political stratification that defines them. There is no more obvious example of this than in how the rulers of these societies are treated in death. The elite classes in state society are buried in a splendor that symbolizes their superior economic, social, and political positions in life.

Consider, for example, the cemetery at the Mesopotamian city of Ur; it contains more than 2,000 graves, only 16 of which were the interments of members of the elite class. The vast majority of the graves are simple, the final resting places of ordinary people. They are little more than holes in the ground with a few personal effects placed in the graves. The burials of the elite are far different, placed in stone chambers with vaulted roofs—one even possessed a dome. One of the tombs, that of a queen called Pu-abi, is emblematic of the royal interments at Ur.

A headdress of gold, festooned with semiprecious stones, was placed on Pu-abi's head. Around her were gold and silver containers, an intricately designed harp, a gaming table, and another 250 or so objects (Figure 11.7). Following a pattern seen among the elite of other early civilizations, humans and animals were sacrificed as part of the royal burial ceremony; in Pu-abi's burial chamber were two female attendants. Just outside the royal chamber were 10 more women (one with a harp—musical accompaniment for the journey), 5 soldiers, and 2 oxen. Beneath Queen Pu-abi's chamber was another tomb— a man's, possibly her husband's. This king was accompanied by 6 soldiers, 19 females wearing gold headpieces, 6 oxen, 2 chariots, a lyre, a gaming table, and an exquisite silver model of a boat. Such were the death settings of Ur nobility. Pu-abi's interment is emblematic of the wealth, power, and social position of the nobility of ancient Mesopotamia and, in fact, all of the other civilizations discussed in this text.

The Beginning of the Written Record

The research of archaeologist Denise Schmandt-Besserat (1992, 1996, 2002) has revealed the most likely scenario for how the use of recorded symbols evolved in Mesopotamia, proposing what is essentially a five-step process.

The first step involved the use of so-called clay **tokens** that, beginning more than 9,000 years ago, litter sites in the Middle East (Lawler 2001). The tokens initially were made in 16 basic shapes, mostly geometric forms like cones, disks, spheres, and cylinders but also stylized animals and some that resemble pottery storage jars (Figure 11.8). Schmandt-Besserat has examined more than 8,000 of these tokens during more than 25 years of research. Some of these artifacts have been found at Hassuna, Samarra, and Halaf, all sites mentioned in Chapter 10 as part of our discussion of early evidence for an agricultural way of life. The tokens appear to have been used as counters for particular goods, symbols of specific products, and, just as important, specific quantities of these items. Schmandt-Besserat (2002) argues, for example, that a cone-shaped token was a counter for recording a small quantity of grain, while a sphere stood for a larger portion of the same material. Tokens have been found primarily in public buildings rather than private residences. Their presence in temples especially suggests their public function as well as the early connection between religion, the religious elite, and control of a food surplus. It would seem that the tokens were used to keep track of food flowing into communal grain-storage facilities or surplus food provided to the temple, perhaps as a tax or tithe.

The second step in Schmandt-Besserat's sequence began about 6,000 years ago when the tokens appear to have experienced an explosion of elaboration, jumping from 16 basic forms to about 300, with various markings etched onto their surfaces to further differentiate their meaning. More forms and the elaboration of marking them meant that more specific and precise record keeping was possible. Instead of simply recording a quantity of a material or product, the increased number and greater complexity of tokens allowed for more detailed records and for distinctions made between raw materials and goods manufactured from those materials.

By about 5,500 years ago, Schmandt-Besserat sees a third step in the development of record keeping in Mesopotamia. The tokens are no longer found as separate, individual counters but, rather, are found stored together in clay containers called **envelopes.** Rather mysteriously, the envelopes were sealed shut, which would seem to negate the purpose of the tokens in record keeping. After all, if the appearance and number of tokens symbolically recorded the quantity of a set of objects, how could tokens still serve this useful function if they were removed from sight, stored in opaque clay containers? The Mesopotamians got around this by first impressing the tokens on the exterior surface of the clay envelope in which they were to be stored when that envelope clay was still moist and soft. So anyone who understood the token code could simply examine the surface of the clay envelope in which the tokens

FIGURE 11.8

These clay tokens with impressed or incised symbols from the Middle East may represent the first evidence for a system of record keeping anywhere in the world. (Courtesy of Département des Antiquités Orientales, Musée du Louvre, Paris. Photograph courtesy Denise Schmandt-Besserat)

were stored to figure out which tokens and how many were housed therein in order to "read" the accounting information inside the container.

It took very little time for the fourth step to occur. No later than 5,200 years ago, record keepers realized that they didn't have to have a large number of individual sets of tokens stored in clay envelopes to represent and record quantities of goods. Instead, they could use a single set of tokens to directly press the information they symbolized onto a flattened piece of clay. The impressed marks on clay were no longer an indirect record of materials, recording the number and kinds of the tokens stored in an envelope, which in turn directly recorded quantities of goods. The impressed marks on slabs of clay now themselves became the direct record of the goods. As Schmandt-Besserat (2002) points out, by eliminating the use of physical objects, the tokens, as counters and by replacing them with marks impressed on soft clay surfaces, the Mesopotamians were producing the world's first texts.

There is one final, fifth step in Schmandt-Besserat's sequence. By 5,100 years ago, the tokens, which originally were the records themselves, and which had then transformed into the tools used to record the information they represented on clay tablets, were dispensed with entirely. With tokens no longer needed in the record-keeping system, scribes now began impressing symbols directly onto soft clay tablets using a pointed tool, a stylus or pen, in a process of free-hand drawing. These markings, called **cuneiform,** allowed for an elaboration of the symbols marked on clay and the creation of a true system of writing (Figure 11.9).

Schmandt-Besserat's view of the origins of a system of record keeping, and, ultimately, record keeping through writing, meshes quite well with the reason why such a system was required by civilized societies. Knowledge is power, and the ability to possess and control knowledge through a system of coded, permanent records gave those who knew the code and kept the records an enormous advantage in their ability to control first the economic system and ultimately the political and social systems. Such a system allows those who keep the records to know precisely which individuals have contributed in the form of food or wealth to the temple or the king—and to know how much more is owed. Originating as a method for keeping track of mundane information, record keeping became a powerful tool for those who controlled it, a way of solidifying the power of the state. A system of record keeping, usually but not universally through writing (see the discussion of the Inca in Chapter 14), played a major role in Mesopotamia and elsewhere in allowing the state to maintain its level of control.

EGYPT OF THE PHARAOHS

Ancient Egypt is, for most people, uniquely illustrative of the mystery and allure of ancient civilization: the great pyramids at Giza, the enigmatic half-human, half-lion that is the Sphinx, and fabulous tombs filled with remarkable treasure. These monuments are all emblematic of the Egypt of the pharaohs and symbolic of the remarkable achievements of ancient Egyptian civilization at its peak. The roots of Egyptian civilization lie in the earliest Neolithic cultures that developed in the Nile Valley (Figure 11.10).

The Egyptian Neolithic

The Greek philosopher Herodotus characterized Egypt as "the gift of the Nile." By this he meant that in a vast, dead desert, the Nile is a vein of life-giving water, its valley a corridor of rich soil fertile enough to nurture the roots of one of humanity's most ancient civilizations.

It is no surprise that along the Nile archaeologists have found evidence of Egypt's first agricultural communities. The shift to agriculture occurred between 7,000 and 5,000 years ago, and the crops (especially wheat and barley) and animals (sheep, goats, and cattle) on which these early communities subsisted were all derived from outside of Egypt, having been used in southwest Asia at an earlier date (see Chapter 10).

Scholars have long recognized that Egypt consists of two primary regions: Upper Egypt, which consists of the majority of the length of the Nile Valley

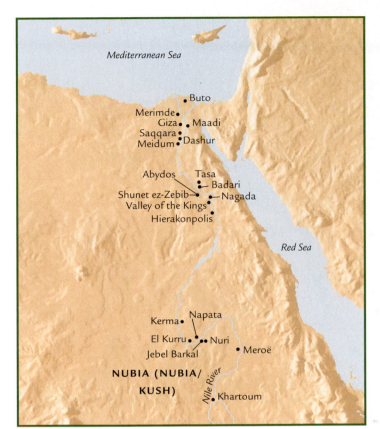

FIGURE 11.10
Archaeological sites in northern Africa where evidence of the evolution of chiefdom and early state-level societies has been found.

("upper" here refers to the flow of the river and signifies upstream and, therefore, is to the *south* because the Nile flows northward) and Lower Egypt (in the north), which is demarcated by the Nile delta, a broad, flat plain spanning about 400 km (248 mi) from east to west and 200 km (124 mi) from the mouth of the river to the south (Figure 11.11). The delta contains more than 60% of the inhabited area of ancient Egypt; the lengthy, narrow valley makes up the remaining 40%. The histories of these two regions are somewhat different and have been divided into a number of sequential components, shown in Table 11.1.

Essentially, between 7,000 and 6,000 years ago, **Badarian** sites to the south and **Fayum/Merimden** sites to the north exhibit mixed economies that included a substantial component of hunting and fishing, supplemented by agriculture. The archaeological sites that mark these periods are relatively small and impermanent and are characterized by insubstantial structures, small oval dwellings likely made of thatch, and thin occupation layers (Brewer and Teeter 1999).

At about 5,750 years ago, **Amratian/Naqada I** sites in the south and **Omari A** sites to the north show a distinct shift in the subsistence focus, with an

FIGURE 11.11
This stunning image from space makes the point clear; the Nile valley and Delta represent a clearly delineated fertile landscape surrounded by an enormous desert. (Jacques Descloitres, MODIS Land Rapid Response Team, NASA/GSFC)

increasing concentration and reliance on domesticated animals, specifically sheep, goats, and cattle. These sites are larger; their occupation layers are thicker, indicating greater permanence; and their houses are more substantial: No longer oval and made of thatch, they are rectangular and made of mud-brick.

Beginning about 5,400 years ago, by **Late Gerzean** (**Naqada II** and **Maadian**) times, the first clear evidence of social inequality appears in Egypt in the form of differentiated burials. It appears that wealth in the form of finely made objects, often made of raw materials not locally available, is becoming concentrated in a nascent elite class who inter these objects with their dead (Bard 2000).

Once wealth, social status, and, perhaps, political influence become concentrated in the hands of a few in a community, jockeying for even greater wealth, status, and influence occurs among the elite; and a single family under a supreme leader may come to dominate. This appears to have happened in Egypt about 5,300 years ago. At this time, in the period labeled **Naqada III** in both the north and the south, true centers of wealth and power developed as characterized by sites like Abydos, Naqada, Maadi, Buto, and, especially, Hierakonpolis. Brewer and Teeter (1999:32-33) liken these communities to city-states, small fiefdoms led by individuals they label "chieftain-kings."

TABLE 11.1

Chronology of Predynastic Egypt

YEARS AGO	UPPER EGYPT	LOWER EGYPT
5,100	Protodynastic	Protodynastic
5,300	Naqada III	Naqada III
5,400	Late Gerzean (Naqada II)	Late Gerzean (Maadian)
5,650	Early Gerzean (Naqada II)	Omari B
5,750	Amratian (Naqada I)	Omari A
6,400	Badarian	
6,800		Merimden
7,200		Fayum A

Though the history of the development of the equivalent of city-states along the Nile seems clear, we are left with vexing questions: Why did power and wealth become concentrated in such places? How did individuals and their families manage to accumulate wealth, obtain power, and achieve a position in society superior to that of the rest of a community's inhabitants? The answers to these questions may be illuminated by the archaeology of one of these communities: Hierakonpolis.

Hierakonpolis

The evidence for the evolution of an increasingly complex society is perhaps clearest at Hierakonpolis, largely due to the diligent efforts of archaeologist Michael Hoffman (1979, 1983). Hierakonpolis began its history nearly 6,000 years ago as a small Neolithic village on the west bank of the Nile. Pottery manufacture became a booming business at Hierakonpolis, and ceramics manufactured in that town's kilns are found up and down the Nile. Though pottery likely originated as a small-scale, family-run affair, here it developed into a specialized craft, and a class of "pottery barons" developed. The burials of these people were larger and far more elaborate than were the interments of the rest of society. Brick-lined tombs cut into the bedrock mark the final resting places of the growing class of pottery makers.

After 5500 B.P., during Nagada II, or Late Gerzean, times, irrigation canals were constructed, likely in response to a change in the local climate. A dry period that began at this time possibly resulted from local deforestation, which in turn resulted from the need to fuel the pottery kilns. The tombs of a developing elite became larger; some include a square stone building called a **mastaba** built on top of a subterranean, brick-lined or rock-cut tomb.

As population along the Nile grew and as competition for resources increased, previously small arguments or perceived injustices among and between neighboring towns grew into full-scale battles for control of the precious land base. Interestingly, the period after 5100 B.P. was marked by the abandonment of small villages located around the central places of Nagada and Hierakonpolis. The populations of the small towns seem to have moved into the larger settlements, making them substantially larger and more complex. Fortifications around Nagada and Hierakonpolis were built and expanded at this time, and the burials of the growing elite became increasingly elaborate (Kemp 1977). At Hierakonpolis, for example, Tomb 100 is brick-lined, is much larger than previous tombs, and has various wall paintings that depict the deceased as a ruler.

First Writing

As discussed earlier in this chapter, large, complex, state societies—what we commonly call "civilizations"—need a way to keep track of wealth, goods, kinship, population, and even history. The Egyptian system of **hieroglyphic** writing is one of the best-known early systems of keeping track of these very things. The earliest evidence for Egyptian writing dates to about 5,200 years ago (Mitchell 1999; Wilkinson 2003a).

The system developed by the ancient Egyptians for recording information is a variety of picture writing. In the Egyptian system, some of the individual pictures represent entire words, others represent particular spoken sounds, and other symbols specify the meaning of the signs that precede them.

Unlike Mesopotamian writing with its long archaeological sequence beginning with clay tokens and culminating in a richly detailed and fully formed script, the origins of Egyptian writing have been difficult to trace. A team led by Egyptologist Gunter Dreyer discovered the oldest evidence of Egyptian hieroglyphics about 400 km (250 mi) south of Cairo at Abydos. Excavating a tomb the team labeled U-j, the final resting place of a leader called "Scorpion I," who ruled 5,200 years ago, Dreyer found about 200 small bone and ivory tags that were attached to containers holding linen and oil (Figure 11.12). The tags were small squares, measuring about 2–3 cm (0.8–1.2 in.) on each side and bearing inscriptions that appear to be symbols documenting the goods, and perhaps indicating their geographic sources (Lawler 2001).

As Egyptologist Toby Wilkinson (2003a) points out, the writing on the tags is purely practical, not lauding the life of the leader with whom they were entombed, not telling great tales of the achievements of the king, of battles won or temples built. The writing on the tags simply represents an accounting of commodities, records of the materials accumulated for placement in the royal grave: how much of what provided by whom and from where.

Though the tags bear the oldest evidence yet discovered of Egyptian record keeping, the writing does not look like the first halting steps of such a system. The hieroglyphs are not primitive, but are fully formed. Either the Egyptians borrowed their system of record keeping from someone else or there are earlier, yet-to-be discovered artifacts that will show more clearly the development of the system through time. The writing seen in Mesopotamia

FIGURE 11.12

These inscribed bone tokens are just a few of the 200 found in the tomb labeled U-j at Abydos, the final resting place of a great leader known as "Scorpion I" who ruled more than 5,200 years ago. The tags were found attached to containers, and the carved images are a form of writing, the earliest hieroglyphs yet found in Egypt, and appear to represent an accounting of goods donated to the king's burial. (© Günter Dreyer/ Deutsches Archäologisches Institut, Kairo)

and discussed previously in this chapter is almost certainly older than the Tomb U-j tags and might chronologically have served as a source, but the symbols on the Abydos tags are quite different from anything seen in the tokens of southwest Asia. Instead, the writing on the tags seems purely Egyptian, with symbols taken, as Wilkinson (2003a:27) points out, from the local environment. This earliest Egyptian writing is far more likely to have been a local development, but only additional discoveries can settle the question.

First Pharaoh

The development of largely autonomous city-states, especially in Upper Egypt, each with its own elite, set the stage for the creation of a unified nation that would become the ancient Egypt with which most people are at least passingly familiar.

Before unification, a number of rulers, notably the locally powerful leaders of the city-states of Abydos, Hierakonpolis, and Naqada, appear to have attempted to unify all of the communities located along the Nile and bring them under their sway as the citizens of a single, enormously powerful nation (Wilkinson 2003b). Abydos, Hierakonpolis, and Naqada each dominated their own segments of territory along the Nile in Upper Egypt and competed amongst each other in the apparent attempt to unify the people in their cities as well as everyone else living up and down the river and to rule over them all (Figure 11.13).

The leaders of these Egyptian city-states had become increasingly powerful and wealthy, and this growing power and wealth are reflected in their treatment upon death. For example, one burial—Tomb U-j, mentioned previously and dating to approximately 5,200 years ago—located in what appears to have been a royal cemetery at the site of Abydos, consists of eight chambers and seems to have been constructed to provide the deceased king with a small-scale model for his afterlife of the royal palace in which he lived in life (Wilkinson 2003b). Trappings of rulership were entombed with the king, and

FIGURE 11.13
Abydos, Nagada, and Hierakonpolis were competing political and economic entities in the centuries before all Egypt was unified under a single pharaoh. This map depicts the probable geographic reaches of each of these predynastic powers.

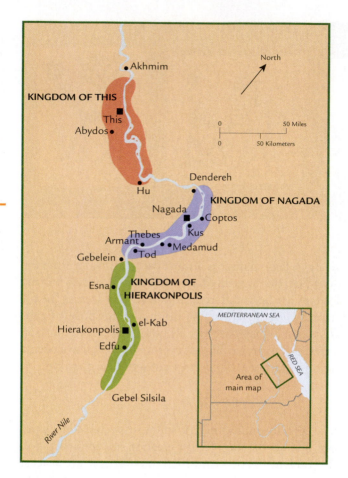

FIGURE 11.13
Abydos, Nagada, and Hierakonpolis were competing political and economic entities in the centuries before all Egypt was unified under a single pharaoh. This map depicts the probable geographic reaches of each of these predynastic powers.

his burial-palace contained items that would have been available only far to the north, in the Delta towns of Lower Egypt. This is interpreted by some to mean that the ruler of Abydos had at least some level of command over the people to the north. Though the name of the leader interred in Tomb U-j is not known, some of the pots he was buried with bear the inscription of a scorpion. Some have, as a result, called him King Scorpion and list him among the first of the rulers over all of Egypt.

A scorpion associated with an important ruler has been found at Hierakonpolis. On a ceremonial mace head, the king is depicted in the act of ritually opening an irrigation canal. He is shown, as was a common convention in Egypt, on a much grander scale than the other people on the mace head, a virtual giant, and he is wearing a crown that is seen in other depictions of kings in Upper Egypt. And there, directly in front of the great ruler's face, is the clear image of a scorpion (Figure 11.14). Some suggest that this depiction indicates that the Abydos leader buried in Tomb U-j—perhaps called King Scorpion— was also considered by the people of Hierakonpolis to be their leader as well.

FIGURE 11.14
Found at the predynastic city-state of Hierakonpolis, the Narmer Macehead shows an oversized king carrying out what appears to be an irrigation rite. Directly in front of the king's face is a scorpion. This has been interpreted as representing the name of the king—King Scorpion—who ruled Hierakonpolis.
(© Werner Foreman/Art Resource, NY)

Based on the work of Manetho, an Egyptian priest who we know lived more than 2,200 years ago, Egyptologists divide Egyptian history into 31 dynasties, which are, in turn, clustered into a number of periods. For a complete enumeration of the dynasties and reigns of all of Egypt's pharaohs, see http://www.touregypt.net/kings.htm. Narmer/Menes is listed as the first true pharaoh, the ruler of the First Dynasty of ancient Egypt. Because King Scorpion predates Narmer, he is sometimes labeled the pharaoh of Dynasty 0.

Archaeologists have recovered a king list, now called the Royal Canon of Turin for the Italian museum where the list is housed, from the New Kingdom (the period 1540–1070 B.C.); it contains the names of about 300 pharaohs (Kemp 1991:23). The list apparently was a virtually complete enumeration of Egyptian rulers to that point in time, providing the duration of their reigns, sometimes to the exact numbers of years, months, and even days. This list traces Egyptian kingship back 958 years, to the rule of the first historically known pharaoh, here called Menes, who united Lower and Upper Egypt. In his role as the first great leader of not just a local chiefdom but also of a geographically extensive state, Menes headed a single political entity that was to become one of the most remarkable of the early civilizations.

A plaque celebrating the unification of Egypt and the ascension of the first pharaoh was discovered at Hierakonpolis. One side depicts a man with a mace or baton raised as if about to strike a kneeling enemy soldier (Figure 11.15).

FIGURE 11.15

The Narmer Palette of Hierakonpolis depicts symbolically the unification of Upper and Lower Egypt under the leadership of Narmer, the first pharaoh, in about 5100 B.P.
(© Giraudon/Art Resource, NY)

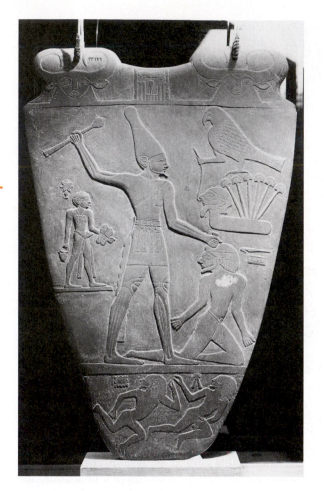

The standing man is wearing a crown that we know from later writing is the symbol of leadership of Upper Egypt. On the obverse of the plaque, the same man is depicted wearing a crown that includes the symbol of kingship of Lower Egypt. We can read his name on the object; it is Narmer. In all likelihood, Narmer is another name for Menes, positioned in the king list mentioned earlier as the first pharaoh of a unified Egyptian state. Narmer's ascension to the throne of Egypt occurred about 5100 B.P., about 100 years after the reign of King Scorpion.

The Flowering of Egypt

After unification under Narmer, the early dynasties of ancient Egypt continued to consolidate their power as they unified the population living along the Nile within an increasingly centralized political and economic entity, the Egyptian state. The ruler, whom we can now legitimately call "pharaoh," was an all-powerful king who presided over a complex and multitiered organization. Individuals who previously had been rulers of autonomous villages or cities now were merely local administrators who owed their allegiance—and likely their continued good health—to the pharaoh. With the labor, agricultural surplus, soldiers, and wealth of not just a local community, but all of the communities along the Nile at his disposal, pharaoh could conscript a vast and powerful army and a huge workforce to dig irrigation canals, construct palaces, and even build huge tombs to house his spirit in the afterlife. Pharaoh fed those thousands of laborers and warriors with the food reserves he accumulated through taxation of the enormous food surplus produced by thousands upon thousands of Egyptian farmers who, it is estimated, made up 75% of the Egyptian population of as many as 3 million people (Brewer and Teeter 1999:34).

The Egyptians continued the precedent they established in their earliest writing in the Abydos tombs of recording through their hieroglyphic writing system many of the mundane aspects of their economic lives, so we know quite a bit about how the system worked. Based on the amount of Nile flooding—those floodwaters irrigated and replenished farmland—state officials estimated regional agricultural productivity. Based on these estimates, they assessed a tax on local farmers, which they paid in bushels of grain.

In return for their contribution to the state in terms of the food surplus they produced, in terms of labor and time contributed to work on state projects, and in terms of sons they provided to the army, local people were members in good standing in what was arguably the single most powerful political entity of the ancient world. Construction of irrigation canals enabled farmers to produce more food and, therefore, greater wealth. A powerful army provided secure borders that led to lengthy periods of peace and security. Participation in the rituals, rites, and obligations commanded by the gods—including working on the eternal resting place of the pharaoh, who was, himself, a god on earth—ensured a place for the individual in eternity.

A religious hierarchy developed to attend to the otherworldly affairs of ancient Egypt. For a vastly polytheistic religion, enormous bureaucracies developed to serve the needs of the gods and the needs of the bureaucracies. Though they had enormous landholdings, temples were exempt from taxation and became powerful and, in a sense, autonomous fiefdoms with agendas often different from that of the pharaoh. It is estimated that, during the Twentieth Dynasty, for example, the priesthood that served Amun, the most powerful god in the Egyptian pantheon, had at their disposal more than 40,000 laborers to tend to their lands, raising their own food and keeping cattle, goats, and fowl (Brewer and Teeter 1999:41).

During Egypt's 31 dynasties, we see a clear pattern marked by a succession of periods of political and economic domination of the rulers' world interspersed with periods of decline when power flowed back into the hands of local administrators or even foreigners.

FIGURE 11.16

The form of the stepped pyramid at Saqqara, built to memorialize the Egyptian pharaoh Djoser in about 4600 B.P., was based on earlier mastaba tombs of Egypt's elite. (M. H. Feder)

The Pyramid Age

Egypt's Third and Fourth Dynasties mark two successive periods of power and domination. This can be seen in the frenzy of construction projects that characterize the period 2686–2498 B.C. Though Egypt continued as a major force in the ancient world for more than a thousand years after this, Egypt's most famous burial monuments were built during this short period of time.

Consider the first truly mammoth pharaonic burial monument, the stepped pyramid of the first pharaoh of the Third Dynasty, Djoser (Figure 11.16). Located at Saqarra and built of clay and stone, Djoser's pyramid rises through six steps to a height of roughly 60 m (197 ft). The base of the stepped pyramid covers a rectangular area exceeding 13,200 m^2 (more than 142,000 ft^2 or about 3.25 acres), and it is the primary element of a gargantuan mortuary complex of structures all built for the pharaoh.

It is in the Fourth Dynasty that an explosion of pyramid building occurs; in fact, the Fourth Dynasty is called "the pyramid age." The Fourth Dynasty's first pharaoh, Sneferu, was responsible for no fewer than three pyramids.

Sneferu's first attempt, at the site of Meidum, was an apparent failure and was abandoned in the middle of the build. Now called the Collapsed Pyramid because only the central core remains (Figure 11.17), the exterior casing was removed long ago and gives the appearance of collapse. Though there is no direct evidence of a catastrophe during construction, the fear of such an event may explain the abandonment of the project. The Collapsed Pyramid was intended not as a stepped monument like that of his predecessor Djoser, but as a true pyramid consisting of four flat triangular faces meeting at a common apex. The slope of each the Collapsed Pyramid's four faces was intended to be an extremely steep 72 to 78 degrees, and Egyptian technology simply was not

FIGURE 11.17
The so-called Collapsed-Pyramid may not be the result of a catastrophic collapse, but does reflect an architectural blunder on the part of Egypt's Fourth Dynasty pyramid builders during the reign of the pharaoh Sneferu. It was built at too steep an angle, so large and dangerous cracks developed in the structure and the project was abandoned. (K. L. Feder)

FIGURE 11.18
The so-called Bent Pyramid represents another error on the part of Sneferu's pyramid builders. Having learned from their mistake with the Collapsed Pyramid, the Bent Pyramid was built at a less steep angle, but cracks appeared in this structure as well. Just a bit more than halfway done, the builders continued construction, but at an even gentler angle. This enabled completion of the project, but the angle change in mid-build gives this pyramid an odd, bent appearance. (K. L. Feder)

up to the task. The enormous weight of the pyramid casing at a very steep angle led to substantial cracks and slumping and likely convinced the builders to try something different.

Sneferu's next attempt, this time to the north of Meidum at Dashur, is called the Bent Pyramid because, unlike a true, geometric pyramid, each face is actually pentagonal rather than triangular (Figure 11.18). When work was

FIGURE 11.19

Sneferu's builders finally got it right here, in the Red Pyramid (top). The faces of this first geometrically true pyramid slope lie at a gentle 43 degrees. The craft of pyramid building reached its apogee later in the Fourth Dynasty at Giza with construction of the truly monumental burial chambers of Khufu, his son Khafre, and his grandson Menkaure (bottom).

(top: K. L. Feder, bottom: Glen Allison/Getty Images)

initiated, the slope of the pyramid was set at 55 degrees, far gentler than what had been planned for the Collapsed Pyramid. Unfortunately, even this gentler slope proved to be too steep, and cracks and distortions appeared at the pyramid base in the middle of construction. The architects and engineers elected not to abandon the project but instead came up with a work-around. They decreased the angle of the top one-third or so of the pyramid slope to an even gentler 43 degrees, thus giving it the bent appearance that gives the pyramid its modern name. Unhappy with this monument, Sneferu had his architects try yet again. This time commencing the project at the same 43 degrees that marks the top of the Bent Pyramid, Sneferu's architects finally got it right with their construction, the so-called Red Pyramid (Figure 11.19).

Sneferu was succeeded by his son, Khufu, whose pyramid has become emblematic of the technological and architectural accomplishments of ancient Egypt (see Figure 11.19). Located north of Dashur, at Giza, Khufu's burial monument was finished in 2566 B.C. Consisting of more than 2.5 million stone blocks, Khufu's is the largest pyramid built in Egypt, a virtual mountain of stone rising to a dizzying height of 146.6 m (481 ft); in fact, it was the tallest human-made structure in the world until the construction of the Eiffel Tower in 1889. Khufu's pyramid is one of the iconic Giza triad of monuments (the other two are the pyramids of Khufu's son Khafre and grandson Menkaure).

In the Eighteenth Dynasty, after the period of pyramid construction had long passed, a young boy ascended to the throne during a period of great turbulence. He ruled for approximately 10 years; he became pharaoh at the age of 9 and died when he was only 19. His name was Tutankhamun, and his splendid burial, which served as a metaphor for ancient civilization in the "Prelude" of this chapter, will likely forever stand as a symbol of ancient Egypt (see Figure 11.2).

OTHER AFRICAN CIVILIZATIONS

Ancient Egypt's influence reached far from its center in northeasternmost Africa. To the south, the ancient civilizations of **Nubia,** initially inspired by the colossus to the north, developed their own uniquely African early civilization.

The Egyptians called the land to the south **Kush.** If you travel south past the so-called first cataract near Aswan in modern Egypt (the first extensive rapids encountered moving along the Nile from north to south) into the modern nation of Sudan, continuing to the sixth cataract, north of the Sudanese city of Khartoum, you have traversed the territory of ancient Nubia (O'Connor 1993).

To be sure, ancient Nubian civilization developed, at least initially, in response to the impact of having one of the world's first great civilizations literally just downstream. But it must be understood that ancient Egyptian civilization was not merely imported upstream, nor do we see Egyptian culture grafted wholesale onto an indigenous population's culture. Rather, developments to the north seem to have inspired the evolution of what was not a pale reflection of ancient Egyptian civilization but rather, as archaeologist David O'Connor (1993) characterizes it in the subtitle of his book, a distinct civilization that was "Egypt's rival" in ancient Africa.

Dating to more than 3,500 years ago, the civilization of Kerma represents the first indigenous complex civilization in Africa south of the ancient Egyptian nation (Connah 1987). The site of Kerma itself is located on the east bank of the Nile, south of the third cataract in Sudan. The site has been called "the earliest city in Africa outside of Egypt" (O'Connor 1993:50). The center of Kerma covered 15–25 acres and was surrounded by a huge wall about 10 m (33 ft) high. Its fortifications included monumental towers called **deffufa,** constructed of mud-brick; the Western Deffufa is an enormous, solid mass of brick some 52 m (170 ft) long and 27 m (88 ft) wide. Today it still stands more than 19 m (62 ft) high, and it was even taller in antiquity.

To the east of the city was a large cemetery, marked by enormous **tumuli**—earth mounds marking the graves of the elite—averaging 88 m (288 ft) in diameter (O'Connor 1993:54). These graves bear witness to the degree of social stratification present in that society. The elite were placed on finely made wooden beds, some encased in gold, and well-crafted items were entombed with them for their enjoyment in the afterlife: bronze swords, bronze razors, fine clothing of leather, fans made of ostrich feathers, and large quantities of pottery. The most impressive grave in the cemetery, Tumulus X, represents the final resting place of an obviously important ruler of Kerma, surrounded by the remains of close to 400 sacrificed people (322 actual remains were found, but the burial was disturbed, and there likely were more burials interred with the primary grave).

After 2800 B.P., the influence of Kerma faded and another Nubian kingdom rose to take its place. Called Napata, it was centered just downstream of the fourth cataract. It likely developed when Egypt's long reach to the south weakened. Social stratification is evident at the cemeteries of El Kurru, Jebel Barkal, and Nuri, where the elite were buried in tombs topped with small pyramids reminiscent of those in ancient Egypt yet clearly of local construction. The main population center of the Napata polity was the very large town of Sanam.

Perhaps the best known of the ancient Nubian cultures is that of Meroë. The Meroitic civilization dates from about 2500 to 2200 B.P. and is clearly the most complex and the most urban of the ancient civilizations south of Egypt (Connah 1987). The city of Meroë was a large settlement covering an area of about 0.75 km^2 (0.3 mi^2). The center of the settlement consisted of a maze of monumental structures made of mud-brick and faced with fired brick. These buildings appear to have been palaces, meeting halls, temples, and residences for nobility and their workers. The central area of Meroë was surrounded by a monumental wall of mud-brick.

In an enormous graveyard excavated to the east of the city were about 600 simple interments of common people. Even farther to the east, in a graveyard called North Cemetery, the tombs of Meroitic nobility were found with small, stone pyramids built on top (Figure 11.20).

Clearly the civilizations of Nubia were at least partially indigenous developments with a heavy dose of influence from the north. Contact with Egypt may have been the catalyst that set local people on the road to great social complexity and technological sophistication. Once the process was initiated, however, Nubians evolved their own, distinct version of civilization.

THE INDUS VALLEY CIVILIZATION

In the broad expanse of the Indus River valley, in the modern nation of Pakistan, developed one of the world's first civilizations, a complex state that controlled an area twice the size of ancient Mesopotamia or Egypt (Allchin and Allchin 1982; Fairservis 1975; Kenoyer 1998; McIntosh 2002; Possehl 1980).

The Indus civilization has been known to scholars in the West only since its two largest cities were first excavated in the early 1920s. The roots of the culture are not nearly as well known as are those of Egypt and Mesopotamia, with only a small handful of pre-Indus sites excavated. In addition, although like Mesopotamia and ancient Egypt, the Indus culture appears to have possessed a written language, the system as yet remains largely undeciphered.

Neolithic Cultures

The roots of the Indus civilization are revealed in a series of archaeological sites located to the west (Figure 11.21). For example, the site of Mehrgarh is located along the course of the Bolan River as it exits the foothills of the mountainous region called Baluchistan. First occupied more than 8,500 years ago, the residents of Mehrgarh survived, in part, by hunting wild animals, especially deer, gazelle, and wild pig, but even in the earliest levels of the site there is evidence that people living at Mehrgarh raised domesticated goats and planted some wheat and primarily barley (Kenoyer 1998). Both the goats and the wheat had been brought in from the west; it would seem that the site's residents borrowed the idea of food production from their neighbors on the western Iranian plateau.

The village grew in size and complexity, and by 8,000 years ago Mehrgarh's residents were building large and compartmentalized facilities of mud-brick in which they appear to have been communally storing their grain (McIntosh 2002). The village included a number of residential units containing between six and nine rooms, probably the homes of individual families.

FIGURE 11.21

Archaeological sites in India, Pakistan, and Afghanistan where evidence of the evolution of chiefdom and early state-level societies has been found.

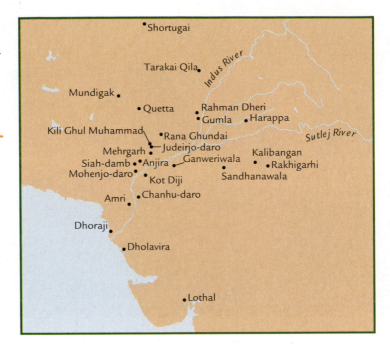

Around this time we also see the elaboration of burial practices, with people being interred with stone tools, bead and shell jewelry, and baby goats. Some of the shell objects found adorning the deceased were produced from conch, whose nearest source would have been the Arabian Sea, about 500 km (310 mi) to the south of the village. Jewelry made from lapis lazuli from Badakshan in northeastern Afghanistan and turquoise from Turkmenia, north of Afghanistan, was found in the burials as well; the sources of these stones are as much as 500 km (310 mi) distant from Mehrgarh.

We also see at this time and accelerating after 7,500 years ago, a decreased reliance on the hunting of wild animals; the frequencies of their bones in hearths and middens drop sharply as those of domesticated goats and cattle dramatically increase, signifying their expanded importance in subsistence at Mehrgarh.

Mehrgarh's location at the zone of transition between the uplands to the west and the floodplain to the east is important in our investigation of the Indus Valley civilization. The Indus is a treacherous river characterized by devastating and unpredictable flooding. Unlike the situation seen in Egypt or Mesopotamia, early Neolithic sites are not found along the river. As archaeologists Bridget Allchin and Raymond Allchin (1982:105) point out, local inhabitants' realization that the Indus system offered incredibly rich agricultural soil, coupled with their development of flood control and protection technology, allowed for the evolution of "an entirely new way of life."

About 1,000 years later, at around 7,000 B.P., a number of other farming villages developed in the Baluchistan Hills. One such site is Kili Ghul Muhammad, a small site covering an area of about 90 m (295 ft) by 55 m (180 ft). The structures at the site were mud-brick, and subsistence included the raising of sheep, goats, and oxen (Allchin and Allchin 1982). The only radiocarbon dates for Kili Ghul Muhammad are between 6400 and 6100 B.P., but these were not derived from the earliest levels at the site. Those levels likely date to a thousand or more years earlier. Another site in the Baluchistan Hills is Rana Ghundai. The houses, again, were of mud-brick, and here, too, sheep and goats were important for subsistence, along with cattle and wild ass.

Trade and competition—perhaps with attendant warfare—appear to have been important factors in the growth of increasingly complex and larger sites in Baluchistan after 6000 B.P. One site, Mundigak, is located on a well-known historical trade route between the Near East and south Asia that apparently was first established at this time. Mundigak was surrounded by enormous defensive walls interrupted with bastions. These walls had a practical purpose; the village was twice destroyed and twice rebuilt during its occupation.

All of these Neolithic sites west of the Indus provide us with a glimpse of the earliest stages of development of the Indus Valley civilization. They all exhibit a reliance on a diverse agricultural base of crops and animals. They show a notable dependence on trade with points as distant as the Arabian Sea and central Asia. They share an architectural form of substantial and planned-out mud-brick houses. And they show a shift through time from the uplands of Baluchistan to the floodplain of the Indus itself. This shift is clearly seen in the archaeological record by about 5500 B.P.

Flood Control and Civilization in the Indus Valley

This shift to the floodplain was the key to the development of civilization in this part of the world. It was made possible by the development of technology for flood control and protection, including the construction of artificial mounds, on which at least a portion of the settlements were built, as well as monumental walls around entire villages for protection from enemies and floodwaters. In this way, villages were protected from the periodic rampages of the Indus by being built, in part, above the floodwaters and by being surrounded by walls higher than those same floodwaters. Dams were built to impound and direct floodwater to storage areas for use in the dry summers that followed wet springs. Also, large tanks or cisterns were constructed to store rainwater for use in the dry season.

The site of Kot Diji is located on the incredibly rich floodplain about 32 km (20 mi) east of the Indus River, immediately adjacent to one of its ancient flood channels (Figure 11.22). The village is surrounded by a huge wall with a limestone rubble foundation and a mud-brick superstructure with bastions upwards of 5 m (more than 16 ft) high. This wall almost certainly served as defense not only against human enemies but also against a natural enemy—the floodwaters of the Indus. To the northeast is another large village called Kalibangan. Here, too, a massive mud-brick wall surrounds the

FIGURE 11.22

Kot Diji, located on an ancient flood channel of the Indus River in Pakistan, was surrounded by a monumental wall whose purpose probably was to keep residents secure from human enemies as well as the floodwaters of the Indus. (Department of Archaeology and Museums, Karachi)

settlement. Other substantial walled villages on the Indus floodplain, dating to the period after 5500 B.P., include the sites of Amri, Gumla, Rahman Dheri, and Tarakai Qila.

Cultural Convergence

An interesting feature of these settlements is the degree of what the Allchins refer to as "cultural convergence" (1982:163) and what Jane McIntosh (2002:48) calls "cultural homogenization." Where previous Neolithic sites in Baluchistan all exhibit their own artifact styles in pottery and items of adornment, as people began moving out onto the floodplain of the Indus, a certain degree of uniformity appears, indicating a greater level of cultural and perhaps political unification. Most significantly, a common image of a horned water buffalo head begins appearing on pottery throughout the area at many of the sites mentioned. Also, terra-cotta statues of women, following a standardized style, appear at many of the sites dating to this period; some archaeologists have dubbed these "mother goddesses," implying a degree of religious unification as well (Allchin and Allchin 1982:163).

A few of these floodplain settlements began undergoing an exponential increase in size sometime after 4800 B.P., culminating in their crossing the boundary between town and true city. Five of these communities expanded in physical size as their populations grew, coming to dominate the physical and cultural landscapes of the Indus Valley. The initially small villages of Ganweri-wala and Rakhigarhi each grew to cover more than 80 hectares (about 200 acres, or the equivalent of the area of about 151 regulation American football fields). Another small village, Dholavira, expanded until it extended across an area of 100 hectares (247 acres, about 187 football fields); located on a now dry channel of the Ravi River, tributary to the Indus, the urban center of Harappa expanded over more than 150 hectares (370 acres, 273 fields); and, located along the southern reaches of the Indus River, the truly gargantuan

FIGURE 11.23
The citadel of Mohenjo-daro (background) looms over the remnants of a neatly gridded layout of streets lined with the houses of the Indus Valley civilization's elite social class.
(© David Agee/ Anthro-Photo)

Mohenjo-daro is estimated to have sprawled out across more than 250 hectares (617 acres; that's more than 467 football fields or about 1 mi^2; all data were taken from Kenoyer 1998:49). Remember, these figures reflect the physical extent only of the urban centers themselves on the basis of the spread of archaeological evidence of houses, temples, streets, industrial zones, and the like. The surrounding hinterlands, populated by farmers whose produce literally fed the growth of the Indus Valley urban centers, were far larger. Kenoyer (1998:50) estimates that each of the five Indus cities just listed dominated an area of between 100,000 km^2 (38,000 mi^2, or an area greater than the state of Indiana, in the case of Ganweriwala) and nearly 170,000 km^2 (66,000 mi^2, or about the size of Washington State, in the case of Mohenjo-daro).

Cities of the Indus

During what specialists refer to as the "Mature Harappan period," lasting for 500 years, from 4500 to 4000 B.P. (Possehl 1980:5), Mohenjo-daro and Harappa developed into complex urban centers, with planned neighborhoods following a rectangular grid pattern, a sophisticated drainage system, communal granaries, bathhouses, and "citadels" consisting of great structures (palaces, temples, or even granaries; their function is not clearly known) built atop artificial mounds (Figure 11.23).

There are no extant census records for Harappa and Mohenjo-daro, so their populations, of course, can only be estimated. Certainly they were in the tens of thousands. Kenoyer (2005:29) suggests that the population of Harappa likely exceeded 40,000 and at its peak (both seasonally and in terms of its overall growth through time) may have been as high as 80,000. For the sake of comparison, that would place the estimated population of Harappa at somewhere between that of the modern American cities of Concord, New Hampshire, and Youngstown, Ohio. Estimates for the more expansive Mohenjo-daro are commensurately larger. Remember again, these estimates apply only to the urban centers themselves. Each Indus city was served by a large and dispersed support population in its surrounding hinterlands living in an estimated 1,500 smaller settlements spread throughout the Indus Valley (Kenoyer 2005:27). Most of these were small agricultural villages with areas of between 1 and 10 hectares (between 2.5 and 25 acres), but there were a few larger villages as well of between 10 and 50 hectares in extent (between 25 and 124 acres).

Even beyond the Indus Valley itself, large frontier settlements show the same material culture and written language. For example, the site of Lothal, located to the east of the Indus, still exhibits many of the architectural characteristics as well as the spatial layout of Mohenjo-daro and Harappa, if on a smaller scale. A full-fledged Indus town, Shortugai, has been found in central Asia, about 1,000 km (621 mi) east of the Indus. Shortugai was a mining settlement where lapis lazuli was collected.

The degree of planning that went into Indus Valley urban sites is unmatched among the earliest civilizations. Mohenjo-daro, Harappa, and Kalibangan follow virtually identical plans (Figure 11.24). There is, as Jane McIntosh (2002:124) phrases it, an "essential unity" to the organization of life in the Indus civilization. In these three cases, a citadel was built up on a platform of mud-brick on the western margin of the city. The citadel was surrounded by large public buildings, including bathhouses and granaries, and this "upper city" was encompassed by a monumental wall. In each of these three cases, the vast expanse of the city—the residential area where tens of thousands of people lived—was spread out to the east of the citadel. The lower city likewise was surrounded by a great wall. In all three cases, it is clear that the cities did not grow simply by accretion, blocks of residences added haphazardly as they were needed in response to population growth. Instead, these cities reflect a pattern of forethought in their construction, with broad main thoroughfares separated by secondary streets, which were, in turn, separated by narrow passageways leading to individual residences. Most of the roads were laid out in an often precise grid of parallel and perpendicular pathways. The alignment of the roads is precisely along the cardinal directions, which likely were determined astronomically (Kenoyer 1998:52). The houses themselves were made of mud-bricks that are so regularly and consistently proportioned (most bricks are made in proportions of 1:2:4—7 × 14 × 28 cm, or 2.75 × 5.5 × 11 in.), it is clear that brick makers, like their modern counterparts in brickyards, adhered to established size and form standards. Standardization extended to issues of water and sewage. Archaeological excavation of housing blocks at Mohenjo-daro has shown that each of those blocks and, in some cases, each individual house, possessed its own source of fresh water in the form of a well. For sanitary disposal, excavations at Harappa show that nearly every house possessed its own latrine. Most of these individual toilets

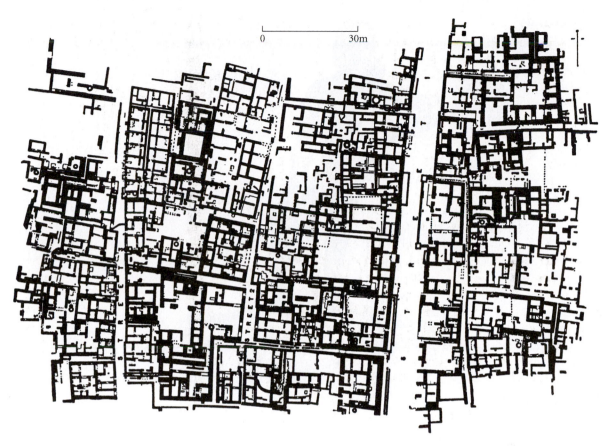

FIGURE 11.24
This map of Mohenjo-daro exhibits the planned nature of the city, with its major avenues, parallel and perpendicular streets, and regularly sized buildings and rooms. (From M. Wheeler 1968. *The Indus Civilization.* New York: Cambridge University Press. Reprinted with permission of the publisher)

led to a large jar with a hole at the bottom to allow waste to drain into the soil. Some were connected to a drain that allowed waste to flow out and away from the house, an early version of a sewer system.

Altogether, the Indus civilizations appear to have been highly centralized and tightly controlled, from the layout of their cities, the shapes of their bricks, and even the organization of their economy, including standardized weights and measures found in excavations at Indus cities. The dwellings in the lower cities of Indus urban centers, however, were not built on a standard plan and, instead, exhibit a wide range in size, from single-room apartments to mansions with dozens of rooms and enclosed courtyards. The size and elaborateness of some residences almost certainly reflect vast differences in the wealth and status of the individuals who lived in them. Certain sections of each of the Indus cities were blocked out for the production of goods by specialist craftspeople. McIntosh (2002) enumerates clusters of specialist workshops throughout Indus cities, including those of potters, flint workers, metal workers, brick makers, shell workers, precious-stone workers, ivory carvers, wood workers, textile makers, and seal makers (Figure 11.25). Other areas of the cities appear to have been the residences of scribes, priests, administrators,

FIGURE 11.25
The bronze dancing girl is a prime example of the unique character of the metallurgical skills of Indus civilization artisans.
(© Scala/Art Resource, NY)

and traders (Allchin and Allchin 1982:185). Add to this workshops in which workers baked bread and others where beads were manufactured and you have a picture of a bustling, busy metropolis.

Indus Valley cities were also trading centers into which exotic and undoubtedly expensive raw materials flowed and in which finely finished goods were produced. Gold, copper, lead, lapis lazuli, turquoise, alabaster, amethyst, agate, chalcedony, and carnelian were brought into the city, although they often originated at sources many hundreds of kilometers distant (Allchin and Allchin 1982:186). Also, some trade was carried out between these Indus Valley cities and the city-states of ancient Mesopotamia. Harappan **seals** have been found in Mesopotamia, and a small number of Mesopotamian **cylinder seals** have been found in Indus Valley sites. The island of Bahrain, located in the Persian Gulf, served as a central point in this intercivilization trade network. In other words, more than 4,000 years ago, Mesopotamia and the Indus Valley were part of an international trading system.

The Indus Script

The discovery of the **Rosetta Stone** in Egypt was the key to deciphering Egyptian hieroglyphs. Carved nearly 2,200 years ago, the Rosetta Stone bore the

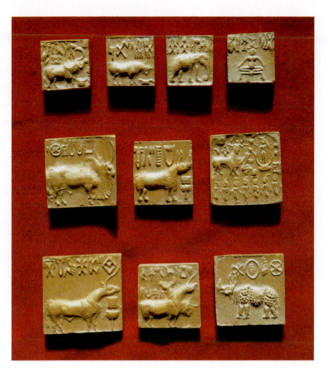

FIGURE 11.26
These inscribed ceramic tiles were found in excavations at the Indus Valley city of Mohenjo-daro and appear to reflect an early, locally developed form of writing. Though not yet deciphered, the writing appears to represent an accounting of lands, goods, and other materials.
(© Charles and Josette Lenars/ Corbis)

same message concerning the wonderful achievements of the pharaoh in three scripts: Greek and two versions of the written language of ancient Egypt, demotic and hieroglyphic. The Greek on the stone was known when the stone was discovered in 1799 and could be read, serving, therefore, as a key to the hieroglyphs. Through study of the Rosetta stone, the Egyptian written language became comprehensible. Unfortunately, there has been no discovery equivalent to the Rosetta Stone in the Indus Valley, and the language remains largely indecipherable.

To date, approximately 4,000 Indus inscriptions have been unearthed. Simple symbols have been found dating to as much as 5,200 years ago, but the script was not in widespread use until 800 years later, about 4,400 years ago. There are between 400 and 450 more or less distinct symbols used in the script, most of them in the form of animal pictographs and abstract geometric patterns (Figure 11.26). Most of the inscriptions have been found on small clay tablets; some are etched into pottery vessels, others on copper tablets. Kenoyer (2005:30) suggests that the context of the inscriptions and the co-occurrence of symbols indicate that, like the earliest Mesopotamian cuneiform and the first of the Egyptian glyphic writing, the Indus script served a rather mundane, economic purpose: keeping count of lands, goods, and other materials, essentially the record keeping of accountants. Kenoyer (2005:28) calls the Indus script "economic documentation" through a shared set of symbols.

A few researchers have argued that the Indus script was not a writing system at all and that the individual elements identified as glyphs are merely marks bearing some magical connotation, but not anything readable, not a comprehensible recording system using consistent symbolic notation (see Lawler 2004). The skeptics have argued that, unlike Mesopotamian cuneiform or Egyptian hieroglyphics, lengthy sequences of the symbols have not been found in the Indus markings—the longest inscription yet found is only 17 symbols in length—and many of the distinct symbols among those identified as elements of the script appear only once or very infrequently in the entire body of inscribed material.

Perhaps it is true that the Indus script was not used to record long-winded testimonials to the king's great achievements in battle, his remarkable intelligence, and his connection to the powers that be, but how long must a sequence of symbols be to record the number of jars of oil sold by a merchant or the amount of real estate owned by a landowner? Not many. A key element of state societies, as mentioned earlier in this chapter, is the ability to keep records—to keep track of wealth, land, and goods—and it seems unlikely that the complex society that developed in the Indus Valley could have functioned without that ability. It very well might not have been a written language in form that we usually think of, but it seems likely that the Indus script served the broader purpose of keeping track, in a more permanent way than mere memory, of those mundane things that civilizations need to keep track of.

"A Peaceful Realm"

The title of archaeologist Jane McIntosh's (2002) wonderful book on the Indus civilization makes an important point about its development as a complex society: *A Peaceful Realm.* There simply is no evidence that organized warfare or armies or the fear of attack played any role in the development of civilization in the Indus Valley. Archaeologists have not found evidence of major military defensive works around Indus cities or villages, no weaponry in the artifact assemblage, no cemeteries filled with skeletons exhibiting mortal wounds that would have resulted from military battles. Though, as we will see in "Issues and Debates" in this chapter, some researchers believe that organized conflict, invasion, and subjugation of a defeated population are key elements in the development of a powerful state society, the Indus Valley civilization provides no evidence to support this scenario. The Indus Valley, indeed, appears to have been a "peaceful realm," showing us that the development of a civilization need not involve the uniquely human invention, war.

ISSUES AND DEBATES

Many issues and debates concerning the evolution of the world's earliest civilizations revolve around two broad questions: (1) Why did state societies develop? and (2) Why do civilized societies collapse? Why states develop is the focus of this chapter's "Issues and Debates" discussion. Why they collapse will be the focus of "Issues and Debates" in Chapters 13 and 14.

WHY DID STATE SOCIETIES DEVELOP?

Living as we do in the modern version of a civilized, complex state society, we may take it for granted that such a condition is intrinsically superior to other, perhaps simpler lifeways. After all, our complex civilization affords us our materially rich lives and provides us with opportunities to follow our own paths—including the pursuit of education.

But there is another perspective to consider, especially when dealing with early civilizations. At least initially, complex state societies offer to only a relatively small proportion of the population the "perks" so many of us expect. For example in discussing the development of civilization in ancient China (discussed in Chapter 12), historian Jacques Gernet points out that the archaeological evidence for most of the people whose work propped up the state organization shows "the existence of a peasantry whose culture and tools (stone knives and wooden spades with curved handles) do not seem to have been very different from those of the Neolithic Age" (1987:44).

Especially in the world's earliest civilizations, most people worked harder than did people who lived in simpler Neolithic villages, and they gave up much of the control they had over their lives. Most people were needed to produce a surplus, part of which they turned over to the temple or the army or the state bureaucracy. Remember the estimate quoted earlier in this chapter: Perhaps as much as 75% of the population of Egypt worked as farmers, providing the state with their agricultural surplus. The peasants, who made up the greatest proportion of the population in all such societies, also provided labor for the state and often sons for military service—and possible death in foreign wars. Finally, as mentioned earlier in this chapter, simpler Neolithic societies probably were largely egalitarian, and most people had the same amount of wealth and about as much control over their lives as everyone else. With social stratification and the attendant evolution of an elite class or classes of kings, nobles, generals, and specialists, most people became second- or third-class citizens of a much larger political entity; archaeologist Thomas Patterson (1993:ix) characterizes the rulers of state societies as "bullies." Considering these factors, it seems reasonable to ask why civilization developed.

Conflict Models

Archaeologist Jonathan Haas (1982) divides explanations for the evolution of the complex civilization into the categories "conflict" and "integration." Conflict-based explanations, which Joseph Tainter (1988) calls "internal conflict" models, propose that complex civilizations evolved as a way to reduce, control, and mediate conflict among people living in a society. The conflict theorists include Lewis Henry Morgan (1877) and Friedrich Engels (1891), archaeologist V. Gordon Childe (1951), and anthropologists Leslie White (1959) and Morton Fried (1967).

Conflict theories, though diverse, have a number of fundamental propositions in common: Civilization is viewed as the outcome of a series of steps that began with the development of an agricultural economy by Neolithic people. In certain areas during the Neolithic, a substantial food surplus was possible. The production of a surplus by an individual or a family resulted in surplus, privately owned wealth. Some people got richer than others as a result of their larger surpluses. This, in turn, led to differences in status and ultimately to conflict between developing social classes. According to Joseph Tainter (1988:33), conflict theorists view the evolution of civilization and the state as the result of "divided interests" leading to domination and exploitation. An organizational solution to these conflicts arose in the form of a bureaucracy that served to validate the existence of social classes and at the same time served to mediate conflicts that arose between them.

Thus, according to the various conflict theories, agriculture led to surplus, which led to wealth, which produced different socioeconomic classes within Neolithic societies. With socioeconomic differentiation came the need to develop institutions that suppressed or mediated conflict between the newborn socioeconomic classes, often by sanctifying and legitimizing the newly evolved nonegalitarian social system. Symbols were needed to justify this new system ritually, and great works of art and architecture were produced. Thus do the social and material trappings of the state appear in the cultural evolutionary record.

Integration Models

Theories of state development that rely on models of integration rather than conflict have been proposed by thinkers as diverse as sociologist Herbert Spencer (1967), anthropologists Elman Service (1975) and Robert Carniero (1970), and historian Karl Wittfogel (1957). Integration theories, also, have a set of core propositions: Integration theories, which Joseph Tainter (1988:32) divides into "managerial" and "external conflict" models, see civilization as evolving from the need for increasingly complex integrative mechanisms in increasingly complex situations (Haas 1982:73). As Tainter (1988) points out, from the integrationist perspective, as the need developed to mobilize large and diverse populations to work together for the good of society, social institutions developed to expedite and at the same time justify, rationalize, codify, legitimize, and sanctify these activities.

From the integrationist perspective, though only a few can inhabit the top of the social, economic, and political pile, most members of civilizations do reap some benefits both directly and indirectly from the complex, stratified social system. The benefits that accrue to the few—great palaces, spectacular tombs, luxurious lifestyles—are viewed as the price paid by society as a whole for the benefits that accrue to everyone as a result of the key social roles played by the elite.

For example, in the view of historian Karl Wittfogel (1957) in his "hydraulic hypothesis," irrigation works played a pivotal role in the development of civilization. The sedentary and secure lifeway made possible by agriculture fostered the growth of human population, and the size of some local populations increased significantly. With growth came the need to produce even greater amounts of food to feed an increasing number of mouths. This need then stimulated the need to increase the productivity of existing farmland and to expand the acreage under cultivation. Along the floodplains of large rivers, this expansion was made possible by the construction of sometimes enormous, complex, and costly (in labor investment) irrigation networks. Such waterworks required not just new technology but also new social and political institutions to organize and coordinate the labor necessary for their construction and maintenance. Consider, for example, the amount of labor, as well as the level of coordination, necessitated by the construction of Mesopotamian canals, some of which were up to 40 km (26 mi) long, or of the enormous walls built around the cities of the Indus Valley to keep out the floodwaters of the river. Of necessity, power was vested in a class of managers who could call up and oversee the labor. Specialist groups who could design irrigation systems were needed. The same social and political apparatus used to organize labor to build canals could also help build defensive works around settlements as competition for land increased. Surplus labor could also be used to construct great homes and tombs for the members of the developing elite class; these material trappings of power developed as powerful symbols that served to legitimize the role of the elite class, further increasing the ability of these people to control the peasants.

Anthropologist Robert Carniero (1970) has suggested another avenue by which Neolithic societies may have crossed the threshold to civilization. Carniero cites the evidence for warfare commonly, though not universally found, in the world's early civilizations. He views this common thread as significant in the development of complex societies.

Though Carniero's use of warfare might seem to imply that his is a conflict-based model for the evolution of the state, in fact his model fits under the integrative approach, Tainter's (1988:32) "external conflict" subset of the integrative model. In Carniero's view, in certain areas agricultural communities developed where their territories were inherently "circumscribed"—that is, geographically or socially restricted, surrounded either by unproductive farmland or productive land already inhabited by another group or groups of people. In such a scenario, once a group's home territory is filled up with a growing population, a rational option is to expand into the surrounding viable farmland or into the next group's territory by taking over their land through wars of conquest. The conquered group then becomes integrated into a larger political entity as second-class citizens. In this way, a system of social stratification develops. Social and political institutions develop to incorporate these people into a growing political unit; symbols of power evolve, legitimizing the control of the victors over the vanquished; and the seeds of civilized life are sown.

Many Paths to Civilization

None of the hypotheses proposed to explain the evolution of the world's first civilizations can be applied universally. There was no unilinear sequence of development reflected in all the cases discussed in this chapter. Not all civilizations responded to the same pressures, not all societies passed through the same sequence of steps.

In some cases (Egypt and the Indus Valley here and lowland Mesoamerica in Chapter 10), rich farmland coupled with the lack of other important resources was key to the evolution of civilization. Social complexity developed in these regions partly because society could produce a food surplus and because they needed to create an effective system of trade. In other regions (early developments at Çatalhöyük and Chavín de Huántar, discussed in Chapter 10, and places like Cerros in the Yucatán, to be discussed in Chapter 13), a rich resource base may have produced nodes of great surplus wealth and a developing social complexity. In some regions, the need to create enormous irrigation networks may have stimulated the growth of social institutions that led to social stratification. In some cases, social stratification and early state institutions may have already existed, but a quantum leap in their power may have occurred with the kind of social control made possible by the reliance on irrigation technology. In other regions, the need for large-scale defensive works may have resulted in the same kinds of changes in society (for example, in Mesopotamia, discussed here, and China, discussed in Chapter 12).

It seems there were many different pathways leading to societies we today recognize archaeologically as possessing the requisite features of what we have defined as civilization. Many cultural evolutionary roads have led to essentially the same place, and it is likely that not one but some—possibly all—of the explanations offered here can help us understand the process in each of the areas discussed. It also is likely that quite different combinations of these explanations can be differentially useful in explaining what transpired in the world's first civilizations. As Egyptologist Barry Kemp has put it: "It is as justifiable to look for 'causes' which slowed down the process in some parts of the world as it is to search for those which allowed its rapid passage in others" (1991:32).

**CASE STUDY
CLOSE-UP**

If you have ever seen the Hollywood epic motion picture, *The Ten Commandments,* with Charlton Heston in the role of the biblical Moses, you are familiar with the notion that the Egyptians relied on slave labor in the construction of their temples and tombs. In this view, under the crack of the overseer's whip, foreigners like the Hebrew immigrants to Egypt mentioned in the Old Testament, large numbers of war captives, and an assortment of criminals serving out their sentences together toiled under the ferocious Egyptian sun, literally worked to death in the service of the state.

The archaeological record, however, is beginning to show something quite different. Remember, thousands, even tens of thousands of people, worked on construction projects like the pyramids; and these workers needed to be housed

FIGURE 11.27

Excavation by Egyptologist Mark Lehner of the remains of the community of pyramid builders belies the common misconception that the tombs of the pharaohs were built by slaves. Lehner has found that the people who worked on the pyramids were well housed and ate better than most other Egyptians of their social class. (© Kenneth Garrett)

and fed. An enormous infrastructure needed to be established to provide all of the support services such a large workforce required. Virtual worker cities must have sprung up around these construction sites, and the archaeology of these communities shows a picture very different from the common conception of the lives of those who built the pyramids and palaces of ancient Egypt.

For example, in 1999, Egyptologist Mark Lehner initiated a major project to excavate one of these worker cities on the Giza Plateau located in the shadow of the three great pyramids of the pharaoh Khufu, his son Khafre, and grandson Menkaure (Figure 11.27). If the workers who built these pyramids had been slaves, one might have expected that their overseers viewed them as largely expendable—with a strategy of treating them just well enough to keep them alive and working, but not expending a substantial amount of effort to keep them comfortable and healthy. Lehner interprets his archaeological research in the city as strongly contradicting this perspective. For example, he has found the remains of food provided to the pyramid workers; and, contrary to what one might expect of a slave class, they were eating better than nearly everybody else in Egypt. Lehner's crew has found and identified in the worker city a prodigious quantity of animal bones, especially of cattle, sheep, and goat, enough to support a crew of several thousand people eating meat every day, something not seen in the average Egyptian community

(Shaw 2003:49). Further, Richard Redding, a faunal analyst examining the bones recovered by Lehner's crew, has determined that the animals being used to feed the pyramid workers had not been old and sick castoffs, as might be expected had the workers been slaves. Instead, the bones indicate that the animals used to feed the workers had been in their prime; much of the cattle bone came from young male animals, under two years of age (Shaw 2003:49).

The archaeological evidence at Giza shows no prison camp or slave compound, but comfortable barracks, looking like oversized Egyptian homes, an abundance of bakeries, and even cemeteries where the dead workers were accorded a level of respect and care in death that would be highly unlikely had they been slaves.

Make no mistake, projects like constructing Khufu's pyramid were back-breaking and dangerous, but Lehner and others are confident that the labor, while likely not entirely voluntary, was, in large measure, considered a sacred duty by the citizens of Egypt. Today, people may complain about paying their taxes and, in the recent past of the United States, they may have worried about their sons being drafted into the Army; but citizens comply, viewing taxation and conscription as the price to be paid for living in a nation that builds roads and schools, protects its citizens and their property from criminals, and guards the borders from the attacks of enemies.

In a few instances, the pyramid workers of ancient Egypt left us messages in their own words, written on the enormous blocks of stone it had been their responsibility to move into place. These messages, perhaps more than anything else, provide us a unique insight into their own perspective of the nature of their labor for the state. Deep within Khufu's pyramid is a stone bearing this message: "We did this with pride in the name of our great King Khnum-Khuf," the formal name of the Pharaoh Khufu (Jackson and Stamp 2003:78). Those are not the words of slaves, but a message of pride by a group of pyramid workers who perceived their labor as the meaningful and necessary contribution of citizens serving their state.

 VISITING THE PAST   Because civilizations produced great works of art as well as monumental and durable works of architecture, many sites have been made readily accessible for tourism, and myriad opportunities exist for you to visit the past of these societies. Most standard tour guides will include information about visiting such sites. Unfortunately, and rather ironically, modern political uncertainties and conflicts make visiting some of the most important and impressive sites of ancient civilizations problematical or even downright dangerous. As with all foreign travel, it is wise for U.S. citizens to contact the State Department for information on travel advisories (see the listing on the State Department's Web site for current travel advisories: http://travel.state.gov/travel/cis_pa_tw/tw/tw_1764.html).

Rather obviously, travel to the hearth of one of the world's first civilizations, Mesopotamia, is not highly recommended; in fact, it's pretty crazy to even think about going. A glance at a world map will show you that Mesopotamia is located in Iraq, a nation still in the throes of terrorism, war, and internecine strife. Egypt, however remains a very popular tourist destination for people all over the world. Egyptians are understandably proud of their ancient heritage, and many appreciate the interest and attention of people from other nations who make a pilgrimage to the land of the pharaohs. Many of the most spectacular of the monuments of ancient Egypt are open to and welcoming of tourists; in fact, many of the photographs of Egyptian sites in this book were taken by my father on my parents' two tourist visits to Egypt. A perusal of the Internet will bring you to many fine travel companies experienced in Egyptian tourism.

Currently, there is an official State Department warning to American citizens about travel to Pakistan, suggesting that nonessential travel there be deferred. Mohenjo-daro and Harappa are spectacular sites and impressive to even the casual visitor; however, it likely is wise to take the counsel of the State Department seriously.

SUMMARY

The Neolithic set the stage for the development of sedentary farming villages in various places in the Old World. In a select few regions, an acceleration of cultural complexity led to the development of a stratified social system that controlled the excess wealth made possible through the ability to produce an agricultural food surplus. Social elites developed as part of a reorganization of society that allowed for orderly and systematic trade, the construction of irrigation canals to increase the food base, and the construction of monumental defensive fortifications. In these same regions, the new way of organizing and controlling human labor was utilized by the developing elite to construct less practical monumental works—temples, palaces, and mortuary features such as pyramids. This kind of monumental construction, today diagnostic of ancient civilizations, was both cause and effect of the new social dynamic of the world's first civilizations. Large, impressive monuments served as dramatic evidence of the power of the elite and symbolized and reified this power at the same time that it magnified it.

In the Old World, the processes that led to the kinds of societies we are calling civilization occurred in Mesopotamia in the Middle East, in the Nile Valley of Egypt and the Sudan, in the Indus Valley of Pakistan all discussed in this chapter, and, in eastern China, in southeastern Europe on Crete, and, later, in southeast Asia, as discussed in Chapter 12.

TO LEARN MORE

Technical Summaries

Ancient Civilizations, by C. C. Lamberg-Karlovsky and Jeremy Sabloff (1995), is an extremely thorough investigation of the origins of civilization in the Middle East and the Indus Valley (and Mesoamerica as well). Thomas C. Patterson's *Archaeology: The Historical Development of Civilizations* (1993) is another terrific source. For a theoretical discussion of the origins of civilization, see Jonathan Haas's *The Evolution of the Prehistoric State* (1982). Joseph Tainter's book, *The Collapse of Complex Societies* (1988), contains a brief and useful discussion of the origins of civilization.

To learn more about the florescence of any of the early civilizations mentioned in this chapter, see the sources cited in each discussion. In particular, for Mesopotamia, see Harriet Crawford's *Sumer and the Sumerians* (1991) and J. N. Postgate's *Early Mesopotamia: Society and Economy at the Dawn of History* (1992). A thorough and detailed exposition of the history of ancient Egypt, beginning in its earliest prehistory, with chapters on each of the important kingdoms and dynasties can be found in *The Oxford History of Ancient Egypt*, edited by Ian Shaw (2000). In their *Egypt and the Egyptians,* Douglas Brewer and Emily Teeter (1999) have written a wonderful and succinct book focusing on life in ancient Egypt. For a detailed chronology of the reigns of each of the pharaohs, see Peter A. Clayton's *Chronicle of the Pharaohs* (1994). If you've ever wondered about how the ancient Egyptians accomplished their heroic feats of engineering and architecture, don't miss Dieter Arnold's *Building in Egypt* (1991). Jonathan Kenoyer's *Ancient Cities of the Indus Valley Civilization* (1998) provides one of the most thorough discussions available on the archaeology of this early state society.

Popular Summaries

To learn more about the discovery of King Tut's tomb, see Brian Fagan's chapter on Howard Carter and Tutankhamun in his book *Quest for the Past: Great Discoveries in Archaeology* (1994). If you are interested in the civilization of Egypt, see Barry Kemp's *Ancient Egypt* (1991). John Romer's *Ancient Lives: Daily Life in Egypt of the Pharaohs* (1984) presents a fascinating account of ordinary occurrences in the lives of ancient Egyptians. For a wonderful chronological treatment of ancient Egypt, see Mark Lehner's *The Complete Pyramids* (1997). A useful work that focuses on the Sphinx but also covers much of Egyptian civilization is Paul Jordan's *Riddles of the Sphinx* (1998). For a quick and very well written treatment of Egyptian architecture, engineering, and construction, especially as these relate to Khufu's Great Pyramid, your best bet is *Building the Great Pyramid* by Kevin Jackson and Jonathan Stamp (2003). For a broad-ranging book on the most popular—and yes, sometimes mysterious—topics surrounding the ancient Egyptian civilization, with articles written by an array of experts, *The Seventy Great Mysteries of Ancient Egypt* (2003), edited by Bill Manley, is informative, well-written, and great fun. Jane McIntosh's *A Peaceful Realm: The Rise and Fall of the Indus Civilization* (2002) is an informative and extremely well written account of that primary civilization.

On the Web

There is an enormous and growing number of sites on the Internet devoted to early civilizations, including scholarly, university, and museum Web sites, sites put up by travel agencies hoping to book you on a tour to an archaeological destination, personal Web pages with tourist-visit photographs of pyramids and temples, and the ever-present New Age Web sites purporting to expose the mystical secrets of ancient societies. I am providing here a very small sample of some of the most informative and accurate sites I have found—one for each of the ancient Old World civilizations discussed in this chapter. Any Internet search engine can help you find lots more for help with a term paper or simply to satisfy your intellectual curiosity about the world's oldest civilizations.

Mesopotamia:
http://www.mesopotamia.co.uk/menu.html

Egypt:
http://guardians.net/egypt

Nubia:
http://www.anth.ucsb.edu/faculty/stsmith/research/nubia_history.html

Indus Valley:
http://www.harappa.com/har/har0.html

Online Learning Center: www.mhhe.com/feder4

The Online Learning Center (OLC) Web companion to *The Past in Perspective* features a variety of supplemental study aids. For each chapter, this free Web site includes

ONLINE LEARNING CENTER

- Self-Quizzes to take as pretests prior to exams
- Interactive Timeline Study Guides for additional review and reinforcement of key information
- Learning Objectives
- Chapter Site links with Web addresses for many of the fossil and archaeological sites mentioned in the text

KEY TERMS

Amratian/Naqada I, 469
Badarian, 469
city-state, 464
civilization, 455
cuneiform, 467
cylinder seal, 490
deffufa, 481
envelope, 466
Fayun/Merimden, 469
hieroglyphic, 472

Kush, 481
Late Gerzean (Naqada II, Maadian), 470
mastaba, 471
monumental work, 456
Naqada III, 470
Nubia, 481
Omari A, 469
Rosetta Stone, 490
seal, 490

social stratification, 457
specialization of labor, 459
state, 454
system of record keeping, 459
token, 466
tumuli, 482
Ubaid, 461

12

An Explosion of Complexity

THE FLOWERING OF CIVILIZATION IN THE OLD WORLD: SHANG, MINOAN, AND KHMER

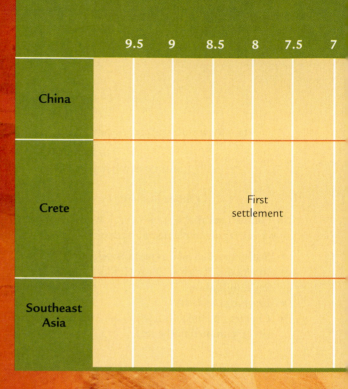

	9.5	9	8.5	8	7.5	7
China						
Crete			First settlement			
Southeast Asia						

CHAPTER OVERVIEW

The pattern of increasing social, economic, and political complexity seen in Mesopotamia, Egypt, and the Indus Valley (Chapter 11) was repeated in several other regions of the Old World. State societies characterized by the concentration of wealth and power in the hands of an elite class, the production of monumental structures, and the creation of fine artwork by a specialist class who served the elite is reflected in the archaeological records of China, Crete, and southeast Asia. The ancient state societies of, respectively, the Shang, Knossos, and the Khmer are described in this chapter.

Thousands of years ago

6.5	6	5.5	5	4.5	4	3.5	3	2.5	2	1.5	1

Ssu-tun (≈5.5)
Ch'eng tzu-yai (≈5.5)
T'a-ssu (≈5.5)
Erh-li-t'ou (≈4.5–4)
Hsi-pei-kang (≈3)
An-yang (≈3)
Hsiao-t'un (≈3)

Agii Theodhori
Amnisos   Mallia
Arkhanes
Katsamba
Kydonia
Phaistos
Knossos (≈5)
Knossos temple (≈4.5)
Thera eruption (≈3.5)

Funan (≈2)
Angkor Wat (≈1.5)
Chenla (≈1.5)
Angkor Thom (≈1.5)

ONLINE
LEARNING
CENTER

Go to **www.mhhe.com/feder4** for an
interactive study guide version of this timeline.

The images presented in the frescoes of Knossos, an impressive and ancient palace/temple on the island of Crete in the eastern Mediterranean are evocative of what appears to be a charming, peaceful, ancient civilization, a culture we now call the Minoans. Graceful and athletic men and women are shown marching and dancing in the paintings. Some seem to be skilled gymnasts and are depicted performing impressive acrobatic movements, going so far as to daringly cartwheel over charging bulls (Figure 12.1). The images are of a vibrant, lively people, citizens of a civilization that we can date to more than 3,800 years ago, 1,000 years before the emergence of the fabled Greek city-states, including Athens and Sparta.

But there is a darker side to these people, as revealed by the archaeology of Knossos, a side of death and horror. In two separate instances, archaeologists have discovered what they believe to be clear evidence of the practice of human sacrifice among the ancient Minoans.

In the first instance, Greek archaeologists Yannis Sakellarakis and Efi Sapouna-Sakellaraki (1981) were excavating a small temple located near the town of Arkhanes, about 7 km (4 mi) from Knossos. The temple had been destroyed by earthquakes that hit Crete in 3650 B.P. The excavators initially thought that they had found the remains of four people killed when the temple collapsed on them during this period of geological instability on the island. On closer examination, however, it turned out that only three had been victims of the earthquake. The fourth appears to have been ritually slaughtered by his comrades, his blood drained from his body, apparently in a last and desperate act of propitiating the angry gods who were causing the earth to shake the great temples of Crete to their foundations.

The body of the sacrifice victim was found in the temple, on a platform commonly used for animal sacrifice by the Minoans. Near the platform was a trough used for catching the blood of the sacrificed for use in ceremonies that followed the ritual killing. A bronze knife used in killing animals being offered up to the gods was found near the altar. Based on the forensic analysis of the skeleton, the human offering had been a healthy and vigorous eighteen-year-old male. Though he died in the ruin of a collapsed temple, his death cannot be ascribed to any kind of accidental trauma. He wasn't killed by a chunk of ceiling falling on his head, nor was he crushed by the building's collapse. The cause of his death almost certainly had been blood loss. His body was being drained of blood at the time of the destruction of the temple. Unfortunately for his friends, his ritual death did little to alter their fates or those of Crete the day the temples collapsed 3,650 years ago.

An even more gruesome scene on Minoan Crete has been reconstructed by archaeologist Peter Warren (1984). Excavating at Knossos itself, in layers dating to the next great natural destruction inflicted by the eruption of the volcano Thera, located 120 km (72 mi) from Crete on the island called Santorini, Warren found the remains of two young children, an 8-year-old and an 11-year-old. Their bones were found in the same room of the temple at Knossos, along with those of a slaughtered sheep.

FIGURE 12.1
This refurbished fresco at Knossos shows a daring gymnast performing a handstand on the back of a charging bull. Bulls are a common theme in paintings and sculptures found at Knossos. (Gustavo Tosich/ Corbis)

The children's bones show them to have been in good health, without any pathologies or sign of disease before their deaths. Furthermore, there is no evidence of trauma in the form of blows from a weapon; these children were not murdered in a fit of violence nor were they killed in some sort of battle. They were not crushed by the building's collapse. In fact, there simply is no natural reason for the deaths of these children. Knife cut marks on their small bones, however, present clear evidence of the painstaking stripping away of the flesh from their bodies. Horribly, the bones of the children bear a striking resemblance to those of animals sacrificed by the Minoans at other sites where animals were flayed as part of their ceremonial killing. Large vessels in the room where the children's bones were found contained shells, the remains of edible snails, and young human phalanges (finger or toe bones) and a human vertebra with a knife cut. Peter Warren interprets this evidence to imply that, not only were the children killed as part of a sacrifice, but their flesh may also have been eaten as part of a practice of ritual cannibalism.

To be sure, the grisly evidence of human sacrifice among the Minoans is quite uncommon. Such killing appears not to have been an everyday practice, but rather a reaction to extreme circumstances. It is likely not coincidental that the evidence for these two sets of ritual human sacrifices are dated to periods of greatest challenge to Minoan Crete, the devastating earthquakes of 3650 B.P. and the volcanic eruption of Thera at 3420 B.P. It bears witness to the terrible steps a people may resort to in their desperate and doomed attempt to avert a natural catastrophe whose ultimate impacts they may have only dimly recognized.

CHRONICLE

In Chapter 11, I presented a chronicle of three of the most impressive of the primary civilizations of the Old World: Mesopotamia, Egypt, and the Indus Valley. Here in Chapter 12, I will chronicle three more ancient Old World civilizations: the Shang, the Minoans, and the Khmer. Two, the Shang and the Khmer are located in eastern Asia, while the Minoans were located in Europe. One, the Shang, was, like the ancient Mesopotamian, Egyptian, and the Indus civilizations, situated largely within the valley of a major river system; and that river had a major influence on the development of its society. Another of the civilizations chronicled in this chapter, the Minoans, was not located along a major river but was, instead, an island nation, perhaps humanity's first maritime civilization. The Khmer were neither riverine nor maritime, but were, instead, situated within a tropical rain forest.

In their similarities and differences, the ancient Old World states discussed in Chapter 11 and to be discussed here in Chapter 12, as well as the state societies that developed in the New World and are to be discussed in Chapters 13 and 14, reflect both the common threads that compose the warp and weft of the evolution of civilizations and the many unique characteristics and histories that contributed to the great diversity seen in the archaeology of the complex societies of the ancient world.

THE CIVILIZATION OF ANCIENT CHINA

The roots of Chinese civilization can be traced back to the Yang-shao culture discussed in Chapter 9. Yang-shao sites are small, and subsistence was based on the cultivation of millet and, only later, rice (Figure 12.2).

The Lung-shan Culture

Chinese archaeologists perceive a change in Yang-shao sometime after 5000 B.P. and define a new culture, the **Lung-shan,** as replacing Yang-shao. A number of new features distinguish Lung-shan sites from earlier Yang-shao sites and presage the development of early Chinese complex civilizations. Rice became the dominant cultigen, and sites are larger and more permanent. For example, at the Lung-shan site of Ch'eng tzu-yai, the village was enclosed by a monumental wall of stamped earth whose size is an indication of the villagers' capacity for communal labor. The Chinese term for the stamped or pounded

FIGURE 12.2
Archaeological sites in China where evidence of the evolution of chiefdom and early state-level societies has been found.

earth technique used in construction is **hang-t'u.** The hang-t'u technique was used frequently in later periods of Chinese history in making house walls as well as in defensive structures.

The wall at Ch'eng tzu-yai is enormous and far beyond the abilities—and needs—of earlier people to muster the labor of a large population. The wall is measured at 390 m (nearly 1,300 ft) by 450 m (nearly 1,500 ft), is 9 m (29 ft) wide at the top, and is 6 m (more than 19 ft) high (Chang 1986:248).

The cemetery at the site reflects another significant element of civilization: status differentiation as reflected in highly differentiated burials. Archaeologist Kwang-chih Chang (1986) notes the existence of a four-tiered burial hierarchy. There are large elaborate graves at the site—high-status tombs where the deceased was interred in a wooden casket and accompanied by fine ceramics. In the same cemetery, there are narrow burial pits barely large enough to hold a human body, with no casket or grave goods. In the typical pattern of a stratified society, there were far fewer members of the elite than of the peasant classes, again as reflected in the burial statistics. From most to least elaborate interments, at Ch'eng tzu-yai there were 5 upper-class burials, 11 second-class, 17 third-class, and 54 fourth-class, or low-class, burials (Chang 1986:249). This ratio compares to socioeconomic class structure as evidenced at the enormous later Neolithic cemetery at T'a-ssu. Of the excavated graves there, 9 were judged to be of the upper class, 80 belonged to a middle tier, and 610 were plain, lower-class interments (Chang 1986:277). Some of the upper-class burials dating to this same period contained an incredible array of rare items that exhibited a high level of artistic sophistication. For example, a young man buried at the site of Ssu-tun was interred with 57 finely carved, intricate jade rings and jade tubes (called *ts'ung*).

Along with monumental village walls, which later became a common feature of Chinese civilization, and status-differentiated burials, the period from 5,000 to 4,000 years ago in China is marked by the appearance of a number of other features that represent key elements in the earliest Chinese civilization. The increasing use of metal, especially copper, and the earliest use of bronze is evidenced during this time. Historian Jacques Gernet (1987) suggests that the sophisticated kilns—capable of producing very high, constant temperatures—used in the Chinese Neolithic to produce the fine ceramics that mark even the early years of that period were an enabling factor in the rapid advancement in metallurgy that marks Chinese civilization. In Gernet's view, the ability to manufacture bronze weapons was a key element in the evolution of Chinese civilization; the development of bronze metallurgy and the rise of China's first civilization do indeed overlap temporally. Gernet proposes that power was invested in those who controlled bronze production and walled cities evolved as a result of competition and warfare.

A number of other identifiable hallmarks of later Chinese civilization appear at this time, between 5,000 and 4,000 years ago. The jade ts'ung tubes and the practice of **scapulimancy**—divining by interpreting the patterns produced by heating animal shoulder blades in a fire—become geographically widespread, indicating a spatially broad sphere of interaction and the initial unification of people into first a religiously defined and ultimately a politically drawn entity. This pattern is highly reminiscent of the development of a common, unifying iconography in Mesoamerica (Olmec) and western South America (Chavin) discussed in Chapter 10 and also reminiscent of the phenomenon of "cultural convergence" seen in the Indus Valley (Chapter 11) immediately prior to the development of civilization there.

In this period we can also perceive evidence of violence on a scale not previously seen in Chinese prehistory. Monumental village walls with ramparts, as well as the skeletal evidence of trauma, imply that institutional violence with armies clashing had already established itself during Lung-shan times.

Acceleration Toward Civilization

The culmination of these early developments can be seen at the site of Erh-li-t'ou, dated to about 3800 B.P. The site itself is an order of magnitude bigger than anything seen previously, covering an area of 2.5 km (1.6 mi) by 1.5 km (a little less than 1 mi). Bronze artifacts are common at the site, as are jade *ts'ung* tubes. Some of the bronzes were utilitarian tools, including knives, chisels, axes, adzes, and arrowheads and other weapons. Many of the bronze artifacts at the site, including disks, fancy drinking vessels, and musical instruments, were ceremonial or ornamental.

FIGURE 12.3
Bronze metallurgy played a significant role in the development of ancient Chinese civilization. This charming casting of a baby elephant perched atop an adult elephant was found at An-yang, a capital city of the Shang civilization. (Freer Gallery of Art, Smithsonian Institution, Washington, D.C.: Purchase, F1936.6a-b)

There are large, impressive burials at Erh-li-t'ou, and some members of what we can confidently call the wealthy, elite class were buried in lacquered coffins. A unique feature at Erh-li-t'ou is seen in the remains of two palaces. These structures are far larger than any of the residences located at the site. One palace was about 100 m (328 ft) on a side; the second was somewhat smaller. The walls of both palaces consisted of thick berms of stamped earth.

The Shang Civilization

The site of Erh-li-t'ou was a precursor to the early florescence of Chinese civilization as represented by the Shang Dynasty. The Shang was China's first true urban civilization. For example, the modern city of An-yang is the site of the ancient city of Yin, a Shang capital city ruled by a succession of 12 kings beginning about 2,400 years ago. Great tombs of the rulers residing at Yin have been found at the sites of Hsiao-t'un and Hsi-pei-kang. These royal interments are enormous and would have required the labor of thousands of peasants. The royal graves are cruciform—in the shape of a giant cross. The king or emperor was buried in the center of the cross, with long, broad access ramps leading to the burial itself. The deceased noble was placed in an elaborate wooden coffin, surrounded by the symbols of rank and wealth that differentiated him or her from the rest of society: jade, bronze, and ceramic artifacts and even chariots and sacrificed horses (Figure 12.3). Along the access ramps

FIGURE 12.4

The burial remains of be-headed people who were sacrificed in ceremonies surrounding the death of a member of the royal class of the Shang civilization in China. (Courtesy of the Institute of History and Philology, Academia Sinica, Taiwan)

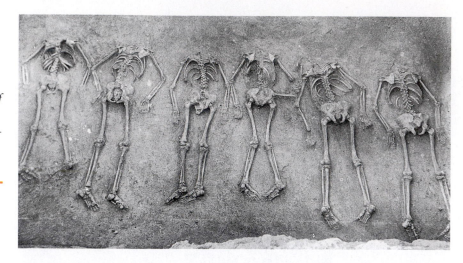

to the royal gravesite were found the remains of dozens of humans sacrificed to accompany their leader into the afterlife, decapitated and laid out neatly in rows along the rampways (Figure 12.4).

It is with the Shang that we enter into the historical period of China's past. A written language containing more than 5,000 characters, only a fraction of which have been translated, has been found at Shang sites. Shang set the stage for all subsequent Chinese civilization (see the "Case Study Closeup" of this chapter for one of the most extraordinary manifestations of ancient Chinese civilization). In at least a symbolic sense, the Chinese emperors who ruled well into the twentieth century were the inheritors of a culture that can be traced back to the time of the first dynasty of the Shang civilization.

MINOAN CRETE

The island of Crete is a tiny jewel in the eastern Mediterranean (Figure 12.5). It is long and narrow, less than 250 km (152 mi) from east to west and not more than 56 km (35 mi) from north to south. Its entire area is barely 8,260 km^2 (3,189 mi^2), equaling, approximately, the combined area of the two smallest states in the United States: Rhode Island and Delaware. Along with being small, Crete is located a great distance from the mainland, and so it was occupied relatively late in prehistory. It was reachable only when the people of the Mediterranean developed seaworthy boats and navigational skills. The oldest occupation of the island dates only to around 8000 B.P.; it was uninhabited by human beings before this time. Yet on this small island, occupied only relatively recently, Europe's first civilization was to develop.

FIGURE 12.5
Archaeological sites in Crete where evidence of the evolution of chiefdom and early state-level societies has been found.

The Rediscovery of Minoan Crete

In the 1890s, archaeologist Sir Arthur Evans discovered the remains of what he labeled the **Minoan** civilization on Crete (Evans 1921–36). Evans had been inspired in his search by the Greek myth of King Minos of Crete, who kept a half-human, half-bull monster called the Minotaur deep in the recesses of a tortuous labyrinth. Until the twentieth century, King Minos and his civilization were assumed by many to be mythological, entirely the product of the imaginations of the myth- and legend-makers of ancient Greece. But some thinkers felt that the Greek myths reflected, in at least some of their particulars, historical truths. In perhaps the best-known example, archaeologist Heinrich Schliemann found the real Troy—assumed by many to be the product of the ancient Greek poet Homer's imagination—by taking Homer literally in his description of that ancient city and its location. In turn, Evans took seriously the core of the story of King Minos and a great civilization on Crete contemporary with or even older than that of ancient Greece.

Evans first visited Crete in 1894, and almost immediately recognized the great archaeological potential of a hillside at **Knossos** on the north-central part of the island. Eventually, Evans was able to purchase the site. In 1900, he initiated excavations and quickly discovered the spectacular remains of a great palace or temple (Figure 12.6; see the chapter titled "Arthur Evans and the Minoans" in Brian Fagan's 1994 book, *Quest for the Past: Great Discoveries in Archaeology*). This seemed to be the remains of King Minos's city, as described by the ancient Greeks. The temple was built up on an artificial mound some 7 m (almost 22 ft) high, composed of the piled-up remains of 10 successive building levels of Neolithic housing dating back to 8000 B.P. (J. D. Evans 1968).

Who Were the Minoans?

The settlers of Crete were people from the mainland of southeastern Europe and southwestern Asia, likely from Greece and Anatolia (Renfrew 1972:1979).

FIGURE 12.6

The temple at Knossos on Crete is the most impressive, though by no means the only, material evidence of the monumental architecture of the ancient Minoan civilization. (M. H. Feder)

Though probably initially discovered by chance, Crete soon was intentionally settled, in the ninth millennium B.P., by people who brought their Neolithic food base with them. Archaeological excavation of Neolithic Crete reveals the presence of emmer and bread wheat, along with sheep, goats, pigs, and cattle, none of which are native to the island (Warren 1987). The Neolithic population grew, and a number of farming villages dotted the island in the millennia following its initial settlement.

Crete was fortuitously positioned geographically, at a crossroads for people sailing between southeastern Europe and the ancient civilizations of the Middle East and ancient Egypt. An influx of wealth from ancient trade between the peoples of three continents seems to have spurred a period of increasing complexity on Crete. The island itself provided perfect conditions for growing olives, and the olive oil produced on Crete and traded throughout the Mediterranean provided even more wealth to the island. A burst of development, centered on the site of Knossos, occurred at about 5000 B.P., beginning with the importation of bronze from the mainland. By about 3880 B.P., the first monumental edifice, the temple discovered and initially excavated by Evans, was constructed at the site of Knossos. The building consisted of a mazelike jumble of rooms, chambers, halls, and corridors. This main temple at Knossos is sometimes called, in fact, the "Labyrinth," a reference to the myth of King Minos's labyrinth with the Minotaur at its core (Castleden 1990a).

Though fueled by trade and contact with older, established civilizations in Africa and the Middle East, civilization on Minoan Crete does not represent the transplantation of an alien culture. Crete benefited from its location, and the ideas and wealth that passed through the island certainly acted as a

FIGURE 12.7
One of the many frescoes depicting everyday life among the Minoans, as reconstructed by the excavator of Knossos, Sir Arthur Evans. (M. H. Feder)

catalyst in the development of Minoan civilization. But as archaeologist Colin Renfrew (1979) points out, Minoan Crete by and large reflects an indigenous European development of civilized life, traceable to evolving complexity that had been going on in the Aegean for 1,000 years.

The Temple at Knossos

The temple at Knossos would at its peak ultimately cover an area of some 20,000 m^2 (more than 210,000 ft^2, or about 5 acres) and would contain about 1,000 separate rooms. The temple included a central courtyard with a pillar-lined hallway, a huge number of storage rooms, a ceremonial bath, and grand staircases leading to upper levels—some parts of the temple possessed three or even four stories. The walls of some of the living quarters and large halls were covered with magnificent fresco paintings of dolphins and especially bulls. The artistic depiction of bulls in ceremonial settings may be connected to the Greek story of the Minotaur. As noted in this chapter's "Prelude," where the Minoans depicted themselves in these paintings, we see a graceful and athletic people (Figure 12.7).

One set of rooms has been interpreted as being the living quarters of the nobility of Knossos, replete with thrones, bathrooms, and a sophisticated drainage system for wastewater. The monumental proportions and complexity of the temple at Knossos are a clear indication of developing complexity in social, political, and economic spheres of the community. Further evidence of Minoan civilization is seen in the form of writing—so-called Linear A, as yet undeciphered.

Developments on Crete were halted, if only temporarily, by the catastrophic earthquake mentioned in the "Prelude" that all but destroyed the temple at Knossos in 3650 B.P. Another impressive temple on Crete at the site of Phaistos was also damaged at this time. That temple later was destroyed utterly in a fire. Remarkably, however, this catastrophe served only to spur further subsequent development on Crete in what is called the **New Temple Period.** Apparently, the wealth still pouring into the island was sufficient to overcome the impact of this natural disaster.

This peak in Minoan civilization occurred during the period 3650 to 3420 B.P. The temple of Knossos was rebuilt and became even larger and more impressive. Paintings and statuettes indicate a developing religion focused on goddesses and priestesses. Though the temple reflects a monumental level of labor on the part of the island's inhabitants and would have been possible only in a socially stratified society, there is little evidence of the kind of personal conspicuous consumption on the part of the societies that marks ancient Egypt, Mesopotamia, or ancient China; there are no overwhelmingly ornate burials of an elite at Knossos or elsewhere on Crete. Small rural farming villages continued to supply their food surplus to support the temples located at Knossos and elsewhere. Large towns developed, each with its own temple and residential areas; Knossos was the largest and most impressive of these, but it was not the only one. At its peak, the population of Knossos and its surrounding "suburbs" may have been close to 100,000 people (Marinatos 1972:709), making it the largest concentration of people anywhere in the ancient world to that point in time.

The Eruption on Thera

This pattern of evolving complexity was brought to a halt by another, even more devastating natural catastrophe. Sometime around 3420 B.P. (perhaps a bit earlier) there was a cataclysmic volcanic eruption on the island today called Santorini (the ancient Greeks called it Thera, and before that it was Kalliste), 116 km (72 mi) north of Crete. The eruption itself, accompanied by severe earthquakes, badly damaged many settlements on Crete. The explosive force of the eruption of Thera has been judged to have been some four times as powerful as the volcanic conflagration of Krakatoa, a historically witnessed eruption in the Dutch East Indies in 1883 (Marinatos 1972:718). That catastrophe killed 36,000 people.

Certainly the damage to Knossos and other communities and the destruction of so many ports were devastating blows to the Minoan polity. The Minoan civilization developed and flourished, at least in part, as a result of trade; the loss of ports through which trade items passed and the probable destruction of the Minoan fleet of trading vessels must have had a tremendous impact on the Minoan economy. Perhaps of even greater significance, however, for the Minoans over the long term was the deposit of poisonous white ash some 20–30 cm (8–12 in.) thick that fell from the sky following the explosive eruption on Thera. This rain of volcanic ash all but destroyed the agricultural economy on Crete for a time. The effects of the volcanic eruption on Thera were so widespread and catastrophic that it may have become the stuff of legend later on in the Mediterranean world; some have argued that Thera was the model for Plato's description of the Lost Continent of Atlantis (see "Issues and Debates" in this chapter; Feder 2007 and Stiebing 1984).

The Minoans were able to survive after Thera's eruption, but it is clear that they never fully recovered from the devastation delivered up by the eruption on Thera. It weakened them sufficiently so that soon after they were conquered by a developing civilization on mainland Greece, the **Mycenaeans,** the precursors to the ancient, historical Greeks. From there the Minoans passed into the stuff of myth and legend until Sir Arthur Evans conducted his archaeological investigation at Knossos at the outset of the twentieth century.

THE KHMER KINGDOM

Henri Mouhot had heard the stories first told by Portuguese traders of great temples in the jungle—fabulous palaces "built by the gods," local people had told them—and was determined to find out if there was any truth to the tales. Exploring in the dense jungle near the town of Siem Reap in Cambodia in the 1860s, Mouhot came upon the spectacular ruins of the ancient **Khmer** civilization. His discovery brought to light the remnants of what had been a remarkable world, previously only the stuff of legend, to Western historians and archaeologists.

Mouhot was to die in the jungle before he could announce his remarkable discovery to the world. He kept a detailed diary, however, and the precise records he had maintained there of his historical research were sent back to his family in France upon his death. When scholars read Mouhot's account, it sparked a flurry of interest and research on the Khmer civilization that has continued to this day, interrupted intermittently, most recently by the tragedy of the Cambodian civil war (see Figure 12.2).

The Roots of Angkor

Archaeologist Charles Higham (2001) traces the roots of the Angkor civilization to the period when settled agricultural villages were established in southeast Asia more than 4,000 years ago. Rice was the key ingredient in the subsistence base of these settlers of the region that would become the modern nations of Thailand, Vietnam, and Cambodia.

The rich, swampy lowlands in which many of these people settled was a perfect habitat for rice cultivation and allowed for the production of a food surplus, which in turn supported the development of economic and social complexity. Technological jumps are also seen; first bronze and then iron metallurgy is evidenced in the archaeological record. Iron spades were especially valuable in tilling the land and directing water through the construction of irrigation networks, increasing agricultural efficiency. Powerful and complex **Iron Age** communities developed throughout southeast Asia soon after 500 B.C.

Funan

The emerging complexity fluoresced in the delta of the Mekong River during the period A.D. 150–550, culminating in the development of the state of **Funan.** Chinese written texts that date to this period describe Funan as a rich nation based on rice agriculture, with cities inhabited by a wealthy nobility living in ornate wooden palaces, slaves serving the needs of the noble class, and an all-powerful king at the top of this social pyramid. These same Chinese texts detail a complex history of growth, of forming alliances, of decay, and of revitalization. Written descriptions of Funan are complemented by the archaeological record of enormous foundations of brick temples and walls and the remains of expansive moats and reservoirs, all attesting to the architectural labors of a large and coordinated workforce. The appearance of exotic materials including coins, glass, and carnelian (a beautiful, reddish-brown stone used to make jewelry) indicates that trade was an important element of the economy (Higham 2001:147). Clearly there was influence from the west; Sanskrit from India was used as the written language of Funan and may have been adopted through contact with Indian traders. Also originating in India, Hinduism became the dominant religion of Funan.

Chenla

Trading patterns changed after A.D. 550, and the Mekong Delta where Funan developed became less important. As a result, wealth and attendant economic complexity, along with political power, shifted upriver, to the north, to the Mekong Valley near the Tonle Sap or "Great Lake" of Cambodia. Here developed the **Chenla** civilization. One of the great rulers of Chenla, Jayavarman I, was responsible for greatly magnifying the social and political complexity of southeast Asian civilization. According to Higham (2001), Jayavarman I created new positions of control with new titles and new trappings of power. Jayavarman I centralized power and control over land and labor, concentrating these in the hands of the elite class he headed.

The Khmer

New capitals were established between the Tonle Sap and the Kulen plateau to the east when a new ruler ascended to the throne. His name was Jayavarman II, and he ruled between A.D. 800 and 850. With his ascension, the kingdom of Angkor was established. Power and wealth, along with social and political control, became increasingly concentrated in his hands. Jayavarman II oversaw the construction of great canals and sandstone, brick, and laterite (a hard, red soil) palaces or "pyramid-temples." These temples were built as homes of the gods and were conscious symbols of the power of the king. The great temples housed not only statues of the various Hindu gods but also thousands of priests who attended to the needs of the gods in their palaces. The temples themselves were built on a plan that reflected Hindu beliefs. In Hinduism, the

FIGURE 12.8
The temple/palace of Angkor Wat represents the culmination of architectural complexity of the ancient Khmer civilization of southeast Asia. (© Kevin R. Morris/Corbis)

gods reside on the mythical Mount Meru. Khmer temples are built up on artificial platforms and have five towers; this is meant to symbolize the location of Mount Meru and to represent its five peaks.

After Jayavarman II's death, the processes of expansion and growth he had initiated were continued. His successors built larger and increasingly spectacular pyramid-temples. By A.D. 944, the capital of the kingdom was moved to Angkor by King Yasovarman I. At that time, Angkor was largely a ceremonial center resided in only by the king, his noblemen and noblewomen, and the temple priests.

Angkor Wat

Angkor Wat, the most impressive and best known Khmer temple, was constructed beginning in A.D. 1113 (Figure 12.8). It has been called the single largest religious structure ever built (Royal Geographical Society 1993a). The temple, with its towers, courtyards, plazas, and intricately carved walls, covers an area of about 2.5 km^2 (almost 1 mi^2). The tallest of its five intricately carved towers rises gracefully to a height of nearly 62 m (more than 200 ft). In the center of the temple complex is a tiny shrine housing the image of Vishnu, the Hindu god to which Angkor Wat is dedicated (Ciochon and James 1994). An outer gallery of Angkor Wat consists of eight enormous sculpted panels, together more than 800 m (nearly half a mile) long. Sculpted in bas-relief are hundreds of figures related to Hindu mythology, including the Hindu creation myth.

Along with the great temples, Angkor Wat and the other Khmer cities are marked by huge artificial reservoirs called **barrays.** The so-called Western

FIGURE 12.9

The Bayon temple at Angkor Thom, built more than 1,000 years ago, is covered with sculpted images of Hindu gods, bas-reliefs, columns, and colonnades.

(© Christophe Loviny/Corbis)

Baray at Angkor Wat is 8 km (5 mi) long and 2.25 km (1.25 mi) wide. It was carved out of the laterite that underlies the site. This quarried laterite may have been used in constructing the foundations of the monuments at Angkor. Allowed to fill with water after quarrying, these barrays then served as reservoirs for storing impounded rainwater that may have been used in rice cultivation (Engelhardt, as cited in Ciochon and James 1994:47–48). Some researchers, including Higham (2001), do not believe that the enormous barrays were functional reservoirs but instead were symbolic of the surrounding ocean.

Angkor Thom was a later Khmer capital, covering 15 km^2 (6 mi^2) and surrounded by a moat (Ciochon and James 1994). The city itself was accessible by any one of five huge bridges crossing the waters of the moat. At the center of the city is an incredible, otherworldly temple called the **Bayon,** covered with sculpted images of Hindu gods, bas-reliefs, columns, and colonnades (Figure 12.9). Most of the buildings in the city were made of sandstone. An incredible amount of this relatively soft rock—estimated in the millions of tons (Ciochon and James 1994:40)—was obtained from a huge quarry at Phnom Kulen, located 40 km (25 mi) to the northeast, where it was floated on rafts or barges down the river to Angkor. Angkor Thom remained the capital of the Khmer kingdom until the thirteenth century (P. White 1986). Today, the ruins of the city mark the center of a 317-km^2 (122-mi^2) archaeological district, littered with several hundred temples, palaces, and other monuments of the Khmer civilization.

The tumultuous history of the Khmer civilization came to an end in the fifteenth century A.D. Alien invaders regularly attacked Angkor, and it was abandoned in 1431. It experienced a renaissance of a sort late in the sixteenth century, only to be abandoned once again. Slowly the magnificent temples were swallowed by the jungle, where they lay buried in the rich flora of the tropical forest until their rediscovery in the nineteenth century. They have inspired wonder and fascination ever since.

WHY WERE THE ELITES OF STATE SOCIETIES SO CONSPICUOUS IN THEIR CONSUMPTION?

ISSUES AND DEBATES

As we have seen in every ancient Old World state society discussed in Chapters 11 and 12 and as will be seen in the ancient New World states to be presented in Chapters 13 and 14, monumentally scaled construction projects are absolutely diagnostic of civilization. Archaeologists have concocted all sorts of names for the end products of these projects, serious-sounding designations like "monstrous visual symbols" or "panoptic monuments." By any name, they clearly are recognizable, even to modern people no longer surprised by the capacity of humans bearing a sophisticated technology to produce great works, as bloody huge and impressive projects that required a large and well-organized workforce conscripted, overseen, and supervised by a technologically sophisticated coordinating authority.

Certainly, monuments like Khufu's Great Pyramid, as well as the pyramids of his son and grandson, the ziggurat at Ur, the temple/palace at Knossos, and the other examples discussed in this book are enormous and awe-inspiring, to the point of extreme and excess. It would seem, from a modern, economically rationalist perspective, that not just an abundance, but an overabundance of the material wealth of ancient states was expended to produce impressive, but otherwise seemingly pointless monuments. It would similarly seem that these same societies simply wasted an enormous portion of their precious treasure by burying hoards of gold and silver, precious and semiprecious stones, ivory, alabaster, ceramics, weavings, finely carved wood, and all the rest of the stuff that was deposited in the tombs of the elite classes. What was the point after all? Does it make any sense for these ancient state societies to have expended what clearly appears to be an excess of their time, energy, and wealth in the apparently wasteful practices of piling up prodigious quantities of stone and essentially throwing wealth away by burying it in the ground? Wouldn't that wealth have been better expended in other ways: on constructing canals, cleaning the streets, arming the military, or feeding the poor?

It may make perfect sense, however, when one considers the following. The elites of state societies are all about excess; in fact, they rely on it literally from birth to death: excess in the size and richness of their domiciles, excess in the number and value of their possessions, excess even in the concentration of wealth accompanying their mortal remains in their tombs. The elites—in antiquity as well as in the modern world—seem to live by the old adage: "If you've got it, flaunt it."

You've probably heard the term "conspicuous consumption," usually referring to people in modern American society who seem compelled to spend money—on houses bigger than they could possibly need and often on more than one of them, on luxurious and overpriced automobiles, yachts, expensive technology, and on and on—if only, perhaps through profligate spending, to show their "superiority" to their friends and neighbors. The elites of ancient societies appear to have been no different. They too were conspicuous consumers and, in a sense, conspicuous material show-offs, boldly, brazenly, and proudly broadcasting their wealth and position through material consumption, by the use of expensive, exotic raw materials, through their possession of finely crafted goods, and by their sponsorship of the construction of enormous monuments. These monuments and possessions reflect something more than simply elites living large because they can. Conspicuous consumption represents not just one of the side benefits of being in an elite class; it appears to be a requirement, even a responsibility. Large homes, luxurious possessions, and grand monuments are symbols necessary to convey a message of superiority to everyone else in the society. Monuments and possessions are, in a sense, badges of office, symbols that not only reflect, but also serve to justify and reify the social inequality on which state societies are based. The masses might not recognize your superiority—and, most dangerously, might not accept it—unless they see it manifested. Conspicuous consumption, in this view, serves as that manifestation, a constant material reminder and reinforcement of that inequality.

WAS MINOAN CRETE ATLANTIS?

When the Greek philosopher Plato (427–347 B.C.) introduced the island nation he called Atlantis in two of his published dialogues, *Timmaeus* and *Critias,* he intended it as a symbol of a nation gone wrong, a representation of an enormously powerful evil empire bent on world domination (Figure 12.10). The Atlanteans are on the verge of successfully achieving this goal when Plato has the hero of the tale, a mythical version of his own city-state, Athens—who just happens to be living a life matching Plato's construct of a perfect society laid out in his most famous work, the *Republic*—single-handedly defeat the Atlanteans in battle. The Atlanteans are economically wealthier, technologically more sophisticated, and militarily more powerful, but the Athenians are victorious nonetheless because their way of life is superior; and, in Plato's story, good triumphs over evil.

Plato was a philosopher, not a historian, and he clearly intended the Atlantis tale to be not a historical treatise, but a moral and political message about how societies should be governed (Jordan 2001a). However, Plato does have Critias, the narrator of the Atlantis tale, preface his remarks by maintaining that the story he is about to tell is true, and some have wondered if

FIGURE 12.10
Based on Plato's written description of Atlantis, artists have attempted to portray what his mythical city may have looked like, ostensibly, 11,000 years ago. These imaginary views bear little resemblance to Minoan Crete. (AKG Images/Peter Connolly)

Plato based the work, at least in part, on some historical event with which he was familiar.

After the Athenian defeat of Atlantis, Plato has the gods of ancient Greece destroy the island nation, sinking it beneath the ocean and, rather inconveniently, erasing any evidence of its existence. Was Plato aware of any great nation in antiquity destroyed by a natural cataclysm, and did he mine that history for the details of his Atlantis story? This is possible, but we need to understand that Atlantis was supposed to have been a continent-sized island (think Australia) placed by Plato in the middle of the Atlantic Ocean. There is no geological evidence whatsoever that any such land mass existed, certainly not in the period of about 11,000 years ago as in Plato's story. But perhaps Plato was exaggerating, or maybe he changed certain elements of the tale. Maybe errors crept in surrounding the details of Atlantis—especially concerning its size, its location, and the age of its culture. Maybe the core of the story—the existence of a highly advanced and sophisticated nation, long before Plato's time, that was destroyed by a natural cataclysm—is based on real history known to Plato.

A number of historians and archaeologists have, in fact suggested that this was the case and that, specifically, Minoan Crete was the model for Plato's Atlantis (Luce 1969; Marinatos 1972; Galanopoulos and Bacon 1969; Castleden 1998). After all, it was ancient even in Plato's time, it likely was the dominant political force in the Mediterranean for centuries, it was militarily powerful, and in some particulars—especially in the use of images of bulls in their art and iconography—Minoan Crete seems to match, at least in a general way, Plato's description of Atlantis. Perhaps most intriguingly, 3,420 years ago it was buffeted by the fallout of an enormous cataclysm, the volcanic eruption of Thera located just 120 km (72 mi) north of Crete.

Unfortunately, you have to do more than just a little hand waving, fudging, and rationalizing to make Atlantis Minoan Crete. As noted, the size, location, and age of the Minoan civilization need to be drastically altered to identify it with Plato's Atlantis. Also, significant aspects of the story told by Plato—for example, the presence of elephants on Atlantis that are nowhere to be found on Crete during Minoan times—need to be ignored. Finally, and most significantly, there is no geological or archaeological evidence that the key elements of the story that Plato has Critias tell, including the military defeat of Atlantis and its absolute destruction in a natural catastrophe, apply to Minoan Crete. There is no evidence of a significant military defeat of the Minoans, by the Athenians or anyone else. Though the Minoans certainly suffered as a result of the massive eruption of Thera—part of its naval fleet may have been destroyed by a tsunami, the ash fall resulting from the eruption likely wrought havoc on their agricultural economy, some buildings were destroyed by accompanying earthquakes, and the populace may have panicked (see this chapter's "Prelude")—archaeological evidence clearly shows a period of renewed vigor and growth at Knossos and elsewhere on Minoan Crete after the Theran eruption. In fact, Minoan civilization thrived for at least a century after the eruption and survived as a viable state for a hundred years more.

It is almost certainly the case that Plato used, in all of his writings, bits and pieces of many historical events with which he was familiar; and it is not impossible that the existence of a highly advanced society long before the Greek city-states as well as a catastrophic event in deep time were at least vaguely known to Plato and that he incorporated these elements into his fiction. But fiction it was; the evidence clearly shows that Minoan Crete cannot be equated with the lost continent of Atlantis.

CASE STUDY CLOSE-UP

THE TERRA-COTTA ARMY OF THE FIRST EMPEROR OF THE QIN DYNASTY

Like Twentieth-Dynasty Egyptian pharaoh Tutankhamun, Ying Zheng ascended to the throne when he was just a child, only 13 when he became emperor of the Chinese state of Qin in 246 B.C. Like another Egyptian pharaoh, Narmer of the First Dynasty, Ying Zheng is credited with having unified an array of fractured city-states—Qin was just one of seven such states in China in the third century B.C.—into a single, hugely powerful kingdom in 221 B.C. Ying Zheng, now titled Qin Shihuang, the First Emperor of the Qin Dynasty, was the first ruler of a united China; and upon his death in 207 B.C., was accorded a memorial the extent and grandeur of which arguably is the most fantastic, the most spectacular, and—following our discussion of the conspicuous consumption that characterizes the elites of ancient as well as modern states—the most excessive investment of time, labor, and treasure for an individual person ever seen before or since.

Located near the Chinese city of Xi'an, Ying Zheng's mausoleum was looted in 206 B.C. and his tomb was pillaged. Fortunately, another part of his mortuary complex remained virtually untouched and was accidentally dis-

FIGURE 12.11

A small phalanx of soldiers in the greater-than-life-size, 8,000-man terra-cotta army created for the burial monument of Ying Zheng, the first emperor of the Qin Dynasty in Xi'an, China, who died in 207 B.C.
(Bettmann/Corbis)

covered by workers only in 1974. There, Ying Zheng's subjects had amassed an astonishing simulated army, a brigade of as many as 8,000 slightly greater than life-sized warriors and horses, all made from the reddish-brown, fire-baked ceramic called terra-cotta (Wu 1986). The men, their horses, and even bronze chariots are arrayed in lengthy columns, an eerily real-looking military formation representing a massive, ceramic army protecting the tomb of the emperor (Figure 12.11).

No standardized molds were used, and each of the clay soldiers excavated and examined to date is unique, each in its own pose. Clay archers kneel in the front of one of the formations, each holding an exquisitely simulated crossbow, while those in the back stand with their weapons, ready to shoot above the heads of their kneeling compatriots in the front. Some of the warriors are depicted wearing armor, others are in clay tunics, and all appear in uniforms that signify their different ranks in the army of the emperor. Perhaps most remarkable of all, just like real people, each terra-cotta warrior has a unique face, each with its own expression (Figure 12.12). It is as if each terra-cotta warrior was not simply an anonymous, imaginary soldier, but the

FIGURE 12.12
Look carefully at the faces of the soldiers in Emperor Ying Zheng's terra-cotta army. Each is unique and distinct, as are the thousands created for the emperor's tomb. The labor expended in the creation of the terra-cotta army is a staggering reflection of the ability of ancient state societies to harness the wealth and labor of their citizens. (© Keren Su/Getty Images/Taxi)

representation of a real living soldier in the emperor's army in the third century B.C. Most of the warrior's hands were shaped to carry weapons and the terra-cotta army clearly was equipped for war. Thousands of weapons have been found with the soldiers including crossbows, longbows, spears, swords, scimitars, battle axes, daggers, and halberds. Many, if not all of the soldiers, were brightly painted.

The terra-cotta army represents a massive, almost incomprehensible investment of time, labor, and treasure, all for nothing more than the burial of a dead king. To be sure, it is a spectacular reflection of the power and, it must be admitted, the artistry, of what a state society can create through its ability to harness, coordinate, control, and even monopolize the talents and time of a huge force of laborers and artisans. At the same time, consider the fact that the unimaginable work involved in producing the thousands of soldiers, horses, and chariots did not help feed the hungry in the emperor's kingdom, it did not result in improved systems of roads for transportation or commerce, it did not make the cities of the empire safer or the lives of its citizens more secure or productive. Clay soldiers, no matter how many or how impressive, could never really protect the kingdom from the depredations of nasty neighbors; they couldn't even protect the emperor's mausoleum, looted barely a year after he was buried. But in the desire and ability reflected in the emperor's decision to built this great tomb for his remains, we see reflected a common pattern exhibited by state societies. We may marvel at the beauty of their works and we may stand in awe of their accomplishments. At the same time we can recognize that these ancient states survived because their citizens accepted the inequality on which their societies were based and that they did so, at least in part, in their own awe at what the emperor or the pharaoh or the king could command and accomplish.

When the terra cotta army of Ying Zheng was discovered in 1974, the Chinese government understood its great archaeological and historical importance. Almost simultaneously, the government also recognized the enormous tourist potential of the site, and it has

VISITING THE PAST

quickly become one of the most important tourist destinations for visitors, both Chinese and foreign, in all of Asia. A huge pavilion was constructed over the part of the site called Vault No. 1 where tourists have an unobstructed view of an impressive formation of soldiers. A separate exhibition hall houses the bronze chariot and horses. All of the descriptions one might read or even the photographs you can see of the terra-cotta army cannot possibly prepare you for its overwhelming presence.

The temple at Knossos on Crete is today a major tourist destination for Mediterranean cruise ships. Earlier in this century, Sir Arthur Evans reconstructed part of the temple, repairing and replacing columns and restoring some of the beautiful frescoes. Though such work is controversial, some of Evans's reconstructions afford the casual visitor the unique opportunity to view at least some of the rooms in the temple as they appeared to the inhabitants more than 3,600 years ago. The museum at Herakleion, Crete, houses most of the impressive artifacts recovered at Knossos and other Minoan sites. In the United States, the University of Pennsylvania Museum in Philadelphia has an extensive collection of Minoan objects.

In the past 25 years, the nation of Cambodia (sometimes called Kampuchea) has been the scene of some of the most terrible genocidal insanity that our species is capable of. For quite some time, the Khmer temples discussed in this chapter were largely ignored by Cambodians, whose collective agony did not afford them the luxury of reflection on their distant past, and foreign scientists were not welcome or safe there. Anthropologist Russell Ciochon (Ciochon and James 1994) reports that when he visited Angkor Wat in 1989 (under the watchful eye of a heavily armed contingent of government soldiers), the place was all but deserted. His more recent visit in 1993 shows that a more stable political situation has brought tourists back to the area. Group tours to Angkor Wat are now available. Though the U.S. State Department does not have any travel warnings currently in place, they strongly recommend that tourists traveling to the area around Angkor Wat do so in groups.

SUMMARY

The Neolithic set the stage for the development of sedentary farming villages in various places in the Old World. In a select few regions, an acceleration of cultural complexity led to the development of a stratified social system that controlled the excess wealth made possible through the ability to produce an agricultural food surplus. Social elites developed as part of a reorganization of society that allowed for orderly and systematic trade, the construction of irrigation canals to increase the food base, and the construction of monumental defensive fortifications. In these same regions, the new way of organizing and controlling human labor was utilized by the developing elite to construct less practical monumental works—temples, palaces, and mortuary features such as pyramids. This kind of monumental construction, today diagnostic of ancient civilizations, was both cause and effect of the new social dynamic of the world's first civilizations. Large, impressive monuments served as dramatic evidence of the power of the elite and symbolized and reified this power at the same time that it magnified it.

In the Old World, the processes that led to the kinds of societies we are calling civilization occurred in Mesopotamia in the Middle East, in the Nile Valley of Egypt and the Sudan, in the Indus Valley of Pakistan discussed in Chapter 11, and, in eastern China, in southeastern Europe on Crete, and, later, in southeast Asia as discussed here.

TO LEARN MORE

Technical Summaries

Though the books listed below under popular summaries are written with a broad audience in mind, any one of them contains a wealth of technical details and arguments on the rise of civilization in China and southeast Asia as well as Crete.

Popular Summaries

K. C. Chang's synthesis work, *The Archaeology of China* (1986) is nearing its twentieth year in print but is still a valuable summary of Chinese prehistory and early history and a good source for information about the Shang Dynasty. Rodney Castleden (1990) is simply a terrific writer on topics related to the ancient world, and his book *Minoans: Life in Bronze Age Crete* is certainly one of the best popular summaries of Europe's first civilization. If you are interested in exploring the possible connection between Minoan Crete and Plato's Atlantis, his book, *Atlantis Destroyed* (1998), supports the notion; but the best book for my money is Paul Jordan's (2001) *The Atlantis Syndrome*. Anyone hoping to show that Plato based his description of Atlantis on Minoan Crete has to overcome Jordan's very convincing argument to the contrary. At least two wonderfully written and profusely illustrated books exist on the topic of the Khmer civilization: Charles Higham's (2001) *The Civilization of Angkor* and Eleanor Mannikka's (1996) *Angkor Wat: Time, Space, and Kingship.*

On the Web

For a site with lots of photographs of the terra-cotta army of Ying Zheng, have a look at http://www.travelchinaguide.com/attraction/shaanxi/xian/terra_cotta_army/. For a very nicely done site put together by tourist visitors to the site, see http://www.anniebees.com/China/China_42.htm. Lots of beautiful images of the palace at Knossos on Crete can be viewed at http://www.culture.gr/2/21/211/21123a/e211wa03.html. A pictorial guide of the site is available at http://www.daedalus.gr/DAEI/THEME/Knossos.htm. For photographs of the Khmer site of Angkor Wat, take a look at http://www.angkorwat.org/. For photographs and brief descriptions of a number of other Khmer sites, visit http://www.theangkorguide.com/introduction.htm.

Online Learning Center: www.mhhe.com/feder4

The Online Learning Center (OLC) Web companion to *The Past in Perspective* features a variety of supplemental study aids. For each chapter, this free Web site includes

ONLINE
LEARNING
CENTER

- Self-Quizzes to take as pretests prior to exams
- Interactive Timeline Study Guides for additional review and reinforcement of key information
- Learning Objectives
- Chapter Site links with Web addresses for many of the fossil and archaeological sites mentioned in the text

KEY TERMS

barrays, 517	Iron Age, 515	Mycenaeans, 515
Bayon, 518	Khmer, 515	New Temple period, 514
Chenla, 516	Knossos, 511	scapulimancy, 508
Funan, 516	Lung-shan, 506	
hang-t'u, 507	Minoan, 511	

13

An Explosion of Complexity

THE FLOWERING OF CIVILIZATION IN THE NEW WORLD: MESOAMERICA

	4,000	3,750	3,500	3,250
Maya	Early Preclassic			
Highland Mexico				

CHAPTER OVERVIEW

"Civilization," including monumental edifices, elaborate burials, large armies, and full-time artisans, developed in some parts of the New World as fewer people were needed in the subsistence quest and as rulers attempted to legitimize and reinforce their position of power and wealth. Highland and lowland Mesoamerica saw the development of some of the first civilizations in the New World. The lowland Maya and highland Teotihuacános and Aztecs of Mesoamerica are discussed in this chapter.

Years ago										
3,000	2,750	2,500	2,250	2,000	1,750	1,500	1,250	1,000	750	500

Middle Preclassic	Late Preclassic	Early Classic	Late Classic	Terminal Classic	Early Postclassic	Late Postclassic

Cerros
Komchén
Dzibilchaltún
Lamanai
El Mirador
Nakbe

Calakmul
Palenque
Copán
Tikal
Uaxactún
Dos Pilas

Xlapak
Chichén Itzá
Tonina
Labna
Sayil
Kabah
Uxmal

Mayapán

Teotihuacán

Toltecs

Aztecs

Monte Alban

Cuexcomate
Capilco
Tenochtitlán

ONLINE
LEARNING
CENTER

Go to **www.mhhe.com/feder4** for an interactive study guide version of this timeline.

PRELUDE

CHAPTER SITES

Pacal the Great was 12, only three years older than Tutankhamun (Chapter 11) and one year younger than Ying Zheng (Chapter 12) when he too ascended to the throne of a great nation. His reign, however, was to last far longer than the Egyptian boy-king's or that of the first emperor of a united China, and he would have a far greater impact on the history of his people. Pacal's story as related here is taken largely from *A Forest of Kings: The Untold Story of the Ancient Maya,* by Mayanists Linda Schele and David Freidel (1990).

Pacal became the ruler of a Maya state centered in the city of Palenque in Chiapas, Mexico, on July 29 in the year A.D. 615. Though from a noble clan, Pacal the Great's father had not been king. Pacal's mother, however, Lady Zac-Kuk, was from a family of kings and had served for three years as the ruler of Palenque, inheriting the throne from her uncle, who likely had no offspring of his own.

Because Maya descent was figured in the male line, it was unusual, but not unheard of, for Pacal to become king. That he did so is largely a testament to the strength and power of his mother, who likely continued to wield great power during the early years of her son's reign. It seems that it was not until after her death in A.D. 640 that the now 37-year-old Pacal fully became king in deed as well as in law. After his mother's death, he initiated a vigorous campaign of construction that saw the completion of some of the most impressive temples and palaces built by an ancient civilization. The marvelous site of Palenque, visited by thousands of tourists each year, is largely the result of Pacal's leadership and that of his two sons (Figure 13.1).

Perhaps the greatest architectural achievement of Pacal's reign was the temple that would serve as his burial place (Figure 13.2). Not just a tomb, the Temple of the Inscriptions was intended to legitimize Pacal's kingship, to make up for the fact that his father had not been king, and to sanctify and confirm the legitimacy of the ascendance of his son, Kan-Xul II, to the kingship after Pacal's death. In an attempt to solidify his claim to the throne, as well as that of his son and his grandsons and great-grandsons yet to be, Pacal had a detailed king list inscribed in the halls of the temple located atop his imposing burial pyramid. This king list elevated Pacal's mother to the status of a virtual goddess, comparable to the mother of the gods in Maya mythology. Just as the three central gods of Maya religion legitimately ascended to their "godship" through the divinity of their heavenly mother, the Temple of the Inscriptions seems to be asserting that so too had Pacal legitimately ascended to his kingship through his earthly mother.

Pacal died on August 31, A.D. 683, at the age of 80, following a 67-year reign. In the ceremonies that marked the king's journey from this life into the next, his body was first brought up the steeply inclined stairway of the pyramid and then into the temple at its apex. Next, the body of the king was carried down into the pyramid itself; the pyramid had actually been constructed around and over Pacal's burial chamber, located down a vaulted, internal stairway leading to a chamber excavated by the Maya beneath the pyramid.

FIGURE 13.1

Pacal the Great ruled over the Maya city of Palenque between A.D. 615 and 683. He oversaw the construction of many of the splendid temples that define this center of Maya civilization. His burial pyramid can be seen in the rear center of this photograph. (© Danny Lehman/Corbis)

At last, the lord and king of Palenque, Pacal the Great, was laid to rest in a sarcophagus carved out of a solid block of limestone. On his face was placed a mask made of obsidian, shell, and jade, bearing a mosaic of Pacal himself. Pieces of jade, a precious stone of enormous significance to the Maya, were placed around the body. The coffin lid is itself an exquisite work of art, depicting Pacal in his journey from life to death. Around the side of the coffin were carved the names of the kings that had preceded Pacal, further emphasizing the legitimacy of his lineage's claim to the kingship of Palenque.

There Pacal rested until 1952, when his burial was discovered and the coffin lid raised. That we can tell his story today, more than 1,300 years after Pacal last looked out upon his city in the jungle, is a testament to the ancient Maya. Though perhaps not in the way they intended, in building the Temple of the Inscriptions to house their king for eternity, in placing the king list inscriptions on the temple walls, and in sealing him in his limestone coffin, they assured Pacal a measure of immortality.

As was the case for Tutankhamun, with the burial pyramid of Pacal, we are faced with the enormous material and social consequences of the evolution of state societies. The description of Pacal's tomb shows quite clearly that complex, stratified societies such as those discussed in Chapters 11 and 12 evolved in the New World as well as the Old. This chapter focuses on the ancient civilizations of Mesoamerica, and Chapter 14 focuses on South America.

When Hernán Cortés entered the Aztec capital city of Tenochtitlán in central Mexico in A.D. 1519, he and his soldiers were astonished by what they saw. Laid out before them was a huge urban sprawl,

CHRONICLE

centered on two islands in the middle of an enormous lake. The islands were connected by numerous bridges and artificial causeways. The city these Spaniards saw and described was a teeming hub of people; modern estimates place the sixteenth-century population of Tenochtitlán at about 200,000 (Adams 1991; Sabloff 1989). Tenochtitlán was an impressive urban center, comparable to Mohenjo-daro and Harappa in the Indus Valley (Chapter 11) in the level of urban planning exhibited, with precisely laid out streets demarcating neighborhoods and plazas. Enormous pyramids and temples defined the architectural style of the city, which was, in turn, surrounded by a huge expanse of raised agricultural fields called **chinampas.** Tenochtitlán obviously was the capital of a New World civilization. The Aztec civilization encountered by the Spanish conquistadors was the product of a lengthy process of cultural evolution: The Aztecs clearly were not the first such society in the New World (Figure 13.3).

THE MAYA

Perhaps the best-known aboriginal civilization in the New World developed far to the south and east of the heartland of the Aztecs. Today we call them the Maya, and their remarkable culture is the focus of numerous popular books and magazine articles—it is almost impossible to pick up an issue of *National Geographic* and not find an article on the Maya—and the Maya have become a frequent focus of science and history documentaries, especially on cable T.V.

Evidence of Maya civilization has been found across a huge swath of Mesoamerica, including the eastern Mexican state of Chiapas, the entirety of

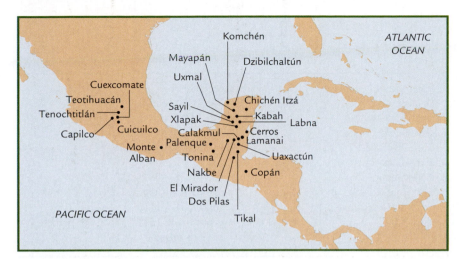

FIGURE 13.3
Archaeological sites in Mesoamerica where evidence of the evolution of chiefdom and early state-level societies has been found.

the Yucatán Peninsula, and the tropical and subtropical lowlands of the modern nations of Guatemala, Honduras, Belize, and El Salvador. Within what was to become, at the peak of the Maya, a territory of about 324,000 km^2 (125,000 mi^2), archaeologists have traced the earliest signs of social and political complexity, reflected by their emerging ability to produce monumental buildings, to more than 2,650 years ago in the tropical lowlands adjacent to those where the Olmec originated (Chapter 10 ; Coe 1993).

Though the popular image of the Maya is that of a dead or extinct culture, it is estimated that today more than 5,000,000 people can rightfully claim to be Maya, speakers of the same language and descendants of those who lived in the splendid cities, built the impressive pyramids, and developed a precise astronomically based calendar—and whose culture dominated the Yucatán and tropical lowlands of Mesoamerica for close to 1,500 years (Webster 2002:39). Archaeologists Jeremy Sabloff (1994) and David Webster (2002) summarize the evidence for the evolution of Maya civilization in this way:

The history of the Maya begins with the earliest settlement of Mesoamerica and, ultimately, with the settlement of the New World; the Maya were and are Native Americans, descendants of the people who migrated to America at the end of the Pleistocene (Chapter 7). Archaeological evidence in what would become the homeland of the Maya indicates settlement as early at 11,000 years ago (Table 13.1). These people and their descendants were hunter-gatherers. The earliest evidence for a reliance on domesticated crops for at least a part of subsistence can be traced to soon after 5,000 years ago in the Maya lowlands. After this, for more than two millennia, little more than small agricultural hamlets dotted the banks of rivers and margins of swamps.

The earliest glimmerings of a social and political trajectory that would culminate in the flowering of Maya civilization can be seen in the archaeological record beginning about 2,650 years ago in what is called the Middle Preclassic

---

TABLE 13.1
Maya Culture Chronology

Paleoindian	Before 9,000 years ago
Archaic	9,000 to 4,500 years ago
Early Preclassic	4,500 to 3,000 years ago
Middle Preclassic	3,000 to 2,400 years ago
Late Preclassic	2,400 years ago to A.D. 250
Early Classic	A.D. 250 to A.D. 600
Late Classic	A.D. 600 to A.D. 800
Terminal Classic	A.D. 800 to A.D. 1000
Early Postclassic	A.D. 1000 to A.D. 1250
Late Postclassic	A.D. 1250 to A.D. 1519 (arrival of Spanish)
Modern	A.D. 1519 to present

---

time period (see Table 13.1). During this period, in Maya communities like Nakbe, El Mirador, Lamanai, Cerros, and Tikal in the south and Dzibichaltún and Komchén in the north, all of which previously had been unremarkable, small farming hamlets, the Maya began building structures that clearly were differentiated from other buildings in terms of both their size and sophistication. These first so-called civic structures are stepped platforms as much as 14 m (46 ft) high, and their surfaces are sometimes elaborated with decoration, especially stucco (plaster) masks (Webster 2002). Clearly these buildings would have required a coordinated labor force with sufficient surplus time to build them and a desire to produce structures approaching monumental proportions (Figure 13.4). These structures likely were related to Maya religion, and these villages, like the ceremonial centers of the Olmec, probably housed members of a nascent religious elite and their attendants. Some geographically advantaged settlements such as Cerros—located on a bay by the mouth of a river—became trading centers where raw obsidian and jade, finely crafted goods from these raw materials, agricultural products like cotton and cacao, and perhaps fine ceramics were distributed, adding to the power of the developing religious elite (Sabloff 1994:115).

A highly productive agricultural system focusing on maize and beans provided food for a growing population. Village population grew, and new villages were established during the period from 2600 to 2300 B.P. As a result of this growth as well as an apparent movement of people from the countryside to the population centers, at this time some of the Maya villages evolved into true urban settlements with large, dense populations.

As population grows, the amount of surplus that can be produced and concentrated in the hands of the elite also grows, as does their ability to solidify, sanctify, and symbolize that power. Monumental, communal construction

FIGURE 13.4
This platform structure, probably used for ceremonial or religious purposes, is in Dzibilchaltún, in the north Yucatán. Dzibilchaltún is an early example of a complex Maya settlement and ceremonial center.
(K. L. Feder)

projects among the Maya, as in other early states, were both a cause and an effect of this process. In the Middle and Late Preclassic the elites had the emerging power to command the construction of monuments; and the construction of monuments, in turn, served to further integrate people into the political entity of the emerging state by engaging them in public projects that reflected the socially and politically stratified structure of Maya society. Communal projects, in other words, were microcosms of life among the Maya. At the same time, monuments provided tangible evidence of the power of the elite, further legitimizing their position of power and enabling them to command the construction of ever more impressive pyramids and temples.

These patterns of the concentration of population in a number of centers along with the concentration of economic resources, social status, and political power in the hands of an elite appear to have accelerated in the period following 2,400 years ago in the Late Preclassic period of Maya history. Monumental construction projects dramatically increased in scope. Trade brought in exotic grave goods, which were crafted into finely finished works that ended up being concentrated in the graves of a small segment of each town's population, the increasingly wealthy and powerful elites. Communities began competing with one another—perhaps for land, raw materials, and even for the allegiance of the people themselves—and there is evidence, in the form of defensive embankments surrounding Maya communities and in Maya art with depictions of individuals wielding weapons against enemies, for warfare, which would eventually become endemic to Maya society.

Agriculture probably intensified at this time. Of necessity, the Maya employed a number of methods, both extensive and intensive, to feed the large and dense populations in their growing urban settlements. In some regions, the Maya practiced slash-and-burn agriculture, where forest land is cut and burned to produce fields that are abandoned after only a short period of use and allowed to grow over, to be used again after a period of agricultural dormancy. In some regions, however, a more energy-intensive agriculture was practiced with the construction of extensive ridged fields. Here, ridges of land were built up in the rich and fertile floodplains of rivers. The artificial high ground remained dry even when the river flooded. Some Maya sites dating to this period show evidence of canals and even swamp-reclamation projects. The Maya also employed a number of other intensive agricultural techniques, including terracing of hill slopes, planting kitchen gardens, and tree-cropping—the specialized use of tree crops in rain forests and within settlements (McKillop 1994).

Maya Writing

The need for ever-increasing control of information in an increasingly complex cultural system may explain the development of a sophisticated system of writing and mathematics that the Maya derived from the Olmec (Coe 1992; Harris and Stearns 1992). In this civilization, the information deemed worthy of recording, as determined by the elite who controlled the writing system, related not to accounting or economics, as was the case, for example, in Mesopotamia. Maya writing focused on the culture's history, often emphasizing kingly succession. The desirability of keeping accurate records of time and the Maya ability to do so led to their development of a highly accurate calendar that was based on sophisticated astronomical observations, particularly of the movements of other planets visible in the night sky (Aveni 1977).

Unfortunately, there has been no Rosetta Stone for Maya writing, no inscribed message in Maya hieroglyphs side by side with the same message in another, known written script (see Chapter 11 for a discussion of the significance of the Rosetta Stone in translating Egyptian hieroglyphs). As a result, translating the Maya written language has been an extraordinarily difficult undertaking. Even more unfortunately, the vast majority of the Maya screenfold books, works called **codices,** that we know existed in the sixteenth century were destroyed in about 1562, burned upon the order of the sixteenth-century Spanish priest who, 10 years later would become installed as the Bishop of the Yucatán, Fray Diego de Landa. Though he could not read the Maya texts, de Landa decided that the books reflected idol worship and had to be eliminated. We simply do not know and cannot even hazard a guess as to the material covered in those books: a history of the Maya in their own words, perhaps, or political records of the alliances and warfare of Maya city-states. Only four Maya books have survived into the present, and these all appear to have been produced just before or, in the case of one of the books, immediately after the arrival of the Spanish (Webster 2002:113). The existing codices reflect bits of Maya history, but focus primarily on arcane matters of creation and worship.

Though most of the books are gone, there are an estimated 15,000 surviving hieroglyphic inscriptions on buildings, monuments, and stelae (Figure 13.5); and these are under the intense scrutiny of archaeologists and epigraphers (Webster 2002:115). The vast majority of the stelae whose inscriptions can be translated tell stories of warfare and ritual; announce marriages, births, and deaths; tell of the founding of great cities and dynasties; and proclaim the military victories of great leaders and the capture of enemies.

Peak of the Maya

As archaeologist David Webster (2002:79-80) states, by the end of the Late Preclassic, about 1,900 years ago, the basic elements of Maya civilization were in place, including a socially stratified society with an elite social class headed by a powerful royal family that had, at its apex, a great king; monumental temples and palaces; stone altars; an art style and iconography that included depictions of death, human sacrifice, and mutilation; a hieroglyphic written language; screenfold, bark paper books bearing lengthy narratives in that written language; stelae—upright stone slabs—also bearing messages in that written language; a written number system; a dual calendar of 365 and 260 days, respectively, that marked time from the beginning of the universe to the end of time or, at least, the end of the current cycle of time as the Maya perceived it; a ritual ball game; a reverence for jade and related green and blue-green semi-precious stones; and the use of chocolate in preparing a ceremonial beverage imbibed by members of the elite class.

With these basic elements in place, the Maya entered into what modern scholars perceive to be the pinnacle of Maya civilization beginning about 1,750 years ago, or A.D. 250 by the reckoning of our modern calendar. This begins the Classic period of Maya history, divided into an Early and Late Classic period (see Table 13.1).

The number of substantial Classic period urban centers, called "regal-ritual cities" by Webster (2002:151)—substantial in terms of their physical, geographic size, their calculated populations, and the magnificence of their monuments—swelled to between 40 and 50. These were more or less autonomous polities, effectively sovereign city-states that marked the capitals of separate Maya states—we might even call them separate "nations." Each was ruled by its own royal dynasties, who lived within the boundaries of the regal-ritual capital of their own states, where they commanded the construction of the impressive pyramids and temples that today so fascinate archaeologists and tourists alike. These Maya cities were not the most highly populated among the ancient urban centers discussed in Chapters 11 and 12 or in this chapter. The most extreme estimates for even the most architecturally impressive of the Maya cities do not exceed several tens of thousands. The population of the urban center of Tikal, for example, located in Guatemala, was likely no more than 60,000 and may have been less than half that size (Figure 13.6). The population in the city was organized into a series of neighborhoods where participants in various crafts lived and produced their goods: stone tools, ceramics, and wooden implements. Copán, another major Maya city-state, may have possessed at its peak an urban population of about 20,000 (Fash 2001). Though not enormous by the standards of other ancient civilizations, the cities of the Maya, nevertheless, relied on the contributions of the substantial human populations in the hinterlands. The residents of these hinterlands included primarily farmers, whose surplus provided the economic basis for the existence of the elites, the construction of their monuments, and trade for their exotic raw materials. Remember our previous estimate that, in order to produce a sufficient food surplus to support the apparatus of the ancient Egyptian state, including pyramids, elite burials, temples, palaces, trade for exotics, the army, and so on, likely up to 75% of the population of ancient Egypt had to be farmers? David Webster (2002:140) estimates that, considering the lower agricultural productivity of the tropical and subtropical lowlands in which the Maya developed, up to 90% of the population had to be

FIGURE 13.6
The impressive Temple I (Temple of the Giant Jaguar) at the Maya site of Tikal in Guatemala. Built around A.D. *700, it towers 45 m (145 ft) above the Great Plaza in this pre-Columbian city of as many as 60,000 people.*
(Cris Wibby)

food producers to support the elements of state societies listed above and shared by ancient Egyptians and Maya alike.

The great Maya centers like Copán, Palenque, and Tikal vied for scarce resources, and bloody wars were waged for control of trade and agricultural land as well as for control of the large populations living in the hinterlands. Luckily for us, as mentioned previously, the Maya wrote about their alliances, treacheries, and wars in their hieroglyphic script, and we are able to read the histories of their conflicts in their own words. For example, a fragmentary and somewhat confusing inscription carved into a series of steps had long been known at the Maya site of Dos Pilas in Guatemala. Recently, a storm uprooted a tree at the site, exposing an additional set of steps with a continuation of the inscription allowing Mayanists to clear up the story (Figure 13.7). The inscription relates the tale of a prolonged and bloody war between the enemy cities of Tikal and Calakmul in the seventh century A.D. The smaller town of Dos Pilas played a fascinating role in the dance for domination played out by its two "superpower" neighbors (Williams 2002).

Dos Pilas is located about 113 km (70 mi) southwest of Tikal and was, at least initially, an outpost of that city, established in the hinterlands of the territory it controlled. When the ruler of Tikal founded Dos Pilas, he installed his own 4-year-old brother, Balaj Chan K'awiil, as its leader, keeping power in the family and ensuring, at least in theory, the allegiance of Dos Pilas to Tikal and maintaining its usefulness as a buffer between Tikal and its powerful enemy, Calakmul. According to the inscription on the steps, this arrangement worked as it was intended for about 20 years when Calakmul's invading army

FIGURE 13.7

The detailed and extensive hieroglyphic text carved onto the stairway at the Maya site of Dos Pilas tells the story of a bloody and protracted war between the enemy cities of Tikal and Calakmul in the seventh century A.D. (© Kenneth Garrett/National Geographic Society Image Collection)

attacked Dos Pilas and quickly overran its military defenders. Balaj Chan K'awiil was allowed to live but forced to shift his allegiance, to become now a mortal enemy of his own brother and the city he ruled. Dos Pilas, now as a client state of Calakmul, and at its behest, initiated the protracted, bloody, decade-long war against Tikal that is memorialized in the stairway inscription. With the backing of its powerful ally, Dos Pilas ultimately defeated the army of Tikal, sacked the city, and took as hostages the rulers of Tikal. The inscription records Balaj Chan K'awiil's dance of victory and the slaughter of Tikal's nobility, including his own brother. As the old saying goes, blood may be thicker than water, but for a chance at life and power, Balaj Chan K'awiil made sure it was his brother's blood that flowed, not his own.

The relationships among the Maya city-states appear always to have been in a state of flux, with fleeting allegiances morphing into states of animosity and then back again to alliance depending on the particular set of circumstances at any given time. Despite the existence of coalitions and partnerships, the Maya city-states appear ultimately, however, always to have been fragmented, always in some state of enmity, friendship, or somewhere in between; warily allied, in the middle of hostilities, or on the way toward one of those extremes. The city-states remained politically autonomous and separate, never coalescing, as was the case in Egypt, into a massive and massively powerful, politically unified nation.

The Maya pattern of competing royal dynasties, each ensconced in its own city-state and overseeing the construction of great temples, pyramids and palaces, erecting stelae festooned with hieroglyphic messages that advertised its achievements in warfare, controlling widespread trading networks, and presiding over a large and urban population—all of this declined dramatically and rather abruptly after A.D. 800. The last inscribed stelae at Tikal bears a date of A.D. 869, and the final known inscribed monument erected by the Maya dates to A.D. 909 at the site of Tonina. Apparently, there were no more great victories to announce, no important births or deaths of royalty

FIGURE 13.8
*The pyramid known as
El Castillo, or the Temple
of the Feathered Serpent,
is located at the site of
Chichén Itzá in the
northern Yucatán.*
(K. L. Feder)

deemed worthy of recording for posterity. Soon thereafter, royal dynasties at least in the southern part of the Maya realm appear largely to have disappeared from the Maya social and political landscape. The last ruler of Copán died in A.D. 820 and was not replaced (see "Issues and Debates," this chapter). During the course of just a few decades following A.D. 800, the majority of the large urban settlements over which those dynasties presided were, again for the most part, abandoned.

Though the Maya world was radically reconfigured at the end of the Classic period, the Maya certainly didn't disappear. In part, their geographic focus shifted to the north where the great Postclassic period centers of Chichén Itzá and Uxmal developed, thrived, engaged in struggles for dominance, and also ultimately collapsed (Figures 13.8 and 13.9). Between A.D. 1250 and 1450, the Maya city of Mayapán was the dominant political entity in the Yucatán, and a number of Maya states continued to thrive outside of Mayapán's reach. Warfare and politics led to the decline of Mayapán, and no single polity rose to take its place in the Yucatán. When the Spanish invaded in the sixteenth century A.D., the much-changed Maya society was largely decentralized and its population was scattered. The construction of great monuments had ceased entirely. There is, of course, no way of knowing what might have developed in the cycle of Maya history had the Spanish not invaded and imposed their will on the native people.

The great "mystery of the Maya," among both archaeologists and a public fascinated by this ancient society, has always concerned this apparently abrupt collapse. Why did what appears to have been a thriving civilization close out

FIGURE 13.9

The 30-m (100-ft) high Pyramid of the Magician at the Maya site of Uxmal, located in the Yucatán peninsula. Typical of Mesoamerican pyramids, the Pyramid of the Magician consists of superimposed stages and has a stairway (actually two, in the case of this monument) leading to a temple at its apex. (K. L. Feder)

its time on history's stage? What caused the Maya to abandon their cities, why did the elites fall from positions of power and disappear, and why did it happen apparently so abruptly? Was it invasion, a drought, an epidemic, a catastrophic earthquake, a revolution—or was the Maya collapse rooted in the ecology of slash-and-burn agriculture in a tropical rain forest? These explanations for the fall of the Maya continue to be debated by researchers in the field. The collapse of the Maya is the focus of this chapter's "Issues and Debates."

TEOTIHUACÁN

Teotihuacán is so fascinating, at least in part, because it seems so different from other early New World state societies. The city itself stands in marked contrast to the pattern of the Maya with their series of discrete, individual city-states, each one, as art historian Esther Pasztory (1997:7) characterizes them, "small and charming," their structures elaborately decorated, and their scale impressive, but quite human. Everything about Teotihuacán, in contrast, is gigantic and singular; its scale is truly monumental, even overwhelming. Again in contrast to the Maya's ritual-regal cities, which were characterized by small urban cores, each surrounded by a vast hinterland of rural farmers, Teotihuacán is all city, all urban core, and no hinterland. The densely packed homes of the city's residents spread out across an expanse of more than 23 km^2 (9 mi^2, or 5,760 acres). At its peak, the population of Teotihuacán was vastly larger—by a factor of two, three, or even four—than what has been suggested for even the largest Maya cities, with estimates reaching as high as 200,000.

Teotihuacán's name and, in fact, the names now applied to most of its monuments, are derived from the Aztecs, described later in this chapter. The Aztecs frequently visited Teotihuacán even though it was in ruins for more than 700 years when they became the dominant political force in the Valley of Mexico. To the Aztecs, the ancient city was so enormous, so impressive, so awe-inspiring, they called it in their language "Teotihuacán," translated as "The Place of the Gods" or, perhaps more accurately, "Where the Gods Are Made" (Pasztory 1997).

Teotihuacán appears to have been a pilgrimage city, a tradition that was practiced both at its peak and even centuries after its abandonment. Archaeological evidence in the form of Aztec sculptures found in proximity to Teotihuacán's most important monuments supports the notion that the Aztecs visited the ruins and viewed it as a sacred place. Some historical records even indicate that Motecuhzoma (Montezuma), the final Aztec ruler, visited the ruins of Teotihuacán every 20 days to perform various rituals to the gods who he likely believed had built the great monuments located there.

The valley in which the city was located is a part of the Basin of Mexico. Though the area presented its inhabitants with rich agricultural soil, timber, obsidian, and other valuable lithic resources, rainfall is unpredictable and its high elevation (over 2,200 m, or 7,000 ft) produces a short growing season for agricultural plants.

Teotihuacán History

A detailed and thorough archaeological survey of the Basin of Mexico directed by archaeologist William Sanders (Sanders, Parsons, and Santley 1979) provides us with a chronology of settlement leading up to the dominance of the Teotihuacán urban center. Between 3500 and 2600 B.P., the basin was lightly occupied by a people increasingly dependent on agriculture for their subsistence. Population increased dramatically after 2600 B.P., and local villages began to be drawn into broader polities, owing their allegiance and labor to developing urban centers: One such village, Cuicuilco, had a population of a few thousand at this time.

Teotihuacán began its history as a small farming village, part of the developing settlement system of the Basin of Mexico. Its location afforded its inhabitants decided advantages over their neighbors. The village was located adjacent to a significant source of obsidian, and the site straddles a major trade route to the south and east. The site is also well suited to irrigation-aided agriculture, and so it was well positioned when overall population growth in the Basin of Mexico strained the ability of simple agriculture to feed the increasing number of people living there.

By 2100 B.P. there were a number of growing population centers, but these were all secondary to Cuicuilco until a series of devastating volcanic eruptions effectively destroyed that site. In the ensuing struggle for dominance in the basin, Teotihuacán was victorious. The key to its success may have been a combination of its location, its resources, the great potential of irrigation, and the evolution of an elite able to take advantage of this constellation of factors.

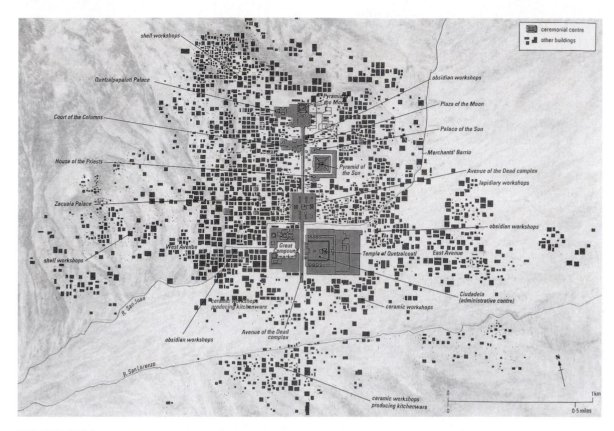

FIGURE 13.10

Compare this site map of the ancient Mexican city of Teotihuacán with that of the Indus Valley city of Mohenjo-daro in Pakistan (Figure 11.24). One city was in the Old World, one in the New World, but both were planned settlements and the capitals of vast ancient states. (Reproduced from *Past Worlds: The Times Atlas of Archaeology* by kind permission of Times Books, Ltd., London)

As Lamberg-Karlovsky and Sabloff (1995) suggest, the growth of Teotihuacán may have been the result of all of these factors, with each enhancing the other. To take advantage of its obsidian resource, miners of the stone, makers of tools, and full-time traders were needed. A greater emphasis on irrigation developed to produce more food, which in turn allowed a greater proportion of the population to engage in specialties related to the obsidian trade. Enormous responsibility and attendant power and wealth rested in the hands of the elite who controlled both trade and irrigation.

A Monumental City

The monuments of Teotihuacán and their positioning clearly were intended to impress both residents and visitors alike. A broad, central avenue more than 3 km (about 2 mi) in length and in places 50 m (164 ft) in width bisects the city (Figure 13.10). Called the Avenue of the Dead by the Aztecs, the roadbed passes through the heart of the city, rising to a summit on top of which, beginning in about A.D. 200, the residents of Teotihuacán built an enormous pyramid. Today it is called the Pyramid of the Moon, again based on its Aztec designation. Its positioning at a naturally high point renders the top of this pyramid a powerful symbol visible from everywhere within the city (Figure 13.11).

FIGURE 13.11
The Pyramid of the Moon is dramatically positioned at a high point in the natural topography of Teotihuacán and at the terminus of the so-called Avenue of the Dead, a broad roadway that bissects the great city. (M. H. Feder)

Off to the side of the Avenue of the Dead is a monument built at about the same time and that dwarfs even the Pyramid of the Moon. Called the Pyramid of the Sun, it measures 250 m (738 ft) on each side and rises to a height of about 70 m (230 ft). The Pyramid of the Sun has about the same sized footprint as the Great Pyramid in Egypt (see Chapter 11), but is only about half as tall. Nevertheless, it contains an enormous volume of more than 1 million cubic meters (1.5 million cubic yards) of material, making it, by most reckonings, the third most massive pyramid in the world (Figure 13.12).

Many of the 600 or so platform monuments and small pyramids built at Teotihuacán were constructed in a characteristic form of alternating steps together called *talud/tablero*. Built as a series of superimposed blocks of diminishing size as one approaches the monument's apex, the levels alternate between a true block shape (these are the *tablero*) with vertical faces (with recessed panels) and horizontal steps, and blocks whose faces are dramatically sloped inward from bottom to top (these are the *talud*), giving them a triangular shape in cross-section. The *talud/tablero* form was used repeatedly in Teotihuacán architecture, rendering the resulting monuments both impressive and visually distinctive (Figure 13.13).

Residences of Teotihuacán's Citizens

Archaeological survey work initiated by René Millon (1967, 1981) in the 1960s revealed Teotihuacán's truly urban character. The work exposed the presence of something on the order of 2,000 substantially scaled, multifamily apartment house compounds, each representing the homes of between 60 and 100 people. These compounds appear to have been built on a consistent and fixed

FIGURE 13.12

The Pyramid of the Sun is truly monumental, the third most massive pyramid produced by any ancient civilization. It is located alongside the Avenue of the Dead at Teotihuacán.

(© Danny Lehman/Corbis)

FIGURE 13.13

A schematic representation of talud/tablero architecture. Characterizing many of the structures at Teotihuacán, the form alternates blocks with vertical faces (the tablero) with blocks whose faces are sloped dramatically inward.

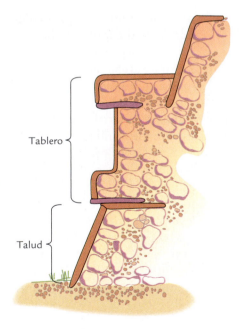

Tablero

Talud

city grid, leaving the clear impression, similar to what is seen in the ancient Indus Valley urban centers (see Figure 11.24), of careful planning and control of housing development on the part of a ruling authority (see Figure 13.10).

It is interesting to point out that until the residential compounds were excavated and carefully investigated, many researchers thought they repre-

FIGURE 13.14
Detailed and colorful wall art decorated the homes of the Teotihuacán elite. This is a reconstruction of a painting likely representing a goddess from whose fingers water droplets are seen flowing. (Gianni Dagli Orti/Corbis)

sented the remains of palaces inhabited only by the high elites of Teotihuacán, because they appeared to be that finely made and appointed. Archaeological evidence, however, shows that the compounds were not palaces but the residences of regular Teotihuacános of most every social rank. That's curious. Consider how very unlikely it would be for a future archaeologist to conclude, on examining the residential buildings in one of our modern cities, including the homes of the poorest citizens, that they were all palaces. This is a reflection of what appears to have been a relatively high standard of living, even among the poor of Teotihuacán.

Of course, economic inequality is reflected in the residential compounds. Many of the rooms in individual family units are large, and some apartments open up onto interior patios. These likely were the domiciles of wealthy, socially and politically important families, perhaps administrators, soldiers of high military rank, and priests (Pasztory 1997). Many, perhaps two-thirds of the residential compounds, were lived in by the poor (Millon 1992); likely they were farmers or craft workers. Their apartments were much smaller, crowded, not as well made, and lack interior patios. But even the smallest, most crowded compounds do not evince abject poverty. Large or small, patios or not, many compounds were beautifully decorated with remarkable, very artfully rendered and colorful wall paintings (Figure 13.14). There are images of jaguars, birds, plumed serpents, lush plant life, and an abundance of images of water, both as flowing streams and as showers of water droplets flowing from the fingers of what is presumed to be a deity.

Though most of Teotihuacán's inhabitants lived in the sprawl of residential compounds, the highest elites had their own, separate and distinct living quarters in a grand palace built on either side of the Temple of the Feathered Serpent. Their homes are positioned within the monumentally scaled Ciudadela compound, a walled fortress or city within the city located off of the Avenue of the Dead, south of the Pyramid of the Sun.

The Reach of Teotihuacán

The social, economic, political, and, perhaps military reach of Teotihuacán was geographically vast. There is archaeological evidence of Teotihuacán-style objects in the burials of even the most powerful Maya rulers whose cities were located hundreds of kilometers from Teotihuacán. There is so much in the way of Teotihuacán material found at the Maya site of Kaminaljuyu in Guatemala that some suggest that it was a vassal state to Teotihuacán.

Also, people throughout Mesoamerica came to Teotihuacán to live and conduct business. A cluster of tombs in the city reflects the cultural practices of people from the ancient city of Monte Alban, located in the Mexican state of Oaxaca. A neighborhood of houses looking markedly different from the standard apartments of most Teotihuacános has been excavated in the eastern part of the city. These houses resemble those found in the Mexican state of Veracruz, located on the Gulf of Mexico; perhaps the people living in these houses were foreign merchants whose business dealings made it sensible for them to live in the big city.

Teotihuacán clearly was a dominant force in ancient Mesoamerica for several hundred years. Its power and impact seem to have diminished after about A.D. 600, and its collapse began to accelerate after A.D. 700, but it is as yet not clear why. There is no indication of a military invasion or a great conflict, but there is some evidence of violence in the form of substantial burning, not in the residential compounds as might be expected in the case of an invader bent on destroying the city, but in ceremonial areas and, especially, in the Ciudadela, the location of what is interpreted to have been the residence of the high elite of the city. Could the end of Teotihuacán have been precipitated by internal social upheaval or even a revolution? Perhaps. After the destruction of the Ciudadela it appears that people simply abandoned the city, occasionally taking the time to burn ceremonial areas, effectively ending Teotihuacán's tenure as Mesoamerica's great urban center.

THE AZTECS

As mentioned previously, the Aztecs were the reigning civilization encountered by the Spanish conquistadors when they entered the Valley of Mexico in

1519. These Spanish invaders wrote detailed historical accounts of sixteenth-century Aztec culture (Soustelle 1964) that have given us the name of the supreme ruler of the Aztec polity: Motecuhzoma (or Montezuma). We also know that he sat atop a multitiered sociopolitical system that included the rulers of city-states that had been incorporated into the Aztec realm; in turn, these leaders ruled over local nobles. As always, at the base of the social, political, and economic pyramid in complex state societies was the vast majority of the population, made up of the commoners whose labor provided the resources that supported the entire system. Motecuhzoma's domain was vast; the Valley of Mexico over which he ruled directly had a population of close to 1 million in the period A.D. 1350–1519. The population of the surrounding territories that can still be considered part of his empire numbered in the millions (M. E. Smith 1997:78). This large population was made possible by an intensive and sophisticated agricultural technology that included substantial irrigation works such as dams and canals. The Aztecs also built walls on hillsides and flattened out slopes naturally too steep for agriculture to produce cultivable terraces. Swamps were drained and artificially raised, and fertilized fields—the *chinampas* mentioned earlier in this chapter—were produced, resulting in one of the most productive farming patterns seen anywhere before the development of modern agricultural techniques.

The ample historical documentation of the Aztec civilization focuses on the final chapter of that culture. Archaeology has given us an appreciation for how Aztec society evolved.

Archaeologist Michael Smith (1997) points out that much of the archaeology conducted in the Aztec realm has focused on the remains discovered at the Aztec capital, Tenochtitlán (Figure 13.15). The capital of the modern nation of Mexico, Mexico City, was built over the remains of the Aztec capital; and, indeed, it seems that in every construction project in the modern nation's city, ancient remains from the previous inhabitants are brought to light. Archaeologists, naturally enough, are drawn to these spectacular artifacts, palaces, and pyramids that reflect the great architectural and artistic achievements of the Aztecs (Figure 13.16). On the other hand, archaeologists realize that an ancient civilization cannot truly be understood without an examination of the lives of the common people who made up the majority population of the society and whose labor made the civilization possible. As a result, Smith has focused his research not on the compounds of the great ruler or the great works of art and architecture but rather on the settlements of the common people living in the hinterlands.

Michael Smith (1997) has excavated at two rural villages: Capilco, with a population of about 135, and Cuexcomate, with about 800 people. Agriculture was intense at both villages; terraced slopes allowed for the increased production of corn, beans, and cotton. This agricultural intensity provided the food surplus that passed into the hands of local nobles and from there to the kings of local city-states and ultimately up the line to support the rulers at Tenochtitlán.

FIGURE 13.15
A computer-graphic reconstruction of the main pyramid located in the central part of the Aztec capital of Tenochtitlán conveys a sense of the beauty and majesty of the brightly painted architecture of this ancient New World city.
(© Taisei Corporation)

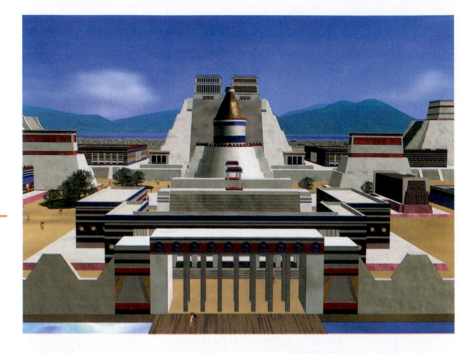

FIGURE 13.16
The so-called Aztec Calendar Stone is not a calendar for keeping track of time in the modern sense. Instead, it depicts the Aztec notion of the cyclical nature of time on a universal scale. The central face on the 23,000-kg (25-ton), painted block of basalt (a hard volcanic rock), 4 m (13.5 ft) in diameter, represents the sun and is surrounded by four other suns that shone in four previous eras of Aztec time.
(© Archivo Iconografico, S.A./Corbis)

The commoners lived in small houses (only about 15 m²—about 160 ft², or a room a little more than 12½ ft on a side). The inhabitants of these houses were, however, part of a complex and interconnected economic system. They produced goods for sale or trade and obtained desired material in exchange. For example, each household grew cotton, and Smith found artifacts used in cotton production (spindle whorls and small bowls used in spinning the cotton) in every excavated house. Cotton textiles were a major product of Aztec peasants and served, for peasants anyway, as the coin of the realm.

Most of the pottery found at Capilco and Cuexcomate had been produced locally, but even the poorest of peasants possessed imported ceramics. Residents also used thousands of obsidian blades, but there is no local source for volcanic glass. It is available 100 km (62 mi) away. Also, though there is no evidence for metallurgy at either site, residents were able to obtain bronze sewing needles, most likely manufactured in western Mexico.

As Smith points out, at least in the outlying sites he excavated, there does not appear to be the kind of grinding poverty that characterizes our modern state societies. In fact, the archaeological record indicates that Aztec commoners did fairly well for themselves. We know from historical records that the Aztecs did not rule with an iron fist; their rule was mostly indirect. As long as each successive rung up the sociopolitical hierarchy received its portion of tribute from those below, people were left alone. In return, they were protected from external threats posed by competitor states, and the goods that people wanted and needed were supplied to the markets.

WHY DID THE MAYA COLLAPSE?

ISSUES AND DEBATES

The common image most of us have of the collapse of an ancient civilization is, perhaps, reflected best in Plato's account of the fictional ancient society of Atlantis—in his story, the dominant social, economic, political, and military force of the world more than 11,000 years ago. In Plato's telling, Atlantis undertook an ambitious military expedition against all of Europe, Africa, and western Asia only to be defeated in battle by a fictionally drawn ancient Athens. The Atlanteans angered the gods by their hubris, and after their military defeat their island home was decimated by a natural catastrophe marked by earthquakes and volcanoes of immense proportions—whereupon this once proud and powerful land sank beneath the roiling waters of the Atlantic over the course of a single day and night (see "Issues and Debates" in Chapter 12).

It's a pretty dramatic image and it certainly adds to Plato's narrative, but this catastrophic view of a civilization's collapse simply doesn't reflect the most common elements of the deaths of most ancient states; they tend to go out with the proverbial whimper rather than the bang. As abruptly as the Maya changed beginning by about A.D. 800, overall, the collapse transpired over the course of a few centuries, and there is no evidence of a dramatic or cataclysmic natural catastrophe at the root of the collapse.

David Webster (2002) proposes, in fact, that the collapse of the Maya was not due to any natural catastrophe, invasion, revolution, or any of the commonly proposed explanations; instead, he ascribes the collapse of the Maya to what might seem like a rather mundane and not terribly dramatic cause: He calls it "an ecological trap of their own making" (p. 255).

Essentially, Webster points out that the homeland of the Maya was not especially well suited to the kind of intensive agricultural system required by a state society. As we have seen in Chapters 11, 12, and 13, and as we will see in Chapter 14, one of the essential foundations of state societies is the production of a food surplus that supports an elite class of people. That elite class must constantly reinforce and legitimize its privileged status through the construction of great monuments, by monopolizing exotic and valuable raw materials, and by its control over a cadre of specialist artisans who manufacture finely made objects from those exotic and valuable raw materials. Craftspeople, construction workers, merchants, and soldiers are all part of the civilization package, and the state must supply these people with the necessities of life, especially food. That food must be provided by a large contingent of farmers who are able to produce far more food than they need to feed their own families.

Some habitats lend themselves to the production of just such a food surplus. For example, in the valleys of major rivers outside of the tropics, soil is replenished by the deposition of alluvium during the yearly flood. In other words, at least to a point and for a time, the nutrients removed by producing food at an ever-escalating rate are restored by a natural process, flooding, that in economic terms doesn't cost anything. The Maya civilization, however, developed in a region that is dominated by a tropical and subtropical forest. Soils in the tropics are relatively nutrient-depleted. Instead of nutrients being stored in the soil and replenished by flooding, nutrients in the tropics are stored in the trees themselves; it is estimated that something like 75% of the nutrients in a tropical forest are stored in the vegetation.

Farmers in the tropics all over the world figured this out and realized that the best way to release the nutrients stored in that vegetation back into the soil where it could be used to sustain agricultural plants was to cut the trees down and burn them. That's why this strategy is given the name "slash-and-burn" agriculture. The problem, however, is that once the nutrients are released into the soil by burning, and once those nutrients are taken up by the crops grown, harvested, and then removed, the soil has become depleted and requires an often lengthy resting or fallow period. During this time the soil nutrients are slowly replenished, vegetation becomes reestablished, nutrients become concentrated in the biomass, and eventually the process can be repeated and another burn can take place and another crop can be planted.

Webster suggests that while the Maya were able to maintain their complex societies based on a system of intensive agriculture for a time, ultimately it was impossible to sustain that system. In this view the Maya were a victim of their own success. The rapacious demands of the elites to sustain their position of power and wealth led to overproduction on thin, depleted soils that were not given sufficient fallow time during which they could replenish their nutrients. This, in turn, led to ever-bloodier conflicts between city-states competing for agricultural lands on which farmers could produce the needed food surplus. Peasant farmers who previously accepted the authority of the elite class and who believed that peace and stability were the result of the sacred legitimacy of the king began to question that legitimacy when crops failed and wars became interminable. Webster (2002:345) goes so far as to suggest that the kings were viewed as being personally responsible when the system failed to provide peace, stability, and food. Without the acquiescence of the peasant farmers, there could be no Maya states; and they may have, in Webster's words, simply voted by their feet and moved beyond the control of the elites living in the regal-ritual centers. The fall of the Maya may have been the result not of a dramatic catastrophe, but of a simple but equally devastating problem: "Too many farmers grew too many crops on too much of the landscape" (Webster 2002:347).

CASE STUDY CLOSE-UP

The great king named Yax Pahsaj Chan Yopat ascended to the throne of the Maya city-state of Copán 1,242 years ago, more precisely on the 2nd of July in the year A.D. 763 (Fash 2001). He was the 16th and final king in Copán's ruling dynasty established by K'inch Yax K'uk Mo' in A.D. 435.

Like his predecessors, Yax Pahsaj recognized the great importance of establishing his legitimacy as ruler of Copán by constructing monumental buildings and erecting stelae verifying, one could even say, advertising, in image and word his relationship to the 15 kings who preceded him and, especially, in emphasizing his direct lineal connection to K'inch Yax K'uk Mo', the first in Copán's kingly line. There is no better example of this than Altar Q, a spectacularly carved, four-sided monument depicting in bas-relief Yax Pahsaj along with the 15 previous rulers of Copán, positioned in chronological sequence around the entire perimeter of the altar (Figure 13.17). In a sense, Yax Pahsaj is located at the end of the succession of rulers but also physically and symbolically at a point back at the beginning, positioned adjacent to both the previous, 15th ruler of Copán on his left, and to the first, K'inch Yax K'uk Mo', on his right. To make the symbolism even more abundantly clear to the citizens of Copán as well as to modern Mayanists, K'inch Yax K'uk Mo' is shown, precisely as in the words of the old cliché, passing the torch to Yax Pahsaj. It is the equivalent of a monument depicting a modern American president being administered the oath of office by George Washington. To make Yax Pahsaj's legitimacy as the rightful heir to the throne of Copán even clearer and to symbolically show his rightful place in the cycle of powerful kings, a crypt was constructed just east of Altar Q in which the skulls of exactly 15 jaguars were entombed, each representing a ruler in the line of succession

FIGURE 13.17

One of the four sides of Altar Q at Copán. The altar depicts each of Copán's sixteen historical kings. The builder of this monument, Yax Pahsaj Chan Yopat (the sixteenth in Copán's kingly succession), is shown here, second from the right, being handed the staff of kingship by a figure representing the first king of Copán.

(© Richard A. Cooke/Corbis)

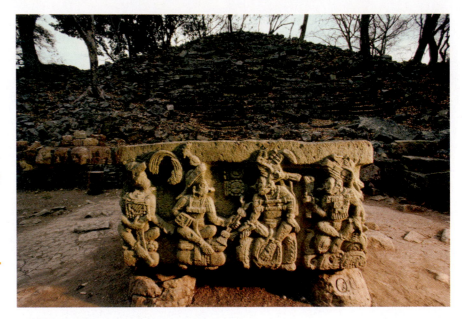

leading up to Yax Pahsaj. Jaguars were viewed by the Maya as protectors of their royal houses.

The spectacular Maya city-state of Copán is located within the borders of the modern nation of Honduras, in an agriculturally extremely rich "pocket" of land carved out by the Copán River (Fash 2001). Along with rich soil, Copán is located close to a significant source of volcanic glass, excellent for making sharp-edged stone tools, and near the largest source of jade in Mesoamerica. Granite used for making grinding stones for milling corn, kaolin for making pottery, and volcanic tuff suitable for sculpting were all abundant in the area around Copán.

At its peak of power and size in the late eighth century A.D., Copán had a population estimated at about 20,000, including a dense urban core. That core is characterized by the presence of pyramids, altars, stelae, the large homes of the elites, and a ballcourt where the Maya played a ceremonial game. (The losing side was sacrificed; according to Mayanist Bill Fash, a lot of the games ended in a tie, which, if you were on one of the teams, you might have found comforting.) This so-called Principal Group of Copán's monumental structures in the urban core covers an area of 12 hectares (about 30 acres; Figure 13.18).

Certainly one the most spectacular of Copán's monuments in the Principal Group is a pyramid, the top of which can be reached by ascending an intensively carved Hieroglyphic Stairway. The hieroglyphs located on the risers of the stairs (the vertical components of the steps) represent the longest continuous written inscription in the New World (Fash 2001:139; Figure 13.19).

FIGURE 13.18
Detail of the principal ground of monuments at the Maya site of Copán. The Principal Group covers an area of about 12 hectares (30 acres) and is surrounded by the primary residential wards of the city.
(© Craig Lovell/Corbis)

The pyramid was constructed by the 13th ruler of Copán over the tomb of the 12th ruler. The detailed message conveyed in the hieroglyphs concerns, as so much of Maya writing seems to, the legitimacy and life histories of the city's rulers, including their births, details of their lineages, their succession to the throne, their important achievements in construction and in war, and then their deaths.

Around the Principal Group archaeologists have found the primary residential wards of Copán where most of the city's population lived. Looking nothing like the regularly laid out neighborhoods of Harappa or Mohenjodaro of the Indus Valley (Chapter 11) or those of highland Mexico, Teotihuacán (this chapter), Copán's neighborhoods appear to have developed in an informal, ad hoc fashion, growing organically rather than according to some master urban plan. Finally, surrounding Copán's religious, political, and urban residential core there is a broad periphery where the more dispersed settlements of farmers who surely viewed Copán as their capital city were located.

During Copán's tenure as a Classic Maya city, there appear to have been at least four distinct social classes, reflected in the sizes of their residences, the proximity of their residences to the Principal Group, and the elaborateness of their burials. From most powerful to least there were (1) the king and his immediate family, (2) a political elite, (3) landed elites, and (4) commoners.

Yax Pahsaj Chan Yopat was the final great ruler of Copán, although at least one additional leader appears to have attempted to succeed him. Bill Fash (2001:178) sees this 17th ruler—if we can really count him on the list—

FIGURE 13.19

The extensively inscribed Hieroglyphic Stairway presents a written history of kingly succession at Copán. It is the longest, continuous, written document ever found in the New World.

(© Craig Lovell/Corbis)

as a rather "tragic figure," an individual who tried to hold Copán together as a great and powerful city-state, but who, in the midst of what appears to be a systemic collapse throughout the Maya world, ultimately failed. Like many of the Maya cities at the end of the ninth and beginning of the tenth century, Copán wasn't destroyed but underwent a dramatic and relatively rapid change, with a large segment of the population moving away from the urban core and even out of the Copán pocket entirely. No more monuments were built, no more stelae were erected, and the royal lineage ended.

VISITING THE PAST

Founded about A.D. 500, Uxmal is located in the northern lowlands of the Yucatán in what is known as the Puuc region. The Maya accomplished a series of truly stunning architectural achievements at Uxmal. The site is dominated by the Pyramid of the Magician, a steep-sided, elliptical structure devoid of right angles; the corners of the pyramid are rounded. A staircase brings the visitor to the top of the pyramid, where, as in most Maya pyramids, a magnificent and intricately designed ceremonial structure was built (see Figure 13.9).

The sound-and-light show at the site is surprisingly well done. But the artificial light show at Uxmal, painting the ruins in shades of blue and red, could not compare with the light show nature had in store during my visit. Standing at the ruin called the "Palace of the Governors," which looks remarkably like a government office building with a broad staircase and imposing façade, one can look down across the main section of the site into the building called the "Nunnery"—four long structures surrounding a massive courtyard—into the ceremonial ballcourt and, to the right, the wonderful Pyramid of the Magician.

As my family and I stood there, literally in awe of the alien beauty of the city, an intensely dark set of rain clouds moved in from the north. Behind us the sun blazed brightly, illuminating the southern face of the pyramid with an eerie glow, while to the north, behind it, the sky turned frighteningly dark. Lightning sparked in the distance. It seemed as if the Mayan rain god Chaac were putting on a spectacular light show for those of us visiting the ancient city.

The great Maya sites of Chichén Itzá, Uxmal, Tikal, and Palenque are relatively accessible and absolutely marvelous places, cities literally carved out of the jungle by the ancient Maya.

SUMMARY

In the New World, just as in the Old, some farming societies eventually developed the ability to produce a food surplus. This surplus enabled the development of social complexity and inequality. Eventually, some of these complex societies developed into true states with a formal government and true power invested in an elite class. The Maya and the complex pre-Aztec cultures of central Mexico, developed independently of Old World civilizations.

Through their concentration of wealth and power and as members of an elite social class in a stratified society, rulers were able to organize the labor of the many to produce the spectacular monuments—the pyramids and temples—that dominate the ancient landscapes of Teotihuacán and the territory of the Maya.

Like the civilizations of the Old World, the complex societies of the New eventually collapsed. Though many suggestions have been proposed to explain the process underlying the fall of ancient civilizations, including resource depletion, environmental catastrophes, invasion, and insurrection, no one of these explanations alone is sufficient. In each case of societal collapse, it is the inability of the society at a particular point in its evolution to respond adequately to a challenge, whatever that challenge may be, that leads to its disintegration.

TO LEARN MORE

Technical Summaries

Once again, *Ancient Civilizations*, by C. C. Lamberg-Karlovsky and Jeremy Sabloff (1995), presents an extremely thorough investigation of the origins of civilization in Mesoamerica (and the Middle East and Indus Valley as well). Thomas C. Patterson's *Archaeology: The Historical Development of Civilizations* (1993) is as valuable for its discussion of New World civilization as it is for the Old World.

Popular Summaries

There is a wealth of good material aimed at a general readership on the Maya of Mesoamerica—in particular, Michael Coe's *The Maya* (1993), Jeremy Sabloff's *The New Archaeology and the Ancient Maya* (1994), T. Patrick Culbert's *The Maya Civilization* (1993), and the wonderfully written *A Forest of Kings,* by Linda Schele and David Freidel (1990). Focusing on seven Maya sites, *The Code of Kings,* by Linda Schele and Peter Mathews (1998), is a marvelously written book on the history of the ancient Maya kingdoms.

Don't let the title fool you; David Webster's (2002) wonderful book, *The Fall of the Ancient Maya,* is about so much more than just the collapse of the Classic Maya civilization after A.D. 800. His is a very well written and inclusive discussion of Maya history from its most ancient origins through its florescence and then on to its collapse, reorganization, and contact with the Spanish invaders. For my discussion of the Maya city of Copán in the "Case Study Close-Up," I relied on the terrific book by William and Barbara Fash (2001), *Scribes, Warriors and Kings: The City of Copán and the Ancient Maya.* For Teotihuacán, I highly recommend a DVD titled *Teotihuacán: City of the Gods* produced by the Educational Video Network and released in 2004. For about the most beautiful and lavishly illustrated book I have seen in a long time on any topic, see *The Aztec Empire,* the published volume that accompanied the Guggenheim Museum's spectacular 2004 exhibit of Aztec and other Mesoamerican art. The book is brimming with incredible photographs of Aztec stonework, metallurgy, and weavings accompanied by short pieces written by experts in Mesoamerican art, history, and archaeology.

On the Web

Of course, there is a wealth of material on the early New World civilizations on the Internet. Type the name of any of the cultures discussed in this chapter in your favorite search engine and you will find lots of sites. For example, a great source on the Web for information about central Mexico's earliest urban center with lots of photos and short movies is Teotihuacán: City of the Gods (http://archaeology.la.asu.edu/teo). One of my favorite sites on the Maya can be found at http://www.halfmoon.org, where you can find a primer in Maya hieroglyphics and download some virtual pyramids that you can walk around, if only on your computer screen. For a Web site with a set of quite beautiful photographs of Maya sites, be sure to visit Barbara McKenzie's Maya Ruins page at http://mayaruins.com/. For an incredibly useful site with links to sites focusing on every imaginable aspect of Aztec culture, visit the Web site put up by the University of Minnesota at Duluth at http://www.d.umn.edu/cla/faculty/troufs/anth3618/maaztec.html. For a brief discussion of the Aztecs, their history, their gods, and their language, see http://www.wsu.edu/~dee/CIVAMRCA/AZTECS.HTM.

Online Learning Center: www.mhhe.com/feder4

The Online Learning Center (OLC) Web companion to *The Past in Perspective* features a variety of supplemental study aids. For each chapter, this free Web site includes

- Self-Quizzes to take as pretests prior to exams
- Interactive Timeline Study Guides for additional review and reinforcement of key information

ONLINE LEARNING CENTER

- Learning Objectives
- Chapter Site links with Web addresses for many of the fossil and archaeological sites mentioned in the text

KEY TERMS

chinampas, 532   codices, 536

14

An Explosion of Complexity

THE FLOWERING OF CIVILIZATION IN THE NEW WORLD: SOUTH AMERICA

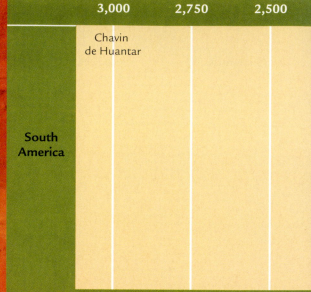

	3,000	2,750	2,500
South America	Chavin de Huantar		

CHAPTER OVERVIEW

"Civilization," including monumental edifices, elaborate burials, large armies, and full-time artisans, developed in some parts of the New World as fewer people were needed in the subsistence quest and as rulers attempted to legitimize and reinforce their position of power and wealth. Western South America saw the development of some of the first civilizations in the New World. The Moche, Tiwanaku, Wari, Sicán, Chimu, and Inca of South America are discussed in this chapter.

Years ago

| 2,250 | 2,000 | 1,750 | 1,500 | 1,250 | 1,000 | 750 | 500 |

Moche
Sipan

Tiwanaku
Pampa Koani

Wari
Azángaro

Sicán
Batán Grande

Chimu
Chan Chan

Inca
Cuzco

ONLINE
LEARNING
CENTER

Go to **www.mhhe.com/feder4** for an
interactive study guide version of this timeline.

Reading the account of his Peruvian expedition, one can clearly sense the excitement of Yale University professor Hiram Bingham when the team he was leading entered into a high-altitude saddle in the "cloud forest" in the mountains of Peru, about 97 km (60 mi) from the ancient Incan capital city of Cuzco (Bingham 1913). It was there, on July 24, 1911, that Bingham led a team of archaeologists, historians, and naturalists into an incredible, hidden archaeological world never before seen by outsiders, a world presenting to its visitors what arguably is the most breathtakingly beautiful setting for any archaeological site anywhere on earth (Figure 14.1).

At an elevation of about 2,400 meters (7,900 feet), enfolded by the nearly vertical, ancient granite peaks of mountains sacred to the Inca, it is no wonder that Bingham surmised, however incorrectly, that the site he had discovered might be a legendary hidden city. When one considers the setting and surroundings of what local people called Machu Picchu, it is understandable that Bingham speculated that it might have been the final redoubt of a clan of royal Inca, a stronghold into which they made their final desperate retreat from the Spanish conquistadors before they vanished into the haze of history.

But Machu Picchu does not represent some romantically doomed last stand of the powerful Incan empire. In fact, it was something far more mundane, though, to be sure, no less fascinating. Machu Picchu simply was a grand royal estate, actually one of many at the disposal of the Inca elite, a "weekend getaway" from the pressures and stresses of running an enormous empire. As

FIGURE 14.1
Though not architecturally the most impressive achievement of the Inca, the setting of Machu Picchu is stunning, located on a ridge at an elevation of more than 2,400 m (8,000 ft) with the majestic peak of Huaynac Picchu looming above. An enormous labor force must have been required to construct this community with its nearly 200 interconnected buildings.
(P. Nute)

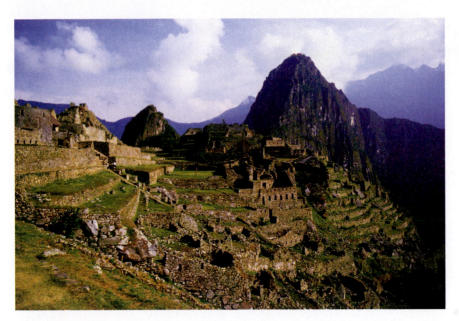

FIGURE 14.2
Finely built walls of precisely carved granite brick literally cling to the steep slopes of Machu Picchu. Though once thought of as a lost city, Machu Picchu was, instead, a royal estate, a retreat for the Inca elite.
(© Royalty-Free/Corbis)

archaeologist Lucy Salazar (2004:27) points out, while modern American presidents have their Camp David retreat, the ancient Inca rulers had Machu Picchu, a place where they could relax and entertain guests, among whom might be political allies and even the rulers of other great nations. Machu Picchu was a place where the Inca emperor and his guests could, essentially, kick back, do a little hunting and fishing, and simply enjoy the stupendous views.

Likely built by the 9th Inca ruler Pachacuti Inca Yupanqui sometime between A.D. 1450 and 1470, Machu Picchu was no lost city but, in fact, a relatively small resort consisting of a series of mostly residential compounds whose walls were constructed with precisely shaped granite bricks (Figure 14.2). Even when the Inca, his family, his entourage, and his guests were in residence, Machu Picchu is unlikely to have housed much more than about 500 people, and certainly not more than 750, less than one-quarter of whom would have been the elite (Salazar 2004:30). Based on the sizes of the residences, Salazar (2004:29) estimates that the elite homes could house no more than between 100 and 120 people at a time.

There are only about 150 individual residences at the site, most with small and not particularly sumptuous living quarters. These likely were lived in year-round primarily by support staff, individuals whose job it was to keep the place in shape for its occasional use by the political and economic elites. Some of the ordinary houses were located away from the main part of the site, near the neatly terraced agricultural fields. These likely were lived in by farmers whose produce ended up on the tables of the elite visitors to the estate.

At least three house clusters or compounds look quite different, consisting of larger, more finely made homes, physically isolated from the clusters of the standard structures, providing their residents better views, direct access to

flowing water in beautifully made fountains, and considerably more privacy. One of the elite compounds, in particular, stands out, also possessing a private bath and even a private garden; pollen analysis indicates that the residents of this compound, called the King's Group, grew food, including beans, corn, and potatoes, as well as a wide array of flowers, in particular, beautiful and colorful orchids.

Along with the houses of royalty and their support staff, there are also a series of 30 shrines and temples at the site, most of which seem to be aligned to the rising of the sun on the summer solstice, the morning on which the sun rises at its northernmost point on the horizon (Figure 14.3). After that day, June 21 or 22, the sun appears to rise successively further to the south along the horizon. Along with the shrines and temples, there are 16 fountains at Machu Picchu whose waters are supplied by natural springs at the site, channeled through a stone-lined canal nearly 750 m (2456 ft) in length.

Machu Pichhu is an amazing place, one that has reached iconic status as a "must-see" tourist destination; a quick glance at Figure 14.1 is all you need to see why. More than 550 years after Machu Picchu was built, it remains, as archaeologist Lucy Salazar (2004:27) phrases it, "a formal architectural symbol of the power of the ruler and his elite." The ability of the elite classes, the royal rulers of an ancient state society, to have constructed their own haven in the sky is just one more material manifestation of the power concentrated in their hands. This chapter focuses on those material manifestations of ancient state societies in South America.

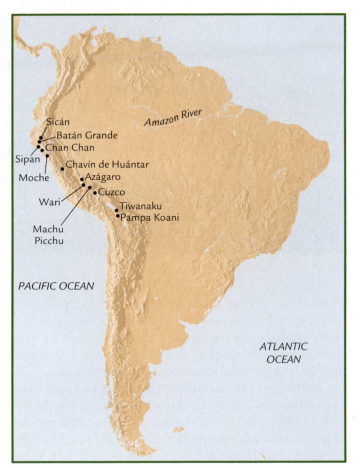

MOCHE

If asked to enumerate the ancient civilizations of pre-Hispanic South America, most of us would be at a loss after we named the builders of Machu Picchu, the Inca. But this largest and best-known South American state society, first encountered by the Spanish in 1532, was only one in a long sequence of impressively powerful civilizations that characterize the history of western South America (Figure 14.4).

For example, about 1,700 years ago, on Peru's northern coast, a culture called Moche developed, with stepped pyramids, hilltop forts, unique pottery styles, and fabulous burials. There are continuities in iconography between Chavín de Huántar (Chapter 10) and Moche, as there are, in fact, between South America's earliest, unifying religious art style and all of the later state societies to be discussed in this chapter.

Beginning construction at their capital in about A.D. 100 and reaching their zenith at about A.D. 400, the Moche produced one of the earliest kingdoms in

CHRONICLE

FIGURE 14.5
The Moche culture Pyramid of the Sun stood over 40 m (135 ft) in height. Begun in about A.D. 100, it consists of more than 143 million adobe bricks.
(© Nathan Benn/Corbis)

South America. With a degree of control across an extent of nearly 600 km (370 mi) of coastline, the Moche state constructed enormous monumental works at its primary city, oversaw an extensive trading network that brought in precious raw materials from all over western South America, and ran a large-scale irrigation system of canals and aqueducts.

Following a pattern in South American complex societies established at Caral more than 2,800 years before, the Moche built the so-called Pyramid of the Sun (Huaca del Sol) at the heart of its urban center. Construction commenced on this monumental project at about A.D. 100; the pyramid was built in eight distinct phases and ultimately was more than 40 m (130 ft) high. The Moche Pyramid of the Sun covers a vast area; along its longer axis it is 342 m (1,122 ft) in length (that's about 3½ football fields) and nearly 160 m (520 ft) wide. In other words, this one monument covers an area of more than 54,000 m² (13.5 acres, or the area covered by more than 12 football fields). Its enormous volume contains 143,000,000 mold-made, sun-dried adobe bricks (Figure 14.5). Its accompanying, smaller Pyramid of the Moon (Huaca de la Luna) is made of 50,000,000 adobe bricks and rises to a height of 20 m (66 ft).

In the interior of the Egyptian pharaoh Khufu's pyramid, work gangs left graffiti, often referring proudly to their role in building the great burial monument to the absolute leader of their society (see Chapter 11). Archaeologists Charles Hastings and Michael Mosely have examined the construction of the Moche pyramids and have found a similar phenomenon. Though none of the pre-Columbian civilizations in South America, including the Moche, possessed a written language, Hastings and Mosely (1975) found more than 100 different kinds of markings on the adobe bricks in the Pyramid of the Sun. They suggest that such markings may have served to record the material contributions of local groups of people to Moche's great leaders for construction of the pyramid. This record keeping, as Hastings and Mosely suggest, implies

FIGURE 14.6
The Moche produced beautiful works of art in clay. Pictured here is a pot made to look like the head of a Moche priest or lord wearing a bird headdress. The part of the pot sticking up out of the head is the spout of the vessel.
(© Gianni Dagli Orti/Corbis)

a complex, hierarchical political organization in which local people were expected to contribute to the needs of the elite—including the monumental construction projects they ordered.

Moche society manifested status differentiation in a definitive way by interring its leaders in a sumptuous splendor that is breathtaking even to our jaded turn-of-the-century sensibilities (Figure 14.6). See the "Case Study Close-Up" in this chapter for a detailed discussion of one remarkable set of Moche elite burials, those of the "Lords of Sipán."

EMPIRES: TIWANAKU

At an elevation of 3,870 m (12,690 ft), the capital of the Tiwanaku civilization, located in Bolivia, just southeast of the enormous and economically productive Lake Titicaca, was one of the highest cities of the ancient world. Beginning in about A.D. 200 and reaching a zenith by about A.D. 400, the builders and sculptors of Tiwanaku constructed a remarkable city encompassing an area of some 4.5 km² (1.74 mi²), filled with a series of palaces,

temples, platforms, and massive monoliths, enormous works crafted from single pieces of stone (Figure 14.7).

The stone used by the builders of Tiwanaku included the hard and dense volcanic rock andesite and the softer sandstone; both were abundant in the Tiwanaku region. Quarrying and transporting this stone, often in enormous blocks—one sandstone monolith moved to the capital weighed 118,000 kg (130 tons)—was a truly monumental undertaking. Andesite was quarried at a site located across the lake from Tiwanaku; it was, in all likelihood, floated over to the city on reed boats. Some of the large sandstone blocks were transported 10 km (6 mi) over land.

The intricately carved Gateway of the Sun, the Ponce Monolith of an enormous Tiwanaku deity, and the Bennett Monolith, a huge sandstone depiction of a Tiwanaku god, are but a small part of the legacy of this civilization (Morris and von Hagen 1993). The amount of labor and the degree of specialization needed to produce these monuments, as well as the impressive architecture of the city of Tiwanaku itself, show just how powerful ancient civilizations can become.

Like all complex state societies, Tiwanaku thrived as the result of a highly productive agricultural system. Though the surrounding territory today seems barren, the farmers of Tiwanaku developed an efficient pattern of raised fields. Through communal labor, they constructed huge platforms of rich soil surrounded by lower swales. The largest of the platforms were 200 m (about 650 ft, or more than two football fields) long and 15 m (50 ft) wide (Morris and von Hagen 1993:105). Excavation of these platforms indicates that they were not simply mounds of earth but carefully engineered agricultural facilities. At one site, Pampa Koani, the platforms were shown to have been built in stages (Kolata 1986). First, a layer of stone cobbles was laid down as a base. The cobbles were covered with a layer of clay, which was in turn covered with three separate sheets of gravel. The productive topsoil was placed on top. The low-lying areas between the raised fields allowed the waters of Lake Titicaca to flow between the plantings. The complex design of these engineered fields ensured that brackish lake water would not percolate up through the mound to damage plants and that the entire facility would be well drained. As with raised fields elsewhere in the New World, the standing water between the platforms produced a rich organic soup that would then be scooped up and laid over the fields to fertilize the soil. This highly productive agricultural system was at the core of Tiwanaku wealth and power.

As in all ancient civilizations, this wealth and power were invested in an elite class who lived in the palaces of Tiwanaku and who ruled over a vast area of hamlets populated by the commoners of Tiwanaku society—the people whose labor made it all possible. And as in all ancient—and modern—civilizations, there had to be a way to legitimize the rule, wealth, power, and comfort of the few over the many. As archaeologist Craig Morris and journalist Adriana von Hagen (1993) point out, legitimization at Tiwanaku was accomplished through religion. The position of the elite class was seen as part of the natural order of things. A complex social and political order was necessary to produce, maintain, and expand the culture's highly engineered agricultural system. That social and political order was reinforced by religious symbolism and monumental construction of palaces, temples, and monoliths.

The influence of Tiwanaku extended across an enormous expanse of South America. Up to 1 million people living in what is now Peru, Bolivia, Ecuador, and Chile were followers of the Tiwanaku state religion.

EMPIRES: WARI

Other civilizations also evolved in highland South America. For example, the Wari developed near the modern Peruvian city of Ayacucho. The Wari partly overlapped with Tiwanaku but peaked later, after A.D. 600. The capital of Wari was an enormous enclosure whose walled neighborhoods covered about 2 km^2 (about three-quarters of a square mile, or nearly 500 acres). The construction is truly monumental; some of the walls are 12 m (40 ft) high and several meters thick and extend for hundreds of meters. Much of the city seems to have been multistoried (Figure 14.8; Morris and von Hagen 1993).

Unlike Tiwanaku or the Aztecs, the Wari were not located on the shores of a lake and did not practice raised-field agriculture. They nevertheless practiced a labor-intensive and highly productive, engineered agricultural system that involved the construction of terraced fields, similar to those seen in Mexico at Teotihuacán. Agriculture also depended on an extensive system of irrigation works, including long canals that brought water from the uplands and

FIGURE 14.8

Located on the southern frontier of Wari territory, the community of Pikillacta was part of the Wari polity and consists of a large number of walled compounds. (Neg. # 334818. Courtesy of Department of Library Services, American Museum of Natural History)

FIGURE 14.9

Ears of corn and the heads of snakes sprout from the head of the Wari sun god, who, in turn, grasps two serpents. (From *The Inca Empire and Its Andean Origins* by Craig Morris and Adriana von Hagen. American Museum of Natural History and Abbeville Press)

distributed it across a complex network of branching secondary canals that led to the terraced fields.

Religious iconography centered at Wari is found represented in textiles and pottery across a broad swath of western South America (Figure 14.9). That the Wari gods appear to have been worshipped in a broad area is an indication of the power and influence of the Wari elite who were identified with those gods. As Morris and von Hagen (1993) point out, one of the most fascinating aspects of Wari is the way in which the leaders maintained their far-

FIGURE 14.10
One-thousand-year-old gold beaker with an image of the Sicán lord.
(© Y. Yoshii/SAP)

flung, religion-based empire. In a pattern that was to be followed again by the Inca, the Wari elite controlled outlying regions, funneling surplus labor and wealth to their capital, by the construction of regional administrative centers across Wari territory. For example, Azángaro, located 15 km northwest of Wari itself, was a walled enclosure built as a smaller version of Wari. Wari pottery is found at Azángaro, and the religious iconography is typically Wari. Other large regional centers scattered throughout Wari territory include Pikillacta and Jincamocco. These regional centers likely served as local offices of the elite, perhaps staffed by Wari nobility, making sure that local populations were participating fully in the Wari state by sending their surplus food to the capital and providing labor for the monumental works required by the elite.

EMPIRES: SICÁN AND CHIMU

Clearly, the Andean region was fertile ground for the development of New World civilizations. After the Moche culture faded along the north coast of Peru after A.D. 700, it was replaced by the culture known as Sicán, which peaked between A.D. 900 and 1100. The Sicán capital city, Batán Grande, also exhibits monumental pyramids and a cemetery for the elite. Everywhere in the iconography seen in textiles and ceramics and on the finely crafted solid gold and gilded objects that typify Sicán, one sees the image of the so-called Sicán lord, presumably the religion's most important god, who ruled a pantheon of other spirit beings (Figure 14.10). Once again, the Sicán empire had at its core a complex agricultural system with enormous irrigation works that

FIGURE 14.11

Aerial view of one of the approximately ten walled palace compounds of the Chimu capital of Chan Chan. Enclosed within its walls were storage areas, government buildings, and burial platforms. (Neg. # 334900. Courtesy of Department of Library Services, American Museum of Natural History)

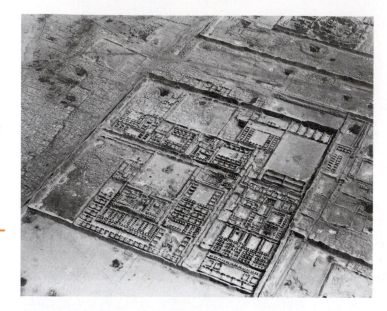

allowed production of a food surplus. This surplus supported an economic system with an elite class; a class of artisans who spent their time manufacturing the ceramic, cloth, and gold artworks that ended up in the hands of the elite; and a large class of commoners whose labor built the monuments and whose sons staffed the military.

Sicán was a significant state society, but it pales in comparison to one of the largest empires ever seen in the ancient New World. The empire of Chimor, or the Chimu, extended across more than 1,300 km (800 mi) of the western coast of South America, essentially the entire northern coast of Peru.

Built beginning sometime before A.D. 900 and expanding at around 1200, the Chimu capital at Chan Chan was one of the most impressive urban centers constructed in the ancient world. From the air it is absolutely remarkable (Figure 14.11). Where Tiwanaku covers an area of 4.5 km^2, Chan Chan's remnants reflect a city some 20 km^2 (almost 8 mi^2) in extent. It is a true city, with neighborhoods divided, in part, according to which crafts were produced by the inhabitants (Topic 1990).

Irrigation was crucial in the development of the Chimu state and was, perhaps, along with the desire of the elite to incorporate surrounding territories into its polity, the reason for its expansion across a huge territory. A sophisticated and monumental complex of irrigation canals produced a rich harvest for the inhabitants of Chan Chan. However, local irrigation in the Moche valley may not have been enough to satisfy the growing population. In addition, as archaeologist Michael Mosely (cited in Morris and von Hagen 1993) points out, irrigated lands build up a concentration of salt, which diminishes harvests and necessitates the incorporation of additional, new lands into the system. Also, as Mosely suggests, the western coast of South America is geologically active. Earthquakes were more than merely a frightening nuisance to the ancient inhabitants of South America, seriously damaging and even destroying irrigation works. Mosely suggests that the Chimu elite found it easier and likely more productive to abandon fields fed by canals if they were destroyed by earthquakes and to annex new territories into their state. This approach would have served the dual purpose of providing more farmland and also new workers—the inhabitants of the annexed territories—for the state.

EMPIRES: THE INCA

As seen in the context of this chapter, the Inca civilization that most people have at least heard of did not arise without antecedents in South America. In fact, the Inca were merely the latest in a series of empires that had achieved prominence and hegemony over the Andean region of South America when the Spanish conquistadors, led by Francisco Pizarro, entered their territory in A.D. 1532. In fact, much of what we know about Incan history and culture we know from the records of the Spanish soldiers, missionaries, and colonists who invaded their territory in the sixteenth and seventeenth centuries (D'Altroy 2003).

The Inca began their historical journey as a small tribe of people living in the region of the modern city of Cuzco in Peru. Cuzco, in fact, became their capital city when their military expansion began in the middle of the fifteenth century A.D. By A.D. 1500, the Inca, who called their nation Tawantinsuyu ("The Four Parts Together"), controlled a broad empire of close to 1 million km^2 (380,000 mi^2), extending across 4,000 km (2,500 mi) of South America's Pacific coast (Figure 14.12). It is estimated that as many as 10 million people were citizens of this empire at its peak (D'Altroy 2003:1).

The capital at Cuzco was typical of the capitals of older Andean states, only bigger. It was filled with palaces, temples, and plazas. The impressive masonry seen at older sites was raised to a level of perfection at Cuzco, home to the elite of Inca society. Enormous stone blocks, often weighing several tons, were carved into various polygonal shapes and then fitted precisely together, much like a jigsaw puzzle.

It is easy to become distracted by the incredibly impressive achievements of Inca architects, but the more mundane engineering accomplishments of the Inca deserve our attention as well. For example, the Inca were an agricultural people living in a largely mountainous region where the low-lying, level fields preferred by farmers in antiquity as well as in the modern world, were limited. Needless to say, agriculture is challenging in regions characterized by the steeply sloping surfaces that dominate many of the areas where the Inca lived. They responded to this challenge by resculpting the land to better suit

FIGURE 14.12
Extent of the Inca empire at its peak.

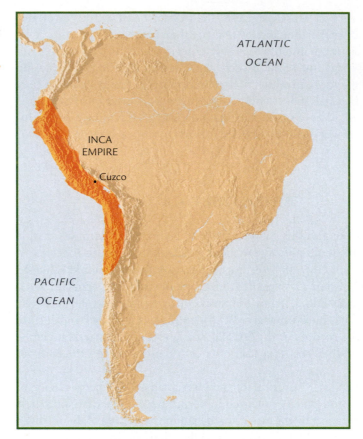

their needs. In what must have represented a tremendous investment of time and labor, the Inca converted steep slopes unsuitable for agriculture into a series of enormously productive flat and fertile steps, or terraces.

An examination of the terraces around Machu Picchu (see the "Prelude" for this chapter), provides a detailed picture of how such fields were engineered (Burger 2004). To produce each individual step in a series of such steps, the Inca began by hauling in and laying down a flat layer of stones to build up and level a sloped surface and to aid in drainage. On top of the stones, they deposited another layer, this time of medium-sized gravel, again to aid in drainage. Above this, they placed a layer of fine sand mixed with gravel for drainage and stability. Finally, as the top layer, the Inca deposited a substantial layer of rich and fertile topsoil extracted from the valley below the slope. Each step in the terrace was held in place by constructing a stone-block retaining wall in the front, giving the entire set-up the appearance of a series of stair steps (Figure 14.13). For increased stability, each retaining wall was built so as to lean into the hill at an angle of about 5 degrees. This intense labor converted acres of unusable, steeply sloping hill and mountainsides into valuable, productive farmland. At Machu Picchu, for example, by construct-

FIGURE 14.13
Aerial view of a system of concentric terracing, an intensive method of farming by which the Inca increased the productivity of their farmland. (© Jeremy Horner/ Corbis)

ing six sets of terraces, the Inca land engineers created, from unusable land, more than 15,000 m^2 (165,320 ft^2, or nearly 3.8 acres) of arable farmland (Zegarra 2004:79). Archaeologist Alfredo Zegarra (2004:79) estimates that this reclaimed land alone would have produced an annual yield of nearly 2,400 kg (5,280 lb) of maize (off the cob), along with small amounts of other agricultural produce. The productive potential of all of the terraces produced by the Inca is enormous.

The Inca Military Empire

Many early state societies fought wars of plunder, attacking their neighbors, appropriating the wealth of the vanquished, and then absconding with their treasure. The Inca employed this practice early in their history, but their empire then evolved a different strategy. As they reached their ascendancy, the Inca became expansionist, and their goal was not just accumulating the spoils of war but also achieving hegemony over their entire region, incorporating the defeated into their empire. In other words, the Inca fought their wars to actually expand their state geographically. Largely through military conquest enabled by an enormous army estimated to have included as many as 80,000 soldiers (D'Altroy 2003:1), the Inca brought together under their rule an enormous and diverse series of cultures and ethnic groups across a broad swath of western South America. Even just the threat of military action on the part of the Inca sometimes was enough to convince a local non-Incan state to acquiesce and join the empire. For example, historical records and oral histories indicate that the Chincha state on Peru's southern coast joined the Tawantinsuyu empire, ostensibly of its own free will. In all likelihood, the rulers of Chincha recognized the clear military superiority of the Inca and the inevitability of Incan control over their territory. Their agreement to join the empire spared their society a war it was bound to lose and likely ensured some level of local control over their nation.

As an expansionist empire that appended the vanquished into their polity, the vast majority of people who were citizens of the Inca state were not culturally or ethnically "Inca." In fact, it is estimated that, at the peak of the empire, those who could claim to be ethnic Incas represented only about 1 percent of the population (D'Altroy 2003: 231). In other words, while they ruled over a vast empire, the Inca themselves were outnumbered in that empire by a ratio of about 100:1. Ultimately, this may have led to their undoing when the Spanish arrived in 1532 and most citizens of Tawantinsuyu were happy to have an invader dismember the empire that had subjugated them.

Certainly, there was a degree of tension between the Inca and the non-Inca people over whom they ruled. Recognizing this tension, the Inca organized their empire into 80 distinct provinces and built administrative centers in the capitals of the states they subdued. In these centers, the Inca appointed one of their own, an ethnic Inca, to the position of provincial governor. In another clever political strategy, representatives of groups subdued in battle were forced to move to and live in Cuzco, the capital of the Inca empire. Many of those removed from their home territories were members of the local political elite. These political leaders likely played a role in administering their home territories for the Inca. In return, they got to continue to breathe and, in all likelihood, lived under conditions far superior to the situation of the folks back home. In other words, as Morris and von Hagen (1993) maintain, these "guests" of the Inca effectively served as hostages, ensuring the obedience of their homelands to Inca rule.

The Inca elites in Cuzco were able to control their vast empire by constructing an incredible system of roads linking the various provinces. Estimates suggest that, altogether, the Inca road system stretched for more than 48,000 km (30,000 mi) connecting even the most distant communities in the Inca empire, passing through deep jungles, over towering peaks, and across rope bridges spanning vast mountain chasms. Though the Inca possessed no special technology for moving along these roads—no llama-drawn wheeled vehicles, for example—the roads ensured that they could move relatively quickly in response to any real threat or rumor of rebellion that faced their empire.

The governor's job included making certain that the empire's subjects continued to farm and to provide a portion of their produce to the Inca elite, allowing them to live in splendor in places like the royal estate of Machu Picchu discussed in the "Prelude" of this chapter. The governor also administered the system by which local people incorporated into the empire contributed their labor and, even at times, their lives to work and fight for the state. Roads, temples, palaces, and royal estates needed to be built and maintained, and wars needed to be fought to continue to grow the empire. The provincial governor made sure that the people over whom he ruled provided the resources that allowed the empire both to thrive and to expand.

All conquered lands became the property of the Inca state. The previous owners became tenants who were allowed to continue to use those lands only at the discretion of the governor and, ultimately, the emperor himself. The "privilege" of being allowed to work the land that had previously belonged to the groups the Inca had subdued was granted only through payment of a tax—not in cash, but in the bushels of maize, potatoes, manioc, quinoa, jícama, cotton, and so forth (see Chapter 9) needed to supply the enormous needs of the Inca state apparatus.

Certainly, Inca wars and the strategy of annexing defeated territories and their people, at least in part, had the practical aim of supplying the state with ever-increasing, secure, consistent, and reliable sources of food, wealth, labor, and soldiers. Territories were selected for invasion and annexation with the goal of supplying the needs of the elites for rare and exotic raw materials, including gold and the brilliantly colored feathers of tropical birds found in the jungles of South America, spondylus shells available along the coast, and various minerals offered by the territories to the south of Cuzco.

Inca wars had another, less material rationale. One way in which individuals could improve their status and position in Inca society was through service in combat. In a sense, in this regard, the Inca weren't that different from us in the modern world. Certainly, it is no coincidence that of the 43 U.S. presidents who have served as this is being written, 30 (70%) served in the military in some capacity and many were veterans of war—their ability to lead, some have argued, forged in the crucible of combat. In 2004, we went through a presidential election in the United States where the military service of both major candidates was a significant point of contention, with the nature of their service being extolled by their supporters or attacked by their opponents. It is clearly the case among the Inca—and, likely among modern Americans—that military service, particularly during times of war, provides an opportunity for individuals to display personal characteristics that may allow them to gain the respect of their fellow citizens and later to rise to power in their society. In fact, among the Inca, war may have become a necessary vehicle to provide opportunities for men to exhibit the courage, heroism, patriotism, and dedication to the state required to attain a high level of status and power.

A State Without Writing?

So far in this book we have talked a bit about the world's most ancient writing systems, specifically, the cuneiform of Mesopotamia, the hieroglyphics of ancient Egypt, the script of the Indus Valley civilization, the bone writing of the Chinese Shang, and the hieroglyphics of the Maya. In some cases, these early systems of record keeping focused on practical economic issues (especially the earliest writing in Mesopotamia and Egypt) amounting to, essentially and rather unromantically, the archives of accountants keeping track of goods, services, and taxes. Other early writing systems, notably that of the Maya, seem far more focused on genealogy and history, validating in a permanent form, the elevated position of the leaders of the Maya city-states. Whatever the particular focus of the specific ancient writing system discussed, they all share the fact that they served the purposes of the state societies in which they were used. Each of the writing systems just mentioned had its own unique way of using conventionalized symbols to keep unambiguous records of things deemed necessary for running the state, intelligible to anyone who knew the code.

Is it possible to have a complex state society in which there was no system of record keeping, no way of keeping track in an unambiguous way, of the production of crops, the manufacture of goods, the payment of taxes, or the lineage and accomplishments of the king? Could the government, bureaucracy, and economy of the United States operate without a writing system; could we function if taxes, laws, business, and banking were all based on the honor system? If the old expression, "knowledge is power," is correct, how can any state society truly possess and wield power if it doesn't have the ability to control the underlying knowledge by codifying it in a clear and concrete way through permanent record keeping?

This question has long vexed those who study the Inca. Clearly the Inca possessed a powerful state society, but there does not appear to have been an Incan writing system. This assertion, however, may reflect our own limited view of what a writing system actually needs to be.

All of the early record keeping systems discussed so far in this book shared several characteristics in common, including one that may seem so obvious to us it barely warrants mentioning; they were all two-dimensional systems. Records were kept by impressing conventionalized shapes onto soft clay tablets, by applying ink to papyrus, paint to bark, or by carving hieroglyphs onto flat stone surfaces. Though it might seem self-evident that writing is, by definition, a two-dimensional system of record keeping—this certainly is the case with our own system of writing—it appears that the Inca used, not a two-dimensional system but a three-dimensional system of record keeping. The Inca did not ink symbols onto paper or papyrus, they did not press standardized marks onto clay, and they did not carve hieroglyphs onto stelae. Instead, the Inca produced what appear to have been conventionalized, rule-bound symbolic records in the form of knotted strings called **khipu,** and

FIGURE 14.14
The Inca had no system of writing, but they did have khipu, a system of knotted strings by which they kept the records of their empire.
(© Peabody Museum, Harvard University, Photo #N21754)

these records could be read by those who understood the underlying code (Figure 14.14). Though it might seem alien to us, that makes the khipu a writing system (Ascher and Ascher 1997; Urton 2003).

The khipu share an unfortunate history with Maya writing; the Spanish missionaries thought they represented idol worship and were banned. Many khipu were destroyed. Nevertheless, today there are about 600 existing khipu in museums and private collections. Some were found individually but some were found in groups; for example, 21 khipu were discovered under the floor of a single house at the site called Puruchuco and likely were the records of what amounts to an individual Inca accountant (Urton and Brezine 2005).

Before they decided they represented the devil's work, the Spanish invaders wrote about the khipu and the way they were read by the record keepers, men called *khipukamayuq*. The Spanish saw the *khipukamayuq* in action, using the khipu, and described the information they clearly seemed to be reading from them: primarily census data, information about quantities of goods in storehouses, amounts of taxes and tribute, calendrical information, and genealogies (Urton 2003:3).

Inca specialist Gary Urton (2003:55) has examined about 450 of the extant khipu and concluded that about two-thirds contain this kind of accounting information. Numbers were coded through the placement of the khipu knots on so-called pendant strings, representing increasing powers of ten as you approach the main string from which the pendant strings are suspended. Urton believes that the other one-third of the khipu he examined may represent actual narratives readable by the *khipukamayuq* in much the same way that an ancient Egyptian or Maya scribe could have read the messages conveyed in their hieroglyphic writing systems.

Though there is, as yet, no equivalent to the Rosetta Stone, no Spanish translation that can be associated with a specific khipu, progress is being made at least in the attempt to figure out the khipu system. In a fascinating approach, Urton suggests that the khipu were written in what amounts to a binary code. In his view, the production and placement of each knot on a khipu involved seven discrete steps—six of these steps involve distinct decisions regarding knot production, each with two possible outcomes (raw material: cotton or wool; yarn or string spinning direction: clockwise or counterclockwise; etc.). Combining these binary steps with a seventh step in the selection of one of the 24 string colors used by the Inca, you come up with more than 1,500 ways to produce and place each knot ($2^6 \times 24$), producing a vocabulary the equal to that of the 1,000 to 1,500 separate cuneiform signs (Mann 2003).

Urton and Brezine (2005:1067) found a consistent feature in the khipu recovered in the excavation of Puruchuco, a series of three figure-eight knots at the beginning of each record. They read this particular series of three knots as the name of the place that the data recorded on the knotted string refer to, in this case Puruchuco. Certainly, a state-required accounting record that enumerates goods or taxes needs to be associated with a particular place and people. Urton and Brezine may have figured out how the khipu accomplished this and, in so doing, they may have translated what amounts to a word written in the khipu's knots: Puruchuco. Though the translation of khipu is only in its infancy, it is hoped that with additional study, the recovery of more of them and, ultimately, the discovery of an actual khipu alongside a Spanish translation, the Inca may someday be able to speak to us in a manner similar to the scribes of the other early civilizations.

The End of The Inca State

In a sense, the rigidly hierarchical political and social system that had been the source of Inca success was turned against them by the Spanish conquistadors when they invaded Inca territory in 1532. Though armed with guns and having the advantage of being on horseback, the Spanish arrived in small numbers—there were only about 180 of them—and could easily have been defeated by the powerful and enormous Inca army, an army that had played a major role in constructing the largest empire seen in the New World. In August 1533, when Pizarro captured the Inca ruler Atawallpa, who, in Inca political culture, was the source of all decisions, the Inca were paralyzed. Though nearly 4,000 Inca soldiers were present when Atawallpa was taken, they were unable to attack the much smaller Spanish force because that would have risked the life of their ruler.

Though the Inca paid a ransom estimated in modern currency to have been the equivalent of 50 million dollars to effect Atawallpa's release (D'Altroy

2003:1), Pizarro realized that in freeing the Inca ruler, he likely would be sealing his own doom. After accepting the ransom, Pizarro killed Atawallpa anyway, throwing the Inca political system into disarray. The empire fell apart as its component parts, always resentful of Inca control, broke away, ending the reign of the most powerful indigenous civilization in the New World.

The world's first civilizations had many features in common. They all were remarkable cultures, spectacularly successful and complex adaptations to their environments. Yet, as successful as they were, all of these early civilizations shared another element that may reflect a fundamental instability in their adaptation. All of these civilizations collapsed.

ISSUES AND DEBATES

WHY DO CIVILIZATIONS COLLAPSE?

In the "Issues and Debates" section of Chapter 13, I presented a number of explanations for the collapse of the Maya civilization. The Maya appear to have been a victim of their own success, generating an extraordinary level of population growth made possible by their complex society, but unsustainable in their environment in the long run. Eventually their ability to produce people outstripped their ability to feed them, and the level of complexity reached during their Classic period could no longer be maintained. As a result, Maya civilization, though it did not disappear or disintegrate, at the very least suffered a serious contraction.

Is the Maya case a model for all collapse, or is it an exception? The broader question is, Why do civilizations, ultimately, almost always fall apart? Is collapse inevitable; is it an intrinsic, unavoidable result of the development of complexity? Is complexity always unsustainable and the disintegration of all civilizations, including our own, just a matter of time? To at least attempt to answer these questions, we need to understand what proximate causes can be determined for societal collapse.

Causes of Collapse

Archaeologist George Cowgill (1988), for example, suggests that state societies historically run into trouble for a number of internal, economic reasons. These societies depend on tax revenues, and through time an increasing number of organizations obtain legal exemptions from taxation, while increasing numbers of citizens may avoid taxes illegally. Expensive bureaucracies proliferate, marked by "increasing corruption, rigidity, incompetence, extravagance, and (perhaps) inefficiency" (Cowgill 1988:263). At the same time, citizens of complex state societies have increasing expectations of services the state should be providing them. All of this sounds disturbingly familiar. How often in our modern civilizations have we heard politicians promising all manner of goods and services to various constituencies—the old, the young, members of the armed forces, educators, students—without any clear proposal for how these goods and services are to be paid for?

Scientist and writer Jared Diamond (2005) makes the point that when complex societies allow for and even perhaps encourage rapid population growth, those societies often need to resort to agricultural intensification to feed the growing number of mouths. Intensification involves an ever-increasing investment of time, energy, and labor—through multiple-cropping, by building irrigation canals, and by expanding cultivation into marginal land—all in an effort to produce more food. These practices of intensification may have unintended consequences including, among others, deforestation, increased soil erosion, and water management problems (Diamond 2005:6). So, while intensification may work for a while, in many circumstances it will be unsustainable, producing a lot of hungry and angry citizens, resulting, ultimately in starvation, emigration, or even revolution.

Archaeologist Joseph Tainter (1988:89–90) has summarized the causes proposed for the collapse of civilizations in this way:

1. *Resource depletion*—The large, dense populations associated with civilizations and their intensive exploitation of the environment lead to the depletion of key resources and the ultimate collapse of the society.
2. *New resources*—The discovery of new resources eliminates the need for the more complex and stratified social hierarchy of civilizations, and this decentralization leads to the dissolution of the society.
3. *Catastrophes*—Natural catastrophes such as hurricanes, earthquakes, and volcanic eruptions are the root cause of the collapse of civilizations.
4. *Insufficient response to circumstances*—As a result of their inherent complexity, civilizations become rigid in their adaptation, and their own inertia makes it difficult, if not impossible, for them to change quickly enough to respond to changes in external or internal conditions.
5. *Other complex societies*—Competition or conflict with other civilizations can lead to the collapse of a civilized society.
6. *Intruders*—Attacks by a more mobile, more aggressive group of intruders can lead to collapse.
7. *Mismanagement*—The elite in a civilization may so abuse their power and direct so much of the surplus wealth and labor of their society to their own benefit that not enough is left for the maintenance of the economic and political system, leading to collapse.
8. *Economic explanations*—Civilizations are expensive to keep going and require increasing amounts of labor and wealth to maintain themselves. As civilizations grow, the upper classes grow—and so does their need for surplus wealth. The overall costs of supporting the system with specialists, servants, slaves, soldiers, police, and so on grow at an increasing rate. Eventually, civilizations simply become top-heavy and economically nonviable. The increasing effort to maintain them produces diminishing returns and leads to their collapse.

As Tainter indicates, most of the enumerated explanations for why civilizations ultimately collapse beg the question. Explanations of environmental catastrophe, the presence of intruders, competition with other civilizations, or resource depletion still leave open the fundamental question: Why can't civilization adequately deal with or respond to such challenges?

The Role of Environment in Collapse

Consider the following question: What would happen, even to our own, technologically very sophisticated society, if the agricultural basis of our subsistence were to be severely disrupted? Since September 11, people whose job it is to think the unthinkable—which very unfortunately after September 11 doesn't seem to be so very unthinkable anymore—have wondered and worried about how vulnerable the very underpinnings of our society, our food supply, might be to a terrorist attack. What would be the result if we no longer could rely on there being a ready, ample, reliable, and marvelously diverse source of food at the supermarket down the street?

It has also occurred to historians, paleoclimatologists, and archaeologists to wonder the same thing about ancient societies who may have faced not terrorist-based but naturally occurring catastrophes to their food supply. In thinking about this possibility, researchers have encountered a number of remarkably timed co-occurrences of environmental downturns and the collapse of ancient civilizations. For example, in Chapter 11 we talked about the rise of urban civilization in Mesopotamia and noted that what appears to be the world's first city, Uruk, developed about 5,500 years ago. At that time, Uruk was a city of at least 10,000 people, thriving as the capital of a vast and powerful city-state whose dominance was made possible by a complex and efficient, irrigation-based, agricultural subsistence system. Yet, at the peak of its development, over the relatively short period of the two centuries between 5,200 and 5,000 years ago, Uruk collapsed into chaos. We may know the reason. Analysis of deep-sea cores in the Gulf of Oman shows a sharp increase in dust blowing off of the land and onto the sea at this time. This has led paleoclimatologists to suggest that a relentless drought afflicted Mesopotamia during this period, one that would have severely impaired any agriculturally based economic system (Weiss and Bradley 2001). Is the co-occurrence between this regional drought and the collapse of a complex society reliant absolutely on a dependable source of water for its crops merely a coincidence, or did the drought cause the societal collapse?

Uruk is not the only such example of the co-occurrence of the collapse of a complex society and drought. In another instance, this one dated to sometime between A.D. 750 and 900, and soon after the war between the superpowers of the Maya world, Tikal and Calakmul (discussed in Chapter 13), the Maya civilization suffered a severe dislocation in its development that can be fairly characterized as a collapse. The Maya stopped building monuments around the same time that lake sediments in their region show a sharp and dramatic change to arid conditions in the Maya's rainforest heartland (Hodell et al. 2001;

deMenocal 2001). Is the seeming correlation of the change to drier conditions and the end of the classic period of Maya development just a coincidence, or did the drought cause, or at least contribute to, the fall of the Maya?

A possible answer to this question has been suggested by a recent analysis of sediment deposition in the Cariaco Basin of Venezuela (Haug et al. 2003). In annually deposited sediments in the basin, researchers discovered that a series of intense, multiyear droughts had afflicted the Caribbean during the ninth and tenth centuries A.D. The peaks of these severe droughts were dated to the years A.D. 810, 860, and 910 (Haug et al. 2003:1734). The Maya depended on rainfall for their agriculture—both directly and through storage of rainfall for later use. It is quite possible that the cumulative effect of these droughts strained their subsistence system to its breaking point, contributing to the overall collapse of their civilization in the tenth century.

A somewhat different scenario is proposed for the Moche of South America (discussed earlier in this chapter). The main Moche site where the inhabitants built the Huaca del Sol was abandoned by about A.D. 600. This abandonment can be shown to correlate with the drying up of their primary irrigation channels, which provided water to the expansive agricultural fields that allowed a large, dense, urban population to exist in this region (deMenocal 2001). Archaeological evidence at Moche shows that the irrigation channels dried up around A.D. 600 and then were covered by shifting sand dunes, signifying their complete abandonment. Interestingly, however, the Moche did not collapse upon the onset of this dry period; instead, they moved. In apparent response to the onset of aridity, the Moche rapidly shifted to sites farther inland and adjacent to rivers whose waters were a more dependable source than rainfall for irrigation. Also, later in South America, Tiwanaku's main urban centers were abandoned by about A.D. 1100, again at a time that also corresponds to the onset of a significant drought (deMenocal 2001).

By just about any measure, the United States in the early twenty-first century is the most powerful economic and political entity ever seen on earth. While tsunamis, earthquakes, droughts, and volcanoes have always had the power to seriously disrupt, even destroy, virtually any other civilization, one might have thought that the United States was exempt from the ravages of nature and, therefore, the exception to the hypothesis that natural disasters can seriously alter the history or even cause the collapse of a society. Our nation has experienced such disasters and, while they have been tragic and deadly on a personal, individual level, for the most part these have left barely a scar on the collective health of the nation. Perhaps, some have thought, we are simply too big and strong for any of these natural catastrophes to truly bring us down.

Anyone who thought that was surely brought up short in the aftermath of Hurricane Katrina, the stupendous storm that battered the American southeast in the summer of 2005. Katrina has been characterized as the single greatest natural disaster ever to strike North America. As I write these words, just four days after Katrina made landfall, it is still uncertain what the precise human toll will be. The mayor of one of the cities most sorely afflicted, New

Orleans, has estimated a death toll in the thousands. In the wealthiest, most powerful, and technologically sophisticated nation on earth, their lives could not be saved and now tens of thousands of survivors are at imminent risk of disease and starvation. Hundreds of thousands are homeless and, perhaps, hopeless. There is little expectation for anything approaching a normal existence, at least anytime soon, across a vast stretch of the United States.

Certainly, Katrina will not destroy the United States, but its effects are rippling across the nation and will, to some extent, change the way we live. New Orleans is a major port; on average, more than 11 million tons of product pass through it. More imported steel and rubber enter New Orleans than any other U.S. port. Thirty percent of the oil consumed in the United States comes from the Gulf of Mexico, and virtually all drilling and refining of this oil has ceased. Given the extent of the tragedy for those who live—or lived—in the region hit directly, it is almost absurdly unseemly to point out the comparatively trivial inconveniences the rest of us will face. For example, within a period of just a few days we saw gasoline prices rocket skyward by more than 13% from an average of about $2.69 to upwards of $3.04 a gallon in the Northeast. The surge in the cost of oil will affect the cost of virtually every item we purchase, certainly any item that travels by truck, rail, or plane. I don't even want to think about how much a gallon of heating oil will cost this winter—but how serious is my complaint when thousands upon thousands no longer have a home to heat? Katrina is having a substantial effect on us all, and suppose the unthinkable were to happen? We are only partway through hurricane season. Suppose another, equally ferocious storm were to hit the United States. How much misery can a nation rebound from? How long would it take for the chaos that has erupted in Katrina's wake to bring down a mighty nation, even our own? There are no definitive answers to these questions, but they certainly force us to consider the possibility that natural disasters have played an important role in the fall of civilizations in antiquity.

In his summary of the collapse of complex societies, modern or ancient, Diamond (2005:11–14) proposes five possible contributing factors: (1) environmental degradation wrought by the practices of those societies; (2) naturally caused climate changes, especially those that might diminish the ability of a group's farmers to produce enough food to feed the citizens of the state, including all those folks who are not food producers but soldiers, merchants, scribes, craftspeople, the idle rich, and the like; (3) the deleterious effects wrought by nasty neighbors (up to and including warfare); (4) the withdrawal of support or vital resources by groups that previously had been allies or partners and had by geographic circumstance been the providers of that support and those resources (think oil embargo); and (5) the ways societies respond to the first four listed contributors to collapse.

Collapse: A Multiplicity of Causes

It is too simple, then, to claim that there is a single, prime mover in societal collapse, a universal cause for why civilizations eventually fall apart. Drought—

or invasion, rebellion, resource depletion, and the rest—cannot act on their own to cause a civilization to decline or, for that matter, to develop in the first place or to thrive. In Diamond's (2005) view, collapse is not inevitable if societies respond (his fifth factor) in such a way as to mitigate the impacts of the first four; he points to historical examples, including the Norse settlers of Iceland and a group of Pacific Islanders—the Tikopians—who rose to the challenges posed by the first four factors and were able to maintain their societies by adjusting their behavior.

State societies are systems that constantly need to respond and adjust to changes they face from external as well as internal sources. A drought may contribute to collapse, as it very well may have, in the case of Uruk or the Maya. But a drought—or a war or an insurrection or whatever—can pose a challenge to a civilization that it may be able to respond to, much in the way the Moche responded to increasing aridity, not by collapsing but by moving to a location where they could continue. The complex interplay between a civilization and its social and physical environment will determine, ultimately, whether that society collapses or endures when faced with the challenge of change. The result will be different in each instance, difficult to explain and perhaps impossible to predict. But the possibility of enduring these changes may give those of us who are members of the modern iteration of civilization cause for at least a little bit of optimism.

CASE STUDY CLOSE-UP

In the village of Sípan, located about 150 km (95 mi) north of the Pyramid of the Sun, are the royal cemeteries of the Moche elite. Initially discovered and looted in 1986–87, the cemeteries caught the attention of the world when the thieves were caught by the police. The violated tomb led archaeologists to excavate in the cemetery, and, remarkably, several other spectacular, unlooted tombs were found and excavated by archaeologists Walter Alva and Christopher Donnan (1993, 1994; Figure 14.15).

The first excavated tomb, dating to about 1,660 years ago, was of a man in his late 30s or early 40s (Alva and Donnan 1994:29). In death he wore an elaborate feathered headdress, nose ornaments, and beaded pectoral ornaments (a chest covering). The tomb was filled with turquoise, copper, silver, and gold jewelry. At his right side lay a gold and silver scepter, and on his left was another scepter of cast silver. Also accompanying this lord of the Moche were hundreds of pottery vessels, some quite elaborate and displaying human shapes; a number were in the form of warriors vanquishing their enemies. The chief resident of the grave did not make his voyage to the Moche version of heaven alone; he was buried with llamas, a dog, two men, three women, and a child. The additional males appear to have been sacrificed as part of the burial ceremony.

It is rare for archaeologists to encounter one such spectacular tomb in a lifetime. Walter Alva and Christopher Donnan were to find two more at the Moche royal cemetery at Sípan. Another royal was found in a plank coffin wearing a headdress of gilded copper. The headdress was in the shape of an owl, with

FIGURE 14.15
View of one of the spectacular burials of a Moche warrior-priest, filled with artifacts of gold and jade.
(© Kevin Shafer/ Corbis)

long hanging bands representing the bird's feathered wings. A final burial was also richly appointed with marvelous gold, silver, and turquoise artifacts.

The royalty buried at Sípan appear to represent a class of warrior-priests. Their clothing, ornamentation, and headdresses match quite closely artistic depictions of great warriors from other Moche sites. In those depictions, victorious warriors are presented with the hands and feet of their enemies as trophies. Alva and Donnan discovered the remains of human hands and feet associated with the major burials at Sípan.

These royal Moche burials are emblematic of civilization. The ability to unify a large population, to control their behavior, and to exploit their labor and wealth were the factors that made possible such sumptuous splendor in death for the Moche lords.

Many of the most impressive sites of the ancient civilizations of South America have become significant destinations for the archaeological tourist. Many travel agencies offer archaeologically themed visits to sites including Chan Chan (the Chimu capital), Moche, Tiwanaku,

VISITING THE PAST

Cuzco, and, especially, Machu Picchu. Many of the pre-Inca and Inca sites have become magnets for people who believe that these are sacred places that reverberate with mystical or spiritual properties lacking in our modern lives. So-called metaphysical tours that involve healing, chanting, channeling, and contacting extraterrestrials—who some in their archaeological delirium believe actually built Machu Picchu, despite the very human burials found at the site—have become popular in recent years (Ochoa 2004). There are hotels located at Machu Picchu (don't ask how much a night for a room at the hotel located at the top costs) and even an ill-conceived scheme to build a cable car to take tourists up the mountain.

SUMMARY

In the New World, just as in the Old, some farming societies eventually developed the ability to produce a food surplus. This surplus enabled the development of social complexity and inequality. Eventually, some of these complex societies developed into true states with a formal government and true power invested in an elite class. The Inca and their predecessors of western South America developed independently of Old World civilizations.

Through their concentration of wealth and power and as members of an elite social class in a stratified society, rulers were able to organize the labor of the many to produce the spectacular monuments—the pyramids and temples—that dominate the ancient landscapes of the Moche, Tiwanaku, Wari, Sicán, Chimu, and the Inca.

Like the civilizations of the Old World, the complex societies of the New eventually collapsed. Though many suggestions have been proposed to explain the process underlying the fall of ancient civilizations, including resource depletion, environmental catastrophes, invasion, and insurrection, no one of these explanations alone is sufficient. In each case of societal collapse, it is the inability of the society at a particular point in its evolution to respond adequately to a challenge, whatever that challenge may be, that leads to its disintegration.

TO LEARN MORE

Technical Summaries

Once again, *Ancient Civilizations,* by C. C. Lamberg-Karlovsky and Jeremy Sabloff (1995), presents an extremely thorough investigation of the origins of civilization in Mesoamerica (and the Middle East and Indus Valley as well). Thomas C. Patterson's *Archaeology: The Historical Development of Civilizations* (1993) is as valuable for its discussion of New World civilization as it is for the Old World.

Joseph Tainter's *The Collapse of Complex Societies* (1988) contains a very detailed presentation on the collapse of such societies.

Popular Summaries

Though its spectacular photographs might give you the impression that it's a coffee-table book, Craig Morris and Adriana von Hagen's *The Inka Empire and Its Andean*

Origins (1993) offers detailed information about the evolution of civilization in South America presented in a nontechnical manner. James B. Richardson's *People of the Andes* (1994) provides a useful summary of the evolution and flowering of state societies in western South America. Terence N. D'Altroy's (2003) *The Incas* is a wonderful summary of the history of the emblematic ancient South American civilization. The book *Machu Picchu: Unveiling the Mysteries of the Incas,* edited by Richard L. Burger and Lucy C. Salazar, that accompanied a museum exhibit at Yale University provides a series of wonderfully informative articles that both describe Machu Picchu in detail and place this incredible site in the firm context of Inca history and civilization.

University of California geography professor Jared Diamond is a scientist, well-respected in his own academic field, and one of the best synthesists of a broad array of scientific data from a host of specialties. His popular book *Collapse: How Societies Choose to Fail or Succeed* (2005) is a thoughtful and insightful discussion of the collapse of civilizations, both ancient and modern.

On the Web

As mentioned in the "Visiting the Past" section of this chapter, there is an enormous amount of popular interest in the archaeological sites left behind by South American civilizations, some of it reflecting a "New Age" view of their significance. It should come as no surprise, therefore, that a host of Web sites espouse all manner of rather, well, interesting claims concerning who "really" built some of these sites (with a common assertion being that it could not have been native people) and when they built them (it is often claimed that the sites are much older than archaeologists believe). I hope that the archaeological data presented in this book might inoculate you against these groundless assertions. If you search under the names of any of the cultures discussed here—New Agers have a special fondness for Tiwanaku—you will find many beautiful photographs of these sites—and much nonsense. For a more sedate virtual visit to Tiwanaku, check out http://www.jqjacobs.net/andes/tiwanaku.html.

For spectacular photos of Machu Picchu, check out http://www.ifip.com/Machupijchu1.htm. The Inca Trail is a modern pathway following an Inca road that passes by several Inca sites and leads the visitor to Machu Picchu. For a virtual photo-journey along the Inca trail, go to http://www.raingod.com/angus/Gallery/Photos/SouthAmerica/Peru/IncaTrail.html.

Online Learning Center: www.mhhe.com/feder4

The Online Learning Center (OLC) Web companion to *The Past in Perspective* features a variety of supplemental study aids. For each chapter, this free Web site includes

ONLINE LEARNING CENTER

- Self-Quizzes to take as pretests prior to exams
- Interactive Timeline Study Guides for additional review and reinforcement of key information
- Learning Objectives
- Chapter Site links with Web addresses for many of the fossil and archaeological sites mentioned in the text

KEY TERM

khipu, 578

15

The Diversity of Complexity

RANK SOCIETIES IN THE OLD AND NEW WORLDS

	5,500	3,250	3,000	2,750
Mound Builders of American Midwest and Southwest	Watson Brake	Poverty Point		
American Southwest				
Zimbabwe				
Northwest Coast of North America				

CHAPTER OVERVIEW

Beginning more than 5,000 years ago, the ancient inhabitants of the American Midwest and Southeast began organizing large labor forces to produce enormous and impressive monuments of earth. The Native Americans who built the mounds were part of a socially, politically, and economically complex society whose great rulers could command the labor of thousands and were, in turn, buried in splendor. In the American Southwest, an entirely different pathway led also to complexity, with clear archaeological evidence for the coordination of large groups of people to construct great edifices of adobe brick, clay, and stone. The Mogollon, Hohokam, and Ancestral Puebloan (Anasazi) cultures have left us an archaeological legacy of great irrigation networks, hundreds of miles

of ceremonial roadways, Great Houses, and remarkable cliff dwellings. In southern Africa, native people constructed an enormous complex of monumental, granite brick buildings and walls. The primary population center of these people was a place that was to lend its name to a modern African nation: Great Zimbabwe. The "affluent foragers" of the northwest coast of North America provide yet another pathway that led to social

590

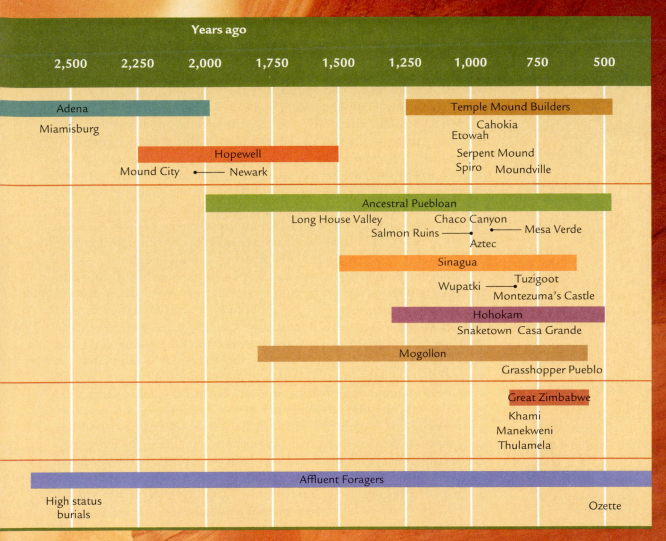

Years ago

| 2,500 | 2,250 | 2,000 | 1,750 | 1,500 | 1,250 | 1,000 | 750 | 500 |

Adena
Miamisburg

Temple Mound Builders
Cahokia
Etowah
Serpent Mound
Spiro   Moundville

Hopewell
Mound City ●———● Newark

Ancestral Puebloan
Long House Valley
Salmon Ruins ———● Chaco Canyon
● ———● Mesa Verde
Aztec

Sinagua
Wupatki ———● Tuzigoot
Montezuma's Castle

Hohokam
Snaketown Casa Grande

Mogollon
Grasshopper Pueblo

Great Zimbabwe
Khami
Manekweni
Thulamela

Affluent Foragers
High status
burials
Ozette

and political complexity, producing a society ruled by powerful chiefs who could organize the labor of an extensive population.

The mound-building societies of the American Midwest and Southeast, the pueblo-dwelling people of the American Southwest, the builders of Great Zimbabwe, and the people of the northwest coast of North America are examples of ancient, complex, non-state societies.

ONLINE
LEARNING
CENTER

Go to **www.mhhe.com/feder4** for an interactive study guide version of this timeline.

If you stand at the apex of the Monks Mound flat-topped pyramid of earth, thousands of acres of floodplain lie at your feet. The soil is rich and dark, the surrounding foliage thick and lush. Construction of this enormous monument in the settlement called Cahokia was begun more than 1,000 years ago by the native inhabitants of what is today Collinsville, Illinois (Figure 15.1).

Monks Mound is impressive, representing a substantial investment of time and energy on the part of the settlement's inhabitants (Figure 15.2, Figure 15.3). The pyramidal mound of earth covers more than 65,000 m^2, or some 16 acres. Its volume of earth totals 623,000 m^3 (22 million ft^3)—moved basketful by basketful by a people who had no animal power or mechanical contrivances. At its summit, the mound stands more than 30 m (100 ft) above the floodplain (all figures for Monks Mound are taken from Fowler 1989 and Silverberg 1989). The huge pile of earth served as the platform for a temple that symbolized the power of the political entity that was Cahokia.

From the summit, you can try to look past the modern suburban sprawl and cut grass, the paved roads, highways, and commercial structures and imagine what the ancient town of Cahokia with Monks Mound as its focal point must have looked like at its peak more than 800 years ago (Figure 15.4). In the year A.D. 1200, from your vantage point atop the great pyramid, you would have gazed down upon a dense settlement of 5,000 and perhaps as many as 10,000 people, buzzing with activity. In front of the great pyramid were smaller but only slightly less impressive earthworks, delineating an expansive rectangular plaza teeming with people. Scattered across the settlement were dozens of other pyramidal and conical mounds of earth, probably more than 100 in total. To the west was an enormous circle of towering logs, the largest located in the precise center of the monument. To the south was the burial of an important ruler, laid to rest wearing a cape of 20,000 finely made mother-of-pearl beads, marked now by only a small earthen mound

FIGURE 15.1
Archaeological sites in North America where evidence of the evolution of chiefdom-level societies has been found.

(Mound 72 in Cahokia's official enumeration). In his tomb were more than 1,000 finely made arrow points, a copper tube, sheets of mica, and shaped stones (called chunky stones), as well as the remains of people sacrificed as part of the ceremony surrounding his interment (Figure 15.5).

Surrounding the main part of the settlement was a log fence or palisade with bastions and watchtowers. The wall of logs enclosed an area of more than 800,000 m² (almost 200 acres), and within it were 18 separate earthen mounds, including Monks Mound. Consisting of an estimated 20,000 logs (and it was rebuilt three times), the huge stockade fence was as monumental a feat as Monks Mound itself, enclosing the central part of the settlement, protecting the homes of Cahokia's elite.

Occupation debris from the sprawl of Cahokia's neighborhoods, suburbs, and satellite communities has been found by archaeologists across an area of about 14 km² (5.4 mi²). As archaeologist Melvin Fowler (1989:207) points

FIGURE 15.2
Monks Mound at Cahokia in East St. Louis served as the platform on which a chief's house or a temple was built. (K. L. Feder)

FIGURE 15.3
Aerial photograph of Monks Mound at Cahokia. (Courtesy of Cahokia Mounds State Historic Site, Collinsville, Illinois)

FIGURE 15.4

Artist's conception of Cahokia at its peak, around A.D. *1150. The dense, near-urban character of the settlement is clearly evident.* (Courtesy of Cahokia Mounds State Historic Site. William R. Iseminger, artist. Reproduced with permission)

FIGURE 15.5

Layout of burials in Mound 72, Cahokia. The primary burial in Mound 72 is that of a young man, laid out on a bed of more than 20,000 mother-of-pearl shell beads. In a practice reminiscent of ancient Egypt, the other interments in Mound 72 are the burials of more than 50 other people, mostly young women, who had been killed, apparently to accompany the primary individual to his afterlife. See Figure 2.12 for a reconstruction of the Mound 72 primary burial.
(Courtesy of William Fowler)

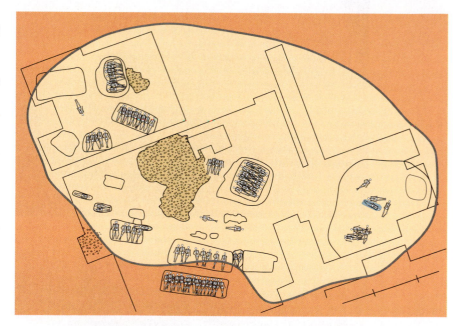

out, "Cahokia is unique. There is nothing else like it, either in size or complexity, representing Native American achievements within the boundaries of the United States."

Today, from the top of the impressive monument that stood at the center of the settlement, you might wonder why people would have devoted their lives to the construction of this impressive but otherwise apparently useless monument. Today, from the top of that same, still impressive structure, you can also look to the west and see the imposing Gateway Arch in downtown St. Louis, its polished steel surface shimmering in the distance. At 192 m (630 ft), the arch is a remarkable feat of engineering and is a modern example of the practice of complex societies to expend an enormous amount of their wealth and labor building monuments to themselves.

COMPLEXITY IN PREHISTORIC AMERICA NORTH OF MEXICO

CHRONICLE

The Development of Complexity

We saw in Chapter 8 that the Archaic period in the American Southeast is marked by the inception of large-scale communal construction projects involving the movement of copious quantities of earth into ridges and mounds. The specific sites mentioned in Chapter 8, including Watson Brake (dating to 5200 B.P.) and Poverty Point (dating to 3200 B.P.), though impressive in their own right and reflecting the ability of their builders to organize the labor of a substantial population, present only a faint hint of the mound-building abilities of the native peoples in the American Southeast and Midwest in the centuries that followed.

Beginning about 2,800 years ago and centered in the Ohio River valley, people bearing a culture today called **Adena** began constructing conical mounds of earth in which a religious and perhaps economic and social elite were buried. Lepper (2004:106) characterizes the period beginning 2,800 years ago as a time of "dramatic, if not revolutionary, cultural transformation." These transformations are, indeed, dramatic; one needs only to examine the remarkable art (Figure 15.6) and impressive earthworks of the Adena that far surpass the art and monuments that preceded them. At the same time, the accomplishments are not really revolutionary but evolutionary. The Adena in the **Early Woodland period** primarily expanded upon and elaborated practices that had their origins in the preceding Archaic; they became more sedentary and built larger and more elaborate earthworks, they increasingly relied on domesticated plants for their subsistence, and they buried their elite dead in increasing splendor.

Somewhat later, at about 2200 B.P., in what is called the **Middle Woodland** period, a different burial-mound-building group, the **Hopewell,** appeared with its own unique set of artifacts (Lepper 1995a). Adena and Hopewell traditions can be said to have overlapped for about 200 years and are differentiated on the basis of certain artifact types. Over that 200-year period of overlap, the Hopewell pattern gradually replaced Adena in the Ohio Valley and then spread far more widely throughout the American Midwest. Again, the changes seen between the Early and Middle Woodland period in the American Midwest were evolutionary, not revolutionary: earthworks

FIGURE 15.6

This marvelous Adena sculpture of a person, replete with headdress, ear spools (large, dangling ear jewelry), and loincloth, is actually a pipe. The bowl is between the man's feet and the smoker would place his or her lips on the head dress where the draw hole can be seen. (Dave Barker, Ohio Historical Society)

FIGURE 15.7
*This enormous Adena bur-
ial mound in Miamisburg,
Ohio, is the largest in that
state, standing 21 m (68 ft)
high.* (K. L. Feder)

became larger, the burials of people who appear to have been part of a growing elite class became increasingly elaborate, and nonlocal raw materials from
which their grave goods were manufactured were brought in from increasing
distances.

There were no great urban centers in Adena or Hopewell society. The residential settlements of both the Adena and Hopewell people generally were
small, consisting of tiny hamlets located across much of southern and central
Ohio and surrounding states to the south and west. The major river valleys in
which the Hopewell lived are enormously rich habitats, and the Hopewell
were expert at exploiting the wild foods of their region. Much of the Hopewell
diet, in fact, relied on these wild foods; they hunted, fished, and collected nuts,
roots, and seeds at a level of intensity that allowed for a large population capable of producing the elaborate earthworks that characterize their society.
The Hopewell produced as well as gathered food by planting many of the
crops independently domesticated by Indians north of Mexico, including sunflower, squash, maygrass, knotweed, and goosefoot (Lepper 1995a; see Chapter 9). The major crop that characterized later Indian agricultural societies
was not an important component of Hopewell subsistence; evidence for maize
agriculture is scanty.

Some of the burial mounds are quite impressive, covering as much as
8,300 m² (2 acres, or more than 1½ football fields) and stretching up to heights
of 21 m (68 ft) (Figure 15.7). For example, Mound 25 at the eponymous
Hopewell site is 150 m (500 ft) long, 55 m (180 ft) wide, and 9 m (30 ft) high.
The volume of earth moved and piled to produce such a monument is enormous and again reflects one of the defining elements of a complex society: its
ability to mobilize a large labor force to produce a monumental structure.

The conical mounds were constructed over the remains of either individuals or groups of people. Finely crafted goods, including many made from ex-

FIGURE 15.8
These carved stone and cut copper (bottom) artifacts reflect the great artistic skill of the ancient Hopewell people. The ability of the makers of objects like these to devote the time necessary to perfect their craft is a hallmark of complex societies. (Tom House/ © Ohio Historical Society)

otic raw materials not native to the core of the Hopewell region, are found in the mound burials. A widespread trade network brought these natural resources to the Hopewell from all over the United States. Copper and silver were brought in from the Great Lakes region. Turtle shells, pearls, fossil shark teeth, alligator teeth, and conch shells from the Gulf of Mexico traveled up the major river systems of eastern North America also to be included in the burials of the Adena and Hopewell. Obsidian from the Rocky Mountains and quartz crystals and mica from the Appalachian Mountains also made long journeys into the hands of the elite of Hopewell society, often being placed in their tombs (Figure 15.8). Objects made from local materials were also found in these burials, and they are often finely made. For example, beautifully made ceramics, intricately flaked lithics far too delicate to have been used as tools, and whimsically carved stone pipes in the form of animals or even people were also included in the burials. In the enormity of the work necessary to build the actual mounds and in the effort expended to obtain raw materials from distant sources, as well as in the care taken in the manufacture of grave goods, Adena and, especially, Hopewell mound interments represent clear archaeological evidence for the existence of an elite or chieftain class of people in burial-mound society.

Some Hopewell earthworks are not mounds but earth-wall-enclosed spaces of unknown purpose. For example, in Newark, Ohio, a series of long, narrow, earthen walls about 1.5 m (5 ft) high enclose an octagonal plot of more than 160,000 m^2 (40 acres), which is in turn connected by two parallel earthen walls to an enormous circular area of more than 80,000 m^2 (20 acres),

FIGURE 15.9
Nineteenth-century map of the extensive prehistoric earthworks seen in Licking County, Ohio, in the vicinity of Newark. The largest of the areas enclosed by the mounded earth in this map is 16 hectares (40 acres), an enormous expanse surrounded by a vaguely square configuration of linear mounds in the upper left of the map. (From *Ancient Monuments of the Mississippi Valley*, AMS Press and Peabody Museum of Archaeology and Ethnology, Harvard University)

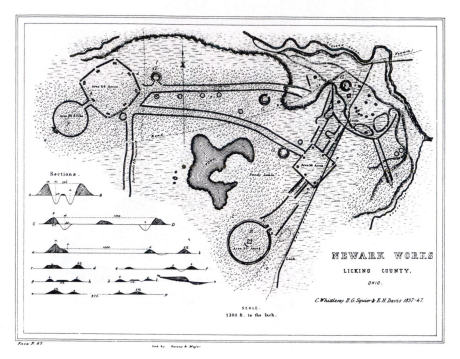

also enclosed with an earth wall more than a meter in height (Lepper 2002; Figure 15.9). This large earthwork is located at the end point of what appears to have been a ceremonial road, 90 km (60 mi) long, demarcated again by two earth walls approximately 60 m (200 ft) apart and several feet—perhaps as much as 2.5–3 m (8–10 ft)—in height (Lepper 1995b). The "Great Hopewell Road" is absolutely straight and seems—geographically and, perhaps, ritually—to connect the earthworks at Newark with a Hopewell necropolis, or "city of the dead," today called Mound City, located in Chillicothe, Ohio (Lepper 1998). Mound City is a square area of about 120,000 m^2 (30 acres) enclosed by an earth wall, containing 23 burial mounds (Figure 15.10). Connecting these sacred or ceremonial mound sites and enclosures, the Great Hopewell Road may have been used by pilgrims visiting these sites for religious observances—perhaps burial ceremonies or worship services. They are yet another example of the ability of the Hopewell to organize a large labor force and produce works of monumental proportions.

As archaeologist Bradley Lepper (1996) suggests, the Great Hopewell Road may have served to formalize connections between groups living along it and practicing what we today identify as Hopewell. Hopewell people lacked the formal government or military apparatus of a true state society (see Chapters 11–14), so symbolic activities like building the road and using it for pilgrimages may have served to make connections between people living at great distances more concrete.

FIGURE 15.10
Mound City in Chillicothe, Ohio, is a virtual necropolis, or city of the dead. The site consists of 23 burial mounds, a few of which can be seen here, within a 5.26-hectare (13-acre) area enclosed by an earth embankment. (K. L. Feder)

Hopewell culture and its construction of enclosures and burial mounds ceased by about 1,500 years ago. Among the numerous possible reasons for Hopewell's decline (Lepper 1995a) are population growth and warfare: Perhaps the largely informal organization of Hopewell society was not up to the task of coordinating the activities of an expanding population, or growing competition among various groups for good farmland may have led to warfare and the subsequent concentration of the previously dispersed Hopewell farmers in dense settlements for protection.

The Mississippian Temple Mound Builders

With the decline in Hopewell, another culture, more formally structured and even more materially impressive, arose in the Mississippi River valley and the American Southeast. This development led to a qualitatively different pattern of social, political, and economic organization, one more complex and more formally and rigidly structured than Hopewell. In fact, it now appears that the Mississippi River valley and the Southeast were the centers of an emerging Native American civilization—how far along that path they were is still a matter of some debate, but certainly these new, major mound-builder sites were the central places of complex chiefdoms.

A cultural pattern evolved in the American Midwest and Southeast that included the construction of large ceremonial and population centers where the pooled labor of a sizable surrounding population was called upon by a religious elite to construct large truncated (cut off at the top) pyramids of earth. Cahokia was the largest and most impressive of these—and the only one with a resident population of a size and density that approaches an urban character (see Figures 15.3 and 15.4). But many others, such as Etowah in Georgia and Moundville in Alabama, although smaller in size and complexity, with

FIGURE 15.11
The flat-topped temple mounds of Moundville served as the platforms on top of which temples or the houses of elite members of society were constructed. Though smaller than Cahokia, Moundville nevertheless was the central place of a mound-building, chiefdom-level society in west-central Alabama. (K. L. Feder)

fewer and smaller monumental earthworks, nevertheless present a fascinating picture of developing complexity and emerging civilization in the period after A.D. 1000 (Figure 15.11).

These temple mound builders were able to maintain their society with a subsistence base primarily of maize and squash agriculture; the use of domesticated beans began relatively later, at about A.D. 1200. Rivers provided fish, and the forests surrounding their habitations provided wild game as well as wild plant foods such as acorn and hickory. Many of the larger, impressive sites—Cahokia in particular—were located on the richest farmland. The enormous food surplus made possible by the agricultural use of these naturally rich "bottom lands" enabled the evolution of a class of priests and an attendant nobility and artisans. As we have seen again and again (in Chapters 11–14, and now here), the ability to produce a food surplus surely was at the heart of the development of stratified, complex societies. The ability of a chief or king to control that surplus is the enabling factor in that leader's amassing of the wealth and power that allow or demand the other characteristics of complex societies.

Cahokia

Archaeologist Timothy Pauketat's (1994) detailed analysis shows that Cahokia was a central place in a three-tiered hierarchy of communities. Cahokia was at the apex of the sociopolitical pyramid, "a paramount center, a qualitatively different place" (Pauketat 1994:73). Beneath Cahokia was a second level of communities with a few small mounds, perhaps the villages of secondary chiefs. Pauketat (1994:76) counts as many as 25 mound sites in the area around Cahokia, at least some of which may have been part of the Cahokia polity. The bottom tier of sites includes numerous farmsteads in the sur-

FIGURE 15.12
A sample of the more than 1,000 finely made stone arrow points recovered in the primary burial in Mound 72 at Cahokia (see Figure 15.5). The amount of labor invested in this enormous assemblage of stone points is an indication of the importance of the young man with whom they were buried. (Courtesy Cahokia Mounds State Historic Site)

rounding hinterlands, inhabited by communities of people who likely supplied most of the food and labor needed to keep the chiefdom running.

The archaeological record at Cahokia shows that craft production was centralized at the site; specialist artisans filled the demands of a powerful elite class for shell and bead pendant necklaces, copper ornaments, fired clay figurines, fine ceramics and lithics, and other items made from exotic raw materials (Pauketat 1994:106; Figure 15.12). The exotic materials from distant sources that made their way into the hands of Cahokia's artisans included copper from Illinois or possibly from as far away as Michigan, shell from the Gulf Coast, and galena (a lead mineral) from the eastern Ozarks (Pauketat 1994). The works of craft and art were produced for the elite class of Cahokians who lived safely within the walls of the palisade and who were buried in the elaborate interments found at the site.

When the Spanish explorer Hernando de Soto and his contingent of more than 600 men traversed much of the American Southeast in the years 1539–43, they encountered the direct descendants of the builders of the prehistoric temple-mound ceremonial centers (de la Vega 1605/1988; Elvas 1611/1966). They may actually have visited the site of Etowah during a late stage of its occupation. De Soto's chroniclers described a number of large settlements they visited as having populations numbered in the thousands. They also described agricultural fields stretching for miles. They even described the native practice of constructing earthen mounds, upon which the chief's house sat.

Ironically, de Soto may have brought more than curiosity and greed with him on his trip. It has been suggested that he and his men unintentionally brought with them infectious diseases (perhaps including smallpox) that the natives had not previously encountered and, as a result, for which they possessed no immunity (Brain 1979; Dobyns 1983; Ramenofsky 1987). Though some of the ceremonial centers had already been abandoned—Cahokia among them—as a result of internal collapse, it is not certain that mound-builder society was destined for disintegration. It may have continued to develop, becoming increasingly complex and more recognizably a civilization. As Timothy Pauketat (1994:6) puts it when assessing the significance of the kind of social stratification and political power evidenced in the archaeological record at Cahokia: "In other regions around the world similar conditions may have been necessary precursors to the rise of early states." But the accidental spread of lethal microbes may have diverted the trajectory of mound-builder culture, and we will never know what might have been.

THE AMERICAN SOUTHWEST

As mentioned in Chapter 9, the Mesoamerican domesticates maize and squash appear in the archaeological record of the American Southwest beginning about 3,200 years ago, and beans show up a bit later (Wills 1988). These domesticates initially served to complement and supplement a highly productive indigenous foraging economy based on local wild crops.

Not until over a thousand years later, at approximately 2000 B.P., did maize-based agriculture replace the traditional foraging subsistence system. A number of different cultural traditions based on agriculture then evolved in the prehistoric Southwest with the development of a new variety of maize, Maize de Ocho, that was better suited to the dry conditions and short growing season of this region. The best known of these cultures were the **Ancestral Puebloan,** or **Anasazi,** in the Four Corners region (the broad area around the intersection of Arizona, New Mexico, Utah, and Colorado), the **Mogollon** in the uplands of New Mexico and northeastern Mexico, the **Hohokam** in southern Arizona, and the **Sinagua** in central Arizona (Cordell 1984; Willey 1966). These cultures vary in pottery styles, geography, and settlement patterns, but all relied to varying degrees on a subsistence base of maize, beans, and squash, and all eventually lived a sedentary lifeway before the coming of the Spanish. One more pattern shared by these cultures is social and political complexity, manifested in the archaeological record by the construction of monumental buildings.

Hohokam

Some nineteenth-century cultural geographers thought that the natural surroundings of each culture determined the degree of complexity and the level of civilization that the culture could achieve. "Environmental determinists" believed that a challenging—but not too demanding—environment produced civilization, whereas other habitats—rain forests and deserts, for example—limited absolutely the level of complexity and cultural achievement that cultures in those environments could attain. The environmental determinists were Europeans who believed, not coincidentally, that the continental climate of Europe provided the perfect context for the evolution of the most "advanced" and civilized nations.

The Sonoran Desert home of the Hohokam (as well as the rainforest home of the Maya; see Chapter 13) belies this outdated notion that any one type of environment spawns complexity while others uniformly produce simple societies. The Sonoran Desert is one rather extreme example of the environmental diversity reflected in the myriad settings of the world's ancient complex societies. In contradiction to the assertions of the environmental determinists, from A.D. 700 to close to A.D. 1000, the dry Sonoran Desert of southern Arizona served as a backdrop for the flowering of a complex society capable of building huge structures and a complex system of irrigation (Reid and Whittlesey 1997).

The settlement pattern of the Hohokam (literally, "those who have gone" in the Pima Indian language) focused on the major river systems of southern Arizona: the Gila, the Salt, and the Santa Cruz. The reason is obvious. The territory of the Hohokam averages less than 30 cm (12 in.) of rain each year. Though the Hohokam included game (deer, bighorn sheep, antelope, and cottontail and jackrabbits) and wild plant foods (mesquite beans and cactus) in their diet, growing corn, beans, and squash was of primary importance and was made possible in this dry environment only by the construction of extensive irrigation networks. The Hohokam irrigated thousands of acres of otherwise dry land through a hierarchical series of canals whose combined length is measured in many kilometers. For example, the Hohokam irrigation network north of the Salt River near modern Phoenix consists of 50 large, primary artificial water channels, hundreds of secondary arteries, and an even greater number of smaller irrigation ditches feeding individual fields (Reid and Whittlesey 1997:76). The labor needed to construct this one irrigation network—and then to maintain it, keeping it clear of clogging silt—must have been enormous and is clear evidence of the Hohokam ability to conscript and organize a substantial workforce far beyond the level of an individual household or family. This, in turn, is a hallmark of social and political complexity.

Hohokam material culture provides additional evidence of the complexity that bloomed in the desert. The Hohokam maintained a trading system that brought in exotic raw materials such as marine shell from the Gulf of California. Hohokam craftspeople produced beautiful and intricate works in carved stone. They also fashioned shell-bead necklaces, shell bracelets, and shell pendants carved into the shapes of animals. They also worked in turquoise and produced an array of finely made ceramics, including red-on-buff painted household wares—a style of pottery that is a defining attribute of Hohokam culture—and whimsical pots in humanlike shapes (Figure 15.13).

Most individual Hohokam villages consisted of multiple sets of separate residential structure clusters called **courtyard groups.** Each courtyard

FIGURE 15.13
Ceramics produced by the Hohokam of the ancient American Southwest were both beautiful and whimsical. (© Richard A. Cooke/ Corbis)

FIGURE 15.14
Casa Grande, a large Hohokam community in southern Arizona. The Great House, shown here, is partially protected from the elements by a large metal superstructure built in the 1930s. (K. L. Feder)

FIGURE 15.15
*Aerial photograph of the
partially excavated ruins of
Snaketown; approximately
60 individual house floors
can be seen.* (© Arizona
State Museum, University of
Arizona; photo by Helga
Teiwes)

group consisted of from 2 to 10 family residences surrounding a common area or courtyard.

The Hohokam also constructed residential compounds called "Great Houses," large apartment buildings that housed most residents of a village. The best example of a Hohokam Great House can be found at the Casa Grande site, located midway between Tucson and Phoenix. Built around A.D. 1350 the main structure at the site is a multistoried, 60-room building surrounded by several smaller adobe structures (Figure 15.14). Casa Grande was built of bricks made of caliche, a desert soil that becomes extremely hard when it dries out. For added strength and stability, the walls of the Great House were massive, 1.2 m (about 4 ft) thick at their base, and set into deep trenches dug into the desert soil. Approximately 600 logs were used in its construction, serving as roof beams and ceilings. An adobe wall more than 2 m (6½ ft) high surrounded the entire complex, enclosing a space of more than 8,000 m^2 (2 acres). Obviously, a large, well-organized labor force was necessary to construct and maintain Casa Grande; it is likely that a few hundred people lived there.

The largest discovered Hohokam village is Snaketown, located on the Gila River; it was the focus of intensive archaeological excavation in the 1930s and then again in the 1960s (Figure 15.15). The ruins at Snaketown cover more than 2.5 km^2 (1 mi^2), and more than 200 family residences have been excavated in this elaborate town. There is a significant irrigation network at the site. Snaketown has also produced evidence of a ceremonial ball game that also was played by the native people of Mesoamerica (Figure 15.16; see Chapter 13). Hohokam ball courts like the one at Snaketown may have been places

FIGURE 15.16

Enclosed ball courts like this one at the Wupatki ruin in north-central Arizona indicate that some groups of ancient inhabitants of the Southwest played a ceremonial ball game similar to one played by the Maya (Chapter 13) to the south.
(K. L. Feder)

where disputes between families or villages were worked out on a ritually sanctified stage.

Clearly, irrigation initially allowed for the development of the agriculture-based Hohokam society in the Sonoran Desert. Intensification of this irrigation technology—building longer and deeper canals that extended the range of arable land ever greater distances from the permanent water-courses—allowed for population growth and the production of a larger food surplus. Elaboration of Hohokam material culture coincided with a probable attendant increase in social and political differentiation among different classes of people as excess wealth became concentrated in the hands of those who controlled, at least to a degree, the irrigation system.

Mogollon

Where the Hohokam were dwellers of the desert, the Mogollon were mountain people, living in the highlands of eastern Arizona and New Mexico— and south into Mexico. Long dependent on hunting and gathering and well adapted to life in the mountains, their shift to agriculture, a sedentary lifestyle, and some degree of social and political complexity occurred rather late in prehistory.

Traced by the diagnostic styles of their artifacts, the Mogollon appear in the archaeological record by about A.D. 200. At this time, they lived in small nomadic groups, hunted deer and turkey, gathered the wild plants that grew abundantly in the mountains, and lived in impermanent villages characterized by small **pit-houses**—semisubterranean structures covered with a thatched roof. Sometime after A.D. 650, the Mogollon began to supplement their diet by farming small garden plots, raising corn, beans, and squash. Not until after A.D. 1150, however, did the Mogollon, probably in contact with the

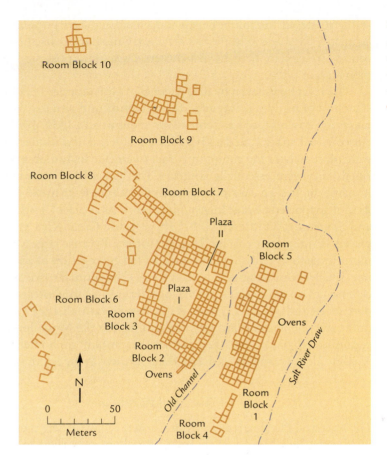

FIGURE 15.17
Map of room distribution at Grasshopper Pueblo, a Mogollon culture site in Arizona.

more complex Ancestral Puebloan culture to the north (discussed later in this chapter) and as the result of a significant drought in about A.D. 1300, give up their nomadic, foraging existence, settle down into permanent habitations, and adopt an agricultural mode of subsistence.

The need to increase the agricultural portion of their diet also caused a shift in settlement patterns among the Mogollon. Although before the drought it had made sense for the Mogollon to spread themselves out across the mountains, after A.D. 1300 it made more sense to settle in at those places that offered good agricultural land. These areas experienced a population explosion or, more precisely, an implosion, as the Mogollon began to concentrate their settlements on arable land.

Grasshopper Pueblo, for example, is a large Mogollon settlement dating to this period, located on the best and most extensive agricultural lands in Mogollon territory (Figure 15.17; Reid 1989). Archaeology around the region of Grasshopper shows that before A.D. 1300 there were a total of only about 200 Mogollon dwellings, located in a series of scattered, impermanent communities. After A.D. 1300 in the same region there were 10 times that number, as the scattered Mogollon began concentrating their population on good farmland (Reid and Whittlesey 1997:156). Grasshopper itself consists of 500 rooms arranged in three distinct clusters. Each block possessed its own common area, or plaza.

Great care was taken by the residents of Grasshopper Pueblo in the construction of buildings intended for ceremony and ritual. One of the large plazas at Grasshopper was roofed over at about A.D. 1330, producing an enclosed ritual space called a **kiva** by the historical and modern Hopi. Kivas were places where the community met to engage in and observe important rituals; they were, essentially, churches. The "Great Kiva" at Grasshopper is, as its name implies, an enormous gathering place some 25 m (82 ft) across, with its roof supported by nine huge juniper posts. As archaeologists Jefferson Reid and Stephanie Whittlesey (1997) suggest, the Great Kiva at Grasshopper played an integrative role in Mogollon society. Because large Mogollon communities such as Grasshopper represent the aggregation of previously separate, smaller communities, it is likely that a shared ritual space and communal ceremonies served to bring people together into a more integrated and complex social and political system. A decrease in rainfall after A.D. 1335 made untenable the agricultural way of life to which the Mogollon had become committed. By A.D. 1400, they had left their mountain homeland, lost their separate identity, and merged with other farmers in the Southwest.

Ancestral Puebloan

The Ancestral Puebloans of the Four Corners region, where the modern states of Arizona, New Mexico, Utah, and Colorado meet at right angles, produced the most spectacular masonry architecture in indigenous North America. The largest prehistoric **pueblos** and incredible settings characterize the Ancestral Puebloans. (You will find these people most commonly referred to as the Anasazi. This term means, literally, "ancient enemies" in the language of another group of Native Americans living in the Southwest, the Navajo, many of whom call themselves the Dineh. Many descendants of the people who built the pueblos object to having their ancestors named by another group, especially a group that they have historically been at odds with. It is with that in mind that we will call their predecessors the Ancestral Puebloans.)

Very early in their sequence, beginning about 2,000 years ago, the Ancestral Puebloans developed a subsistence system that while including a broad array of wild plants and animals, depended quite heavily on maize agriculture. The most diagnostic elements of their culture at this point were baskets, textiles, and nets used in hunting. In fact, the early years of Ancestral Puebloan development are divided into periods called Basketmaker I and II (500 B.C. to A.D. 600) and III (A.D. 600–800).

The florescence of Ancestral Puebloan culture occurred after A.D. 1000. A burst of social and political complexity is demonstrated by the construction of monumental residential structures, including Great Houses exponentially

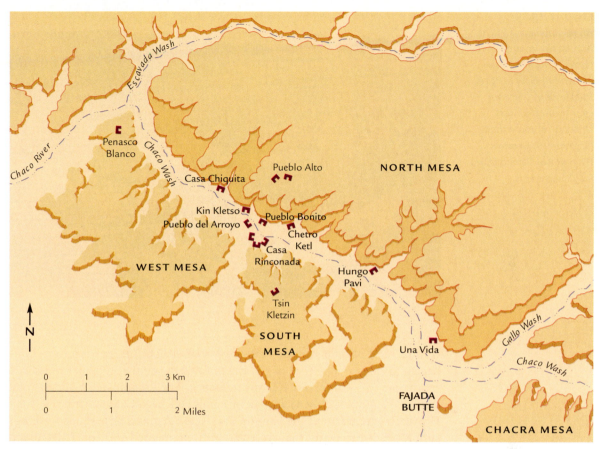

FIGURE 15.18
Locations of the Great Houses of Chaco Canyon in New Mexico.

larger than the Great Houses of the Hohokam, remarkable and beautiful cliff dwellings, and enormous ceremonial buildings in the form of Great Kivas. Chaco Canyon is the most obvious manifestation of such complexity; nine Great Houses were built at the base of the cliffs demarcating the margins of the arable land along the Chaco River (Figure 15.18). The largest of these, Pueblo Bonito, was a single immense structure made from millions of quarried sandstone blocks (Figure 15.19). Altogether, Pueblo Bonito consisted of about 800 rooms in its five stories (Figure 15.20). Roofs and ceilings were constructed from thousands of trees cut down and transported from forested areas as much as 80 km (50 mi) distant. The Great Houses at Chaco are monumental structures but likely were not the residences of huge numbers of people. Rather, the Great Houses may have been a kind of public architecture intended by the Ancestral Puebloans, on the practical side, for storage (see the "Case Study Close-Up" in this chapter) and also, in a metaphorical sense, as symbols of the power of their societies.

In all, about 75 substantial settlements and more than 300 smaller communities have been found that were part of the Chaco Ancestral Puebloan

FIGURE 15.19

An aerial view of Pueblo Bonito, the greatest of the Great Houses of Chaco Canyon in New Mexico. Pueblo Bonito was an enormous, five-story structure of more than 800 rooms. (Courtesy National Park Service, David Six photographer)

culture, most of them outside of the canyon itself. The major towns were connected to Chaco by a series of roads 9 m (30 ft) wide that together measured more than 650 km (about 400 mi) in length. The longest single Chaco road traversed approximately 68 km (42 mi), linking Chaco Canyon with the Great Houses to the north at the Salmon and Aztec Ruins. These roads were not simply timeworn trails; they were carefully engineered and constructed and traveled in quite straight lines. Chaco roads never avoided steep slopes but simply climbed them. Where the roads traveled over bare rock, walls were built to demarcate them.

The Chaco road system may have served an economic purpose, allowing for the transportation of precious raw materials and finely made art objects within the Chaco sphere; but as archaeologist John Kantner (1996) points out, a detailed analysis of the paths taken by the roads shows that most were not even close to providing the most efficient or fastest travel between Chaco villages. He feels that the roads played a far more important role in ritually and symbolically uniting the far-flung communities in the Chaco universe. Whatever the case, there is little doubt that economically, politically, and ritually, as more than one writer has put it, "all roads led to Chaco."

Chaco Great Houses and Great Kivas are enormously impressive, the product of a large, coordinated labor force. If cultural complexity can be assumed to be directly proportional to the massiveness of construction projects as manifested in the archaeological record, then the inhabitants of Chaco represent the most complex of the indigenous people of the American Southwest.

Though smaller than Chaco's Great Houses, the cliff dwellings of Mesa Verde in southwestern Colorado, built during a 100-year period beginning at

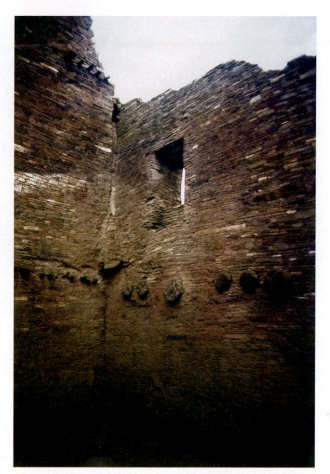

FIGURE 15.20
*A small section of Pueblo
Bonito, the largest of the
Ancestral Puebloan Great
Houses. Pueblo Bonito is
one of more than a dozen
Great Houses built at
Chaco Canyon.* (K. L. Feder)

the tail end of the twelfth century A.D., are even more striking. These houses
look like fairy castles, set into natural depressions in the cliffs that characterize
the region (Figure 15.21). There are more than 600 such cliff dwellings at Mesa
Verde. Most are quite small, but some consist of a series of residences and storage rooms constructed with stone blocks and stretching across cliff faces more
than 100 m (330 ft) in length, with delicate four-story square bastions and
graceful round towers (Figure 15.22). It is not clear why the residents of Mesa
Verde built their homes in such difficult, inaccessible, though visually striking
locations. Perhaps defense from marauding outsiders explains their location,
or perhaps it was protection from the elements or ease of access to fresh water
seeping through the cliff face. Whatever the case, it is clear that their construction required careful planning and the communal effort of a large force of people. Though there is little evidence at Mesa Verde for the presence of an elite
class, certainly the size of their dwellings and the difficulty posed by their construction are material evidence of the complexity of their society.

FIGURE 15.21
Mesa Verde contains some of the most spectacular and monumental of the cliff dwellings. Cliff Palace is a remarkable town built into the side of a mountain.
(K. L. Feder)

A combination of factors may have precipitated abandonment of the majestic cliff homes by the later thirteenth century, soon after Mesa Verde's population peaked. The population of Mesa Verde may have outstripped the environment's ability to support it, especially during the great drought that afflicted the area in the last quarter of the thirteenth century. Shortages of wood for fuel and construction may have played a role. It is also possible that a new religion may have attracted the Mesa Verdeans to the south. The inhabitants of Mesa Verde did not become extinct. They merely moved and today live in modern Hopi villages in New Mexico (see "Issues and Debates" in this chapter).

NORTHWEST COAST OF NORTH AMERICA

In their wide-ranging book, anthropologists Kenneth Ames and Herbert Maschner (1999:13) summarize succinctly European fascination with the native cultures of the northwest coast of North America: These native people simply "contradicted many of the basic assumptions that Europeans held about human societies, particularly the ones that linked cultural complexity with agriculture."

It was apparent from the very earliest contact between Europeans and the native peoples who lived along the coasts of Oregon, Washington, Vancouver Island, and British Columbia in the late 1700s that the aboriginal inhabitants had long lived in large, sedentary villages with populations as high as 2,000 people, where specialists produced splendid works of art, especially carved

FIGURE 15.22
The Square Tower House ruin, nestled in a niche at the base of a cliff in Mesa Verde in Colorado. With names such as "Cliff Palace," "Balcony House," and "Square Tower House," the cliff dwellings of Mesa Verde were the product of a sophisticated complex society that flourished more than 800 years ago in the American Southwest. (K. L. Feder)

and painted objects of wood, including **totem poles** (Figure 15.23). It was also clear to early European observers that the inhabitants of the northwest coast, including people who called themselves the Haida and the Kwakwaka'wakw (Kwakiutl), developed a complex political system headed by powerful, hereditary chiefs and that they lived in a stratified society consisting of two classes: free people and slaves. Free people were further divided into three ranks including an upper rank of noblemen and women, a middle rank of people with some prestige and official titles, and a third rank of common people. Slaves, often captives from wars fought with neighboring groups, represented the bottom of the social hierarchy. These social categories were largely hereditary; if you were born a slave, your descendants would be slaves, and if you were born to nobility, your descendants would be of noble standing.

No one got blindingly wealthy in native Northwest Coast societies. In fact, increased prestige and status was achieved by redistributing excess wealth and not by hoarding it, by, essentially, giving it away in enormous celebrations called **potlatches.** Though historical eyewitnesses to the character of native Northwest Coast societies described no absolute rulers, no one with the all-encompassing power of a King Tut (Chapter 11) or of a Pacal (Chapter 13), clearly Northwest Coast natives had produced a complex society in which authority, privilege, and, to a certain extent, wealth were invested in the hands of a noble class headed by a chief.

What was surprising to the Europeans who first encountered these societies continues to cause anthropologists to write clarifying footnotes disclaiming the otherwise seemingly valid generalization that before social and

political complexity can evolve, a people must develop a productive system of agriculture. Simply stated, contrary to all the other socially and politically complex societies described in Chapters 11–14, and here in 15 of this book, Northwest Coast economies were based not on agriculture but rather on hunting and gathering.

What made it possible for large, dense, sedentary populations to develop along the northwest coast of North America was the fact that the natural environment of the coast was so fabulously productive, it enabled the kind of food surplus that elsewhere was possible only by artificially raising food productivity through the practice of agriculture. In the terminology of anthropology, the native peoples of the northwest coast of North America were "**affluent foragers,**" living in an environment so rich as to allow large, dense, sedentary human populations to thrive there and to develop complex patterns of the production and distribution of wealth and the organization of labor and authority. The forests of the Northwest provided a wide variety of foods including roots, bulbs, berries, acorns, and hazelnuts. Elk, two species of deer, and numerous smaller mammals were hunted, and their meat provided a significant source of protein. Intertidal flats, estuaries, marshes, rocky shores, and extensive shallows attracted a diverse array of birds, fish, and land and sea mammals that were exploited by people living along the coast (Ames and Maschner 1999:47). Fish, especially salmon and marine mammals, including harbor seals, sea lions, porpoises, and gray whales, were hunted as well. Ames and Maschner (1999) suggest that it was the mixture of a diversity of productive food sources that provided the capacity for the production of a rich food surplus—the equivalent of what can be produced by agriculture—that led to the richness and complexity of Northwest Coast culture.

The origins of social ranking in the southern segment of the northwest coast can be traced in the archaeological record to at least 2,650 years ago. Beginning at this time, about 15% of the human interments that have been excavated archaeologically show evidence of differential wealth and deduced higher status. These high-status burials contain grave goods including things like beads, sometimes in the thousands, made from dentalium shells (a white mollusk); copper artifacts; pendants; rattles; and large stone spearpoints (Ames and Maschner 1999:187). The amount of labor that went into these finely crafted goods signifies their value and reflects the status of the individuals in whose burials such goods were concentrated. It is also important to point out that there were no age restrictions in terms of high-status burials, suggesting that status was inherited, not achieved. Children received high-status interments, almost certainly not because they attained high status through their accomplishments in life but simply because their parents were high-status individuals and this high status was passed down to their offspring.

Ethnographically, much of the architecture and finely and artistically produced work of the Northwest Coast people was made of wood, which preserved very poorly in their wet environment. In one instance, fortunately, this was not the case. Located on the Olympic Peninsula in Washington State, the Ozette site was a village where five houses were destroyed virtually in an instant by a mudslide dated to about A.D. 1491 (Pascua 1991). Ozette was a large and complex village, stretching nearly a mile against the coast (Figure 15.24). The encasing wet slurry of mud prevented aerobic bacteria from eating the organic objects produced by the village's inhabitants. Archaeologists recovered more than 50,000 artifacts in their excavation of the site, including finely made baskets, mats, wooden bowls, and an astonishing block of red cedar, carved into the shape of a whale's dorsal fin, inlaid with more than 700 otter teeth.

An important lesson can be gleaned from the complex societies that developed along the northwest coast of North America. A prerequisite in the development of social, economic, and political complexity is the ability to produce

FIGURE 15.24

FIGURE 15.24
This artist's conception of the 500-year-old Ozette village is based on the archaeological and ethnographic records. Ozette was destroyed in a mudslide that, ironically, contributed to the remarkable preservation of the material culture of the inhabitants. (© Richard Schlecht/National Geographic Society Image Collection)

a food surplus. That surplus certainly is facilitated by the development of an agricultural economy. However, though agriculture may facilitate increasing complexity, it is not the only way in which a substantial food surplus can be produced. Some world areas, like the northwest coast of North America (coastal Japan is another example), are so naturally productive that social stratification, wealth differentiation, and political inequality can develop. The fascinating cultures of the northwest coast attest to this alternative pathway to complexity.

GREAT ZIMBABWE

For the Europeans who first encountered its ruins in southern Africa in the late nineteenth century, Great Zimbabwe was an enigma. Its name was taken from the local Shona people who called the ruin, appropriately, *dzimbabwe*, "houses of stone." Indeed, these first European visitors were impressed by the immensity of its stone construction—the huge number of carefully shaped granite bricks used to build the walls that enclosed parts of the site and the majestic beauty of its dry-laid masonry (Figure 15.25). Clearly, the people who had built the great walls and enclosures of Zimbabwe had been a technologically and architecturally sophisticated people. Equally clearly, a complex social system must have been necessary to organize and oversee the labor needed to construct the very impressive remains.

FIGURE 15.25
Made of thousands of precisely cut granite bricks, the monumental stonework at Great Zimbabwe reflects a level of labor organization and coordination that is the hallmark of a complex society. (© Robert Holmes/Corbis)

The first Europeans to investigate Zimbabwe found it inconceivable that local Africans had been responsible for building the site. Their racist assumption was that sub-Saharan Africans were incapable of such a complex undertaking. As archaeologist Graham Connah (1987:183) points out, the European colonizers of Africa sought to deny the indigenous people of that continent their rightful cultural heritage. Some went so far as to suggest that Zimbabwe was associated with Solomon's Temple in Jerusalem, implying that Zimbabwe had been built not by native Africans but by interlopers from the Middle East.

Such nonsense persisted for more than a century. Even into the 1960s and 70s, attempts were made to disassociate ancient Zimbabwe from the modern inhabitants of sub-Saharan Africa (see the discussion in Garlake 1973). But the archaeological record is quite clear on this point. The builders of Great

FIGURE 15.26
Site map of Great Zimbabwe.

Zimbabwe and a large number of smaller sites of the same cultural tradition were the ancestors of the contemporary people of south-central Africa. More than 700 years ago, the people of Great Zimbabwe had produced their own indigenous complex society, inspired primarily by their own ability.

The Glory of Zimbabwe

Great Zimbabwe itself consists of an impressive set of stone-brick structures demarcating the central or elite precinct of a large town that likely also served as a ceremonial center for a widespread rural population, a residence for their gods as well as their chiefs. Massive and impressive, Great Zimbabwe grew by accretion as its population expanded and as its role as the central place of a developing complex society changed through time (Figure 15.26; Ndoro 1997).

Great Zimbabwe is the largest of close to 200 settlements built in the same style in an area known geologically as the Zimbabwe Plateau. A greater number of smaller sites in Botswana and South Africa without impressive

FIGURE 15.27
Archaeological sites in southern Africa associated with Great Zimbabwe.

stonework—for example, Danamombe, Khami, Manekweni, and Thulamela—likely represent the remains of villages that were part of a large and impressive chiefdom with Great Zimbabwe as its focal point, dating to A.D. 1100–1600 (Ndoro 1997; Figure 15.27). While these secondary sites cover tens or even hundreds of acres, Zimbabwe is larger by at least an order of magnitude, with its stone structures spread out over more than 7 km^2 (close to 3 mi^2, or nearly 1,800 acres).

Zimbabwe-style architecture includes large, dry-laid stone walls made of rectangular granite "bricks." Zimbabwe-style walls are massive and broad, with bastions, stepped platforms, towers, and large monoliths (massive, upright, single stones) incorporated into their construction (Figure 15.28). Some wall sections are ornately designed with the granite bricks laid in chevron and herringbone patterns. The monumental granite brick walls served as enclosures for a small part of the population, likely the elite of Zimbabwe society. Their homes were constructed of an extremely high quality clay locally called **dagga.**

The two main structures at Great Zimbabwe—the "Hill Ruin" and the "Great Enclosure"—are the most imposing of the monuments built by these people (Figure 15.29). The Hill Ruin is the smaller of the two, yet its walls stand some 11 m (nearly 37 ft) high. The Hill Ruin actually consists of two separate enclosures connected by a narrow passageway walled in with granite bricks. Altogether, the long axis of the Hill Ruin is more than the length of a football field, about 100 m (328 ft) long and 45 m (148 ft) wide.

FIGURE 15.28
This stone tower, an example of the beautiful masonry used in Zimbabwe construction, is located within one of the enormous granite brick enclosures at the site. (© J. Laure/Woodfin Camp and Associates)

The Great Enclosure is larger still, an elliptical wall some 244 m (nearly 800 ft) in circumference, 5 m (16 ft) thick, and 10 m (33 ft) tall, enclosing a space with a maximum diameter of nearly 90 m (almost 300 ft). This truly monumental construction project required nearly 1 million granite bricks for its completion. More than simply massive, the masonry of the Great Enclosure is the finest in ancient Africa outside of Egypt. The bricks fit together virtually seamlessly; the walls are imposing yet, in places, delicately graceful. Interior walls demarcate space within the Great Enclosure, and there is, again, extensive evidence of dagga huts throughout. It has been suggested by some researchers that the Great Enclosure housed the elite of Zimbabwe society and that it was, in fact, a palace (Ndoro 1997).

Early archaeology at Great Zimbabwe centered on the great enclosures. Only recently have archaeologists turned their attention to the zone surrounding the enclosures. There they have found the remains of extensive settlements of dagga huts, likely the houses of people of lower status than those residing within the walled compounds. The community had a dense, near-urban character; even the most conservative estimate puts Zimbabwe's population at its peak at about 2,000 adults (Ndoro 1997). Some have gauged the total population of Great Zimbabwe to have been as high as 18,000 at its peak (Connah 1987:184).

By one interpretation, Great Zimbabwe was the capital of a far-reaching chiefdom, sitting atop a hierarchy that included a middle level of smaller towns; there, secondary, regional elites lived within stone enclosures. A third level included small peasant villages without monumental stonework. Those living outside of the enclosures and those living in smaller villages provided

the necessary economic support for the sociopolitical system by growing surpluses of sorghum and millet and by raising sheep, goats, and cattle.

The peasants provided food for the elite living in the enclosures. Archaeological faunal evidence implies that the elite had a diet different from that of
the masses. For example, at the Zimbabwe site of Manekweni, it is apparent
that those living outside of the enclosure were limited in their diet, with sheep
and goat providing the bulk of their meat, whereas those living inside the enclosure, though they produced no food, were provided with beef for their
subsistence (Barker 1978).

Zimbabwe's location may have been the key to its growth and complexity. Its location took strategic advantage of a number of trade routes, including those along which valuable ivory moved during the occupation of the site.
Also, like the inhabitants of Çatalhöyük (Chapter 10), who were located near
a precious and valuable resource (obsidian) and who could amass wealth as a
result of controlling that resource, Great Zimbabwe was located near a significant natural source of gold and likely came to dominate in its trade. The Zimbabwe elite may have derived and maintained their position as a class above
the masses on the basis of the wealth they were able to accumulate through all

manner of trade but, perhaps, especially this gold. That trade was widespread is evidenced in the archaeological record. Glass from Syria, faience (tin-glazed earthenware) bowls from Persia, and even Chinese celadon dishes (finely made ceramics with an olive, gray, or blue glazing) have been found at Zimbabwe (Ndoro 1997).

The walls of Great Zimbabwe and related settlements today are the most conspicuous evidence of the power of the elite in that society. It is likely that as trade in gold and other commodities served to enrich some families on the Zimbabwe Plateau, these families became economically and socially distinguished from everybody else. These elites were able to have the enclosures constructed, setting them physically apart from the great mass of people and reinforcing the fact that they were economically and socially apart from these people as well. Today the silent walls speak volumes to the archaeologist and historian, telling us that enormous power was invested in the elite of this chiefdom society to direct and control the labor of the great mass of people.

ISSUES AND DEBATES

IS THE STATE INEVITABLE?

As we saw in Chapter 10, social and political complexity was not inevitable. Some societies, primarily hunter-gatherers, maintained a relatively simple form of social and political organization virtually up to the **ethnographic present.** For example, though their societies certainly did not remain static, the residents of the Kalahari Desert in South Africa, the people who lived in the heart of the Australian desert, and the Inuit people of the Arctic maintained much of their traditional social and political organization for thousands of years, right up to and past their contact with societies having a more complex form of organization, such as the Europeans who first came into contact with them. Their social structures remained largely egalitarian: Virtually all individuals within the same age/sex category had equal wealth and a fair degree of control over their own lives. Authority was vested in families, not in a political structure imposed from above. There were no social classes and no all-powerful chiefs or kings, and no one was buried in sumptuous style.

Just as social and political complexity itself was not an inevitable development in the historical trajectories of all people, rank societies or chiefdoms did not lead inevitably to state societies. In fact, some complexly organized people remained as rank societies or chiefdoms for millennia. For example, the megalith builders of western Europe discussed in Chapter 10, though clearly a complex culture capable of marshaling the forces and coordinating the work of a large group of laborers to construct the monuments that give the society their modern name, never developed some of the diagnostic characteristics of state societies. There apparently was no formal government, no highly and formally organized political bureaucracy, and no hierarchy separating rigidly defined social classes.

The cultures discussed in this chapter similarly may best be characterized as complex, non-state societies. Such societies do not necessarily represent a step on some cultural evolutionary ladder to an inevitable state level of organization. Instead, they reflect a different way in which people constructed and organized their societies.

THE MYTH OF THE MOUND BUILDERS

The first Europeans to encounter the impressive ruins at Great Zimbabwe presumed that indigenous Africans were not capable of producing such sophisticated and complex architecture. Zimbabwe certainly was not the only instance in which Europeans were confronted by archaeological evidence that the ancestors of people they wished desperately to believe were inferior had produced a sophisticated culture. Actually, the European response to Zimbabwe is part of a general pattern whereby Europeans denied civilized status to many of the non-European people they encountered in their exploration of the world in the fifteenth through nineteenth centuries. The story of the European reaction to the mound builders of North America is an example of this form of racism in its extreme.

Robert Silverberg's book *The Mound Builders* (1989) is a wonderful treatment of this sorry saga in American history (also see chapters in Feder 2007 and Williams 1991 for summaries of this issue). In the eighteenth and nineteenth centuries, European settlers of the North American continent were confronted with clear evidence, in the form of monumental works (the mounds themselves) and sophisticated artifacts found in and around the mounds, of the previous existence of an advanced, "civilized" culture in the heartland of the continent. Rather than conclude from this that the ancient native people of North America, the descendants of whom those European settlers were displacing and whose cultures they were destroying, had been responsible for the clearly impressive achievements of the mound builders, instead a myth of a "vanished race" was concocted. This vanished race, many believed, *not* the Indians, had built the mounds and manufactured the beautiful artifacts found in association with them. This myth took hold, despite the complete lack of evidence for the existence of anyone but the Indians and their ancestors on this continent. And it took hold even though historical records clearly described mound-building Indians living in dense settlements in the sixteenth century, before their populations were decimated by diseases introduced by European explorers and colonists (de la Vega 1605/1988; Elvas 1611/1966).

The controversy concerning the source of mound-builder culture was a vigorous one until relatively recently. It was an issue of great concern to the Smithsonian Institution, which funded a number of major investigations into the mound-builder question in the nineteenth century. More than 100 years ago a federal agency, the Bureau of American Ethnology, published researcher

Cyrus Thomas's (1894/1985) voluminous work on the topic. During the course of his study, Thomas and his assistants examined 2,000 mound sites, collected over 40,000 artifacts, and examined countless historical documents and accounts. Not a shred of the evidence they examined supported the hypothesis of some vanished race of mound builders. Everything showed conclusively that the people who had built the mounds, the people who had produced the sophisticated material culture, the people who had developed the complex society that left these things behind had been none other than the American Indian. Stereotypes of primitive, nomadic tribes of Native Americans were hard to break, but break them Cyrus Thomas did. It is remarkable to think that this issue was resolved just over 100 years ago. Today, Cahokia is included on the World Heritage Site list, an honor roll kept by the United Nations of significant archaeological sites worldwide. Its inclusion on this list memorializes the marvelous cultural achievements of the Native Americans who built it.

WHAT HAPPENED TO THE ANCESTRAL PUEBLOANS?

We saw that Mesa Verde was abandoned in the beginning of the fourteenth century. The reason for this abandonment remains a mystery. In a fascinating bit of analysis on population size, movement, and settlement abandonment by another group of Ancestral Puebloans, researchers produced a computer simulation of population fluctuations in Long House Valley located in northeastern Arizona that is relevant to this question (Axtell et al. 2002; and see Diamond 2002 for a summary).

The simulation began with a small virtual human population of households in A.D. 800 that was programmed to grow or decline at a rate commensurate with fluctuating food availability. As discussed in this chapter, Ancestral Puebloans were agriculturalists and their primary food, both historically and in the simulation, was maize. Yearly variations in probable maize yields were determined for the valley and input into the simulation on the basis of actual, historically determined, yearly rainfall fluctuations. Yearly amounts between A.D. 800 and 1300 could be measured relatively precisely on the basis of tree-ring widths dendrochronologists have determined for the area. So based on the amount of rain falling in a given year, determined by how thick the tree rings in Long House Valley were for that year, the number of bushels of maize that could have been produced by the valley residents was estimated. Thicker rings meant more rain, which in turn meant higher maize yields. Based on ethnographic data, the researchers assigned an average amount of maize needed to sustain an individual during the course of a year. With this in mind, researchers could estimate the total human population in the valley for a given year by dividing the total maize output by the number of bushels needed to sustain an individual for a year.

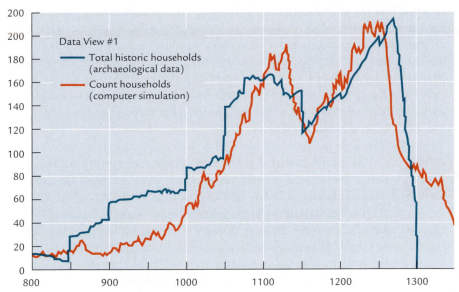

FIGURE 15.30
Graph showing the results of a simulation of population growth and contraction among the Anasazi of Long House Valley. By experimenting with the variables in the simulation, the authors of the study were able to produce a population graph that closely resembles the actual population curve derived from the archaeological analysis of the valley. (From Axtell et al. 2002)

The next step involved actually running the simulation and determining the fluctuating size of the human population dependent on maize, sustainable each year in the valley. In the mathematical model used in the simulation, the initial, small population could grow, as long as the people could produce sufficient food to feed the increasing population based on potential yields that were determined by the amount of rainfall for each given year. The population in the simulation would fall when the potential maize yield fell below that which would have been required to sustain the level the population had grown to.

The final step in the analysis lay in comparing the simulation's predicted human population curve between A.D. 800 and 1300 and the population curve determined archaeologically by counting the number of residences in the valley. The resulting comparison is breathtaking. The two curves—one representing the best estimate determined by archaeological research and the other based on the output of the simulation—are almost identical. In other words, the simulation predicts nearly perfectly the population curve deduced from the archaeological record (Figure 15.30).

Interestingly, the two curves diverge significantly only toward the end of the 1200s, at about the time the Ancestral Puebloans abandoned Long House Valley. Herein lies an interesting lesson. Although, on the basis of the archaeological record, the actual population in the valley declines to effectively zero, the simulation indicates that after A.D. 1270, a reduced but still sizable human population could have survived there. In other words, as the researchers conclude, though rainfall patterns certainly affected crop yield, which then affected human population size, something other than reduced crop yield factored into the abandonment of the valley. The researchers suggest that the final abandonment was a conscious choice on the part of residents, based not on purely economic considerations—they wouldn't have starved but could have survived with a reduced level of population. Sociocultural issues must have affected the choice to abandon Long House Valley, and this must be considered in the case of Mesa Verde as well. Modeling those factors—religious issues or social alliances—however, will be far more difficult to simulate than economic factors like crop yields.

CASE STUDY CLOSE-UP

Chaco in particular, but other areas of the prehistoric Southwest as well, shows extensive evidence of monumental architecture and social stratification, implying a level of organization beyond that of simple, egalitarian societies. Archaeologist Lynne Sebastian (1992) suggests an explanation for the development of this complexity, at least as it relates to the Chaco Anasazi. (This term is so ingrained that we will continue to use it here, with no disrespect intended to the Pueblo people.) She sees a shift in the settlement pattern in the area occurring between A.D. 700 and 900 from small, largely undifferentiated settlements to larger, more monumental construction. Sebastian feels that the excess labor available for these large construction projects resulted from a shift in subsistence strategies.

The Southwest is an arid climate prone to prolonged periods of dought. Agriculture is an iffy proposition under such conditions, and years of low agricultural yields are always a possibility. This situation may explain why for such a long time farming merely supplemented the subsistence system in this region. As population increased, however, there was a shift toward agriculture and greater sedentism. But herein a problem arose. Certainly in good years, more mouths could be fed through agriculture, but a greater reliance on farming brought with it the potential for greater possible disaster from a bad year with little rainfall and low crop yields.

In Sebastian's (1992:100) opinion, the strategy at Chaco to cope with just such a problem was the *overproduction* of food—the intentional production of a surplus through intensification of the agricultural system—in good years. The surplus could then be stored for distribution in bad crop years. Indeed, there is a marked increase in storage areas in villages during the period A.D. 700–900. There is also evidence of the construction of water-management facilities, providing for the capture and distribution of rainwater—in other words, irrigation technology. In Sebastian's view, groups living in hydraulically privileged areas, such as Chaco Canyon, were able to produce food surpluses through water management. In her model, large construction projects resulting in some of the impressive structures at Chaco had the goal of producing large storage areas for the food surplus.

The distribution of that surplus in bad years resulted in a large population being obliged to the people at Chaco who produced, stored, maintained, and then distributed the food. In Sebastian's (1992:123) words, it is possible that "the great house residents were able to convert long-term patterns of

FIGURE 15.31
Casa Rinconada, associated with the settlement of Pueblo Bonito, is one of the Great Kivas in Chaco Canyon, New Mexico.
(K. L. Feder)

power and obligation into permanent status and roles of leadership." She further suggests that they cemented and rationalized this power through Ancestral Puebloan religion. People able to produce a large food surplus and then distribute it during lean times may have been thought to have supernatural connections. Sebastian relates this religious link to the mid-eleventh-century construction of Great Kivas at Chaco, structures of great religious significance in Ancestral Puebloan and later cultures (Figure 15.31).

Roads were built connecting the main settlements in Chaco; an extensive trading network is evidenced by the use of exotic raw materials; and some of the material culture, especially the pottery, was quite elaborate and sophisticated. This exotic material was used in religious ceremonies, and some of it ended up in the burials of powerful people, likely providing further legitimacy for their privileged position. When the overall climate improved between A.D. 1050 and 1130, the capacity for the production of a food surplus increased and the power of those who produced and controlled food became even greater.

I first visited Cahokia in 1976 while I was in nearby St. Louis for an archaeology conference. I had great trouble getting to the site at the time; nobody in the hotel had even heard of the place, much less knew how I might get there. Through sheer perseverance I made it to the site, where I found what was essentially an empty state park with a tiny, cinder-block museum. When I next visited, in 1991, there was a splendid, multimillion-dollar museum that receives tens of thousands of visitors each year. Cahokia is a place of wonder; the mounds are impressive, as are the artifacts housed in the museum, and the audiovisual presentation in the museum is informative and extremely beautiful. If you are in the area don't miss it! If you're not planning a trip to St. Louis, you can undertake a virtual visit of

VISITING THE PAST

Cahokia. The official Cahokia Web site presents a wealth of information including an interactive map and detailed information about each of the mounds at the site (http://www.cahokiamounds.com/cahokia.html.

Etowah in Georgia, Moundville in Alabama, and Spiro in Oklahoma are just three of the many additional fascinating temple mound sites open to the public. For Adena and Hopewell cultures, there is no better place to visit than the Ohio Historical Society's museum in Columbus (http://www.ohiohistory.org/places/ohc). Many mound sites have been preserved and are maintained by the Society; places like the enormous Miamisburg Mound in Miamisburg and Serpent Mound in Peebles are open to the public and more than worth the trip.

Many of the most spectacular of the complex sites in the American Southwest are on federal land or Indian reservations. Many of the most impressive are readily accessible to even the casual tourist. Mesa Verde in southwestern Colorado offers probably the best views and walk-throughs of cliff dwellings. Chaco Canyon is accessible only via a dirt road, but it is well worth the bumpy trip; a series of pueblo structures, including the most monumental of the Ancestral Puebloan buildings, are located within a short drive of each other. See David Grant Noble's (1991) book, *Ancient Ruins of the Southwest: An Archaeological Guide,* for maps, descriptions of many of the most important sites in the Southwest, and a practical guide for visiting them.

The Makah Nation maintains a cultural and research center in Neah Bay, Washington. Some of the finest examples of artifacts recovered at the Ozette site are on display there along with a full-scale replica of a native house.

The political situation in southern Africa since the dissolution of the apartheid governments of Rhodesia and South Africa has improved greatly. The modern nation of Zimbabwe (formerly Rhodesia) was named for the African civilization discussed here. Great Zimbabwe is protected and administered by a government agency, the National Museums and Monuments of Zimbabwe. The site has been designated a World Heritage Site, one site on a worldwide honor roll of significant historical sites. Tourist visits to Great Zimbabwe are possible; there is even a hotel within walking distance of the ruins.

By visiting any one of the cultural sites discussed in this chapter, you can achieve a visceral appreciation for the power of rank and chiefdom societies to mobilize great numbers of people for communal projects and to produce social systems in which some are afforded an opportunity to devote their lives to the perfection of an artistic or scientific specialty.

SUMMARY

Complex societies developed in places where a food surplus could be produced, allowing for the development of wealth that could then be concentrated in the hands of an elite rank or class. In most cases, the ability to produce a food surplus was made possible by the adoption of an agricultural economy where the few could feed the many. However, in some areas the natural food base was so rich, a large, dense, sedentary population developed with attendant cultural complexity without the benefit of agriculture.

In some world areas, the development of social complexity, political inequality, and the concentration of wealth culminated in the evolution of state societies as described in Chapters 11–14. In some cases, though, society became divided into classes and further subdivided into various levels of noble and common ranks, and the power to completely control the lives of the commoners didn't develop. Leaders in such societies maintained a level of power, not so much by concentrating wealth but by serving as channels for redistribution of that wealth within their societies. We give these societies a separate designation—chiefdoms—but there certainly is a continuum from chiefdoms to state societies.

The burial and temple mound builders of the Midwest and Southeast, the Ancestral Puebloans of the American Southwest, the native people of the northwest coast of North America, and the builders of Great Zimbabwe are just a few examples of the various expressions of cultural complexity that developed in the ancient world.

TO LEARN MORE

Technical Summaries

For details on Cahokia archaeology, see Melvin Fowler's *Cahokia Atlas: A Historical Atlas of Cahokia Archaeology* (1989). An extremely valuable book is Timothy Pauketat's *The Ascent of Chiefs* (1994), a theoretical look at the evolution of a stratified social system at Cahokia. Jefferson Reid and Stephanie Whittlesey have written a broad overview of the American Southwest titled *The Archaeology of Ancient Arizona* (1997). Lynne Sebastian's highly readable, theoretical look at the origins and evolution of Ancestral Puebloan society at Chaco Canyon is titled *The Chaco Anasazi: Sociopolitical Evolution in the Prehistoric Southwest* (1992). On Great Zimbabwe and its place in the development of complex societies in Africa, see Graham Connah's book *African Civilization: Precolonial Cities and States in Tropical Africa; an Archaeological Perspective* (1987).

Popular Summaries

For the mound builders at Cahokia and the history of their acceptance as an indigenous American civilization, see Robert Silverberg's wonderful historical summary, *The Mound Builders* (1989). Focusing on the archaeology of Ohio, Brad Lepper's (2004) splendidly illustrated book, *Ohio Archaeology: An Illustrated Chronicle of Ohio's Ancient American Indian Cultures* is both beautiful and enormously informative with lots of material about the Adena and Hopewell mound builders. David Roberts's book, *In Search of the Old Ones: Exploring the Anasazi World of the Southwest* (1997) provides a detailed look at this region. In the Smithsonian Institution's series, Exploring the Ancient World, Linda S. Cordell's *Ancient Pueblo Peoples* (1994) is an overview of prehistory in the Southwest. For the peoples of the northwest coast, Kenneth Ames and Herbert Maschner's wonderful book titled *Peoples of the Northwest Coast: Their*

Archaeology and Prehistory (1999) is a great source of information and a great read. Webber Ndoro's *Scientific American* article, "Great Zimbabwe" (1997), is a terrific place to start learning more about this complex society in southern Africa.

On the Web

The Cahokia site has its own home page located at http://www.cahokiamounds.org/cahokia.html. Along with photographs, maps of the mounds, and lots of text, this site lists the various activities conducted at the site, including excavations, lectures, hands-on programs, powwows, and so forth.

For an overview of the various cliff dwellings at Mesa Verde, visit the National Park Service's page devoted to this national monument at http://www.nps.gov/meve/home.htm. For an excellent and very thorough site covering many issues related to the ancient inhabitants of Chaco Canyon, there is no better place on the Internet than another National Park Service site, located at http://www.nps.gov/chcu. Be sure to click on the "Traditions of the Sun" button for an interactive virtual visit to Chaco.

For some terrific historic images from the northwest coast, especially photographs of those emblems of the sophisticated art of the native peoples of that region, totem poles, go to http://content.lib.washington.edu/aipnw/wright.html.

For a site with several stunning photographs of Great Zimbabwe architecture and stonework, go to art history professor Dr. George Landow's Web site at http://www.scholars.nus.edu.sg/landow/post/zimbabwe/art/greatzim/gz1.html. The PBS science show *Nova* maintains a very nice site that deals with Zimbabwe at http://www.pbs.org/wgbh/nova/israel/zimbabwe.html.

Online Learning Center: www.mhhe.com/feder4

The Online Learning Center (OLC) Web companion to *The Past in Perspective* features a variety of supplemental study aids. For each chapter, this free Web site includes

- Self-Quizzes to take as pretests prior to exams
- Interactive Timeline Study Guides for additional review and reinforcement of key information
- Learning Objectives
- Chapter Site links with Web addresses for many of the fossil and archaeological sites mentioned in the text

KEY TERMS

Adena, 595
affluent forager, 614
Ancestral Puebloan (or Anasazi), 602
courtyard group, 603
dagga, 619
Early Woodland period, 595

ethnographic present, 622
Hohokam, 602
Hopewell, 595
kiva, 608
Midddle Woodland, 595
Mogollon, 602
pit-house, 606

potlatch, 613
pueblo, 608
Sinagua, 602
totem pole, 613

Evolutionary Epilogue

CHAPTER OVERVIEW

Our story began with the birth of the universe, the origin of life, the evolution of the primates, and the florescence of the apes. We saw one ape species pushed out onto the savanna at the end of the Miocene—able to survive as a result of its unique ability to walk on two legs. We witnessed the enormous success of this species' descendants as their brains expanded and as they relied increasingly on the intellectual power of those big brains to invent tools, tame fire, domesticate plants and animals, and develop complex societies.

We have reached a milepost in our investigation of the human past, where we literally have caught up with ourselves on the human evolutionary pathway. We can gaze back, as we have in this book, along its winding and serendipitous route, and in the distance we can see, if only dimly, our ancient evolutionary ancestors. Ahead, we can imagine our species racing forward to some unknown and unfathomable point on the horizon of our own future.

PAST PERSPECTIVES, FUTURE DIRECTIONS

This book has chronicled our species' long and exciting journey as revealed through the scientific investigation of the period of time literally before history. Together we have traveled a pathway paved with the material remains of those who have passed here before us. Littering the trail have been their bones and their trash, their tools and their monuments. These are the things that have informed us of their story. And *their* story has been *our* story, the physical and cultural evolutionary history of all humankind. It is a tale yet unfolding and of which we are all a part.

The Human Adaptation

As we have seen, 2.5 million years ago our human ancestors crossed an intellectual threshold that would forever determine the focus of the human adaptation. In our species' African nursery was born our unique reliance on *culture*—our ability to conceive strategies for survival intellectually, to implement those plans, and to teach our children, who in turn teach theirs. Using the intellectual potential conferred on us by our expanding brains, our *Homo habilis* ancestors initiated a pattern that has continued to define the hominid line. Though nature has not endowed us with great strength or speed, though we lack wings to fly and powerful jaws to bite, though our senses are muted in comparison with those of other animals, we nevertheless have become a hugely successful species. What makes us unique and constitutes the foundation of our success is our intellectual capacity and the manifold cultural adaptations we have invented out of our creative imaginations. Our intelligence enables us to define our evolutionary destinies. We needn't wait for natural selection to slowly shift our adaptations to match our environments. We change ourselves and simultaneously construct our environments, all in the time it takes to formulate a thought or to express an idea.

This process began when *Homo habilis* first visualized a sharp, durable edge within a dull, round rock. A few carefully placed, sharp blows with another stone, and the visualized edge became an actual one, capable of cutting, slicing, or chopping more effectively than any of the bodily "tools" nature had given us. In that instant our ancestors had evolved the equivalent of more powerful, piercing canine teeth, razor-sharp slicing claws, and rock-solid fists. It took no genetic mutation; it merely required the unique genius of our evolutionary family line.

In a sense, all human history is based on the Oldowan stone-tool industry, and all human achievement has been but a series of variations on the theme established 2.5 million years ago on the African savanna. The Acheulean handaxe of *Homo erectus,* the Levallois and Mousterian industries associated with anatomically archaic varieties of our own species, *Homo sapiens,* and even cave paintings and barbed harpoons, domesticated plants and animals, socially stratified societies and walled cities—in fact, civilization itself—all of these things are mere variations on the theme established in the Oldowan tools of the Lower Paleolithic. Throughout our stay on earth, human beings have perceived the need and possessed the intellectual capacity to develop new ways of gathering resources, manipulating the environment, recording and transmitting information, organizing labor—in essence, of living our lives. And cultural adaptation continues today to distinguish us from all other life on the planet.

From Stone Tools to Star Trek

February 1, 2003, began for me as a quiet Saturday morning at home. My wife was at work, and both of my kids were off doing assorted weekend kid things. At last I had been afforded a continuous stretch of quiet time to work on the final stages of the previous (3rd) edition of *The Past in Perspective*. It was only a bit after 9:00 A.M. here on the east coast, but I had already gotten a lot done and was taking a break when I grabbed the remote and flipped the TV on to CNN.

At first, I only half-comprehended the scroll at the bottom of the screen: "NASA has declared an emergency." So blasé have we become about spaceflight, it took that message for me to remember that the space shuttle *Columbia* was just finishing a mission in space and due to return to earth. Though, like many, I can be characterized as an enthusiastic but only casual follower of the space program, it was immediately obvious to my untrained eyes that the cluster of blindingly bright balls of light, streaking in tandem across the sky in replay after replay, could not be good. Though NASA officially still held out hope as I watched the TV, it seemed clear that something serious and horrible had happened to the space shuttle *Columbia* and its crew as it had reentered the earth's atmosphere across an arc of brilliantly blue Texas sky. And indeed, as we soon came to understand, the space shuttle and its crew of seven explorers—Rick Husband, William McCool, Michael Anderson, David Brown, Kalpana Chawla, Dr. Laurel Clark, and Ilan Ramon—were gone.

In the hours and then days that followed, the age of the *Columbia* was considered as a contributing factor in the accident. In fact, the *Columbia* had been the very first orbiter in the shuttle fleet to fly; its initial foray into space took place on April 12, 1981—more than 21 years before its blazing destruction in 2003.

It was probably not an exaggeration when writers described *Columbia*, this "artifact" of the late twentieth century, as the "single most complex machine ever built by man" (Melvyn Smith 1985:120). The *Columbia*, in its original configuration, weighed 75,000 kg (more than 82 tons) and possessed 49 rocket engines, 4 online computers and 1 backup, 23 antennas, sophisticated fuel cells to provide electrical energy for all of the machinery on board, and literally millions of interworking, individual parts (all space shuttle statistics taken from Gurney and Forte 1988). The entire shuttle consisting of the delta-winged orbiter along with the booster rockets that placed the orbiter and two

The space shuttle Columbia blasts off on its maiden voyage, April 12, 1981. (NASA Marshall Space Flight Center NASA-MSFC)

astronauts into space on that April morning weighed about 2 million kilograms (4.5 million pounds).

Though *Columbia* carried no payload and circled the earth only 36 times in a little more than 2 days, its successful flight ushered in a new era of space exploration. That new era would include the deployment of a series of satellites enabling us to better investigate the earth and its weather patterns, resource concentrations, and even the impacts of our own civilization on the ecological balance of the planet. The shuttle also enabled the deployment of a defective Hubble Space Telescope—and also its ultimate in-space repair—that has added immeasurably to our understanding of the universe. The shuttle has carried into orbit large sections of a multinational, permanent space station that will allow human beings to live and work together in space over extended periods, providing humanity with the ultimate bird's-eye view of our home planet and a small window into the infinite universe.

In fact, *Columbia* paved the way for the regular and almost routine return to space. And although tragedies like the *Challenger* disaster in 1986 and the destruction of the *Columbia* itself in 2003, have occurred, the shuttle pro-

Space exploration, one of the truly monumental undertakings of twentieth- and twenty-first century civilization, has provided a unique perspective for all of us inhabitants of the earth. (Courtesy NASA)

gram has experienced both small and large triumphs of the human will to expand beyond the bonds of our own planet, representing some of the first faltering steps our species has taken to become constituents not just of the small planet that gave us life but also citizens of the universe.

All of these space accomplishments have taken place in little more than 50 years. Humans did not evolve an ability to live in the cold, dark airless vacuum of space in that short period of time. This accomplishment is entirely a result of our ability to think. Given a few more generations, perhaps our children's children will be exploring farther into our universe and actually fulfilling the fictional promise of Captain James T. Kirk and Captain Jean-Luc Picard of the Starship(s) *Enterprise:* "to boldly go where no one has gone before."

Many Pathways

The space shuttle, as complex as it is, is simply a tool, a point along a continuum of complexity that began with Oldowan. The simple stone tool took our hominid ancestors where they had not gone before as surely as has the space shuttle, our computers, and all the other tools we have invented to allow us more effectively to feed ourselves, provide for our physical necessities, and explore the world and ourselves.

I am comparing Oldowan tools and the space shuttle because, though incredibly different in scale, they bespeak a common bond between our modern civilization and our ancient hominid forebears. But this implies no inevitable sequence of change, no inexorable "march of progress" from ancient hominids to Western society. When in this book we have looked back along our evolutionary pathway, we have seen that the pathway is, in actuality, made up of many intersecting and diverging avenues. There is no single highway of change leading inevitably to Western civilization, no necessary trail from stone tools to spacecraft. Our society represents merely one point along one of many possible pathways, one of many possible modes of adaptation, not better or more "evolved" than any others and in no way an inevitable outcome of cultural evolution.

This is a difficult but crucial point to make. Many of us in the West view history as an endless upward spiral of material progress, an inevitable pathway of "improvement" of the human condition leading necessarily to us, to Western civilization. We also often view history as teaching moral lessons—history as a tale of good guys versus bad guys, with the good guys (that would be us) always coming out on top and their destiny being realized.

The belief that all of human prehistory and history followed a single, inevitable pathway—the perspective of **orthogenesis**—provides the philosophical underpinning for a hypothesis of **unilineal evolution** (see the discussion of cultural evolutionist Lewis Henry Morgan in Chapter 1). The view of the universality of cultural evolutionary sequences may be a popular one, but it is not the only view. The ancient Egyptians discussed in Chapter 11, for example, perceived history quite differently. As Egyptologist Barry Kemp (1991) points out, the Egyptians saw history not as a trajectory leading somewhere but as a constant, ordered, linear series of transitions from pharaoh to pharaoh. History, for the ancient Egyptians, leads nowhere in particular but proceeds along a constant line of kingship. When Egyptians wrote their own history, there was no search for meaning or pattern, no saga of a destiny fulfilled. For them, history simply was a list of kings, a succession of rulers.

Anthropologists view history differently. History for us is played out on an evolutionary stage where there is no necessary direction, only a common, underlying theme of change and adaptation. We view the ancient past neither as a continual parade of divine and semidivine leaders nor as a parable of the inevitability of material progress. We see a unique series of winding cultural pathways reflecting the myriad ways by which people adapted to their environment and constructed a way of life.

If a pattern leading to increasing technological complexity has been one of the cultural evolutionary pathways followed by our species and navigated in this book, it must be remembered that this has been neither the only nor the inevitable avenue traced by human beings. The trajectories seen in this book exhibit tremendous cultural diversity. Such diversity in the evolutionary pathways followed by human beings may be a key to our species' survival.

"Diversity" has become an American buzzword nowadays in an ongoing argument about what our nation has become and what it should be. Often it refers to so-called racial diversity in neighborhoods, schools, and businesses. But I mean the term to signify variation on a broader geographic and temporal scale, a worldwide and "timewide" diversity of human cultural adaptation, from Arctic hunters to tropical rainforest horticulturists, from desert wanderers to seafaring islanders, from megalith-building farmers to grassland hunters, from urban nation-states to tribal societies. It may take the collective wisdom of the cultures of all these people to ensure the survival of the species, ironically at the very time when cultural homogenization—the Westernization of the world—seems to be overtaking us.

I began this epilogue by likening the human story to a lengthy journey. Now, at last, in this book we have reached a milepost in our investigation. We have literally caught up with ourselves on the human evolutionary pathway; we have reached our present location on the trail. We can gaze back, as we have in this book, along the tortuous, serendipitous route and in the distance see, if only dimly, our ancient evolutionary ancestors. Ahead, we can imagine our species racing forward to some unknown, unfathomable point on the horizon of our future. Though the twists and turns will almost certainly bring us to a point that anthropologists have never even considered, we can all be certain of one thing: The journey will take us where no one has gone before.

KEY TERMS

orthogenesis, 636   unilineal evolution, 636

Glossary

Abejas phase   The period of time in the **Tehuacán** Valley in highland Mexico from 5400 to 4300 B.P. Characterized by increased **sedentism** and the first appearance of **domesticated** maize, beans, and squash.

absolute date   Any date where a year or range of years can be applied to a site or an artifact, as opposed to a **relative date,** where only a chronological order can be established.

accelerator mass spectrometry (AMS) dating   A variety of **radiocarbon dating.** In conventional radiocarbon dating, the amount of carbon-14 left in a sample is measured indirectly by the amount of radioactivity the sample gives off. In AMS dating, the amount of carbon-14 left in a sample is measured directly by an actual count of atoms. AMS can be applied to much smaller samples than conventional radiocarbon dating.

Acheulean handaxe   Symmetrical stone tool of the later **Lower Paleolithic.** The bifacially flaked, teardrop-shaped, all-purpose handaxe dates to as early as 1.4 million years ago in Africa. There, and after about 1.0 million B.P. in Europe, the handaxe was manufactured by members of the species *Homo erectus.*

activity area   A place where an activity or group of activities were carried out in the past. The activity area is transformed into an archaeological **feature** by the loss or discard of material items used in the activity—stone toolmaking, cooking, butchering, burial—that was carried out there.

adaptation   A mode or strategy for survival. An adaptation can be a physical characteristic; for example, the thick fur of a polar bear is a physical adaptation for life in the Arctic. Adaptation can also be a cultural behavior; for instance, the material culture of the Inuit people (Eskimos), including harpoons, igloos, parkas, and dog sleds, are their invented, cultural adaptations to life under very cold environmental conditions.

adapted   The state of being biologically or culturally prepared to survive in a given environment.

Adena   A burial-mound-building culture centered in the Ohio River valley. Beginning about 2,800 years ago, this culture developed at the **chiefdom** level of sociopolitical integration, often building impressive tombs for its chiefs.

affluent foragers   Though social, political, and economic complexity is commonly fueled by an agricultural subsistence system, the wild food resource base in some areas is so rich and abundant, complexity may develop without the adoption of food production. People who live in these resource-privileged regions are called affluent foragers. The **Jomon** of Japan and the native people of the northwest coast of North America are examples of affluent foragers.

Agricultural Revolution   Period of fundamental change in human economy marked by a shift from foraging wild foods to the production of **domesticated** plants and animals. This revolution in subsistence occurred in multiple world areas beginning after about 12,000 years ago. This term is synonymous with **Neolithic Revolution** and **Food-Producing Revolution.**

Ajalpán phase   The period of time in the **Tehuacán** Valley in highland Mexico from 3500 to 2850 B.P. Characterized by increased **sedentism** and increasing reliance on **domesticated** maize, beans, and squash, though still more than half of the diet consisted of wild foods.

Ajuereado phase   The period of time in the **Tehuacán** Valley in highland Mexico from 12,000 to 9000 B.P. Human groups in the valley lived in small, nomadic **microbands** of fewer than 10 people, subsisting on wild plant and animal foods.

altricial   The condition of being born at an immature stage of development. The term originated in ornithology to describe bird species in which hatchlings are entirely dependent on one or both parents for all of their needs for an extended period. Used here to describe a similar circumstance in hominid species, both ancient and modern.

Amratian/Naqada   Time period in predynastic Egypt. The Amratian/Naqada I represents the time period between 5,750 and 5,650 years ago in Upper Egypt (the southern part of the Egyptian realm).

anatomically modern *Homo sapiens*   Human beings anatomically indistinguishable from those living today. They are found in the paleoanthropological record dating to soon after 200,000 years ago in Africa.

Ancestral Puebloan   A prehistoric culture centered in the Four Corners region of the American Southwest. The Ancestral Puebloans sometimes constructed large and impressive structures that housed the population of the village. Formerly called Anasazi.

anthropological linguistics   The subfield of anthropology that studies language.

anthropology   The study of humanity. A broad social science with varied foci on human biological and cultural adaptations, human origins, biological and cultural evolution, and modern cultures.

arboreal   Life in the trees. **Primates,** for the most part (our species is a notable exception), possess an arboreal adaptation.

archaeological site   A place where people lived and/or worked and where the material objects that they made, used, lost, or discarded can yet be recovered and analyzed.

archaeology   The study of humanity through the analysis of the material remains of human behavior: the study of the things that people made and used in the past and that have fortuitously preserved. Archaeologists often focus on human cultural evolution.

archaeomagnetism   Orientation of the earth's magnetic field can become fixed in relatively recent cultural deposits like the sediments in a canal or the clay in bricks lining a kiln. The date of a site can be determined where that orientation points to a location of magnetic north already fixed in space and time along a geographical and chronological curve.

Archaic   The chronological period in the New World that follows the **Paleoindian** period, begins at the end of the **Pleistocene,** and represents a period of cultural adaptation to the new, postglacial environment by Native Americans.

archaic *Homo sapiens*   Extinct varieties of humanity that share much in common with modern *Homo sapiens* or **anatomically modern *Homo sapiens*** but that commonly retain primitive skeletal features and possess a somewhat smaller mean cranial capacity than do modern people. The Neandertals are the best-known archaic variety of the human race. Also called **premodern *Homo sapiens.***

articular surfaces   The surfaces of two adjacent bones marking the point at which they attach or "articulate." By examining the articular surfaces of a bone, scientists can determine the mechanics of joint movement.

artifact   Anything manufactured by a human being or human ancestor but usually a portable object like a stone spearpoint or a clay pot, as distinguished from larger, more complex archaeological **features.**

artificial selection   The process used in the **domestication** and refinement of plants and animals by which human beings select which members of a species will live and produce offspring. Humans make such decisions on the basis of their needs or desires concerning the form or behavior of the species—for example, plants that produce larger seeds, animals that produce woollier coats, or animals that produce more milk.

association   The spatial relationships among archaeological **artifacts, ecofacts,** and **features.** Objects found in proximity to each other are said to be in association.

Aurignacian   A lithic tool technology associated with anatomically modern human beings in Europe dating from 34,000 to 27,000 years ago. Includes long, narrow blade tools.

Aurignacian blade   A **blade** tool produced in the **Aurignacian** technology dating between 34,000 and 27,000 years ago.

Australian Small Tool Phase   Cultural phase beginning in Australia around 6,000 years ago and becoming widespread within about a thousand years. The phase is marked by the production of blade tools, reflecting a more efficient use of stone than in earlier technologies.

australopithecine   Any member of the genus *Australopithecus,* including several species: *anamensis, afarensis, garhi, africanus, robustus, boisei,* and *aethiopicus.* The oldest members of the genus date back to about 4.2 million years ago. The genus became extinct by 1 million years ago and was characterized by an ape-sized brain but also by the modern human behavioral trait of bipedal locomotion.

backed blade   A stone blade tool in which one edge has been dulled, or "backed," so it can more readily be held in the hand during use.

Badarian   Time period in predynastic Egypt. The Badarian represents the time period between 6,400 and 5,750 years ago in Upper Egypt (the southern part of the Egyptian realm).

barray   Large reservoir constructed by the ancient Khmer people in their elaborate ceremonial centers such as Angkor Wat and Angkor Thom. Initially resulting from sandstone quarrying for the construction materials for Khmer temples, these large depressions filled with water and probably served as reservoirs.

basicranium   The bones of the base of the cranium. Because the soft parts of hominid anatomy involved in the production of sound are connected to the base of the skull, the basicranium is a crucial part of the anatomy when assessing the ability of human ancestors to produce human speech.

Bayon   The spectacular temple complex in the center of the ancient Khmer city of Angkor Thom that is covered with images of Hindu gods, bas-reliefs, columns, and colonnades.

Beringia, or **Bering Land Bridge**   A broad piece of land, measuring more than 1,500 km (1,000 mi) from north to south, that connected northeastern Asia with northwestern North America during periods of sea-level depression in the **Pleistocene.** People living in Asia walked east across the land bridge or rafted along the land bridge coast into the lands of the Western Hemisphere at least 15,000 years ago and possibly earlier.

bipedal locomotion   The ability to walk on two feet. With a few notable exceptions (such as some dinosaurs and birds), the **hominids** are the only creatures who habitually and efficiently walk on two feet.

blade   A long, thin stone flake, commonly twice as long as it is wide, that represents an efficient use of stone, producing a high proportion of edge for the amount (weight) of stone used.

brachiating   Moving through the trees by swinging, arm over arm. Many **primates** are expert brachiators.

burin   A sharp and durable stone tool used in engraving to etch out thin slivers of antler or bone, which then were modified to make awls and needles.

C3 pathway   The photosynthetic process employed by most trees, whereby a radioactive **isotope** of carbon—^{13}C—is differentially filtered out.

C4 pathway   The photosynthetic process employed by most grasses and sedges, whereby a radioactive **isotope** of carbon—^{13}C—is more readily used than in plants that follow the **C3 pathway.**

cache   A stash of stuff placed away for safekeeping by ancient people. When the archaeologist is lucky, a cache was not returned to in the past and whatever was stored therein was not retrieved. A cache becomes the equivalent of an unintentional time capsule, providing a cluster of **artifacts** representing a single time period.

calibration curve   Curve resulting from the graphing of dendrochronologically derived dates for an extensive series of tree rings and the carbon dates determined for each of those same rings. See also **dendrochronology.**

calvarium   The top part of a skull minus the lower jaw (mandible) and facial bones.

camelid   A large, ruminant animal, including bachtrian and dromedary camels in the Old World and llamas, alpacas, guanacos, and vicuñas in the New World.

Capsian   A culture in northwestern Africa dating to after 10,000 B.P. and characterized by hunting of wild sheep, collecting of shellfish and snails, and harvesting of wild grains.

carbon dating   See **radiocarbon dating.**

carbon isotope analysis   Analysis of the proportion of ^{12}C and ^{13}C in a bone or soil sample. Useful in dietary and environmental reconstruction because different groupings of plants use carbon compounds containing ^{12}C and ^{13}C differentially.

carrying capacity   The number of organisms a given region or habitat can support without degrading the environment.

catastrophist   A person who believes that the current appearance of the earth can be explained best as having resulted from a series of natural catastrophes—for example, floods and volcanoes. Catastrophism was quite popular prior to the nineteenth century and lent support to the claim of a recent age for the earth.

central place   As used in the field of cultural geography, the geographic focal point of a political entity. A large city or ceremonial center with religious structures often are central places for **states** or **chiefdoms.**

cereals   Plants, especially grasses, that produce starchy grains. These were among the first domesticated foods produced during the **Neolithic.**

Châtelperronian   A lithic technology that includes the use of blades and appears to be intermediate in form and time between **Mousterian** and **Aurignacian.** Associated with some late populations of Neandertals following contact with modern *Homo sapiens.*

Chavin   A distinctive art style that developed in western South America beginning about 3,000 years ago. The religious iconography of Chavin seems to have served as a unifying influence, setting the stage for the later development of geographically broad empires.

Chenla Civilization in Cambodia that predates the **Khmer.** Located in the Mekong Valley near the Great Lake (Tonle Sap). Jayavarman I, the great ruler of Chenla, centralized power and control over land and labor, concentrating these in the hands of the elite class.

chiefdom A level of sociopolitical integration more complex than the tribe but less complex than the **state.** The social system is ranked, not **egalitarian.** Individuals are placed in a hierarchy of power and prestige. Chiefdoms are less rigidly structured than state societies, and a chief's power is less than that of a king or a pharaoh.

chinampas Artificial islands in lakes and swamps produced by the Aztecs of central Mexico for intensive farming.

city-state A political entity characteristic of some early civilizations, especially in **Mesopotamia.** A central population center dominates the surrounding hinterlands. The wealth of the countryside flows into the city, where it is concentrated in the hands of the elite classes.

civilization As used here, cultures exhibiting social stratification, a formal government, labor and craft specialization, a food surplus that supports a political and/or religious elite, monumental construction, and a system of record keeping.

clay tokens Small geometric shapes of clay, some bearing impressed symbols, dating back to 10,000 years ago in the Middle East that appear to represent an early system of record keeping that led ultimately to a system of writing.

Clovis A **fluted point** type of the Paleoindians. Large, laurel-leaf-shaped stone blades exhibiting a channel, or "flute" (as in a fluted column), on both faces to aid in hafting the stone point onto a wooden shaft. The channel begins at the base and generally extends from one-third to no more than one-half the length of the point. Clovis points date from about 11,500 to 10,000 B.P. (Compare to **Folsom.**)

codices (sing., codex) The screenfold books of the Maya. Written in their hieroglyphic language, the vast majority of the codices were collected and destroyed by the Spanish in A.D. 1562. Only four codices survived this tragic period of book burning.

complex foraging A system of hunting animals and gathering wild plants in which subsistence is focused on a few highly productive resources. These foods are collected and stored, allowing for a more sedentary settlement system. (Compare to **simple foragers.**)

complex societies Societies organized beyond the level of the household, family, or local community. Complex societies exhibit differences in social status, political power, and wealth.

Cordilleran The **Pleistocene** ice mass in North America centered in the Rocky Mountains.

core In stone-tool manufacturing, the stone nodule from which flakes or blades are removed. In manufacturing a core tool like an **Acheulean handaxe,** the stone nodule becomes the tool. In a core-and-blade or core-and-flake technology, the core is merely the source for numerous sharp flakes or blades that are then used as is or modified into tools.

cortex The exterior surface or rind of a **core,** usually removed in the process of stone-tool manufacturing.

courtyard groups Clusters of separate residential structures in **Hohokam** villages surrounding a common area or courtyard. Most individual villages consisted of multiple courtyard groups. Each courtyard group consisted of from 2 to 10 family residences.

Coxcatlán phase The period of time in the **Tehuacán** Valley in highland Mexico from 7000 to 5400 B.P. that is characterized by a reliance on wild foods.

cranial suture The lines of connection between cranial bones, which appear as a squiggly line on both the interior and the exterior surfaces of the skull. Cranial sutures progressively disappear with age and can be used to provide a general estimate for age at death.

craniometrics Measurement of the shape of the cranium.

cranium The bones of the head and face (excluding the lower jaw).

creationist One who believes that the universe, the earth, life, and humanity are the creation of an all-powerful god.

culture The invented, taught, and learned patterns of behavior of human groups. The extrasomatic (beyond the body or beyond the biological) means of **adaptation** of a human group.

cuneiform An early form of written records in **Mesopotamia,** involving the impression of standardized symbols on wet clay. Dating to close to 6,000 years ago, cuneiform is the earliest writing in the world.

cylinder seal   Mesopotamian system of impressing symbolic notation onto wet clay with a marked cylinder.

dagga   A high-quality, clay-based building material used in southern Africa. Dagga construction is commonly found in the homes of the people of Great Zimbabwe.

deciduous dentition   The baby teeth.

deffufa   Monumental mud-brick towers built by the inhabitants of the ancient Nubian civilization of Kerma located south of the third cataract of the Nile in modern Sudan. Kerma dates to more than 3,500 years ago.

Denali Complex   A lithic technology seen in the Arctic and consisting of **wedge-shaped cores, microblades,** bifacial knives, and **burins.** Dating to about 10,000 years ago, several features of the Denali Complex are reminiscent of elements of older complexes in northeastern Asia, particularly that of Dyuktai Cave.

dendrochronology   Tree-ring dating. By placing a tree section found at an archaeological site within a **master sequence** of tree-ring widths through time, the year when the tree died or was cut down can be determined and associated with the site.

diaphysis   The shaft of a long bone. On either end of the diaphysis is an **epiphysis.**

diastema   A gap between the teeth of both the mandible (lower jaw) and the maxilla (upper jaw). The large canine teeth of apes fit into the diastemas of their opposing jaws when those jaws are closed.

DNA (deoxyribonucleic acid)   The genetic code; the genetic instructions for each life-form on the planet.

dolmen   Standing stones found throughout western Europe, erected by the same Megalithic culture that produced Stonehenge. Though they range widely in size, dolmen can be quite tall and heavy stones that must have taken an enormous effort to move into place and then to erect.

domesticated   A plant or animal that has been altered by human beings through selective breeding. Some plants and animals have been so altered in this way, they can no longer survive without human intervention.

domestication   Through **artificial selection,** the production of new species of plants and animals that owe their existence to human intervention. Some **domesticated** species become so highly specialized to the demands of human beings that they can no longer survive and propagate without human assistance.

Early Woodland   Time period in ancient eastern North America, usually dated between 3,000 and 2,200 years ago.

ecofact   An element found in an archaeological context that exhibits human activity but that was not made by people and so is not, strictly speaking, an **artifact.** Burned wood in a fireplace, butchered animal bone in a trash pit, and charred seeds or nuts in a midden are all ecofacts.

egalitarian   Social systems in which all members of the same age/sex category are equal in the sense that they all possess the same wealth, social standing, and political influence.

einkorn   A variety of wheat, *Tripsicum monococcum,* that possesses hulled grains and was an important domesticate in the **Neolithic.** Today it is not a significant agricultural crop. (Compare to **emmer.**)

ejecta   All the material thrown out of a volcano during an eruption.

electron spin resonance dating (ESR)   A radiation-damage dating technique based on measurement of the buildup of electrons in crystalline materials. It can be applied to sites more than a few thousand years old. The upper limit of the technique is estimated to be more than 10 million years.

El Riego phase   The period of time in the **Tehuacán** Valley in highland Mexico from 9000 to 7000 B.P., which was characterized by a subsistence focus on wild plants, including squash, beans, chili peppers, amaranth, and avocado. During this period, people traveled in microbands for part of the year but gathered in macrobands in the spring and summer months.

emmer   A variety of wheat, *Tripsicum turgidum,* that became the primary stock of early agricultural wheat. It is the source of cultivated wheat in the modern world. (Compare to **einkorn.**)

enamel hypoplasia   A medical condition affecting the outside layers of teeth. Horizontal imperfections develop on the enamel in individuals who have experienced malnutrition during their early years.

endocast   A mold of the brain produced naturally when sediment enters the skull and then mineralizes. Also produced artificially by coating the inside of the skull with a latex-based material. Endocasts can exhibit features of the exterior surface of the brain.

envelope Name given to clay containers used to store **clay tokens** in the Middle East beginning 5,500 years ago. The clay tokens were of various shapes and used as an information storage system, the different shapes representing different categories of goods—jars of oil, sheep, cattle, and so on. Markings were made on the clay envelope to indicate the kind and number of tokens they contained. Ultimately, the tokens were eliminated and these markings developed into the world's first writing system.

epiphyseal fusion The **epiphyses** of each long bone join to the **diaphysis** during physical maturation. The age of death of a juvenile individual can be assessed by reference to the degree of epiphyseal fusion exhibited.

epiphysis (pl., *epiphyses*) The long-bone endcap. The epiphyses join at the ends of the **diaphysis** of each long bone.

epistemology The study of knowledge; how you know what you know.

erosion The disintegration and transportation of geological material by wind, water, or ice.

ethnoarchaeology The archaeological study of a living group of people that often focuses on the processes by which human behavior becomes translated into the archaeological record.

ethnographer A cultural anthropologist who lives among a group of people or a cultural group and interacts with them daily, often for an extended period of time, observing their behavior.

ethnographic present The ethnographic present includes that period of time when Western people have been in contact with, studying, and writing about traditional cultures.

ethnology The comparative study of culture. Ethnologists study human behavior cross-culturally, looking for similarities and differences in how people behave: how they raise their children, how they treat elders, how they organize their labor, and so forth.

evolution The systematic change through time of biological organisms or human cultural systems.

experimental replication The reproduction, under laboratory conditions, of facsimiles of archaeological artifacts. A process employed to analyze ancient technology.

faunal assemblage The animal bones found at a site and the species represented by those bones.

Fayum/Merimden Time period in predynastic Egypt. The Fayum/Merimden represents the time period between 7,200 and 6,400 years ago in Lower Egypt (the northern part of the Egyptian realm).

feature The combination of **artifacts** and/or **ecofacts** at a site, reflecting a location where some human activity took place. Features include fireplaces, **middens,** burials, cooking hearths, **activity areas,** and buildings. Also defined as nonportable, complex artifacts.

femur The upper leg bone.

Fertile Crescent A crescent-shaped region extending from the Mediterranean coast of modern Israel, Lebanon, and Syria, north into the Zagros Mountains and then south toward the Persian Gulf (see Figure 9.4), marked by an abundance of wild cereal grain at the beginning of the **Holocene epoch.** Not coincidentally, this region is where some of the world's first domestication of plants took place.

fire-cracked rock Rock that has been heated to a high temperature in, for example, a fireplace or hearth and that has fractured as a result. Large quantities of fire-cracked rock in a given location are often diagnostic of an archaeological site.

fission-track dating A radiation-damage dating technique that measures the age of an **artifact** as a function of the amount of physical damage in the form of tracks left in a material by radioactive decay.

flake A stone fragment removed from a **core** by the force of a **hammerstone,** antler baton, or pressure flaker. The flake can be discarded, used as is, or further modified for use as a specific tool.

fluted point Projectile point made by Paleoindians in the New World between 11,500 and 10,000 B.P. Exhibits a distinctive channel, or "flute" (as in a fluted column), on both faces. These channels aided in hafting the spearpoint onto its wooden shaft. The two major forms of fluted point are **Clovis** and **Folsom.**

Folsom A **fluted point** type of the Paleoindians. Generally smaller than **Clovis** points, Folsom points are also later in time, dating to after 10,000 B.P. Clovis points have been found in association with the bones of extinct elephants, whereas Folsom points have been found in association with the bones of bison. Folsom points are fluted, with the channels commonly extending nearly the entire length of the point.

Food-Producing Revolution   Period of fundamental change in human economy marked by a shift from foraging wild foods to the production of **domesticated** plants and animals. This revolution in subsistence occurred in multiple world areas beginning after about 12,000 years ago. This term is synonymous with **Neolithic Revolution** and **Agricultural Revolution.**

foraging   A subsistence system based on the collection of wild foods, including any combination of hunting wild game, gathering wild plants, fishing, and shellfish collecting.

foramen magnum   Large hole at the base or back of the skull through which veins, arteries, and nerves pass. The location of the foramen magnum in a fossil skull is an indicator of how the skull was attached to the vertebral column and, by inference, the form of locomotion employed by the creature.

foraminifera   Microscopic marine organisms whose exoskeletons are used in the analysis of the oxygen isotope ratio in seawater. This ratio varies in proportion to the amount of the earth's water that is contained in land-based ice fields.

Funan   The name given to the earliest civilization in Southeast Asia, established in Cambodia during the first century A.D. by merchants from India.

gene flow   The movement and exchange of genetic material among populations of a species through interbreeding.

gene pool   All of the genetic variants in a population.

genera (sing., *genus*)   The level in biologic taxonomy between family and species. For example, chimpanzees are classified as *Pan troglodytes,* whereas their cousins, the bonobos, are classified as *Pan paniscus;* they are members of the same taxonomic family, the Pongidae, the same genus, *Pan,* but different species, *troglodytes* and *paniscus.*

Geometric Kebaran   Pre-**Neolithic** culture in the Middle East, dating to the period 14,500–12,500 B.P. Located in the moist Mediterranean woodlands of the central **Levant** and extending into the margins of the Negev and Sinai Deserts and across southern Jordan, subsistence was based on **foraging.**

glacial   Period of ice advance during the **Pleistocene epoch.** Glacials generally last many thousands of years. Cold glacials were interrupted by equally long warmer periods called **interglacials.**

glacier   A massive body of ice that, through a number of processes, can expand and move.

glume   The case in which an individual **cereal** grain is enclosed.

glyph   A carved figure or symbol that is part of a written language.

gracile   Lightly constructed, as referring to the overall appearance of a **hominid** skeleton. Modern humans are gracile, and when the term is applied to the fossils of extinct hominids, it is in reference to their appearance relative to anatomically modern human beings. Bones that are more massive than those of modern humans are said to be **robust.**

grave goods   Cultural materials placed into a grave, sometimes in a conscious attempt to provide the deceased with items it is believed are needed in the afterlife.

Gravettian   Toolmaking tradition of the **Upper Paleolithic,** characterized by the production of small **blades** and denticulate knives (with projections, or "teeth," along the cutting edge). Dated from 27,000 to 21,000 B.P.

Halafian   A culture in Mesopotamia dating from 7500 to 6700 B.P. Halafian sites generally are small farming villages.

half-life   The amount of time it takes for half of the radioactive **isotope** in a given sample to decay into a stable form. The half-life of radiocarbon, for example, is 5,730 years and that of radioactive potassium is 1.3 billion years.

Hamburgian   A culture of the northern European **Upper Paleolithic.**

hammerstone   In stone toolmaking, the lithic tool used in percussion flaking to remove **flakes** or **blades** from a **core** or to detach additional flakes from flakes or blades.

hang-t'u   The Chinese term for stamped or pounded and compacted earth used to make structures.

haplogroup   A cluster of DNA variants that are found together in individual members of a population. Five major mitochondrial haplogroups have been identified among Native Americans; all five are also found in central and eastern Asian populations.

Harris lines   Longitudinal cracks located at the ends of long bones; indicative of dietary stress during physical development. Also called by the more descriptive term "growth arrest lines."

Hassunan   A culture in **Mesopotamia** dating from 8000 to 7200 B.P. that was characterized by small farming villages where subsistence was based on the growing of wheat, barley, peas, and lentils. Hunting supplemented the diet.

hieroglyphic   A writing system in which pictorial symbols are used to convey a particular sound, object, or idea—or some combination of these three things.

Hoabinhian   Southeast Asian **Mesolithic** stone-tool tradition based on the manufacture of tools from chipped pebbles.

Hohokam   A culture in the American Southwest centered in southern Arizona. The Hohokam people constructed irrigation canals to water the fields in which they grew maize, beans, and squash.

Holocene epoch   The recent and current geological epoch. The Holocene followed the **Pleistocene** and represents a break with glacial climates.

Holocene Warm Maximum   Period when worldwide temperatures rose beginning about 8,700 years ago. Depending on your location, temperatures were between 0.5°C (0.9°F) and 3°C (5.4°F) higher than they are currently.

hominid   Any creature believed to be in the direct human line, a member of the taxonomic family Hominidae. **Bipedal locomotion** is the common characteristic of the hominids.

Hopewell   Burial-mound-building culture centered in the Ohio River valley. Beginning about 2,200 years ago, this culture developed at the **chiefdom** level of sociopolitical integration, sometimes building impressive tombs for their chiefs. Hopewell is generally later than **Adena.**

humerus   The upper arm bone.

hypothesis   A proposed explanation for some phenomenon that may be derived initially from empirical observation of the phenomenon by the process called induction. A hypothesis must be tested; predictions are deduced about what new data must be found if the hypothesis is to be supported. When data are found that contradict these predictions, the hypothesis is rejected or modified.

Iberomaurusians   A culture in northwestern Africa dating to after 16,000 B.P. that inhabited the coastal plain and interior of modern Tunisia and Morocco. Subsistence was based on hunting wild cattle, gazelle, hartebeest, and Barbary sheep and collecting marine mollusks.

ice-free corridor (or **McKenzie corridor**)   A proposed route of safe passage between the farthest-west extent of the **Laurentide** ice field and the farthest-east extent of the **Cordilleran** glacier. Paleoindians may have traveled down this corridor from the western Arctic into the heartland of America.

ilium   The upper blade of the pelvis.

impact wear   Distinctive damage scars on stone tools that can be experimentally shown to have resulted from the tool's use as a projectile.

innominate   The left or right side of the pelvis that consists of the **ilium,** the **ischium,** and the pubis.

interglacial   A period during the **Pleistocene** when glacial ice melted and temperature ameliorated. Interglacials lasted for thousands of years and were preceded and followed by **glacials.**

interstadial   A short period during a glacial when glacial ice melted and temperature increased.

Iron Age   The final of the three periods in the National Museum of Denmark's C. J. Thomsen's **three-age system.** Period of time in human history when the iron metallurgy became the dominant technology for producing metal tools.

ischium   The bottom rear portion of the **innominate** bone of the pelvis.

isotope   A variety of an element's atomic form. Isotopes of individual elements are distinguished by the number of neutrons in their atomic nuclei. Some isotopes are unstable and decay into other forms; these are said to be radioactive. Some radioactive isotopes can be used in dating paleontological or archaeological material.

Jomon   Ancient Japanese culture dating from 13,000 years ago. The Jomon people were foragers, relying on hunting wild animals, gathering wild plants, and, especially, collecting food from the sea. The earliest pottery in the world has been found at Jomon sites dating to more than 11,000 years ago. The rich resource base exploited by the Jomon allowed for dense population and complex social patterns before their adoption of agriculture.

K/Ar dating   Potassium/argon dating. The **half-life** of radioactive potassium has been measured as 1.3 billion years. Because potassium is an abundant element in the earth's crust and argon collects in rock solely as a result of the decay of radioactive potassium, this technique is widely applicable as a form of geological dating.

Karim Shahirian   Pre-**Neolithic** culture located in the foothills of the Zagros Mountains in modern Turkey.

khipu   A record-keeping system of the Inka in which a series of knotted strings were used as mnemonic devices to help record keepers keep track of information.

Khmer   Local name given to the civilization of Southeast Asia dating to after A.D. 800. The great temple cities of Angkor Thom and Angkor Wat represent the culmination of this civilization after A.D. 1000.

Kibish formation   Ancient stratum in Ethiopia in which the Omo I and Omo II crania were found. The specific part of the stratum (Member I) in which the crania were recovered has now been dated to 195,000 years ago, making Omo I the oldest anatomically modern human cranium yet found and dated.

kiva   A structure, usually round, used in religious ceremonies by Native American societies in the Southwest. Most kivas are relatively small, but so-called Great Kivas are enormous. Casa Rinconada in Chaco Canyon, for example, is nearly 20 m (63.5 ft) across.

knapper   One who makes stone tools. To *knapp* is to make stone tools through the application of percussion and pressure.

Knossos   An enormous and impressive site representing the culmination of **Minoan** civilization. The temple at Knossos was built beginning in 3880 B.P. and at its height covered an area of about 20,000 m^2 (close to 5 acres) and had 1,000 rooms built up to three stories and, in some sections, four stories high.

Kush   The Egyptian name for the land south of their territory. Kush began at the first cataract of the Nile in southern Egypt and extended to the sixth cataract, near the modern Sudanese city of Khartoum.

lacustrine   Having to do with lakes.

Lake Forest Archaic   An **Archaic** culture of eastern North America centered in, though not restricted to, the region of the Great Lakes. Lake Forest people exploited the food resources of the large lakes of eastern North America.

Lapita   A pottery style known from the inhabited Pacific Islands. The movement of people from the western to the eastern Pacific can be traced by the presence and spread of Lapita pottery.

Late Gerzean   Time period in predynastic Egypt. The Late Gerzean (Nagada II) represents the time period between 5,400 and 5,300 years ago in Upper Egypt (the southern part of the Egyptian realm). The Late Gerzean (Maadian) represents the time period between 5,400 and 5,300 years ago in Lower Egypt (the northern part of the Egyptian realm).

Laurentide   The massive continental ice sheet of **Pleistocene** North America, centered in central northeastern Canada.

legume   A large family of flowering plants, all of which produce fruits that grow in the form of a pod that splits along its seams when mature and opens to reveal the seeds. Garden peas, snap beans, lima beans, lentils, and chickpeas are all legumes domesticated during the **Neolithic.**

Levallois   Stone tool technology involving the production of consistently shaped flakes from carefully prepared **cores.** Levallois technology is associated with archaic forms of *Homo sapiens.*

Levant   The name applied to the areas along the eastern shore of the Mediterranean, including present-day Greece, Turkey, Syria, Lebanon, Israel, and Egypt.

Levantine Corridor   A natural geographic passageway of low-lying land hugging the eastern margin of the Mediterranean, linking Africa, Asia, and Eurasia.

Linienbandkeramik (LBK)   An early **Neolithic** culture of central Europe dating to about 6500 B.P. The subsistence base was domesticated **emmer** wheat, barley, and pulses.

lintels   Horizontal cross-members of the Stonehenge monument. The 30 lintels at Stonehenge rest on top of and connect the 30 upright **sarsens.**

littoral   Related to the seashore.

logistical collecting   A settlement-subsistence strategy that involves the movement of a group in a fixed seasonal round. Logistical collectors plan the movements of their settlements to coincide with the availability of food resources in their territory.

Lower Paleolithic   Period from 2.5 million years ago to 250,000 years ago that encompasses the stone tool industries of *Homo habilis* and *Homo erectus.*

luminescence dating   Determining the age of an object by releasing as light the energy it has accumulated since a fixed point in time. The amount of light it emits in this process is directly proportional to its age. Light (**optically stimulated luminescence**) or heat (**thermoluminescence**) can be used to release this energy.

Lung-shan   A Chinese culture that followed the **Neolithic Yang-shao.** Dated to 5000 B.P., Lung-shan sites are larger, with evidence of substantial **hang-t'u** construction. Lung-shan cemeteries have produced clear evidence of a socioeconomically stratified society. Lung-shan laid the foundation for China's first complex state, the Shang.

Maadian   Time period in predynastic Egypt. The Late Gerzean (Maadian) represents the time period between 5,400 and 5,300 years ago in Lower Egypt (the northern part of the Egyptian realm).

macrobands Hunter-gatherers often arrange themselves into communities or "bands" of 25 to 75 people. A group of bands of people who interact on a regular basis—they may intermarry, conduct group hunts, share resources—is called a macroband. Compare to **microbands.**

Magdelanian **Upper Paleolithic** culture in Europe dating from 16,000 to 11,000 B.P. Known from sites primarily in France and Spain, Magdelanian material culture included finely made barbed harpoons, carved decorative objects, and cave paintings.

Maglemosian An early **Mesolithic** culture of Europe adapted to a forest and lakeside environment. The famous site of Star Carr is a Maglemosian site.

mandible The lower jaw. (Compare to **maxilla.**)

Maritime Archaic An **Archaic** period culture of northeastern North America centered along the coast of northern New England and the Canadian Maritime provinces. The subsistence focus was on the sea, fishing and hunting sea mammals. Burials with elaborate grave goods mark the Maritime Archaic.

mastaba Mud-brick structures built over the tombs of the deceased members of a developing elite class in Egypt before the pharaohs. They became larger through time, were stacked on top of each other, and ultimately evolved into the pyramid tomb emblematic of ancient Egyptian civilization.

master sequence The regional pattern of yearly variation in tree-ring width. The master sequence for the American West extends back close to 11,000 years ago. When an archaeological tree-ring section can be placed within the master sequence, it can be dated directly, and this date can be associated with the archaeological site at which it was found.

Mast Forest Archaic An **Archaic**-period culture of northeastern North America centered in central and southern New England. Subsistence focus was on the interior forest of New England, especially on the resources of the mast forest: nut foods such as acorn, hickory, chestnut, and walnut, and animals, especially deer.

mattock A digging tool with a working blade set at right angles to the handle. Antler mattocks have been found in European **Mesolithic** sites such as Star Carr.

maxilla The upper jaw. (Compare to **mandible.**)

McKenzie corridor See **ice-free corridor.**

megafauna Very large animals; commonly used to describe the large, now-extinct herbivores of the **Pleistocene** world.

megaliths Large stone monuments. The Megalithic culture erected thousands of these monuments beginning more than 5,000 years ago. Stonehenge is the most famous of the Megalithic monuments.

Melanesia Islands located north of New Guinea in the western Pacific.

Mesolithic The culture period after the Paleolithic and before the **Neolithic;** a period of the proliferation of many regional adaptations and an explosion of local cultural diversity.

Mesopotamia The land between the Tigris and Euphrates Rivers in modern Iraq. The world's first cities and complex civilization developed in Mesopotamia.

metatarsal Any of the long bones of the feet, located between the bones of the ankles and the toes.

microbands Small cohabiting groups, commonly 10 to 15 people, who move together seasonally and nomadically. (Compare to **macrobands.**)

microblade A very small stone blade, often with very sharp cutting edges. Groups of microblades often were set into wooden, bone, or antler handles.

microcephaly A congenital condition characterized by a very small head and incomplete development of the brain. Some suggested, at least initially, that the cranium found on the island of Flores and called the Hobbit was not an ancestral form of hominid but a pathological individual, a victim of microcephaly.

microlith A very small stone tool. Microliths were usually used in groups, set into wood, bone, or antler handles.

Micronesia Small islands in the western Pacific, east of New Guinea.

midden An archaeological **feature** that consists of a refuse heap. A preserved pile of trash, often food remains.

Middle Paleolithic The Middle Stone Age, the period after the **Lower Paleolithic** and before the **Upper Paleolithic.** Covers the span from 250,000 to 40,000 years ago and includes the cultures of premodern and modern varieties of human beings.

Middle Woodland Time period in ancient eastern North America, usually dated between 2,200 and 1,600 years ago.

Minoan The name given by Sir Arthur Evans to the early European civilization that evolved on the island of Crete. The temple at **Knossos** is the best-known manifestation of this culture.

Miocene epoch   The period of time from 25 million years ago to 5 million years ago. Forests were more extensive during the Miocene than they are today. A broad array of **arboreally** adapted ape species thrived during this epoch; most became extinct at the end of the Miocene, when the forests diminished in geographic extent.

mitochondrial DNA (mtDNA)   Genetic material located in the mitochondria of cells. Analysis of mtDNA has proven useful in assessing evolutionary relationships among existing species.

mobiliary art   Art that is portable. Mobiliary art made during the **Upper Paleolithic** includes **Venus figurines,** animal carvings, and geometrically incised bone and antler.

Mogollon   A prehistoric culture located in the American Southwest, centered in the uplands of New Mexico and northeastern Mexico. The Mogollon people grew maize, beans, and squash, relying mostly on rainfall agriculture.

monumental works   Large-scale communal construction projects characteristic of complex societies.

morphology   Literally, the study of form. An analysis of the shape and form of skeletons or **artifacts.**

mosaic   Environments characterized by patches of different habitats rather than a single, homogeneous habitat. It is believed that the first **hominids** lived in a mosaic environment characterized by a mixture of woodlands and savannas.

Mousterian   The stone-tool tradition of the Neandertals and early anatomically modern human beings. A **core-and-flake** technology in which a series of different, standardized tool types were produced from stone flakes struck from cores.

Movius line   Geographic boundary, running through central India, that marks the break between the manufacture of handaxes by *Homo erectus* populations to the west and less symmetrical chopping tools to the east.

multiregional (or **regional continuity**) **model**   The view that anatomically modern *Homo sapiens* evolved from premodern humans in several regions simultaneously.

musculoskeletal hypertrophy   Great size and associated strength in the muscles and bones of a species or individual. Among recent human ancestors, the Neandertals exhibit an extreme level of musculoskeletal hypertrophy.

Mushabian   Pre-**Neolithic** culture located in the steppe and arid zones of the Negev and Sinai Deserts in modern Israel and Egypt. Contemporary with the **Geometric Kebaran,** dating from 14,500 to 12,500 B.P.

Mycenaeans   A southern European civilization that followed the **Minoans** and preceded the Greeks.

Naqada II   Time period in predynastic Egypt. The Early Gerzean/Nagada II represents the time period between 5,650 and 5,300 years ago in Upper Egypt (the southern part of the Egyptian realm).

Naqada III   Time period in predynastic Egypt. The Nagada III represents the time period between 5,300 and 5,100 years ago in both Upper (southern) and Lower (northern) Egypt.

Natufian   A Middle Eastern culture dated from 13,000 to 9000 B.P., located in the Mediterranean woodland zone. The Natufian reliance on wild wheat and barley set the stage for the **Neolithic.**

natural selection   The process proposed by Charles Darwin for how species evolve: Those individuals in a species that possess advantageous characteristics are more likely to survive, have offspring, and pass on those characteristics to those offspring than are individuals that do not possess them.

Nenana Complex   Perhaps the oldest stone tool complex identified in Alaska dating from 11,800 to 11,000 B.P. Predating the **Denali Complex,** Nenana includes bifacially flaked, unfluted spearpoints. Nenana bifaces are similar and perhaps related to tools made in eastern Russia about 11,300 years ago.

Neolithic   The "New Stone Age." In the past, Neolithic was defined on the basis of the appearance of ground-stone tools as opposed to chipped-stone tools. Today, Neolithic refers to the period after 12,000 years ago when food producing through the domestication of plants and animals replaced foraging as the dominant mode of subsistence.

Neolithic Revolution   Period of fundamental change in human economy marked by a shift from foraging wild foods to the production of **domesticated** plants and animals. This revolution in subsistence occurred in multiple world areas beginning after about 12,000 years ago. This term is synonymous with **Agricultural Revolution** and **Food-Producing Revolution.**

neoteny   The apparent retention, in adults of one species, of juvenile physical characteristics of an evolutionarily related species. For example, physical features of adult human beings are similar to those of juvenile chimpanzees, which is an indication of our species neoteny.

neutron activation analysis Form of **trace element analysis.** The precise and unique chemical make-up of numerous raw material sources have been determined through neutron activation analysis. Archaeological **artifacts** can be analyzed for their chemical makeup as well. When the artifact's chemistry matches that of a source area, it is concluded that the ancient people obtained the material from the chemically matching source.

New Temple Period The culture period for **Minoan** Crete dating from 3650 to 3420 B.P. It followed a catastrophic earthquake that badly damaged the temple at **Knossos** and marks a florescence of Minoan culture.

niche The actual physical area occupied by an organism as well as its functional role in a community of organisms. Sometimes referred to as an organism's ecological address.

Nubia The territory south of the ancient Egyptian nation, primarily between the first and sixth cataracts of the Nile, from southern Egypt to Sudan. The ancient Egyptians called this area **Kush.**

nuclear DNA The genetic instructions contained in the nucleus of the cell that determine the biological makeup of the organism.

object piece In the manufacturing of stone tools, the stone that is being worked through the application of either percussion or pressure.

obsidian hydration A dating method based on the rate at which a freshly exposed surface of obsidian begins to alter physically by chemically combining with water in the air or soil. The thickness of the hydration layer that develops in a given environment is a factor of time.

obtrusiveness Term that describes the archaeological record. People who lived in permanent settlements and built large structures from durable raw material produce a highly obtrusive archaeological record. People who are nomadic and make only small objects from impermanent material produce sites that are much less obtrusive. Archaeologists design surveys for a region, in part, on the level of archaeological obtrusiveness.

occipital The area at the rear of the skull. In ancient **hominids,** the occipital area tends to be massive and **robust.** In anatomically modern human beings, the occipital tends to be smooth and **gracile.**

Oldowan The earliest stone tools, simple chopping tools and sharp flakes, dated to 2.4 million years ago, that were probably made by *Homo habilis.*

Olmec An ancient culture of lowland Mesoamerica dating to 3,200 years ago. The Olmec produced a number of large ceremonial centers where they created great earthworks, finely carved jade sculptures, and massive basalt carvings of human heads. The religious iconography of Olmec art seems to have served as a unifying element in ancient Mesoamerica.

Omari A Time period in predynastic Egypt. The Omari A represents the time period between 5,750 and 5,650 years ago in Lower Egypt (the northern part of the Egyptian realm).

opportunistic foragers Groups that follow a subsistence pattern in which they take advantage of whatever resources become available without much patterning or planning in advance.

optically stimulated luminescence Method of **luminescence dating** in which the time-dependent energy stored in an archaeological specimen is released by the application of laser light.

orthogenesis The invalid notion of a predestined and progressive pattern of evolutionary change.

osteological Related to bones.

osteological comparative collection A bone library; a collection of bones used as models to aid in identifying the bones (species, sex, anatomical part) recovered in a paleontological or archaeological excavation.

paleoanthropology Anthropological study of the evolution of our species. Paleoanthropologists study the skeletal remains and cultures of ancient hominids.

Paleo-Arctic tradition Stone-tool tradition in the Arctic dating to the period before 9,000 years ago. The technology involved the production of **microblades** detached from **wedge-shaped cores.**

paleoecological Reference to the relationship between an ancient organism and its environment.

Paleoindian The period and culture in the New World dating from about 11,500 B.P. to about 10,000 B.P. **Fluted points** are the most distinctive element in the Paleoindian stone **tool kit.** Paleoindians hunted the late **Pleistocene** megafauna of the New World as part of their subsistence pattern.

paleomagnetic dating A dating method based on the movement of the earth's magnetic poles.

paleopathology   The study of ancient disease, trauma, or dietary deficiency, of which hominid skeletons often bear evidence.

palynology   The identification of plants through the remains of their pollen grains. Pollen is morphologically species-specific; the pollen grains of each species are recognizably different from the pollen of all other plant species. Recovery at an **archaeological site** of the preserved pollen of particular species allows for the reconstruction of the plant community present when the site was occupied, which can, in turn, inform us of the climate at the time.

paradigm   An overarching perspective, a broad view that underlies a scientific discipline.

parietal art   Art on the walls of a cave, like the cave paintings of the **Upper Paleolithic.**

pastoralists   People who raise and tend livestock, such as sheep or cattle, as the focus of their subsistence.

pedestrian survey   A systematic walkover of an area in the search for archaeological remains. A pedestrian survey is a useful tool in the search for sites especially where ancient people built structures with durable materials, where natural processes did not cover up materials on the ground, and where natural or cultural processes have exposed buried layers on the surface.

Peiligang   Earliest **Neolithic** culture in northern China, with well-established farming villages dating to 8,500–7,000 years ago.

pelagic   Anything related to or that lives in the open sea, far from shore.

petroglyph   A design etched into a rock face. Darker, weathered rock surface is removed, creating a design or pattern by exposing lighter-colored rock beneath.

photosynthesis pathways   Different specific modes of photosynthesis that various plant groups employ in the production of energy from sunlight. Most trees employ one such photosynthesis pathway (called **C3**); most grasses another (called **C4**).

phylogeny   The evolutionary histories of different kinds of organisms and their relationships to each other. A phylogeny can be a chart showing the evolutionary connections among organisms as well as the timing of those connections.

phytolith   Microscopic, inorganic particles produced by plants. Phytoliths are extremely durable and species-specific. Enormous databases have been compiled allowing researchers to identify the species from which the phytoliths originated.

pit-houses   Semisubterranean houses constructed by the ancient inhabitants of the American Southwest. Pit-houses commonly were circular pole-and-mud-covered residences.

Pleistocene epoch   The geological epoch beginning about 1.7 million years ago and ending about 10,000 years ago. It was marked by a succession of colder periods, or **glacials,** interrupted by warmer periods, or **interglacials.**

Pliocene   Geological epoch of the Tertiary Period, following the **Miocene epoch** and preceding the **Pleistocene epoch** of the Quaternary Period. The Pliocene is defined as beginning about 5 million years ago and lasting until about 1.7 million years ago.

pluvial   A period of increased rainfall in areas far south of large glacial masses during the **Pleistocene.**

pollen   Pollen grains are the male gametes in plant sexual reproduction. They are durable and morphologically species-specific. When they are preserved at or near an **archaeological site** and recovered from the same stratigraphic level as a site, it is possible to construct a general picture of the local plant community present when the location was occupied.

pollen rain   The overall count or percentage of pollens of different plant species falling at a particular place and time.

Polynesia   Islands of the central and eastern Pacific; they are volcanic in origin.

pongid   A member of the taxonomic family Pongidae; an ape.

postcranial   Referring to the skeleton, all of the bones below the cranium.

potlatch   Celebrations held by chiefs among the native peoples of the northwest coast of North America in which much of their wealth—in the form of food, animals skins and furs, and so on—is distributed to members of the group. Potlatches allowed for the redistribution of wealth, conferred increased status on chiefs, and, at the same time, prevented individual chiefs from accumulating a permanent reservoir of wealth.

preform   A partially worked **core, flake,** or **blade.** In a preform, the first general steps have been made in producing a tool.

premodern *Homo sapiens*   Extinct varieties of humanity that share much in common with modern

Homo sapiens or **anatomically modern** *Homo sapiens* but that commonly retain primitive skeletal features and possess a smaller mean cranial capacity than modern people. The Neandertals are the best-known premodern variety or subspecies of the human race. Also called **archaic** *Homo sapiens.*

primary refuse Archaeological artifacts and ecofacts left at the place they were used or produced.

primate A member of the taxonomic order Primates: prosimians, monkeys, and apes. An animal with grasping hands and feet, stereoscopic vision, and a relatively large brain (in proportion to body size). Most, but not all, primates have nails instead of claws, tails, and an **arboreal** adaptation.

primatologist A person who studies **primates.**

prognathous Having a forward-thrusting lower face. Apes are prognathous, as are extinct **hominids. Anatomically modern human beings** tend to have flat, nonprognathous faces.

pubic symphysis The point of articulation between the two pubic bones of the pelvis. Changes in the appearance of the pubic symphysis occur fairly regularly during an individual's life and so can be used to determine the age of death.

pueblo Apartment-house-type structure of the ancient, and some modern, inhabitants of the American Southwest that were constructed of adobe brick, rubble, and shaped stone.

pumice A light and porous volcanic rock. Pumice forms when a glassy molten froth cools and solidifies quickly.

punctuated equilibrium A mode of evolution in which long periods of stasis or equilibrium in a species are interrupted by short, relatively rapid bursts (punctuations) of great change, producing a new species.

Purrón phase The period of time in the **Tehuacán** Valley in highland Mexico from 4300 to 3500 B.P. Little is known about this period in terms of subsistence. Pottery was used for the first time by valley inhabitants.

pyroclastic A swiftly flowing mass of ash, molten rock, and gas spewing from an erupting volcano. Essentially a burning avalanche, the pyroclastic flow that overwhelmed the Roman cities of Pompeii and Herculaneum traveled at speeds of up to 200 kmh (almost 125 mph).

Qadan Sites along the Nile in Egypt dating to the period 15,000 to 11,000 years ago. Evidence at Qadan sites shows a reliance on fishing, hunting, and the collection of wild grains. **Micro-blades** found at Qadan sites exhibit polish that may indicate their use in the harvesting of wild **cereal** crops.

rachis The area of attachment between seeds and other seeds or between seeds and other parts of the plant. A brittle rachis is an adaptive feature under natural conditions, but because it makes harvesting more difficult, it is selected against by humans through **artificial selection.**

radiocarbon dating **Radiometric** dating technique based on the decay of a radioactive isotope of carbon: ^{14}C, or radiocarbon. Carbon dating can be applied to virtually anything that was once part of a living organism, within a range from about 300 to 40,000 years ago. Also called **carbon dating.**

radiometric Referring to any dating technique based on the measurement of radioactive decay.

rank societies Societies characterized by a few sociopolitical levels filled by a relatively small number of people.

regal-ritual cities Term used by archaeologist David Webster (2002) to describe Maya population centers. These centers were the home of Maya nobility and served also as the central location for Maya religion and ritual.

relative date A date that places a fossil or an archaeological site or artifact in a sequence with other specimens but does not allow for the assignment of an age in terms of years or even a range of years. (Compare to **absolute date.**)

remote sensing A procedure that allows for the discovery of archaeological sites or artifacts without digging and that may include aerial photography and a number of technologies that allow for scanning below ground without disturbing the soil (proton magnetometry, electrical resistivity survey, and ground penetrating radar).

replacement model The view that anatomically modern *Homo sapiens* evolved from premodern humans in one place at one time (usually Africa between 100,000 and 200,000 years ago) and spread out from that point of origin, replacing premodern human beings as they encountered them especially in Asia and Europe.

robust A term applied to skeletal features that are heavily built.

Rosetta Stone Discovered in 1799, the Rosetta Stone bore the same message in three scripts: Greek and two versions of the written language of ancient

Egypt, demotic and hieroglyphic. The Greek on the stone was known when the stone was discovered and provided, therefore, a key to deciphering the Egyptian written language.

sagittal crest   A ridge of bone that runs along the top of the skull from front to back and that provides added surface area for the attachment of powerful temporalis muscles that attach to the jaws. Male gorillas and some ancient hominid fossils possess a sagittal crest.

Sahul   The land mass of "Greater Australia," including Australia proper, New Guinea, and Tasmania. During periods of **glacial** maxima in the **Pleistocene,** these three islands were combined in the single land mass of Sahul.

Samarran   Neolithic culture of southern **Mesopotamia** dating to after 7500 B.P. Samarran sites are located on the floodplain of the Tigris and Euphrates Rivers. There is evidence of communal works, including the construction of irrigation canals, fortification walls, and communal grain storage structures.

sarsen   The 30 upright stones at Stonehenge are called the sarsens. Each sarsen is over 4 m (13 ft) tall and weighs 25,000 kg (55,000 lb).

savanna   Grasslands. The replacement of the **Miocene** forests of Africa with savannas set the stage for the success of an upright primate adapted for life under conditions of flat, open expanses and few trees.

scapulimancy   A process of divining the future, popular in ancient China, in which the scapulae (shoulder blades) of animals are burned and the pattern of burning and breakage is "read" by a diviner.

seal   A carved or molded symbol (on a ring, stamp, or cylinder) that was impressed into soft clay to leave one's official mark. Used in early **Mesopotamia** as a system of record keeping. (See also **cylinder seal.**)

secondarily altricial   Human infants are born at an advanced—precocial—state in terms of sensory and brain development but at an immature and dependent—**altricial**—state physically. This combined condition is labeled secondarily altricial.

secondary refuse   Archaeological **artifacts** and **ecofacts** that were removed by the people who made, used, or produced them from the place where they were made, used, or produced to a designated refuse area or areas—for example, a trash pile or pit.

sedentism   A pattern of settlement in which a community of people tends to remain in one place over the course of a year or years. A sedentary settlement pattern differs from nomadism, in which a community may move seasonally, following the availability of resources.

seedbed selection   Process wherein the seeds of wild plants are tended in planted seedbeds. As later-germinating and slower-growing plants are weeded out of the seedbed, plants that sprout and grow quickly because they have larger seeds and thinner seed coats are selected for unintentionally. This can be a first step in the domestication of plants.

settlement pattern   The location, size, function, and seasonality of the various communities or activity areas within a given cultural system. The pattern of land use.

sexual dimorphism   Differences in the form and size of the two sexes. Among most **primates,** the male tends to be larger and physically more powerful than the female.

simple foragers   Hunters and gatherers with no particular focus on or commitment to any one food source.

Sinagua   Literally "without water," refers to a prehistoric culture group in the American Southwest, especially in central Arizona.

site   A place where people lived and/or worked and where the physical evidence of their existence, in the form of **artifacts, ecofacts,** and **features,** can be or has been recovered.

social stratification   A pattern of social integration in which individuals are placed into a hierarchy of social levels. The presence of a hierarchy of differences in status and wealth in a society.

Solutrean   The stone-toolmaking tradition of the European **Upper Paleolithic** dating from 21,000 to 16,000 B.P. Solutrean bifaces include exquisitely made, symmetrical, leaf-shaped projectile points.

spear-thrower   A tool used to increase the range and accuracy of the hand-thrown spear. It is a straight rod or board with a hook at one end that articulates with the end of the spear and effectively increases the length of the arm of the individual throwing the spear.

specialization of labor   A cultural pattern in which some individuals can focus all or most of their labors on some specialty: metalworking, pottery manufacturing, stoneworking, weaving, architectural design, and so on. By specializing, these individuals can become quite proficient at their craft, art, or science. The specialization of labor is characteristic of complex civilizations.

stadial   A short period of increased glaciation. Stadials can occur during either **glacials** or **interglacials** and are separated by **interstadials.**

starch grains   Small fragments of starch produced by plants. Starch grain shapes are unique to individual plant species. As a result, when starch grains preserve on tools used to process plants, they can be recovered and the plant species identified.

state   A class society, often rigidly stratified into social levels. The ruling class controls the populace not by consensus but by coercion and force. The rulers in a state society have the powers to levy and collect taxes, to establish and enforce laws, and to conscript people to do the work of the state.

stratigraphic (stratigraphy)   Related to the geological or cultural layer in which something has been found. Stratigraphic layering represents a relative sequence of geological time and/or cultural chronology.

striking platform   Where a stone **core** or worked **flake** is struck with a **hammerstone** or antler hammer to remove a flake.

Sunda (or Sundaland)   The combined land mass of the modern islands of Java, Sumatra, Bali, and Borneo. These islands became a single, continuous land mass during periods of glaciation and attendant lowered sea level during the **Pleistocene.**

supraorbital torus   A continuous, projecting ridge of bone above and across the eye orbits. Commonly seen in modern apes and in ancient hominids, it is lacking in anatomically modern human beings, though less conspicuous brow ridges are present in some individuals.

system of record keeping   Any symbolic system that usually, but not always, involves some form of writing for keeping track of economic transactions, historical events, religious rules, and the like. A fundamental need in complex civilizations.

talus   A large bone in the ankle that articulates the tibia with the bones of the foot.

taphonomic   Referring to how materials become part of the paleontological or archaeological record.

taphonomy   The study of how materials become part of the paleontological or archaeological record.

taro   Tropical plant with edible roots and leaves.

Tehuacán   A valley in central highland Mexico that was the focus of a multidisciplinary research project that produced important archaeological data concerning the **domestication** of plants in the New World, particularly the domestication of maize and squash.

teosinte   The wild ancestor of **domesticated** maize; grew and grows wild throughout the American tropics. The mutation of a very few teosinte genes changes the spikey stem, with its small, encased seeds, into a cob with a larger number of bigger, naked kernels.

test pit   A hole or boring into soil in the search for archaeological evidence. In some parts of the world, a pattern of test pits spread out across an area is a primary method by which archaeological sites are searched for and by which the spatial distribution of buried materials at a site is first identified.

thermoluminescence (TL)   A trapped-charge, radiation-damage technique for dating archaeological objects. Energy produced by natural radiation in soil becomes stored in nearby objects. The amount of stored energy is a function of the background radiation level (which can be measured) and time. Once the level of background radiation at a particular place is known, how much has accumulated in an archaeological object can be measured, and from that the age of the object (how long it has been accumulating the energy) can be determined.

tholoi   An architectural form seen at **Halafian** sites in **Mesopotamia** dating to after 7500 B.P. Tholoi appear to have been communal storage facilities for **Neolithic** people and may also have served as burial chambers for a growing class of socioeconomically important individuals.

three-age system   The chronological breakdown of the history of human culture into a Stone Age, a Bronze Age, and an Iron Age, developed in 1836 by J. C. Thomsen, of the Danish National Museum, as part of a guidebook for the archaeological collections at the Danish National Museum.

three-dimensional computed tomography   Technique for producing a three-dimensional virtual image. This technique has been used to produce a virtual image of the interior of hominid crania and, in this way, a three-dimensional image of the exterior surface of hominid brains, which can then be compared to the brain of modern *Homo sapiens.*

tibia   The larger of the two long bones making up the lower leg; the shin bone.

token   Small pieces of shaped clay (southwest Asia) or inscribed tags of bone or ivory (Egypt) that represent early steps in the development of a written language. The clay tokens of southwest Asia date to 9,000 years ago and appear to have been used to tabulate amounts of goods.

tool kit   A set of tools used together in performing a single task (for example, a butchering tool kit for dismembering an animal carcass). A tool kit can also refer to the entire range of tools used at a particular site or during a given time period or produced by a particular group of hominids.

totem pole   A wooden pole, along which have been carved and painted the images of animals or mythical beasts that are a family's or clan's symbol, or "totem." Totem poles are emblematic of the native peoples of the northwest coast of North America.

trace element analysis   Determining the geographic source of the materials used by an ancient people through the analysis of small, or trace, concentrations of elements or chemicals in those raw materials. The levels measured in archaeological artifacts are compared to the levels present in various possible sources. Where the concentrations in an artifact and a source closely match, it is suggested that the prehistoric people obtained the raw material from that source.

trilithon   Set of three stones, two uprights and one lintel, at Stonehenge. There are five trilithons at Stonehenge. The largest of the trilithon uprights stand about 8 m (24 ft) above the surface, with an additional 2 m (6 ft) of stone nestled in the ground. The largest of the trilithon uprights weighs 45,000 kg (nearly 100,000 lb) and the associated lintel weighs 9,000 kg (nearly 20,000 lb).

tuber   A relatively short, fleshy, usually underground stem of a plant, often rich in starch and carbohydrates. Tubers have long contributed to the human food quest.

tumuli (sing., *tumulus*)   An artificial pile of earth, often placed over an individual's grave.

Ubaid   The name given to the culture of southern **Mesopotamia** at 6300 B.P. Irrigation canals constructed by the Ubaidic people made agriculture possible, and larger settlements grew up in the Mesopotamian floodplain at this time. Evidence of the growing power of the religious elite is seen at Ubaidic sites, with wealth becoming concentrated in the temples.

ulna   One of the bones of the forearm. The ulna is the more interior bone, closer to the body, whereas the radius is the more exterior bone (on the thumb side).

Umm Dabaghiyah   A **Neolithic** culture in northern **Mesopotamia** dating to more than 8,000 years ago and characterized by a subsistence base of wheat, barley, sheep, and goats. Hunting was still important, and their settlements were small.

uniformitarianism   The belief that the appearance of the earth could be understood as resulting from the slow action of known processes over a very long period of time. This belief, first championed in the late eighteenth and early nineteenth centuries, allowed for a great age of the earth.

unilineal evolution   Discredited view that all cultures pass through the same stages of development and that some cultures may become stuck at a given stage.

Upper Paleolithic   The final phase of the Paleolithic, dating to after 40,000 years ago and associated with anatomically modern human beings in Europe.

varve   Layers of sediment laid down annually in a body of water, usually a lake. Varves may preserve evidence of yearly fluctuations in the environmental conditions in and around the body of water in which they were deposited.

Venus figurines   **Upper Paleolithic** sculptures of females, often, but not always, with exaggerated secondary sexual characteristics. They have been found in geographic clusters in western, central, and eastern Europe, usually dated to the narrow time span between 25,000 and 23,000 years ago.

visibility   In archaeological terms, a measure of the degree to which natural processes serve to expose or hide archaeological material in a given region. A dry area with little vegetation and few or slow-acting processes of soil formation has high visibility. An area with lots of vegetation and quick soil formation and rapid deposition has low visibility. Archaeologists design surveys for a region, in part, on the level of archaeological visibility.

Wallacea   The name given to the sea over the **Wallace Trench.**

Wallace Trench   An undersea chasm located between New Guinea/Australia and Java/Borneo and nearly 7,500 m (25,000 ft) deep. It was not breached during periods of lowered Pleistocene sea levels, so population movement from southeast Asia to **Sahul** was accomplished, of necessity, via water.

wear patterns   Characteristic and diagnostic traces of damage or polish left on stone tools as a result of their use. Analysis of wear patterns can often tell the researcher how a tool was used and on what material.

weathering The decomposition and disintegration of rock, usually at or near the earth's surface.

wedge-shaped cores **Cores** shaped like wedges from which blades are struck; found as part of the **Paleo-Arctic tradition** in northeastern Asia and also found as part of the **Denali Complex** in the American Arctic.

X-ray fluorescence A technique for identifying the chemical makeup of a raw material. For example, each chemical element in the raw material of an **artifact**—for example, a flint spearpoint—gives off a unique set of energies when bombarded with X-rays. The energies released can be read and then used to determine the precise elemental composition of the raw material. The geographic source of the raw material can be determined when its composition as determind by X-ray fluorescence is

similar to the composition of a possible source determined in the same way.

Yang-shao An early **Neolithic** culture of China, dating to about 7000 B.P. Yang-shao settlements appear to have been planned out. Subsistence was based on the cultivation of foxtail millet. Domesticated rice, initially a minor dietary component, becomes an important part of the diet at this time.

Younger Dryas The name given in Europe to a cold period that lasted from 12,600 years ago to 11,450 years ago. Though a relatively short interlude of renewed glacial expansion during a general warming trend at the end of the **Pleistocene,** the Younger Dryas may have been severe enough to have caused the temporary abandonment by humans of much of northwest Europe.

Zarzian A pre-**Neolithic** culture identified in the foothills of the Zagros Mountains in Turkey.

References

Adams, Richard E. W. 1991. *Prehistoric Mesoamerica.* Norman: University of Oklahoma Press.

Adams, R. McC., and H. J. Nissen. 1972. *The Uruk Countryside.* Chicago: University of Chicago Press.

Adovasio, J., O. Soffer, and B. Klíma. 1996. Upper Paleolithic fibre technology: Interlaced woven finds from Pavlov I, Czech Republic, c. 26,000 years ago. *Antiquity* 70:269.

Adovasio, J. M., J. Donahue, and R. Stuckenrath. 1990. The Meadowcroft Rockshelter radiocarbon chronology—1975–1990. *American Antiquity* 55:348–53.

Adovasio, J. M., et al. 1979–80a. Meadowcroft Rockshelter—Retrospect 1977: Part 1. *North American Archaeologist* 1(1):3–44.

———. 1979–80b. Meadowcroft Rockshelter—Retrospect 1977: Part 2. *North American Archaeologist* 1(2):99–138.

Agenbroad, Larry D. 1988. Clovis people: The human factor in the Pleistocene megafauna extinction question. In *Americans Before Columbus: Ice-Age Origins,* edited by R. C. Carlisle. 63–74. Vol. 12 of Ethnology Monographs. Pittsburgh: University of Pittsburgh.

Agnew, N., and M. Demas. 1998. Preserving the Laetoli footprints. *Scientific American* 279(3):44–55.

Ahler, S. R. 1993. Stratigraphy and radiocarbon chronology of Modoc Rockshelter, Illinois. *American Antiquity* 58:462–89.

Aiello, L. C. 1994. Variable but singular. *Nature* 368:399–400.

Aiello, L. C., and M. Collard. 2001. Our newest oldest ancestor? *Nature* 410:526–27.

Allchin, Bridget, and Raymond Allchin. 1982. *The Rise of Civilization in India and Pakistan.* Cambridge: Cambridge University Press.

Allison, Marvin J. 1984. Paleopathology in Peruvian and Chilean populations. In *Paleopathology at the Origins of Agriculture,* edited by M. N. Cohen and G. J. Armelagos. 515–29. New York: Academic Press.

Allsworth-Jones, P. 1990. The Szeletian and the stratigraphic succession in central Europe and adjacent areas: Main trends, recent results, and problems for resolution. In *The Emergence of Modern Humans: An Archaeological Perspective,* edited by P. Mellars. 160–242. Ithaca: Cornell University Press.

Alroy, J. 2001. A multispecies overkill simulation of the end-Pleistocene megafaunal mass extinction. *Science* 292:1893–96.

Alva, Walter, and Christopher B. Donnan. 1993. *Royal Tombs of Sípan.* Los Angeles: Fowler Museum of Culture History.

———. 1994. Tales from a Peruvian crypt. *Natural History* 103:26–34.

Ames, K. M., and H. D. G. Maschner. 1999. *Peoples of the Northwest Coast: Their Archaeology and Prehistory.* London: Thames and Hudson.

An, Zhimin. 1989. Prehistoric agriculture in China. In *Foraging and Farming,* edited by D. R. Harris and G. C. Hillman. 643–49. London: Unwin Hyman.

Anderson, David. 1990. The Paleoindian colonization of eastern North America. *Research in Economic Anthropology* Supplement 5:163–216.

Anderson, Douglas D. 1968. A Stone Age campsite at the gateway to America. *Scientific American* 218(6):24–33.

———. 1970. Microblade traditions in northwestern Alaska. *Arctic Anthropology* 7(2):2–16.

Anderson, Edgar. 1956. Man as a maker of new plants and new plant communities. In *Man's Role in Changing the Face of the Earth,* Vol. 2, edited by W. L. Thomas. 767–77. Chicago: University of Chicago Press.

Ardrey, Robert. 1961. *African Genesis: A Personal Investigation into the Animal Origins and Nature of Man.* New York: Dell.

Arensburg, Bernard, L. A. Schepartz, A. M. Tillier, B. Vandermeersch, and Yoel Rak. 1990. A reappraisal of the anatomical basis for speech in Middle Paleolithic hominids. *American Journal of Physical Anthropology* 83:137–46.

Arnheim, R. 1956. *Art and Visual Perception: A Psychology of the Creative Eye.* London: Faber and Faber.

Arnold, D. 1991. *Building in Egypt: Pharaonic Stone Masonry.* Oxford: Oxford University Press.

Arsuaga, Juan-Luis. 2002. *The Neanderthal's Necklace: In Search of the Fast Thinkers.* New York: Four Walls Eight Windows Press.

Arsuaga, Juan-Luis, Ignacio Martinez, Ana Garcia, José-Miguel Carretero, and Eudald Carbonell. 1993. Three new human skulls from the Sima de los Huesos Middle Pleistocene site in Sierra de Atapuerca, Spain. *Nature* 362:534–37.

Ascher, M., and R. Ascher. 1997. *Mathematics of the Incas: Code of the Quipu.* Mineola, New York: Dover.

Asfaw, Berhane, Yonas Beyene, Gen Suwa, Robert Walter, Tim White, Giday WoldeGabriel, and Tesfaye Yemane. 1992. The earliest Acheulean from Konso-Gardula. *Nature* 360:732–35.

Asfaw, Berhane, W. H. Gilbert, Y. Beyene, W. K. Hart, P. R. Renne, G. WoldeGabriel, E. S. Vrba, and T. D. White. 2002. Remains of *Homo erectus* from Bouri, Middle Awash, Ethiopia. *Nature* 416:317–19.

Ashmore, Wendy, and Robert J. Sharer. 2000. *Discovering Our Past: A Brief Introduction to Archaeology.* 3rd ed. New York: McGraw-Hill.

Aveni, Anthony, ed. 1977. *Native American Astronomy.* Austin: University of Texas Press.

Axtell, R. L., J. M. Epstein, J. S. Dean, G. J. Gumerman, A. C. Swedlund, J. Harburger, S. Chakravarty, R. Hammond, J. Parker, and M. Parker. 2002. Population growth and collapse in a multiagent model of Kayenta Anasazi in Long House. *Proceedings of the National Academy of Sciences* 99:7275–79.

Bahn, J., and J. Vertut. 1997. *Journey Through the Ice Age.* Berkeley: University of California Press.

Bahn, Paul G. 1994. *Homo erectus* in Europe. *Archaeology* 47:25.

———. 1996. Further back down under. *Nature* 383:577–88.

———. 1998. Neanderthals emancipated. *Nature* 394: 719–21.

Bailey, G. N. 1978. Shell middens as indicators of postglacial economies: A territorial perspective. In *The Early Postglacial Settlement of Northern Europe: An Ecological Perspective,* edited by P. Mellars. 37–63. Pittsburgh: University of Pittsburgh Press.

Balter M. 1998. Why settle down? The mystery of communities. *Science* 282:1442–45.

———. 2000. Paintings in Italian cave may be oldest yet. *Science* 290:419–21.

———. 2001. Stone Age artists—or art lovers—unmasked. *Science* 294:31.

———. 2002. What made humans modern? *Science* 295: 1219–25.

———. 2004a. Dressed for success: Neandertal culture wins respect. *Science* 306:40–41.

———. 2004b. Earliest signs of human-controlled fire uncovered in Israel. *Science* 304:663–665.

———. 2005. *The Goddess and the Bull: Çatalhoyuk: An Archaeological Journey to the Dawn of Civilization.* New York: Free Press.

Balter, M., and A. Gibbons. 2000. A glimpse of humans' first journey out of Africa. *Science* 288:948–50.

Barbetti, M., and H. Allen. 1972. Prehistoric man at Lake Mungo, Australia, by 32,000 years B.P. *Nature* 240:46–48.

Bard, K. A. 2000. The emergence of the Egyptian state (c. 3200–2686 BC). In *The Oxford History of Ancient Egypt,* edited by I. Shaw. 61–88. Oxford: Oxford University Press.

Barker G. 1978. Economic models for the Manekweni Zimbabwe, Mozambique. *Azania* 13:71–100.

Barlow, Nora, ed. 1958. *The Autobiography of Charles Darwin.* London: Collins.

Barnosky, A. D., P. L. Koch, R. S. Feranec, S. L. Wing, and A. B. Shabel. 2004. Assessing the causes of Late Pleistocene extinctions on the continents. *Science* 306:70–75.

Bartstra, G. J., S. Soegondho, and A. V. D. Wijk. 1988. Ngandong Man: Age and artifacts. *Journal of Human Evolution* 17:325–37.

Bar-Yosef, Ofer. 1998. The Natufian culture of the Levant, threshold to the origins of agriculture. *Evolutionary Anthropology* 6(5):159–77.

Bar-Yosef, Ofer, and D. Pilbeam. 2000. *The Geography of Neandertals and Modern Humans in Europe and the Greater Mediterranean.* Peabody Museum Bulletin 8. Cambridge: Peabody Museum of Archaeology and Ethnology.

Bar-Yosef, Ofer, B. Vandermeersch, B. Arensburg, A. Belfer-Cohen, P. Goldberg, H. Laville, L. Meignen, Y. Rak, J. D. Speth, E. Tchernov, A-M. Tillier, and S. Weiner. 1992. The excavations in Kebara Cave, Mt. Carmel. *Current Anthropology* 33:497–534.

Beadle, G. 1977. The origin of *Zea mays.* In *The Origins of Agriculture,* edited by C. A. Reed. 615–35. The Hague: Mouton.

Beaumont, Peter, H. de Villiers, and J. C. Vogel. 1978. Modern man in sub-Saharan Africa prior to 49,000 B.P.: A review and evaluation with particular reference to Border Cave. *South African Journal of Science* 74:409–19.

Bednarik, Robert G. 1993. Oldest dated rock art in the world. *International Newsletter on Rock Art* (4):5–6.

Begun, David R. 1992. Miocene fossil hominids and the chimp-human clade. *Science* 257:1929–33.

———. 2003. Planet of the apes. *Scientific American* 289(2):74–83.

———. 2004. The earliest hominins—Is less more? *Science* 303:1478–1480.

Begun, David R., and Alan Walker. 1993. The endocast. In *The Nariokotome* Homo erectus *Skeleton,* edited by A. Walker and R. Leakey. 326–58. Cambridge: Harvard University Press.

Beja-Pereira, A., et al. 2004. African origins of the domestic donkey. *Science* 304:1781.

Belfer-Cohen, Anna, and N. Goren-Inbar. 1994. Cognition and communication in the Levantine Lower Paleolithic. *World Archaeology* 26:144–57.

Belfer-Cohen, Anna, and Erella Hovers. 1992. In the eye of the beholder: Mousterian and Natufian burials in the Levant. *Current Anthropology* 33:463–71.

Ben-Itzhak, S., P. Smith, and R. A. Bloom. 1988. Radiographic study of the humerus in Neandertals and *Homo sapiens sapiens. American Journal of Physical Anthropology* 77:231–42.

Benson, E. P., B. de la Fuente, and M. Castro, eds. 1996. *Olmec Art of Ancient Mexico.* Washington, D.C.: National Gallery of Art.

Bermúdez de Castro, J. M., J. L. Arsuaga, E. Carbonell, A. Rosas, I. Martinez, and M. Mosquera. 1997. A hominid from the lower Pleistocene of Atapuerca, Spain: Possible ancestor to Neandertals and modern humans. *Science* 276:1392–95.

Binford, Lewis. 1978. *Nunamiut Ethnoarchaeology.* New York: Academic Press.

———. 1984. *Faunal Remains from Klasies River Mouth.* Orlando: Academic Press.

———. 1987a. *Bones: Ancient Men and Modern Myths.* New York: Academic Press.

———. 1987b. Were there elephant hunters at Torralba? In *The Evolution of Human Hunting,* edited by M. H. Nitecki and D. V. Nitecki. 47–105. New York: Plenum Press.

Binford, Lewis, and Sally Binford. 1966. A preliminary analysis of functional variability in the Mousterian of Levallois facies. *American Anthropologist* 68:239–95.

Binford, Sally. 1968. Variability and change in the Near Eastern Mousterian of Levallois facies. In *New Perspectives in Archaeology,* edited by L. Binford and S. Binford. 49–60. Chicago: Aldine.

Bingham, H. 1913. The discovery of Machu Picchu. *Harper's Monthly* 127:709–719.

Birdsell, Joseph H. 1977. The recalibration of a paradigm for the first peopling of Greater Australia. In *Sunda and Sahul: Prehistoric Studies in Southeast Asia, Melanesia, and Australia,* edited by J. Allen, J. Golson, and R. Jones. 113–67. New York: Academic Press.

Bischoff, James L., Narcis Soler, Julià Maroto, and Ramon Julià. 1989. Abrupt Mousterian/Aurignacian boundary at c. 40 ka bp: Accelerator ^{14}C dates from l'Arbreda Cave (Catalunya, Spain). *Journal of Archaeological Science* 16:563–76.

Bjorck, S. 2001. High resolution analyses of an early Holocene climate event may imply decreased solar forcing as an important climate trigger. *Geology* 29:1107–10.

Blackwell, L. R., and F. d'Errico. 2001. Evidence of termite foraging by Swartkrans early hominids. *Proceedings of the National Academy of Sciences* 98:1358–63.

Blomster, J. P., H. Neff, and M. D. Glascock. 2005. Olmec pottery production and export in ancient Mexico determined through elemental analysis. *Science* 307:1068–1072.

Blumenschine, Robert J. 1987. Characteristics of an early hominid scavenging niche. *Current Anthropology* 28: 383–407.

———. 1989. A landscape taphonomic model of the scale of prehistoric scavenging opportunities. *Journal of Human Evolution* 18:345–71.

Blumenschine, Robert J., and Fidelis T. Masao. 1991. Living sites at Olduvai Gorge, Tanzania? Preliminary landscape archaeology results in the basal Bed II lake margin zone. *Journal of Human Evolution* 21:451–62.

Boëda, E., J. M. Geneste, C. Griggo, N. Mercier, S. Muhesen, J. L. Reyss, A. Taha, and H. Valladas. 1999. A Levallois point embedded in the vertebra of a wild ass (*Equus africanus*): Hafting projectiles and Mousterian hunting weapons. *Antiquity* 73:394–402.

Bonnichsen, Rob, and A. L. Schneider. 2001–02. The case for a pre-Clovis people. *American Archaeology* 5(4):35–39.

Bonnichsen, Rob, and K. L. Turnmire, eds. 1991. *Clovis: Origins and Adaptations.* Corvallis, Ore.: Center for the Study of the First Americans.

Bordaz, J. 1970. *Tools of the Old and New Stone Age.* New York: Natural History Press.

Bordes, François. 1961. Mousterian cultures in France. *Science* 134:803–10.

———. 1972. *A Tale of Two Caves.* New York: Harper and Row.

Bordes, François, and J. Labrot. 1967. La stratigraphie du gisement de Roc de Combe et ses implications. *Bulletin de la Société Préhistorique Française* 64:15–28.

Borziyak, Ilia A. 1993. Subsistence practices of Late Paleolithic groups along the Dnestr River and its tributaries. In *From Kostenki to Clovis: Upper Paleolithic-Paleoindian Adaptations,* edited by O. Soffer and N. Preslov. 67–84. New York: Plenum.

Boule, Marcellin, and H. V. Vallois. 1923. *Fossil Men.* New York: Dryden Press.

Bowdler, Sandra. 1974. Pleistocene date for man in Tasmania. *Nature* 252:697–98.

———. 1977. The coastal colonisation of Australia. In *Sunda and Sahul: Prehistoric Studies in Southeast Asia, Melanesia, and Australia,* edited by J. Allen, J. Golson, and R. Jones. 205–46. New York: Academic Press.

———. 1990. Peopling Australasia: The "Coastal Colonization" hypothesis re-examined. In *The Emergence of Modern Humans: An Archaeological Perspective,* edited by P. Mellars. 327–43. Ithaca: Cornell University Press.

Bower, B. 1992a. Early hominid's diet expands. *Science News* 141:253.

———. 1992b. *Erectus* unhinged. *Science News* 141:408–409, 411.

———. 1993a. Ancient American site identified in Alaska. *Science News* 143:215.

———. 1993b. Fossil jaw offers clue to human ancestry. *Science News* 144:277.

———. 1993c. Fossil may extend antiquity of human line. *Science News* 141:134.

———. 1993d. Lucy's new kin take a powerful stand. *Science News* 144:324.

———. 1994a. Asian hominids make a much earlier entrance. *Science News* 145:150.

———. 1994b. Neandertal tot enters human-origins debate. *Science News* 145:5.

———. 1994c. Siberian site cedes stone-age surprise. *Science News* 145:84.

———. 1996. Visions on the rocks. *Science News* 150: 216–17.

———. 1997a. Ancient human saunters into limelight. *Science News* 152:117.

———. 1997b. Ancient roads to Europe. *Science News* 151:12–13.

———. 1997c. Early humans make their marks as hunters. *Science News* 151:222.

———. 2000a. Early farmers crop up in Jordan. *Science News* 158:280.

———. 2000b. Early New World settlers rise in the east. *Science News* 157:244.

————. 2000c. The "Y guy" steps into human-evolution debate. *Science News* 158:295.

————. 2003a. *Erectus* ahoy: Prehistoric seafaring floats into view. *Science News* 164:248–250.

————. 2003b. Stone age code red. *Science News* 164:277–278.

Bowlby, John. 1990. *Charles Darwin: A New Life.* New York: Norton.

Bowler, J. M., H. Johnston, J. M. Olley, J. R. Prescott, R. G. Roberts, W. Shawcross, and N. A. Spooner. 2003. New ages for human occupation and climatic change at Lake Mungo, Australia. *Nature* 421:837–40.

Bowler, J. M., Rhys Jones, Harry Allen, and A. G. Thorne. 1970. Pleistocene human remains from Australia: A living site and human cremation from Lake Mungo, western New South Wales. *World Archaeology* 2:39–60.

Bowler, J. M., and J. McGee. 2000. Redating Australia's oldest human remains: A sceptic's view. *Journal of Human Evolution* 38:719–26.

Bowler, J. M., A. G. Thorne, and H. A. Polach. 1972. Pleistocene man in Australia: Age and significance of the Lake Mungo skeleton. *Nature* 240:48–50.

Bradley, D. G., R. T. Loftus, P. Cunningham, and D. E. MacHugh. 1998. Genetics and domestic cattle origins. *Evolutionary Anthropology* 6(3):79–86.

Braidwood, Robert. 1960. The agricultural revolution. *Science* 203:130–48.

————. 1975. *Prehistoric Men.* Glenview, Ill.: Scott, Foresman.

Brain, J. P. 1979. *Tunica Treasure.* Cambridge, Mass.: Peabody Museum of Archaeology and Ethnology Papers 71.

Bramble, D. M., and D. E. Lieberman. 2004. Endurance running and the evolution of *Homo. Nature* 432:345–352.

Bräuer, Günter. 1984. A craniological approach to the origin of anatomically modern *Homo sapiens.* In *The Origins of Modern Humans: A World Survey of the Fossil Evidence,* edited by F. H. Smith and F. Spencer. 327–410. New York: Liss.

————. 1992. Africa's place in the evolution of *Homo sapiens.* In *Continuity or Replacement: Controversies in* Homo sapiens *Evolution,* edited by G. Bräuer and F. Smith. 83–98. Rotterdam: Balkema.

Bräuer, Günter, Hilary J. Deacon, and Friedrich Zipfel. 1992. Comments on the new maxillary finds from Klasies River Mouth, South Africa. *Journal of Human Evolution* 23: 419–22.

Bräuer, Günter, and Emma Mbua. 1992. *Homo erectus* features used in cladistics and their variability in Asian and African hominids. *Journal of Human Evolution* 22:79–108.

Bräuer, Günter, and Klaus W. Rimbach. 1990. Late archaic and modern *Homo sapiens* from Europe, Africa, and Southwest Asia: Craniometric comparisons and phylogenetic implications. *Journal of Human Evolution* 19: 789–807.

Bräuer, G., Y. Yokoyama, C. Falguères, and E. Mbua. 1997. Modern human origins backdated. *Nature* 386:337.

Brennan, M. U. 1991. *Health and Disease in the Middle and Upper Paleolithic of Southwestern France: A Bioarchaeological Study.* Ph.D. diss., New York University.

Brewer, D. J., and E. Teeter. 1999. *Egypt and the Egyptians.* Cambridge: Cambridge University Press.

Brice, William R. 1982. Bishop Ussher, John Lightfoot, and the age of creation. *Journal of Geological Education* 30: 18–24.

Brooks, Alison S., and Bernard Wood. 1990. The Chinese side of the story. *Nature* 344:288–89.

Brown, Frank, John Harris, Richard Leakey, and Alan Walker. 1985. Early *Homo erectus* skeleton from west Lake Turkana, Kenya. *Nature* 316:788–92.

Brown, K. 2001. New trips through the back alleys of agriculture. *Science* 292:631–33.

Brown, Michael. 1990. *The Search for Eve.* New York: Harper and Row.

Brown, P. 2000. The first Australians: The debate continues. In *Australasian Science,* May, pp. 28–31.

Brown, P., T. Sutikna, M. J. Morwood, R. P. Soejono, Jatmiko, E. W. Saptomo, and R. A. Due. 2004. A new small-bodied hominin from the Late Pleistocene of Flores, Indonesia. *Nature* 431:1055–1061.

Bruhns, Karen Olsen. 1994. *Ancient South America.* Cambridge World Archaeology. Cambridge: Cambridge University Press.

Brunet, M., F. Guy, D. Pilbeam, D. E. Lieberman, A. Likius, H. T. Machaye, M. S. P. d. Leon, C. P. E. Zollikofer, and P. Vignaud. 2005. New material of the earliest hominid from the Upper Miocene of Chad. *Nature* 434:752–755.

Buckley, Tom. 1976. The discovery of Tutankhamun's tomb. In *The Treasures of Tutankhamun,* edited by K. S. Gilbert, J. K. Holt, and S. Hudson. 9–18. New York: Metropolitan Museum of Art.

Buikstra, Jane E. 1984. The lower Illinois River region: A prehistoric context for the study of ancient diet and health. In *Paleopathology at the Origins of Agriculture,* edited by M. N. Cohen and G. J. Armelagos. 215–34. New York: Academic Press.

Bunn, Henry, and Ellen Kroll. 1986. Systematic butchery by Plio-Pleistocene hominids at Olduvai Gorge, Tanzania. *Current Anthropology* 27:431–52.

Burger, Richard L. 1988. Unity and heterogeneity within the Chavin horizon. In *Peruvian Prehistory,* edited by R. W. Keatinge. 99–144. Cambridge: Cambridge University Press.

————. 1995. *Chavin and the Origins of Andean Civilization.* London: Thames and Hudson.

————. 2004. Scientific insights into daily life at Machu Picchu. In *Machu Picchu: Unveiling the Mystery of the Incas,* edited by R. L. Burger and L. C. Salazar. 85–106. New Haven: Yale University Press.

Burger, Richard L., and R. B. Gordon. 1998. Early central Andean metalworking from Mina Perdida, Peru. *Science* 282:1108–11.

Burl, Aubrey. 1995. *A Guide to the Stone Circles of Britain, Ireland, and Brittany.* New Haven: Yale University Press.

———. 1999. *Great Stone Circles.* New Haven: Yale University Press.

Burley, D. V., and W. R. Dickinson. 2001. Origin and significance of a founding settlement in Polynesia. *Proceedings of the National Academy of Sciences* 98:11829–31.

Burns, James A. 1990. Paleontological perspectives on the ice-free corridor. In *Megafauna and Man: Discovery of America's Heartland,* edited by L. D. Agenbroad, J. I. Mead, and L. W. Nelson. 61–66. Hot Springs, S.D.: The Mammoth Site of Hot Springs and Northern Arizona University.

———. 1996. Vertebrate paleontology and the alleged ice-free corridor: The meat of the matter. *Quaternary International* 32:107–112.

Callen, E. O. 1967. Analysis of the Tehuacán coprolites. In *Prehistory of the Tehuacán Valley,* Vol. 1—*Environment and Subsistence,* edited by D. Byers. 261–89. Austin: University of Texas Press.

Carbonell, E., J. M. Bermúdez de Castro, J. L. Arsuaga, J. C. Diez, A. Rosas, G. Cuenca-Bescós, R. Sala, M. Mosquera, and X. P. Rodriguez. 1995. Lower Pleistocene hominids and artifacts from Atapuerca–TD 6 (Spain). *Science* 269:826–30.

Carlisle, R. C., and J. M. Adovasio, eds. 1984. *Meadowcroft: Collected Papers on the Archaeology of Meadowcroft Rockshelter and the Cross Creek Drainage.* Pittsburgh: University of Pittsburgh, Department of Anthropology.

Carniero, Robert. 1970. A theory of the origin of the state. *Science* 169:733–38.

Carrier, D. R. 1984. The energetic paradox of human running and hominid evolution. *Current Anthropology* 25:483–495.

Carter, R. J. 1997. Age estimation of the roe deer (*Capreolus capreolus*) mandibles from the Mesolithic site of Star Carr, Yorkshire, based on radiographs of mandibular tooth development. *Journal of the Zoological Society of London* 241:495–502.

Caspari, R., and S.-H. Lee. 2004. Older age becomes common late in human evolution. *Proceedings of the National Academy of Science* 101(30):10895–900.

Castellani, F. 2005. Historical monuments: The film crew. *Nature* 433:100–1.

Castleden, Rodney. 1987. *The Stonehenge People: An Exploration of Life in Neolithic Britain 4700–2000* B.C. London: Routledge.

———. 1990a. *The Knossos Labyrinth.* London: Routledge.

———. 1990b. *Minoans: Life in Bronze Age Crete.* London: Routledge.

Catto, Norm, and Carole Mandryk. 1990. Geology of the postulated ice-free corridor. In *Megafauna and Man: Discovery of America's Heartland,* edited by L. D. Agenbroad, J. I. Mead, and L. W. Nelson. 80–85. Hot Springs, S.D.: The Mammoth Site of Hot Springs and Northern Arizona University.

Cerling, Thure, Yang Wang, and Jay Quade. 1993. Expansion of C4 ecosystems as an indicator of global ecological change in the late Miocene. *Nature* 361:344–45.

Cerling, T. E., et al. 1997. Global vegetation change through the Miocene/Pliocene boundary. *Nature* 389:153–58.

Chang Kwang-chih. 1968. *The Archaeology of Ancient China.* 2nd ed. New Haven: Yale University Press.

———. 1986. *The Archaeology of Ancient China.* 4th ed. New Haven: Yale University Press.

Chapman, Jefferson, and Gary D. Crites. 1987. Evidence for early maize (Zea mays) from Icehouse Bottom Site, Tennessee. *American Antiquity* 52:318–29.

Chard, Chester. 1974. *Northeast Asia in Prehistory.* Madison: University of Wisconsin Press.

Charteris, J., J. C. Wall, and J. W. Nottrodt. 1981. Functional reconstruction of gait from the Pliocene hominid footprints at Laetoli, northern Tanzania. *Nature* 290:496–98.

Chase, Philip G. 1991. Symbols and Paleolithic artifacts: Style, standardization, and the imposition of arbitrary form. *Journal of Anthropological Archaeology* 10:193–214.

Chase, Philip G., and Harrold L. Dibble. 1987. Middle Paleolithic symbolism: A review of current evidence and interpretations. *Journal of Anthropological Archaeology* 6:263–96.

Chauvet, J.-M., Éliette Deschamps, and Christian Hillaire. 1996. *Dawn of Art: The Chauvet Cave.* New York: Abrams.

Chen Tiemei, Yang Quan, and Wu En. 1994. Antiquity of *Homo sapiens* in China. *Nature* 368:55–56.

Chen Tiemei and Zhang Yinyun. 1991. Paleolithic chronology and possible coexistence of *Homo erectus* and *Homo sapiens* in China. *World Archaeology* 23(2):147–54.

Childe, V. Gordon. 1942. *What Happened in History.* Baltimore: Pelican Books.

———. 1951. *Man Makes Himself.* New York: Mentor Books.

———. 1953. *New Light on the Most Ancient East.* New York: Norton.

Chippindale, Christopher. 1983. *Stonehenge Complete.* Ithaca: Cornell University Press.

Churchill, S. E., and F. H. Smith. 2000. Makers of the early Aurignacian of Europe. *Yearbook of Physical Anthropology* 43:61–115.

Churchill, Steven E., and Erik Trinkaus. 1990. Neandertal scapular glenoid morphology. *American Journal of Physical Anthropology* 83:147–60.

Cinque-Mars, J. 1978. Bluefish Cave I: A late Pleistocene eastern Beringian cave deposit in the northern Yukon. *Canadian Journal of Anthropology* 3:1–32.

Ciochon, Russell, and Jamie James. 1994. The glory that was Angkor. *Archaeology* 47(2):38–49.

Claassen, C. 1996. A consideration of the social organization of the Shell Mound Archaic. In *Archaeology of the Mid-Holocene Southeast,* edited by K. E. Sassaman and D. G. Anderson. 235–258. Gainesville: University Press of Florida.

Clark, Grahame. 1980. *Mesolithic Prelude.* Edinburgh: University of Edinburgh Press.

Clark, J. D., Y. Beyene, G. WoldeGabriel, W. K. Hurt, P. R. Renne, H. Gilbert, A. Defleur, G. Suwa, S. Katoh, K. R.

Ludwig, J.-R. Boisserie, B. Asfaw, and T. D. White. 2003. Stratigraphic, chronological and behavioural contexts of Pleistocene *Homo sapiens* from Middle Awash, Ethiopia. *Nature* 423:747–52.

Clark, J. G. D. 1971. *Excavation at Star Carr.* Cambridge: Cambridge University Press.

Clarke, R. J. 1990. The Ndutu cranium and the origin of *Homo sapiens. Journal of Human Evolution* 19: 699–736.

Clayton, Peter A. 1994. *Chronicle of the Pharaohs: The Reign-by-Reign Record of the Rulers and Dynasties of Ancient Egypt.* London: Thames and Hudson.

Clottes, J., J. Courtin, and M. Garner, trans. 1996. *The Cave Beneath the Sea: Paleolithic Images at Cosquer.* New York: Abrams.

Clottes, J., and D. Lewis-Williams. 1998. *The Shamans of Prehistory: Trance and Magic in the Painted Caves.* New York: Harry N. Abrams.

Coe, Michael. 1968. *America's First Civilization.* New York: Van Nostrand.

———. 1992. *Breaking the Maya Code.* New York: Thames and Hudson.

———. 1993. *The Maya.* New York: Thames and Hudson.

———, ed. 1996. *The Olmec World: Ritual and Rulership.* Princeton, N.J.: Art Museum at Princeton University.

Cohen, Mark. 1977. *The Food Crisis in Prehistory.* New Haven: Yale University Press.

Cohen, Mark Nathan, and George J. Armelagos. 1984. Paleopathology at the origins of agriculture: Editors' summation. In *Paleopathology at the Origins of Agriculture,* edited by M. N. Cohen and G. J. Armelagos. 585–601. New York: Academic Press.

Coltorti, M., M. Cremaschi, M. C. Delitala, D. Esu, M. Fornaseri, A. McPherron, M. Nicoletti, R. van Otterloo, C. Peretto, B. Sala, V. Schmidt, and J. Sevink. 1982. Reversed magnetic polarity in an early Paleolithic site in central Italy. *Nature* 300:173–76.

Conkey, Margaret. 1978. Style and information in cultural evolution: Towards a predictive model for the Paleolithic. In *Social Archaeology: Beyond Subsistence and Dating,* edited by C. Redman, M. J. Berman, E. V. Curtin, W. T. Langhorne, N. M. Versaggi, and J. C. Wanser. 61–85. New York: Academic Press.

———. 1980. The identification of prehistoric hunter-gatherer aggregation sites: The case of Altamira. *Current Anthropology* 21:609–30.

———. 1981. A century of Paleolithic cave art. *Archaeology* 34(4):20–28.

Connah, Graham. 1987. *African Civilization: Precolonial Cities and States in Tropical Africa; An Archaeological Perspective.* Cambridge: Cambridge University Press.

Conrad, N. J. 2003. Paleolithic ivory sculptures from southwestern Germany and the origins of figurative art. *Nature* 426:830–832.

Conroy, G. C., G. W. Weber, H. Seidler, P. V. Tobias, A. Kane, and B. Brunsden. 1998. Endocranial capacity in an early hominid cranium from Sterkfontein, South Africa. *Science* 280:1730–31.

Constable, George, and the Editors of Time-Life Books. 1973. *The Neanderthals.* New York: Time-Life.

Conyers, L. B. 2004. *Ground Penetrating Radar for Archaeology.* Walnut Creek, Calif.: AltaMira Press.

Cook, J., C. B. Stringer, A. P. Currant, H. P. Schwarz, and A. G. Wintle. 1982. A review of the chronology of the European Middle Pleistocene hominid record. *Yearbook of Physical Anthropology* 25:19–65.

Cooley, A. E. 2003. *Pompeii.* London: Duckworth.

Cope, J. 1998. *The Modern Antiquarian.* London: Thorsons.

Coqueugniot, H., J.-J. Hublin, F. Veillon, F. Houet, and T. Jacob 2004 Early brain growth in *Homo erectus* and implications for cognitive ability. *Nature* 431:299–302.

Cordell, Linda. 1984. *The Archaeology of the Southwest.* New York: Academic Press.

———. 1994. *Ancient Pueblo Peoples.* Exploring the Ancient World series. Washington, D.C.: Smithsonian Books.

Cosgrove, Richard, Jim Allen, and Brendan Marshall. 1990. Paleo-ecology and Pleistocene human occupation in south-central Tasmania. *Antiquity* 64:59–78.

Cowgill, George L. 1988. Onward and upward with collapse. In *The Collapse of Ancient States and Civilizations,* edited by N. Yoffe and G. L. Cowgill. 244–76. Tucson: University of Arizona Press.

Crawford, Gary W. 1992. Prehistoric plant domestication in East Asia. In *The Origins of Agriculture: An International Perspective,* edited by C. W. Cowan and P. J. Watson. 7–38. Washington, D.C.: Smithsonian Institution Press.

Crawford, Harriet. 1991. *Sumer and the Sumerians.* New York: Cambridge University Press.

Crelin, Edmund S. 1987. *The Human Vocal Tract: Anatomy, Function, Development, and Evolution.* New York: Vantage.

Crompton, Robin H., Li Yu, Wang Weijie, Michael Günther, and Russell Savage. 1998. The mechanical effectiveness of erect and "bent-hip, bent-knee" bipedal walking in *Australopithecus afarensis. Journal of Human Evolution* 35(1):55–74.

Culbert, P. 1993. *Maya Civilization.* Exploring the Ancient World series. Washington, D.C.: Smithsonian Books.

Cummins, John, ed. 1992. *The Voyage of Christopher Columbus: Columbus' Own Journal of Discovery.* New York: St. Martin's Press.

Dalrymple, G. Brent, and Marvin A. Lanphere. 1969. *Potassium-Argon Dating: Principles, Techniques, and Applications to Geochronology.* San Francisco: W. H. Freeman.

Dalton, R. 2003. Lion man takes pride of place as oldest statue. *Nature* 425:7.

———. 2005. Skeleton keys. *Nature* 433:454–56.

D'Altroy, T. N. 2003. *The Incas.* Oxford: Blackwell

Daniel, Glyn, and Colin Renfrew. 1988. *The Idea of Prehistory.* Edinburgh: Edinburgh University Press.

Darwin, Charles. 1845. *Journal of Researches into the Natural History and Geology of the Countries Visited During the*

Voyage of H.M.S. Beagle *Round the World.* 2nd ed. London: John Murray.

———. 1859. *The Origin of Species by Means of Natural Selection.* 1952 ed. Chicago: Encyclopaedia Britannica.

Darwin, Sir F., ed. 1961. *Charles Darwin's Autobiography.* New York: Collier Books.

David, B., R. Roberts, C. Tuniz, R. Jones, and J. Head. 1997. New optical and radiocarbon dated from Ngarrabullgan Cave, a Pleistocene archaeological site in Australia: Implications for the comparability of time clocks and for the human colonization of Australia. *Antiquity* 71: 183–88.

Davis, M. B. 1969. Climatic changes in southern Connecticut recorded by pollen deposition at Rogers Lake. *Ecology* 50:409–22.

Day, M. H. 1969. Omo human skeletal remains. *Nature* 222:1135–38.

Day, Michael H. 1986. *Guide to Fossil Man.* Chicago: University of Chicago Press.

Day, Michael, and E. H. Wickens. 1980. Laetoli Pliocene hominid footprints and bipedalism. *Nature* 286:385–87.

Dayton, L. 2003. Tracing the road down under. *Science News* 302:555–56.

Deacon, Hilary J., and Ria Shuurman. 1992. The origins of modern people: The evidence from Klasies River. In *Continuity or Replacement: Controversies in* Homo sapiens *Evolution,* edited by G. Bräuer and F. Smith. 121–30. Rotterdam: Balkema.

Dean, C., M. G. Leakey, D. Reid, F. Schrenk, G. T. Schwartz, C. Stringer, and A. Walker. 2001. Growth processes in teeth distinguish modern humans from *Homo erectus* and earlier hominins. *Nature* 414:628–31.

Dean, M. C., C. B. Stringer, and T. G. Bromage. 1986. Age at death of the Neandertal child from Devil's Tower, Gibraltar, and the implications for students of general growth and development in Neandertals. *American Journal of Physical Anthropology* 70:301–9.

Deino, A., P. R. Renne, and C. C. Swisher III. 1998. ^{40}Ar/^{39}Ar dating in paleoanthropology and archaeology. *Evolutionary Anthropology* 6(2):63–75.

de la Vega, Garcilaso. 1988. *The Florida of the Inca.* Translated by John Varner and Jeannette Varner. Austin: University of Texas Press. (Original work published 1605)

deMenocal, P. 2001. Cultural responses to climate change during the Holocene. *Science* 292:667–72.

Denham, T. P., S. G. Haberle, C. Lentfer, R. Fullagar, J. Field, M. Therin, N. Porch, and B. Winsborough. 2003. Origins of agriculture at Kuk Swamp in the highlands of New Guinea. *Science* 301:189–93.

Denison, S. 1995. Mesolithic food industry on Colonsay. *British Archaeology* 5.

Dennell, Robin. 1986. Needles and spear-throwers. *Natural History* 95(10):70–78.

———. 1992. The origins of crop agriculture in Europe. In *The Origins of Agriculture: An International Perspective,* edited by C. W. Cowan and P. J. Watson. 71–100. Washington, D.C.: Smithsonian Institution Press.

Derenko, M. V., T. Grzybowski, B. A. Malyarchuk, J. Czarny, D. Miscicka-Sliwka, and I. A. Zakharov. 2001. The presence of mitochondrial haplogroup X in Altaians from south Siberia. *American Journal of Human Genetics* 69:237–41.

De Tapia, Emily McClung. 1992. The origins of agriculture in Mesoamerica and South America. In *The Origins of Agriculture: An International Perspective,* edited by C. W. Cowan and P. J. Watson. 143–71. Washington, D.C.: Smithsonian Institution Press.

Dettwyler, K. A. 1991. Can paleopathology provide evidence for "compassion"? *American Journal of Physical Anthropology* 84:375–84.

Diamond, Jared. 1987a. How do flightless mammals colonize oceanic islands? *Nature* 327:324.

———. 1987b. The worst mistake in the history of the human race. *Discover* 8:50–60.

———. 1994. How to tame a wild plant. *Discover* 15: 100–106.

———. 2002. Life with the artificial Anasazi. *Nature* 419:567–69.

———. 2004. The astonishing micropygmies. *Science* 306:2047–48.

———. 2005. *Collapse: How Societies Choose to Fail or Succeed.* New York: Penguin.

Dibble, Harold. 1987. The interpretation of Middle Paleolithic scraper morphology. *American Antiquity* 52: 108–18.

Dickson, D. Bruce. 1990. *The Dawn of Belief: Religion in the Upper Paleolithic of Southwestern Europe.* Tucson: University of Arizona Press.

Diehl, Richard A. 1989. Olmec archaeology: What we know and what we wish we knew. In *Regional Perspectives on the Olmec,* edited by R. J. Sharer and D. C. Grove. 17–32. New York: Cambridge University Press.

———. 2004. *The Olmecs: America's First Civilization.* London: Thames and Hudson.

———. 2005. Patterns of cultural primacy. *Science* 307:1055–56.

Dikov, N. N. 1978. Ancestors of Paleoindians and proto-Eskimo-Aleuts in the Paleolithic of Kamchatka. In *Early Man in America From a Circum-Pacific Perspective,* edited by A. L. Bryan. 68–69. Edmonton, Canada: Archaeological Researches International.

DiLeo, Joseph H. 1970. *Young Children and Their Drawings.* New York: Brunner/Mazel.

Dillehay, Tom D. 1987. By the banks of the Chinchihuapi. *Natural History* 96(4):8–12.

———. 1989. *Monte Verde: A Late Pleistocene Settlement in Chile.* Vol. 1—*Paleoenvironment and Site Context.* Washington, D.C.: Smithsonian Institution Press.

———. 1997a. The battle of Monte Verde. *The Sciences* (January/February):28–33.

———. 1997b. *Monte Verde: A Late Pleistocene Settlement in Chile.* Vol. 2—*The Archaeological Context and Interpretation.* Washington, D.C.: Smithsonian Institution Press.

Dillehay, Tom D., and Michael B. Collins. 1988. Early cultural evidence from Monte Verde in Chile. *Nature* 332:150–52.

Dincauze, Dena. 1993. Fluted points in the eastern forests. In *From Kostenki to Clovis: Upper Paleolithic-Paleoindian Adaptations,* edited by O. Soffer and N. Preslov. 279–92. New York: Plenum.

Dixon, E. J. 1993. *Quest for the Origins of the First Americans.* Albuquerque: University of New Mexico Press.

———. 1999. *Bones, Boats, and Bison: Archaeology and the First Colonization of Western North America.* Albuquerque: University of New Mexico Press.

Dobyns, H. 1983. *Their Numbers Became Thinned.* Knoxville: University of Tennessee Press.

Doebley, J., A. Stec, and L. Hubbard. 1997. The evolution of apical dominance in maize. *Nature* 386:485–88.

Duarte, C., J. Maurîcio, P. B. Pettitt, P. Souto, E. Trinkaus, H. van der Plicht, and J. Zilhão. 1999. The early Upper Paleolithic human skeleton from the Abrigo do Lagar Velho (Portugal) and modern emergence in Iberia. *Proceedings of the National Academy of Sciences* 96:7604–09.

Dubois, Eugene. 1894. *Pithecanthropus erectus.* Eine Menschenähnliche Übergangsform Aus Java. Batavia: Landers-druckerei.

Duhard, Jean-Pierre. 1993. Upper Paleolithic figures as a reflection of human morphology and social organization. *Antiquity* 67:83–91.

Eighmy, J. L., and J. B. Howard. 1991. Direct dating of prehistoric canal sediments using archaeomagnetism. *American Antiquity* 56:88–102.

Eighmy, J. L., and R. S. Sternberg, eds. 1990. *Archaeomagnetic Dating.* Tucson: University of Arizona Press.

Eldredge, Niles, and Stephen Jay Gould. 1972. Punctuated equilibrium: An alternative to phyletic gradualism. In *Models in Paleobiology,* edited by T. S. Schopf. 82–115. San Francisco: Freeman, Cooper.

Elias, S. A., S. K. Short, C. H. Nelson, and H. H. Birks. 1996. Life and times of the Bering Land Bridge. *Nature* 382: 60–63.

Elvas, Gentleman of. 1966. *The Discovery and Conquest of Tierra Florida by Don Ferdinando de Soto and Six Hundred Spaniards, His Followers.* New York: Burt Franklin.

Engels, Friedrich. 1891. *The Origins of the Family, Private Property, and the State.* 1972 ed. Chicago: Kerr.

EPICA. 2004. Eight glacial cycles from an Antarctic ice core. *Nature* 429:623–28.

Eshed, V., A. Gopher, T. B. Gage, and I. Hershkovitz. 2004. Has the transition to agriculture reshaped the demographic structure of prehistoric populations? New evidence from the Levant. *American Journal of Physical Anthropology* 124:315–29.

Evans, Arthur. 1921–36. *Palace of Minos.* 4 vols. Oxford: Oxford University Press.

Evans, J. D. 1968. Neolithic Knossos: The Growth of a Settlement. *Proceedings of the Prehistoric Society* 37(2): 95–117.

Excoffier, Laurent, and André Langaney. 1989. Origin and differentiation of human mitochondrial DNA. *American Journal of Human Genetics* 44:73–85.

Fagan, Brian M. 1994. *Quest for the Past: Great Discoveries in Archaeology.* Prospect Heights, Ill.: Waveland Press.

———. 1998. *Eyewitness to Discovery.* New York: Oxford University Press.

———. 2000a. *Ancient North America: The Archaeology of a Continent.* 3rd ed. London: Thames and Hudson.

———. 2000b. *In the Beginning: An Introduction to Archaeology.* 10th ed. Englewood Cliffs, N.J.: Prentice Hall.

———. 2002. Everything new is old again. *American Archaeology* 6(3):20–25.

———. 2003. *Archaeology: A Brief Introduction.* 7th ed. New York: Longman.

Fairservis, William. 1975. *The Roots of India.* Chicago: University of Chicago Press.

Falk, Dean. 1984. The petrified brain. *Natural History* 93(9):36–39.

Falk, D., C. Hildebolt, K. Smith, M. J. Morwood, T. Sutikna, P. Brown, Jatmiko, E. W. Saptomo, B. Brunsden, and F. Prior. 2005. The brain of LB1, *Homo floresiensis. Science* 308:242–45.

Farnsworth, Paul, James E. Brady, Michael J. DeNiro, and Richard S. MacNeish. 1985. A re-evaluation of the isotopic and archaeological reconstruction of diet in the Tehuacán Valley. *American Antiquity* 50:102–16.

Fash, W. L. 2001. *Scribes, Warriors, and Kings: The City of Copan and the Ancient Maya.* New York: Thames and Hudson.

Feder, Kenneth L. 2002. *Frauds, Myths, and Mysteries: Science and Pseudoscience in Archaeology.* 4th ed. Mountain View, Calif.: Mayfield.

———. ed. 1999. *Lessons from the Past: A Reader in Introductory Archaeology.* Mountain View, Calif.: Mayfield.

———. 2007. *Frauds, Myths, and Mysteries: Science and Pseudoscience in Archaeology.* 5th ed. New York: McGraw-Hill.

Fedoroff, N. V. 2003. Prehistoric GM corn. *Science* 302: 1158–59.

Feibel, C. S., F. H. Brown, and I. McDougal. 1989. Stratigraphic context of fossil hominids from the Omo Group deposits: Northern Turkana Basin, Kenya, and Ethiopia. *American Journal of Physical Anthropology* 78:595–622.

Fiedel, S. J. 1999. Older than we thought: Implications of corrected dates for Paleoindians. *American Antiquity* 64:95–115.

Flannery, Kent V. 1968. Archaeological systems theory and early Mesoamerica. In *Anthropological Archaeology in the Americas,* edited by B. Meggars. 67–87. Washington, D.C.: Anthropological Society of Washington.

———. ed. 1986. *Guilá Naquitz: Archaic Foraging and Early Agriculture in Oaxaca, Mexico.* New York: Academic Press.

Fleagle, John. 1988. *Primate Adaptation and Evolution.* New York: Academic Press.

Flint, Richard Foster. 1971. *Glacial and Quarternary Geology.* New York: Wiley.

Ford, R. 1985. Patterns of prehistoric food production in North America. In *Prehistoric Food Production in North America,* edited by R. Ford. 341–64. Vol. 75 of Anthropological Papers. Ann Arbor: University of Michigan, Museum of Anthropology.

Foster, Nelson, and Linda S. Cordell, eds. 1992. *Chilies to Chocolate: Food the Americas Gave the World.* Tucson: University of Arizona Press.

Fowler, Melvin. 1959. *Summary Report of Modoc Rockshelter: 1952, 1953, 1955, 1956.* Report of Investigations 8. Springfield: Illinois State Museum.

———. 1989. *The Cahokia Atlas: A Historical Atlas of Cahokia Archaeology.* Studies in Illinois Archaeology 6. Springfield: Illinois Historic Preservation Agency.

Franciscus, R. G., and Eric Trinkaus. 1988. Nasal morphology and the emergence of *Homo erectus. American Journal of Physical Anthropology* 75:517–27.

Frayer, David W., Milford H. Wolpoff, Alan G. Thorne, Fred H. Smith, and Geoffrey G. Pope. 1993. Theories of modern human origins: The paleontological test. *American Anthropologist* 95:14–50.

Freeman, Leslie. 1973. The significance of mammalian faunas from Paleolithic occupations of Cantabrian Spain. *American Antiquity* 38:3–44.

Frere, John. 1800. Account of flint weapons discovered in Hoxne in Suffolk. *Archaeologia* 13:204–5.

Freud, Sigmund. 1976. *Introductory Lectures on Psychology.* Translated by J. Strachey. Harmondsworth, England: Penguin.

Fried, Morton H. 1967. *The Evolution of Political Society: An Essay in Political Anthropology.* New York: Random House.

Frink, D. S. 1997. OCR carbon dating of the Watson Brake mound complex. Paper presented at the 53rd annual meeting of the Southeastern Archaeological Conference, Birmingham, Alabama.

Frison, George C. 1974a. Archaeology of the Casper site. In *The Casper Site: A Hell Gap Bison Kill on the High Plains,* edited by G. C. Frison. 1–112. New York: Academic Press.

———. ed. 1974b. *The Casper Site: A Hell Gap Bison Kill on the High Plains.* New York: Academic Press.

Fritz, Gayle. 1994. Are the first American farmers getting younger? *Current Anthropology* 35(3):305–9.

Gabunia, L., A. Vekua, D. Lordkipanidze, C. Swisher III, R. Ferring, A. Justus, M. Nioradze, M. Tvalchrelidze, S. C. Antón, G. Bosinski, O. Jöris, Marie-A.-deLumley, G. Majsuradze, and A. Mouskhelishvili. 2000. Earliest Pleistocene cranial remains from Dmanisi, Republic of Georgia: Taxonomy, geological setting, and age. *Science* 288: 1019–25.

Galanopoulos, A. G., and E. Bacon. 1969. *Atlantis: The Truth Behind the Legend.* Indianapolis: Bobbs-Merrill.

Galik, K., B. Senut, M. Pickford, D. Gommery, J. Treil, A. J. Kuperavage, and R. B. Eckhardt. 2004. External and internal morphology of the BAR 1002'00 *Orrorin tugenensis* femur. *Science* 305:1450–53.

Galinat, Walton C. 1992. Maize: Gift from America's first people. In *Chilies to Chocolate: Food the Americas Gave the World,* edited by N. Foster and L. S. Cordell. 47–60. Tucson: University of Arizona Press.

Gamble, Clive. 1982. Interaction and alliance in Paleolithic society. *Man* 17:92–107.

———. 1986. *The Paleolithic settlement of Europe.* Cambridge, Mass.: Cambridge University Press.

Gardner, Howard. 1980. *Artful Scribbles: The Significance of Children's Drawings.* New York: Basic Books.

Gargett, Robert H. 1989. The evidence for Neandertal burial. *Current Anthropology* 30:157–77.

Garlake, P. S. 1973. *Great Zimbabwe.* London: Thames and Hudson.

Garn, S. M., A. B. Lewis, K. Koski, and D. Polachesk. 1958. The sex difference in tooth calcification. *Journal of Dentistry Research* 37:561–67.

Gernet, Jacques. 1987. *A History of Chinese Civilization.* Cambridge: Cambridge University Press.

Gero, J., and M. Conkey, eds. 1990. *Engendering Archaeology.* Cambridge: Basil Blackwell.

Gibbons, A. 1993. Geneticists trace the DNA trail of the first Americans. *Science* 259:312–13.

———. 1996a. Did Neandertals lose an evolutionary "arms" race? *Science* 272:1586–87.

———. 1996b. The peopling of the Americas. *Science* (274):31–33.

———. 1998. Mother tongues trace steps of earliest Americans. *Science* 279:1306–7.

———. 2001. The riddle of coexistence. *Science* 291: 1725–29.

———. 2002. In search of the first hominids. *Science* 295:1214–19.

Gifford-Gonzalez, Diane. 1993. You can hide, but you can't run: Representation of women's work in illustrations of Paleolithic life. *Visual Anthropology Review* 9(1):23–41.

Gingerich, P. D. 1986. *Plesiadapis* and the delineation of the order Primates. In *Major Topics in Primate and Human Evolution,* edited by B. Wood, L. Martin, and P. Andrews. 32–46. Cambridge: Cambridge University Press.

Glob, P. V. 1969. *The Bog People.* New York: Ballantine.

Glover, Ian C. 1993. Tools and cultures in Late Paleolithic southeast Asia. In *The First Humans: Human Origins and History to 10,000 B.C.,* edited by G. Burenhult. 128–30. San Francisco: HarperSanFrancisco.

Goebel, Ted, Roger Powers, and Nancy Bigelow. 1991. The Nenana Complex of Alaska and Clovis origins. In *Clovis: Origins and Adaptations,* edited by R. Bonnichsen and K. L. Turnmire. 49–79. Peopling of the Americas. Corvallis, Ore.: Center for the Study of the First Americans.

Goebel, T., M. R. Waters, and M. Dikova. 2003. The archaeology of Ushki Lake, Kamchatka, and the Pleistocene peopling of America. *Science* 301:501–6.

Gonzalez-Jose, R., A. Gonzalez-Martin, M. Hernandez, H. M. Pucciarelli, M. Sardi, A. Rosales, and S. V. d. Molen. 2003. Craniometric evidence for Paleoamerican survival in Baja California. *Nature* 425:62–65.

Goodall, Jane. 1986. *The Chimpanzees of Gombe: Patterns of Behavior.* Cambridge, Mass.: Belknap Press.

Goodman, A. H., and George Armelagos. 1985. Disease and death at Dr. Dickson's mound. *Natural History* 94(9): 12–18.

Goodyear, A. C. 1999. Results of the 1999 Allendale Paleoindian expedition. *Legacy* 4(1–3):8–13.

Goren-Inbar, N., N. Alperson, M. E. Kislev, O. Simchoni, Y. Melamed, A. Ben-Nun, and W. Werker. 2004. Evidence of hominin control of fire at Gesher Benot Ya'aqov, Israel. *Science* 304:725–27.

Goren-Inbar, N., G. Sharon, Y. Melamed, and M. Kislev. 2002. Nuts, nut cracking, and pitted stones at Gesher Benot Ya'aqov, Israel. *Proceedings of the National Academy of Sciences* 99:2455–60.

Gorman, Charles, 1972. Excavations at Spirit Cave, North Thailand: Some interim impressions. *Asian Perspectives* 13:79–107.

Gould, Stephen Jay. 1977. Human babies as embryos. In *Ever Since Darwin.* 70–75. New York: Norton.

———. 1988. A novel notion of Neanderthal. *Natural History* 97(6):16–21.

———. 1991. Fall in the house of Ussher. *Natural History* 100(11):12, 14–16, 18–21.

———. 1994. Lucy on the earth in stasis. *Natural History* 103(9):12, 14, 16, 18–20.

Gowlett, John. 1984. Mental abilities of early man. In *Hominid Evolution and Community Ecology,* edited by G. N. Bailey and P. Callow. 169–92. London: Academic Press.

———. 1986. Culture and conceptualisation: The Oldowan-Acheulian gradient. In *Stone Age Prehistory: Studies in Memory of Charles McBurney,* edited by G. N. Bailey and P. Callow. 243–60. Cambridge: Cambridge University Press.

Gramly, Richard Michael. 1982. *The Vail Site: A Palaeo-Indian Encampment in Maine.* Bulletin of the Buffalo Society of Natural Sciences 30. Buffalo, N.Y.: Buffalo Society of Natural Sciences.

———. 1993. *The Richey Clovis Cache.* Buffalo: Persimmon Press.

Gray, D. 1996. Champion of Aboriginal art. *Archaeology* 46(4):44–47.

Grayson, Donald K. 1983. *The Establishment of Human Antiquity.* New York: Academic Press.

———. 1987. Death by natural causes. *Natural History* 96(5):8, 10, 12–13.

———. 1991. Late Pleistocene mammalian extinction in North America: Taxonomy, chronology, and explanations. *Journal of World Prehistory* 5(3):193–231.

Grayson, D. K., and D. J. Meltzer. 2002. Clovis hunting and large mammal extinction: A critical review of the evidence. *Journal of World Prehistory* 16:313–59.

Greene, J. C. 1959. *The Death of Adam: Evolution and Its Impact on Western Thought.* Ames: Iowa State University Press.

Grine, F. E. 1987. The diet of South African australopithecines based on a study of dental microwear. *L'Anthropologie* 91:467–82.

Groube, Les, John Chappell, John Muke, and David Price. 1986. A 40,000-year-old human occupation site at Huon Peninsula, Papua New Guinea. *Nature* 324:453–55.

Grove, D. 1996. The Olmec. Unpublished manuscript.

Grove, Jean. 1988. *The Little Ice Age.* London: Methuen.

Grün, Ranier. 1989. Electron spin resonance (ESR) dating. *Quaternary International* 1:65–109.

———. 1993. Electron spin resonance dating in paleoanthropology. *Evolutionary Anthropology* 2(5):172–81.

Grün, Ranier, Peter B. Beaumont, and Christopher B. Stringer. 1990. ESR dating evidence for early modern humans at Border Cave in South Africa. *Nature* 344: 537–39.

Grün, R., J. S. Brink, N. A. Spooner, L. Taylor, C. B. Stringer, R. G. Franciscus, and A. S. Murray. 1996. Direct dating of Florisbad hominid. *Nature* 382:500–1.

Grün, Ranier, Nicholas J. Shackleton, and Hilary J. Deacon. 1990. Electron-spin-resonance dating of tooth enamel from Klasies River Mouth cave. *Current Anthropology* 31(4):427–32.

Grün, Ranier, and Christopher B. Stringer. 1991. Electron spin resonance dating and the evolution of modern humans. *Archaeometry* 33:153–99.

Gurney, Gene, and Jeff Forte. 1988. *Space Shuttle Log: The First 25 Flights.* Blue Ridge Summit, Penn.: Aero.

Guthrie, R. Dale. 1990. Late Pleistocene faunal revolution—New perspective on the extinction debate. In *Megafauna and Man: Discovery of America's Heartland,* edited by L. D. Agenbroad, J. I. Mead, and L. W. Nelson. 42–53. Hot Springs, S.D.: The Mammoth Site of Hot Springs and Northern Arizona University.

Gutin, J. 1995. Archaeology: Do Kenya tools root birth of modern thought in Africa? *Science* 270:1118–19.

Haas, Jonathan. 1982. *The Evolution of the Prehistoric State.* New York: Columbia University Press.

Haas, J., W. Creamer, and A. Ruiz. 2004. Dating the Late Archaic occupation of the Norte Chico region of Peru. *Nature* 432:1020–24.

Hager, Lori D. 1994. Fashioning the primitive: 100 years of looking at Neandertals, looking at us. Paper presented at the Annual meeting of the Society for American Archaeology, Anaheim, California.

Haile-Selassie, Y. 2001. Late Miocene hominids from the Middle Awash, Ethiopia. *Nature* 412:178–81.

Haile-Selassie, Y., G. Suwa, and T. D. White. 2004. Late Miocene teeth from Middle Awash, Ethiopia, and early hominid dental evolution. *Science* 303:1503–05.

Halvorson, John. 1987. Art for art's sake in the Paleolithic. *Current Anthropology* 28:63–71.

Hanotte, O., D. G. Bradley, J. W. Ochieng, Y. Verjee, E. W. Hill, and J. E. O. Rege. 2002. African pastoralism: Genetic imprints of origins and migrations. *Science* 296:336–39.

Hansen, J. M. 1981. *The Paleoethnobotany of Franchthi Cave, Greece.* Bloomington: Indiana University Press.

Hanson, B. 2001. Dating Nanjing Man. *Science* 291:947.

Hard, Robert J., and John R. Roney. 1998. A massive terraced village complex in Chihuahua, Mexico, 3,000 years before present. *Science* 279:1661–64.

Harlan, Jack. 1992. Indigenous African agriculture. In *The Origins of Agriculture: An International Perspective,* edited by C. W. Cowan and P. J. Watson. 59–70. Washington, D.C.: Smithsonian Institution Press.

Harris, John F., and Stephen K. Stearns. 1992. *Understanding Maya Inscriptions.* Philadelphia: University of Pennsylvania, the University Museum.

Harrold, Francis B. 1980. A comparative analysis of Eurasian Palaeolithic burials. *World Archaeology* 12:195–211.

———. 1989. Mousterian, Châtelperronian, and Early Aurignacian in western Europe: Continuity or discontinuity? In *The Human Revolution: Behavioural and Biological Perspectives in the Origins of Modern Humans,* edited by P. Mellars and C. Stringer. 677–713. Princeton, N.J.: Princeton University Press.

———. 1992. Paleolithic archaeology, ancient behavior, and the transition to modern *Homo.* In *Continuity or Replacement: Controversies in* Homo sapiens *Evolution,* edited by G. Bräuer and F. Smith. 219–30. Rotterdam: Balkema.

Harter, A. V., K. A. Gardner, D. Falush, D. L. Lentz, R. A. Bye, and L. H. Rieseberg. 2004. Origin of extant domesticated sunflowers in eastern North America. *Nature* 430:201–4.

Hasten, L., ed. 2005. *Annual Editions: Archaeology.* Guilford, Conn.: Dushkin/McGraw-Hill.

Hastings, M. C., and M. Mosely. 1975. The adobes of Huaca del Sol and Huaca de la Luna. *American Antiquity* 40:196–203.

Haug, G. H., D. Günter, L. Peterson, D. M. Sigman, K. A. Hughen, and B. Aeschlimann. 2003. Climate and the collapse of Maya civilization. *Science* 299:1731–53.

Haury, Emil W., E. B. Sayles, and William W. Wasley. 1959. The Lehner Mammoth site, southeastern Arizona. *American Antiquity* 25:2–30.

Hay, R. L., and Mary Leakey. 1982. The fossil footprints of Laetoli. *Scientific American* 246:50–57.

Haynes, C. Vance. 1964. Fluted projectile points: Their age and dispersion. *Science* 145:1408–13.

———. 1980. The Clovis culture. *Canadian Journal of Anthropology* 1:115–21.

———. 1982. Were Clovis progenitors in Beringia? In *Paleoecology of Beringia,* edited by D. M. Hopkins, J. V.

Matthews, Jr., C. E. Schweger, and S. B. Young. 383–98. New York: Academic Press.

———. 1987. Clovis origins update. *The Kiva* 52(2):83–93.

———. 1992. Contributions of radiocarbon dating to the geochronology of the peopling of the New World. In *Radiocarbon Dating After Four Decades: An Interdisciplinary Perspective,* edited by R. R. Taylor, A. Long, and R. S. Kra. 355–74. New York: Springer-Verlag.

Heinzelin, Jean de, J. D. Clark, T. White, W. Hart, P. Renne, G. WoldeGabriel, Y. Beyenne, and E. Vrba. 1999. Environment and the behavior of 2.5-million-year-old Bouri hominids. *Science* 284:625–29.

Heiser, Charles B., Jr. 1990. *Seed to Civilization: The Story of Food.* Cambridge, Mass.: Harvard University Press.

Heizer, R. F., and L. K. Napton. 1970. Archaeology as seen from Lovelock Cave, Nevada. *University of California Research Facility Contributions* 10(1).

Helbaek, Hans. 1965. Early Hassunan vegetable food at Tell es-Sawwan near Samarra. *Sumer* 20:45–48.

Henning, G. J., W. Herr, E. Weber, and N. I. Xirotiris. 1981. ESR-dating of the fossil hominid cranium from Petralona Cave, Greece. *Nature* 292:533–36.

Henry, Donald O. 1989. *From Foraging to Agriculture: The Levant at the End of the Ice Age.* Philadelphia: University of Pennsylvania Press.

Henshilwood, C., and J. Sealy. 1997. Bone artifacts from the Middle Stone Age at Blombos Cave, Southern Cape, South Africa. *Current Anthropology* 38:890–95.

Henshilwood, C. S., F. d'Errico, C. W. Marean, R. G. Milo, and R. Yates. 2001. An early bone tool industry from the Middle Stone Age at Blombos Cave, South Africa: Implications for the origins of modern human behaviour, symbolism, and language. *Journal of Human Evolution* 41:631–78.

Henshilwood, C., F. d'Errico, M. Vanhaeren, K. van Niekerk, and Z. Jacobs. 2004. Middle Stone Age shell beads from South Africa. *Science* 304(404).

Henshilwood, C. S., F. d'Errico, R. Yates, Z. Jacobs, C. Tribolo, G. A. T. Duller, N. Mercier, J. C. Sealy, H. Valladas, I. Watts, and A. G. Wintle. 2002. Emergence of modern human behavior: Middle Stone Age engravings from South Africa. *Science* 295:1278–80.

Heun, M., R. Schäfer-Pregl, D. Klawan, R. Castagna, M. Accerbi, B. Borghi, and F. Salamini. 1997. Site of einkorn wheat domestication identified by genetic fingerprinting. *Science* 278:1312–13.

Higham, Charles. 1989. *The Archaeology of Mainland Southeast Asia.* Cambridge: Cambridge University Press.

———. 2001. *The Civilization of Angkor.* Berkeley: University of California Press.

Hill, Andrew, Steven Ward, Alan Deino, Garniss Curtis, and Robert Drake. 1992. Earliest *Homo. Nature* 355:719–22.

Hodder, I. 2005. Women and men at Çatalhöyük. *Scientific American: Special Edition* 15(1):35–41.

Hodder, I., and C. Cessford. 2004. Daily practice and social memory at Çatalhöyük. *American Antiquity* 69:17–40.

Hodell, D. A., M. Brenner, J. H. Curtis, and T. Guilderson. 2001. Solar forcing of drought frequency in the Maya lowlands. *Science* 292:1367–70.

Hoffman, Michael A. 1979. *Egypt Before the Pharaohs: The Prehistoric Foundations of Egyptian Civilization.* New York: Knopf.

———. 1983. Where nations began. *Science '83* 4(8):42–51.

Holden, C. 1999. Making Neandertals part of the human family. *Science* 284:737.

———. 2001. Ancient stepping-stones to Australia. *Science* 292:47.

———. 2002a. Cave paintings in jeopardy. *Science* 297:47.

———. 2002b. Very old tools. *Science* 295:795.

———. 2003a. Dmanisi hominids get legs. *Science* 301:1469.

———. 2003b. Leftovers spur edible debate. *Science News* 300:1653.

Hole, Frank, Kent Flannery, and James A. Neely. 1969. *Prehistory and Human Ecology of the Deh Luran Plain: An Early Village Sequence from Khuzistan, Iran.* Ann Arbor: University of Michigan Press.

Holliday, V. T. 2003. Where have all the mammoths gone? *Science* 300:1373–74.

Holloway, Ralph. 1980. Indonesian "Solo" (Ngandong) endocranial reconstructions: Preliminary observations and comparisons with Neandertal and *Homo erectus* groups. *American Journal of Physical Anthropology* 53:285–95.

———. 1981. The Indonesian *Homo erectus* brain endocasts revisited. *American Journal of Physical Anthropology* 55:503–21.

Hoppe, Kathryn. 1992. Antiquity of oldest American confirmed. *Science News* 142:334.

Hovers, E., S. Ilani, O. Bar-Yosef, and B. Vandermeersch. 2003. An early case of color symbolism: Ochre use by early modern humans in Qafzeh Cave. *Current Anthropology* 44:491–522.

Howell, F. C. 1960. European and northwest African Middle Pleistocene hominids. *Current Anthropology* 1:195–232.

Hublin, J.-J., F. Spoor, M. Braun, F. Zonneveld, and S. Condemi. 1996. A late Neanderthal associated with Upper Paleolithic artefacts. *Nature* 381:224–26.

Huddleston, Lee. 1967. *Origins of the American Indians: European Concepts 1492–1729.* Austin: University of Texas Press.

Hughes, Robert. 1995. Behold the Stone Age. *Time* 145:52–57, 60, 62.

Hurst, W. J., S. M. Tarka, Jr., T. G. Powis, F. Valdez, Jr., and T. R. Hester. 2002. Cacao usage by the earliest Maya civilization. *Nature* 418:289–90.

Hutton, James. 1795. *Theory of the Earth: With Proofs and Illustrations.* 2 vols. 1959 ed. Weinheim, Germany: H. R. Engelmann (J. Cramer) and Wheldon & Wesley.

Ikeya, M. 1982. Petralona Cave dating controversy: Response to Henning et al. *Nature* 299:281.

Iriarte, J., I. Holst, O. Marozzi, C. Listopad, E. Alonso, A. Rinderknecht, and J. Montana. 2004. Evidence for cultivar adoption and emerging complexity during the mid-Holocene in the La Plata basin. *Nature* 432:614–17.

Irwin, Geoffrey. 1993. *The Prehistoric Exploration and Colonisation of the Pacific.* Cambridge: Cambridge University Press.

Irwin, Geoffrey, S. H. Bickler, and P. Quirke. 1990. Voyaging by canoe and computer experiments in the settlement of the Pacific. *Antiquity* 64:34–50.

Isaac, Glynn. 1977. *Olorgesailie: Archaeological Studies of a Middle Pleistocene Lake Basin in Kenya.* Chicago: University of Chicago Press.

Jackson, K., and J. Stamp. 2003. *Building the Great Pyramid.* Buffalo: Firefly Books.

Jaenicke-Despres, V., E. S. Buckler, B. D. Smith, M. Gilbert, A. Cooper, J. Doebley, and S. Paabo. 2003. Early allelic selection in maize as revealed by ancient DNA. *Science* 302:1206–08.

James, Steven R. 1989. Hominid use of fire in the lower and middle Pleistocene. *Current Anthropology* 30(1):1–26.

Janus, Christopher, and William Brashler. 1975. *The Search for Peking Man.* New York: Macmillan.

Jelinek, A. J. 1994. Hominids, energy, environment, and behavior in the late Pleistocene. In *Origins of Anatomically Modern Humans,* edited by M. Nitecki and D. Nitecki. 67–92. New York: Plenum.

Jia Lanpo and Huang Weiwen. 1990. *The Story of Peking Man.* New York: Oxford University Press.

Jian Guan and J. A. Rice. 1990. The dragon bones of Tongxin. *Natural History* 99(9):60–67.

Jochim, Michael. 1983. Paleolithic cave art in ecological perspective. In *Hunter-Gatherer Economy in Prehistory: A European Perspective,* edited by G. Bailey. 212–19. Cambridge: Cambridge University Press.

Jochim, M. A. 1998. *A Hunter-Gatherer Landscape: Southwest Germany in the Late Paleolithic and Mesolithic.* New York: Plenum.

Johanson, Donald. 1993. A skull to chew on. *Natural History* 102(5):52–53.

Johanson, Donald, and Maitland Edey. 1981. *Lucy: The Beginnings of Humankind.* New York: Warner Books.

Johanson, Donald, and B. Edgar. 1996. *From Lucy to Language.* New York: Simon and Schuster.

Johanson, Donald, Lenora Johanson, and Blake Edgar. 1994. *Ancestors: In Search of Human Origins.* New York: Villard.

Johanson, Donald, and James Shreeve. 1989. *Lucy's Child: The Discovery of a Human Ancestor.* New York: Morrow.

Johanson, D. C., F. T. Masao, G. G. Eck, T. D. White, R. C. Walter, W. H. Kinbel, B. Asfaw, P. Manega, P. Ndessokia, and G. Suwa. 1987. New partial skeleton of *Homo habilis* from Olduvai Gorge, Tanzania. *Nature* 327:205–9.

Johnson, E. 1991. Late Pleistocene cultural occupation on the southern Plains. In *Clovis: Origins and Adaptations,* edited by R. Bonnichsen and K. L. Turnmire. 215–36. Corvallis, Ore.: Center for the Study of the First Americans.

Jones, Rhys. 1987. Pleistocene life in the dead heart of Australia. *Nature* 328:666.

———. 1989. East of Wallace's Line: Issues and problems in the colonisation of the Australian continent. In *The Human Revolution: Behavioural and Biological Perspectives in the Origins of Modern Humans,* edited by P. Mellars and C. Stringer. 741–82. Princeton, N.J.: Princeton University Press.

———. 1992. The human colonisation of the Australian continent. In *Continuity or Replacement: Controversies in* Homo sapiens *Evolution,* edited by G. Bräuer and F. Smith. 289–301. Rotterdam: Balkema.

Jordaan, H. V. F. 1976. Newborn:adult brain ratios in hominid evolution. *American Journal of Physical Anthropology* 44:271–78.

Jordan, P. 1998. *Riddles of the Sphinx.* New York: New York University Press.

———. 2001a. *The Atlantis Syndrome.* Phoenix Mill, England: Sutton.

———. 2001b. *Neanderthal.* London: Sutton.

Kantner, J. 1996. An evaluation of Chaco Anasazi roadways. Available at http://sipapu.ucsb.edu/roads/.

Kaplan, Lawrence. 1981. What is the origin of the common bean? *Economic Botany* 35:241–54.

Kaplan, Lawrence, and Lucille N. Kaplan. 1992. Beans of the Americas. In *Chilies to Chocolate: Food the Americas Gave the World,* edited by N. Foster and L. S. Cordell. 61–79. Tucson: University of Arizona Press.

Kaplan, Lawrence, Thomas F. Lynch, and C. E. S. Smith, Jr. 1973. Early cultivated beans (*Phaseolus vulgaris*) from an intermontaine Peruvian valley. *Science* 179:76–77.

Kappelman, John. 1993. The attraction of paleomagnetism. *Evolutionary Anthropology* 2(3):89–99.

Karl, W., and Lorenz Bruchert. 1997. Spearthrower performance: Ethnographic and experimental research. *Antiquity* 71:890–97.

Kasnakoglu, H. 2004. *FAO Yearbook: Production 2003.* Vol. 57, No. 177. Rome: Food and Agriculture Organization of the United Nations.

Keefer, D. K., S. D. deFrance, M. E. Moseley, J. B. Richardson III, D. R. Satterlee, and A. Day-Lewis. 1998. Early maritime economy and El Niño events at Quebrada Tacahuay, Peru. *Science* 281:1833–35.

Keeley, Lawrence. 1980. *Experimental Determination of Stone Tool Use: A Microwear Analysis.* Chicago: University of Chicago Press.

Keeley, Lawrence, and Nicholas Toth. 1981. Microwear polishes on early stone tools from Koobi Fora, Kenya. *Nature* 293:464–65.

Kemp, Barry J. 1977. The early development of towns in Egypt. *Antiquity* 51:185–99.

———. 1991. *Ancient Egypt.* New York: Routledge.

Kennedy, Kenneth A. R., Arun Sonakia, John Chiment, and K. K. Verma. 1991. Is the Narmada hominid an Indian *Homo erectus? American Journal of Physical Anthropology* 86:475–96.

Kenoyer, J. M. 1998. *Ancient Cities of the Indus Valley Civilization.* Oxford: Oxford University Press.

———. 2005. Uncovering the keys to the lost Indus cities. *Scientific American: Special Edition* 15(1):24–33.

Kent, J. 1987. The most ancient south: A review of the domestication of the South American camelids. In *Studies in the Neolithic and Urban Revolutions,* edited by L. Manzanilla. 169–84. Vol. 349 of BAR International Series. Oxford: British Archaeological Review.

Kenyon, Kathleen. 1954. Ancient Jericho. *Scientific American* 190:76–82.

Kiernan, Kevin, Rhys Jones, and Don Ranson. 1983. New evidence from Fraser Cave for glacial age man in southwest Tasmania. *Nature* 301:28–32.

Kimbel, William H., Donald C. Johanson, and Yoel Rak. 1994. The first skull and other new discoveries of *Australopithecus afarensis* at Hadar, Ethiopia. *Nature* 368:449–51.

Kind, C.-J. 2001. The Mesolithic sites of Siebenlinden. Baden-Württemberg. http://www.landesdenkmalamt-bw.de/ english/archaeol/siebenlinden/index.php

Kirch, Patrick Vinton. 1984. *The Evolution of Polynesian Chiefdoms.* Cambridge: Cambridge University Press.

Kislev, M. E., and N. D. Carmi. 1992. Epi-Paleolithic (19,000 B.P.) cereal and fruit diet at Ohalo II, Sea of Galilee, Israel. *Review of Paleoethnobotany and Palynology* 71:161–66.

Kitagawa, H., and J. van der Plicht. 1998. Atmospheric radiocarbon calibration to 45,000 B.P.: Late glacial fluctuations and cosmogenic isotope production. *Science* 279:1187–90.

Klein, Richard G. 1969. *Man and Culture in the Late Pleistocene: A Case Study.* San Francisco: Chandler.

———. 1977. The ecology of early man in Southern Africa. *Science* 197:115–26.

———. 1983. The stone age prehistory of southern Africa. *Annual Review of Anthropology* 12:25–48.

———. 1989. *The Human Career: Human Biological and Cultural Origins.* Chicago: University of Chicago Press.

———. 1993. Hunter-gatherers and farmers in Africa: The transformation of a continent. In *People of the Stone Age: Hunter-Gatherers and Early Farmers,* edited by G. Burenhult. 39–47, 50–55. San Francisco: HarperSanFrancisco.

———. 1994. The problem of modern human origins. In *Origins of Anatomically Modern Humans,* edited by M. Nitecki and D. Nitecki. 3–17. New York: Plenum.

Klein, Richard G., and B. Edgar. 2002. *The Dawn of Human Culture.* New York: John Wiley and Sons.

Knecht, Heidi, Anne Pike-Tay, and Randall White. 1993. Introduction. In *Before Lascaux: The Complex Record of the Early Upper Paleolithic,* edited by H. Knecht, A. Pike-Tay, and R. White. 1–4. Boca Raton: CRC Press.

Kolata, A. 1986. The agricultural foundations of the Tiwanaku state: A view from the heartland. *American Antiquity* 51:748–62.

Kopper, P. 1986. *The Smithsonian Book of North American Indians Before the Coming of the Europeans.* Washington, D.C.: Smithsonian Books.

Krings, Matthias, A. Stone, R. W. Schmitz, H. Krainitzki, M. Stoneking, and S. Pääbo. 1997. Neandertal DNA sequences and the origin of modern humans. *Cell* 90(1): 19–30.

Krogman, Wilton Marion. 1973. *The Human Skeleton in Forensic Medicine.* Springfield, Ill.: Thomas.

Kromer, B., and M. Spurk. 1998. Revision and tentative extension of the tree-ring-based ^{14}C calibration, 9200–11,855 cal. B.P. *Radiocarbon* 40:1117–26.

Krotova, Aleksandra A., and Natalia G. Belan. 1993. Amvrosievka: A unique Upper Paleolithic site in eastern Europe. In *From Kostenki to Clovis: Upper Paleolithic-Paleoindian Adaptations,* edited by O. Soffer and N. Preslov. 125–42. New York: Plenum.

Kunzig, R. 1997. Atapuerca: The face of an ancestral child. *Discover* 18(12):88–101.

Kurtén, Björn. 1976. *The Cave Bear Story: Life and Death of a Vanished Animal.* New York: Columbia University Press.

———. 1980. *Dance of the Tiger.* New York: Pantheon.

Lahdenpera, M., V. Lummaa, S. Helle, M. Tremblay, and A. F. Russel. 2004. Fitness benefits of prolonged postreproductive lifespan in women. *Nature* 428:178–81.

Lamberg-Karlovsky, C. C., and Jeremy A. Sabloff. 1995. *Ancient Civilizations: The Near East and Mesoamerica.* 2nd ed. Prospect Heights, Ill.: Waveland Press.

Larick, R., R. L. Ciochon, Y. Zaim, Sudijono, Suminto, Y. Rizal, F. Azizi, M. Reagan, and M. Heizler. 2001. Early Pleistocene 40Ar/39Ar ages for Bapang Formation hominids, Central Java, Indonesia. *Proceedings of the National Academy of Sciences* 98:4866–71.

Lawler, A. 2001. Writing gets a rewrite. *Science* 292:2418–20.

———. 2004. The Indus script: Write or wrong. *Science* 306:2026–29.

Leakey, Mary. 1971. *Olduvai Gorge 3.* Cambridge: Cambridge University Press.

Leakey, Mary, and Alan Walker. 1997. Early hominid fossils from Africa. *Scientific American* 276(6):74–79.

Leakey, M. D., and R. L. Hay. 1979. Pliocene footprints in the Laetoli Beds at Laetoli, northern Tanzania. *Nature* 278:317–23.

Leakey, M. G., C. S. Feibel, I. McDougall, and A. Walker. 1995. New four-million-year-old hominid species from Kanapoi and Allia Bay, Kenya. *Nature* 376:565–71.

Leakey, M. G., C. S. Feibel, I. McDougall, C. Ward, and A. Walker. 1998. New specimens and confirmation of an early age for *Australopithecus anamensis. Nature* 393: 62–65.

Leakey, M. G., F. Spoor, F. H. Brown, P. N. Gathogo, C. Klarie, L. N. Leakey, and I. McDougall. 2001. New hominin genus from eastern African shows diverse middle Pliocene lineages. *Nature* 410:433–40.

Leakey, Richard, and Roger Lewin. 1992. *Origins Reconsidered: In Search of What Makes Us Human.* New York: Doubleday.

Leakey, Richard, and Alan Walker. 1985a. A fossil skeleton 1,600,000 years old: *Homo erectus* unearthed. *National Geographic* 168(5):624–29.

———. 1985b. Further hominids from the Plio-Pleistocene of Koobi Fora, Kenya. *American Journal of Physical Anthropology* 64:135–63.

Lebel, S., E. Trinkaus, M. Faure, P. Fernandez, C. Guérin, D. Richter, N. Mercier, H. Valladas, and G. A. Wagner. 2001. Comparative morphology and paleobiology of Middle Pleistocene human remains from the Bau de l'Aubesier, Vaucluse, France. *Proceedings of the National Academy of Sciences* 98:11097–102.

Lee, Richard. 1979. *The !Kung San: Men, Women, and Work in a Foraging Society.* Cambridge: Cambridge University Press.

Lehner, M. 1997. *The Complete Pyramids.* New York: Thames and Hudson.

Leigh, Steven R. 1992. Cranial capacity evolution in *Homo erectus* and early *Homo sapiens. American Journal of Physical Anthropology* 87:1–13.

Leonard, J. A., R. K. Wayne, J. Wheeler, R. Valadez, S. Guillén, and C. Vilà. 2002. Ancient DNA evidence for Old World origin of New World dogs. *Science* 298:1613–16.

Lepper, Bradley T. 1995a. *People of the Mounds: Ohio's Hopewell Culture.* Hopewell, Ohio: Hopewell Culture National Historical Park.

———. 1995b. Tracking Ohio's Great Hopewell Road. *Archaeology* 48(6):52–56.

———. 1996. The Newark earthworks and the geometric enclosures of the Scioto Valley: Connections and conjectures. In *A View from the Core: A Synthesis of Ohio Hopewell Archaeology,* edited by P. Pacheco. 226–41. Columbus: Ohio Archaeological Council.

———. 1998. The archaeology of the Newark Earthworks. In *Ancient Earthen Enclosures of the Eastern Woodlands,* edited by R. C. Mainfort, Jr., and L. P. Sullivan. 114–34. Gainesville: University Press of Florida.

———. 2002. *The Newark Earthworks.* Columbus: Ohio Historical Society.

————. 2004. *Ohio Archaeology: An Illustrated Chronicle of Ohio's Ancient American Indian.* Wilmington, Ohio: Orange Frazer Press.

Leroi-Gourhan, André. 1968. The evolution of Paleolithic art. *Scientific American* 218(2):58–70.

————. 1982. *The Dawn of European Art: An Introduction to Paleolithic Cave Painting.* Cambridge: Cambridge University Press.

Lewin, Roger. 1987. *Bones of Contention: Controversies in the Search for Human Origins.* New York: Simon and Schuster.

Lewis, D. 1988. *The Rock Paintings of Arnhem Land: Sociological, Ecological and Material Culture Change in the Post-glacial period.* Oxford: British Archaeological Reports.

Lewis-Williams, J. D., and T. A. Dowson. 1988. The signs of all times. *Current Anthropology* 29(2):201–17.

Lieberman, Philip. 1984. *The Biology and Evolution of Language.* Cambridge: Harvard University Press.

————. 1992. On Neanderthal speech and Neanderthal extinction. *Current Anthropology* 33:409–10.

Lieberman, Philip, Edmund Crelin, and D. H. Klatt. 1972. Phonetic ability and related anatomy of the newborn and adult human, Neanderthal Man, and the chimpanzee. *American Anthropologist* 74:287–307.

Lieberman, Philip, Jeffrey T. Laitman, J. S. Reidenberg, and P. J. Gannon. 1992. The anatomy, physiology, acoustics, and perception of speech: Essential elements in analysis of the evolution of human speech. *Journal of Human Evolution* 23:447–67.

Lippert, D. 1997. In front of the mirror: Native Americans and academic archaeology. In *Native Americans and Archaeologists: Stepping Stones to Common Ground,* edited by N. Swindler, K. E. Dongoske, R. Anyon, and A. S. Downer. 120–127. Walnut Creek, Calif.: AltaMira.

Li Tianyuan and D. A. Etler. 1992. New Middle Pleistocene hominid crania from Yunxian in China. *Nature* 357:404–7.

Lloyd, Seton. 1961. *Art of the Ancient Near East.* New York: Praeger.

Long, A., B. Benz, J. Donahue, A. Jull, and L. Toolin. 1989. First direct AMS dates on early maize from Tehuacán, Mexico. *Radiocarbon* 31:1035–40.

Lourandos, H. 1997. *Continent of Hunter-Gatherers.* Cambridge: Cambridge University Press.

Lovejoy, Owen C. 1981. The origin of man. *Science* 211:341–50.

————. 1984. The natural detective. *Natural History* 93(10):24–28.

————. 1988. Evolution of human walking. *Scientific American* 259(5):118–25.

Lovejoy, Owen C., K. G. Heiple, and Albert Burnstein. 1973. The gait of *Australopithecus. American Journal of Physical Anthropology* 38:757–80.

Lowe, Gareth W. 1989. The heartland Olmec: Evolution of material culture. In *Regional Perspectives on the Olmec,* edited by R. J. Sharer and D. C. Grove. 33–67. New York: Cambridge University Press.

Lowenthal, D. 1988. *The Past Is a Foreign Country.* Cambridge: Cambridge University Press.

Luce, J. V. 1969. *Lost Atlantis: New Light on an Old Legend.* New York: McGraw-Hill.

Luikart, G., L. Gielly, L. Excoffier, J.-D. Vigne, J. Bouvet, and P. Taberlet. 2001. Multiple maternal origins and weak phylogeographic structure in domestic goats. *Proceedings of the National Academy of Sciences* 98:5927–32.

Lundelius, Ernest L., Jr. 1988. What happened to the mammoth? The climatic model. In *Americans Before Columbus: Ice-Age Origins,* edited by R. C. Carlisle. 75–82. Vol. 12 of Ethnology Monographs. Pittsburgh: University of Pittsburgh.

Lu Zun'e. 1987. Cracking the evolutionary puzzle: Jinniushan Man. *China Pictorial* 4:34–35.

Lyell, Charles. 1830. *Principles of Geology; Being an Attempt to Explain the Former Changes of the Earth's Surface, by Reference to Causes Now in Operation.* 1990 ed. 2 vols. Chicago: University of Chicago Press.

————. 1863. *The Geological Evidences of the Antiquity of Man.* London: Murray.

Lynch, Thomas F., R. Gillespie, John A. J. Gowlett, and R. E. M. Hedges. 1985. Chronology of Guitarrero Cave, Peru. *Science* 229:864–67.

MacDonald, G. F. 1985. *Debert: A Paleo-Indian Site in Central Nova Scotia.* Buffalo: Persimmon Press.

MacNeish, Richard S. 1964. Ancient Mesoamerican civilization. *Science* 143:531–37.

————. 1967. An interdisciplinary approach to an archaeological problem. In *Prehistory of the Tehuacán Valley:* Vol. 1—*Environment and Subsistence,* edited by D. Beyers. 14–23. Austin: University of Texas Press.

Magnusson, M., and H. Paulsson. 1965. *The Vinland Sagas.* New York: Penguin.

Maisels, Charles Kenneth. 1990. *The Emergence of Civilization: From Hunting and Gathering to Agriculture, Cities, and the State in the Near East.* New York: Routledge.

Malek, J. 2000. The Old Kingdom (c. 2686–2125 BC). In *The Oxford History of Ancient Egypt,* edited by I. Shaw. 89–117. Oxford: Oxford University Press.

Mandryk, Carole A. 1990. Could humans survive the ice-free corridor? Late-glacial vegetation and climate in west-central Alberta. In *Megafauna and Man: Discovery of America's Heartland,* edited by L. D. Agenbroad, J. I. Mead, and L. W. Nelson. 67–79. Hot Springs, S.D.: The Mammoth Site of Hot Springs and Northern Arizona University.

Manley, B., ed. 2003. *The Seventy Great Mysteries of Ancient Egypt.* London: Thames and Hudson.

Mann, C. C. 2003. Cracking the khipu code. *Science* 300:1650–51.

————. 2005. Oldest civilization in the Americas revealed. *Science* 307:34–35.

Mannikka, E. 1996. *Angkor Wat: Time, Space, and Kingship.* Honolulu: University of Hawai'i Press.

Marean, C. W., and S. Y. Kim. 1998. Mousterian large-mammal remains from Kobeh Cave: Behavioral implications for Neanderthals and early modern humans. *Current Anthropology* 39:S79–113.

Marinatos, Spyridon. 1972. Thera: Key to the riddle of Minos. *National Geographic* 141(5):702–26.

Marks, Anthony E. 1990. The Middle and Upper Paleolithic of the Near East and the Nile Valley: The problem of cultural transformations. In *The Emergence of Modern Humans: An Archaeological Perspective*, edited by P. Mellars. 56–80. Ithaca: Cornell University Press.

———. 1993. The early Upper Paleolithic: The view from the Levant. In *Before Lascaux: The Complex Record of the Early Upper Paleolithic*, edited by H. Knecht, A. Pike-Tay, and R. White. 5–21. Boca Raton: CRC Press.

Marshack, Alexander. 1972. Upper Paleolithic notation and symbol. *Science* 178:817–28.

———. 1976. Some implications of the Paleolithic symbolic evidence for the origin of language. *Current Anthropology* 17:274–82.

Marshall, E. 2001. Pre-Clovis sites fight for acceptance. *Science* 291:1730–32.

Martin, Paul S. 1967. Prehistoric overkill. In *Pleistocene Extinctions: The Search for a Cause*, edited by P. S. Martin and H. E. Wright. 75–120. New Haven: Yale University Press.

———. 1973. The discovery of America. *Science* 179: 969–74.

———. 1982. The pattern and meaning of holarctic mammoth extinction. In *Paleoecology of Beringia*, edited by D. M. Hopkins, J. V. Matthews, Jr., C. E. Schweger, and S. B. Young. 399–408. New York: Academic Press.

———. 1987. Clovisia the beautiful. *Natural History* 96: 10–13.

Martin, Paul S., and John E. Guilday. 1967. A bestiary for Pleistocene biologists. In *Pleistocene Extinctions: The Search for a Cause*, edited by S. Martin and H. E. Wright. 1–62. New Haven: Yale University Press.

Martin, P. S., and H. E. Wright, eds. 1967. *Pleistocene Extinctions: The Search for a Cause*. New Haven: Yale University Press.

Martin, Robert D. 1989. Evolution of the brain in early hominids. *Ossa* 14:49–62.

Matsuoka, Y., Y. Vigouroux, M. Goodman, J. Sanchez G., E. Buckler, and J. Doebley. 2002. A single domestication for maize shown by multilocus microsatellite genotyping. *Proceedings of the National Academy of Science* 99:6080–84.

Maureille, B. 2002. A lost Neanderthal neonate found. *Nature* 419:33.

McBrearty, S., and A. S. Brooks. 2000. The revolution that wasn't: A new interpretation of the origin of modern human behavior. *Journal of Human Evolution* 39: 453–563.

McCamant, John F. 1992. Quinoa's roundabout journey to world use. In *Chilies to Chocolate: Food the Americas Gave the World*, edited by N. Foster and L. S. Cordell. 123–41. Tucson: University of Arizona Press.

McDermott, F., R. Grün, C. B. Stringer, and C. J. Hawkesworth. 1993. Mass-spectrometric U-series dates for Israeli Neanderthal/early modern hominid sites. *Nature* 363:252–55.

McDougall, I., F. H. Brown, and J. G. Fleagle. 2005. Stratigraphic placement and age of modern humans from Kibish, Ethiopia. *Nature* 433:733–36.

McHenry, Henry M. 1991. Sexual dimorphism in *Australopithecus afarensis*. *Journal of Human Evolution* 20:21–32.

McIntosh, J. R. 2002. *A Peaceful Realm: The Rise and Fall of the Indus Civilization*. Boulder, Colo.: Westview Press.

McKillop, H. 1994. Ancient Maya tree-cropping. *Ancient Mesoamerica* 5:129–40.

Megaw, J. V. S., and D. D. A. Simpson, eds. 1979. *Introduction to British Prehistory*. Leicester: Leicester University Press.

Mehringer, Peter J., and Franklin F. Foit, Jr. 1990. Volcanic ash dating of the Clovis cache at East Wenatchee, Washington. *National Geographic Research* 6(4):495–503.

Meiklejohn, Christopher. 1978. Ecological aspects of population size and growth in late-glacial and early postglacial northwestern Europe. In *The Early Postglacial Settlement of Northern Europe: An Ecological Perspective*, edited by P. Mellars. 65–79. Pittsburgh: University of Pittsburgh Press.

Mellaart, James. 1965. *Earliest Civilizations of the Near East*. London: Thames and Hudson.

Mellars, Paul. 1978. Excavation and economic analysis of Mesolithic shell middens on the Island of Oronsay (Inner Hebrides). In *The Early Postglacial Settlement of Northern Europe: An Ecological Perspective*, edited by P. Mellars. 371–96. Pittsburgh: University of Pittsburgh Press.

———. ed. 1990. *The Emergence of Modern Humans: An Archaeological Perspective*. Ithaca: Cornell University Press.

———. 1996. *The Neanderthal Legacy: An Archaeological Perspective from Western Europe*. Princeton, N.J.: Princeton University Press.

———. 2004. Neanderthals and the modern human colonization of Europe. *Nature* 432:461–65.

Mellars, Paul, and P. Dark. 1998. *Star Carr in Context*. Cambridge: McDonald Institute for Archaeological Research.

Meltzer, David J. 1989. Why don't we know when the first people came to North America? *American Antiquity* 54:471–90.

———. 1993a. Is there a Clovis adaptation? In *From Kostenki to Clovis: Upper Paleolithic-Paleoindian Adaptations*, edited by O. Soffer and N. Preslov. 293–310. New York: Plenum.

———. 1993b. Pleistocene peopling of the Americas. *Evolutionary Anthropology* 1(5):157–69.

———. 1993c. *Search for the First Americans*. Smithsonian: Exploring the Ancient World series. Washington, D.C.: Smithsonian Books.

———. 1997. Monte Verde and the Pleistocene peopling of America. *Science* 276:754–55.

Menon, S. 1997. Neanderthal noses. *Discover* 18(3):30.

Mercader, J., M. Panger, and C. Boesch. 2002. Excavation of a chimpanzee stone tool site in the African rainforest. *Science* 296:1452–55.

Mercier, N., H. Valladas, J.-L. Joron, J.-L. Reyss, F. Léveque, and B. Vandermeersch. 1991. Thermoluminescence dating of the late Neanderthal remains from Saint-Césaire. *Nature* 351:737–39.

Merpert, N. Y., and R. M. Munchaev. 1987. The earliest levels at Yarim Tepe I and Yarim Tepe II in northern Iraq. *Iraq* 49:1–36.

Midant-Reynes, B. 2000. The Naqada period (c.4000–3200 BC). In *The Oxford History of Ancient Egypt*, edited by I. Shaw. 44–60. Oxford: Oxford University Press.

Miller, G., M. L. Fogel, J. W. Magee, M. K. Gagan, S. J. Clarke and B. J. Johnson. 2005. Ecosystem collapse in Pleistocene Australia and a human role in megafaunal extinction. *Science* 309:287–90.

Miller, Naomi. 1992. The origins of plant cultivation in the Near East. In *The Origins of Agriculture: An International Perspective*, edited by C. W. Cowan and P. J. Watson. 39–58. Washington, D.C.: Smithsonian Institution Press.

Millon, René. 1967. Teotihuacán. *Scientific American* 216: 38–49.

———. 1981. Teotihuacán: City, state, and civilization. In *Supplement to the Handbook of Middle American Indians*. Vol. 1, edited by J. Sabloff. 198–243. Austin: University of Texas Press.

———. 1992. Teotihucan residential architecture. Paper presented at the Society for American Archaeology.

Minnis, Paul E. 1992. Earliest plant cultivation in the desert borderlands of North America. In *The Origins of Agriculture: An International Perspective*, edited by C. W. Cowan and P. J. Watson. 121–41. Washington, D.C.: Smithsonian Institution Press.

Mitchell, L. 1999. Earliest Egyptian glyphs. *Archaeology* 52(2):28–29.

Moeller, Roger. 1980. *6LF21: A Paleo-Indian Site in Western Connecticut*. Washington, Conn.: American Indian Archaeological Institute.

Molnar, Stephen, and I. M. Molnar. 1985. The incidence of enamel hypoplasia among the Krapina Neandertals. *American Anthropologist* 87:536–49.

Monastersky, Richard. 1994a. Staggering through the ice ages. *Science News* 146:74–75.

———. 1994b. How stable is the current climate? *Science News* 146:75.

———. 1998. Children of the C4 world. *Science News* 153:14–15.

Moore, P. D. 1996. Hunting ground for farmers. *Nature* 382:675–76.

Moorrees, M. A., E. A. Fanning, and E. E. Hunt. 1963. Age variation of formation stages for the permanent teeth. *Journal of Dental Research* 42:1490–1502.

Morgan, Lewis Henry. 1877. *Ancient Society*. 1964 ed. Cambridge, Mass.: Belknap Press.

Morgan, Michèle, John Kingston, and Bruno Marino. 1994. Carbon isotope evidence for the emergence of C4 plants in the Neogene from Pakistan and Kenya. *Nature* 367:162–65.

Morlan, Richard E. 1970. Wedge-shaped core technology in northern North America. *Arctic Anthropology* 7(2): 17–37.

Morris, Craig, and Adriana von Hagen. 1993. *The Inka Empire and Its Andean Origins*. New York: American Museum of Natural History.

Morris, Henry. 1974. *The Troubled Waters of Evolution*. San Diego: Creation Life Publishers.

Morwood, M. J., P. Brown, Jatmiko, T. Sutikna, E. W. Saptomo, K. E. Westaway, R. A. Due, R. G. Roberts, T. Maeda, S. Wasisto and T. Djubiantono. 2005. Further evidence for small-bodied hominins from the Late Pleistocene of Flores, Indonesia. *Nature* 437:1012–17.

Morwood, M. J., P. B. O'Sullivan, F. Aziz, and A. Raza. 1998. Fission-track ages of stone tools and fossils on the east Indonesian island of Flores. *Nature* 392:173–76.

Morwood, M. J., R. P. Soejono, R. G. Roberts, T. Sutikna, C. S. M. Turney, K. E. Westaway, W. J. Rink, J.-X. Zhao, G. D. v. d. Bergh, R. A. Due, D. R. Roberts, M. W. Moore, M. I. Bird, and L. K. Fifield. 2004. Archaeology and age of a new hominin from Flores in eastern Indonesia. *Nature* 431:1087–91.

Mosimann, James E., and Paul S. Martin. 1975. Simulating overkill by Paleoindians. *American Scientist* 63:305–15.

Mowat, Farley. 1987. *Woman in the Mists*. New York: Warner Books.

Müller-Beck, Hansjürgen. 1967. On migrations of hunters across the Bering Land Bridge in the upper Pleistocene. In *The Bering Land Bridge*, edited by D. M. Hopkins. 373–408. Stanford: Stanford University Press.

Mulvaney, J., and J. Kamminga. 1999. *Prehistory of Australia*. Washington, D.C.: Smithsonian Institution Press.

Napier, J. 1967. The antiquity of human walking. *Scientific American* 216:56–66.

Napier, J. R., and P. H. Napier. 1967. *A Handbook of Living Primates*. New York: Academic Press.

Ndoro, W. 1997. Great Zimbabwe. *Scientific American* 277(5): 94–99.

Nelson, Sarah Milledge. 1993. *The Archaeology of Korea*. Cambridge: Cambridge University Press.

Newcomer, Mark. 1971. Some quantitative experiments in handaxe manufacture. *World Archaeology* 3:85–94.

Nichols, J. 1990. Linguistic diversity and the first settlement of the New World. *Language* 66:475–521.

Niewoehner, W. A. 2001. Behavioral inferences from the Skhul/Qafzeh early modern human hand remains. *Proceedings of the National Academy of Sciences* 98: 2979–84.

Noble, David Grant. 1991. *Ancient Ruins of the Southwest: An Archaeological Guide*. Flagstaff: Northland.

Normille, D. 1997. Yangtze seen as earliest rice site. *Science* 275:309.

Oates, Joan. 1973. The background and development of early farming communities in Mesopotamia and the Zagros. *Proceedings of the Prehistoric Society (London)* 39:147–81.

Ochoa, J. A. F. 2004. Contemporary significance of Machu Picchu. In *Machu Picchu: Unveiling the Mystery of the Incas,* edited by R. L. Burger and L. C. Salazar. 109–123. New Haven: Yale University Press.

O'Connell, J. F., and J. Allen. 1998. When did humans first arrive in Greater Australia and why is it important to know? *Evolutionary Anthropology* 6(4):132–46.

O'Connor, David. 1993. *Ancient Nubia: Egypt's Rival in Africa.* Philadelphia: University of Pennsylvania, University Museum.

O'Connor, S. 1995. Prehistoric occupation of the Kimberly region, W.A. *Australian Archaeology* 40:58–59.

Oglivie, Marsha D., Bryan K. Curran, and Erik Trinkaus. 1989. Incidence and patterning of dental enamel hypoplasia among the Neandertals. *American Journal of Physical Anthropology* 79:25–41.

Ohnuma, K., and C. A. Bergman. 1990. A technological analysis of the Upper Paleolithic levels (XXV–VI) of Ksar Akil. In *The Emergence of Modern Humans: An Archaeological Perspective,* edited by P. Mellars. 91–138. Ithaca: Cornell University Press.

Oliva, Martin. 1993. The Aurignacian in Moravia. In *Before Lascaux: The Complex Record of the Early Upper Paleolithic,* edited by H. Knecht, A. Pike-Tay, and R. White. 37–55. Boca Raton: CRC Press.

Ovchinnikov, I. V., A. G. Götherström, G. P. Romanova, V. M. Kharitonov, K. Lidén, and W. Goodwin. 2000. Molecular analysis of Neanderthal DNA from the northern Caucasus. *Nature* 404:490–93.

Ovey, C., ed. 1964. *The Swanscombe Skull: A Survey of Research on a Pleistocene Site.* Occasional Paper 20. London: Royal Anthropological Institute of Great Britain and Ireland.

Owen, Roger C. 1984. The Americas: The case against an Ice-Age human population. In *The Origins of Modern Humans: World Survey of the Fossil Evidence,* edited by F. H. Smith and F. Spencer. 517–64. New York: Liss.

Page, Cynthia, and Julia Cort. 1997. Secrets of lost empires: Stonehenge. *Nova.* Television documentary. Boston: WGBH.

Parés, J. M., and A. Pérez-González. 1995. Paleomagnetic age for hominid fossils at Atapuerca archaeological site, Spain. *Science* 269:830–32.

Parfit, M. 2000. The hunt for the first Americans. *National Geographic* 198(6):35–39.

Pascua, M. P. 1991. A Makah village in 1491: Ozette. *National Geographic* 180(4):38–53.

Pasztory, E. 1997. *Teotihuacan: An Experiment in Living.* Norman, Okla.: University of Oklahoma Press.

Patterson, Thomas C. 1993. *Archaeology: The Historical Development of Civilizations.* Englewood Cliffs, N.J.: Prentice-Hall.

Pauketat, Timothy R. 1994. *The Ascent of Chiefs: Cahokia and Mississippian Politics in Native America.* Tuscaloosa: University of Alabama Press.

Pavlov, P., J. I. Svendsen, and S. Indrelid. 2001. Human presence in the European Arctic nearly 40,000 years ago. *Nature* 413:64–68.

PBS. 1980. Other people's garbage. *Odyssey.* Television documentary, Public Broadcasting Service.

Pearsall, Deborah. 1992. The origins of plant cultivation in South America. In *The Origins of Agriculture: An International Perspective,* edited by C. W. Cowan and P. J. Watson. 173–205. Washington, D.C.: Smithsonian Institution Press.

Pennisi, E. 2002. A shaggy dog history. *Science* 298:1540–42.

Pfeiffer, John E. 1982. *The Creative Explosion: An Inquiry into the Origins of Art and Religion.* New York: Harper and Row.

Philip, Lieberman, Edmund Crelin, and D. H. Klatt. 1972. Phonetic ability and related anatomy of the newborn and adult human, Neanderthal man, and the chimpanzee. *American Anthropologist* 74:287–307.

Phillipson, David W. 1993. *African Archaeology.* 2nd ed. Cambridge: Cambridge University Press.

Piaget, Jean, and B. Inhelder. 1969. *The Psychology of the Child.* London: Routledge and Kegan Paul.

Pickford, M. 1983. Sequence and environments of the lower and middle Miocene hominoids of western Kenya. In *New Interpretations of Ape and Human Ancestry,* edited by R. L. Ciochon and R. S. Corruccini. 421–38. New York: Plenum.

Pineda, Rosa Fung. 1988. The late Preceramic and Initial Period. In *Peruvian Prehistory,* edited by R. W. Keatinge. 67–96. Cambridge: Cambridge University Press.

Piperno, D., and K. Flannery. 2001. The earliest archaeological maize (*Zea mays* L.). *Proceedings of the National Academy of Sciences* 98:2101–03.

Piperno, D., and K. A. Stothert. 2003. Phytolith evidence for early Holocene *Cucurbita* domestication in southwest Ecuador. *Science* 299:1054–57.

Piperno, D. R., and D. M. Pearsall. 1998. *The Origins of Agriculture in the Lowland Neotropics.* Orlando: Academic Press.

Piperno, D. R., A. J. Ranere, I. Holst, and P. Hansell. 2000. Starch grains reveal early root crop horticulture in the Panamanian tropical forest. *Nature* 407:894–97.

Piperno, D. R., E. Weiss, I. Holst, and D. Nadel. 2004. Processing of wild cereal grains in the Upper Paleolithic revealed by starch grain analysis. *Nature* 430:670–73.

Pitulko, V. V., P. A. Nikolsky, E. Y. Girya, A. E. Basilyan, V. E. Tumskoy, S. A. Koulakov, S. N. Astakhov, E. Y. Pavlova, and M. A. Anismov. 2004. The Yana RHS site: Humans in the Arctic before the last glacial maximum. *Science* 303:52–56.

Pohl, M. E. D., K. O. Pope, and C. von Nagy. 2002. Olmec origins of Mesoamerican writing. *Science* 298:1984–88.

Ponce de Léon, M., and C. Zollikofer. 2001. Neanderthal cranial ontogeny and its implications for late hominid diversity. *Nature* 412:534–38.

Pope, G. 1989. Bamboo and human evolution. *Natural History,* October, pp. 50–54.

———. 1992. Craniofacial evidence for the origin of modern humans in China. *Yearbook of Physical Anthropology* 35:243–98.

Pope, K. O., M. E. D. Pohl, J. G. Jones, D. L. Lentz, V. von Nagy, F. J. Vega, and I. R. Quitmyer. 2001. Origin and environmental setting of ancient agriculture in the lowlands of Mesoamerica. *Science* 292:1370–73.

Possehl, Gregory L. 1980. *Indus Civilization in Saurashtra.* Delhi: B. R. Publishing.

Postgate, J. N. 1992. *Early Mesopotamia: Society and Economy at the Dawn of History.* New York: Routledge.

Potts, R. 1996. Evolution and climate variability. *Science* 273:922.

Potts, R., A. K. Behrensmeyer, A. Deino, P. Ditchfield, and J. Clark. 2004. Small mid-Pleistocene hominin associated with East African Acheulean technology. *Science* 305:75–77.

Potts, Richard, and Pat Shipman. 1981. Cutmarks made by stone tools on bones from Olduvai Gorge, Tanzania. *Nature* 291:577–80.

Poulianos, A. N. 1971–72. Petralona: A Middle Pleistocene cave in Greece. *Archaeology* 24/25:6–11.

Powell, E. 2005. The turquoise trail. *Archaeology* 58(1):24–29.

Powers, William Roger, and Thomas D. Hamilton. 1978. Dry Creek: A late Pleistocene human occupation in central Alaska. In *Early Man in America from Circum-Pacific Perspective,* edited by A. L. Bryan. 72–77. Edmonton, Canada: Archaeological Researches International.

Powers, William R., and John F. Hoffecker. 1989. Late Pleistocene settlement in the Nenana Valley, central Alaska. *American Antiquity* 54:263–87.

Price, A. Grenfell, ed. 1971. *The Explorations of Captain James Cook in the Pacific: As Told by Selections of His Own Journals 1768–1779.* New York: Dover Publications.

Price, T. Douglas. 1987. The Mesolithic of western Europe. *Journal of World Prehistory* 1:225–305.

———. 1991. The view from Europe: Concepts and questions about terminal Pleistocene societies. In *The First Americans: Search and Research,* edited by T. D. Dillehay and D. J. Meltzer. 185–208. Boca Raton: CRC Press.

———, ed. 2000. *Europe's First Farmers.* Cambridge: Cambridge University Press.

Price, T. D., and A. B. Gebauer, eds. 1995. *Last Hunters-First Farmers: New Perspectives on the Prehistoric Transition to Agriculture.* Santa Fe, N. Mex.: School of American Research.

Pringle, Heather. 1997. Ice Age communities may be earliest known net hunters. *Science* 277:1203–4.

———. 1998a. New women of the Ice Age. *Discover* 19(4): 62–69.

———. 1998b. Traces of ancient mariners found in Peru. *Science* 281:1775–77.

———. 2001. The first urban center in the Americas. *Science* 292:621–22.

Quade, J., N. Levin, S. Semaw, S. Sileshi, R. Dietrich, P. Renne, M. Rogers, and S. Simpson. 2004. Paleoenvironments of the earliest stone tool makers, Gona, Ethiopia. *Geological Society of America Bulletin* 116:1529–44.

Quilter, Jeffrey, Bernardino Ojeda E., Deborah M. Pearsall, Daniel H. Sandweiss, John G. Jones, and Elizabeth S. Wing. 1991. Subsistence economy of El Paraíso, an early Peruvian site. *Science* 251:277–83.

Raloff, Janet. 1993. Corn's slow path to stardom. *Science News* 143:248–50.

Ramenofsky, Ann F. 1987. *Vectors of Death.* Albuquerque: University of New Mexico Press.

Ramirez Rozzi, F. V., and J. M. Bermudez de Castro. 2004. Surprisingly rapid growth in Neanderthals. *Nature* 428:936–38.

Raven, C. E. 1950. *John Ray, Naturalist: His Life and Works.* London: Cambridge University Press.

Ray, John. 1691. *The Wisdom of God Manifested in the Works of the Creation.* 1974 ed. New York: Verlag.

Reid, J. 1989. A Grasshopper perspective on the Mogollon of the Arizona Mountains. In *Dynamics of Southwest Prehistory,* edited by L. S. Cordell and G. J. Gummer-man. 65–97. Washington, D.C.: Smithsonian Institution Press.

Reid, J., and S. Whittlesey. 1997. *The Archaeology of Ancient Arizona.* Tucson: University of Arizona Press.

Reimer, P. J., et al. 2004. Radiocarbon calibration from 0-26 cal kyr BP. *Radiocarbon* 46:1029–58.

Relethford, J. 2001. *Genetics and the Search for Modern Human Origins.* New York: Wiley-Liss.

Renfrew, Colin. 1972. *The Emergence of Civilization.* London: Methuen.

———. 1979. *Before Civilization: The Radiocarbon Revolution and Prehistoric Europe.* Cambridge: Cambridge University Press.

Renfrew, Colin, and Paul Bahn. 1996. *Archaeology: Theories, Methods, and Practice.* New York: Thames and Hudson.

Rice, Patricia. 1981. Prehistoric Venuses: Symbols of motherhood or womanhood. *Journal of Anthropological Research* 37:402–14.

Rice, Patricia, and Ann Paterson. 1985. Cave art and bones: Exploring the interrelationships. *American Anthropologist* 87:94–100.

———. 1986. Validating the cave art-archaeofaunal relationship in Cantabrian Spain. *American Anthropologist* 88:658–67.

———. 1988. Anthropomorphs in cave art: An empirical assessment. *American Anthropologist* 90:664–774.

Richards, M. P., P. P. Pettitt, E. Trinkaus, F. H. Smith, M. Paunovi, and I. Karavani. 2000. Neanderthal diet at Vindija and Neanderthal predation: The evidence from stable isotopes. *Proceedings of the National Academy of Sciences* 97:7663–66.

Richards, M. P., R. J. Schulting, and R. E. M. Hedges. 2003. Sharp shift in diet at onset of Neolithic. *Nature* 425:366.

Richardson, J. B. III. 1994. *People of the Andes*. Exploring the Ancient World series. Washington, D.C.: Smithsonian Books.

Riel-Salvatore, J., and G. A. Clark. 2001. Middle and Upper Paleolithic burials and the use of chronotypology in contemporary Paleolithic research. *Current Anthropology* 42:449–80.

Rightmire, G. Philip. 1979a. Cranial remains of *Homo erectus* from Beds II and IV, Olduvai Gorge, Tanzania. *American Journal of Physical Anthropology* 51:99–116.

———. 1979b. Implications of Border Cave skeletal remains for later Pleistocene evolution. *Current Anthropology* 20:23–35.

———. 1981. Patterns in the evolution of *Homo erectus*. *Paleobiology* 7(2):241–46.

———. 1984. *Homo sapiens* in sub-Saharan Africa. In *The Origins of Modern Humans: A World Survey of the Fossil Evidence*, edited by F. H. Smith and F. Spencer. 295–326. New York: Liss.

———. 1985. The tempo of change in the evolution of mid-Pleistocene *Homo*. In *Ancestors: The Hard Evidence*, edited by E. Delson. 255–64. New York: Liss.

———. 1990. *The Evolution of* Homo erectus: *Comparative Anatomical Studies of an Extinct Human Species*. New York: Cambridge University Press.

———. 1991a. Comparative studies of late Pleistocene human remains from Klasies River Mouth, South Africa. *Journal of Human Evolution* 20:131–56.

———. 1991b. The dispersal of *Homo erectus* from Africa and the emergence of more modern humans. *Journal of Anthropological Research* 47:177–91.

Rindos, David. 1984. *The Origins of Agriculture: An Evolutionary Perspective*. New York: Academic Press.

Ritchie, William A. 1971. *A Typology and Nomenclature for New York State Projectile Points*. Albany: University of the State of New York, New York State Museum, Bulletin 384.

Roach, Mary. 1998. Ancient altered states. *Discover* 19(6):52–58.

Roberts, David. 1993. The Ice Man: Voyager from the Copper Age. In *National Geographic* 183(6):36–67.

———. 1997. *In Search of the Old Ones: Exploring the Anasazi World of the Southwest*. New York: Simon and Schuster.

Roberts, R., T. F. Flannery, L. K. Ayliffe, H. Yoshida, J. M. Olley, G. J. Prideaux, G. M. Laslett, A. Baynes, M. A. Smith, R. Jones, and B. L. Smith. 2001. New ages for the last Australian megafauna: Continent-wide extinction about 46,000 years ago. *Science* 292:1888–92.

Roberts, Richard G., Rhys Jones, and M. A. Smith. 1990. Thermoluminescence dating of a 50,000-year-old human occupation site in northern Australia. *Nature* 345:153–56.

Romer, John. 1984. *Ancient Lives: Daily Life in Egypt of the Pharaohs*. New York: Holt, Rinehart and Winston.

Roosevelt, A. C., et al. 1996. Paleoindian cave dwellers in the Amazon: The peopling of the Americas. *Science* 272:373–84.

Rose, Mark. 1993. Early skull found in Java. *Archaeology* 46(5):18.

———. 1995. The last Neandertals. *Archaeology* 48(5):12–13.

Rosenberg, Karen R. 1992. The evolution of modern human childbirth. *Yearbook of Physical Anthropology* 35:89–124.

Ross, Philip E. 1991. Mutt and Jeff: Did Cro-Magnons and Neanderthals co-exist? *Scientific American* 265(3):40–48.

Royal Geographical Society. 1993a. *Angkor Wat*. San Francisco: InterOptica. CD-ROM.

———. 1993b. *The Egyptian Pyramids*. San Francisco: InterOptica. CD-ROM.

———. 1993c. *Inca Ruins*. San Francisco: InterOptica. CD-ROM.

Ruff, Christopher B. 1993. Climatic adaptation and hominid evolution: The thermoregulatory imperative. *Evolutionary Anthropology* 2(2):53–60.

Ruff, Christopher B., Erik Trinkaus, Alan Walker, and Clark Spencer Larsen. 1993. Postcranial robusticity in *Homo*. I: Temporal trends and mechanical interpretation. *American Journal of Physical Anthropology* 91:21–53.

Ruggles, Clive. 1996. Stonehenge for the 1990s. *Nature* 381:278–79.

Ruspoli, Mario. 1986. *The Cave of Lascaux: The Final Photographs*. New York: Abrams.

Russo, M. 1996. Southeastern Archaic mounds. In *Archaeology of the Mid-Holocene Southeast*, edited by K. E. Sassaman and D. G. Anderson. 259–87. Gainesville: University Press of Florida.

Sabloff, Jeremy A. 1989. *The Cities of Ancient Mexico: Reconstructing a Lost World*. New York: Thames and Hudson.

———. 1994. *The New Archaeology and the Ancient Maya*. New York: Scientific American Library.

Sakellarakis, Yannis, and Efi Sapouna-Sakellaraki. 1981. Drama of death in a Minoan temple. *National Geographic* 159(2):205–22.

Salazar, L. C. 2004. Machu Picchu: Mysterious royal estate in the cloud forest. In *Machu Picchu: Unveiling the Mystery of the Incas*, edited by R. L. Burger and L. C. Salazar. 21–47. New Haven: Yale University Press.

Sanders, William, J. R. Parsons, and R. Santley. 1979. *The Basin of Mexico: The Cultural Ecology of a Civilization*. New York: Academic Press.

Sandweiss, D. H., H. McInnis, R. L. Burger, A. Cano, B. Ojeda, R. Paredes, M. Sandweiss, and M. D. Glasscock. 1998. Quebrada Jaguay: Early South American maritime adaptations. *Science* 281:1830–32.

Santa Luca, A. P. 1980. The Ngandong fossil hominids: A comparative study of a Far Eastern *Homo erectus* group. *Yale University Publications in Anthropology* 78:1–175.

Saunders, J. J. 1977. Lehner Ranch revisited. *The Museum Journal* 17:48–64.

Saunders, J. W., et al. 1997. A mound complex in Louisiana at 5,400–5,000 years before the present. *Science* 277:1796–99.

Saura Ramos, P. A. 1998. *The Cave of Altamira.* New York: Harry N. Abrams.

Savolainen, P., Ya-ping Zhang, J. Luo, J. Lundeberg, and T. Leitner. 2002. Genetic evidence for an East Asian origin of domestic dogs. *Science* 298:1610–13.

Scala Archives. 1994. Voyage in Egypt: A Virtual Journey Through Ancient Egypt. Acta-Emme. CD-ROM.

Schele, Linda, and David Freidel. 1990. *A Forest of Kings: The Untold Story of the Ancient Maya.* New York: Morrow.

Schele, Linda, and Peter Mathews. 1998. *The Code of Kings: The Language of Seven Sacred Maya Temples and Tombs.* New York: Scribner.

Schick, Kathy D., and Nicholas Toth. 1993. *Making Silent Stones Speak: Human Evolution and the Dawn of Technology.* New York: Simon and Schuster.

Schiffer, M. B. 1976. *Behavioral Archaeology.* New York: Academic Press.

Schiffer, M. B., A. P. Sullivan, and T. C. Klinger. 1978. The design of archaeological surveys. *World Archaeology* 10(1):1–28.

Schmandt-Besserat, Denise. 1992. *Before Writing: From Counting to Cuneiform.* 2 vols. Austin: University of Texas Press.

———. 1996. *How Writing Came About.* Austin: University of Texas Press.

———. 2002. Signs of life. *Odyssey* 6–7 (January/February): 63.

Scholz, M., L. Bachmann, G. J. Nicholson, J. Bachmann, I. Giddings, B.Rüschoff-Thale, A.Czarnetzki, and C. M. Pusch. 2000. Genomic differentiation of Neanderthals and anatomically modern man allows a fossil DNA-based classification of morphologically indistinguishable hominid bones. *American Journal of Human Genetics* 66:1927–32.

Schrenk, F., Timothy Bromage, Christian Betzler, Uwe Ring, and Yusuf Juwayayi. 1993. Oldest *Homo* and Pliocene biogeography of the Malawi Rift. *Nature* 365:833–36.

Schwartz, J. H. 2004. Getting to Know *Homo erectus. Science* 305:53–54.

Sebastian, Lynne. 1992. *The Chaco Anasazi: Sociopolitical evolution in the prehistoric Southwest.* Cambridge: Cambridge University Press.

Semaw, S., P. Renne, J. W. K. Harris, C. S. Feibel, R. L. Bernor, N. Fesseha, and K. Mowbray. 1997. 2.5-million-year-old stone tools from Gona, Ethiopia. *Nature* 385:333–36.

Semaw, S., S. W. Simpson, J. Quade, P. R. Renne, R. F. Butler, W. C. McIntosh, N. Levin, M. Dominguez-Rodrigo, and M. J. Rogers. 2005. Early Pliocene hominids from Gona, Ethiopia. *Nature* 433:301–5.

Serre, D., A. Langaney, M. Chech, M. Teschler-Nicola, M. Paunovic, P. Mennecier, M. Hofreiter, G. Possnert, and S. Paabo. 2004. No evidence of Neandertal mtDNA contribution to early modern humans. *PLoS Biology* 2(3):e57.

Service, Elman. 1975. *The Origins of the State and Civilization: The Process of Cultural Evolution.* New York: Norton.

Settegast, Mary. 1987. *Plato Prehistorian: 10,000 to 5000 B.C. in Myth and Archaeology.* Cambridge, Mass.: Rotenberg Press.

Severinghaus, J. P., T. Sowers, E. J. Brook, R. B. Alley, and M. L. Bender. 1998. Timing of the abrupt climate change at the end of the Younger Dryas interval from thermally fractionated gases in polar ice. *Nature* 391:141–46.

Shackleton, Nicholas, and Neil Opdyke. 1973. Oxygen isotope and paleomagnetic stratigraphy of equatorial Pacific core V28-238: Oxygen isotope temperatures and ice volumes on a 10^5 and 10^6 year scale. *Quaternary Research* 3:39–55.

———. 1976. Oxygen-isotope and paleomagnetic stratigraphy of Pacific core V28–239 late Pliocene and latest Pleistocene. In *Investigation of Late Quaternary Paleoceanography and Paleoclimatology,* edited by R. M. Cline and J. Hays. 449–64. Vol. 145. New York: Geological Society of America.

Shackleton, Nicholas, J. Backman, H. Zimmerman, D. V. Dent, M. A. Hall, D. G. Roberts, D. Schnitker, J. G. Baldauf, A. Despraires, R. Homrighausen, P. Huddleston, J. B. Keene, A. J. Kaltenback, K. A. O. Krumsiek, A. C. Morton, J. W. Murray, and J. Westberg-Smith. 1984. Oxygen isotope calibration of the onset of ice-rafting and history of glaciation in the North Atlantic region. *Nature* 307:620–23.

Shapiro, B., et al. 2004. Rise and fall of the Beringian steppe bison. *Science* 306:1561–65.

Shapiro, Harry L. 1974. *Peking Man.* New York: Simon and Schuster.

Sharer, Robert, and D. Grove. 1989. *Regional Perspectives on the Olmec.* New York: Cambridge University Press.

Sharer, Robert J., and Wendy Ashmore. 1993. *Archaeology: Discovering Our Past.* 2nd ed. Mountain View, Calif.: Mayfield.

Shaw, I., ed. 2000. *The Oxford History of Ancient Egypt.* Oxford: Oxford University Press.

Shaw, J. 2003. Who built the pyramids. *Harvard Magazine* July/August:43–49, 99.

Shea, John J. 1989. A functional study of the lithic industries associated with hominid fossils in Kebara and Qafzeh Caves, Israel. In *The Human Revolution: Behavioural and Biological Perspectives in the Origins of Modern Humans,* edited by P. Mellars and C. Stringer. 611–25. Princeton, N.J.: Princeton University Press.

———. 1990. A further note on Mousterian spear points. *Journal of Field Archaeology* 17:111–14.

———. 1992. Lithic microwear analysis in archaeology. *Evolutionary Anthropology* 1(4):143–50.

———. 1998. Neandertal and early modern human behavioral variability: A regional-scale approach to lithic evidence for hunting in the Levantine Mousterian. *Current Anthropology* 39:S45–61.

Shipman, P. 2001. *The Man Who Found the Missing Link: Eugene Dubois and His Lifelong Quest to Prove Darwin Right.* New York: Simon and Schuster.

Shipman, Pat. 1983. Early hominid lifestyle: Hunting and gathering or foraging and scavenging? In *Animals and Archaeology,* edited by J. Clutton-Brock and C. Grigson. 31–49. Vol. 1 of International Series 163. London: British Archaeological Association.

———. 1984. Scavenger hunt. *Natural History* 93(4):20–27.

———. 1986. Scavenging or hunting in early hominids: Theoretical framework and tests. *American Anthropologist* 88:27–43.

———. 1990. Old masters. *Discover* 11(7):60–65.

———. 2000. Doubting Dmanisi. *American Scientist* 88(6):491.

Shipman, Pat, and Jennie Rose. 1983. Evidence of butchery and hominid activities at Torralba and Ambrona; An evaluation using microscopic techniques. *Journal of Archaeological Science* 10:465–74.

Shouse, B. 2001. For Ice Man the band plays on. *Science* 293:2373.

Shreeve, J. 1995. *Neanderthal Enigma.* New York: Harper Collins.

———. 1996. New skeleton gives path from trees to ground an odd turn. *Science* 272:654.

Shreeve, James. 1993. As the old world turns. *Discover* 14(1):24–28.

Sillen, Andrew, and C. K. Brain. 1990. Old flame. *Natural History* 99(4):6–10.

Silverberg, Robert. 1989. *The Mound Builders.* Athens: Ohio University Press.

Simek, Jan F. 1992. Neanderthal cognition and the Middle to Upper Paleolithic transition. In *Continuity or Replacement: Controversies in* Homo sapiens *Evolution,* edited by G. Bräuer and F. Smith. 231–46. Rotterdam: Balkema.

Simmons, Alan H. 1986. New evidence for the early use of cultigens in the American Southwest. *American Antiquity* 51:73–89.

Sinclair, A. 2003. Art of the ancients. *Nature* 426:774–75.

Singer, Ronald, and John Wymer. 1982. *The Middle Stone Age at Klasies River Mouth in South Africa.* Chicago: University of Chicago Press.

Sjøvold, Torstein. 1992. The Stone Age Iceman from the Alps: The find and the current status of investigation. *Evolutionary Anthropology* 1(4):117–24.

Smith, B. Holly. 1993. The physiological age of KNM-WT 15000. In *The Nariokotome* Homo erectus *skeleton,* edited by A. Walker and R. Leakey. 195–220. Cambridge, Mass.: Harvard University Press.

Smith, Bruce. 1989. Origins of agriculture in eastern North America. *Science* 246:1566–70.

———. 1992a. Prehistoric plant husbandry in eastern North America. In *The Origins of Agriculture: An International Perspective,* edited by C. W. Cowan and P. J. Watson. 101–19. Washington, D.C.: Smithsonian Institution Press.

———. 1992b, ed. *Rivers of Change.* Washington, D.C.: Smithsonian Institution Press.

———. 1995. *The Emergence of Agriculture.* New York: Scientific American Library.

———. 1997. The initial domestication of Cucurbita pepo in the Americas 10,000 years ago. *Science* 276:932–34.

———. 1998. Between foraging and farming. *Science* 279:1651–52.

Smith, Christopher. 1992. *Late Stone Age Hunters of the British Isles.* London: Routledge.

Smith, Fred H. 1991. The Neandertals: Evolutionary dead ends or ancestors of modern people? *Journal of Anthropological Research* 47(2):219–38.

———. 1992. The role of continuity in modern human origins. In *Continuity or Replacement: Controversies in* Homo sapiens *Evolution,* edited by G. Bräuer and F. Smith. 145–58. Rotterdam: Balkema.

———. 1994. Samples, species, and speculations in the study of modern human origins. In *Origins of Anatomically Modern Humans,* edited by M. Nitecki and D. Nitecki. 227–52. New York: Plenum.

Smith, Fred H., Anthony B. Falsetti, and Steven M. Donnelly. 1989. Modern human origins. *Yearbook of Physical Anthropology* 32:35–68.

Smith, Fred H., E. Trinkaus, P. B. Pettitt, I. Karavani, and M. Paunovic. 1999. Direct radiocarbon dates for Vindija G1 and Velika Peina late Pleistocene hominid remains. *Proceedings of the National Academy of Sciences* 96:12281–86.

Smith, Grafton Elliot. 1927. *Essays on the Evolution of Man.* London: Oxford University Press.

Smith, M. A. 1987. Pleistocene occupation in arid Central Australia. *Nature* 328:710–11.

Smith, Melvyn. 1985. *An Illustrated History of the Space Shuttle.* Newbury Park, Calif.: Haynes.

Smith, Michael E. 1997. Life in the provinces of the Aztec Empire. *Scientific American* 277(3):76–83.

Smith, Pat. 1972. Diet and nutrition in the Natufians. *American Journal of Physical Anthropology* 37:233–38.

Smith, Pat, Ofer Bar-Yosef, and A. Sillen. 1985. Archaeological and skeletal evidence for dietary change during the late Pleistocene/early Holocene in the Levant. In *Paleopathology at the Origin of Agriculture,* edited by M. N. Cohen and G. J. Armelagos. 101–30. New York: Academic Press.

Snow, Dean. 1980. *The Archaeology of New England.* New York: Academic Press.

Soffer, Olga. 1992. Social transformations at the Middle to Upper Paleolithic transition. In *Continuity or Replacement: Controversies in* Homo sapiens *Evolution,* edited by G. Bräuer and F. Smith. 249–59. Rotterdam: Balkema.

———. 1993. Upper-Paleolithic adaptations in central and eastern Europe and man-mammoth interactions. In *From Kostenki to Clovis: Upper Paleolithic-Paleoindian Adaptations,* edited by O. Soffer and N. Preslov. 31–50. New York: Plenum.

———. 1994. Ancestral lifeways in Eurasia: The Middle and Upper Paleolithic record. In *Origins of Anatomically Modern Humans,* edited by M. Nitecki and D. Nitecki. 101–19. New York: Plenum.

Solecki, Ralph. 1971. *Shanidar: The First Flower People.* New York: Knopf.

Solis, F., ed. 2004. *The Aztec Empire.* New York: Solomon R. Guggenheim Foundation.

Solis, R. S., J. Haas, and W. Creamer. 2001. Dating Caral, a preceramic site in the Supe Valley on the central coast of Peru. *Science* 292:723–26.

Souden, D. 1997. *Stonehenge Revealed.* New York: Facts on File.

Soustelle, J. 1964. *The Daily Life of the Aztecs.* London: Pelican.

Spencer, Herbert. 1967. *The Evolution of Society* [selections from *Principles of Sociology:* Vol. 1, 1876; Vol. 2, 1882; Vol. 3, 1896]. Chicago: University of Chicago Press.

Spencer-Wood, S. 1991. Toward an archaeology of materialistic domestic reform. In *The Archaeology of Inequality,* edited by R. H. McGuire and R. Paynter. 231–86. Cambridge, Mass.: Basil Blackwell.

Spindler, Konrad. 1994. *The Man in the Ice.* New York: Harmony Books.

Staeck, J. 2002. *Back to the Earth: An Introduction to Archaeology.* New York: McGraw-Hill.

Stager, J. C., and P. A. Mayewski. 1997. Abrupt early to mid-Holocene climatic transition registered at the equator and the poles. *Science* 276:1834–36.

Stanford, D., and B. Bradley. 2000. The Solutrean solution: Did some ancient Americans come from Europe? *Discovering Archaeology* 2(1):54–55.

Stern, Jack T., and Randall L. Susman. 1983. The locomotor anatomy of *Australopithecus afarensis. American Journal of Physical Anthropology* 60:279–317.

Stewart, T. 2002. Mesoamerican source determined for Mississippian scraper. *American Archaeology* 6(2):7.

Stiebing, William H., Jr. 1984. *Ancient Astronauts, Cosmic Collisions, and Other Popular Theories About Man's Past.* Buffalo: Prometheus Press.

———. 1993. *Uncovering the Past: A History of Archaeology.* New York: Oxford University Press.

Stiles, Daniel. 1991. Early hominid behaviour and culture tradition: Raw material studies in Bed II, Olduvai Gorge. *The African Archaeological Review* 9:1–19.

Stiner, M. 1994. *Honor Among Thieves: A Zooarchaeological Study of Neandertal Ecology.* Princeton, N.J.: Princeton University Press.

Stokstad, E. 2000. "Pre-Clovis" site fights for recognition. *Science* 288:247.

Stone, Anne C., and Mark Stoneking. 1993. Ancient DNA from a pre-Columbian Amerindian population. *American Journal of Physical Anthropology* 92:463–71.

Straus, Lawrence Guy. 1989. Age of the modern Europeans. *Nature* 342:476–77.

———. 2000. Solutrean settlement of North America? A review of reality. *American Antiquity* 65:219–26.

Stringer, Christopher B. 1988. The dates of Eden. *Nature* 331:565–66.

———. 1990. The emergence of modern humans. *Scientific American* 263:1263–68.

———. 1992a. Reconstructing recent human evolution. *Philosophical Transactions of the Royal Society of London (B)* 337:217–24.

———. 1992b. Replacement, continuity, and the origin of Homo sapiens. In *Continuity or Replacement: Controversies in* Homo sapiens *Evolution,* edited by G. Bräuer and F. Smith. 9–24. Rotterdam: Balkema.

———. 1993. Secrets of the pit of the bones. *Nature* 362:501–2.

———. 1994. Out of Africa: A personal history. In *Origins of Anatomically Modern Humans,* edited by M. Nitecki and D. Nitecki. 149–74. New York: Plenum.

Stringer, C. 2003. Out of Ethiopia. *Nature* 423:692–95.

Stringer, Christopher B., and Philip Andrews. 1988. Genetic and fossil evidence for the origin of modern humans. *Science* 239:1263–68.

Stringer, Christopher, and W. Davies. 2001. Those elusive Neanderthals. *Nature* 413:791–92.

Stringer, Christopher, and Clive Gamble. 1993. *In Search of the Neanderthals.* New York: Thames and Hudson.

Stringer, Chris B., and Ranier Grün. 1991. Time for the last Neandertals. *Nature* 351:701–2.

Stringer, Christopher B., R. Grün, H. P. Schwarcz, and P. Goldberg. 1989. ESR dates for the hominid burial site of Es Skhul in Israel. *Nature* 338:756–58.

Stringer, Christopher, and R. McKie. 1996. *African Exodus.* New York: Henry Holt.

Struever, Stuart, and Felicia Antonelli Holton. 1979. *Koster: Americans in Search of Their Prehistoric Past.* Garden City, N.Y.: Anchor.

———. 2000. *Koster: Americans in Search of Their Prehistoric Past.* 2nd ed. Prospect Heights, Ill.: Waveland Press.

Susman, Randall L. 1994. Fossil evidence for early hominid tool use. *Science* 265:1570–73.

Susman, Randall L., Jack T. Stern, and William L. Jungers. 1984. Arboreality and bipedality in the Hadar hominids. *Folia Primatologica* 43:113–56.

Suwa, G., B. Asfaw, Y. Beyene, T. D. White, S. Katoh, S. Nagaoka, H. Nakaya, K. Uzawa, P. Renne, and G. WoldeGabriel. 1997. The first skull of *Australopithecus boisei. Nature* 389:489–92.

Svoboda, Jirí. 1993. The complex origin of the Upper Paleolithic in the Czech and Slovak Republics. In *Before Lascaux: The Complex Record of the Early Upper Paleolithic,* edited by H. Knecht, A. Pike-Tay, and R. White. 23–36. Boca Raton: CRC Press.

Swisher, C. C., G. H. Curtis, T. Jacob, A. G. Getty, A. Suprijo, and Widiasmoro. 1994. Age of the earliest known hominids in Java, Indonesia. *Science* 263:1118–21.

Swisher, C. C., G. H. Curtis, and R. Lewin. 2000. *Java Man: How Two Geologists Changed the History of Human Evolution.* New York: Scribner.

Swisher, C. C., W. J. Rink, S. C. Antón, H. P. Schwarcz, G. H. Curtis, A. Suprijo, and Widiasmoro. 1996. Latest *Homo erectus* of Java: Potential contemporaneity with *Homo sapiens* in Southeast Asia. *Science* 274:1870–74.

Sykes, B. 2001. *The Seven Daughters of Eve.* New York: W. W. Norton.

Tague, Robert G., and C. Owen Lovejoy. 1986. The obstetric pelvis of A. L. 288-1 (Lucy). *Journal of Human Evolution* 15:237–55.

Tainter, Joseph. 1988. *The Collapse of Complex Societies.* New York: Cambridge University Press.

Tankersley, Kenneth B. and Cheryl Ann Munson. 1992. Comments on the Meadowcroft Rockshelter radiocarbon chronology and the recognition of coal contaminants. *American Antiquity* 57:321–26.

Tanner, Nancy. 1981. *On Becoming Human.* Cambridge: Cambridge University Press.

Tattersall, Ian. 1995a. *The Last Neanderthal: The Rise, Success, and Mysterious Extinction of Our Closest Human Relatives.* New York: Macmillan.

———. 1995b. *The Fossil Trail: How Do We Know What We Know About Human Evolution?* New York: Oxford University Press.

———. 1998. Neanderthal genes: What do they mean? *Evolutionary Anthropology* 6(5):157–58.

———. 1999. *Becoming Human: Evolution and Human Uniqueness.* Orlando: Harcourt.

Tattersall, I., and J. H. Schwartz. 1999. Hominids and hybrids: The place of Neanderthals in human evolution. *Proceedings of the National Academy of Sciences* 96: 7117–19.

———. 2000. *Extinct Humans.* New York: Westview Press.

Taylor, R. E. 1991. Frameworks for dating the Late Pleistocene peopling of the Americas. In *The First Americans: Search and Research,* edited by T. D. Dillehay and D. J. Meltzer. 77–111. Boca Raton: CRC Press.

Templeton, Alan. 2002. Out of Africa again and again. *Nature* 416: 45–51.

Terrell, John. 1986. *Prehistory in the Pacific Islands.* Cambridge: Cambridge University Press.

Thieme, H. 1997. Lower Paleolithic hunting spears from Germany. *Nature* 385:807–10.

Thomas, Cyrus. 1985. *Report on the Mound Explorations of the Bureau of American Ethnology.* Washington, D.C.: Smithsonian Institution Press. (Original work published 1894)

Thomas, David Hurst. 1998. *Archaeology.* 3rd ed. New York: Harcourt Brace.

———. 1999. *Archaeology: Down to Earth.* 2nd ed. New York: Harcourt Brace.

———. 2000. *Skull Wars: Kennewick Man, Archaeology, and the Battle for Native American Identity.* New York: Basic Books.

Thomas, Glyn V., and Angèle M. J. Silk. 1990. *An Introduction to the Psychology of Children's Drawings.* New York: New York University Press.

Thorne, Alan G. 1977. Separation or reconciliation? Biological clues to the development of Australian society. In *Sunda and Sahul: Prehistoric Studies in Southeast Asia, Melanesia, and Australia,* edited by J. Allen, J. Golson, and P. Jones. 187–204. New York: Academic Press.

Thorne, Alan G., R. Grün, G. Mortimer, N. A. Spooner, J. J. Simpson, M. McCulloch, L. Taylor, and D. Curnoe. 1999. Australia's oldest human remains: Age of the Lake Mungo 3 skeleton. *Journal of Human Evolution* 36:591–612.

Thorne, Alan G., and Milford H. Wolpoff. 1992. The multiregional evolution of humans. *Scientific American* 264(4):76–83.

Tianyuan, Li and Dennis A. Etler. 1992. New Middle Pleistocene hominid crania from Yunxian in China. *Nature* 357:404–7.

Tiemei Chen and Zhang Yinyun. 1991. Paleolithic chronology and possible coexistence of *Homo erectus* and *Homo sapiens* in China. *World Archaeology* 23(2):147–54.

Todd, I. A. 1976. *Çatal Hüyük in Perspective.* Menlo Park: Benjamin/Cummings.

Topic, J. 1990. Craft production in the kingdom of Chimor. In *The Northern Dynasties: Kingship and Statecraft in Chimor,* edited by M. Moseley and A. Cordy-Collins. 145–76. Washington, D.C.: Dumbarton Oaks.

Toth, Nicholas. 1985. The Oldowan reassessed: A close look at early stone artifacts. *Journal of Archaeological Science* 2:101–20.

———. 1987. The first technology. *Scientific American* 256: 112–21.

Trigger, B. G. 1983. The rise of Egyptian civilization. In *Ancient Egypt: A Social History,* edited by B. G. Trigger, B. J. Kemp, D. O'Connor, and A. B. Lloyd. 1–70. New York: Cambridge University Press.

Trinkaus, Erik. 1983a. Neandertal postcrania and the adaptive shift to modern humans. In *The Mousterian Legacy.* 165–200. Vol. 164 of British Archaeological Reports, International Series. Oxford.

———. 1983b. *The Shanidar Neandertals.* New York: Academic Press.

———. 1985. Pathology and the posture of the La Chapelle-aux-Saints Neandertal. *American Journal of Physical Anthropology* 15:193–218.

———. 1986. The Neandertals and modern human origins. *Annual Review of Anthropology* 15:193–218.

———. 1989. The upper Pleistocene transition. In *The Emergence of Modern Humans: Biocultural Adaptations in the Later Pleistocene,* edited by E. Trinkaus. 42–46. Cambridge: Cambridge University Press.

Trinkaus, Erik, and Pat Shipman. 1993. *The Neandertals: Changing the Image of Mankind.* New York: Knopf.

Trinkaus, Erik, and D. D. Thompson. 1987. Femoral diaphyseal histophometric age determinators for the Shanidar 3, 4, 5, and 6 Neandertals and Neandertal longevity. *American Journal of Physical Anthropology* 72:123–29.

Trinkaus, Erik, and Isabelle Villemeur. 1991. Mechanical advantages of the Neandertal thumb in flexion: A test of an hypothesis. *American Journal of Physical Anthropology* 84:249–60.

Troy, C. C., D. E. MacHugh, J. F. Bailey, D. A. Magee, R. T. Loftus, P. Cunningham, A. T. Chamberlain, B. C. Sykes, and D. G. Bradley. 2001. Genetic evidence for Near Eastern origins of European cattle. *Nature* 410:1088–91.

Tylor, Edward. 1865. *Researches into the Early History of Mankind and the Development of Civilization.* London: J. Murray.

———. 1871. *Primitive Culture: Researches into the Development of Mythology, Philosophy, Religion, Language, Art, and Custom.* London: J. Murray.

Unger-Hamilton, Ramona. 1989. The epi-Paleolithic southern Levant and the origins of cultivation. *Current Anthropology* 30:88–103.

Urton, G. 2005. *Signs of the Inka Khipu.* Austin: University of Texas Press.

Urton, G., and C. J. Brezine. 2005. Khipu accounting in ancient Peru. *Science* 309:1065–67.

Valdes, Victoria Cabrera, and James L. Bischoff. 1989. Accelerator ^{14}C dates for early Upper Paleolithic (Basal Aurignacian) at El Castillo Cave (Spain). *Journal of Archaeological Science* 16:577–84.

Valladas, H., J. Clottes, J.-M. Geneste, M. A. Garcia, M. Arnold, H. Cachier, and N. Tisnérat-Laborde. 2001. The evolution of prehistoric cave art. *Nature* 413:479.

Valladas, H., J. L. Reyss, J. L. Joron, G. Valladas, O. Bar-Yosef, and B. Vandermeersch. 1988. Thermoluminescence dating of Mousterian "Proto-Cro-Magnon" remains from Israel and the origin of modern man. *Nature* 331:614–16.

Van Der Veen, M., ed. 1999. *The Exploitation of Plant Resources in Ancient Africa.* New York: Kluwer Academic Publishers.

Van Peer, Philip, and Pierre M. Vermeersch. 1990. Middle to Upper Paleolithic transition: The evidence for the Nile Valley. In *The Emergence of Modern Humans: An Archaeological Perspective,* edited by P. Mellars. 139–59. Ithaca: Cornell University Press.

Van Riper, A. Bowdoin. 1993. *Men Among the Mammoths: Victorian Science and the Discovery of Human Prehistory.* Chicago: University of Chicago Press.

Vekua, A., D. Lordkipanidze, G. P. Rightmire, J. Agusti, R. Ferring, G. Maisuradze, A. Mouskhelishvili, M. Nioradze, Maria Ponce de Leon, M. Tappen, M. Tvalchrelidze, and C. Zollikofer. 2002. A new skull of early *Homo* from Dmanisi, Georgia. *Science* 297:85–89.

Vercors. [Jean Bruller]. 1953. *You Shall Know Them.* Translated by Rita Barisse. Boston: Little, Brown.

Vietmeyer, Noel. 1992. Forgotten roots of the Incas. In *Chilies to Chocolate: Food the Americas Gave the World,* edited by N. Foster and L. S. Cordell. 95–104. Tucson: University of Arizona Press.

Vilà, C., P. Savolainen, J. Maldonado, I. R. Amorin, J. E. Rice, R. L. Honeycutt, K. A. Crandall, J. Lundeberg, and R. K. Wayne. 1997. Multiple and ancient origins of the domestic dog. *Science* 276:1687–89.

Villa, Paola. 1990. Torralba and Aridos: Elephant exploitation in middle Pleistocene Spain. *Journal of Human Evolution* 19:299–309.

Walker, Alan, and Richard Leakey, eds. 1993. *The Nariokotome* Homo erectus *Skeleton.* Cambridge: Harvard University Press.

Walker, A., R. E. Leakey, J. M. Harris, and F. H. Brown. 1986. 2.5 Myr *Australopithecus boisei* from west of Lake Turkana, Kenya. *Nature* 322:517–22.

Walker, A., and P. Shipman. 1996. *The Wisdom of the Bones.* New York: Vintage.

Wallace, D. C., K. Garrison, and W. C. Knowler. 1985. Dramatic founder effects in Amerindian mitochondrial DNAs. *American Journal of Physical Anthropology* 68:149–55.

Wang, H., T. Nussbaum-Wagler, B. Li, Q. Zhao, Y. Vigouroux, M. Faller, K. Bomblies, L. Lukens and J. F. Doebley. 2005. The origin of the naked grains of maize. *Nature* 436:714–19.

Warren, Peter. 1984. Knossos: New excavations and discoveries. *Archaeology* 37(4):48–55.

———. 1987. Crete: The Minoans and their gods. In *Origins: The Roots of European Civilisation,* edited by B. Cunliffe. 30–41. Chicago: Dorsey Press.

Weaver, Kenneth. 1985. The search for our ancestors. *National Geographic* 168(5): 560–623.

Webster, D. 2002. *The Fall of the Ancient Maya: Solving the Mystery of the Maya Collapse.* London: Thames and Hudson.

Weiner, Steve, Qinqi Xu, Paul Goldberg, Jinyi Liu, and Ofer Bar-Yosef. 1998. Evidence for the use of fire at Zhoukoudian, China. *Science* 281:251–53.

Weiss, H., and R. S. Bradley. 2001. What drives societal collapse. *Science* 291:609–10.

Wendorf, Fred, Angela E. Close, Romuald Schild, Krystyna Wasylikowa, Rupert A. Housley, Jack R. Harlan, and Halina Królik. 1992. Saharan exploitation of plants 8000 years B.P. *Nature* 359:721–24.

Wendorf, Fred, Romauld Schild, and Angela E. Close. 1989. Loaves and fishes: *The Prehistory of Waddi, Kubbaniya.* Dallas: Southern Methodist University, Dept. of Anthropology.

Wendorf, Fred, R. Schild, N. El Hadidi, A. Close, M. Kobusiewicz, H. Wieckowska, B. Issawa, and H. Hass. 1979. Use of barley in the Egyptian Late Paleolithic. *Science* 205:1341–47.

Wendt, W. E. 1976. Art mobiler from the Apollo 11 Cave, South West Africa: Africa's oldest dated works of art. *South African Archaeological Bulletin* 31:5–11.

West, Frederick Hadleigh. 1967. The Donnelly Ridge site and the definition of an early core and blade complex in central Alaska. *American Antiquity* 32:360–82.

———. 1975. Dating the Denali complex. *Arctic Anthropology* 11(1):76–81.

———. 1981. *The Archaeology of Beringia*. New York: Columbia University Press.

———. 1996. *American Beginnings: The Prehistory and Palaeoecology of Beringia*. Chicago: University of Chicago Press.

Wheeler, M. 1968. *The Indus Civilization*. New York: Cambridge University Press.

Wheeler, P. E. 1991. The thermoregulatory advantages of hominid bipedalism in open equatorial environments: The contribution of increased convective heat loss and cutaneous evaporative cooling. *Journal of Human Evolution* 21:107–15.

Whiston, William. 1696. *A New Theory of the Earth*. London.

White, J. Peter. 1993. The settlement of ancient Australia. In *The First Humans: Human Origins and History to 10,000 B.C.,* edited by G. Burenhult. 147–51, 153–57, 160–65. San Francisco: HarperSanFrancisco.

White, J. Peter, and James F. O'Connell. 1982. *A Prehistory of Australia, New Guinea, and Sahul*. New York: Academic Press.

White, Leslie. 1959. *The Evolution of Culture: Civilization to the Fall of Rome*. New York: McGraw-Hill.

White, Peter W. 1986. The Temples of Angkor: Ancient glory in stone. *National Geographic* 161(5):552–89.

White, Randall. 1982. Rethinking the Middle/Upper Paleolithic transition. *Current Anthropology* 23:169–92.

———. 1986. *Dark Caves, Bright Visions: Life in Ice Age Europe*. New York: American Museum of Natural History.

———. 1993. Technological and social dimensions of "Aurignacian-age" body ornaments across Europe. In *Before Lascaux: The Complex Record of the Early Upper Paleolithic,* edited by H. Knecht, A. Pike-Tay, and R. White. 277–99. Boca Raton: CRC Press.

White, T. D. 2003. Early hominids—diversity or distortion. *Science* 299:1994–97.

White, T. D., B. Asfaw, D. DeGusta, H. Gilbert, G. D. Richards, G. Suwa, and F. C. Howell. 2003. Pleistocene *Homo sapiens* from Middle Awash, Ethiopia. *Nature* 423:742–47.

White, Tim. 1980. Evolutionary implications of Pliocene hominid footprints. *Science* 208:175–76.

White, Tim, and Pieter A. Folkens. 1991. *Human Osteology*. San Diego: Academic Press.

White, Tim D., and Gen Suwa. 1987. Hominid footprints at Laetoli: Facts and interpretations. *American Journal of Physical Anthropology* 72:485–514.

White, Tim D., Gen Suwa, and Berhane Asfaw. 1994. *Australopithecus ramidus,* a new species of early hominid from Aramis, Ethiopia. *Nature* 371:306–12.

Whittle, Alasdair. 1985. *Neolithic Europe: A Survey*. New York: Cambridge University Press.

Wildman, D. E., L. I. Grossman, and M. Goodman. 2001. Human and chimp functional DNA shows they are more similar to each other than either is to other apes. Paper presented at the Development of the Human Species and Its Adaptation to the Environment, Cambridge, Massachusetts. Available online at http://www.uchicago.edu/aff/mwc-amacad/biocomplexity/conference_papers/papers.html.

Wilford, J. N. 2004. The oldest Americans may prove even older. *New York Times,* November 18, p. 24.

Wilkinson, T. 2003a. Did the Egyptians invent writing? In *The Seventy Great Mysteries of Ancient Egypt,* edited by B. Manley. 24–27. London: Thames and Hudson.

———. 2003b. Who were the first kings of Egypt? In *The Seventy Great Mysteries of Ancient Egypt,* edited by B. Manley. 28–32. London: Thames and Hudson.

Willey, Gordon R. 1966. *An Introduction to American Archaeology* 1: North and Middle America. Englewood Cliffs, N.J.: Prentice-Hall.

Williams, A. R. 2002. A new chapter in Maya history: All-out war, shifting alliances, bloody sacrifice. *National Geographic* 202(4): Geographica.

Williams, Stephen. 1991. *Fantastic Archaeology: The Wild Side of North American Prehistory*. Philadelphia: University of Pennsylvania Press.

Willis, Delta. 1989. *The Hominid Gang: Behind the Scenes in the Search for Human Origins*. New York: Viking.

Willoughby, C. C. 1935. *Antiquities of the New England Indians*. Cambridge, Mass.: Peabody Museum of Archaeology and Ethnology.

Wills, W. H. 1988. *Early Prehistoric Agriculture in the American Southwest*. Santa Fe: School of American Research.

Wilmsen, Edwin. 1974. *Lindenmeier: A Pleistocene Hunting Society*. New York: Harper and Row.

Wilson, Allan C., and Rebecca L. Cann. 1992. The recent African genesis of humans. *Scientific American* 266(4): 68–73.

Wing, Elizabeth. 1977. Animal domestication in the Andes. In *Origins of Agriculture,* edited by C. A. Reed. 837–60. The Hague: Mouton.

Wittfogel, Karl. 1957. *Oriental Despotism: A Comparative Study of Total Power*. New Haven: Yale University Press.

Wolpoff, Milford H. 1984. Evolution in *Homo erectus:* The question of stasis. *Paleobiology* 10(4):389–406.

———. 1989a. Multiregional evolution: The fossil alternative to Eden. In *The Human Revolution: Behavioural and Biological Perspectives in the Origins of Modern Humans,* edited by P. Mellars and C. Stringer. 62–108. Princeton: Princeton University Press.

———. 1989b. The place of the Neandertals in human evolution. In *The Emergence of Modern Humans: Biocultural Adaptations in the Later Pleistocene,* edited by E. Trinkaus. 97–141. Cambridge: Cambridge University Press.

———. 1992. Theories of modern human origins. In *Continuity or Replacement: Controversies in* Homo sapiens *Evolution,* edited by G. Bräuer and F. Smith. 25–64. Rotterdam: Balkema.

Wolpoff, Milford, and R. Caspari. 1997. *Race and Human Evolution.* New York: Simon and Schuster.

Wolpoff, Milford H., Alan G. Thorne, Fred H. Smith, David W. Frayer, and Geoffrey G. Pope. 1994. Multiregional evolution: A worldwide source for modern human populations. In *Origins of Anatomically Modern Humans,* edited by M. Nitecki and D. Nitecki. 175–99. New York: Plenum.

Wolpoff, Milford H., X. Z. Wu, and Alan G. Thorne. 1984. Modern *Homo sapiens* origins: A general theory of hominid evolution involving the fossil evidence from East Asia. In *The Origins of Modern Humans: A World Survey of the Fossil Evidence,* edited by F. H. Smith and F. Spencer. 411–84. New York: Liss.

Woo Ju-kang (Wu-Rukang). 1966. The skull of Lantian Man. *Current Anthropology* 7(1):83–86.

———. 1985. New Chinese *Homo erectus* and recent work at Zhoukoudian. In *Ancestors: The Hard Evidence,* edited by E. Delson. 245–48. New York: Liss.

Wood, Bernard. 1992a. Early hominid species and speciation. *Journal of Human Evolution* 22:351–65.

———. 1992b. Origin and evolution of the genus *Homo. Nature* 355:783–90.

Wright, G. 1971. Origins of food production in southwestern Asia: A survey of current ideas. *Current Anthropology* 12:447–77.

Wright, H. E., Jr. 1991. Environmental conditions for Paleoindian immigration. In *The First Americans: Search and Research,* edited by T. D. Dillehay and D. J. Meltzer. 113–35. Boca Raton: CRC Press.

Wu Rukang (Woo Ju-kang), and Xingren Dong. 1982. Preliminary study of *Homo erectus* remains from Hexian, Anhui. *Acta Anthropological Sinica* 1(1):2–13.

Wu, Z. 1986. *Terra-cotta Figures and Bronze Chariots and Horses at Qin Mausoleum.* Museum of the Emperor, Xian, China.

Yamei, H., R. Potts, Y. Baoyin, G. Zhengtang, A. Deino, W. Wei, J. Clark, X. Guangmao, and H. Weiwen. 2000. Mid-Pleistocene Acheulean-like stone technology of the Bose Basin, South China. *Science* 287:1622–26.

Yarnell, R. 1974. Plant food and cultivation of the Salts Caverns. In *Archaeology of the Mammoth Cave Area,* edited by P. J. Watson. 113–22. Orlando: Academic Press.

———. 1977. Native plant husbandry north of Mexico. In *Origins of Agriculture,* edited by C. A. Reed. 861–78. The Hague: Mouton.

Yellen, John E., Alison S. Brooks, Els Cornelissen, Michael J. Mehlman, and Kathlyn Stewart. 1995. A Middle Stone Age worked bone industry from Katanda, Upper Semliki Valley, Zaire. *Science* 268:553–56.

Yi Seonbonk, and Geoffrey Clark. 1985. The "Dyuktai Culture" and New World origins. *Current Anthropology* 26:1–13.

Yokoyama, Y., K. Lambeck, P. D. Deckker, P. Johnston, and L. K. Fifield. 2000. Timing of the Last Glacial Maximum from observed sea-level minima. *Nature* 406:713–16.

Zeder, Melinda A. 1994a. After the revolution: Post-Neolithic subsistence in northern Mesopotamia. *American Anthropologist* 96:97–126.

———. 1994b. New perspectives on agricultural origins in the ancient Near East. *AnthroNotes* 16(2):1–7.

Zeder, Melinda, and B. Hesse. 2000. The initial domestication of goats (*Capra hircus*) in the Zagros Mountains 10,000 years ago. *Science* 287:2254–57.

Zegarra, A. V. 2004. Recent archaeological investigations at Machu Picchu. In *Machu Picchu: Unveiling the Mystery of the Incas,* edited by R. L. Burger and L. C. Salazar. 71–82. New Haven: Yale University Press.

Zhu, R. X., K. A. Hoffman, R. Potts, C. L. Deng, Y. X. Pan, B. Guo, C. D. Shi, Z. T. Guo, B. Y. Yuan, Y. M. Hou, and W. W. Huang. 2001. Earliest presence of humans in northeast Asia. *Nature* 413:413–17.

Zhu, R. X., R. Potts, F. Xie, K. A. Hoffman, C. L. Deng, C. D. Shi, Y. X. Pan, H. Q. Wang, R. P. Shi, Y. C. Wang, G. H. Shi, and N. Q. Wu. 2004. New evidence on the earliest human presence at high northern latitudes in northeast Asia. *Nature* 431:559–62.

Zihlman, A. and N. Tanner. 1979. Gathering and the hominid adaptation. In *Female Hierarchies,* edited by L. Tiger and H. M. Fowler. Chicago: Beresford Book Service.

Zilhao, J. 2001. Radiocarbon evidence for maritime pioneer colonization at the origins of farming in west Mediterranean Europe. *Proceedings of the National Academy of Sciences* 98:14180–85.

Zilhao, J., and E. Trinkaus, eds. 2003. *Portrait of the Artist as a Child: The Gravettian Human Skeleton from the Abrigo do Lagar Velho and its Archaeological Context.* Instituto Portugues de Arqueologia.

Zimmer, C. 2004. Faster than a hyena? Running may make humans special. *Nature* 306:1283.

Zohary, D., and M. Hopf. 2001. *Domestication of Plants in the Old World: The Origin and Spread of Cultivated Plants in West Asia, Europe, and the Nile Valley.* Oxford: Oxford University Press.

Zollikofer, C. P. E., M. S. Ponce de Leon, D. E. Lieberman, F. Guy, D. Pilbeam, A. Likius, H. T. Machaye, P. Vignaud, and M. Brunet. 2005. Virtual cranial reconstruction of *Sahelanthropus tchadensis. Nature* 434:755–59.

Zubrow, Ezra. 1989. The demographic modeling of Neanderthal extinction. In *The Human Revolution: Behavioural and Biological Perspectives in the Origins of Modern Humans,* edited by P. Mellars and C. Stringer. 212–31. Princeton: Princeton University Press.

Zun'e Lu. 1987. Cracking the evolutionary puzzle. Jinniushan Man. *China Pictorial* 4:34–45.

Index

Page numbers in *italic* type indicate figures.